Step inside the world of a small company with a big business mission. **JAGGED EDGE MOUNTAIN GEAR**, owned by twin sisters Margaret and Paula Quenemoen, manufactures and sells mountain climbing and other outdoor gear. This growing entrepreneurial company is based in Telluride, Colorado, and does business throughout the United States and Asia.

The owners and employees of **JAGGED EDGE** embody the concept of the person-organization fit. **JAGGED EDGE**'s culture encourages employees to pursue their passion for outdoor sports which, in turn, creates a sense of teamwork and shared goals, and contributes to both individual and organizational effectiveness.

That's why **JAGGED EDGE** is profiled in a continuing video case that closes each part of *Organizational Behavior: The Person-Organization Fit.* This inside look at the people of **JAGGED EDGE** shows how OB topics link together, and how OB can make a difference in business success.

Jagged Edge
Mountain Gear

ORGANIZATIONAL BEHAVIOR

The Person-Organization Fit

Afsaneh Nahavandi
Arizona State University West

Ali R. Malekzadeh
St. Cloud State University

Prentice Hall, Upper Saddle River, New Jersey 07458

Acquisitions Editor: Stephanie K. Johnson
Developmental Editor: Charlotte Morrissey
Editorial Assistant: Hersch Doby
Editor-in-Chief: Natalie E. Anderson
Marketing Manager: Tamara Wederbrand
Production Editor: John Roberts
Permissions Coordinator: Monica Stipanov
Managing Editor: Dee Josephson
Manufacturing Buyer: Kenneth J. Clinton
Manufacturing Supervisor: Arnold Vila
Manufacturing Manager: Vincent Scelta
Formatting Supervisor: Christy Mahon
Electronic Art Supervisor: Warren Fischbach
Senior Manager of Production & Technology: Lorraine Patsco
Senior Designer: Cheryl Asherman
Design Manager: Patricia Smythe
Interior Design: Donna Wickes
Photo Research Supervisor: Melinda Lee Reo
Image Permission Supervisor: Kay Dellosa
Photo Researcher: Teri Stratford
Cover Design: Cheryl Asherman
Front Cover/Front Endpaper Photos: Bill Hatcher/National Geographic Society
Back Cover Photo: Don Mason/The Stock Market

Library of Congress Cataloging-in-Publication Data
Nahavandi, Afsaneh.
    Organizational behavior: the person-organization fit / Afsaneh
Nahavandi, Ali R. Malekzadeh
        p.   cm.
    Includes bibliographical references and index.
    ISBN 0-13-285982-3
    1. Organizational behavior.   I. Malekzadeh, Ali R.   II. Title.
HD58.7.N34   1998   98-21488
658—dc21   CIP

Prentice-Hall International (UK) Limited, London
Prentice-Hall of Australia Pty. Limited, Sydney
Prentice-Hall Canada, Inc., Toronto
Prentice-Hall Hispanoamericana, S.A., Mexico
Prentice-Hall of India Private Limited, New Delhi
Prentice-Hall of Japan, Inc., Tokyo
Pearson Education Asia Pte. Ltd., Singapore
Editora Prentice-Hall do Brasil, Ltda., Rio de Janeiro

Printed in the United States of America

10   9   8   7   6   5   4   3   2

To my parents and my sister Firouzeh—AN
To my parents and my brother Ahmad Reza—ARM

BRIEF CONTENTS

CONTENTS

3   CULTURE IN ORGANIZATIONS   73

PREFACE

Perpetual motion: It's a reality for people in organizations. Managers in particular tackle many jobs at once. They have to harness creativity, learn faster, stay flexible, be team oriented, lead well, and think like customers. Fierce global competition, demographic and social changes, technological innovation, and more demanding customers mean that organizations must manage change to keep pace or risk failure. As a result, organizations experiment with different structures, strategies, and technology and try new methods of working and decision making. All these activities affect people in organizations, often in unexpected ways.

Organizational Behavior: The Person-Organization Fit reflects the reality of managing people in today's organizations. Through research, market feedback, and our own experience in the classroom, we've tried to make this text more current in approach and relevant to students than any OB book we've seen. We know that you have many OB textbooks to choose from, so why consider this one? Here are five reasons why you'll want to give *Organizational Behavior: The Person-Organization Fit* a try:

▌ REASON 1: EXPERIENCE
▌ A WORLDVIEW THAT NO OTHER TEXT OFFERS

To succeed, managers must deal effectively with people from many cultures in the workplace and in the business environment. So how does our text help prepare students for a global, diverse work world? Our text goes beyond superficial international coverage—such as boxed features of cultural "do's and don'ts" and examples sprinkled throughout the text. Instead, we hope to set a new standard for meaningful cultural coverage. Take a look at chapter 3, which examines national culture and diversity in depth. There we explore guiding principles and current research findings that prepare future managers to anticipate, identify, and cope with cultural challenges. Then we seamlessly weave relevant cultural principles into every chapter's text discussion. No other text has this type of integration. In addition to integrating cultural principles throughout the text, we reinforce the principles with a plethora of international and diversity applications from more than forty different countries. These examples and applications range from companies such as Ecover, a "green" manufacturer of cleaning products in Belgium, to Cirque du Soleil, a Canadian circus troupe with employees from seventeen countries, who speak a total of thirteen different languages and work in places as varied as Latvia and Luxembourg.

REASON 2: LEARN TO THINK "BIG PICTURE" IN ALL SITUATIONS

Businesses expect employees to go beyond their job description—they want people to think like owners. Will introducing new technology lead to work stress? Is our organization's culture stifling honest communication? Can the company mission actually motivate people? Will a change to team-based decision making improve the effectiveness of our organization?

To fully understand people and manage them well, managers must grasp how the "big picture" affects individuals, groups, and organizational processes. If that's the reality of business, then why treat all macro topics as if they were something disconnected from individual and group topics? To avoid this artificial separation, we give a brief overview of the context of organizations and their managers in chapters 2 and 3, introducing such topics as the environment, structure, and culture.

Then we integrate these topics in appropriate depth throughout the rest of the text in special "In Context" segments. This way, students can see the interplay between macro topics that affect individuals (part II), groups and teams (part III), organizational processes (part IV), and personal and organizational effectiveness (part V). We also examine the strategic implications of OB in "Big Picture" cases at the end of each chapter in parts II–V.

REASON 3: GET AN EDGE—THE JAGGED EDGE

It's easy for students to lose sight of the course goals, especially when they're learning new terms and concepts and unlearning certain misconceptions. To provide a thread that ties everything together, we stepped inside the world of a small company with a big business mission. Jagged Edge Mountain Gear, owned by twin sisters Margaret and Paula Quenemoen, manufactures and sells mountain climbing and other outdoor gear. This growing entrepreneurial company is based in Telluride, Colorado, and does business throughout the United States and Asia. The owners and employees of Jagged Edge embody the concept of the person-organization fit. The organization's culture allows employees the freedom to pursue their passion for the outdoors and extreme sports such as rock climbing, mountaineering, skiing, and mountain biking. This, in turn, creates a sense of teamwork and shared goals, and contributes to both individual and organizational effectiveness.

A Jagged Edge case closes each part of the text and integrates themes from several chapters. Our Jagged Edge video (made exclusively for this book) expands and enhances the running case. Through the Jagged Edge, we show students not only how OB topics link together, but also how OB makes a difference in business success.

REASON 4: EXPLORE OUR UNIQUE CHAPTER ON THE PERSON-ORGANIZATION FIT

Our final chapter explores the relationship between personal and organizational effectiveness. For personal effectiveness, the chapter examines careers in the twenty-first century and individual stress. Then the chapter investigates views of organizational effectiveness. The chapter closes by examining how to find the right fit between you and an organization and why a fit leads to more effectiveness on both sides.

REASON 5: CONSIDER THAT PRACTICE MAKES PERFECT—IN ALL TYPES OF MEDIA

OB is a discipline that requires much more than common sense to master. But how can we convince students that the current and classic OB theories are worth learning? The answer is, give a practical context that will engage students. We do that in the text, on the videos, and over the World Wide Web.

- *In-Text:* The text is full of hundreds of examples that show rather than tell why the concepts and theory are crucial. The profiled companies range from small, cutting-edge firms to large multinationals that span the globe.
- *Videos:* We support the text with a range of quality videos that are second to none. In addition to the "On Location" Jagged Edge video that links to part-ending cases, we also offer fifteen separate video segments that help bring the topics of each chapter to life. These include videos filmed exclusively for Prentice Hall as well as videos from the "Small Business 2000" series as seen on PBS.
- *The Internet:* We support the text examples and concepts with an extensive Web site on PHLIP (Prentice Hall's Learning on the Internet Partnership). PHLIP is a content-rich, multidisciplinary business education Web site created by professors for professors and their students. See the section below on "Instructor and Student Resources" for detailed information on how PHLIP can help you integrate technology into your course.

OTHER HIGHLIGHTS: TEXT FEATURES AND ANCILLARY SUPPORT

We want you to have as much support as possible in both the text and ancillaries. The text features and ancillaries make teaching and learning from *Organizational Behavior: The Person-Organization Fit* a multidimensional experience that should appeal to a broad audience.

In-Text Pedagogy

Pedagogy in each chapter includes clearly identified learning objectives, summary points that link directly to those objectives, easy-to-find definitions in the margin, in-margin cross-references to other pages, end-of-chapter key terms that link to page references, and review and discussion questions. We also include the following features that distinguish us from other texts:

- The "Managerial Challenge," "A Look Back," "Point of View" exercises, and Web exercises fit together. No matter how engaging chapter openers are, students tend to skip them. Because we believe the vignettes we've selected are more than entertainment, we've integrated the opening Managerial Challenge into the chapter in four meaningful ways. First, the challenge leaves several questions unanswered so that we can develop the example throughout the chapter. Second, we answer the questions posed in depth in a chapter-ending "Look Back" feature. Third, related "Point of View" exercises ask students to think like both a manager and an employee as they solve two hypothetical problems from the profiled company. Fourth, we tie Web exercises to the Managerial Challenge. These Web exercises are posted on our Web site at www.prenhall.com/nahavandi.
- "Change Challenge" and "Team Challenge" segments illustrate the importance of innovation and change and the use of teams in today's organizations. These features give examples of state-of-the-art management methods that various organizations use to tackle change- or team-related issues. One of these features is in every chapter.
- Two "Advice from the Experts" features in every chapter help build students' career portfolios. "Career Advice from the Experts" gives tips on many aspects of career skills, and "Management Advice from the Experts" gives practical, how-to advice on managing people. Combined with the self-assessments in

every chapter, these features expose students to the skills they must develop to excel at work.

- Two "Question of Ethics" scenarios help make students aware of ethical challenges in organizations. These short scenarios ask students to answer questions that they may face in the workplace, especially the tough ones that don't have one "right" answer.
- "Student Summary Points" close each section within chapters. They give a brief recap of the material in outline form so students can assess their understanding of key points as they read.
- End-of-chapter Skills Exercises build individual and team skills. In addition to the individual Point of View exercises, we offer (1) self-assessments, (2) a team exercise, and (3) a Web link that directs students to exercises on our Web site.
- "Up Close" and "Big Picture" Cases follow the exercises and give students the chance to explore a case that requires critical thinking skills. The Up Close case applies the concepts of the chapter to a scenario. The Big Picture case examines the strategic implications of the chapter concepts in a real-world setting.

Instructor and Student Resources

We want to make teaching and learning OB a successful experience. We designed each supplemental resource to work hand-in-glove with the text and add extra value.

- The Instructor's Resource Manual (IRM) adds extra value. We offer transition notes that help make your transition to this text a seamless one. We also offer traditional but necessary features such as a chapter overview, chapter outline and objectives, a summary and suggested answers to all features and exercises, cases notes, key figures and tables, and a chapter summary. We distinguish ourselves by offering extra lecture enhancers and tips, additional international examples, extra group and individual exercises, a guide to integrating all supplements, and a video guide.
- The Test Bank provides a file of approximately 1,500 questions. The question types include multiple choice, true/false, short answer, and essay. Some of these questions target issues from the Managerial Challenges. The questions also indicate the level of difficulty—easy, moderate, and challenging.
- Prentice Hall Custom Test for Windows is a state-of-the-art test-generation program that gives you complete flexibility, allowing you to customize tests to suit your course needs. Its user-friendly, powerful test-creation features also mean that you can develop tailor-made tests quickly and simply without error. You also have the options of administering your exams traditionally or on-line, evaluating and tracking student results, and analyzing the success of the exam.
- Color Transparencies and Electronic PowerPoint Slides give you visual aids for any size of class. We offer more than 250 PowerPoint slides and 100 color transparencies covering the major concepts of each chapter.
- The Video Package, developed by Rob Panco of Baruch University, answers professors' concerns about having ample variety, length options, and quality subject matter in the package. In addition to the five-part integrative video case on Jagged Edge Mountain Gear, we offer fifteen additional video segments (one for each chapter) from such sources as "Small Business 2000" (as seen on PBS) and Prentice Hall's "On Location" videos. Video notes found in the Instructor's Resource Guide offer a summary of each video with discussion points and suggested responses.

Prentice Hall's Learning on the Internet Partnership

The PHLIP Web Site (www.prenhall.com/nahavandi), developed by Professor Dan Cooper at Marist College, provides academic support for faculty and students using this text. PHLIP is divided into a faculty page and a student page. The faculty page helps professors prepare lectures, integrate technology into the classroom, and enhance in- and out-of-class learning with industry examples as current as today's world news. Features include:

- Text-specific Faculty Resources, including downloadable supplements (Instructor's Manual, Technology Resource Manual, and PowerPoint presentations) and on-line faculty support for the student page (including additional cases, articles, links, and suggested answers to the questions posted on the student page).
- "Talk to the Team" is a moderated and password-protected conference and chat room system that allows faculty the opportunity to ask questions, make suggestions, and explore new teaching ideas.
- The "Teaching Archive" features teaching resources submitted by instructors throughout the world, and includes tips, techniques, academic papers, and sample syllabi for traditional classroom presentations and for integrating technology in and out of the classroom.
- "Help with Computers" provides tips and links to tutorials to help you master spreadsheets, word processing, and presentation software.
- "Internet Skills" offers beginner and advanced advice, tips, and tutorials for using the Internet.

The student page supports students through an Interactive Study Guide, Current Events Cases and Exercises, Study Skills, and Writing and Research Assistance. Features include:

- "Student Study Hall" helps develop students' study skills through the following resources: "Ask the Tutor" serves as virtual office hours, allowing students to post questions or comments to the threaded message board and receive responses from both the PHLIP faculty and the entire learning community. This feature is monitored by Professor Dan Cooper to maintain quality. The "Writing Center" provides links to on-line dictionaries, writing tutors, style and grammar guides, and additional tools to help students develop their writing skills. The "Study Skills Center" helps students develop better study skills. The "Career Center" encourages students to investigate potential employers, get career information and advice, view sample resumés, and even apply for jobs on-line. The "Research Center" provides tips and resources that make it easy to harness the power of the Internet as a research tool through tutorials and descriptive links to virtual libraries and a wealth of search engines.
- Numerous "Current Events" articles and exercises with every chapter keep your class up to date. Each current event item is a summary and analysis of a current news event written by our PHLIP faculty provider and supported with links to the text, discussion questions, group activities, background/historical information, a glossary, a bibliography, and links to related news sources. Whenever possible, there is a link to the original article itself. New current event items are added every two weeks (past current event items remain on the site until they are no longer useful or valid).

- "Interactive Study Guide" offers multiple-choice and true/false questions for every chapter of this text. Students submit responses to the server, which scores them and provides immediate feedback, including additional help and page references linked to the text. Test scores can be sent to as many as four e-mail addresses.
- "Internet Resources" provide links to helpful Web sites, complete with an "Info" button that offers professors and students a description of each site.

ACKNOWLEDGMENTS

A book like this is a major undertaking. This text went through an extensive review process at all stages. Special thanks go to the faculty that reviewed multiple drafts of the manuscript and to those that attended focus groups to help us develop the project in the right direction:

Cheryl L. Adkins, Louisiana State University
Peggy Anderson, University of Wisconsin–Madison
Ed Arnold, Auburn University
Debra Arvanites, Villanova University
Joy K. Benson, University of Illinois at Springfield
Anthony F. Buono, Bentley College
Rudy Butler, The College of New Jersey
Sharon K. Clinebell, University of Northern Colorado
Anne C. Cowden, California State University–Sacramento
Joseph Garcia, Western Washington University
Paul A. Fadil, Valdosta State University
Judson C. Faurer, Metropolitan State College of Denver
Lisa L. McConnell, Oklahoma State University
Dean B. McFarlin, Marquette University
Jeffrey A. Miles, University of the Pacific
Janet P. Near, Indiana University
Philip Pettman, Mankato State University
Dale E. Rude, University of Houston
Melvin E. Schnake, Valdosta State University
Ronald R. Sims, College of William and Mary
Shanthi Srinivas, California State Polytechnic University–Pomona
William E. Stratton, Idaho State University
Ram Subramanian, Grand Valley State University
James K. Swenson, Moorhead State University
Steven L. Thomas, Southwest Missouri State University
Ed Ward, St. Cloud State University
Edward Wertheim, Northeastern University
Bobbie W. Williams, Georgia Southern University

The people at Prentice Hall also deserve accolades for their hard work and vision. Our thanks go to Editor-in-Chief Natalie E. Anderson, for having the vision to see the book before it existed, and to Senior Acquisitions Editor Stephanie K. Johnson, who jumped in with both feet, adopted us as her own, and made sure every detail was in place to make the book a success. Thanks also to Editorial Director Jim Boyd and Business Division President Sandy Steiner for their support. Our appreciation also goes to Assistant Editor Shane Gemza, who handled the supplements process with care and attention to detail, and Editorial Assistants

Hersch Doby and Dawn-Marie Reisner, who managed hundreds of key details with speed and aplomb.

We owe a very special thanks to Charlotte Morrissey, Senior Development Editor, who went well beyond the call of duty. Her creativity and intelligence added immeasurable value to every aspect of this project. Many thanks to Steve Deitmer, Director of Development, for supporting and staffing the project to our benefit.

Kudos to the efforts of our marketing team and the special efforts of the Prentice Hall sales force—you really are the best in the business. Some standout efforts are noteworthy. Thanks especially to Marketing Manager Tamara Wederbrand, whose input, smarts, and energy played a key role in planning and defining a message strategy for this text. Patti Arneson, Senior Marketing Research Analyst, helped craft a survey and focus group that provided critical feedback. Finally, to Brian Kibby, Director of Marketing, thank you for supporting the project and managing such terrific people.

The hard work of two other teams was essential to this text. First, the production team of John Roberts (we couldn't have asked for a better production editor!), Dee Josephson, Joanne Jay, Ken Clinton, Arnold Vila, Vincent Scelta, Cheryl Asherman, Pat Smythe, Christy Mahon, David Salierno, Veronica Schwartz, and Lorraine Patsco made sure that the design and production value of the text were second to none. Second, the marketing communications team of Janet Ferruggia, Eve Adams, Mara Surrey, and Julia Meehan communicated the message of the text in a simple, creative way.

We would also like to thank our graduate assistants Violetka Vanderlip, James Finnegan, and Judd Wasden for help on the research for the book. Special thanks to Victoria McWilliams of Villanova University and Thomas McWilliams of Drexel University for their support and friendship. Thank you to our colleagues and the staff at Arizona State University West School of Management and St. Cloud State University.

Finally, a very warm thank you to Margaret and Paula Quenemoen and all the folks at Jagged Edge Mountain Gear; Hattie Bryant, Bruce Camber, and the staff of Small Business 2000; Dan Cooper; Marian Wood; and Rob Panco. Your help in making this text come alive was pivotal. Your time and effort made a difference!

—Afsaneh Nahavandi
Ali R. Malekzadeh

ABOUT THE AUTHORS

Afsaneh Nahavandi

Dr. Afsaneh Nahavandi received her B.A. in Psychology and French from the University of Denver and her M.A. and Ph.D. in Social Psychology from the University of Utah. An award-winning teacher and author, Dr. Nahavandi taught at the School of Business at Northeastern University in Boston and then moved to Arizona State University West as one of the founding business faculty in 1987. In addition to her teaching and research responsibilities, she directed Arizona State University's MBA program. Her teaching interests include organizational behavior, organization theory, leadership, and cultural diversity. Her research focuses on leadership, teams, and organizational culture. Dr. Nahavandi has done consulting and training work in the areas of leadership, teams, and culture for many organizations, including AT&T and Honeywell. Her numerous articles have been published in journals such as the *Academy of Management Review, Group and Organization Studies,* the *Journal of Management Studies,* and the *Academy of Management Executive.* Her article about teams was selected as the *Academy of Management Executive* best article in 1994. Dr. Nahavandi is also the author of *The Art and Science of Leadership* (1997) and co-author of *Organizational Culture in the Management of Mergers* (1993).

Ali R. Malekzadeh

Dr. Ali R. Malekzadeh received his B.S. and MBA at the University of Denver and his Ph.D. in Business Strategy from the University of Utah. He taught at Northeastern University's School of Business and then at Arizona State University West in 1987, where he also served as President of the Faculty Senate and Associate Vice Provost for Graduate Programs. He is currently Professor and Dean of the College of Business at St. Cloud State University in Minnesota. His teaching interests include strategic management and global business. His research interests include mergers and acquisitions and corporate control. He has done strategic management consulting for many businesses, including Honeywell and Sea Ray. Dr. Malekzadeh is co-author of *Organizational Culture in the Management of Mergers* (1993) with Dr. Nahavandi and has written articles in journals such as the *Academy of Management Review, Entrepreneurship,* the *Journal of Applied Business Research,* and the *Journal of Management Studies.*

Drs. Nahavandi and Malekzadeh are married and have two daughters. They have extensive international experience and have traveled throughout Europe and the Middle East. Dr. Nahavandi is fluent in French and Farsi and trained in Spanish. Dr. Malekzadeh is fluent in Farsi and trained in French. The whole family holds black belts in Tae Kwon Do.

THE CHALLENGE OF MANAGING PEOPLE AND ORGANIZATIONS

LEARNING OBJECTIVES

1. Define organizational behavior (OB) and identify its three levels of analysis.
2. Summarize the functions, roles, and skills that managers must perform in organizations.
3. Describe the open systems view of organizations and outline the elements of the contingency approach to management.
4. Highlight the four major challenges that organizations face today and explain organizations' response to those challenges.
5. Explain how managers must respond to the four challenges of organizations.

MANAGERIAL CHALLENGE

Starbucks Goes Global

Starbucks has changed the coffee-drinking habits of millions, bringing lattes and espresso into the mainstream through more than 1,500 trendy coffee retail locations stretching from Seattle to Singapore. Java king Howard Schultz's secret weapon? His employees. "Starbucks store managers and workers have been the best ambassadors for the brand," he recently said. "They make personal attachments with customers, who have spread the word."[1]

Three entrepreneurs opened the original Starbucks store in Seattle in 1971, selling only gourmet coffee beans and accessories. After Howard Schultz was hired in 1982 to handle marketing, he came back from a trip to Italy with the vision of opening coffee bars across the United States. However, the founders opted to concentrate on coffee roasting. In 1987 Schultz, along with some investors, purchased the six Starbucks stores and followed through on his dream of national expansion. Within ten years, the company had outlets in 28 states as well as in Asia, brewing up nearly $1 billion in annual sales.[2]

Schultz calls his 25,000 employees *partners*, an apt title given their important contribution to Starbucks's success. The average age of employees is 26; many have attended college and all are positively evangelistic about great coffee. They are paid well (compared with other food-service outfits), receive health insurance benefits, and can earn valuable stock options over time. New employees attend training in the company's three Star Skills: maintain and enhance self-esteem; listen and acknowledge; and ask for help. Because chief executive officer (CEO) Schultz and his executives act quickly on comments received through e-mail, suggestion cards, and open forums, employees also see that their ideas can make a real difference.[3]

What next for Starbucks? Schultz is aiming for 2,000 stores by the beginning of the twenty-first century, and he has several new products in the works.[4] But can he sustain the company's rapid growth—and his employees' enthusiasm?

■ Questions

1. What key challenges must Schultz address to maintain the momentum of Starbucks's success?
2. What managerial skills are most important for Schultz to apply as he responds to these challenges?

Starbucks's success depends on its employees' ability to work well together. In any organization, few tasks are accomplished by just one person. Most tasks can't be completed unless people work together to finish them. In business, organizations of all sizes around the world produce the products and services that we depend on and consume every day. These organizations range in size from small businesses run by a few people to multinational corporate giants that have tens of thousands of employees, many layers of management, and operations that span several continents. Regardless of size, all organizations face the challenge of managing people.

Royal Dutch/Shell is one of the world's corporate giants. Managers of the $128 billion-a-year oil company supervise 101,000 employees working in offices in 130 countries, 54 refineries, and over 47,000 gas stations worldwide. The company is so large that it has two headquarters—one in The Hague in the Netherlands and one in London—to better serve its customers.[5] Federal Express, based in Memphis, Tennessee, is another example of a complex business organization. With 140,000 employees in 2,000 offices scattered throughout the world, FedEx managers rely on advanced information systems to coordinate the activities of their employees and keep track of the millions of packages they handle.[6]

Though often less complex in structure than their multinational counterparts, small and medium-size businesses still need to coordinate the activities of their employees to reach their goals. Consider Marc Brownstein, president of a family-owned advertising agency in Philadelphia. Brownstein manages his workforce through careful planning, goal setting, and restructuring to keep pace with changes in the advertising world. In these ways, the organization can continue to offer topnotch service to clients such as AT&T and Hallmark. Not one to waste time, Brownstein begins each day during his drive to work: "I turn the radio off and think, 'What are the first three things I need to get done this morning, or what are things I need to do today over everything else?'"[7] He knows that if he prioritizes his management responsibilities, his employees can perform more effectively.

Just as organizations have changed, so too have the functions, roles, and skills of managers.[8] The speed and constancy of change, new competitors, employee diversity, rapid technological advances, and a global economy require that managers continually retrain and reeducate themselves. Only then can they work successfully with others around the world, manage diverse teams, handle complicated information systems, fill in for laid-off workers as needed, and assist with their companies' strategic plans. In short, managers must be skilled and versatile enough to handle the business demands and human behavior in today's modern organizations.

Understanding organizations and how people behave and function in them is essential to your personal career success as future managers. Helping you understand people and organizations is our goal. In this text, we examine how to manage people effectively by examining the behavior of people, groups, and organizational processes. This chapter explains what organizational behavior is and investigates the changing jobs and roles of managers today. We also discuss the *open system model* of organizations and the elements of the *contingency approach* to management. Finally, we consider business challenges and organizations' response to those challenges.

WHAT IS ORGANIZATIONAL BEHAVIOR?

Organizations are groups of two or more people who cooperate and coordinate their activities in a systematic manner to reach their goals. Churches, social and sports groups, and businesses are all types of organizations. In all types of organizations, people work toward common goals. **Organizational behavior** (OB) is the study of how people behave in organizations as individuals and as teams and how organizations structure human resources (their employees and managers) to achieve their goals. The purpose of OB is to understand people in organizations, provide practitioners and managers with the tools to manage people more effectively, and help organizations achieve their goals.

The OB field is broad. It includes the following areas of study:

- Managing individual differences to achieve performance
- Motivating employees
- Managing teams
- Using power and leading people and organizations
- Decision making
- Communicating inside and outside the organization
- Managing conflict and negotiating
- Implementing change.

Because of its broad scope, OB helps us understand all types of organizations: nonprofit, governmental, social, school, and business. Our focus in this text is on business organizations.

Three Levels of Analysis

To give you a complete picture of this field of study, we analyze three levels of OB in this text, as shown in Figure 1.1. The first level of analysis, called *micro OB*, studies the individual. It is the smallest possible level of analysis in organizations and includes topics such as perception, personality, motivation, and learning. The second and middle level of analysis in OB is the *small group* that is made up of individual employees within an organization. These groups can be as small as two people or larger, depending on the group's goals and tasks. The study of small groups in OB includes issues of group size and composition, cohesion, trust, conflict management, team building, small-group decision making, and leadership.

The third level of analysis in OB, called *macro OB*, is concerned with larger groups, such as departments, and organizational processes. Macro OB topics include issues such as the design and structure of organizations, organizational culture and strategy, organizational power and politics, change, and organizational effectiveness. Managers must understand their organization at all three levels of analysis to meet the daily challenges they face. For instance,

Organizations
Groups of two or more people who cooperate and coordinate their activities in a systematic manner to reach goals

Organizational behavior (OB)
The study of how people behave in organizations and how organizations structure their human resources to achieve goals

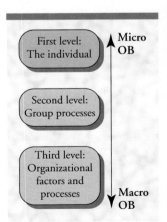

FIGURE 1.1
The Three Levels of Analysis in Organizational Behavior

Starbucks managers work with individual employees and with groups. They interview and select the best people to work in their stores and train them to work as teams to serve customers. Managers must also understand how their organization functions and how events around the country and around the world affect how they do business. For example, changes in U.S. labor safety laws in the food service industry affect how all U.S. Starbucks stores operate. Similarly, Starbucks managers need to understand how changes in the world market for coffee beans affect their pricing at the local level.

Related Management Fields

Though the study of OB is essential to managers' effectiveness, it is only one of several management fields. Other areas also concentrate on individuals, groups, or organizational processes. Three areas most closely related to OB are organization theory, human resource management, and strategic management. Each area offers insights that can help managers perform their jobs more effectively.

Organization Theory (OT) The study of organizational processes at the macro level of analysis

Organization Theory   **Organization Theory** (OT) is the study of organizational processes at the macro level of analysis. The goal of OT is understanding organizations from a broad perspective. OT includes topics such as organizational environment, design and structure, and control systems. It also includes topics that we study in OB: conflict, change, decision making, and power and politics. Drawing the line between OB and OT is difficult because the difference is primarily the level of analysis rather than the content. For example, the topic of conflict can be considered from an OB point of view by considering conflict in small groups. If we were to study conflict in OT, we'd analyze conflict among different departments. In this text we discuss OT topics that overlap with OB and provide a context for understanding individual and small group behavior.

Human Resource Management (HRM, or personnel management) The procedural, technical, and legal aspects of recruiting, placement, training, evaluation, and development of the employees of an organization

Human Resource Management   **Human Resource Management** (HRM, also known as personnel management) deals with the procedural, technical, and legal aspects of employee recruiting, placement, training, evaluation, and development. HRM studies employee compensation, benefits, and labor relations. The goal of HRM is to ensure that the organization has access to an appropriate pool of skilled employees who help the organization reach its goals.

The fields of HRM and OB are closely linked. OB's emphasis on individuals and groups helps managers create and implement human resource policies and procedures. For instance, a manager can use her knowledge of motivation (an OB topic) to conduct better performance reviews (an HRM topic). However, the orientation of HRM is typically more technical and procedural than OB. Because of the close links between the two fields, we cover many issues that affect and apply to HRM, such as motivation, career development, and stress.

Strategic Management The study of how upper management sets the general course for the business and how it uses human, financial, and operational resources to achieve company goals

Strategic Management   **Strategic Management** (also called business policy) focuses on how upper management sets the general course for the business and uses human, financial, and operational resources to achieve company goals. Strategic management relies on many OB topics, particularly in implementing strategies to achieve goals. These issues are relevant to managers. Why? Today's managers can't operate in a vacuum and expect to succeed.

First, managers must understand the organization's goals to make sure that their activities support and do not conflict with those goals. For instance, if the company plans to implement new information systems to speed customer service, managers should spend time training employees to use the new system. Second, managers need to understand the context in which people and groups function and organizational processes occur. It's tough to motivate employees when the business is considering layoffs. It's also hard to encourage quick, creative decision making when the organization requires approval for even the smallest decision and is slow to give it. In this text we examine key strategic management issues where appropriate to provide a "big picture" view of organizations.

The major difference between OB and the other three disciplines is OB's focus on people, groups, and the general structure of organizations. The other three disciplines shy away from individual concerns and either have a more organizational or more technical focus.

No matter what you do, whether you are an accountant or an engineer, you need to understand how to manage people and organizations. Say that you work as a sales manager in the marketing department. You rely on your marketing knowledge to lead your sales force. In addition, you will use your knowledge of OB and other management disciplines to motivate your sales associates, propose a strategic plan to your boss, change the structure of your department, and recruit and train the appropriate sales force.

Common Roots

OB is a relatively young discipline. To understand people and organizations, OB researchers and practitioners rely on information from many different disciplines. Information from these other disciplines allows us to study how people function in organizations in a systematic way that moves beyond intuition. We discuss the contributions of other social sciences to OB next.

Interdisciplinary Contributions   OB is a social science that analyzes human behavior. It is an interdisciplinary field that shares concepts and research methods with several other social sciences, as Figure 1.2 illustrates. Though many disciplines influence OB, psychology and sociology have the strongest influences. Psychology helps OB practitioners understand the micro issues in OB such as perception, motivation, learning, decision making, and small-group dynamics. Social psychological theories explain group behavior, power and leadership, conflict, work stress, and performance appraisal. Sociology affects OB mostly at the macro level through the field of OT. As such, sociology helps us understand the organization's environment, technology, structure, culture, conflict, and adaptability to change.

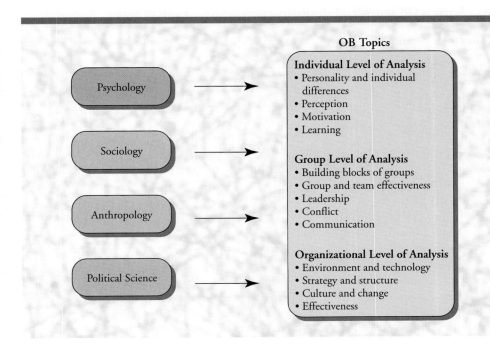

OB Topics

Individual Level of Analysis
• Personality and individual differences
• Perception
• Motivation
• Learning

Group Level of Analysis
• Building blocks of groups
• Group and team effectiveness
• Leadership
• Conflict
• Communication

Organizational Level of Analysis
• Environment and technology
• Strategy and structure
• Culture and change
• Effectiveness

Psychology

Sociology

Anthropology

Political Science

FIGURE 1.2
The Social Sciences That Contribute to Organizational Behavior

In some instances, we can trace directly the influence of a particular branch of social science. For example, our understanding of organizational structure is almost exclusively related to sociology. However, in most cases several fields contribute to our understanding of OB issues. The topic of conflict is an excellent illustration. Psychology helps us understand conflict at the micro level by explaining individual differences in conflict management. Sociology helps us analyze organizational and departmental sources of conflict. Anthropology contributes to a cultural analysis of conflict, and political science takes a look at political and interorganizational conflict sources. Just as OB borrows concepts from various social science fields, it also borrows research methods from the social sciences to help practitioners learn about people and organizations.

Interdisciplinary Research Methods   OB relies on the scientific method, which is based on observation, prediction, and measurement. The scientific method helps us to explain and predict the behavior of people in organizations. Appendix 2 highlights the various scientific methods used in OB.

Why is the use of the scientific method so important? It provides predictability and the ability to generalize from one situation to another. Use of the scientific method also allows OB practitioners to study issues systematically rather than rely solely on intuition. Although intuition is helpful in many managerial situations, used alone it can lead to serious error.

One reason for such potential error is that OB research findings are often counterintuitive. One of the best illustrations is the relationship between employee satisfaction and performance. Common sense and intuition suggest that satisfaction leads to good performance—meaning that happy employees produce more. However, as we see in chapter 5, the link between satisfaction and performance is far from direct. To safeguard against such errors, managers need to rely on a combination of the scientific method, experience, and intuition to make effective decisions.

Summary Point 1.1   **What Is OB and What Is Its Relationship to Other Fields of Study?**

- OB is the study of how people behave in organizations as individuals and as teams and how organizations structure their human resources (their employees and managers) to achieve company goals.
- OB has three levels of analysis: the individual or micro level, the group or middle level, and the organizational or macro level.
- OT, the study of organizational processes, provides a big picture perspective for managers.
- HRM deals with the procedural, technical, and legal aspects of managing the employees of an organization. This field helps managers recruit, train, and motivate employees.

- Strategic Management studies how top-level managers and executives set the general course for the business. This field helps managers set more effective goals for employees and understand the context in which their employees operate.
- Knowledge and information from psychology, sociology, anthropology, and political science all contribute to our understanding of OB.
- OB relies on the scientific process of observation, prediction, and measurement to learn about people and organizations.

The goal of OB is to understand people and organizations. Because this is a complex task, OB takes an interdisciplinary perspective that relies on contributions from the content and methods of a number of social science fields. These contributions provide OB with a rich, multilevel perspective that allows for a thorough analysis and understanding of managing people in organizations. Next we discuss the job of managers in today's organizations.

THE JOB OF A MANAGER

Organizations first used the concept of professional *managers*, people whose major role is to organize and supervise the activities of others, during the industrial revolution. Extensive research about the role of managers allows us to outline the traditional roles and functions of managers. Today, however, managers' jobs are undergoing tremendous change in response to business trends. In the sections that follow, we investigate traditional and current views of managers' tasks, roles, and skills. We also analyze trends that will affect the careers of future managers.

Managerial Functions and Roles: The Traditional View

According to the traditional view of management, managers have several formal functions, tasks, and roles to perform. We briefly examine these three items next.

Managerial Functions   As we see in Figure 1.3, the four principal functions or tasks of managers are to plan, organize, lead, and control so that employees can do the actual work. **Planning** is the process of setting goals and deciding how to allocate resources to achieve those goals. When Lou Gerstner became the CEO of IBM in 1993 he set a clear goal for the business: Rejuvenate the aging company.[9] IBM managers then set specific goals that supported Gerstner's goal. For instance, managerial goals included producing marketable mainframe systems with useful features and delivery targets that met customer needs. Gerstner then allocated resources to the departments based on their contribution to the overall company goal. Gerstner states: "Every single unit has clear goals. It has to grow as fast as its relevant competition . . . and when we are not a leader, we're withdrawing from those markets or not funding them the way we used to."[10]

Planning is a major part of Marc Brownstein's job at his Philadelphia advertising agency, but Brownstein doesn't want to plan alone. He meets biweekly with department managers and monthly with the entire staff to listen to their suggestions, plan the ad agency's activities, and decide how to allocate resources. He wants his employees "to get more involved in business."[11]

The second managerial function is to organize people. **Organizing** is the process of assigning tasks, establishing procedures, and setting deadlines to reach goals. Gerstner reorganized the structure of IBM to emphasize mainframes. He set specific deadlines for introduction of new products and assigned a mix of IBM veterans and outsiders to manage key divisions.[12] Brownstein took a different approach to organize his workforce. "I kept hearing we don't have enough structure. I wasn't sure I knew how to solve it."[13] After listening to what his employees wanted, he asked them to rewrite the employee manual to bring more organization and clarity to their tasks and procedures.

Leading is the third managerial function. It involves motivating and encouraging employees to perform their assigned work on schedule, helping them resolve conflict, and ensuring that they coordinate their efforts to achieve the organization's goals. Gerstner motivates IBM employees through a mix of focus, discipline, nurturing, mentoring, and conflict resolution.[14] Brownstein informs employees about the company's financial situation and motivates them by letting them make many of the decisions he used to make. For instance, employees vote on whether to take on a new client even though their vote sometimes means losing a potentially lucrative client.[15]

The final management function is controlling. **Controlling** is the process of monitoring, measuring, and evaluating employees' performance based on set goals. Gerstner sets high standards for managers and expects them to perform. He rewards them lavishly with bonuses when they meet their goals. In a year in which managers met most of their goals, for instance, Gerstner gave the managers the largest bonuses in the history of IBM.[16]

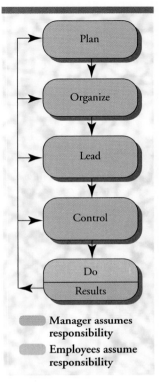

FIGURE 1.3
Traditional Managerial Functions

Planning
The process of setting goals and deciding on how to allocate resources to achieve those goals

Organizing
The process of assigning tasks, establishing procedures, and setting deadlines to reach the goals

Leading
Motivating and encouraging employees to perform work on schedule, helping to resolve conflict, and ensuring that employees coordinate efforts to achieve company goals

Controlling
The process of monitoring, measuring, and evaluating employees' performance based on the set goals

Controlling often leads to changing initial plans, adjusting organizational processes, or trying out new leadership methods. Brownstein changed his leadership methods when his managers told him that he did not give them enough feedback about their performance. He now listens more and gives managers greater decision-making power. The results have been impressive. The company is making more money than ever, the employees are happier, and turnover is down. David Hofrichter, vice president of a major human resource consulting firm, attributes much of the success to Marc Brownstein's management.[17]

Managerial Roles and Skills Managers assume a variety of roles when they perform their four basic functions. **Roles** are predetermined sets of behaviors, tasks, and actions that managers are expected to perform. Table 1.1 describes some of the most common roles managers perform on the job.

Interpersonal roles are those in which managers communicate with employees and peers. *Informational roles* focus on managers as the center of information for the organization. *Decisional roles* are those in which managers make decisions regarding people and resources. Because of work demands, managers often play multiple roles each day while they plan, lead, control, and organize. Managers, then, should become adept at performing all managerial roles and functions if they want to succeed.

To perform the managerial functions and roles well, managers must develop the three main skills summarized in Table 1.2. A **skill** is an acquired talent that a person develops related to a specific task. These three managerial skills are technical, human, and conceptual. **Technical skills** consist of the specialized know-how, the tools, and the methods needed to perform a certain task. For example, a marketing manager should have knowledge of marketing and sales methods and techniques. A manager of a department store must know how to open and close registers, enter sales, and keep track of inventory and employee hours. These are examples of technical skills necessary for managers to plan and organize the work of others.

Role
Predetermined set of behaviors, tasks, and actions that managers are expected to perform as they work

Skill
An acquired talent related to a task

Technical skill
The know-how to perform a certain task

T a b l e 1 . 1 MANAGERIAL ROLES

Managerial Role	Description of the Role
Interpersonal Roles	
Figurehead	Is the legal authority for the organization and performs ceremonial duties such as meeting with visitors
Leader	Motivates the employees to achieve the goals of the organization
Liaison	Acts as a link in the organization's communication chain, both horizontally and vertically
Informational Roles	
Nerve Center	Receives all types of information from every part of the organization
Disseminator	Sends specific information to people in the organization
Spokesperson	Sends specific information to people outside the organization
Decisional Roles	
Entrepreneur	Makes decisions about changes in the organization
Disturbance Handler	Resolves conflict
Resource Allocator	Decides on the amount of resources each unit will receive
Negotiator	Acts on behalf of the organization in any negotiations with outside parties such as suppliers

Source: Adapted from Henry Mintzberg, *The Nature of Managerial Work* (New York: HarperCollins, 1973), 54–94.

Table 1.2   MANAGERIAL SKILLS

Managerial Skills	Description
• Technical Skills	Technical know-how to perform a task; knowledge of job-related methods and procedures
• Human Skills	Know-how to work with and through others and to manage another's performance
• Conceptual Skills	Know-how to analyze different situations and to solve problems

Human skills involve the know-how to work with and through others to achieve results. Managers use these skills to manage conflict, motivate, provide feedback, and correct the actions of employees. Furthermore, as shown previously in Table 1.1, managers act as a liaison or negotiator with internal and external groups. These two roles also require mastery of human skills. The skills are most relevant to managers' controlling and organizing functions. However, managers spend the majority of their time working with others, so developing and refining human skills are key to managers' on-the-job success.

Conceptual skills relate to problem solving and learning. Being able to understand various situations and problems that organizations face, and plan and implement solutions require conceptual skills. Managers apply these skills when they assist with strategic planning or help develop a human resource plan to ensure that the organization can attract and retain well-qualified employees.

Managers must have technical, human, and conceptual skills to perform their jobs. Traditionally, as managers moved up through the organization, they needed more conceptual skills and fewer technical skills. For instance, no one expects Phil Condit, CEO of Boeing, to have the technical skills to weld an airplane wing. Instead, the organization relies on his knowledge and expertise in strategic management.[18]

Today's organizations increasingly require their managers at all levels to use more conceptual skills. Furthermore, high-level managers who traditionally only supervised the work of others are now required to contribute through actual work. Why have such changes occurred? External pressures from global competition and internal changes in organizations have forced managers to do more with less, to continually learn new skills, to delegate more tasks, and to encourage employees to work smarter rather than simply harder. As a result, the roles and functions of managers are expanding and are no longer clear-cut.

Human skills
The ability to work with and through others to achieve results

Conceptual skills
The ability to analyze various situations, solve problems, and learn

---

Summary Point 1.2   What Are Traditional Managerial Functions, Roles, and Skills?

- Planning, organizing, leading, and controlling are the four main managerial functions.
- Three key types of roles that managers play include interpersonal, informational, and decisional roles.
- Managers need technical, human, and conceptual skills to perform their functions and roles.

Changes in the Roles and Functions of Managers

In response to the complexity of the world they face, the traditional roles and functions of managers are changing.[19] Consider the fact that 20 years ago, a textbook in management would not have been considered complete without a discussion of the concept of "motivation to manage."[20] According to this concept, successful managers needed to be competitive, in charge, and willing to dominate others. OB practices have certainly changed.

Rethinking Managerial Functions   Look back at Figure 1.3 and the four traditional managerial functions it presents. To plan, organize, lead, control, and have complete accountability for results, managers do need to be in full control and have a strong desire to be in charge of others. Now take a look at Figure 1.4. It presents the current view of managerial functions. The central role for managers is to provide leadership and direction.[21] Managers and employees now share the responsibility for the other traditional managerial functions.

In addition to their supervisory functions, many managers produce goods and services. For example, managers may handle several clients or help design a product or provide a service. At Southwest Airlines, managers perform any function necessary to serve the customer. If a baggage handler is overloaded with work, the manager chips in and loads the baggage into the planes. Even Southwest's president, Herb Kelleher, has been known to load luggage on busy days. Perhaps the flexibility Southwest expects of its managers contributes to the company's ranking as number one among *Fortune* magazine's top 100 companies to work for in America.[22]

In some businesses, teams of employees also handle the controlling and monitoring functions, which for years were the exclusive domain of management. The teams monitor their own progress and take corrective action as needed. For example, many organizations use **Total Quality Management** (TQM), a management concept popularized by W. Edwards Deming of the United States that focuses on customer satisfaction through continuous improvement of business processes. **Continuous improvement** is a practice in which everyone engages in activities needed to improve the quality of products or services on an ongoing basis. In effect, managing quality becomes everyone's job, not just the managers'.

Ford has relied on TQM to produce its Taurus line of cars in the United States.[23] At Ford, teams of managers, engineers, suppliers, and assembly line workers design and build cars. Every single process involved in building a car—from design to testing to manufacturing—is continuously reviewed and improved. The teams perform the traditional managerial roles of planning, organizing, and controlling. The result? The Ford Taurus has been one of the best-selling sedans in the United States.

We've seen that managers and employees now share traditional managerial functions. Next, we discuss the new roles for managers.

New Roles for Managers   The changes in how we view and define the functions of a manager have also changed the roles managers play. One of the key changes is a new role that man-

Total Quality Management (TQM)
A management concept that focuses on customer satisfaction through continuous improvement of business processes

Continuous improvement
A practice in which everyone engages in activities needed to improve the quality of products or services on an ongoing basis

FIGURE 1.4
Changing Managerial Functions

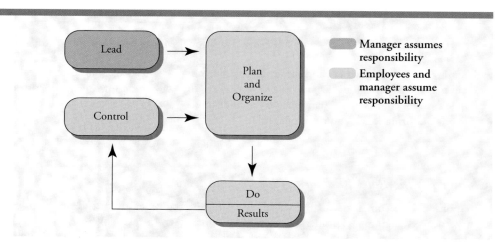

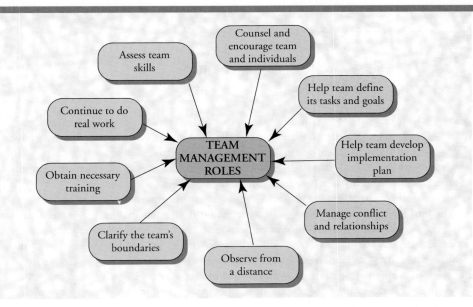

FIGURE 1.5
Team Managerial Roles

agers must perform—that of team manager or facilitator. A **team manager/facilitator** is a team member who helps the team move forward but is not single-handedly responsible for the team's results. All team members share that accountability. With increased use of teams in organizations, managers are more and more required to be facilitators for their teams. As a result, managers must understand the different challenges that managing teams poses because team behavior differs from individual behavior. Figure 1.5 outlines the team management roles.

The new role of team leader is closely associated with that of resource provider and negotiator. One of the primary functions of a team leader is to assure that team members have the resources, technology, and training they need to do their jobs. Obtaining these resources requires skillful negotiations inside and outside the organization.

Team manager/facilitator
A team member who is responsible for helping the team move forward but is not single-handedly responsible for the outcome

New Skills for Today's Managers   The new skills managers must master to succeed in today's organizations are managing change, managing one's career, managing diverse relationships, and delegation and empowerment, as we see in Table 1.3. We briefly discuss each of the new skills next.

T a b l e 1 . 3   NEW MANAGERIAL SKILLS

New Managerial Skills	Description
Managing change	Ability to recognize and adapt to new trends
Managing one's career	Ability to take responsibility for one's career by taking advantage of training and education and by thinking creatively about career track
Managing diverse relationships	Ability to successfully guide and control diverse professional and personal relationships within and outside the organization
Delegation and empowerment	Ability to assign tasks and to delegate the responsibility and authority for the tasks to employees and team members

Team Challenge

ORGANIZATIONS LOOK FOR TEAM LEADERS IN MANY WAYS

T raditionally, U.S. organizations have looked for employees with strong academic credentials, who demonstrate a potential for learning and success, and who have a combination of individual traits that indicate their ability to perform well. These characteristics are still important. However, as organizations move away from traditional structures, managers must also demonstrate their potential for teamwork.

Rosembluth International, a Philadelphia-based travel management company, seeks employees who are nice, can get along with others, and have good manners. They test their potential executives' niceness and ability to work in teams by sending them to repair fences or drive cattle in their North Dakota ranch. Worthington Industries, a steel processor in Ohio, also focuses on a potential employee's teamwork. People are placed in teams for a probationary period. When that period ends, co-workers vote to keep or oust the new team member.[a]

As future managers develop various skills, they must complement their technical and conceptual skills with the human skills required in working well with others and in facilitating teams.

a. J. Martin, "So You Want to Work for the Best . . . ," *Fortune* 137, no. 1 (1998): 77–78.

Change is a constant in organizations worldwide. Managers, then, must be able to *manage change*—that is, be able to recognize and adapt to new trends. Today's managers need to analyze business, social, cultural, and political trends; understand their implications for the organization; and adapt to them. The ability to manage change is a complex, difficult skill to master. It's worth the effort, though, if you want to seize opportunities in today's fast-paced business environment.

To illustrate this point, consider Dell Computer. A few years ago, even though most PC manufacturers sold their products through retail outlets such as CompUSA, Dell decided to sell its PCs directly to consumers via the telephone. Customers could call Dell and custom order the exact computer they wanted. Dell then built the product to order and mailed it to the customer. Then came the Internet. CEO Michael Dell spotted the possibilities immediately: Dell could transfer the build-to-order strategy to the Internet. Dell had a Web page and staff handling Internet computer orders when its competitors were still trying to figure out how to use the Internet to market products. As a result of Dell's ability to implement change quickly, the company reaped Internet sales revenues of $1 million a day in 1997 and grew twice as fast as its nearest competitor, Compaq.[24] Dell's ability to recognize the need for change and take advantage of new technology has made the company highly successful.

Along with the ability to manage change, businesspeople must *manage their careers* through creative career planning and by actively seeking training, education, and new learning opportunities. Why is career management an important new managerial skill? The traditional vertical career ladder is becoming increasingly rare. Few organizations promise their employees and managers stable, long-term employment these days. In the past, AT&T always prided itself in providing lifetime employment. Today, AT&T tries to enhance its workers' employability, but employees assume responsibility for managing their own careers.

Bill Applegate, the CEO of AG Communication, a telecommunication company, bluntly states that his organization cannot guarantee anyone a job. However, he promises that AG employees will maintain high technical competence that will make it easier for them to find new jobs.

Managing careers is now each employee's responsibility. However, many businesses try to keep their employees "employable" by regularly updating their skills. Some also go one step further and help employees who lose their jobs because of the fast-changing business environment. For example, recently, AT&T, Du Pont, Johnson & Johnson, GTE, TRW, Lucent Technologies, and several other companies formed the nonprofit Talent Alliance, an organization designed to help employees plot their careers.[25] The Alliance's goals include helping employees find continuous employment but not necessarily with the same company. It offers career counseling, job bulletin boards, a Web site, and chat rooms designed to help employees find jobs that match their skills and interests. Employees are matched with training and education programs available through Alliance member companies and through various universities. John McMorrow, who heads the Alliance, believes that the organization's unique and unprecedented collaborative effort among many companies provides employees with timely, real, and relevant information about jobs.

As we see later in the text, changes in organizations can provide opportunities for creative employees to craft their own career path. In fact, many organizations view **knowledge workers**—employees whose greatest value to the business is their expertise and knowledge—as critical company assets.[26] Such workers have advanced technical skills, creativity, a desire for autonomy, and self-motivation; they recognize that they must actively manage their own careers.

Knowledge workers
Employees whose value for the organization is their expertise and knowledge

Another important skill for future managers is the capability to establish and manage strong relationships with people inside and outside the organization. The skill of *managing relationships* is the ability to guide and control personal and work relationships effectively. Today's managers not only supervise their employees, they are also in constant interaction with their external customers, suppliers, and many other outsiders. The organization may also expect them to take active roles in their communities as members of charitable, civic, or busi-

John McMorrow heads the Talent Alliance, a nonprofit organization that helps employees retrain and retool so they can have continuous employment, though not with the same company.

ness organizations. This active management of relationships puts particular emphasis on developing human skills to manage internal and external relationships. As a result, all employees, not only those who are managers, need to have good human skills.

The last new skill required of managers is the ability to delegate tasks and empower employees and team members. *Delegation* refers to assigning various tasks to employees. **Empowerment** goes one step further. The manager turns over the responsibility and *authority* to complete the task. The manager therefore empowers—that is, gives power to—an employee to be in charge of the job.

For example, the purchasing department at Aetna Inc., the Hartford-based health care company, empowered its clerical workers to make many decisions previously made by managers. Purchasing clerks were trained to become purchasing consultants who could serve as advisers and problem solvers to other employees and to outside vendors. The results were considerable cost cutting and a striking 88 percent reduction in the purchasing staff.[27] This type of change requires that managers move beyond the traditional functions and roles and improve their delegation and empowerment skills.

Because of many changes in organizations and the job of managers, if you plan to manage others, a specialization such as majoring in accounting will only help you get your first job. Once managers are on the job, organizations expect them to learn new skills, rethink their careers, and adapt to new requirements and situations quickly. Though the many changes in managers' jobs may be stressful, the opportunities for learning and growth are an exciting part of today's dynamic business careers.

Empowerment
The process of giving power to others

CAREER ADVICE
from the Experts

TAKING ADVANTAGE OF THE REBIRTH OF MIDDLE MANAGEMENT

During the 1990s, many companies laid off thousands of workers. In 1997 alone, companies such as Kodak, Boeing, and GM reduced their workforce by more than 35,000 employees. Middle managers were often the victims of these layoffs. The cuts went too deep, and the trend has reversed. Organizations are now desperate to hire middle managers. Even with increased demand and limited supply, companies look for particular characteristics in their new managers. What follows are some tips that may help you join the ranks of the much-wanted new middle managers.

- Focus on developing your leadership knowledge and skills through education, training, and reading.
- Build and maintain professional relationships.
- Build and maintain communication skills.
- Become an expert at project and team management.
- Keep up with your education and your computer skills.

Sources: G. Colvin, "Revenge of the Nerds," *Fortune* 137, no. 4 (1998): 223–224; see also N. Munk, "The New Organization Man," *Fortune* 137, no. 5 (1998): 63–74.

Summary Point 1.3   **What Are the New Functions, Roles, and Skills for Managers?**

- New managerial functions focus on sharing traditional functions with employees and team members.
- A new managerial role is that of team manager and facilitator.

- New management skills include change, career, and relationship management; delegation; and empowerment.

Global and internal pressures have forced organizations to change their views of managerial functions, roles, and skills. These changes are some of the most distinct features of today's complex organizations. Before we consider the challenges that today's organizations face, we discuss how organizations function as systems.

ORGANIZATIONS AS SYSTEMS AND THE CONTINGENCY APPROACH

The concepts that you read in this text, whether the latest trends or "golden oldies," are guided by common assumptions of modern management. These assumptions are rooted in the history of the field (see Appendix 1) and continue to influence how we think about management. Two essential concepts in our study and understanding of organizations are open systems and the contingency approach. We explore these two topics next.

Definition of Open Systems

Open systems are complex systems made up of interrelated parts that continuously interact with one another and with their external environment. Such systems include inputs, processes, and outputs. *Inputs* are all the resources that enter the organization. These include people, capital, and materials. Open systems take inputs from their environment and transform them through various processes. *Processes* are all the activities that use and change the inputs in some way. They include all the tools, actions, and knowledge applied to transform inputs to manufactured products or to deliver services. Through processes, organizations transform their inputs into outputs. *Outputs* are all the products and services that an organization gives its customers. Figure 1.6 depicts an open system.

The concept that "the whole is greater than the sum of the parts" is an integral part of the open systems view of organizations. That view assumes that the organization consists of more than individual parts; it also consists of relationships and interactions among the parts.[28]

Open systems
Complex systems made up of interrelated parts that continuously interact with one another and with their external environment

---

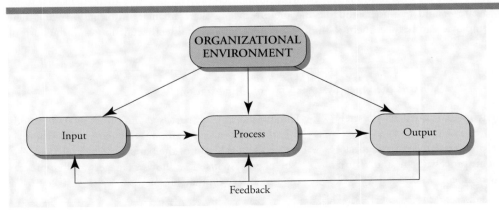

FIGURE 1.6
The Open System

Understanding any one part is necessary, then, but not sufficient for understanding the system. For example, understanding several individual employees' work styles is necessary but not sufficient to assess whether they will make an effective team. For a full picture, we must consider the relationships among the employees when working on the team.

All organizations are open systems that interact with their environment. The environment can limit the inputs that an organization receives, change the processes used, and reject the outputs. As outputs are rejected, they, in turn, impact inputs and processes, as we see in Figure 1.6. For example, if consumers find the products of an organization to be unsafe, they will not buy them and may even boycott the company. The decrease in sales and negative publicity affect whether the company can obtain future funding or attract high-quality employees. Furthermore, the company is likely to change its products and the way they are produced and marketed. In this example we see how the environment can affect all elements of the organization.

The open systems view is a comprehensive one that requires an internal and external focus. Starbucks is a business that changes as it interacts with its environment. For instance, when Starbucks expanded to Canada, it had to offer salaries comparable to its competition because of union activity.[29]

Why Open Systems?

The open systems model assumes an active relationship between the organization and its environment, as well as a complex set of relationships among the various parts of the organization. However, it is difficult to look at all the parts of the system at once. In this book, for example, we will look at various parts of organizational systems in turn, not at the whole system, to foster learning. Similarly, most managers and employees do not think of organizations as open systems on a day-to-day basis. However, if you keep in mind that organizations are open systems, you can manage and work more effectively.

Employees and managers at all levels need to consider a system view. At the upper level of organizations, one of the main jobs of chief executive officers (CEOs) and other top managers is to set the strategic direction of an organization. To do so, they need to assess and understand the environment and the internal processes of their organization. Thus, they always need to take a system view.[30] Middle and lower-level managers can similarly make better decisions by looking at the big picture. For example, if a manager takes a simple view of a poorly performing employee and labels her lazy and unmotivated, he will ignore many factors that affect her performance. By using a systems approach, the manager would consider the employee's personality, her hostile co-workers, poor leadership, fear of layoffs, a particularly rude customer, lack of training, and a number of other complex personal and organizational factors. This approach would take into account the employee and the processes that affect her output. Thus, the manager using the systems approach is likely to make a better decision about this employee.

Today's organizations are requiring all their employees, not only their managers, to be aware of and to understand the big picture. Many share financial information with their employees and expect them to understand how their work directly contributes to the bottom

---

Summary Point 1.4   **What Is the Open Systems View of Organizations?**

- Organizations are open systems that interact with their environment.
- Open systems are made up of interrelated parts that take inputs from the environment, process them, and return them as outputs to the environment.

- Understanding each part is as important as understanding the relationships among the parts (the whole is greater than the sum of the parts).
- The open systems view allows managers and employees to keep an eye on the "big picture."

line. Medtronics, a medical-products organization in Minneapolis, provides its employees with an open systems view by inviting patients and others whose lives were saved by Medtronics products to its annual meeting. The patients' stories demonstrate to employees how the products they invent and produce save lives and thereby provide employees with a broad view of the importance of their work.[31]

Contingency View

In the early days of scientific management and during the human relations movement of the middle part of the twentieth century, theories of management and organizations focused on providing managers with the one right answer. During the scientific management era, this answer was a control and command management style that focused on standardization of all tasks. Later, the human relations movement focused on giving employees opportunities for self-actualization and growth. In both cases, the approach to management was to find universal truths and provide managers with "golden rules" that they could apply to all situations.

As organizations and their environments have become more complex, the solutions proposed by both approaches appear overly simplistic. There are few golden rules that apply in all situations. Each employee is different, as is each business problem. In addition, golden rules for one culture may not apply to another. What works in the United States may not work in Mexico, Japan, or Singapore.

As a result of the awareness of the complexity of organizations, individuals, and cultures, modern management is guided by the concept of contingency.[32] The **contingency approach** suggests that what works depends, or is contingent, on the situation. The contingency view further recognizes that people's behaviors change so employees can learn new skills and behaviors. For example, the command and control management style of the scientific management era may work better with unskilled workers than with educated professionals. Money may motivate some people more effectively than others, depending on their career stage and financial needs. In some cultures, authoritarian leadership is more appropriate whereas in others, leaders are expected to consult with their followers before making decisions.

Because each situation requires different responses, managers must learn to understand the various contingency factors of each situation so they can respond appropriately. Compared to earlier management approaches that offered clear but overly simplistic answers, the contingency approach provides a complex and more realistic view of people and organizations.

The contingency approach is compatible with the open systems approach because it encourages managers to consider the many factors that affect behavior in organizations. Also, the contingency view allows for better decision making just as the open systems approach does. In contrast to the open systems view, however, many practitioners use the contingency approach on a daily basis. Managers can consider several factors in a situation more easily than they can consider all elements of a system at all times.

The contingency view of organizations strongly dominates our current views of people and organizations. We see its influence in all the individual, team, and organizational processes covered in this text. We next consider the major challenges that organizations and their managers face.

Hot ▼ Link

For more detail on the history of these OB theories, see Appendix 1.

Contingency approach
A view of management suggesting that what works depends, or is contingent, on the situation

---

Summary Point 1.5   What Is the Contingency View of Organizations?

The contingency view recognizes the following points:

- People and organizations are complex.
- What works depends on the situation.

- Understanding situations and people is central to effective management.

▮ CHALLENGES FOR TODAY'S ORGANIZATIONS

Pick up a newspaper, cruise the Internet, or listen to the radio. Chances are that you will learn about myriad changes in business. Though the specifics may seem like a quagmire, several key themes emerge. In the next section we examine the four key challenges that organizations face, as shown in Figure 1.7: globalization and cultural diversity, the rapid pace of change, customer demands for quality and efficiency, and multiple stakeholders. We also explore how organizations respond to these four challenges.

Managing Globalization and Culture

Globalization
The interconnectedness of people and organizations around the world

A factor that makes managing a more rigorous, complex task is globalization. **Globalization** refers to the interconnectedness of people and organizations around the world. All sizes of organizations face the challenges of operating in a fast-changing world and a global economy. The manager of an agricultural products company in the American Midwest needs to monitor political upheavals in India, Russia, or China where some major suppliers and customers are located. Political events affect the flow of supplies and products and can increase or decrease prices. Similarly, a small air-conditioner manufacturer in Mexico with clients from the Middle East will be affected by events in that part of the world. If you work in clothing manufacturing, you are likely to use laborers in developing countries, so you must monitor the political climate and changing labor laws in those countries.

Large corporations such as GM, IBM, and Boeing have seen their profits and market shares threatened by foreign competitors that manufacture cheaper, higher-quality, and more innovative products. For instance, Boeing dominated the airplane industry for decades, holding a 90 percent market share with its successful products, such as Boeing 737 and 747 airplanes. However, in the mid-1970s it started losing market share to Airbus, a consortium of French, British, and other European companies with financial backing from their governments. Because of the Airbus, Boeing's market share has declined to around 50 percent of world markets.[33]

Globalization has many direct and indirect effects on businesses. As a result of shrinking domestic markets and considerable growth of other countries' economies, U.S. corporations and others around the world look outside their borders to expand their markets.[34] In 1991, the international sales figures for U.S. multinational corporations were $1.2 trillion, accounting for 29 percent of the companies' revenues.[35] Twenty years ago, the world's volume of trade—the total dollar amount of all imports and exports around the world—was about $2 trillion. Now it has surpassed $7 trillion per year.[36]

As the per capita income of many nations rises, opportunities for trade increase. Countries such as India, China, Indonesia, Singapore, Brazil, and South Africa are experienc-

FIGURE 1.7
Four Challenges Facing Today's Organizations

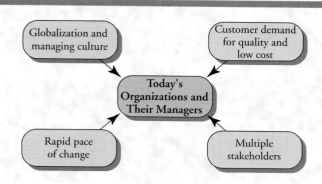

ing considerable economic growth and are expanding their trade worldwide. In addition, many governments now view trade as a means of raising the living standards of their populations, so they lower trade barriers. A *trade barrier* is any tax, tariff, or restriction imposed by a government on import of foreign goods and services.

Though the world is becoming more interconnected, cultural, political, or religious obstacles can prevent easy interaction. For example, to control the flow of information, China does not allow satellite dish imports and Turkey prohibits cell phones. Because of high standards of health and safety, Denmark restricts agricultural imports. For religious reasons, Saudi Arabia bans the import and sale of alcoholic beverages. To overcome such obstacles, companies and nations rely on international agreements that specify guidelines to manage globalization.

International Cooperation and Trade Agreements To manage the globalization process more effectively, countries are signing agreements aimed at reducing tariffs (taxes on imports), subsidies, quotas, and other obstacles to business interaction and cooperation. One of the most significant and highly publicized international agreements affecting the United States and its neighbors is the North American Free Trade Agreement (NAFTA) signed by Canada, Mexico, and the United States in 1993. NAFTA removed trade barriers among the three countries and allowed the free movement of goods and services. Negotiations for linking all American countries through a similar agreement are scheduled to continue well into the beginning of the twenty-first century.

The European Union (EU), created in 1992, is another example of international cooperation aimed at increased interaction and free trade. The EU already has in place a European government staffed by appointed and elected officials from all member countries. The EU passport has replaced individual country passports, and work on a common European currency, called the Euro, continues with the EU appointing Dutchman Wim Duisenberg to run the European Central Bank.[37] The 15 member countries are Austria, Belgium, Denmark, Finland, France, Germany, Great Britain, Greece, Ireland, Italy, Luxembourg, the Netherlands, Portugal, Spain, and Sweden. Combined, these countries include close to 320 million people.

Other countries have forged similar agreements to promote interaction and trade. ASEAN (Association of Southeast Asian Nations) is an agreement made in 1992 between Singapore, the Philippines, Malaysia, Thailand, Brunei, and Indonesia. It aspires to promote

The European Union is one of the most publicized international cooperative agreements in the world. Blending the interests and cultures of all members is often a difficult balancing act where there is much at stake.

free trade among the member countries. The trade agreements and transnational and regional unions help businesses function in a global environment. As a manager in any part of the world, your success depends on your awareness of the cultural issues that arise in this global environment.

Learning to operate in a global market is one of the major challenges that managers face. Being successful on a global scale requires many skills. Managers have to understand international trade issues, the political environments, the social problems, and the cultural values of different countries.

A QUESTION OF ETHICS

Ethics and Globalization

Companies face considerable challenges in going global. Although moving manufacturing operations overseas saves costs and allows companies to keep prices low, organizations also face criticism. First, some people believe that firms should not export jobs to other countries. Second, many countries that offer cheaper labor have less restrictive labor, environmental, and safety standards than the home country. Particularly, critics have accused businesses such as Nike and WalMart of using child labor to manufacture products. How can managers balance the need for globalization with the ethical challenges they face abroad? What ethical guidelines should they follow?

Managing Culture As people move around the world and companies step outside their national borders, managers now supervise employees who are not like them. They have to learn to adapt and change their managerial practices to fit other cultures. For example, U.S. managers operating in China must change many behaviors and practices to adapt to the Chinese cultural and political values. They do so by paying attention to relationship building and maintaining appropriate protocol, two factors that are more important in China than they are in the United States. Similarly, successful European managers moving from one country to another even within the European Union have learned to adjust their styles and expectations to match the culture of their host countries. Italians adjust to the formal German style, Swedes moderate their need for team decision making and consensus building when working with the French, and so forth.

Companies that can take advantage of the massive world market have a better chance for success. Managers, then, should actively seek international opportunities and develop an understanding of the cultural challenges they may face. McDonald's has succeeded in the global marketplace in part because of its managers' cultural understanding.[38] As the U.S. fast-food market has become saturated by fierce competition, McDonald's has franchised its fast-food operations all over the world. For instance, its Moscow restaurant serves more than 50,000 customers a day and is the busiest in the world.[39] McDonald's also opened stores in India—a predominantly vegetarian country where many consider cows to be sacred animals. The Indian burgers are made of vegetable products or lamb, not beef. In India, you can order a "Maharaja-Mac" that meets the religious standards and taste preferences of a predominantly vegetarian nation. Again in response to cultural values, McDonald's in Saudi Arabia has two dining halls, one for men and one for women and children. "Wine with your Big Mac, Madame?" *"Oui!"* if you are in a McDonald's restaurant in France.

Cultural adaptations such as those made by McDonald's are essential for success in the global economy. Organizations that lack understanding of cultural differences often face trouble. Mitsubishi, for instance, attracted considerable negative publicity in the United States because of accusations of cultural insensitivity and sexual harassment. Experts claimed that Mitsubishi was unable to attract top local talent in its foreign operations, particularly in the United States, because of such sexual harassment complaints and lawsuits.[40]

MANAGERIAL ADVICE
from the Experts

MANAGING ACROSS CULTURES 101

Today's managers can expect to work with individuals from different cultures either in their own country or when sent on foreign assignments. Thorough preparation should be the goal. However, you can reduce the potential for conflict by following some basic rules:

- Do not assume anything! People's actions and words that appear simple and familiar may have considerably different meanings in different cultures.
- Listen very carefully to verbal messages and pay attention to nonverbal cues.
- Accept responsibility for effective interaction. Be proactive in addressing issues and solving problems.
- Ask questions. Check your understanding and ask for help from people who know the culture.
- Expect misunderstandings, mistakes, and conflicts. Deal with them patiently and use them as learning opportunities without blaming others.

Sources: L. H. Chaney and J. S. Martin, *Intercultural Business Communication* (Englewood Cliffs, NJ: Prentice Hall, 1995); C. Rodrigues, *International Management: A Cultural Approach* (Minneapolis/St. Paul, MN: West, 1996), 265–345.

Another aspect of managing culture is dealing with diverse cultures within a country. **Cultural diversity** refers to differences due to individual and group factors such as ethnicity, religion, gender, age, physical attributes, sexual orientation, regional differences, functional specialization, and so forth. We consider the challenge of managing other cultures in detail in chapter 3.

Cultural diversity
Differences due to individual and group factors such as ethnicity, religion, gender, age, physical attributes, sexual orientation, regional differences, and so forth

Rapid Pace of Change

The Boeing example used earlier illustrates not only the impact of globalization but also the rapid pace of change in today's business. In the span of a few years, that company went from dominating the market with a 90 percent share to a position of equality with Airbus with only a 50 percent share. To regain market share, Boeing has redesigned its planes, introduced more economical models, and is changing its internal structure to become more efficient.[41] It also merged with McDonnell Douglas, its major U.S. competitor, to produce some planes jointly. Boeing felt that it could not by itself continue to compete successfully with Airbus.[42] The European monetary unification, the potential protectionism of EU nations, and the increasing rate of technological change in the airframe industry created a fast-changing environment, challenging the managers of Boeing to keep pace.

Technology is one factor that changes at an extremely fast rate. Consider the changes in information technology. Developments in computer hardware and software allow business to manufacture products and deliver services faster than ever before. These changes raise our expectations of employees, suppliers, and others who affect the business.

Technological changes have also triggered an explosion of widely available information. Satellite technology, cell phones, the Internet, pagers, and fax machines generate a worldwide market for information. Such technology creates a fast-changing environment. With Motorola's Iridium system of 66 satellites orbiting the earth, cell phones will be able to connect managers any time, anywhere. Another technological marvel is the advent of *Rapid Prototyping (RP)*.[43] These desktop manufacturing machines turn computer-generated designs of products into an actual prototype. We discuss RPs and other technological changes and their effect on organizations in detail in the next chapter.

Other changes that affect business are political changes around the world. On the one hand, the fall of communism has given rise to many new democracies with considerable opportunity for social renewal and business growth. For instance, the former East Germany's entire industrial structure needs to be rebuilt. On the other hand, the spread of the fundamentalist Islamic movement, which started in Iran in 1978, has affected many countries such as Afghanistan, Sudan, Algeria, and other predominantly Moslem nations and threatened the flow of oil and the profits of major oil companies. The movement has also caused internal strife and unrest in countries such as France and Germany that rely on imported workers from Muslim countries.

Managing the many changes that are happening around the world is another challenge that today's organizations and their managers face. If well managed, change can be turned into opportunities for growth; if ignored or poorly guided, change can have devastating effects on any organization.

Quality and Efficiency

Because of competition and increased access to information, businesses can succeed only if they are responsive to customers' needs. Managers must constantly evaluate how to respond well to consumers who demand better quality products and lower prices. The challenge to deliver quality at a lower cost has forced organizations around the world to seek ways to cut costs and become more efficient.

Efficiency is defined as the most economical method to produce a good or service, using the least amount of resources. The need for quality and efficiency is a driving force in all industries because of consumer demands and global competition. These two factors are forcing businesses to find ways to do more with less. Any organization today that fails to provide a quality product at a reasonable price will be challenged, often from across the globe, as illustrated by the banking industry in the United States. Bank of America for decades was the number one bank in the world. However, in the 1980s it failed to provide its customers with valuable products at low cost. Soon, Japanese, European, and other U.S. banks such as Citicorp and Chase displaced Bank of America from the top spot, relegating it to number 19 in the world.[44] Even in Los Angeles, the home turf of Bank of America, Japanese banks such as Sumitomo have built grand office buildings and are providing worldwide banking services to California customers.

Multiple Stakeholders: Ethics and Social Responsibility

The last challenge that organizations face creates an interesting dilemma. Although businesses must respond to the global challenge, manage change, and deliver better quality more efficiently at lower cost, they also have to remain responsive to external and internal stakeholders. **Stakeholders** are individuals and groups who have some interest or stake in the organization.

The stakeholders of a publicly held corporation include its shareholders, employees and managers, suppliers, customers, and the local community. All have a stake in what the organization does and how well it does it. However, what may be in the best interest of one group of stakeholders may hurt another group. For instance, a firm that faces bankruptcy often must act by closing unprofitable operations. Shareholders may then benefit if the company cuts its labor costs by laying off employees. However, the employees, their families, and even the local community will be hurt. If the business doesn't take drastic action, it may fail and hurt all stake-

Stakeholders
Individuals and groups who have some interest or stake in the organization

holders. To balance the needs of multiple stakeholders while running a successful enterprise, managers must analyze the implications of business decisions and often make tough choices.

Today, more than ever, businesses are required to behave in accordance with both legal and ethical standards. Ethical standards are the principles of morally acceptable behavior—what is right and correct regardless of legal definition. For example, although it may be legal in some countries to provide gifts to customers or suppliers to secure business, many U.S. and Canadian companies have ethical codes that forbid such actions.

In addition to ethical conduct, multiple stakeholders often demand that businesses behave in socially responsible ways. Social responsibility requires that an organization consider its responsibility to all local and global stakeholders when making business decisions. For example, U.S. tobacco companies have consistently satisfied their shareholders with good financial returns. However, they have been accused of being socially irresponsible by marketing and selling a product associated with numerous health problems. Managers make decisions every day that have implications for society, and now more than ever they are held to a high standard of ethics and of social responsibility.

The four major challenges just described are interrelated. Although some businesses may be affected by one more than others, it is difficult to separate them. For instance, an organization that responds to global challenges and opens a new plant outside its national boundaries must adapt its management practices to the new culture. It also needs to devise new ways to maintain quality and remain efficient while it also may face ethical challenges in another part of the world.

Summary Point 1.6   What Are Four Challenges That Businesses Face?

- Increased globalization
- The rapid pace of change

- Customer demands for high quality at low cost
- Balancing the needs of multiple stakeholders

How Organizations Are Responding

In response to global competition, fast-paced change, the demand for high quality at low cost, and stakeholder needs, organizations are changing the way they operate. Although the changes in large corporations such as GM, IBM, and AT&T are most publicized, all large and small organizations are changing.[45] Managers test new management methods, put in place new human resource (HR) policies and structures, implement new production methods, and explore new markets. We provide many examples of these practices throughout the text. Next, we examine the organizational responses to these four challenges, as shown in Figure 1.8.

Going Global and Managing Culture   To respond to the challenge of globalization, organizations are expanding their markets and operations to all parts of the world and establishing partnerships with others in different countries. For example, since the early 1980s, hundreds of U.S. businesses have opened operations in China. Thousands of others have expanded to Eastern European countries. Though many such ventures are risky and some have failed, others are thriving and providing major opportunities for growth for U.S. organizations.

Another common response to global competition has been for organizations to become more diverse internally and train managers to handle cultural differences effectively. Companies with operations abroad hire managers from host countries. These managers bring knowledge of the general and business cultures and social and political issues. Firms also provide cultural sensitivity training to their employees to make them aware of internal cultural differences and to

FIGURE 1.8
Organizational Responses to the Four Challenges

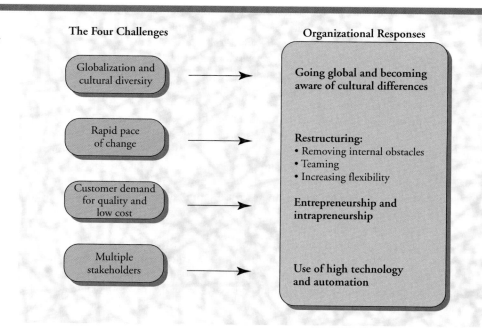

become more effective in managing across cultures. Internally, many organizations are handling cultural diversity through training and the implementation of new policies.

For example, Eli Lilly, a major drug manufacturer in the United States, has changed its HR practices to manage and take advantage of the cultural diversity of its employees and managers. It offers progressive benefit packages, including a generous leave policy for new parents, child-care benefits, time off for taking care of family members—both children and elderly parents—and benefits for spouses and partners. Randall Tobias, the CEO of Eli Lilly, believes that although these HR policies are expensive, they are essential because they address the needs of the company's diverse workforce and build loyalty that leads to higher productivity.[46]

Restructuring   To face the global, quality, and efficiency challenges, many organizations have restructured.[47] **Restructuring** refers to changing the way the human resources of an organization are organized. For example, an organization may break up several departments and create new ones. It may close old offices or add new divisions, resulting in the reshuffling of people and the tasks that they perform (more about structure in chapter 2). *Delayering, right-sizing, downsizing* are all terms that organizations use to describe their restructuring efforts. The goals of restructuring are increased flexibility, quicker response to external changes, and more fluid structures that combine jobs and tasks to create more challenge for individual employees.

In many cases, structural changes start with the process of **reengineering**, a practice of redesigning an organization around basic processes to become more effective and more efficient.[48] A major guiding theme is to break down barriers that prevent people from doing their jobs and to make the organization more efficient and more effective. To that end, organizations are using teams made up of employees and managers from different areas. We discuss the use of teams in today's organizations in more detail in chapters 2 and 8.

In spite of some success, restructuring often leads to massive layoffs.[49] IBM laid off 60,000 employees in 1993; GM, 74,000 in 1991; Sears, 50,000 in 1993; and AT&T, 40,000 in 1995 and another 40,000 in 1997.[50] Even Japanese firms that traditionally have prided themselves in never laying off employees have started to restructure and lay off their workers. Although restructuring is essential for businesses to maintain their competitiveness, layoffs are

Restructuring
Changing the way the human resources of an organization are organized

Reengineering
Redesigning an organization around basic processes to become more effective and more efficient

not. Managers can often find a better solution than laying off valued employees. Consider the case of 3M, which in 1996 restructured and eliminated 7,000 positions, but laid off only 100 employees.[51] The others were absorbed throughout the organization.

Layoffs have drastic effects on those who are retained as well as those who leave. The remaining employees face increased workloads, survivor guilt, and the stress and anxiety that come from broken trust and from waiting for the next wave of layoffs to hit. Needless to say, morale, job satisfaction, productivity, and quality all can suffer.

Many organizations replace laid-off employees with temporary workers or outside contractors. The process of hiring outsiders to do various tasks is called **outsourcing**. Outsourcing is key to several of the new organizational structures that we discuss in the next chapter.

Outsourcing
The process of hiring outsiders to do various tasks

A QUESTION OF ETHICS

Effect of Restructuring	The search for the perfect structure has led to a wave of restructuring and inevitably to layoffs. What are the ethical issues involved in these restructurings? What are businesses' social responsibilities?

Entrepreneurship and Intrapreneurship   Small businesses are a major contributor to many economies. Let's look at the impact of entrepreneurial firms and how they have forced large organizations to create their own brand of entrepreneurship next.

Although many of you may see your future with the IBMs of the world, chances are that you will be working for a small or medium-size business instead. Don't be fooled into thinking that small size means small profits. Many small businesses, once established, are extremely profitable, and turn into Microsoft and Dell. Close to 80 percent of all businesses in the United States are classified as small, meaning that they have less than 500 employees. The number of small businesses is continually growing, even though less than 20 percent of new small businesses survive beyond the first few years. Why? The appeal of being one's own boss and the potential for creativity and personal achievement attracts many individuals. Additionally, many talented individuals have been forced to start new careers due to corporate restructuring, so they opt to become *entrepreneurs*, those who start their own companies.

Entrepreneurs provide considerable competition for large businesses. The small organizations are free of bureaucratic red tape and are more connected to their customers. As a result, they are flexible enough to "turn on a dime" when a new opportunity or challenge comes up. Plus, they can address the needs of customers in ways that many larger businesses cannot.

Consider the case of Trend Micro, a Taiwan-based software company owned by Steve Chang. The company decided to specialize in antivirus software when market demand and software trends indicated that quality virus protection programs were hot products. The company's engineers now create programs to fight about 200 new strains of virus that infect the programs of computer users, mostly through the Internet. Its products are of such high quality that Netscape and Microsoft use them. Chang, a graduate of Lehigh University in Pennsylvania, is one of many highly successful entrepreneurs.[52]

The flexibility, creativity, and responsiveness of entrepreneurial firms are benefits that many large businesses try to harness by encouraging intrapreneurs. **Intrapreneurs** are employees in a large organization that have the drive, creativity, and flexibility of entrepreneurs.[53] Business organizations that want to encourage intrapreneurship must have clear goals and reward systems and must remove bureaucratic obstacles. Managers need to provide support, time, resources, and opportunities for free exchange of ideas among employees. One of the goals of reengineering efforts is to allow intrapreneurship to flourish.

One of the best-known organizations for its ability to encourage intrapreneurs is 3M.[54] Through innovative management techniques that allow employees to experiment without the

Intrapreneurship
The drive, creativity, and flexibility that characterize small entrepreneurial firms within a large business

Entrepreneur Steven Chang owns Trend Micro, a firm that specializes in sophisticated antivirus protection programs. His small firm caters to high-power clients such as Netscape and Microsoft.

burden of red tape, and through generous profit sharing with those who come up with new ideas, the company has been able to maintain its creative and innovative edge. Technical employees are encouraged to spend 15 percent of their time on ideas for new products. The story of yellow 3M Post-its, notes that are now as common as pencils in all offices and homes, and its inventor Arthur Fry are part of business legend. Another 3M success story is the scientist who spent 15 percent of his time to develop a promising line of microstructured abrasives, called Apex, which allow for very quick finishing of a metal piece.[55]

Bell Atlantic calls its intrapreneurship program Champion. Jack Copley used the Champion program to develop his idea for a new graphic software called Thinx. Because of the Champion program, Copley was able to harness the talent of a 20-member team that developed, tested, and prepared Thinx for the market.[56] Managers at 3M and Bell Atlantic point out that for every successful Post-it, Apex, or Thinx, there are many failures that become learning opportunities to encourage further experimentation and creativity.

Use of High-Technology Tools

To address the challenges of globalization, rapid change, and customer demands for quality and efficiency, many businesses rely on technology and automation. Computer networks, state-of-the-art hardware and software, information technology and telecommunication tools, automation, and robotics are all part of the latest and newest high technology that allows organizations to do more in less time.

For example, many financial institutions use on-line services, telecommunication technology, and automatic teller machines (ATMs) to compete more efficiently and flexibly in the global market. Banks can offer worldwide service to customers through the use of ATMs, which replace branch offices. Customers also bank directly from home at any time through the use of on-line services. They can check their balance or secure a loan through sophisticated telecommunication systems.

High-technology tools further allow organizations to address their employees' diverse needs. Working parents or employees who live far from the office can telecommute by work-

Thinx, a graphic software program, would never have been developed without Bell Atlantic's intrapreneurship program. That program provides resources and helps intrapreneurs cut through red tape to get a product to market quickly.

ing at home. Managers reduce additional travel time because of technology that connects employees in various locations such as e-mail, teleconferencing, and document sharing.

In this section, we explored the challenges that organizations face and several ways businesses are responding to those challenges. We next consider how future managers should respond to the four challenges to be effective.

Summary Point 1.7   **What Are Organizations' Responses to the Challenges?**

- Organizations are opening themselves up to new global markets and adjusting their internal policies to the needs of diverse employees.
- Organizations are restructuring to become more efficient and more flexible.

- Entrepreneurial organizations can address challenges and customer demands because of their size and flexibility. Larger organizations try to capture an entrepreneurial spirit by encouraging intrapreneurship.
- Through the use of high technology, business organizations can become more efficient and flexible.

HOW SHOULD MANAGERS RESPOND TO THE FOUR CHALLENGES OF ORGANIZATIONS?

The four key challenges of organizations provide a blueprint for what future managers must know to be successful. First, to meet the challenge of globalization and diversity, managers must learn to handle these issues effectively to maximize potential benefits and avoid missteps. Second, managing change is pivotal to managing well. Change is part of everyday life in organizations—whether it is change in the general economy, managerial techniques, the structure of an organization, the use of teams, or the use of technology. Managers must learn to identify, respond to, and harness the inherent opportunities created by change. Third, customer demands for efficiency, quality, and low cost require that managers be flexible, adaptable, efficient, and capable of managing others and themselves to deliver high-quality products and services. Those managers who can learn quickly and think broadly and creatively will be better equipped to meet this challenge. Fourth, managers must think and act in ways that are sensitive to multiple stakeholder interests. To do so, managers must have a broad, big-picture view of their roles and functions in the organization. We highlight these four challenges and the ways the text can prepare you to meet these challenges in Table 1.4.

Accurately predicting the future is not an easy task. Few visionaries among us are able to do so. However, if you can understand and master the skills of the four themes we've outlined, you will be a more effective manager. In every chapter in the text, you will find the four themes either integrated through discussions and specific segments such as the "Change Challenge" or "Question of Ethics," or in examples, cases, and end-of-chapter materials. Every chapter also includes practical career advice, self-assessments, and managerial tips to help you manage your career and bridge the gap between theory and practice.

To help you develop a broad OB perspective, we use an hourglass organizational approach that lets us investigate the big picture view of organizations and the people in them. Part I provides an overview of macro OB topics such as organizational environment, technology, strategy, structure, and culture. Part II moves to a micro OB analysis, covering such issues as individual differences, perception, motivation, and learning. Part III focuses on a middle-level analysis of groups and teams. Part IV takes a detailed view of organizational processes such as decision making, conflict management, and organizational change. Part V blends micro and macro topics to show how the person and organization fit together. This approach will allow you to develop a well-rounded view of organizations and prepare you for the challenges that managers face.

Table 1.4   **HOW MANAGERS MUST RESPOND TO THE FOUR CHALLENGES OF ORGANIZATIONS**

Four Challenges	Description	Where to Find It in the Text
Globalization and cross-cultural issues	Managers must learn to work with people from other countries effectively and manage diverse cultures inside and outside the organization.	• Cross-cultural and global issues integrated with other material throughout every chapter • Examples, cases, and exercises
The rapid pace of change	Because change is a constant in today's business, managers must learn to recognize, adapt to, and reap the inherent benefits of change.	• "Change Challenge" features • "Team Challenge" features • Change coverage integrated with other material throughout chapters • Examples, cases, and exercises
Customer demand for quality and efficiency	To respond to customer demands, managers must learn quickly, adjust to new situations, respond to organizational and customer demands efficiently, and think broadly and creatively.	• Management Advice from the Experts, Career Advice, and end-of-chapter self-assessments • "Team Challenge" features that highlight ways teams can help businesses stay flexible and be more adaptable • Point of View exercises and Big Picture cases in end-of-chapter materials
Keeping a broad perspective that considers the interests of multiple stakeholders	Managers must learn to work with a diverse workforce, be socially responsible and aware of ethical issues, and consider the effects of business activities on multiple stakeholders.	• Cross-cultural and global focus throughout the book • "Question of Ethics" features in chapters • Exercises that spotlight ethical issues • "In Context" segments • "Big Picture" cases that help develop a broad perspective

For updated information on the topics in this chapter, Web exercises, links to related Web sites, an on-line study guide, and more, visit our companion Web site at:

http://www.prenhall.com/nahavandi

A Look Back at the

MANAGERIAL CHALLENGE

Starbucks Goes Global

At end of the 1990s, an estimated 8,000 coffee outlets were catering to U.S. coffee lovers, an incredible 40-fold increase from the 200 such outlets operating in 1989. The biggest winner in the java wars was Starbucks, which expanded from its Seattle base to open coffee bars across the country and then around the world. Under CEO Howard Schultz, the company has launched a series of new products, including a frozen cappuccino beverage, premium coffee ice creams, and packaged coffee beans—all developed especially for sale in supermarkets.[57]

Globalization and cultural diversity continue to be key challenges facing Schultz. After opening stores in Japan and Singapore, he was determined to plant the green-and-white Starbucks logo in downtown areas throughout the Pacific Rim, including Hong Kong and China. He teamed up with basketball great Magic Johnson in a joint venture to bring Starbucks stores to major inner-city areas around the United States.[58]

In his role as CEO, Schultz is ultimately responsible for managing relationships with a wide variety of organizational stakeholders. These include managers and employees, suppliers, customers, community groups, government regulators, and—after Starbucks became a publicly traded corporation in 1992—stockholders and industry analysts. Maintaining these relationships requires Schultz to apply his well-honed human skills.

Because Starbucks operates in a dynamic global environment, Schultz needs to apply his conceptual skills to the company's ever-changing circumstances and problems. Even though his company is the undisputed market leader, the CEO is keenly aware that past success does not guarantee future success. "I believe the way to stay on top is to continually reinvent yourself," he observes, "and that is exactly what Starbucks does with its brand and products."[59]

■ **Point of View Exercises**

You're the Manager: As the manager of a local Starbucks store, you supervise 25 employees. Choose one of the three types of managerial roles—interpersonal, informational, or decisional—and explain how this role applies to your position.

You're the Employee: As a weekend employee at the local Starbucks, you have been studying the company's specialty coffees, and you've mastered the precise brewing instructions. Are these brewing skills technical, human, or conceptual skills? How might these skills help you advance to a management position at Starbucks? What else do you need to learn?

SUMMARY OF LEARNING OBJECTIVES

1. **Define the field of organizational behavior and identify its three levels of analysis.** Organizational behavior (OB) is the study of how people behave in organizations as individuals and as teams and how organizations structure their human resources to achieve their goals. OB's purpose is to understand people in organizations and provide practitioners and managers with the tools to manage people more effectively. OB consists of three levels of analysis. The first level, micro OB, focuses on understanding the individual. This level is the smallest possible level of analysis in organizations. The second and middle level of analysis in OB is the small group, which consists of individual employees in an organization. The third level of analysis in OB, called macro OB, concentrates on larger groups such as departments and on organizational processes.

2. **Identify the functions, roles, and skills that managers must perform in organizations.** Planning, organizing, leading, and controlling are the four main functions of managers. In today's organizations, however, teams now perform many of the planning, organizing, and controlling functions of managers. Managers play many roles in their daily routines, such as interpersonal, informational, decisional, and team facilitator roles. To perform well, managers need technical, human, and conceptual skills. Some new skills required for managerial success in today's organizations include managing change, managing one's career, managing diversity, delegation, and empowerment.

3. **Describe the open systems view of organizations and outline the elements of the contingency approach to management.** The open systems view of organizations, which we take in this text, assumes that organizations are complex systems made up of interrelated parts that continuously interact with one another and with their external environment. It also assumes that organizations have inputs, processes, and outputs. Inputs are all the resources that enter the organization. Open systems take inputs from their environment and transform them through various processes. Processes are all the activities that use the inputs and change them in some form. Through processes, organizations transform their inputs into outputs. Outputs are all the products and services that an organization provides to its customers.

   Modern management is guided by the concept of contingency, which suggests that what works depends, or is contingent, on the situation. The contingency approach provides a realistic, complex, and situational view of people and organizations. The contingency view is compatible with the open systems approach.

4. **Highlight the four major challenges that organizations face today and explain organizations' response to those challenges.** Globalization and managing culture, rapid pace of change, customer demand for quality and low cost, and multiple stakeholders are the major challenges facing today's organizations and their managers. Most businesses are affected by all these issues. Organizations are responding to these challenges by going global and implementing diversity programs, restructuring, implementing entrepreneurship and intrapreneurship programs, and using high-technology tools and automation.

5. **Explain how managers must respond to the four challenges.** Managers must be able to think globally and manage diversity effectively. They must also be able to manage change, be flexible and adaptable, learn quickly, and think in a broad, creative manner. This text helps managers respond to these four challenges in chapter discussion, features, and exercises.

KEY TERMS

conceptual skills, p. 9

contingency approach, p. 17

continuous improvement, p. 10

controlling, p. 7

cultural diversity, p. 21

empowerment, p. 14
globalization, p. 18
Human Resource
   Management, p. 4
human skills, p. 9
intrapreneurship, p. 25
knowledge workers, p. 13
leading, p. 7
open systems, p. 15

organizational behavior,
   p. 3
organizations, p. 3
Organization Theory, p. 4
organizing, p. 7
outsourcing, p. 25
planning, p. 7
reengineering, p. 24
restructuring, p. 24
role, p. 8

skill, p. 8
stakeholders, p. 22
Strategic Management,
   p. 4
team manager/facilitator,
   p. 11
technical skill, p. 8
Total Quality
   Management, p. 10

REVIEW QUESTIONS

1. Provide a definition of OB and compare and contrast it to other management disciplines.
2. What are the different managerial functions, roles, and skills?
3. Provide an example of the components of an open system.
4. Describe the four major challenges that today's organizations face.
5. How have today's organizations responded to the challenges they face?

DISCUSSION QUESTIONS

1. Explain why we need to understand organizations from the three levels of individual, group, and organization.
2. The job of managers has changed significantly in the last two decades. What are some of challenges that these changes pose for today's students of management?
3. Discuss how managers can use an open system view of organizations to understand and manage organizations better.
4. What are the benefits and disadvantages of taking a contingency view of organizations?
5. What can you do to prepare yourself to face the challenges of managing organizations in the future?

▶ SELF-ASSESSMENT 1
Is It Time to Consider a Career Move?

Constant change is one of the defining characteristics of today's careers. Knowing when to undertake a change is key to making the right moves. Whether you are considering looking for another job or giving up work for a while to go to school full time, the questions that follow can help you in your decision. You'll find a scoring key in Appendix 3 of this book.

1.	Are you learning new skills?	Yes	No
2.	Is you salary stagnating?	Yes	No
3.	Is your company doing well?	Yes	No
4.	Do you enjoy going to work?	Yes	No
5.	Are you excluded from decision making?	Yes	No
6.	Do people like you?	Yes	No
7.	Are you being challenged with interesting assignments?	Yes	No
8.	Does your boss seek your input?	Yes	No

9. Is the company stable (as compared to being targeted
    for major cuts or a merger, for example)?   Yes   No
10. Do you feel that you belong?   Yes   No

▶ TEAM EXERCISE 1
Old Wines and New Skins

This exercise is designed to highlight the changes between new and old styles of managing people in organizations.

1. **PREPARE AND PRESENT**

    The class will be divided into two sections and each section is assigned one of two tasks.

    - Prepare a three- to five-minute presentation about the traditional ways people are managed. Focus on issues such as how managers and employees interact, what the responsibilities for each are, how decisions are made, and so forth. Consider the benefits of the traditional management styles and explore the reasons that change may be needed.

    OR

    - Prepare a three- to five-minute presentation about the newer ways people are managed. Focus on issues such as how managers and employees interact, what the responsibilities for each are, how decisions are made, and so forth. Consider the potential benefits of the current approaches and the challenges they pose for managers and for organizations.

2. **CLASS DISCUSSION**

    After presentation of the two sides, the class discussion should focus on the following:

    - The situations that warrant change to "New Skins"
    - Situations that make drastic transitions too difficult
    - Individual students' preferences for "Old Wines" or "New Skins" as
      a. managers
      b. employees

Source: Adapted with permission from Afsaneh Nahavandi, *The Art and Science of Leadership* (Upper Saddle River, NJ: Prentice Hall, 1997), p. 42.

UP CLOSE

▶ Promotion at Central Insurance

Central Insurance company has 40 employees including sales agents, adjusters, and managerial and office staff who work in two different locations in a large metropolitan area. The employees come from a diverse background reflecting the high level of diversity of this metropolitan city. Each of the two locations operates independently with its own staff and managers. Roberto Salazar is the office manager for one of the offices. Like Cynthia Baxter, the other office manager, he is primarily responsible for the office staff consisting in his case of one clerical worker, two data entry specialists, and three secretaries. He takes care of their scheduling, vacations, pay, and other paperwork and is responsible for assuring that the office has proper coverage at all times. He also manages the office budget and orders supplies.

Roberto is originally from Costa Rica. He has been in the United States for almost ten years. He has an easy-going, soft-spoken style that has made him very popular with his staff. He is flexible when it comes to scheduling, is willing to work with them to solve their problems, listens to their concerns, and runs interference for them with the insurance agents and adjusters as needed. He always has time to listen to the personal problems of his staff and remembers to ask his staff about the welfare of their family members. Although some of the agents complain that Roberto is sometimes too flexible with the office staff, they like him and consider him to be effective. The flexibility means that people are sometimes not in the office on a fixed schedule, but the staff always pitch in during a crunch and get things done. Many willingly stay after hours to finish their work or help out others. The turnover in the office staff has been negligible and the staff is dedicated and loyal. To allow for more flexibility, Roberto often uses temporary workers thereby increasing his labor costs. Roberto states: "The staff are great people. Money is not the issue here. They do their job, they are loyal, and they take care of the company as long as the company takes care of them. We are a family."

Cynthia Baxter, Roberto's counterpart in the other office, runs a very different operation. She supervises nine staff members and she runs a tight ship. She does not have much time and patience for what she calls whining and lack of responsible behavior. The schedules are fixed and there is little room for negotiation. The work hours are set, and overtime is kept at a minimum; the office rarely needs to hire temporary help. Cynthia's office has a 20 percent annual turnover that leads to considerable recruitment and training costs. She considers these expenses to be part of the cost of doing business. She has an excellent knowledge of the technical side of the insurance business and seems to anticipate problems before they occur. The agents who work with Cynthia consider her highly efficient, although not approachable. The staff members complain that she does not respond to their personal problems and that she has little flexibility. Overall, the staff do not particularly like her and are unwilling to take any extra steps to help her out. They have left her in a pinch on several occasions when overtime work was needed to finish the job.

The volume of business has been growing at a very fast pace for Central Insurance, and the two locations have quickly outgrown their current office space. To handle the growth and to cut costs, Central Insurance is planning to combine the two offices into one larger location that it has recently purchased. The managers of the company feel that having one location will allow them to provide better service for the customers, who are mostly located near the new office. The plan is to retain all the agents and staff, and to promote one of the two office managers to business manager, with the other one reporting to him or her. The new location will be highly automated and one of the new responsibilities of the business manager will be to coordinate the work of several new part-time salespeople. The owner of Central Insurance is considering Roberto and Cynthia for the promotion. Both are equally educated and generally qualified.

Questions

1. If you were the owner of Central Insurance, what factors would you consider in your decision regarding the business manager?
2. Which one of the two candidates should get the promotion? Why?
3. Are there any other options?

NOTES

1. Lori Ioannou, "Making Customers Come Back for More," *Fortune* (March 16, 1998): 156J.
2. Jennifer Reese, "Starbucks: Inside the Coffee Cult," *Fortune* (December 9, 1996): 190–200; Ioannou, "Making Customers," 156J–156L.
3. Reese, "Starbucks."
4. Lee Moriwaki, "Starbucks, Magic Johnson Join to Open Inner-City Stores," *Knight-Ridder Tribune* (February 5, 1998), accessed on-line at http://www.hotel-online.com/Neo/News/1998_Feb_05/K.00r.886784862; Martin Wolk, "Starbucks to Begin Grocery Sales of Coffee Beans," *Yahoo! Reuters News* (February 6, 1998), accessed online at http://204.71.177.75/headlines/980206/business/stories/starbucks_1; Sabrina Thompson, "The Starbucks Juggernaut," *Sky* (January 1998): 25–27.
5. J. Guyon, "Why Is the World's Most Profitable Company Turning Itself Inside Out?" *Fortune* 136, no. 3 (August 4, 1997): 120–125.
6. R. Levering and M. Moskowitz, "The 100 Best Companies to Work for in America," *Fortune* 137, no. 1 (January 12, 1998): 84–95.
7. H. Stout, "Self-Evaluation Brings Change to a Family's Ad Agency," *Wall Street Journal*, January 6, 1998, p. B2.
8. For examples of new management styles in various companies, see J. Huey, "The New Post-Heroic Leadership," *Fortune* 129, no. 4 (1995): 42–50.
9. Betsy Morris, "Big Blue," *Fortune* (April 14, 1997): 68–81.
10. Peter Petre, "Gerstner Talks Tech," *Fortune* (April 14, 1997): 73.
11. Stout, "Self-Evaluation."
12. Morris, "Big Blue."
13. Stout, "Self-Evaluation."
14. Morris, "Big Blue."
15. Stout, "Self-Evaluation."
16. Morris, "Big Blue," 80.
17. Stout, "Self-Evaluation."
18. See R. Henkoff, "Boeing's Big Problem," *Fortune* 137, no. 1 (January 12, 1998): 96–103.
19. For an example, see P. deValk, "Managing Change and All That Jazz," *Management–Auckland* 40, no. 10 (1993): 83–85.
20. J. B. Minor and N. R. Smith, "Decline and Stabilization of Managerial Motivation over a 20-Year Period," *Journal of Applied Psychology* (June 1982): 298.
21. For examples of modern approaches to management, see P. Block, *The Empowered Manager* (San Francisco: Jossey-Bass, 1987); P. Block, *Stewardship: Choosing Service over Self-Interest* (San Francisco, CA: Berrett-Koehler, 1994); and J. R. Katzenbach and D. K. Smith, *The Wisdom of Teams* (New York: Harper Business, 1992).
22. R. B. Lieber, "Why Employees Love These Companies," *Fortune* 137, no. 1 (January 12, 1998): 72–74.
23. See J. B. Quinn, "Ford: Team Taurus," in H. Mintzberg and J. B. Quinn, *The Strategy Process* (Upper Saddle River, N.J.: Prentice Hall, 1996).
24. Eryn Brown, "First: Could the Very Best PC Maker Be Dell Computer?" *Fortune* (April 14, 1997): 26–27; Lawrence M. Fisher, "Fourth-Quarter Net Soared 52% at Dell Computer," *New York Times*, February 19, 1998, p. C1.
25. Hall Lancaster, "Companies Promise to Help Employees Plot Their Careers," *Wall Street Journal*, March 11, 1997, B1; Ellen Graham, "Their Career: Count on Nothing and Work like a Demon," *Wall Street Journal*, October 31, 1995, B1, B7.
26. For a detailed discussion of the concept of knowledge worker, see P. Drucker, *Post-Capitalist Society* (New York: HarperCollins, 1993); J. B. Quinn, P. Anderson, and S. Finklestein, "Managing Professional Intellect: Making the Most of the Best," *Harvard Business Review* 74, no. 2 (March/April 1996): 71–80.
27. S. Barr, "Advantage Aetna," *CFO*, 12, no. 11 (November 1996): 35–36.
28. J. D. Thompson, *Organizations in Action* (New York: McGraw-Hill, 1967), 4–13.
29. Lee Moriwaki, "Starbucks Protest in Vancouver Spotlights Risks of International Expansion," *Seattle Times*, May 25, 1997, accessed on-line at www.seattletimes.com/sbin.iarecor.
30. See P. M. Senge, "The Leader's New Work: Building Learning Organizations," *Sloan Management Review* (Fall 1990): 7–23.
31. Lieber, "Why Employees Love These Companies," 74.
32. For some of the earliest studies on the concept of contingency, see K. Lewin, R. Lippit, and R. K. White, "Patterns of Aggressive Behavior in Experimentally Created Social Climates," *Journal of Social Psychology* 10 (1939): 271–301.
33. J. Guyon, "The Sole Competitor," *Fortune* 137, no. 1 (January 12, 1998): 102.
34. "The International Giants with Impressive Statistics," *Forbes* (July 23, 1990): 318; E. S. Hardy, "Is There Life in the Laggards?" *Forbes* (July 17, 1995).
35. E. James, "Why Overseas? 'Cause That's Where the Sales Are," *Business Week* (January 10, 1994): 62–63.
36. See *International Financial Statistics Yearbook, 1996*, vol. 49 (U.S. Department of Commerce, International Trade Administration), p. 7.
37. T. Kamm, B. Coleman, and C. Rohwedder, "EU Takes First Step Toward Single Currency," *Wall Street Journal*, May 4, 1998, A17.
38. F. Trompenaars, *Riding the Waves of Culture: Understanding Diversity in Global Business* (New York: Irwin, 1994).
39. C. M. Solomon, "Big Mac's McGlobal HR Secrets," *Personnel Journal* 75, no. 4 (April 1996): 46–54.
40. E. Updike, "Mitsubishi and the 'Cement Ceiling,'" *Business Week* (May 13, 1996): 62.
41. Henkoff, "Boeing's Big Problem."
42. Ibid.
43. G. Bylinsky, "Industry's Amazing Instant Prototypes," *Fortune* 137, no. 1 (January 12, 1998): 120B–120D.
44. L. Colby, "The Fortune Global Five Hundred," *Fortune* 136, no. 3 (August 4, 1997): F1–F28.
45. J. R. Galbraith and E. E. Lawler III, "Effective Organizations: Using the New Logic of Organizing," in *Organizing for the Future: The New Logic for Managing Complex Organizations*, ed. J. R. Galbraith, E. E. Lawler III, and associates (San Francisco: Jossey-Bass, 1993): 290–92.
46. Levering and Moskowitz, "The 100 Best Companies," 84.
47. H. Sirkin and M. A. Miles, "The Reorganization Crutch," *Across the Board* 30, no. 9 (1993): 52–53.
48. H. Hammer and James Champy, *Reengineering the Corporation* (New York: HarperBusiness, 1993); James Champy, *Reengineering Management: The Mandate for New Leadership* (New York: HarperBusiness, 1996).
49. For more information on the impact of restructuring, see M. Hitt, B. W. Keats, H. F. Harback, and R. D. Nixon, "Rightsizing: Building and Maintaining Strategic Leadership and Long-Term Competitiveness," *Organizational Dynamics* 23 (Autumn 1993): 18–32; S. J. Tolchin, "Pain, No Gain Feeds Anger," *The Arizona Republic*, October 27, 1996, H5.
50. T. Steward, "Watch What We Did, Not What We Said," *Fortune*, April 15, 1996, 140–141; S. J. Tolchin, "Pain, No Gain"; Robert E. Allen, "The Anxiety Epidemic," *Newsweek*, April 8, 1996, 15.
51. Levering and Moskowitz, "The 100 Best Companies," 88.
52. Louis Kraar, "A World of Cool Companies," *Fortune*, October 28, 1996, pp. 162–163.
53. "Intrapreneurs Go Official," *Management Today* (November 1995): 13–17; D. F. Kuratko, J. S. Hornsby, D. W. Naffziger, and R. V. Montagno, "Implementing Entrepreneurial Thinking in Established Organizations," *SAM Advanced Management Journal* 58, no. 1 (1993): 28–33.
54. J. W. Duncan, P. M. Ginter, A. C. Ruchks, and T. D. Jacobs, "Intrapreneurs and the Reinvention of the Corporation," *Business Horizons* 31, no. 3 (May/June 1988): 16–21; "Lessons from a Successful Intrapreneur," *Journal of Business Strategy* 9, no. 2 (March/April 1988): 20–24.
55. T. E. Schellhardt, "David in Goliath," *Wall Street Journal*, May 23, 1996, p. R14.
56. Ibid.
57. Wolk, "Starbucks to Begin Grocery Sales"; Ioannou, "Making Customers."
58. Moriwaki, "Starbucks, Magic Johnson."
59. Ioannou, "Making Customers."

UNDERSTANDING THE CONTEXT OF ORGANIZATIONS

LEARNING OBJECTIVES

1. Identify the five contextual forces that influence organizations.
2. Describe the organizational environment and define enactment and uncertainty.
3. Define technology and explain types of technologies and their effect on organizations.
4. Discuss the relationship among mission, goals, and strategy and outline the strategic management process of formulation and implementation.
5. Describe organizational structure, its basic components and elements, and contrast traditional and new structural options.
6. Highlight the importance of the fit among the strategic contextual forces and how they affect organizations.

MANAGERIAL CHALLENGE

McCormick & Company

"Make the best—someone will buy it" has long been the motto of McCormick & Company, the global spice maker based in a suburb of Baltimore, Maryland. In fact, many people were buying McCormick's best: $4 out of every $10 spent on spices and food flavorings went into the company's coffers. Yet even with the company's annual sales approaching $2 billion, CEO Robert J. Lawless has a plateful of potential problems to consider.[1]

One issue is a change in consumer lifestyles and tastes across the United States. Two-career families are spending less time in the kitchen and cooking up fewer fancy feasts with special spices. In addition, more people are eating out, which hurt retail sales of herbs and spices in supermarkets and food stores. At the same time, increased diversity in the U.S. population and the influx of international cuisine are fueling demand for curry, red pepper, and many other fiery spices—products that McCormick did not promote aggressively.[2]

Another issue is competition. It heated up when Australia's Burns, Philp & Company mounted an aggressive challenge to McCormick's dominance of the spice market. Burns, Philp bought two well-known spice brands, Durkee and Spice Islands, and offered supermarkets higher fees for prominent display space on store shelves. As a result, McCormick was forced to pay higher fees to ensure good shelf position and defend its share of market. These increasing costs have sliced into McCormick's earnings, which were already being hurt by the escalating cost of black pepper, the company's most important product. Without question, the environmental situation facing McCormick's CEO is extremely difficult.[3]

■ Questions

1. What opportunities and threats would Robert Lawless have to consider when developing a strategy for the company?
2. What company strengths could he use in his strategy for coping with a dynamic environment?

McCormick & Company is not alone in facing a changing environment. Organizations all over the world are changing at a pace that may only be comparable to transformations they experienced during the industrial revolution of the early 1900s. Changes include new organizational structure and management styles, a strong customer orientation, alliances with competitors, and new views on the social responsibilities of business. Why are the changes taking place? Simply because the environment demands them.

To illustrate, consider these examples. Investors call for higher returns so managers restructure their organizations and set a new mission based on efficiency. Employees from diverse backgrounds and generations ask for participation, flexibility, and autonomy. In response, managers involve employees in decision making and rely more heavily on teams and empowerment. Consumers demand high-quality, safe products at low cost so businesses innovate to address these concerns. As domestic markets for goods and services shrink, companies look outside their national borders to grow and expand markets. Communities demand fair treatment, ethical conduct, and environmentally safe products, so businesses develop social responsibility programs to address these needs. These examples show the many factors that affect today's organizations and how managers must understand these forces to work effectively.

In the next two chapters, we examine the context in which individuals, teams, and organizations function. We'll see how the context influences all behaviors and decisions in a business. In this chapter we start by defining the five key ingredients that form the context of organizations: the environment, technology, strategy, structure, and culture. This chapter considers the first four topics. Because of the complexity and importance of culture, we devote all of chapter 3 to that topic.

■ THE MANAGER'S FRAMEWORK OF FIVE FORCES

The context in which organizations function includes the five contextual, strategic forces illustrated in Figure 2.1. The forces of environment, technology, strategy, structure, and culture are *contextual* because they form the context and the background within which individuals and groups operate. We also call these forces *strategic* because they have broad, long-term implications for the organization. These five forces are interrelated and all affect organizations. Let's first define each force.

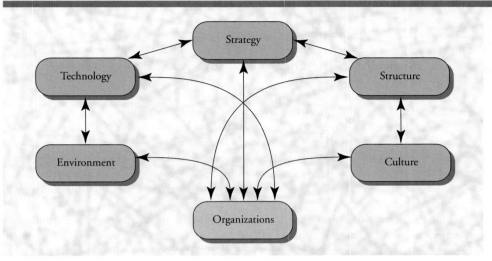

FIGURE 2.1
Five Contextual Strategic Forces

The **environment** of an organization is made up of all external factors that have the potential to affect the organization. **Technology** is the knowledge, tools, techniques, and processes used to create the goods and services of an organization by transforming inputs into outputs. The **strategy** of a firm is how it achieves its mission and goals.[4] **Structure** refers to how people are organized to achieve the company's mission.[5] **Culture** is defined as values commonly held among a group of people. This group may be a country, an ethnic group, an organization, or a group of people with similar interests.[6]

Managers need to monitor all five forces, recognizing that they are closely interrelated. Because the forces influence one another, change in one often affects the others. In addition, different forces become important in different situations. For instance, changes in the business environment affect the way McCormick is managing its organization. Changes in demographics and global competition are also forcing McCormick to change its strategies. Furthermore, as McCormick loses customers, it may reduce its workforce and restructure its organization. These contextual changes affect managers' jobs in these companies.

Managers need to understand how each contextual strategic force affects their organization. The simultaneous management of these contextual strategic forces is the essence of managing in an open system. We use the five forces throughout the text to explain how the context affects people and organizations. The first contextual strategic force we explore is the external environment.

Environment
All external factors that have the potential to affect the organization

Technology
The knowledge, tools, techniques, and processes used to create the goods and services of an organization

Strategy
How a business achieves its mission and goals

Structure
How people are organized to achieve the company's mission

Culture
The values commonly held among a group of people

Summary Point 2.1 **What Are the Five Contextual Strategic Forces?**

- Five forces—environment, technology, strategy, structure, and culture—make up the context of organizations.

- Managers need to understand and simultaneously manage the five contextual strategic forces.

THE ENVIRONMENT OF ORGANIZATIONS

Organizations do not function in a vacuum. As open systems, they interact with their environment by taking inputs, changing their internal processes and technologies because of environmental requirements, and giving outputs to the environment. The environment, then, is a key factor in understanding organizations. But what constitutes the environment?

Defining the Environment

Recall that an organization's environment is all the factors outside the organization that have the potential to affect it. For example, the presence of competitors and changes in consumer tastes and lifestyles are major environmental factors that have a significant effect on McCormick & Company.

The environment does not consist of every external factor—only those that can affect the organization. Accordingly, an airline and a restaurant franchise will not have identical environments even though they may operate in the same location and cater to similar customers. The airline's environment includes factors such as engine part suppliers, the pilot's union, other airline competitors, and airline regulatory agencies. These factors do not affect the restaurant franchise and are therefore not part of its environment. In the following sections, we examine the process managers use to define their environment and ways of defining environmental uncertainty.

Many elements make up the environment of an organization. The range of environmental elements that businesses must consider is shown in Figure 2.2. Note, however, that although all organizations have the society, the national culture, and the economic situation as part of their environment, elements such as organized labor or certain demographic groups are not relevant for all organizations. In addition, even when the elements are the same, the importance an organization gives to each varies and depends on the organization's mission and strategy.

The General and Business Environments

General environment
Societal, demographic, and cultural trends; the political climate; and historical and religious influences

Environmental elements can be grouped into two broad categories. The first category is the **general environment.** It includes elements such as general societal, demographic, and cultural trends; the political climate; and historical and religious influences. These elements affect how organizations are run at a broad, general level. For instance, the societal trend of increasing numbers of women and minorities entering the workforce affects the availability and the composition of the labor force in the United States. The same trends also affect some companies' sales, as they did McCormick's spice sales. The decrease in sales of spices was partly based on the increasing number of women joining the workforce and changing food tastes in the United States toward ethnic, spicier food. The company has been slow to respond to customer taste changes, as evidenced by the few ethnic recipes it offers the company's Web site visitors.[7]

Business environment
Customers, competitors, human resources, suppliers, financial institutions, governmental regulations, the economy, and technology

The second category in the environment is the **business environment,** which consists of specific elements such as customers, competitors, human resources, suppliers, financial

FIGURE 2.2
Elements of the Environment

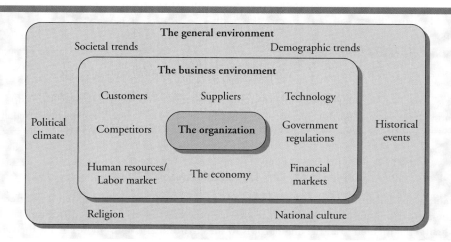

institutions, governmental regulations, the economy, and technology. These are elements that managers typically deal with on a day-to-day basis. For example, changes in interest rates affect businesses directly because they change managers' ability to obtain a loan and the short-term and long-term costs of those loans. Similarly, when a competitor declares bankruptcy, it affects other organizations in that industry as do customer preferences and satisfaction. In addition to changing demographics, McCormick faced fierce competition from the Australian company Burns, Philp.[8] However, Burns, Philp's financial trouble gave McCormick an opportunity to win back some of its edge in the spice market. Managers, then, should monitor the elements of the business environment often.

Two particularly important elements of the environment deserve special attention. Within the general environment, national and ethnic culture play key roles. Today's managers need to have an in-depth understanding of the effect of culture to be effective. Within the business environment, technology has a strong impact on managerial decision making and management practices. Because of the significance of these two elements, we consider them to be distinct strategic contextual forces and discuss them separately in this chapter, in chapter 3, and throughout the text.

Not all elements of the general or business environment affect all organizations at one time or to the same extent. For example, although Estee Lauder and Hard Candy are both cosmetics companies and have many common environmental elements, each prioritizes environmental elements differently because of their size, the markets each targets, and differences in product lines.

Estee Lauder has an extensive line of skin care products, targets an older market, and has a strong global presence. In contrast, Hard Candy emphasizes the younger generation and focuses on trendy products, rather than a broad line of skin care products. In spite of being in the same industry, therefore, the two companies have different environments.

Enacting the Environment

Once managers understand the range of elements in the general and business environments, they must identify those that are relevant to their organization. This important process, known as **enactment**, defines the environment of the organization.[9] Just how critical is this process? Consider an auto manufacturer that decides global competition is not a relevant element of the firm's environment. The decision to disregard global competition may sound ludicrous to those of you who drive foreign cars, but it is exactly what the U.S. automakers did in the 1970s and 1980s. In addition, they ignored several social, economic, and political elements of their environment. The results were disastrous.

In the 1970s, GM, Chrysler, Ford, and American Motors did not pay attention to their Japanese competitors; ignored their customers' demands for smaller, cheaper, more reliable cars; and overlooked the economic and global political signals that pointed to an increase in gasoline prices. The U.S. auto manufacturers misread their environment and did not enact their environment accurately. As a result, they lost market share to foreign competitors that marketed smaller, more efficient, higher quality cars. The loss was so great that Chrysler teetered on the edge of bankruptcy and American Motors filed for bankruptcy.

Inaccurate enactment is a common pitfall in a fast-changing environment. Many U.S. car dealerships failed to consider competition from on-line car-buying services, such as Auto-by-Tel, as part of their relevant environment. As a result, hundreds of dealerships have closed in recent years because their prices weren't competitive and their sales processes were too time-consuming for customers.[10]

Correct enactment is a process that is part art, part science, and part luck. It requires careful gathering and interpretation of data and sound judgment. Education and experience can help business leaders develop such skills, but in today's world they cannot guarantee suc-

Enactment
The process of identifying relevant environmental elements to define the environment of the organization

cess. Business managers must also be able to predict trends accurately by analyzing an environment that is often uncertain.

Environmental Uncertainty

Environmental uncertainty
Unpredictability in the environment

Rate of change
The speed at which various elements in the environment change

Environmental complexity
The number of elements an organization has to consider in its enactment process

Why is enacting and defining the environment so difficult? The major reason is that the environment is unpredictable. This unpredictability is called **environmental uncertainty**. Most organizations must cope with uncertain general and business environments. Two factors combine to make the environment uncertain. First is the rate of change and second is the complexity within the environment.[11]

The **rate of change** refers to the speed at which various elements in the environment change. Changes can relate to the general environment, such as broad demographic changes, or to the business environment, such as changes in government regulations, customer demands, or competitors' actions. The **complexity** of the environment refers to the number of elements an organization has to consider in its enactment process. Organizations that have a simple environment deal with only a few elements at any one time. Organizations that have a complex environment must juggle many different elements at once. Generally, the more complex the environment, the more complicated the manager's job is.

Rate of change and complexity combine to create different levels of environmental uncertainty. Table 2.1 shows four general levels. If the environment has few elements that do not change frequently, then the level of uncertainty is low. An environment with many elements that don't change often has a low-to-moderate level of uncertainty. An environment that has few elements that change frequently is one with a moderate-to-high level of uncertainty. A highly uncertain level is one in which there are many elements that change often and unpredictably.

Many of today's organizations face an uncertain environment that they can neither predict nor control. The four challenges we discussed in chapter 1—globalization, rapid change, customer demands for quality and low cost, and multiple stakeholders—contribute to uncertainty.

What are the effects of uncertainty? First, uncertainty creates stress for managers who rarely have complete information to make decisions. Second, it makes planning difficult because there are many unstable factors to consider. Third, the chances of error increase as do

Table 2.1 LEVELS OF ENVIRONMENTAL UNCERTAINTY

	Level of Complexity (Number of Elements)	
	Low (few elements)	**High (many elements)**
Low	*STABLE + SIMPLE = LOW UNCERTAINTY*	*STABLE + COMPLEX = LOW/MODERATE UNCERTAINTY*
	Small number of external factors that change slowly	Large number of external factors that change slowly
	Example: Packaging industry	Examples: Refrigeration and trucking industries
Rate of Change		
	HIGH RATE OF CHANGE + SIMPLE = MODERATE/HIGH UNCERTAINTY	*HIGH RATE OF CHANGE + COMPLEX = HIGH UNCERTAINTY*
	Small number of external factors that change quickly	Large number of external factors that change quickly
High	Example: Toys; Fashion	Examples: Computers, airlines

Source: Based on R. B. Duncan, "Characteristics of Perceived Environments and Perceived Environmental Uncertainty," *Administrative Science Quarterly* 17, no. 3 (1972): 313–27.

CAREER ADVICE
from the Experts

MANAGING YOUR CAREER IN UNCERTAIN ENVIRONMENTS

Uncertainty not only affects organizations; it also affects your career. As organizations change to adapt to their environment, they force their employees to change as well. Here are some pointers on how to manage uncertainty and build a productive career.

- If you are good at what you do today, tomorrow is much more likely to take care of itself. Focus on developing and demonstrating competence.
- Gain international experience. In many businesses it is a requirement, not an option. Volunteer for foreign assignments; take courses and training.
- Move across different job areas, not only up. Take on assignments in other functional areas and think of your career as a web or circle rather than a ladder.
- Create new opportunities for your organization; it can open up new doors for you.
- Learn new management skills and new technology continuously. Continue taking college courses and take advantage of company training.
- Take care of people. Be compassionate of others, make strong connections, and build a wide network.

Source: Based on Anne Fisher, "Six Ways to Supercharge Your Career," *Fortune* (January 13, 1997): 46–48.

the risks associated with making a bad decision. For example, as the environment changes, competitors change their organizational structures. Investors then become edgy, so managers feel compelled to restructure their organization to keep up. The decision to restructure the organization in an uncertain environment is risky because there are no guarantees that the managers have selected the appropriate structure.

Managers can define the environment for their organization by assessing environmental uncertainty and evaluating its effect on the organization. The next step is to manage that environment. In the remainder of the chapter, we examine the ways managers use technology and design strategies and structures to manage their environment. First, we turn our attention to technology, an environmental element that increasingly affects people in organizations at all levels.

Summary Point 2.2   **How Do Managers Define the Environment and Environmental Uncertainty?**

- The environment of an organization is defined as all the general and business elements outside the organization that have the potential to affect it.
- Managers use the enactment process to select the environmental elements that are relevant to their business.

- Managers assess environmental uncertainty by examining the relationship between the rate of change (the pace at which the environment changes) and complexity (the number of relevant elements in the environment).

▉ TECHNOLOGY

Technology is the knowledge, tools, techniques, and processes that organizations use to create goods and services. Technology functions as the heart of an organization in an open system. Just as a heart takes incoming blood from the veins, transforms it, and sends it out through the arteries, technology takes inputs, processes them, and transforms them into outputs. Because technology changes rapidly and is central to the organization, it is a contextual strategic force that managers must be aware of and must manage well.

Manufacturing firms
Business organizations that produce tangible goods

Service firms
Business organizations that deliver a service rather than a tangible product

Types of technology differ according to the type of organization. **Manufacturing firms** produce an actual product, such as shoes, steel pipes, or desks. That is, their output is tangible. Manufacturing technology involves the tools, machines, and knowledge used to create the output. **Service firms** deliver a service rather than a tangible product. The technology of service firms includes the processes and knowledge involved in the creation and delivery of the service. The outputs are intangible: Customers use the service as it is delivered, and service providers deliver the service directly to the customer. For instance, a financial consultant offers advice to clients directly and the customer receives the advice at the moment the provider offers it. Examples of service organizations include banks, consulting firms, health care providers, and the hospitality industry.

Technology is the main link between the organization and its environment whether the business is a manufacturing or a service organization. Managers can either buy the technology they need to produce their products and services or develop it internally through research and development. *Research and development* (R&D) is the process by which organizations search for information and create techniques to improve their products and services. For example, a company that needs new computer software for its accounting department can either buy that technology from another firm or develop the software internally through research and development.

Changing Technology

Technological changes force organizations to reconsider how they transform their inputs into outputs. Here we consider four major technological changes and their effect on organizations.

High Technology The term *high technology* (more commonly known as high tech) refers to the latest and newest technological developments. Firms use high technology to improve their products, services, or processes. Today's companies rely more and more on high technology to distinguish their business from competitors. They do so through a strong focus on R&D and an extensive use of computers, satellites, and other high-tech tools. The use of high technology requires constant monitoring of the environment and continual training and retraining of employees.

Motorola's Iridium project highlights how high technology can lead to changes. Motorola, the world leader in cellular phone technology, set the goal of providing a comprehensive global service to its customers, allowing them to use their cell phone from anywhere in the world. The company and its partners designed 66 satellites that orbit the earth. The satellites are connected to hundreds of ground stations in various countries. The technology allows Motorola's customers to call anyone from anywhere in the world. High technology helped Motorola deliver a service that only a few years ago was considered an impossible dream.

The Iridium project doesn't just affect Motorola and its customers, however. In response to the project, Motorola's competitors are changing and expanding their line of products and services. Several small businesses that worked with Motorola on the project have seen new business opportunities crop up. For example, the Iridium project satellites need to be replaced beginning in 2001. Kelly Space & Technology signed an $89 million contract with Motorola

Rapid prototypes, such as the one shown here, allow organizations to cut down their costs and increase the speed of innovation. The result? Companies can respond to environmental changes more quickly.

that requires Kelly to send spacecraft to orbit and replace the aging satellites. Kelly may also launch hundreds of new satellites to support Motorola's various voice and data communication systems.[12]

New Manufacturing Technology and Automation   Today's organizations face the challenge of implementing new manufacturing technologies. One of the most striking examples is rapid prototypes (RP), desktop manufacturing machines that turn computer-generated designs into an actual prototype. Using laser technology, the machines bind powdered steel, ceramics, and other material into molds that are used directly for manufacturing specific products. 3M uses the RP technology in products ranging from respirators to tape dispensers. Marge Hartfel, 3M's senior engineer, speculates about the potential of RP: "We could have naval ships carry not an inventory of parts but their images digitized on 3.5-inch diskette, plus a bag of powdered metal and a rapid manufacturing machine."[13]

Computer-assisted design (CAD) and Computer-assisted manufacturing (CAM) are two other manufacturing technologies that organizations use to help design and manufacture new products. CAD/CAM technologies allow managers to integrate information about needed materials, design products on the computer, and simulate situations in which consumers may use products. Leading companies in the transportation industry, such as Boeing and Ford Motor Company, and those in the chip manufacturing and telecommunication industries all use CAD/CAM to improve their products and to become more efficient.[14]

Another tool organizations use is automation. **Automation** is the process of replacing human resources with machines. Robots already perform manufacturing jobs in many industries. People monitor the machines instead of actually manufacturing the products. For example, Toyota pioneered the use of robots in the assembly line. Many functions people performed were repetitive, were subject to high error rates, and required a great deal of labor. Toyota replaced people with robots that could do the work more efficiently. Now most automobile manufacturers use robotics in several segments of the manufacturing process.

Another example of automation is the use of laser sensors in sensitive, high-speed processes. Perceptron, a small company based in Plymouth, Michigan, has developed a laser-guided machine used by paper- and log-cutting companies. The Perceptron system scans a log's density and decides on the best way to cut the log into various shapes and sizes. Manager Griff Stanley uses Perceptron machines to cut 3,000 logs a day in his log-cutting business. He

Automation
The process of replacing human resources with machines

states: "We used to make all these decisions using plain old human judgment. There's no doubt that the machinery's smarter most of the time."[15]

Information Technology   Advances in information technology allow people to communicate with one another and to access information at all times. **Information technology** consists of communication hardware and software that allow us to interact with one another. Examples of information technology include teleconferencing, e-mail, document sharing, use of the Internet, fax machines, and telephone systems. Information technology allows managers to stay in touch with their company and their environment. Managers can conduct electronic brainstorming sessions with team members around the globe, send data and information in the blink of an eye, and negotiate face-to-face with potential partners thousands of miles away.

Many organizations have taken advantage of the information technology revolution. Connectix, a small U.S.-based company, developed a $130 videoconferencing system that allows users to receive live audio and video signals through the Internet.[16] Titleist & Foot-Joy Worldwide, a golf equipment company, uses automation and information technology to custom-design golf gloves. Customers insert their hands into a laser scanner that accurately measures dimensions. The data are then sent to Thailand where manufacturers custom-make the gloves. Soon, the company plans to have computer-controlled sewing machines available in numerous locations to create the gloves.[17] By using sophisticated technologies, large and small organizations have shifted from selling mass-produced goods to custom products that meet the exact demands of the customer.

Expert Systems   The fourth technological change that affects many organizations is the development of **expert systems**—computer systems and software designed to help decision makers improve the quality and efficiency of their decisions. Expert systems developers create programs based on accumulated experience, knowledge, decision rules, and options that help managers evaluate alternatives, consider consequences, and make more objective decisions at lower cost. For example, flight simulators used in training fighter pilots rely on expert systems. The system assesses the pilot's weaknesses and adjusts its program to provide training that addresses those shortcomings.

Effects of Changing Technologies

How do these fast-changing technologies affect people in organizations? The technologies change the way we work, manage people, and view organizations, as depicted in Figure 2.3. First, new technologies can help businesspeople become more productive and efficient.

Second, new technologies create more options for organizing people. For example, telecommuting is possible only because of information technology tools, such as e-mail and videoconferencing. Those same technology tools help managers to supervise employees, suppliers, or temporary workers that they don't see on a daily basis. In addition, new technologies give businesses more options for structuring the organization. For instance, organizations can have more team-based structures because high technology and information technology tools can be used to support them and make staying in touch easier.

Third, changing technologies require that managers and employees learn continuously. The need for constant updating of skills can be a mixed blessing. On the one hand, managers must keep up with, use, and be prepared to train others to use changing technology to function effectively in their organizations. In fact, the pace of change is so rapid that many organizations, such as Intel and Arthur D. Little, have their own "universities" that teach employees new technologies. On the other hand, although employees are developing new skills, they often feel the pressure of always having to stay ahead of the curve. Similarly, organizations benefit from well-trained employees, but they have to shoulder the high costs of training.

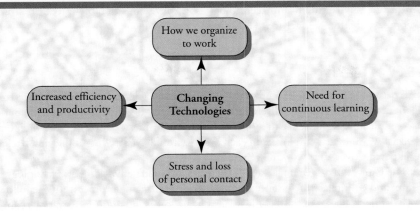

FIGURE 2.3
Effects of Changing Technologies

Changes in technology also have negative effects. First, many employees and managers feel pressure to master and improve their technological skills continuously in the midst of busy schedules. Some employees can't keep pace, and they struggle as a result. Second, high technology often replaces personal contact with other employees and managers. Though employees are connected electronically, they interact less with others and may feel isolated.

Managers must weigh the potential advantages of new technologies against the potential disadvantages. If technology suits the business and is well managed and well implemented, it can reduce costs, free workers of repetitive and menial tasks, put them in touch with managers and others across the world, and open up new opportunities to do business. Many successful organizations continue to operate successfully by using traditional and relatively low-technology tools and practices. For example, Tootsie Roll, the U.S. candy maker, although not relying extensively on high-technology, continues to be very successful.

Whether the changing technologies excite or threaten you, they are a fact of business. Managers consider the environment and technology as they set the direction for their

Summary Point 2.4   **What Are Key Changes in Technology and Their Effects?**

- Technology is the knowledge, tools, techniques, and processes used to create the goods and services of an organization.
- Major changes in technology in organizations include high technology, new manufacturing technology and automation, information technology, and expert systems.

- New technologies affect organizations in positive and negative ways. Technology can increase productivity and efficiency, give more options for organizing people, require that individuals learn continually, create stress, and decrease personal contact with others.

A QUESTION OF ETHICS

Electronic Monitoring | With high-technology tools, organizations can now monitor employees at all levels through the use of hidden cameras and e-mail and telephone tracking systems. A major Fortune 500 company fired one of its executives for accessing what the company considered inappropriate Web sites from work. If you were a manager, what level of monitoring, if any, would you consider acceptable? Do you think organizations have an ethical obligation to inform employees that they might be monitored? Why?

organization. Environment and technology both have considerable effect on strategy, the next contextual strategic factor we examine.

 STRATEGY

No two organizations are exactly alike. As we have seen, each organization responds to its environment and uses technology differently. Moreover, each organization has a different purpose and accomplishes that purpose in a distinct manner. Businesses also structure their employees in a special way. Finally, employees in each organization have varying skill levels, backgrounds, cultural perspectives, and working relationships.

The choices managers make about their organization's environment, technology, strategy, structure, and culture are the essence of the strategic management process. In the following section, we define strategy, the third contextual strategic force, and examine its various components.

The Basics: Mission, Goals, and Strategy

Mission
A statement of the organization's purpose and reason for existence

Mission is a statement of the organization's purpose and reason for existence. The mission provides the general direction for the organization and keeps all managers and employees in sync. To achieve its mission, a company sets goals—objectives that specify what needs to be achieved and when. The organization tries to achieve short-term goals within one year. Long-term goals are those that extend beyond one year. A firm's strategy is a comprehensive road map that states how a firm can reach its goals and achieve its mission within a set time frame.[18] Figure 2.4 illustrates the relationship among mission, goals, and strategy.

Mission Each organization has a unique mission. Some missions are comprehensive, formal, and frequently mentioned in business discussions. Others may be informal and brief. Regardless of their format, mission statements provide a sense of direction for the organization. Odwalla, the natural fruit juice manufacturer based in Washington, defines its mission as "Creating the best tasting, most nutritious fruit and vegetable juices."[19] Shell Oil Company's mission states: "Shell's main business is drawing stored energy from earth—as oil, gas and coal—and getting it in a useful form to where people want it."[20] Hewlett-Packard (H-P) wants "to provide products and services of the highest quality and the greatest possible value to our customers, thereby gaining and holding their respect and loyalty."[21]

Through the mission statement, each of these companies is not only defining its reason for existence but also enacting its environment and identifying its important stakeholders. Recall that stakeholders are groups or individuals who have a direct or an indirect interest in the success of the organization. Mission statements give priority to one group of stakeholders over others. For example, H-P clearly targets its customers as key stakeholders. Shell Oil emphasizes both its customers and the engineers who extract the oil. One company's mission may refer to the financial success of the company, thus acknowledging the importance of the company's shareholders; another company, such as Tom's of Maine, may state that serving the community is a key focus.

Mission statements should ideally create a sense of excitement for the organization's employees. When you walk into an organization with a well-defined and broadly accepted mission, you get a sense that everyone working there knows what the mission is, believes in it, takes pride in it, and practices it. Such an organization has a good chance of being successful. Although having a well-defined and broadly accepted mission is not a guarantee of success, it helps employees work toward the same goals. For example, employees at Medtronics, a medical products company located in Minneapolis, Minnesota, are inspired by the mission of the organization: "Restoring patients to full life." Bill George, the CEO of Medtronics, believes that patients come before profit, and his message is a source of pride for the employees.[22]

FIGURE 2.4
The Relationships Among Mission, Goals, and Strategy

Dilbert reprinted by permission of United Feature Syndicate, Inc.

Goals   Organizational goals, based on the mission, can be both financial and nonfinancial. For instance, achieving a 20 percent return on investment within the next three years is a financial goal. Achieving a 10 percent reduction in absenteeism per year is a nonfinancial goal, although it has financial implications. Organizations set goals for every possible activity, then measure their performance against those goals. The challenge for managers is to ensure that organizational goals do not conflict with the direction specified by the mission statement.

For instance, if the mission statement refers to the affordable cost of the products for consumers, then the manufacturing department's managers must set their goals to keep the cost of production low. Otherwise, the goals will not match the mission statement. Similarly, if a promise of high-quality products is part of the mission statement, several organizational goals should focus on improving product quality.

Strategy   Managers can choose from many different strategies to achieve goals. Their strategy, however, must support the company's mission and goals. If the goal is to keep the cost of the product affordable, then managers might select a strategy to produce a limited array of products with just a few options. That way, they minimize production costs. If quality is the aim, then managers could choose a strategy of manufacturing a wide variety of products with multiple options and instituting extra quality control programs.

Let's look at an example that illustrates the relationship among mission, goals, and strategy. A new rock group may define its mission as becoming the most successful group in music history. The short-term goal would be to have its newest CD hit the top of the charts within three months, and its long-term goal may be to have a platinum CD in its first five years. The strategies to achieve these goals may include conducting market research about the band's target audience and creating a specific marketing campaign to promote the band. The campaign may consist of a video directed by a successful director; increased play time on popular radio and TV stations around the country; public relations interviews, appearances, and tours of major cities; and an image developed through advertising that appeals to the 15- to 18-year-old market. The band should also plan to develop high-quality songs that appeal to its market so that its CDs become platinum sellers.

To be effective, all managers and employees should know not only their organization's mission but also its short- and long-term goals and the specific strategies the business plans to use to achieve the goals. Various departments and individuals take ownership of the goals and are responsible for their achievement. In more traditional organizations, top leaders and managers set goals and are held accountable for them.

Increasingly, everyone in the business helps develop goals. This participation is due in part to the use of teams in business and to new management techniques such as "open book management," discussed in the Change Challenge segment in this chapter. The participation increases the sense of ownership and makes more people accountable and responsible for accomplishing goals. However, organizations must assign a goal to a specific person or group; otherwise they cannot be sure that the goal will be accomplished.

Summary Point 2.5   **What Are Mission, Goals, and Strategy?**

- Mission is the organization's purpose.
- Goals are the means used to achieve the mission.
- Strategy is a comprehensive road map that states how a firm can reach its goals and achieve its mission within a set time frame.

- An organization's goals and strategies should support and not conflict with the company's mission.

Managing Strategy

Strategy formulation
The process of forging a cohesive, integrated set of strategies designed to deal with the environment and achieve the business mission and goals

Strategy implementation
Actions the organization takes to execute its strategies

Strategic management process
The combined processes of strategy formulation and implementation

SWOT analysis
An analysis of a company's internal strengths and weaknesses and the opportunities and threats in the organization's environment

Managers evaluate the contextual strategic forces and then design strategies to take advantage of business opportunities. **Strategy formulation** is the process of forging a cohesive, integrated set of strategies designed to deal with the environment and achieve the business mission and goals. **Strategy implementation** is the actions the organization takes to execute the strategy it has formulated. The **strategic management process** consists of strategy formulation and implementation processes.

To formulate strategy, managers analyze the strengths and weaknesses of their organization relative to their competitors and examine the opportunities and threats in their environment.[23] This analysis is called a **SWOT analysis** (*s*trengths, *w*eaknesses, *o*pportunities, and *t*hreats). A SWOT analysis is an evaluation of the organization's environment for opportunities and threats and how those match with the company's internal strengths and weaknesses. The SWOT analysis is the first step in the strategic management process, as we see in Figure 2.5. Once a company conducts a SWOT analysis, its managers can design specific strategies to exploit strengths and minimize weaknesses to achieve the organization's mission and goals.[24]

Assume that you want to open a bookstore in the United States. First, you should analyze the business and general environment of bookstores. You will find a highly competitive industry dominated by national chains such as Barnes & Noble and Borders. After doing a SWOT analysis and considering the hefty resources needed to compete with these chains, you decide that your company's strengths are its small size, flexibility, and up-to-date technology. The competition's main weaknesses are their inability to provide personalized services to customers and their expensive inventory of unsold books. Because of your analysis, you decide not to open stores across the United States as the bigger players have done. Instead, you formulate a strategy to sell on-line and bypass the traditional outlets for selling books.

Amazon.com followed such a strategy. The company sells books over the Internet at some of the lowest prices available.[25] Amazon.com takes your order, adds it to all other orders for the book, buys the exact number of books needed, and mails the book to you within three to five days. As a result of its process, it has guaranteed sales and few returns. The company has sales of $10 million per year, no stores, and no inventory. Instead of putting resources into hiring managers and sales staff, the company's 32-year-old CEO Jeff Bezos focuses on keeping up with the newest technology and invests in hiring computer programmers.

The company's strategy stems from the SWOT analysis and the enactment of the environment. Bezos has enacted his company's environment as primarily including technology. Because of Bezos's strategy, he doesn't consider the competition with large bookstores too threatening. Instead, he feels his major threat is another entrepreneur, like himself, who may devise an even brighter idea to take advantage of unknown opportunities while working out of a garage or home office.

Though it may appear that the strategic formulation and implementation process is sequential, businesses seldom develop strategy and then implement it in a step-by-step man-

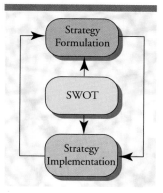

FIGURE 2.5
The Strategic Management Process

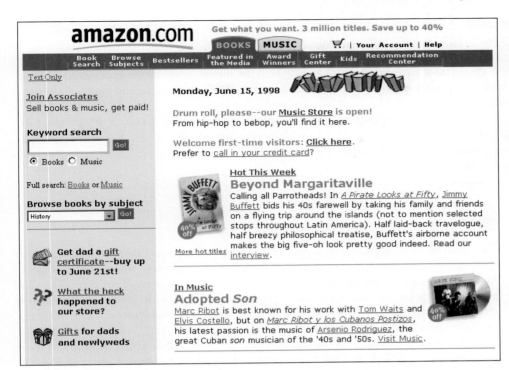

How do you take on big competitors? Amazon.com did so by using web technology to compete with large book sellers without having to go head to head with them.

ner. Formulation and implementation occur simultaneously. In addition, realized strategies may or may not resemble the intended strategy.[26] During formulation and implementation, managers modify most strategies, discontinue some, and create new ones. The contextual strategic factors, such as environment and technology, that influence the choice of strategy continue to impact how strategy is implemented. As the environment and the technology change, the strategy changes as well. In addition, internal organizational forces such as structure and culture affect how a strategy is implemented.

Formulating the right strategy for the organization is as much art as it is science. Consider the case of Honda.[27] When Mr. Soichiro Honda created a strategy to start exporting small Honda motorcycles to the United States in 1959 to achieve Honda's growth goals, the Japanese government advised him not to do so. According to Japanese government analysts, the United States environment was not suitable for small bikes. Motorcycle manufacturers such as Harley Davidson dominated the market with large, powerful bikes. The analysts perceived American motorcycle customers as leather-jacket-wearing riders interested only in big bikes. The Japanese government did not believe that moving to the U.S. market would be a wise strategy. Mr. Honda disagreed. He envisioned millions of young Americans riding his small bikes for fun around their neighborhoods.

After some initial setbacks, Honda's strategy of focusing on young people paid off. Its logo of "You meet the nicest people on a Honda," and ads showing casually dressed young couples riding Honda Scooters contributed to the phenomenal success that Honda motorcycles became. With low prices and a clear image that set it apart from the big bikes, the company established a strong foothold in the U.S. market. This success eventually led to the export of small Honda cars to the United States, with the Honda Accord becoming one of the best-selling U.S. car brands.

Now that we have discussed environment, technology, and strategy, we turn our attention to the fourth contextual strategic force: organizational structure.

Summary Point 2.6   **How Do Organizations Manage Strategy?**

- Strategy formulation is the design of a cohesive, integrated strategy to deal with the environment and to achieve the mission and goals.
- Strategy implementation is the actions the organization takes to execute the integrated strategy.
- The strategic management process consists of strategy formulation and strategy implementation processes.

- SWOT is the analysis of the internal strengths and weaknesses and external opportunities and threats of the organization.
- The strategic management process is highly dynamic and rarely occurs sequentially.

THE ORGANIZATION'S STRUCTURE

The structure of an organization refers to the way human resources are organized to achieve the company's mission. Who is responsible for what; who reports to whom; and how information moves up, down, and across the organization are all aspects of structure. The simplest way to assess the structure of an organization is to look at its chart (see examples of charts in Figures 2.6 to 2.10 on pages 55–59). An **organizational chart** is a diagram of the organization's skeletal structure.

Organizational chart
A diagram of the basic structure of the organization

Structure is central to an organization's effectiveness. The structure must fit the environment, use technology in a productive way, and support the company's strategy and culture. An organization that doesn't have the appropriate structure is unlikely to achieve its mission and goals easily. We stress the word *appropriate* because there is no best way to structure the human resources of an organization. What works depends on many factors, such as the organization's environment, use of technology, strategy, culture, and size. For instance, smaller businesses tend to organize employees in simpler ways than larger organizations because an increase in size means that it's harder for people to interact. For example, Amazon.com is a relatively small business that has a simple structure. The company relies on technology to achieve its mission. Managers, then, must adjust structure to cope with communication issues.

Basic Components of Structure

What makes up the structure of an organization? Structure has five basic components:[28]

- *Reporting relationships:* a specification of who reports to whom; the pecking order of the organization
- *Span of control:* an allocation of authority determined by the number of people who report to each manager
- *Departmentation:* a designation of how people are grouped into teams, departments, or sections
- *Allocation of responsibilities:* the assignment of duties, responsibilities, and authority for each task
- *Coordination:* a plan that establishes how people interact and work with each other to accomplish tasks

The structure of an organization clarifies the organization's hierarchy (its power structure). That is, it informs employees who their supervisors are and lets managers know who reports to them. It also shows employees and managers how they link up with others in different departments throughout the organization.

Summary Point 2.7   **What Is Structure and What Are Its Components?**

- Structure is defined as the way the organization's human resources are organized to achieve its mission.

- The five key components of structure are reporting relationships, span of control, departmentation, allocation of responsibilities, and coordination.

Structural Elements

Being aware of the five components that define structure is the first step in understanding the structure of an organization. The second step is analyzing how organizations differ in structuring employees to achieve business goals. To analyze how each organizational structure differs, we need to examine the seven structural elements defined in Table 2.2: formalization, specialization, standardization, hierarchy, centralization, differentiation, and integration.[29] Organizational structures differ according to what choices the business makes about each of these elements.

Because every organization combines these seven elements differently, every organization's structure is unique. Employees in an organization such as Union Pacific Railway, which has a tall hierarchy with centralized decision making and a high degree of specialization, formalization, and standardization, will behave and feel differently from those in an organization

Table 2.2   SEVEN STRUCTURAL ELEMENTS

Structural Elements	Description
Degree of Formalization	The number of formal, written documentation relating to organizational procedures, activities, and behaviors. A formalized organization clearly describes all activities in writing.
Amount of Specialization	The degree to which each individual, department, or team performs special, narrow tasks as compared to a broad set of tasks. High specialization means that individuals perform specific limited tasks.
Degree of Standardization	The degree to which similar activities are performed in a standardized, similar way. In a standardized organization, all individuals performing similar tasks perform them the same way.
Hierarchy	The number of reporting relationships and the span of control of managers. *Tall hierarchies* have many different levels of power and an individual manager at each level has only a few people reporting to him or her.
Degree of Centralization	The extent to which decisions are made at either the top or at other levels of the organization. In a centralized organization a few people at the top make most decisions.
Extent of Differentiation	The extent of difference in approaches among people with different specialties. Differentiated organizations have clearly separate departments or groups that deal with different aspects of organizational goals and processes.
Extent of Integration	The quality and degree of cooperation among departments. In well-integrated organizations, differentiated departments or groups with different goals cooperate extensively and share resources and information to accomplish overall goals.

such as Southwest Airlines, which has few levels in the hierarchy, decentralized decision making, and a low degree of specialization and formalization.

Similarly, organizations that are highly differentiated organize people in clearly defined departments that can create barriers among employees.[30] In highly differentiated organizations, such as in Toyota Corp., market researchers are clearly separate from salespeople. In less differentiated organizations, such as in Amazon.com, employees' functions and tasks aren't as clearly defined and separated. Many new or small businesses are less differentiated. The same people, often the small business owner and one or two partners, take care of many different functions. Each person may be involved in production, accounting, marketing and sales, payroll management, and customer service. As departments become more differentiated, they need to be able to coordinate their activities well.

Good integration mechanisms are essential to an effective and productive organization. The essence of an organization is people who cooperate to tackle complex problems. If people handle cooperation and integration of activities poorly, they threaten the existence of an organization. A business can achieve integration through simple programs, such as informal weekly meetings, or through a complex structure that includes numerous teams and task forces. The key challenge of designing the structure of an organization is to use the integration tools that allow employees to do their job well and allow access to the information they need when they need it.[31]

Consider the case of W. L. Gore and Associates and its unusual and highly effective structure. The company makes all types of outdoor, camping, medical, and other products based on the Gore-Tex® membrane, a flexible, water-resistant material. Most outdoor enthusiasts own some of the company's camping gear and numerous hospitals use medical supplies made with Gore-Tex® products.[32]

The unique structure at W. L. Gore is called a lattice organization.[33] Each of the company's plants has only about 200 employees, a number that founders Bill and Vieve Gore felt encouraged a sense of belonging and flexibility. No one has a formal title; employees are simply called associates. The company does not establish clear lines of hierarchy or assign authority to specific people. There are no bosses, only "sponsors" who help others learn new tasks. Associates often change positions through what the company calls natural leadership and followership.

W. L. Gore and Associates uses the unique and creative lattice to organize its employees to address its needs for innovation and flexibility.

The organization doesn't have differentiated departments. Instead, the structure integrates various activities and encourages person-to-person communication and participatory decision making. The company doesn't assign tasks and functions to formal departments. Rather, teams and committees that operate in a nonhierarchical structure accomplish tasks and functions. The owners encourage experimentation, realize that mistakes will happen and accept this, expect associates to ask questions, and do not tolerate poor performance.

Through the unique combination of informal processes, low specialization, low standardization, decentralized decision making, and well-integrated teams, W. L. Gore has created a structure that supports the company's mission of innovation, world-class quality, and customer satisfaction. Employees also rate it as one of the top 100 U.S. companies to work for.[34]

Organic and Mechanistic Organizations

When managers combine the basic components and elements of structure, the resulting structure has certain characteristics. One method of understanding these characteristics is through the concepts of organic and mechanistic organizations. **Organic** organizations are informal; they have a low degree of specialization and standardization, decentralized decision making, and well-integrated activities. Organic organizations are most appropriate when the environment is uncertain.[35] Loose structures, decentralized decision making, and good integration give organizations the flexibility to deal with fast-paced environmental change and many different elements.

W. L. Gore is organic. A consulting firm serves as another example of an organic organization. The environment of consulting firms changes rapidly because these firms solve client's unique problems as they arise. Because consulting firms do not know in advance what types of projects they may have, they form teams according to customer needs. Consulting firms have few rules and regulations and decisions are usually made at the team level as issues develop and based on client requests.

Organizations that have centralized decision making and formal, standardized control systems are **mechanistic**.[36] Such organizations work well in stable, simple environments. Managers integrate the activities of clearly differentiated departments through formal channels and in formal meetings. An example of a highly mechanistic organization is a **bureaucracy**— an organization that has a highly formalized, specialized, standardized, centralized structure with many layers and a focus on hierarchical reporting relationships.[37] General Motors (GM) is an example of a bureaucracy. GM has a formalized, specialized, standardized, and centralized structure. Its six divisions have many layers with hierarchical reporting relationships.

For another example, let's say that you need a driver's license, so you visit a drivers' license bureau anywhere in the United States. With some minor state differences, you'll move through the following process: After checking in, someone verifies your identity, charges you a fee, and hands you a standard written exam. If you pass the written test, you take a standard driving test in which you must perform a long list of driving activities at a basic skill level. If you once again pass, you take an eye test and have your picture taken. Roughly two hours after entering the bureau, a clerk hands you your new driver's license. Every step of this process is standardized, formalized, specialized, centralized, hierarchical, differentiated, and integrated. The reason is simple: Every person who applies for a driver's license has to be treated exactly the same way. Imagine finding out that a neighbor who just received his license didn't have to take the driving test, or that another one paid no fee, and a third one had only her left eye examined! The mission of any drivers' license bureau is to make sure that every person who receives a license knows the rules, can drive safely, and is fit to do so. The mechanistic structure of the bureaucracy structure supports that mission.

Most organizations fall somewhere in between the two extremes of organic and mechanistic. Table 2.3 highlights the differences between the two types of organizations. Although they provide some clear advantages, mechanistic organizations are also inflexible and slow to

Organic organization
Organization with a low degree of formality, specialization, and standardization; decentralized decision making; and well-integrated activities

Mechanistic organization
An organization that has centralized decision making and formal, standardized control systems

Bureaucracy
Organization with a highly formalized, specialized, standardized, centralized structure with many layers and hierarchical reporting relationships

Table 2.3   MECHANISTIC AND ORGANIC ORGANIZATIONS

Mechanistic	Organic
• Specialized tasks	• General tasks
• Well-defined departments with clear hierarchy	• Loosely defined departments with loosely defined hierarchy
• Centralized decision making by a few people	• Decentralized decision making by many individuals
• Integration achieved by relying on formal meetings among managers	• Integration achieved by employees and managers interacting and exchanging information as needed
• Clear and efficient reporting relationships	• Flexibility and capability for rapid change

change. An organization like W. L. Gore can respond to change quickly by reassigning employees whereas a bureaucracy cannot. Each organization designs its structure to address its mission, goals, and strategy. If the structure fits with other contextual elements, the organization has a better chance of being effective.

Now that we have defined structure, analyzed potential structural features, and examined organic and mechanistic organizations, we turn to the traditional and current structural options available to managers.

Summary Point 2.8   **What Are the Elements of Structure and What Are Organic and Mechanistic Organizations?**

- Formalization, specialization, standardization, hierarchy, centralization, differentiation, and integration are the key elements of structure.
- Organic organizations are informal, with low standardization and specialization, and decentralized decision making.

- Mechanistic organizations are formal, standardized, specialized, and have centralized decision making. Bureaucracies are an example of mechanistic organizations.

Traditional Structural Options

The four traditional structural options are the functional, product/divisional, hybrid, and matrix. As managers organize their employees to accomplish the organizational mission and goals, these traditional structures can offer a starting point. Each has certain advantages and disadvantages and each fits a certain organizational size and mix of contextual factors.

Functional Structures   The simplest form of structure is to group employees by their functional specialization. In a **functional structure**, people who perform the same function are in the same groups, teams, or departments. Such an organization would, for example, have accounting, marketing, production, and human resources departments. Figure 2.6 presents a simple functional structure.

Functional structure
One in which people who perform the same function are in the same groups, teams, or departments

The functional structure is one of the most commonly used designs and is usually the starting point for most organizations. Large firms such as Microsoft, American Airlines, Compaq, and Merck all started with a functional structure.

The functional structure is generally appropriate in a low uncertainty environment, and for a small to medium-size organization that focuses on control and efficiency. The biggest

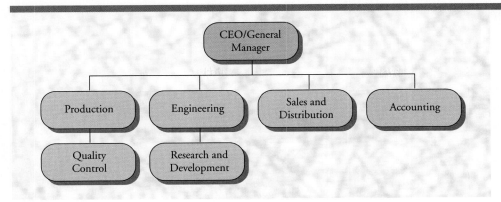

FIGURE 2.6
The Functional Structure

challenge for a functional structure is how to encourage different functional departments to interact and to focus on the mission of the organization rather than on how each department can get more resources to achieve its individual goals.

Product Structures   The second traditional structure, depicted in Figure 2.7, is **product or divisional structure**. It groups people by the products or services they work on, or according to geographic region. For example, employees working in the northeastern United States or in central Canada are part of one division. The product structure is appropriate for large organizations that face an uncertain environment, have demands for quick response to customers, and command considerable resources. Such organizations typically have decentralized leadership with a mission of customer satisfaction and flexibility. Although integration among departments tends to be good, organizations with this type of structure can lose sight of overall organizational goals and the latest developments in the environment. Why? Because each product group or division becomes a kingdom unto itself. The challenge in the product/divisional structure, then, is to integrate the various goals and activities of the divisions in a meaningful way.

GM used a product structure for many years. The original five divisions of GM competed with one another and lost sight of the external environment and their foreign competition. The whole corporation suffered until the 1980s when the structure was redesigned to

Product or divisional structure
One that groups people by the products or services they work on

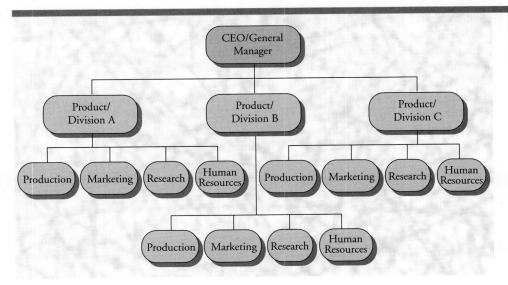

FIGURE 2.7
The Product/Divisional Structure

FIGURE 2.8
The Hybrid Structure

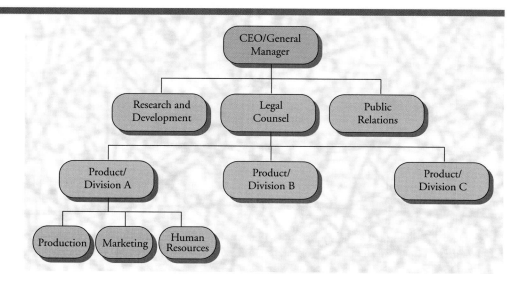

focus on the external market and a specific group of customers. The current structure reduces the competition among the divisions.

Hybrid Structures

Hybrid structure
Combines the functional and product structures

As organizations grow and neither the functional nor the product structure allows them to be effective, they look for other structural options. One option available to very large organizations that operate in many different locations is to combine the functional and product structure to form a **hybrid structure**, as we see in Figure 2.8. The hybrid organization has headquarters that provide several functions to all divisions. The divisions then specialize either by product or by region. Because the hybrid structure can work for large organizations, many multinational organizations such as Exxon, AT&T, Nestlé, and Bayer use it.

The hybrid generally has both the disadvantages and the advantages of the functional and product structures. The hybrid provides many advantages such as flexibility, greater ability to deal with an uncertain environment, and responsiveness to customers. However, the hybrid has the disadvantage of requiring extensive resources because the organization duplicates many departments and functions in each product group or region.

Matrix Structures

Matrix structure
Uses project teams of both functional specialists and product/project specialists

The final traditional form of organizations is the matrix. The matrix structure was originally developed to address the problems associated with the other three structures and to respond to environmental uncertainty and customer demands for efficiency, flexibility, and high quality.[38] As we see in Figure 2.9, the **matrix structure** uses in a flexible manner project teams that include both functional specialists and product or project specialists. The goal of the matrix is to provide a high level of integration between function and product and to do so without using extensive resources.

Cross-functional teams
Teams of people from different departments

The matrix is appropriate for organizations that face a highly uncertain environment and are under pressure both to be efficient and to respond to their customers quickly. The organization creates and disbands project teams as needed to address customer needs. In fact, if an organization constantly creates teams of people from different departments, also referred to as **cross-functional teams**, and those teams never seem to disband, the matrix may be the next step.

Many project-related businesses such as software companies, consulting firms, defense contractors, construction companies, and research and development firms use matrix structures. By pulling experts from their functional departments and putting them, temporarily, on a certain project, the organizations use their expertise wisely. These project teams can be responsive to a specific customer's needs.

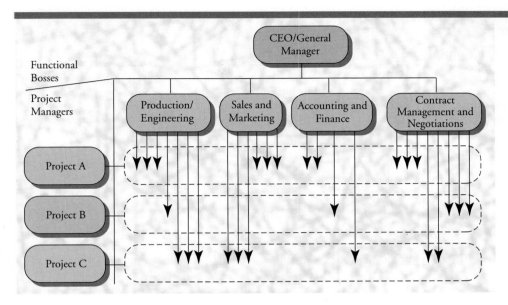

FIGURE 2.9
Matrix Structure

The matrix structure can address integration problems. Since employees and managers from different functions work together on projects, they can easily coordinate their activities. For example, Boeing produces new airplanes using a matrix structure. When the company designed its 777 jetliner, managers, engineers, designers, marketers, and hundreds of other specialists were pulled from their functional departments and put on the 777 team. Team members were able to coordinate their activities relatively easily.

Organizations must also recognize some of the drawbacks of the matrix structure. First, organizations need expertise in managing teams before they can implement this structure effectively. Second, the matrix structure puts a lot of pressure on project managers to make sure the job is done on time and within budget. Third, people from different functional areas often have difficulty working well together. Fourth, project teams spend considerable time and resources coordinating and integrating their activities and training people to work in teams.

None of the four basic structural options is perfect. Table 2.4 presents a summary analysis of the advantages and disadvantages of the four traditional structures. Whether a structural option works for an organization depends on the fit among the contextual strategic factors of environment, technology, strategy, and culture. Knowing the advantages and disadvantages of each of the traditional structures and being aware of the effect of the contextual factors on the choice of structure can help managers make good decisions about how to organize people. In

---

Summary Point 2.9   **What Are the Four Traditional Structures?**

- The functional structure organizes people based on their business functional area. It is most appropriate for organizations that face a certain environment, are small in size, and have limited goals or products.
- The product/divisional structure organizes people based on the product on which they work. It is most appropriate for an organization that faces an uncertain environment, is large in size, and needs to handle multiple goals or products.

- The hybrid structure combines the functional and product structure with several functions dominating the products or divisions. It is most appropriate for organizations with large resources that have many goals and products.
- The matrix structure creates temporary departments based on both function and product. It is most appropriate for organizations with equal demand for efficiency and high quality in uncertain environments with limited resources.

Table 2.4 THE FOUR TRADITIONAL STRUCTURAL OPTIONS

	When Appropriate	Advantages	Disadvantages
Functional	• Environment is certain • Organization is small to medium size • Focus is on efficiency and specialization • Business has few goals	• Is efficient • Provides functional specialization	• Has poor integration among functional departments • Is inflexible • Can't handle multiple goals or change easily
Product/Divisional	• Environment is uncertain • Organization is large • Focus is on customer satisfaction • Business has multiple goals	• Has good integration inside divisions • Can handle multiple goals and environmental demands	• Requires considerable resources • Duplicates effort across divisions • Fosters competition among divisions
Hybrid	• Environment is uncertain • Organization is large • Business has multiple goals	• Can help manage large organizations • Can address multiple goals	• Requires considerable resources • Duplicates effort across divisions • Fosters poor coordination among departments
Matrix	• Environment is uncertain • Customers demand efficiency, quality, and flexibility • Business does project-type work	• Fosters good integration of departments • Handles multiple goals, products, or projects • Uses limited resources efficiently	• Requires considerable coordination • Creates potential for stress due to multiple demands • Can be inefficient with too much time spent on process

addition to these four traditional structures, today's organizations also are experimenting with new structural forms.

The New Structural Options

We learned in chapter 1 that many organizations throughout the world are restructuring. As we've seen, businesses that restructure must examine how they organize reporting relationships, departments, responsibilities, and integration mechanisms. Today's organizations are using many innovative structures to become more effective. The new structural options focus on better integration and more flexibility.[39] In this section, we investigate five new structures: virtual, team-based, boundaryless, spaghetti, and network organizations.

Virtual organizations
Organizations that function with a limited, relatively small core of permanent employees and facilities

Hot ▼ Link

We defined outsourcing in chapter 1, p. 25.

Virtual Organizations **Virtual organizations** are those that function with a limited, relatively small core of permanent employees and facilities. They then rely on a large number of full- and part-time outside contractors and production and service facilities. The process of hiring outside contractors, known as *outsourcing,* is one of the major business trends of the last decade.[40] All parts of the virtual structure are connected through a network of computers and electronic communication devices.

Figure 2.10 shows an example of a virtual organization chart. Note the absence of clear departments and vertical and horizontal lines linking people. Instead, employees and outsiders interact as needed. The structure works well if the organization can establish extensive cooperative links with its various partners. The virtual organization structure is nonhierarchical with few levels and few departments. The resulting flexibility is the key to virtual organizations.

Aside from increased flexibility, the potential advantages of this structure include reduced human resource costs through outsourcing and use of part-time workers. Although contractors may cost more per hour than permanent employees, they receive no benefits and can be terminated with a moment's notice. The virtual organization can also be more innovative because the outside talent that it seeks may offer a wide variety of perspectives and isn't as likely as permanent employees might be to do things "the corporate way."

An example of a successful virtual organization is Pittsburgh-based Super Bakery, a doughnut maker. Super Bakery set up various accounting, monitoring, and feedback systems that allow it to control the performance of its contractors closely.[41] The result? The business generates $9 million per year. Another example of a successful virtual organization is the AeroTech Service Group. That business built a model virtual factory with McDonnell Douglas Aerospace (now part of Boeing). AeroTech's success was to a great extent due to the sophisticated information technology networks that, as in the Super Bakery case, allowed for close communication and contact with its partners.[42]

Although the trend toward using virtual organizations seems here to stay, it has many critics.[43] While contracting allows firms to remain flexible, contractors do not develop a sense of loyalty toward the organization. The danger is that they may do just the minimum amount required and not go "the extra mile" for their temporary employer. Worse, the contractors may not deliver what they promise. Managers may also find the constant negotiation with and monitoring of contractors burdensome.

In just such an example, manufacturer AC International followed the virtual corporation trend and signed a number of agreements with varied contractors for producing its products: a line of bicycle tire-liners that prevent flat tires. After two years of mounting costs and missed deadlines, the firm decided to manufacture most of its products internally so that it would have control over the quality and cost.[44]

Virtual organizations are redefining the concept of organizations, leadership, and management. How is a manager supposed to motivate a "virtual employee" who is an independent outside contractor? If an organization is a group of people working toward a common goal, then what is a virtual organization where contractors work on different goals based on their contracts with different companies? And how does the manager ensure that confidentiality of the organization's trade secrets and processes is maintained? These challenges continue to face today's managers in virtual organizations.

For some employees, particularly those who need autonomy and independence, virtual organizations are ideal. For others, they can be a nightmare. Some feel isolated and lose touch with the business. In most cases, managers must learn to manage both the technology of telecommuting and a dispersed set of people. In all cases, virtual organizations can be successful only if they achieve integration and coordination through intense negotiations, careful management of relationships, constant contact, and trust. Like the traditional structural options, the virtual organization is neither an ideal design nor a cure-all. It is an option that some organizations implement to adapt to extreme uncertainty, limited resources, and a high need for flexibility to achieve the business mission.[45]

Team-Based Structures It is almost impossible to open a business magazine or newspaper without reading about how organizations use teams effectively. Teams can't function independently, however, unless the organization *empowers* them to act. **Empowerment** is the act of giving power to employees at various levels of the organization so they are able to make autonomous decisions about their tasks.[46] Though most organizations are starting to use teams in some fashion, not all are empowering employees.

Those organizations that have a team-based structure often use cross-functional teams to make and implement decisions, work on a task, or solve a problem. Teams may include individual employees and managers with different expertise and different levels of responsibility.[47] When an organization has empowered teams in place, managers' roles changes from command and control to providing support, securing resources, and removing obstacles for the team.

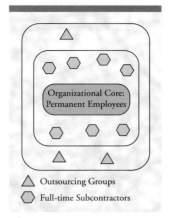

FIGURE 2.10
The Virtual Organization

△ Outsourcing Groups
⬡ Full-time Subcontractors

Empowerment
Giving power to employees at various levels of the organization

Hot ▼ Link

We discussed empowerment in chapter 1, p. 14.

The use of a team-based structure is a central feature of many modern organizations. Think back to W. L. Gore's lattice structure. It relies on teams and committees to make decisions. Many other organizations such as Rubbermaid, Honeywell, Intel, and Ford also rely on teams to varying degrees. At Intel, team members have considerable input about who gets hired. Rubbermaid considers teams to be its source of innovation and success. Ford relied on teams as the cornerstone of its revival in the 1980s and its continued success in the 1990s. In spite of increased use, team-based organizations are far from ideal structures. They are difficult to manage and have not always lived up to their promise.

Boundaryless, Spaghetti, Network, and Other Structural Experiments The changing environment, new technologies, global competition, and the creativity of entrepreneurs are some of the many factors that threaten the success and dominance of well-established organizations. As a result, many businesses are looking for ways to survive and thrive.

Small entrepreneurial firms have the distinct advantage of being able to change easily. Because these firms are small and have little formal structure, they tend to be well integrated, flexible, and able to respond quickly to change. In contrast, the world's largest corporations—such as GM, IBM, or Sumitomo—change more slowly. The pace slows down because large organizations often spend years planning, researching the effects of, making decisions about, and implementing the changes.

Change Challenge

OPEN-BOOK MANAGEMENT

Some organizations are implementing a new approach based on full employee involvement and participation in all aspects of a business. The approach, called open-book management, is attributed to executives of the Johnsonville Sausage Corporation and to Ricardo Semler, a highly successful young Brazilian entrepreneur and president of Semco, a manufacturing organization.[a] Johnsonville and Semco opened their financial records, strategic management process, and all other information about the company to their employees. Then they trained employees to understand these processes fully.

Although not all employees were directly involved in financial and strategic planning, knowledge about these issues increased the participants' sense of involvement and helped them see how their performance related to the organization's performance. Other firms, such as Corning, Herman Miller, and TDI, have started to use open-book concepts. A small Dallas-based installer of air conditioners, TDI has monthly meetings for employees to explain the financial results of the past month. One worker explains: "This company makes you feel like a human being again."[b]

The key to open-book management is well-designed training that allows employees to understand and use financial data and strategic management concepts. This type of understanding can help broaden both their feeling of ownership and their sense of responsibility.

a. J. Case, "The Open Book Revolution," *Inc* (June 1995): 25–50; V. Griffith, "Knowledge of the Company Accounts Is Believed to Improve Employee Performance," *Financial Times*, July 1995, 7; and R. Semler, *Maverick! The Success Story Behind the World's Most Unusual Workplace* (London: Century, 1993).

b. R. Levering and M. Moskowitz, "The 100 Best Companies to Work for in America," *Fortune* 137, no. 1 (January 12, 1998): 84.

Organizations have devised new structural forms to address the need to be flexible in an environment that changes rapidly. The **boundaryless organization** is a team-based structure designed to reduce or remove obstacles to free interaction among people, departments, and various organizational levels.[48] The structure eliminates departments, replaces them with cross-functional teams, and simplifies the chain of command by empowering employees. To succeed, boundaryless organizations require considerable training and resource investment.

Boundaryless organization
A structure designed to reduce or remove obstacles to free interaction among departments and people, and between different organizational levels

General Electric, under the leadership of Jack Welch, has been one of the most celebrated examples of boundaryless structures. Welch aimed at eliminating all internal and external barriers among employees and with customers and suppliers to allow productive and effective interactions.[49] Several other large organizations such as Hewlett-Packard and Motorola have implemented at least some elements of a boundaryless structure. These organizations changed their structure considerably by reducing vertical and horizontal barriers that prevent coordination and integration.

Other notable examples of new structures include the "spaghetti" organization that Oticon, a Danish hearing-aid manufacturer, has adopted.[50] Oticon had a functional structure that managers believed prevented it from responding to its competitors and customers. Managers discarded the existing structures, including job descriptions and physical structures such as office walls and furniture.

Instead the spaghetti structure organizes employees by project rather than by department. Oticon managers assigned employees to projects and let them invent the jobs that needed to be done. Instead of assigning employees to offices, the business organized them around workstations that allowed them to complete their tasks. The new structure allowed Oticon's employees to interact with people of different expertise and to focus on its customers' needs more efficiently.

Other businesses have developed other new structures to suit their needs. Asea Brown Boveri (ABB) is a giant multinational that has experimented successfully with a network structure.[51] ABB is one of the world's largest organizations, with $30 billion in sales and over 215,000 employees. It has 1,300 units that operate in over 140 countries to provide industrial, environmental, power generation, and mass transit services to local customers. ABB's CEO and a committee of 12 members, representing seven different nationalities, manage the company. This network of top executives meets every three weeks in different locations around the world to coordinate their goals and strategies.

Beneath this coordinating committee is a loose matrix structure, representing world geographic areas and the global business segments of ABB. Each segment is a small, highly autonomous profit center within the larger organization. As the name suggests, a profit center is responsible for its own profits and losses. These centers require intense cooperation, coordination, information and resource exchange, and continuous feedback and adjustment. ABB has been able to achieve major efficiencies in its businesses because of its network structure, even though its operations are scattered around the world.

The common themes for the spaghetti, network, and other new structures are simplification, decentralization, low formalization and low specialization, integration, and open exchange of information. Such structures enable managers to cope with rapidly changing environments more effectively because they can adjust to the mission, goals, and strategy and remain competitive and flexible.

Although the effects are often positive, the new structures' success does not come without pain. Particularly, these new structures have eliminated jobs and triggered layoffs. For example, General Electric eliminated 100,000 jobs in the 1980s when it implemented its boundaryless structure.[52] ABB's new network structure also led to the elimination of many jobs across Europe. Furthermore, these new structures continue to be experiments. Managers and employees often do not know how to make them work and, as a result, often feel frustrated and stressed.

Summary Point 2.10   **What Are the New Structures?**

- Virtual organizations function with a limited and relatively small core of employees and facilities and rely on a large number of outside contractors.
- Team-based structures are on the rise, such as those that use cross-functional teams to make and implement decisions.

- New structures such as the boundaryless, spaghetti, and network structures all rely on simplification, decentralization, integration, and open exchange of information.

Regardless of the structure managers select, for an organization to be effective its structure has to support its mission, goals, and strategy. Furthermore, the structure must fit the environment and the technology. In this final section, we consider the important links among the strategic contextual forces of environment, technology, strategy, and structure.

■ MANAGING IN AN UNCERTAIN ENVIRONMENT TO STAY COMPETITIVE: JUGGLING THE FIVE FORCES

To keep the organization competitive, managers need to monitor the contextual strategic forces of environment, technology, strategy, structure, and culture, and the ways they influence one another. The fit among the contextual strategic factors is key to an effective organization.[53] Monitoring the environment is the starting point because environmental changes dictate the types of adjustments the organization must make to stay competitive. Managers can respond to environmental changes through a number of activities, such as using new technology, designing a new strategy, or altering organizational structure.

For instance, in the early 1980s when the price of crude oil was rising, chemical companies, such as DuPont, faced an uncertain environment. They did not know whether the flow of oil would continue or how its price would fluctuate. To reduce environmental uncertainty, a number of chemical firms altered their structure by merging with oil companies. The new structure guaranteed a stable source of oil.

Managers can respond to an uncertain environment in three general ways:

- *Gather information* about environmental elements to monitor changes
- *Change their internal structures* to be more responsive to the environment
- *Change their environment* through lobbying and strategic alliances

Gathering Information

An organization needs complete, reliable information so that its managers can conduct a SWOT analysis, formulate and implement strategy, assess technological needs, and ensure that its structure will be responsive enough to environmental changes, including customers' and other stakeholders' demands. There are two methods managers can use to gather information:

- *Environmental scanning* is the systematic gathering of information about the environment, its elements, and characteristics. Examples include market research and competitive analyses or searching for new technologies.
- *Boundary spanning* is the process of interacting with the environment to accomplish the twin goals of gathering information and informing the environment about the organization's activities. A *boundary spanner* is the person or department with the responsibility for interacting with the environment to gather and disseminate information.[54] Spanners often conduct environmental scanning. Salespeople and public relations departments who exchange information with the environment are examples. Similarly, employees involved in

research and development look for and design new technologies and products to make the organization more effective and efficient.

The information that organizations gather from their environment through various methods is used to make decisions regarding use of technology, strategy, and structure. For example, environmental scanning allows managers to identify upcoming technological advances. Similarly, gathering information is key to analysis of opportunities and threats in SWOT.

Adapting Internal Structures

The second action managers can take to manage uncertainty is to adapt internal organizational structures. Remember that there isn't one "perfect" structure. The structure must fit the other contextual strategic forces. An uncertain environment requires a more organic structure, whereas a certain environment can allow a mechanistic structure to work well. Similarly, a functional structure is appropriate for a certain environment when the organization is focused on efficiency, whereas the matrix can address the needs of multiple constituents and is appropriate for organizations with limited resources. The new structures allow organizations to respond to global competitive pressures for quality. In general, uncertain environments create the need for high levels of integration and flexibility.

Using Strategy to Change the Environment

In addition to gathering information and changing internal structures to respond to environmental pressures, many organizations take the further step of changing or controlling their environment through lobbying and strategic alliances. By changing or controlling the environment, managers can not only manage uncertainty but also increase the resources available to their organization.

Lobbying   *Lobbying* involves active interaction and exchange with government officials with the goal of influencing their decisions and thereby changing the environment, eventually decreasing uncertainty. Large organizations either have their own lobbyists or rely on industry lobbyists hired by several companies in the same industry. Alternatively, businesses join trade organizations that provide strong lobbying representation for a group of organizations with similar objectives. For instance, small U.S. manufacturers can join the National Association of Manufacturers and be represented by the association's lobbyists who promote U.S. manufacturing interests in Washington, D.C.

The primary goal of lobbying is to reduce uncertainty by changing various elements of the environment to provide more control to the organization and its managers. For example, through lobbying, paper product companies can reduce environmental restrictions on logging and thereby assure a continued supply of timber. Managers can also use lobbying to prevent the effect of technological advances on an organization. For instance, an industry that relies on burning coal may lobby to slow down regulation requiring use of the latest pollution control technology.

A QUESTION OF ETHICS

Lobbyists   Many organizations use lobbyists to gather and disseminate information and to change the political and regulatory environment to benefit the organization's shareholders and investors. Is it ethical to use lobbyists to obtain favorable treatment? What lobbying tactics would you consider unethical? Do you think it is fair for large, wealthy organizations to have stronger lobbying capabilities than smaller businesses?

Strategic Alliances   The strategy that managers set helps them change their environment. Particularly, by entering into alliances with other organizations, they can control suppliers, competitors, and customers. There are three types of strategic alliances:

1. *Joint contracts* are temporary agreements organizations make with others for specific tasks or resources. By joint contracting with a supplier, a company reduces its risk of resource shortage. By controlling its resources, it reduces uncertainty.
2. In a *joint venture*, two or more companies join to create a subsidiary company. Managers create joint ventures for a specific purpose, such as sharing of technologies, and dismantle or spin them off after a certain period of time. Usually each partner in a joint venture invests a certain amount of resources and expects to receive a proportionate return on that investment.
3. *Mergers and acquisitions* are legal processes in which one company purchases or combines with another to become one entity that shares resources, technologies, and profits.

Table 2.5 presents the benefits and disadvantages of these different strategic alliances and examples for each.

As managers and employees of organizations deal with environmental uncertainty, they need to look for threats and opportunities for the firm. As one product is discontinued or one organization fails, multiple others rush in to take advantage of the gap in the market. The law that makes certain activities illegal opens the door for new and innovative products. For example, in the United States, environmental regulations limit and control air pollution, making older, high-pollution machinery unusable. These regulations also create opportunities for companies manufacturing environmentally friendly equipment.

Successful organizations manage all the contextual strategic forces to provide a good fit. Managers cannot expect a free flow of ideas and creative decision making in an organization that is centralized and formalized. The strategy and structure have to fit with and make use of technology. An innovative mission that requires creativity and flexibility does not fit with a mechanistic structure. New structures need to respond to environmental demands and technological changes. Furthermore, there must also be a fit among the organization, its con-

T a b l e   2 . 5   STRATEGIC ALLIANCES

Methods	Benefits and Disadvantages	Example
Joint contracts	• Access to resources; shared costs and risks • Time-consuming procedure; no long-term commitment to success	IBM and Motorola have agreements with several companies to share resources and technologies. These contracts give them early or exclusive access to technological breakthroughs.
Joint ventures	• Access to resources; shared costs and risks • Commitment to long-term success • Risk of losing control over company secrets and technologies	IBM, Siemens, and Toshiba entered a joint venture to manufacture a new semiconductor chip. The estimated cost to reach production was $2 billion.
Mergers and acquisitions	• Immediate access to resources of both companies • Reduction of competition • Costly and risky implementation • Potential decline in productivity • Lack of focus	Compaq acquired Digital Equipment Corporation to gain access to DEC's mainframe market. Compaq reduced competition with this acquisition.

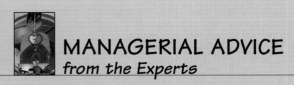

MANAGERIAL ADVICE
from the Experts

MANAGING UNCERTAIN ENVIRONMENTS

Managers can take these specific additional steps to manage the organization's environment:

- Gather and analyze extensive information about events outside your organization. Track business and economic news, pertinent government reports, industry and trade journals.
- Keep abreast of general management trends by reading academic and practitioner literature.
- Stay close to your community; maintain ties with stakeholders.
- Join trade organizations, attend chamber of commerce events, and participate with other organizations that have political and economic relevance to your business.
- Network with people inside and outside your industry. Focus on suppliers and other firms that affect your business.

Source: Based partially on information in P. Drucker, E. Dyson, C. Handy, P. Saffo, and P. M. Senge, "Looking Ahead: Implications for the Present," *Harvard Business Review* (September–October 1997): 18–32.

text, and the employees and managers. Without a good fit, the organization will struggle to be effective.

In the next chapter, we focus on culture as the fifth force in understanding the context of managing people and organizations.

Summary Point 2.11   **How Do the Contextual Strategic Forces Interrelate?**

Organizations manage their environment and reduce their uncertainty in these ways:

- Gathering information about the environment through environmental scanning and boundary spanning
- Changing their internal structures to be more responsive by differentiating departments, increasing integration mechanisms, and changing their internal control from mechanistic to organic

- Changing their environment through lobbying and strategic alliances such as joint contracts, joint ventures, and mergers and acquisitions

---

For updated information on the topics in this chapter, Web exercises, links to related Web sites, an on-line study guide, and more, visit our companion Web site at:
http://www.prenhall.com/nahavandi

A Look Back at the

MANAGERIAL CHALLENGE

McCormick & Company

Changing consumer lifestyles and tastes, demographic shifts, aggressive competition, and soaring costs for a key product are all changing McCormick's environment. The company has had to manage its competition actively while also addressing evolving consumer needs. CEO Robert Lawless has been changing the company's strategy while continuing to pursue its mission of quality.

One of McCormick's strengths is the firm's financial capabilities. Lawless has persevered in the battle to defend against the challenge of rival Burns, Philp, by paying as much as $200 million annually to protect its spice products' positions on supermarket shelves. The costly battle weakened Burns, Philp financially, causing the competitor to ease off on its attacks. As a result, McCormick was able to reduce the amount of annual fees it spent for supermarket shelf space to about $120 million.

Another strength is the company's expertise in all types of food flavorings, not just pepper and traditional spices. "People say we're an herbs-and-spices company," Lawless said, "but I say we're a flavoring company."[55] This strength has helped the CEO prepare a strategy for turning the threat of changing consumer lifestyles into a definite opportunity. Seeing that time-pressed families wanted help in streamlining meal preparation, McCormick began promoting its many seasoning mixes, products that cut cooking time while enhancing meat dishes. In one year, Lawless designated almost $25 million for advertising the entire product line.[56] These strategies allowed the company to take advantage of environmental changes.

Still, the CEO cannot afford to ignore the environmental threat posed by fewer cooks in the kitchen. His response has been to put more emphasis on sales to industrial customers such as restaurants, a business that has great potential—even though its profit margins are lower than in the consumer business.[57] Knowing that lifestyles, tastes, costs, and other environmental elements will surely continue to evolve, Lawless has to remain alert for environmental changes that require a change in McCormick's strategy.

■ **Point of View Exercises**

You're the Manager: As a senior manager in McCormick's strategic planning group, you are considering the company's options for organizational structure. In light of the firm's environment, its large number of employees, and its many global offices, would a mechanistic or an organic organization work best? Explain your answer.

You're the Employee: As a new college graduate, your first job is as a market analyst for McCormick's strategic planning staff, where you look at the sales and profit potential of new markets. Would you prefer to work in a mechanistic or an organic structure? Would your answer be different if you had much more work experience? Explain your answers.

SUMMARY OF LEARNING OBJECTIVES

1. **Identify the five contextual strategic forces that influence organizations.** The context in which organizations and people operate includes five forces: the environment, technology, strategy, structure, and culture.

2. **Describe the organizational environment and define enactment and uncertainty.** The environment of an organization includes the external elements that are outside the organization and that have the potential to affect it. The general environment consists of cultural, economic, political, and social elements. The business environment includes customers, competitors, human resources, suppliers, financial institutions, governmental agencies, and technology. Enactment is the process of selecting which environmental elements are relevant to an organization. Environmental uncertainty is defined as the rate of change and complexity. The rate of change refers to how fast or how dynamic or stable the various elements are. Complexity refers to the number of environmental elements that an organization has to take into account.

3. **Define technology and explain types of technologies and their effect on organizations.** Technology is made up of the tools, techniques, and processes people use to create the goods and services of an organization. The use of high-technology tools and new manufacturing methods can increase businesspeople's productivity and efficiency, affect how managers organize workers, increase the need to learn continuously, heighten the level of stress, and decrease personal contact among employees.

4. **Discuss the relationship among mission, goals, and strategy and outline the strategic management process of formulation and implementation.** Mission is a statement of the organization's purpose and reason for existence. To achieve its mission, a company sets goals. Goals state what needs to be achieved and when. Strategy is a comprehensive road map that states how a firm can reach its goals and achieve its mission. The strategic management process consists of strategy formulation and strategy implementation. To formulate strategy, managers develop a cohesive, integrated set of strategies designed to deal with the environment and achieve the mission and goals. To help with the strategy formulation process, managers conduct a SWOT analysis that considers the strengths and weaknesses of their organization relative to their competitors' and examines the opportunities and threats in their environment. Strategy implementation includes actions the organization's members take to execute the strategy.

5. **Describe organizational structure, its basic components and elements, and contrast the traditional and new structural options.** The structure of an organization refers to the way human resources are organized to achieve the company's mission. The components of structure are reporting relationships, span of control, departmentalization, allocation of responsibilities, and coordination. In addition, each organization's structure differs in terms of degree of formalization, specialization, standardization, hierarchy, centralization, differentiation, and integration.

   Traditional organizational forms include functional, product/divisional, hybrid, and matrix structures. Newer structures—such as virtual, team-based, network, and boundaryless organizations—focus on increasing integration, removing unnecessary barriers, and creating flexible organizations that respond well to changes in their environment.

6. **Highlight the importance of the fit among the contextual strategic forces and how they affect organizations.** Effective organizations focus on finding a fit among the environment, technology, strategy, structure, and culture and between the organization and people. Managers respond to uncertain environments by gathering information through environmental scanning and boundary spanning, by adjusting their internal structures, and by attempting to change the environment. Various structural forms can be used to

find a fit between the structure and other organizational and external forces. Organizations control their environment through their lobbying efforts and by implementing strategies that create strategic alliances with other organizations.

KEY TERMS

automation, p. 42
boundaryless organization,
   p. 61
bureaucracy, p. 53
business environment, p. 38
cross-functional teams,
   p. 56
culture, p. 37
empowerment, p. 59
enactment, p. 39
environment, p. 37
environmental complexity,
   p. 40
environmental uncertainty,
   p. 40

expert systems, p. 44
functional structure, p. 54
general environment, p. 38
hybrid structure, p. 56
information technology,
   p. 44
manufacturing firms, p. 42
matrix structure, p. 56
mechanistic organization,
   p. 53
mission, p. 46
organic organization, p. 53
organizational chart, p. 50
product or divisional
   structure, p. 55

rate of change, p. 40
service firms, p. 42
strategic management
   process, p. 48
strategy, p. 37
strategy formulation, p. 48
strategy implementation,
   p. 48
structure, p. 37
SWOT analysis, p. 48
technology, p. 37
virtual organizations, p. 58

REVIEW QUESTIONS

1. What are the five contextual strategic forces that affect organizations?
2. How do organizations define their environment and assess the level of uncertainty?
3. Why is technology important? How does it affect organizations?
4. Provide an example of how mission, goals, and strategy are linked.
5. What are the five components of structure?
6. What are the major advantages and disadvantages of the four traditional and the current structures?

DISCUSSION QUESTIONS

1. Why is it important for managers to understand the context of their organization?
2. Can a manager be "too responsive" to the environment? Provide examples to support your answer.
3. What is the role of managers in helping their employees manage technological change?
4. What are the arguments for and against employees' involvement in setting the mission, goals, and strategy?
5. Would you like to work in a boundaryless organization? Why or why not?

▶ **SELF-ASSESSMENT 2**
Personal Acceptance of Change

The following questionnaire will help you assess your personal tolerance for change. Consider carefully the following list of changes. List any others that are applicable. Which of these changes have occurred in your life in the past five years? As you consider each change, recall your resistance to change when it happened. In column A, place a number reflecting your resistance at the time of the change. Next, in column B, place a number reflecting your current level of acceptance of that change. If you did not experience the change, place a "0" in both columns. See Appendix 3 for a scoring key.

Scale A: No Resistance   1   2   3   4   5   Strong Resistance
Scale B: No Acceptance   1   2   3   4   5   Strong Acceptance

A   B

_____ _____   1. You were married or engaged.
_____ _____   2. There was a death in your immediate family.
_____ _____   3. You moved to a new location.
_____ _____   4. You enrolled in a college or university.
_____ _____   5. You had a personal health problem.
_____ _____   6. You began work at a new job.
_____ _____   7. An important relationship in your life changed.
_____ _____   8. Your income level changed by over $10,000 a year.
_____ _____   9. You were divorced or separated.
_____ _____   10. A close friend or relative was divorced or separated.
_____ _____   11. Other (list):

Source: Robert E. Quinn, Sue R. Faerman, Michael P. Thompson, and Michael R. McGrath, *Becoming a Master Manager: A Competency Framework* (New York: Wiley, 1990): 238–239. Adapted with permission.

▶ **TEAM EXERCISE 2**
Reengineering Your Organization

Reengineering is the process of redesigning an organization around its core business processes. To that end, the core business processes and the most important technologies have to be identified first. Second, you could start with a blank sheet of paper and ask the question, "What is the best way to do what we want to do?" The answer to this question should be the start of the reengineering process. Obviously, few if any organizations have the luxury of starting completely from scratch. The goal of this exercise is to give you a chance to reengineer an organization or department where you have worked.

1. **DESCRIBE AND SELECT TARGET DEPARTMENT OR ORGANIZATION**

- In groups of three to six people, discuss each member's various work experiences.
- Select one job to be reengineered; it could be a whole organization or just one department. You should select a job that most of you understand well and that currently has some problems and inefficiencies. In other words, do not pick a department that is running well or one about which you have limited information.

- Fully describe the current processes used in the department/organization so that all team members understand them well. To achieve this, the team members may want to interview the person whose job has been selected.

2. BASIC QUESTIONS

Once your team has selected the department/organization to be reengineered, discuss the answer to the following questions:

- What is the mission of the department/organization?
- Who are the primary customers?
- What is the current structure? How are people organized to get their work done?
- What are the current problems?

3. REENGINEERING ALTERNATIVES

The next step is for the team to answer the question, "If we were to have total freedom and could start from scratch, what would be the best way to achieve the mission and to serve the customers of this department/organization?" The goal is to develop a number of alternatives to the current work processes and structures.

4. EVALUATE AND SELECT SOLUTION

Once your team has developed a number of alternatives for reengineering the department/organization, you need to examine and evaluate each alternative carefully. The following questions need to be addressed:

- What are the benefits and disadvantages of each alternative?
- Who will be affected? Consider employees, customers, managers, suppliers, and so forth.
- What are the obstacles? What elements may help implement the alternative?

Based on your analysis and evaluation, select one alternative for reengineering your target job.

5. TEAM PRESENTATION

Each team makes a 5-minute presentation that discusses the current target job and presents and justifies the reengineering proposal.

UP CLOSE

► ## AirMega's Dilemma in the European Airline Market

David has a good job. Actually, he has a great job. His official title is Senior Strategist for AirMega, one of the largest European airlines. His job is to make sure that AirMega stays ahead of its competition in everything it does. Until today, David has accomplished his task. AirMega is a successful, full-service airline that provides travelers with an extensive array of amenities. This morning, things began to change.

Dr. Christine Andersen, the founder and the president of AirMega, walked into David's office and turned his life upside down. She calmly stated that while he has been keeping his eyes on the large European airlines, such as Lufthansa, British Airways, and Air France, the smaller airlines have been gaining ground on AirMega. She informed him that some of these smaller regional airlines just offered very low prices and that travelers are rushing to buy their cheap tickets. She asked him to design a strategy to counteract the low price strategy of these regional airlines.

David knows that it will not be easy to match their low prices. Everything his company does is based on the premise of high quality. And quality costs money. The aircraft that AirMega recently purchased is the most expensive Airbus aircraft in the world. The pilots and the flight attendants receive some of the highest wages in the industry, and the mechanics are paid high salaries as well because they are some of the best and most experienced in Europe. In addition, the several layers of managers and supervisors who oversee the operations of the company have high seniority and are considered the best in the industry. Everybody who works in AirMega has a specific job assignment and specializes in that task.

The services that the airline provides are known to be high quality. A French magazine rated the food the company serves its passengers "superb." No luggage is ever lost. No trip is overbooked. An Italian designer recently designed the uniforms of all the airline's personnel. Each person is trained extensively to provide a high degree of comfort to the customers. The reservation system is state-of-the-art, and a fully automated system guides the routing and scheduling of airplanes. Because bad weather in Europe often causes delays and long waits, AirMega leases finely furnished lounges in most of the European airports for the exclusive use of its customers. These services cost money.

Although David dismisses the strategy of the low-cost airlines, he is fully aware of how they achieve their success. He knows that most follow the strategy of Southwest Airlines, the "crown jewel" of discount airlines. "Why didn't Herb Kelleher open a discount doughnut shop, instead of an airline where everyone, including Herb, did everything?" David thought. "Why couldn't he have left us alone? And why are all these European airlines downgrading the fine tradition of quality travel in Europe and turning it into a bus trip, as has happened in the United States?"

David knows that regardless of his misgivings, AirMega needs a plan, and needs it now, if he is to remain the Senior Strategist.

Questions

1. What is your analysis of the situation?
2. What are the current strategy and structure at AirMega?
3. Should the company try to become another Southwest Airlines?
4. What would be the implications of this new strategy on the structure and technology of AirMega?

NOTES

1. Constance L. Hays, "Trouble in Spice World," *New York Times*, February 20, 1998, C1, C5.
2. Ibid.
3. Ibid.; see also "McCormick History," McCormick & Company Web site, accessed on-line at http://www.mccormick.com.
4. J. B. Quinn, *Strategies for Change: Logical Incrementalism* (Homewood, IL: Irwin, 1980).
5. For the traditional definition of *structure*, see D. Pugh, D. J. Hickson, and C. R. Hinings, "An Empirical Taxonomy of Structure of Work Organizations," *Administrative Science Quarterly* 14 (1969): 115–26. For a definition relating structure to mission, see T. L. Wheelen and J. D. Hunger, *Strategic Management and Business Policy* (Reading, MA: Addison-Wesley, 1998).
6. E. H. Schein, *Organizational Culture and Leadership* (San Francisco, CA: Jossey-Bass, 1985).
7. C. L. Hays, "Trouble in Spice World: McCormick Faces Changing Demographics, Changing Tastes," *New York Times*, February 20, 1998, C1, C5.
8. Ibid.
9. K. Weick, *The Social Psychology of Organizing*, 2d ed. (Reading, MA: Addison-Wesley, 1979).
10. K. Bradsher, "A New Era of Wheeling and Dealing," *New York Times*, January 1, 1998, C1, C4.
11. H. Aldrich, *Organizations and Environments* (Englewood Cliffs, NJ: Prentice Hall, 1979).
12. E. Schonfeld, "Blasting Off the Cheap Way," *Fortune* 137, no. 2 (February 2, 1998): 140.
13. G. Bylinsky, "Industry's Amazing Instant Prototypes," *Fortune* 137, no. 1 (January 12, 1998): 120B–D.
14. Ibid.
15. S. F. Brown, "Giving More Jobs to Electronic Eyes," *Fortune* 137, no. 3 (February 16, 1998): 104B–D.
16. M. J. Himowitz, "Long-Distance Eye Contact Made Easy," *Fortune* 137, no. 2 (February 2, 1998): 137.
17. Brown, "Giving More Jobs."
18. For an excellent discussion of mission, goals, and strategy, see T. L. Wheelen and J. D. Hunger, *Strategic Management and Business Policy*, 5th ed. (Reading, MA: Addison-Wesley, 1995).
19. See Odwalla's Web page at www.enw.com/odwalla.
20. See Shell's Web page at www.shell.com.
21. See Hewlett-Packard's mission statement at its Web page at www.hp.com.
22. R. B. Lieber, "Why Employees Love These Companies," *Fortune* 137, no. 1 (January 12, 1998): 74.
23. J. B. Barney, *Gaining and Sustaining Competitive Advantage* (Reading, MA: Addison-Wesley, 1997): 145–64.
24. For an excellent discussion, see Wheelen and Hunger, *Strategic Management and Business Policy*, 81–105.
25. M. H. Martin, "The Next Big Thing: A Bookstore?" *Fortune* (December 9, 1996): 168–70.
26. See Henry Mintzberg and J. A. Waters, "Of Strategies, Deliberate and Emergent," *Strategic Management Journal* 6 (1985): 257–72.
27. R. T. Pascale, "Perspectives on Strategy: The Real Story Behind Honda's Success," *California Management Review* 26, no. 3 (1994): 47–72.
28. J. Child, *Organization* (New York: Harper & Row, 1977).
29. Much of the research about structural elements was done by D. Pugh, D. J. Hickson, and C. R. Hinings. For example, see "An Empirical Taxonomy;" H. Mintzberg, *Structure in Five's: Designing Effective Organizations* (Englewood Cliffs, NJ: Prentice Hall, 1983).
30. P. R. Lawrence and J. W. Lorsch, *Organization and Environment* (Homewood, IL: Irwin, 1969).
31. See Mintzberg, *Structure in Five's*.
32. See the W. L. Gore Web page at www.gore.com.
33. For a description of how the company sees its structure and culture, see the W. L. Gore Web page at www.gore.com.
34. See Lieber, "Why Employees Love These Companies," 74.
35. T. Burns and G. M. Stalker, *The Management of Innovation* (London: Tavistock, 1961).
36. Ibid.
37. Ibid.; G. Zaltman, R. Duncan, and J. Holbeck, *Innovation and Organizations* (New York: Wiley, 1973).
38. M. S. Davis and P. R. Lawrence, *Matrix* (Reading, MA: Addison-Wesley, 1977).
39. C. A. Bartlett and S. Ghoshal, "Beyond the M-form: Toward a Managerial Theory of the Firm," *Strategic Management Journal* 14 (special issue, 1993): 23–46; R. G. Ligus, "Enterprise Agility: Maneuverability and Turbo Power," *Industrial Management* 35, no. 6 (1993): 27; D. Staunton, "The Siren Call of Complacency," *CMA Magazine* 67, no. 10 (1993): 27.
40. M. Upton and A. McAfee, "The Real Virtual Factory," *Harvard Business Review* 74, no. 4 (July/August 1996): 123–33.
41. T. R. V. Davis and B. L. Darling, "How Virtual Corporations Manage the Performance of Contractors: The Super Bakery Case," *Organizational Dynamics* 24, no. 1 (1995): 70–75.
42. Upton and McAfee, "The Real Virtual Factory."
43. For an example, see R. Kirk, "It's About Control," *Inc.* 16, no. 8 (August 1994): 25–26.
44. Ibid.
45. For more information on virtual organizations, see J. King, "Network Tools of the Virtual Corporation," *Network World* (April 4, 1994): 28–30; M. Menagh, "Virtues and Vices of Virtual Corporations," *Computerworld* (November 13, 1995): 134; Kirk, "It's About Control;" Upton and McAfee, "The Real Virtual Factory."
46. P. Block, *The Empowered Manager* (San Francisco: Jossey Bass, 1987); J. A. Conger and R. Kanungo, "The Empowerment Process: Integrating Theory and Practice," *Academy of Management Review* 13, no. 3 (1988): 471–82; J. A. Conger, "Leadership: The Art of Empowering Others," *Academy of Management Executive* 3, no. 1 (1989): 17–24.
47. The use of empowerment and teams has roots in the perception of Japanese management style and in the use of quality circles in many organizations in the 1960s. For a review, see E. E. Lawler III and S. A. Mohrman, "Quality Circles: After the Honeymoon," *Organization Dynamics* (Spring 1987): 42–54; G. E. Ledford, E. E. Lawler III, and S. A. Mohrman, "The Quality Circle and Its Variations," in J. R. Campbell and associates (eds.), *Productivity in Organizations* (San Francisco, CA: Jossey-Bass, 1988): 255–94.
48. R. Ashkenas, D. Ulrich, T. Jick, and S. Kerr, *The Boundaryless Organization: Breaking the Chains of Organizational Structure* (San Francisco: Jossey-Bass, 1995).
49. J. Curran, "GE Capital: Jack Welch's Secret Weapon," *Fortune* 136, no. 9 (November 10, 1997): 116–34.
50. T. Peters, "Structural Entrepreneurship at Oticon," *Forum* 2 (1994): 16–17; T. Peters, *Tom Peters Seminar: Crazy Times Call for Crazy Organization* (New York: Vintage, 1994).
51. T. Lester, "The Rise of the Network," *International Management* (June 1992): 72–73; see also C. M. Solomon, "Transplanting Corporate Cultures Globally," *Personnel Journal* (October 1993): 89; W. Taylor, "The Logic of Global Business: An Interview with ABB's Percy Barnevik," *Harvard Business Review* (March/April 1991): 91–105.
52. Lester, "The Rise of the Network."
53. Mintzberg, *Structure in Five's*.
54. D. Jemison, "The Importance of Boundary Spanning Roles in Strategic Decision Making," *Journal of Management Studies* 21 (1984): 131–52.
55. Hays, "Trouble in Spice World," C7; also see "Post 200: Top 30 Maryland Public Companies," *Washington Post*, April 28, 1997, accessed on-line at http://www.washingtonpost.com/wp-srv/business/longterm/post200/data/bfmc005.
56. Hays, "Trouble in Spice World."
57. Ibid.

CULTURE IN ORGANIZATIONS

LEARNING OBJECTIVES

1. Define culture and describe national culture, cultural diversity, and organizational culture.
2. Outline four models that help managers classify national cultural values.
3. Discuss the nature and role of cultural diversity in organizations and analyze approaches to managing diversity.
4. Describe the effect and development of organizational culture.
5. Explain how culture fits with the contextual strategic forces.

MANAGERIAL CHALLENGE

Cirque du Soleil

The "Circus of the Sun"—known as the Cirque du Soleil—is a world-class entertainment company that caters to the imaginations of young and old around the world. More than 15 million people in 123 cities have witnessed the spectacular feats of this Montreal-based circus troupe, which shatters preconceived notions about the circus. You won't find any bears, lions, and dancing elephants at the Cirque. This award-winning "reinvented circus" relies solely on human performers who deliver an innovative blend of theater, street performance, and Broadway show. Acrobats, jugglers, and mimes dress in breathtaking costumes and perform amid sets, music, and lighting that create magical, fairytale effects.[1]

The Cirque du Soleil started in 1984 as a group of young street performers in Quebec, Canada. The business now employs more than 1,250 people, including 210 performers, who hail from 17 different countries and speak in 13 different languages. The organization has four headquarters, the main one in Montreal and others in Amsterdam, Las Vegas, and Singapore. This multinational structure supports the Cirque's diverse employees as they perform in cities such as Los Angeles, Chicago, Tokyo, Osaka, Hong Kong, Paris, London, Vienna, and Berlin.[2]

Marc Gagnon, vice president for human resources, faces a key challenge: keeping the company neighborly no matter how big it gets.[3] He believes the Cirque owes much of its success to its strong sense of community, so he works hard to integrate workers' diverse cultures and talents. He starts by carefully and thoroughly screening candidates (the business receives 30 to 50 unsolicited résumés a day) to find those whose personal goals, talents, and values mesh with the company's values and goals.[4] He also helps Cirque employees develop a sense of togetherness despite their far-flung locations by building global conversations among employees and with company executives. Three company publications keep everyone informed, spread the news, and encourage an exchange of ideas. One of the publications contains a column called "Culture Shock," a forum in which Cirque employees share the challenges, obstacles, and benefits of working all over the world with a multicultural workforce.[5]

■ Questions

1. What role does culture play in the success of the Cirque du Soleil?
2. What are the cultural challenges the organization faces?

The Cirque du Soleil's challenges in managing different cultures are common in today's global business environment. If you live in the United States or Canada, you are as likely to drive a Japanese car as an American car. Most television sets and compact disc players are built in Japan or Korea. Your clothes are likely to have been made in Southeast Asia and Central or South America. There are probably several foreign students in your class who have traveled to gain access to educational opportunities. The other students around you probably come from a variety of ethnic backgrounds and vary in age and gender. The world is indeed getting smaller! With easier travel, satellites, computers, and the extensive use of information technology, it is hard to ignore the rest of the world.

Because the world is so interconnected, business organizations must learn to manage culture effectively. Today's managers work with people from different countries and cultures either in their own countries or on international assignments. Even within an organization, different groups approach issues in different ways. The key to managing these cross-country and cross-cultural differences is understanding the nature of culture.

In this chapter we examine culture—the fifth contextual strategic factor—at three levels. We consider national culture; diversity due to different cultures in a nation through, for example, ethnic and gender differences; and organizational culture. Although organizational culture has the most immediate impact on managerial decisions, today's managers cannot ignore the effects of national culture and cultural diversity on their employees and their organization's performance.

 DEFINING CULTURE

Culture is defined as the values commonly held among a group of people. It is a set of norms, customs, values, and assumptions that guides the behavior of a particular group of people. Culture gives each group its uniqueness and differentiates it from other groups. We are strongly influenced by our culture. It determines what we consider right and wrong, it influences what and who we value, what we pay attention to, and how we behave. Culture not only affects values and beliefs but also influences management and interpersonal styles; it also affects simple things such as clothing styles and food preferences. We learn about culture formally through various teachings and informally through observation.[6] The family, educational, social, and religious institutions are the major teachers of culture.

Culture exists at three levels presented in Figure 3.1. The first level of culture is national culture. **National culture** is a set of values and beliefs shared by people within a nation. Because national culture addresses many different aspects of life, it has a strong and pervasive influence on people's behavior, both in everyday activities and in organizations.

In addition to an overall national culture, there may be ethnic and other cultural groups within each nation. Although these groups share national cultural values, they also have their unique culture. The ethnic or group cultures form the second level of culture. Some nations and cultures have many such subcultures; others do not. National cultures that have many different subcultures are **heterogeneous.** The United States, Canada, and Indonesia are examples of nations with heterogeneous cultures. Many different cultural, ethnic, and religious groups are part of the overall culture of these nations, leading to considerable cultural diversity. **Homogeneous** cultures have only one or few subcultures. Japan and Scandinavian countries are two examples.

People within ethnic or other subgroups share worldviews, norms, values, beliefs, and behaviors that differentiate them from others and make them unique. Such groups can be based on ethnicity and race such as African-Americans or Hispanics within the United States, or on other factors such as gender or geographic location. We therefore consider gender, for example, to be a cultural factor that influences people's behavior. Similarly, Southerners in the United States are to some extent different from New Englanders or Midwesterners. All of us belong to more than one culture. We are Americans, Australians, Malaysian, Italians, and so forth. But we are also male or female, have different regional cultures, belong to different ethnic groups, and embrace different religions. Each of these subcultures further influences our values and behaviors.

The third level of culture is organizational culture. **Organizational culture** is the set of values, norms, and beliefs shared by members of an organization. Given time, all organizations develop a unique culture or character. Employees share common values and beliefs about work-related issues. These shared elements make them unique and set them apart from employees in other organizations. Similar to national cultures, some organizational cultures are homogeneous while others are heterogeneous with many subcultures.

The influence of organizational culture is generally limited to work-related values and behaviors. However, organizational culture is strongly influenced by both national culture and cultural diversity. For instance, all French companies share some characteristics that make them different from companies in other countries. Compared to their Swedish counterparts,

National culture
A set of values and beliefs shared by people within a nation

Heterogeneous cultures
Cultures that have many different subcultures

Homogeneous cultures
Cultures that have only one or very few subcultures

Organizational culture
The set of values, norms, and beliefs shared by members of an organization

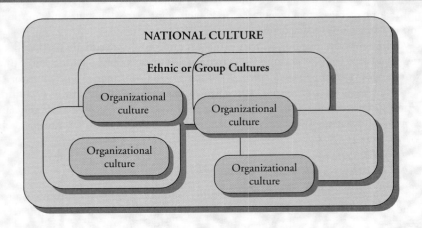

FIGURE 3.1
Three Levels of Culture

French companies are more hierarchical and status oriented and rely more on managers' individual decisions rather than group decision making.

Because of globalization and increased cultural diversity within nations, today's managers confront many cultural issues that they need to understand and manage on a daily basis. Culture is therefore a key contextual strategic force that affects managers and organizations. In this chapter, we first consider national cultural values, then cultural diversity, and finally organizational culture.

Summary Point 3.1 What Is Culture?

- Culture is a set of norms, customs, values, and assumptions that guides the behavior of a particular group of people.
- National culture is shared by members of a nation.

- Subgroups within a nation that share common beliefs, customs, and values based on factors such as ethnicity, gender, and religion create cultural diversity.
- Organizational culture is shared by members of an organization.

 # UNDERSTANDING NATIONAL CULTURE

Expatriates
Individuals who leave their own country to work

How can managers learn about national culture? First, they can learn through exposure by visiting a country or through secondary sources by studying and reading about the different values, social and religious beliefs, and traditions. A company may send a manager to Singapore to train her in language skills, religious practices, social norms, arts, and so on. Such training is necessary for **expatriates**, individuals who leave their own country to work. It is, however, impossible for any one person to learn about all the national cultures that he or she is likely to encounter.

Second, managers can learn about classifications of national cultures, gleaned from research results, particularly as they apply to a nation's business organizations. Each country and region in the world has developed a particular organizational and management style largely based on national culture. This style is called the *national organizational heritage*. Although there are many differences from one organization to another and from one manager to another, research indicates that this heritage is noticeable and distinct.[7]

Managers can begin to understand the national organizational heritage of a country by studying research that classifies that culture. They can and should supplement this general knowledge with firsthand interaction. Why? Because general classifications cannot and do not apply to every person in a country because of individual differences. Relying on general classifications alone can lead to stereotyping, a dangerous practice that can result in discrimination and prevent sound management.

We consider next four models that managers can use to understand and classify national cultures. These are Hall's high/low-context cultural framework, Kluckhohn and Strodbeck's values orientation, Trompenaars's cultural groupings, and Hofstede's dimensions of cultural values. Rather than attempting exact description of all individuals within a culture, each model provides general descriptions of cultural value systems. In spite of their generality, the models are useful starting points in understanding how national culture influences behavior.

Hall's High-Context and Low-Context Cultural Framework

One of the simplest models used to differentiate communication styles within cultures is the high- and low-context model.[8] In this model, context refers to the environment and the information that provide the background for interaction and communication. Members of

CAREER ADVICE
from the Experts

PREPARING TO BE A GLOBAL MANAGER

Students of business can use their education as a starting point for becoming a global manager. Some steps include the following:

- Increase your "book" knowledge of global international issues. Read the foreign press, visit international Web sites, check out your library's international holdings.
- Visit museums, listen to international music, visit international enclaves in your city.
- Take courses in foreign languages, focusing on becoming fluent in at least one.
- Take advantage of cultural exchange programs at your university.
- Go on "study abroad" trips when available.
- Join various foreign cultural organizations in your city.
- Take international politics, culture, and history courses.

Sources: Partially based on P. Guptara, "New Approaches and Radical Innovations in Developing Cross-cultural Managers," *Forum* 1 (1994): 40–42; T. Lester, "Pulling Down the Language Barrier," *International Management* (July–August 1994): 42–44.

high-context cultures rely heavily on the context, nonverbal cues, and situational factors to communicate with others and understand the world around them. They rely on personal relationships to establish communication. Members of **low-context cultures** focus on explicit, specific verbal and written messages to understand people and situations.[9]

For example, Saudi Arabia, Italy, France, Vietnam, Korea, and China all have high-context cultures where subtle body posture, tone of voice, detailed rituals, and a person's title and status all convey strong messages that determine behavior and its interpretation. Communication does not always need to be explicit and specific. Trust is often viewed as more important than written communication or legal contracts. In low-context cultures, such as those of Germany, Scandinavia, Switzerland, the United States, England, and Canada, people pay attention to the verbal message. What is said or written is more important than nonverbal messages or the situation. People are therefore specific and clear in their communication with others.

The difference between high and low context can explain many cross-cultural communication problems that managers face around the world. The low-context European and North American managers may get frustrated with their high-context Asian or Middle Eastern partners' lack of preciseness. Whereas managers from low-context cultures focus on specific agreements and contracts, those from high-context cultures aim at developing relationships. The high-context managers may be offended at low-context Westerners' directness, which they interpret as rudeness.

The high-low context model, though simple, can help managers understand national culture and its effect on communication styles and organizational behavior. We explore three models that offer more complex cultural heritage information next.

High-context cultures
Cultures that rely heavily on the context, nonverbal cues, and situational factors to communicate with and understand others

Low-context cultures
Cultures that focus on explicit verbal and written messages to understand people and situations

Summary Point 3.2   What Is the High/Low-Context Model?

- The high/low-context model classifies cultures by examining the importance of context in communication.

- High-context cultures rely on nonverbal cues and situational factors to communicate.
- Low-context cultures focus on verbal and written messages.

Kluckhohn and Strodbeck's Values Orientation

Kluckhohn and Strodbeck propose that cultures differ in terms of how they approach the six basic dimensions presented in Table 3.1.[10] First, cultures differ in their *relationship to nature*. Some see nature as a force to respect whereas others consider it an obstacle to master. For example, some nations focus on mastering nature through efforts such as dam construction, irrigation, landfills, and land reclamation. Others focus on combining man-made elements effectively with nature. Other cultural groups, such as the Inuit Eskimos, have a third type of relationship to nature, one in which its members believe that nature subjugates and dominates people.

Second, cultures differ in their *time orientation*. Some cultures focus on the past and on traditions; others stress the present and short-term performance and results; and still others look to the future and long-term performance. According to theorists, the United States focuses more on the present and the future than does Japan, a nation that tends to concentrate more on learning from the past. Interestingly, the United States is also short-term oriented.

The third dimension in the values model concerns *views of human nature*. This dimension examines whether the culture views people as basically good, evil, or neutral. Views of human nature as good lead to a willingness to trust and cooperate, whereas views of people as evil lead to suspicion and control. The fourth dimension, *activity orientation*, relates to the degree to which people within a culture are proactive, reactive, or controlling. According to the Kluckhohn and Strodbeck classification, people from the United States are generally proactive, Indians and Mexicans are reactive, and the French and Germans are controlling.

The fifth dimension relates to *relationships among people*. Some cultures, like that of the United States, focus on individuals and individual achievements and performance. Others, like the Korean culture, emphasize group harmony and performance. Still some cultures view social relationships as hierarchical and based on well-established rank and order. Several Central and South American cultures fall in this category.

Table 3.1   KLUCKHOHN AND STRODBECK'S VALUE ORIENTATIONS

Cultural Dimensions	Description
Relation to nature: subjugation, harmony, or mastery	Views of nature and its relationship to people as either an object to be controlled or as a force with which to live in harmony
Time orientation: past, present, or future	Focus on past, present, or future
Basic human nature: evil, neutral, good	Views of human nature as positive or negative
Activity orientation: being, controlling, doing	Views on level or type of activity and being proactive or reactive to events
Relationship among people: individualistic, group, or hierarchy	Views relating to how people interact as individuals and groups and hierarchical relationships in society
Space orientation: private, mixed, or public	Views of ownership of private and public space

Sources: Based on information in F. Kluckhohn and F. L. Strodbeck, *Variations in Value Orientations* (Evanston, IL: Peterson, 1961); H. W. Lane, J. J. DiStefano, and M. L. Maznevski, *International Management Behavior*, 3d ed. (Malden, MA: Blackwell, 1997).

The last dimension deals with *views of personal space*. In some cultures, such as those of many Western European and North American nations, there is a strong sense of privacy and private ownership of personal space. In others such as the Japanese culture, space is commonly shared. Many cultures fall in the middle category with a combination of public and private views of space.

Few cultures can be clearly classified in any one of the value-orientation dimensions. Most have mixed approaches that, for example, value both present and future, or see society as both group oriented and hierarchical. The value orientations affect work-related behaviors. For instance, managers are likely to be proactive and focused on individual short-term performance if their national culture values mastery of the environment, a present time orientation, the individual, private space, and proactivity.

As with the other cultural models we discuss, the Kluckhohn and Strodbeck value-orientations model provides a basic explanation of cultural differences to help people manage others from different national cultures. The model does not propose clear applications to management, and the orientations are not clearly defined. The Trompenaars model, which we examine next, builds on Kluckhohn and Strodbeck's value orientations and applies the orientations directly to organizational behavior.

Summary Point 3.3   **What Is the Cultural Value-Orientation Model?**

Relation to nature, time orientation, views of basic human nature, activity orientation, relationships among people, and space orientation are value orientations that theorists and practitioners use to explain cultural heritage differences.

Trompenaars's Seven Dimensions of Culture

Dutch consultant and researcher Fons Trompenaars provides a complex model that helps managers understand national culture and its effect on business practices.[11] He developed the model after surveying 15,000 people in organizations in 47 cultures. Trompenaars suggests that cultures differ on seven dimensions, shown in Table 3.2. The first five dimensions focus on how people interact with and relate to one another. The last two dimensions of relation to time and to nature are similar to those used by Kluckhohn and Strodbeck.

The first five dimensions focus on how we relate to others. They are critical to organizations because an understanding of these dimensions helps managers see how culture affects people's behavior in organizations. To illustrate, in universalist, individual, emotionally neutral, specific, and achievement-oriented cultures, relationships at work are likely to be clearly defined, objective, and unrelated to personal feelings. In a particular, collectivist, emotional, diffuse, and ascriptive culture, work relationships are likely to be ruled by personal feelings, to carry to other aspects of life, to affect the whole group, and to be influenced by social class in addition to performance.

Once we know that U.S. business behavior tends to be more like the former example than the latter, we can make some predictions. For one, managers in the United States who give negative feedback to an employee during a performance appraisal are more likely to continue having a good working relationship with that employee than are managers in a country that is more emotional, diffuse, and ascriptive. Furthermore, in the United States individual performance and achievement rather than family background and clan membership are likely to be the basis for status and success.

The sixth dimension of time orientation helps managers understand how national culture affects organizational behavior. In some cultures time is circular—that is, in the cultural

Table 3.2   TROMPENAARS'S CULTURAL DIMENSIONS

Dimensions and Countries	Description
• Universalism versus particularism *Universal cultures: United States, Switzerland, Germany, Sweden* *Particular cultures: France, Italy, Spain, the Middle East*	Universalist cultures develop rules that apply to all relationships and situations. Particularistic cultures focus on the uniqueness of each situation.
• Individualism versus collectivism *Individualist cultures: Canada, United States* *Collectivist cultures: Kuwait, South Korea, Singapore*	In individualism, value is placed primarily on the individual rather than on the community. Collectivist cultures place more value on the group than on the individual.
• Neutral versus emotional *Neutral cultures: Japan, United Kingdom, Indonesia* *Emotional cultures: Italy, France*	Interactions are based on objectivity and neutrality, or they are based on emotional bonds.
• Specific versus diffuse *Specific cultures: United States, Australia, Netherlands* *Diffuse cultures: France, Italy, Japan, Mexico*	Relationships are specific to situations or generalize to different situations.
• Achievement versus ascription *Achievement-based cultures: United States, Canada, Norway, Sweden, United Kingdom* *Ascription-based cultures: Middle East, Eastern Europe, France*	People's worth is judged by their recent performance and achievement or by an ascribed status based on other factors such as birth or social class.
• Perception and use of time *Present based and linear: United States, Germany* *Past and circular: Mexico*	Focus and value are placed on the present, the past, or the future.
• Perceptions of physical environment *Environment to be used: Brazil, Portugal, South Korea* *Environment to be respected: Japan, Egypt, Singapore, Sweden*	Either the individual or the environment is seen as dominant; the environment is either used or respected.

Source: F. Trompenaars, *Riding the Waves of Culture: Understanding Culture and Diversity in Business* (London: Nicholas Brealey, 1994).

view, present, past, and future are interrelated. Other cultures view the present as separate from the past. Managers from the first type of culture focus on history and are likely to engage in long-term planning; managers from the second type of culture focus on short-term performance.

The last dimension, how people perceive the physical environment, describes whether people think the environment is an object to use or a force to respect. Brazilians, for example, try to dominate the environment and make full use of it as an object. This cultural value is partially responsible for the extensive deforestation of the Amazon. Swedes have the opposite view, which explains their involvement in many ecological endeavors.

The use of Trompenaars's national cultural groupings relates cultural differences to organizational style more directly than the two previous models we examined. The particular focus on relationships among people is also useful in managing across cultures.

Summary Point 3.4   **How Do Managers Use Trompenaars's Seven Dimensions?**

• Managers can use Trompenaars's seven cultural dimensions to explain cross-cultural differences in managing people and organizations.

• The seven dimensions are universalism/particularism, individualism/collectivism, neutral/affective, specific/diffused, achievement/ascriptive, perception and use of time, and perception of the physical environment.

Hofstede's Five Dimensions

Researcher Geert Hofstede developed one of the best-known classifications of culture, known as Hofstede's dimensions. Hofstede originally conducted more than 100,000 surveys of IBM employees in 40 countries, later supplementing those with another scale based on Confucian dynamism. He used the results to develop the five cultural dimensions described and defined in Table 3.3.[12] Hofstede's classifications relate directly to people and organizations.

According to Hofstede, the United States is low on **power distance**, meaning that relative to other countries, the United States has a narrow gap between those who have power and those who do not. This low power distance is consistent with U.S. history and its political system. The United States ranks moderate to low on **uncertainty avoidance**. This rating indicates that the nation tolerates uncertainty and does not have a strong focus on finding absolute truths. The uncertainty-avoidance ranking of the United States is consistent with the ethnic, religious, and cultural diversity of the country.

The United States ranks at the top of the scale on **individualism**. That is, the nation values individual achievements and focuses on preserving individual rights. The historical, political, and social systems of the United States are consistent with this value. The United States ranks in the middle-to-high end of the scale on **masculinity**. The nation values assertiveness, material goods, ambition, and independence, even though gender roles are not as differentiated as they are in some other cultures. Finally, the United States ranks toward the bottom on long-term orientation because of the nation's focus on short-term results, such as daily stock and quarterly company performance reports.

The country rankings on each of the dimensions give a broad overview of cultural values. Keep in mind that there are many differences in each country. For example, in the United States, certain ethnic groups might be higher on power distance and lower on individualism than the mainstream culture. Similarly, in other culturally heterogeneous countries such as Indonesia, speaking of general "Indonesian" cultural values may be highly misleading.

We show Hofstede's scores for 10 countries in Table 3.4. Note that the United States (along with Australia, which is not shown) ranks highest on individualism. This contrasts with Scandinavian, Asian, and some Central and South American countries that rank high on col-

Power distance
The size of the gap between those who have a lot of power and those who have little power

Uncertainty avoidance
The extent to which uncertainty is tolerated and finding absolute truths is important

Individualism/collectivism
The extent to which individuals or closely knit social structures such as the extended family are the basis for social systems

Masculinity
The amount of value placed on assertiveness, material goods, ambition, and independence

Table 3.3   HOFSTEDE'S FIVE CULTURAL DIMENSIONS

Power Distance	The extent to which people accept unequal distribution of power. In higher power distance cultures, there is a wider gap between the powerful and the powerless.
Uncertainty Avoidance	The extent to which the culture tolerates ambiguity and uncertainty. High uncertainty avoidance leads to low tolerance for uncertainty and to a search for absolute truths.
Individualism	The extent to which individuals or closely-knit social structures such as the extended family (collectivism) are the basis for social systems. Individualism leads to reliance on self and focus on individual achievement.
Masculinity	The extent to which assertiveness and independence from others is valued. High masculinity leads to high sex-role differentiation, focus on independence, ambition, and material goods.
Long-Term Orientation	The extent to which people focus on past, present, or future. Present orientation leads to a focus on short-term performance.

Sources: G. Hofstede, *Culture's Consequences: International Differences in Work-related Values* (Thousand Oaks, CA: Sage, 1980); G. Hofstede, "Cultural Constraints in Management Theories," *Academy of Management Executive* 7, no. 1 (1993): 81–94.

T a b l e 3.4 CULTURAL DIMENSION SCORES FOR TEN COUNTRIES

	Power Distance	Individualism	Masculinity	Uncertainty Avoidance	Long-term Orientation
USA	40L	91H	62H	46L	29L
Germany	35L	67H	66H	65M	31M
Japan	54M	46M	95H	92H	80H
France	68H	71H	43M	86H	30L*
Netherlands	38L	80H	14L	53M	44M
Hong Kong	68H	25L	57H	29L	96H
Indonesia	78H	14L	46M	48L	25L*
West Africa	77H	20L	46M	54M	16L
Russia	95H*	50M*	40L*	90H*	10L*
China	80H*	20L*	50M*	60M*	118H

Note: The numbers are the scores for each country on each dimension. The letter by each number indicates the comparative rankings for each country. H = top third, M = medium third, L = bottom third (among 53 countries for the first four dimensions; among 23 countries for the fifth dimension).

* estimate

Source: Adapted with permission from A. M. Francesco and B. A. Gold, *International Organizational Behavior: Text, Reading, Cases, and Skills* (Upper Saddle River, NJ: Prentice Hall 1998), 27.

lectivism (the opposite of individualism). Hofstede's classifications do not replace the intimate, personal knowledge that managers need to be effective in another culture. However, the scores provide a broad view that helps them begin to understand and compare cultures.

Managers can use the cultural dimensions to understand and predict organizational and management styles. For example, in countries with collectivist cultures, such as Japan and Sweden, team efforts are generally easier than in individualist cultures, such as the United States and France. Similarly, a participative management style—one in which managers delegate decision making to employees—may be hard to implement in cultures with high power distance, such as Malaysia or the Philippines, even though both countries value collectivism. Cultural dimensions can further be used to understand certain countries' focus on long-term strategic planning.

Hofstede's dimensions provide managers with general information about five cultural dimensions. They are a good starting point for learning about other cultures but should not be used as the sole means of understanding the organizational behavior of another culture. Managers can use a combination of the four models to develop a general understanding of cultures that differ from their own. No one model is best; each applies to different situations. Managers should then seek personal experience to develop a rich understanding of the cultures

Summary Point 3.5 **How Do Hofstede's Cultural Dimensions Help Managers?**

- Hofstede's five dimensions help managers classify cultures and predict organizational and management styles. The dimensions are power distance, uncertainty avoidance, individualism, masculinity, and long-term orientation.
- The United States ranks low on power distance, moderate-to-low on uncertainty avoidance, high on individual-

ism, moderate-to-high on masculinity, and low on long-term orientation.
- Though Hofstede's classifications provide a general ranking for a country, there may be many differences among the groups within a country.

with which they will interact. The cultural training provides the background; the direct personal experience completes the understanding. Kristi Conlon, senior training specialist at Intel, became acutely aware of this issue when she was sent to conduct training for project managers for warehouse employees in Costa Rica. She had received specific training about the Costa Rican culture at Intel University before she left. However, she says, "I ran into things that I really did not anticipate."[13] As a result of her experience, she believes that direct experience must supplement classroom training. Similarly, the employees at the Cirque du Soleil manage cultural challenges on a daily hands-on basis.

Team Challenge

HAWORTH AND RHONE POULENC

Working in teams is hard enough when team members share the same language and culture. Imagine the obstacles teams may face when members come from a variety of national cultures with different values, national organizational heritages, and corporate national cultures. Consider the two examples of Haworth, the Michigan-based office furniture manufacturer, and Rhone Poulenc, the French chemical maker. Both companies actively acquire companies outside their national borders so their managers work with people from different cultures.

Haworth has successfully acquired companies in many European countries including France, Portugal, and Germany.[a] Patience, a hands-off policy, and the creation of a multinational, 11-member team headed by Mr. Von Prondzinski, the company's German vice president of European operations (who is fluent in four languages), have helped Haworth overcome cultural obstacles.[b] For instance, Haworth has dealt with ingrained French cultural stereotypes about Portuguese cultural inferiority. The company has also recognized and coped with different perceptions of management approaches, such as Germans who thought U.S. managers with a participative, hands-off style were poor leaders. Haworth approaches working with other cultures like a slow courtship and focuses on building long-term relationships to make them feel part of a team.[c]

Conversely, Rhone Poulenc has been unsuccessful in managing its U.S. acquisition of a drug manufacturer because French executives lacked an understanding of U.S. markets and management practices, and were often insensitive to cultural differences. They imposed hierarchical, formal French systems on all U.S. managers. The French wanted a strongly centralized organization. In contrast, the U.S. managers wanted independence and autonomy. The lack of attention to cultural integration both at the national and organizational level created a crisis that prevented the acquisition from reaching its goals. Rhone Poulenc's difficulty in moving across cultures and Haworth's success demonstrate the importance of patience, consideration, and understanding when working in teams with people from different cultures.[d]

a. Gregory L. Miles, "The Trials of Two Acquirers," *International Business* (February 1995): 34–46.
b. Richard G. Haworth, "The Mid-Sized Firm as a Global Acquirer: Haworth, Inc.," *Merger & Acquisitions* 29, no. 4 (January–February 1995): 31–33.
c. Miles, "The Trials."
d. Ibid.

The four national culture models we examined help explain cross-national differences. Another key issue to understanding culture and its role in organizations is to consider cultural subgroups in a country, also known as cultural diversity.

A QUESTION OF ETHICS

| *Investing in Dictatorships Abroad* | Should you invest in a company with a global interest and partners in third world dictatorships? On the one hand, the investment allows for betterment of social and economic conditions; on the other hand, it supports a dictatorship. What is the ethical approach? |

Hot ▼ Link

We discussed cultural diversity in chapter 1, p. 21.

■ CULTURAL DIVERSITY

In the previous section, we analyzed several general models that help identify the effects national culture has on people in organizations. However, countries are culturally heterogeneous, so managers must also understand the different ethnic and other group cultures that affect their organization. Such cultures may be based on religion, gender, age, physical attributes, sexual orientation, regional differences, functional specialization, and so on. The differences and similarities of these subgroups are the source of a nation's cultural diversity. Although the concept of *cultural* diversity applies most directly to national or ethnic differences, each distinct group develops its own worldview and unique values and norms.

All countries and organizations are to some extent culturally heterogeneous and multicultural. Workers and managers travel to work in different countries because of increased globalization and international cooperation, which leads to more cultural diversity. The diversity is evident at all levels of organizations. Consider the top executives in companies such as the cosmetic manufacturer L'Oreal, food companies Heinz and Nestlé, and the consulting firm McKinsey. L'Oreal is headed by Lindsay Owen-Jones who is Welsh. Irishman Tony O'Reilly runs the all-American Heinz, while Swiss Nestlé is headed by a German. Rajat Gupta, an Indian, is McKinsey's CEO.[14] In addition to diverse top executives, these companies deal with many different cultures across the globe and their workforce reflects these cultural differences. The Cirque du Soleil has successfully integrated cultures and was recognized for its successes in that area when it won the Optima Award from *Workforce* magazine.[15]

Many people believe that unique cultures within a country or an organization are valuable and should be preserved. Recognition and preservation of cultural differences is at the heart of the cultural diversity movement. Having employees and managers with diverse worldviews, different approaches to problem solving, and distinct styles is one way businesses can address the complex problems they face. Several companies, such as Citibank and Procter & Gamble, put this belief into practice: Over half the senior managers at these two U.S. companies are non-Americans.[16] Procter & Gamble chairman John Pepper declared that whatever the U.S. laws governing racial quotas, his company will continue to promote diversity aggressively. Pepper is such a believer in the importance of diversity that it was the focus of his first act as chairman of Procter & Gamble.[17]

Many other countries also have diverse workforces. For example, Malaysia's population is divided into two general groups. The Bumiputera population consists of the original inhabitants of the peninsula; it includes the aborigines, the Malay, and the Malay-related diverse populations. The second group, the non-Bumiputera, consists of Chinese, Indians, Arabs, Sinhalese, Eurasians, and Europeans.[18] Singapore similarly is made up of many different ethnic groups and nationalities. Its population of 3 million includes 78 percent Chinese, 14 percent Malays, 7 percent Indians, and 1 percent Eurasians.[19] The country has four official lan-guages—English, Malay, Mandarin, and Tamil. Most Singaporeans are fluent in at least two. With the strong Chinese presence, Mandarin is often the business language, although many other Chinese dialects are used as well. Managers in countries with such cultural diversity must learn to understand and manage culture.

Furthermore, cultural diversity is important to managers around the world because of globalization, the heterogeneity of the workforce, and social and demographic changes. For instance, less than 25 years ago, U.S. organizations were populated with a clear majority of male Euro-Americans. Since that time, the percentage of employees with European origins has decreased relative to those of other backgrounds and will continue to decrease. By 2050, the average and most common U.S. resident will be from a non-European background.[20] Specifically, 25 percent of the U.S. population will be Hispanic with an estimated spending power of $650 billion.[21]

Although women hold only 10 percent of the executive positions in the United States, they make up almost half the workforce, currently hold half the lower- to mid-management jobs in several industries, and are staying in organizations longer than they did in the past.[22] By some estimates, by the year 2000 women will comprise more than 50 percent of the U.S. workforce.[23] The end result is that women will constitute a larger group with seniority that will be harder to ignore.[24] There are similar trends in many other countries where the number of women in the workforce has been steadily increasing. For example, in spite of cultural and religious pressures for women to continue fulfilling traditional roles in Turkey, 35 percent of professionals are now women.[25]

The age of the workforce can also create diversity issues. Although the percentage of young people in the 16–24 age range in the United States is expected to drop 16.3 percent by 2005, the percentage of people 55 and older is projected to grow by 15 percent.[26] Although several other Western industrialized countries such as Belgium face similar challenges, many developing countries have the opposite problem with a very young population. The diverse ages of workforce members has serious implications for business in the areas of training, lead-ing, motivation, and career advancement opportunities.

Whatever the cause of workforce diversity, managers cannot simply assume that all employees want the same thing and can be managed the same way.[27] Instead, managers must understand how cultural diversity affects the expectations and behavior of people in their orga-nization. The challenge of managing an increasingly diverse workforce is to provide a work-place where diversity is recognized and valued and where productivity is fostered. In the next section, we investigate ways to manage diversity effectively.

Summary Point 3.6   **What Is Cultural Diversity?**

- Cultural diversity consists of subgroups within a country, each of which has unique norms and values. These groups may form their own culture based on ethnicity, age, gen-der, religion, physical attributes, sexual orientation, regional differences, functional specialization, and so on.

- Cultural diversity is important to managers because of globalization, the heterogeneity of nations, and changes in demographics and social issues that affect the compo-sition of the workforce.

Managing Diversity in Organizations

How can managers focus on the special needs of diverse groups, yet treat the entire workforce consistently and fairly? An organization must manage diversity fairly or risk causing conflict, distrust, and poor communication between diverse groups. If diversity is managed well, organizations can benefit.

The Benefits of Managing Diversity

Why should managers be so concerned with managing diversity effectively? Our national culture, race, ethnicity, age, gender, sexual orientation, physical ability, and other individual differences determine how we view the world. Without active management these differences can lead to misunderstandings, conflicts, and poor productivity. They can even result in legal and public relations crises and the loss of talented employees.

For instance, the news that some Texaco Oil executives used racist language about African-Americans and apparently discriminated against minorities in hiring and franchising practices cost the company over $140 million in legal settlement costs. In addition, the negative publicity tarnished Texaco's image.[28] Many other companies, such as GE, Xerox, Digital, and Pacific Bell, have received positive publicity from their diversity management efforts.[29]

The five key reasons managers should learn to manage diversity effectively are increased creativity, employee recruitment, flexibility, better marketing, and cost savings.[30]

- *Increased creativity.* Employees from diverse backgrounds can provide varied viewpoints and solutions to complex problems. As a result, heterogeneous teams and organizations tend to have better problem solvers and more creative workers.
- *Flexibility.* The presence of different viewpoints creates a more flexible organization that can respond effectively to varied environmental demands.
- *Recruiting employees.* A reputation for managing diversity well helps a company attract and retain a wide variety of talented individuals, giving the organization access to a better human resource pool. Hewlett-Packard CEO Lewis Platt believes that diversity "allows us to tap a broad range of human potential."[31]
- *Marketing.* A diverse workforce improves a company's ability to market its products and services to a broad customer base.
- *Cost savings.* Effective management of and positive response to a diverse workforce reduce the cost of turnover, absenteeism, and litigation, thereby allowing an organization to lower some of its labor costs.

Some businesspeople fear that valuing diversity will compromise performance because they believe businesses must lower their hiring standards to accommodate women, minorities, the physically disabled, and other groups. Instead, cultural diversity often improves performance standards and helps businesses develop new opportunities.

As an example, because of gender-neutral hiring practices, women lead half of Kraft Foods' U.S. operating units.[32] The presence of senior women executives has made it easier for Kraft to market its products to its primary customers: women. Another example is Voice Processing Corp., a company that makes voice command software. The company has been able to globalize more effectively because its culturally diverse managers, which as a group speak 30 different languages, have broader views and knowledge of different cultures.[33] J.C. Penney is another company that concentrates on diversity in its promotion practices. The company chairperson states: "If we don't have people of diverse backgrounds in the back, how in the world can we satisfy the diversity of people coming in through the front door?"[34]

Many organizations find that they benefit from diversity because they need different types of leaders to cope with the challenges of today's organizations. For instance, in an empowered, team-oriented environment, leaders must be able to delegate, share power, network, and build relationships. Jessica Lipnack, author of *The Age of the Network*, states: "In a network, all you have is influence. That's all you've got. And extensive shared commitment to a purpose. Trust is what it all comes down to. In a hierarchy the CEO is always a CEO, but in networks leadership is always shifting."[35]

Because the workforce of many U.S. organizations is still dominated by Euro-American males, effective inclusion of other diverse groups is likely to enrich organizations. Diversity gives businesses access to broader, more diverse ideas and markets and increases overall effectiveness in a complex, multicultural world. Proper management of cultural diversity can provide an organization with a distinct competitive advantage.[36]

Acculturate Diverse Groups to Manage Diversity   There are various ways to manage cultural differences. The process of diverse groups working together and resolving their differences to greater or lesser degrees is called **acculturation**. Figure 3.2 shows the four main approaches to acculturation. The difference in the four approaches is the extent to which the minority or smaller group is attracted to the larger group, and the extent to which members want to preserve their own culture.

The first type of acculturation represents the general model for cultural diversity. With the **integration** approach, the smaller-minority group preserves its uniqueness but also adopts some of the values of the dominant group. There is extensive contact and considerable exchange and sharing of ideas and cultural elements such as beliefs, values, traditions, and so forth.[37] Current immigration practices in the United States and Canada focus on integration of cultures. An analogy for the integration model of acculturation is a "salad," in which all elements retain their uniqueness and contribute to the overall flavor.

Assimilation is the second type of acculturation. Here the smaller group willingly gives up its culture to fit in with and adopt the culture of the more dominant group. The immigration policies in the United States in the early part of the twentieth century focused on assimilation of immigrants into the mainstream American culture. An appropriate analogy for assimilation is the "melting pot," in which all elements are mixed so they become a smooth, homogeneous entity with no unique group standing out.

Another example of assimilation is the treatment of women in the U.S. workforce in the 1960s and 1970s. Businesses encouraged women to blend in, dress like their male counterparts, ignore their feminine sides, and generally try to become as "male" as possible. Businesswomen accepted this model, believing it was their best chance for success.

The third approach to acculturation is **separation.** With this approach, smaller minority groups advocate separation from the dominant culture and refuse to interact and exchange cultural elements. Because of limited interaction and isolation, separation creates resentment, stereotyping, and conflict. For example, before J.C. Penney established its new diversity program, the organization conducted a survey of its employees. Many stereotypes became evident: Men mentioned that women were not as serious about their careers as men were; women and

Acculturation
The process of diverse groups working together and resolving differences to greater or lesser degrees

Integration
The smaller minority group preserves its uniqueness but also adopts some of the values of the dominant group

Assimilation
The smaller minority group willingly gives up its culture and adopts the culture of the more dominant group

Separation
The smaller minority groups advocate separation from the dominant culture and refuse to interact and exchange cultural elements

	Preserving Unique Elements of Smaller Culture	
	high low	
Smaller Group's Attraction to Dominant Culture high	**Integration** Smaller/Minority group keeps most of its culture and there is equal exchange between groups	**Assimilation** Smaller/Minority group willingly gives up most of its culture and adopts the dominant culture
low	**Separation** Smaller/Minority group keeps most of its culture and stays separate from dominant culture	**Deculturation** Smaller/Minority group is forced to give up most of its culture without adopting the dominant culture

FIGURE 3.2
Acculturation Models

Source: Based on information in J. Berry, "Acculturation: A Comparative Analysis," in R. J. Samuda and S. L. Woods (eds.), *Perspectives in Immigrant and Minority Education* (Lanham, MD: University Press of America, 1983): 66–77.

minorities stated that the upper management, mostly white males, were not comfortable being seen socializing with women and minorities.[38] As a result, the various cultural groups remained separate.

Deculturation
The process of forcing one group to give up its culture entirely without fully allowing it to adopt the culture and practices of the dominant group

The fourth approach is **deculturation,** which is the process of forcing one group to give up its culture entirely without fully allowing it to adopt the culture and practices of the dominant group. Deculturation leads to a loss of identity and increased stress, as evidenced by the treatment of the indigenous populations in Canada, the United States, and Australia. Either because of limited interaction or because one group's unique contributions are destroyed, separation and deculturation models do not allow organizations to take full advantage of cultural diversity. Managing cultural diversity effectively, then, depends on using either the integration or assimilation approach.

Practical Tips for Managing Diversity   Given that diversity exists in the workplace, it is up to organizations to learn to manage it well and to benefit from it.[39] First, managers must identify the various workforce cultures, analyze the similarities and differences among the cultures, and decide how the organization can deal with the diversity in the most advantageous way. For instance, diverse cultures often have diverse expectations about work, organizations, and management. Dual-career couples expect their employers to accommodate their specific needs with increased flexibility and nontraditional career paths. Younger workers tend to expect quick promotions, autonomy, and participation in decision making to a greater extent than their older counterparts.[40] Employees with family responsibilities often seek flexibility and family-related benefits to help balance their work and personal lives.

Many organizations are changing their practices to address these expectations. For example, some companies are implementing family-friendly policies. Managers at Corning (the company that invented fiber-optic cables and the TV picture tube) try to hire couples whenever they have job openings. Marc Whalen, a recent hire whose spouse also received an offer from Corning, states: "I think Corning realizes that happy people tend to be more productive."[41] FelPro, a Skokie, Illinois, maker of car gaskets with $500 million in sales in 1997, also has a pronepotism policy. Over two-thirds of its 1,900 employees have relatives in the organization. Both Corning and FelPro were named among the top 100 best companies to work for in the United States, partly because of these policies.

Still other companies implement practices to harness the talent of each generation. The New York advertising agency Avrett, Free and Ginsberg is putting younger and older employees to work in teams. That way, everyone benefits from the fresh ideas of the young and the experience of the veterans.[42]

Organizations such as Corning, FelPro, Motorola, Colgate-Palmolive, and Hoechst Celanese are known for their effective management of diversity. They share several characteristics, highlighted in Figure 3.3, that provide practical guidelines for other organizations and managers to follow.

- *Strong support from the top levels of the organization.* The values, beliefs, and behaviors of the top leadership of the organization set the tone for others and create a domino effect. The leadership's strong commitment to diversity signals its importance in the organization. For instance, Motorola created a high-level position for its new vice president and director of diversity, Roberta Gutman, who reports directly to the CEO. The Diversity Advisory Group at Coopers & Lybrand is chaired by company CEO Nicholas Moore.
- *Clear and consistent application of diversity principles in personnel decisions.* Managers need to "walk the diversity walk" through their recruitment, hiring, and promotion practices. The presence of a generally diverse workforce at all levels sends a clear signal about what the organization values. Colgate-Palmolive

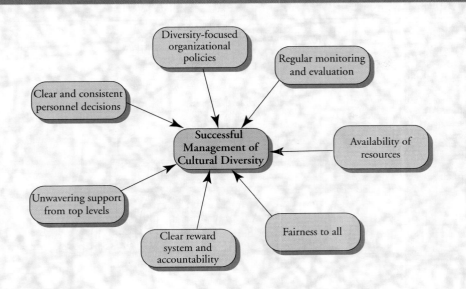

FIGURE 3.3
Factors in Successful Diversity Management

invests heavily in diversity programs and has been successful in attracting women and minorities.

- *Diversity-focused organizational policies.* Organizational benefits and practices such as flexible schedules and access to day care, support groups, mentoring programs, and so forth are all essential. Hoechst Celanese, the chemical giant, has a formal mentoring program that pairs its high-potential women and minority employees with successful executives in the company.[44]

- *Appropriate reward systems and accountability.* Managers and other employees must be rewarded for their efforts in promoting diversity and held accountable in their performance regarding such efforts. Hoechst Celanese ties about 25 percent of managers' bonuses to their efforts in promoting diversity.

- *Access to resources to support training and other activities.* Organizations need to train all managers and employees in the skills required to manage diversity and to deal with inevitable conflicts and disagreements. Colgate-Palmolive has a mandatory two-day diversity training for all employees. Employees who want to miss the training must call Executive Vice President Lois Juiber directly and explain why.[45] American Express managers have access to a "Diversity Toolbox" that includes a collection of videotapes and activities they can use to facilitate discussions about diversity.[46]

- *Fairness to all.* Special attention should focus on supporting all employees, including the members of majority groups and on recognizing individual differences that cross many cultural boundaries. Diversity programs should focus on benefiting the whole organization, not just a few members. To foster greater understanding of others' perspectives, Silicon Graphics Inc. encourages all employees to attend seminars offered by its women's-issues groups.[47]

- *Regular monitoring and evaluation.* The effectiveness of diversity programs and their success should be monitored and regularly evaluated through interviews, focus groups, and surveys. Mobil has an assessment program called "scoreboard" that keeps track of the company's performance on diversity issues.[48]

Diversity audits
Evaluations of the organization's diversity performance and suggestions for future action

These **diversity audits** review the organization's performance on diversity and suggest future courses of action.

Having access to the different points of views and approaches that spring from diversity in the organization is key to the success of today's complex organization. Such diversity can flourish and provide the organization with a clear competitive advantage only if all managers and employees generally accept the value of diversity. This acceptance must be an aspect of the organization's culture. James Houghton, the CEO of Corning Inc., emphasizes his organization's commitment to diversity: "To attract the best talent, we must show that we believe in and practice diversity in the workplace. Talented individuals will not enlist if they don't see a friendly environment where everyone has a chance to succeed. . . . They will not be attracted

A QUESTION OF ETHICS

Diversity Quotas

To achieve cultural diversity, some organizations set specific targets for how many women and minorities should be hired. What are the ethical, social, and organizational implications of using such targets to increase the number of women and minorities in organizations? What about the possible backlash from other groups? How can managers balance the need for diversity and equality?

Summary Point 3.7   **What Are the Benefits of and Methods for Managing Diversity?**

- Managing diversity well can benefit businesses through increased creativity, recruiting of employees, flexibility, better marketing, and cost saving.
- Acculturation is the process of diverse groups working together and resolving their differences to greater or lesser degrees. It can take place through integration, assimilation, separation, or deculturation.

- Managing cultural diversity effectively depends on using either integration or assimilation.
- Managing diversity successfully requires unwavering support from top management, clear and consistent personnel decisions, diversity-focused policies, a supportive reward system and accountability, availability of resources, fairness, and regular monitoring and evaluation.

by homogeneity but by cultural diversity."[49] Lou Noto, Mobil's chair and CEO, states, "Our culture must allow and encourage high performance from everyone—regardless of race, gender, national origin, or other individual differences."[50]

So far, we have examined national culture and ethnic or group culture and diversity. Next we explore organizational culture—its purpose and how it develops.

■ MANAGING ORGANIZATIONAL CULTURE

Just as countries and groups have their distinct cultures and individuals have unique personalities and styles, so do organizations. Organizational culture, also known as corporate culture, is the shared values and beliefs that guide the behavior of members of an organization. Culture allows one organization to distinguish itself from others. In the sections that follow, we examine the purpose of organizational culture, its nature and components, how it develops, and its impact on organizations.

Purpose of Culture

The culture of an organization provides a sense of stability and order.[51] It helps an organization's members maintain a sense of purpose in times of crisis. It provides a sense of direction and helps organize activities and set priorities. It tells people what is important and what is not.

One of the marks of a successful organization is a corporate culture that supports its mission and encourages employees and managers to engage in behaviors that will achieve that mission.[52] By helping the organization define itself, organizational culture helps the organization adapt to its environment and maintain smooth internal functioning.

Consider an example. Pepsi has for many years attempted to overtake Coca-Cola as the number one soft drink in the world. Being number one has become the mission of Pepsi's managers and executives. To achieve this mission, they have created a hard-driving, competitive, and win-at-all-costs organizational culture. Anything that Coke does, Pepsi tries to do better. For instance, Pepsi immediately matches any pricing strategy or promotional program that Coke unveils. Overall, Pepsi's focus on its competition creates a culture that has a clear direction. Beating Coke is the top priority of Pepsi's mission.

Organic Online, a 56-person business that creates Web sites for big companies such as Nike and McDonalds, is another case in point. The firm is one of the few start-up companies related to the Internet that has made money. It has been successful in achieving its mission

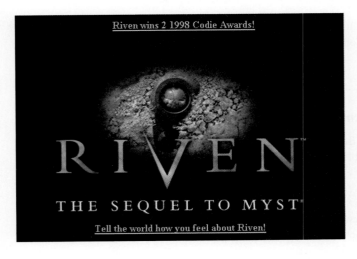

Jon Nelson, owner of Organic Online, tries to create a corporate culture of high-tech, empowerment, and flexibility. His mission is to keep the company responsive to its environment and to develop creative Web sites, such as this one for Riven. Organic Online's profitable bottom line shows that the match between culture and mission is a good one.

© 1997 Cyan, Inc. Riven® is a registered trademark of Cyan, Inc.

because its culture supports it. Jonathan Nelson, the 29-year-old founder and CEO, has created a culture in which employees have the freedom to do their jobs and are empowered to make decisions. With a simple and flexible structure to match its strategy and factors such as extensive health benefits, including benefits for domestic partners, top-of-the-line technology, and bagels in the morning, the company tries to create a supportive and innovative environment. Nelson states: "Fundamentally, I think I've built a very caring company. . . . And I'm having a blast."[53]

Just as corporate culture can support a company's mission and strategy, it can also work against effectiveness. For example, as Eastern European companies are moving toward a market economy, they find that organizational cultures that developed to deal with Soviet-style government and management are not adapting quickly.[54] The old cultures, based on minimal performance and precise implementation of centrally imposed plans, did not encourage initiative, speed, or creativity. Instead, conformity and lack of individual responsibility—typical reactions in autocratic systems—were the norm. The cultures of many Eastern European organizations still reflect these values and, as a result, the organizations struggle to support the new missions and strategies that are performance based.

Eastern European organizations are not alone in their cultural inflexibility. The well-established culture of any organization can prevent it from adapting quickly to environmental changes. It takes a lot of effort from managers to change the shared norms and values of an organization's members. Despite managers' efforts, ingrained inflexibility often leads to restructuring and layoffs in times of crisis. The leader of AT&T, C. Michael Armstrong, laid off 40,000 additional workers in 1997, in part to redirect the "sluggish, incompetent, boring" culture of AT&T toward a new mission.[55]

Managers need to be aware of their organization's culture as a contextual strategic force, particularly in light of increased diversity. Michael Schell, president of the Windham Group, a consulting firm in New York, and Charlene Solomon, contributing editor for *Workforce,* state: "Since organizations no longer will be ethnically uniform, corporate culture will take a far more important meaning. . . . That corporate culture, together with its norms, will unify an organization's workforce, enhance communication and enable global teams to work together to achieve a single common purpose."[56] Recall the Cirque du Soleil, profiled in the Managerial Challenge. Its organizational culture, one that is based on creativity, cooperation, respect, and community service, unifies employees from many national cultures.

Summary Point 3.8   **What Is Organizational Culture and What Is Its Purpose?**

- Organizational culture brings a sense of stability and order to a business by allowing for external adaptation and smooth internal functioning.

- Organizational culture should support the other contextual strategic forces.
- Organizational culture can also work against effectiveness and change.

Nature and Components of Organizational Culture

Organizational culture has three major components, depicted in Figure 3.4.[57] The most obvious component is observable aspects of culture, followed by shared values and beliefs, and finally basic assumptions.

Observable Cultural Elements   Observable components of culture are visible to insiders and outsiders. They are cultural elements such as the company dress code, the jargon used, the formality of interaction, the office setting, the decorations, and the tone of company social events. Other aspects of observable culture include company stories and rituals. Stories are often about the organization's founders and other critical events and incidents. These stories tell members which behaviors are rewarded, how to achieve success, what can get them in trouble, and so forth.

Stories about Intel's CEO, Andy Grove, explain much about the culture of Intel. Named by *Time* as the 1997 Person of the Year, Grove is legendary for demanding discipline and performance. "Andy Grove had no tolerance for people who were late or meetings that ran on without a purpose," states John Doerr, a former Intel employee.[58] In 1981, Grove decided that to increase productivity, every Intel employee needed to work two extra hours a day for free—a 25 percent increase. This solution became the legend of "125 percent," sending a message that hard work is part of the culture of the organization.[59]

Rituals are prescribed ceremonies that members perform at certain times. A company with a ritual that reflects its culture is Medtronic, the Minneapolis-based medical products organization we mentioned in chapter 2. Every December the company gives a holiday party and invites not only all its employees but also patients and their families. During the party, patients whose lives were saved because of Medtronic's heart pacemakers or other products get up and thank the employees. "I remember going to my first holiday party, and someone asked me if I had brought my Kleenex. I assumed I'd be fine, but then these parents got up with their daughter who was alive because of our product. Even the surgeons who see this stuff all the time were crying," explains Art Collins, Medtronic's president.[60] This emotional ritual gives Medtronic employees and managers a feeling that they are working for an important organization.

Shared Values and Beliefs   The second component of culture is not easily observable, though most organizational members are aware of it and can describe it. It includes the core values and beliefs shared by members of the organization about what is important and what is not. For instance, Body Shop's values include these: "We are against animal testing in the cosmetics industry. We campaign for human and civil rights."[61] Shared values address questions such as, What do we stand for? What is our organization about? What do we value in our employees and managers? Other values include the importance of social responsibility, the respect the

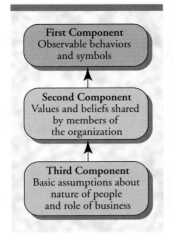

FIGURE 3.4
Components of Culture

Medtronic's corporate culture includes observable rituals to reinforce the belief that its products make a difference in many people's lives. Anjanette Schmeltzer of Medtronic's marketing management team believes the company's culture makes her job more rewarding.

customer deserves, or the value of turning out a high-quality product or service. The shared values and beliefs are typically expressed in the company's mission statement.

At Medtronic, every new employee is given a medallion inscribed with the mission statement: "to alleviate pain, restore health, and extend life."[62] The organization makes sure its employees are constantly reminded about the organization's values. In time, the values become an integral component of the culture of the organization.

Basic Assumptions   The third component of culture is the hardest to observe.[63] It comprises basic assumptions that are at the root of values and behaviors shared by the organization's members. These assumptions deal with general philosophical issues that are not always directly related to business. They form the **management philosophy**, which is the system of values about the nature of people and organizations and how the organization should conduct business.

Management philosophy
The system of values about the nature of people and organizations and how the organization should conduct business

Basic assumptions reflect the values of justice, honesty, fairness, humility, beneficence, compassion, individual dignity, and frugality.[64] Andy Grove of Intel has a management philosophy based on hard work, frugality, and an insatiable drive to excel. This philosophy has roots in his struggle as a child and young man to survive the Nazi and Soviet occupations of Hungary, his immigration to the United States, his hard work to earn a Ph.D. from the University of California–Berkeley, and his dream to help Noyce and Morris found Intel. He still works in a small 8-by-9-foot cubicle, just like everyone else at Intel.

Organizational Culture Components and National and Ethnic Cultures   The three components of organizational culture are closely tied to national, ethnic, and other group cultures. An organization's management philosophy often reflects its national heritage. Corporate cultures in the United States, for instance, often reflect the country's low-context culture with attention to specific verbal and written communication.

Similarly, the French cultural value of high power distance is evident in that country's hierarchical, formal organizational structures and cultures. Asian organizations reflect the cultural values of long-term orientation and collectivism, as shown in their emphasis on long-term performance and team management structures.

Ethnic and other group cultures have a similar influence on organizational culture. Organizations located in California are known to be more informal and laid back than businesses located in New York, for instance. Similarly, the organizational culture can reflect gender differences. Many organizations headed by women are known for having more "feminine" cultures. For example, at Avon, where a strong majority of women are in managerial ranks, courtesy is a requirement. Offices are decorated with needlepoint sayings and playing golf is not required for corporate success.[65]

Summary Point 3.9   **What Are the Components of Organizational Culture?**

- The first component of organizational culture is the observable elements such as stories and rituals, dress code, the jargon used, the formality of interaction, the office setting, the decorations, and the tone of company social events.
- The second component of organizational culture includes the values and beliefs shared by members of the organization about what is important and what is not.

- The third level of organizational culture includes the basic assumptions that form the management philosophy of an organization.
- An organization's culture reflects national, ethnic, and group cultures.

How Organizational Culture Develops

The culture of an organization starts forming as soon as the organization is created. It takes some time to shape and develop clear components. However, once formed, the culture has a strong impact on the organization and is difficult to change. In the following sections, we investigate how organizations create and maintain culture.

In the Beginning: Creating the Culture of an Organization   The culture of an organization develops over time and is strongly influenced by the organization's founders who leave an indelible mark on it.[66] Through stories, rituals, dress codes, and other means, founders help shape the culture of the organization. Think how much today's Disney corporation is a reflection of Walt Disney himself. He was adamant that every Disney employee be friendly, cheerful, and clean. He mandated that men had to shave every day, have no mustache, and have short hair. Four decades later, Walt's wishes still dictate many rules of behavior for Disney employees.

Disney is not alone in having its founder influence its culture. For many years, IBM was a reflection of J. Watson's personality. Southwest Airlines is made in Herb Kelleher's image. Mary Kay Cosmetics' culture reflects its founder's faith and beliefs. Microsoft's culture represents Bill Gates's intellectual, demanding, and perfectionist personality. Oprah Winfrey, the first African-American and the third woman to own a TV and film production studio with over $100 million in sales, runs an organization that reflects her high-energy, nurturing style. As organizations grow, if the values and assumptions support the organization's success and effectiveness, they will be reinforced and passed on to newcomers through socialization.

Maintaining Culture Through Socialization   New employees access all levels of an organization's culture formally through various teachings and informally through observation and interaction with other employees.[67] The formal teaching occurs as employees attend orientation programs and training courses, read employee manuals, and experience the formal evaluation process. The informal teaching occurs through observation, conversations, and interactions with other employees and managers. The process by which employees learn about the culture of an organization is called **organizational socialization**.[68]

The three stages of socialization are presented in Figure 3.5. During the first stage of *anticipatory socialization,* potential job candidates who are not yet members of the organization gather information about the company. If they are interested in the organization, some degree of early socialization takes place as they assess how well they match job requirements and fit the culture. By reading the organization and its culture well and presenting themselves accordingly, job candidates increase their chance of getting hired. For example, potential and

Organizational socialization
The process by which employees learn about the culture of an organization

TV and film production studio founder Oprah Winfrey has left a distinct impression on her organization's culture. The culture mirrors her nurturing, inclusive, and energetic style.

FIGURE 3.5
Stages of Socialization

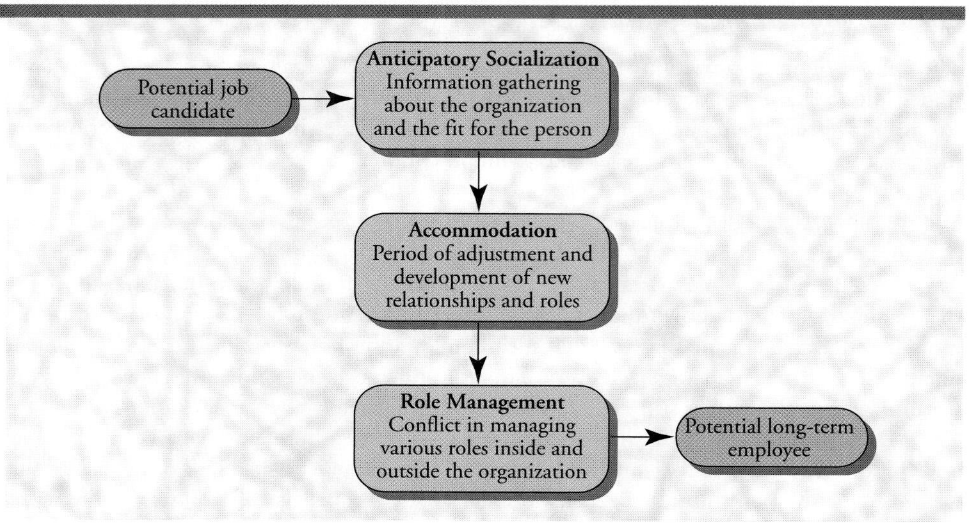

new employees are encouraged to go to the Cirque du Soleil's performances to become familiar with the company.

Similarly, organizations have many different methods for assessing whether a candidate fits with their culture. Formal interviews provide technical information; informal interactions, including discussion over meals, give further information about fit.

The second stage of socialization, *accommodation*, starts when the new employees join the organization and adjust their expectations, values, and behaviors to the organizational culture. The organization provides formal and informal training that informs the new members about the various components of its culture. In some cases, the employees continue to perceive a good fit and are able to adjust well. In other cases, there may be a poor fit between a new employee and the organization, eventually causing the employee to resign or be terminated.

The third stage of socialization is *role management*. During the role management stage, employees encounter conflicts between their roles inside and outside the organization. Successful and long-term employees manage these role conflicts well and become fully socialized into the organizational culture. Less successful employees continue to struggle in their attempt at accommodation and role management.

In some organizations, the process of socialization is formal and detailed, involving in-depth training programs. Wal-Mart expends considerable resources to train new employees about its corporate culture. In other organizations, the socialization process is informal: A new employee learns by watching others, listening to conversations and stories, participating in rituals, getting advice, making mistakes, and being corrected. Socialization becomes crucial for organizations that want to retain their best talents. At J.C. Penney, upper-management candidates are socialized through a formal mentoring program, regular meetings, discussion groups, and lunches with the top managers. The program has been successful for female executives, who now represent 26.6 percent of the managerial positions, up from 18.9 percent just a few years ago. Hoechst Celanese pairs top-level male executives with talented, promising women or minority managers. "These young fast-trackers gain exposure to the company's decision makers, while the mentors learn to be more comfortable working outside all-male cliques."[69]

Regardless of the degree of formality of the socialization process, the goal is to inform employees about the organization's culture and to achieve some level of agreement over basic assumptions and values. The extent of agreement and the degree to which employees are expected to adopt a uniform culture depends on the organization. Culture provides the con-

MANAGERIAL ADVICE
from the Experts

SOCIALIZING EMPLOYEES INTO THE CULTURE

Building a strong organizational culture requires that all employees agree with the basic assumptions that guide organizational actions. Here are some tips for socializing employees:

- Provide potential employees with accurate and thorough information about the company, the job, and the culture.
- Design formal orientation programs such as seminars or programs that orient employees to work with different people.
- Match new employees with others who have similar interests and skills.
- Listen to employee needs and work on matching them with organizational goals through training, transfers, and new assignments.
- Rely on existing employees to recruit their friends and socialize them into the organization.
- Provide flexibility in schedules and work assignments to allow employees to juggle their work and personal responsibilities and to further align employee needs with organizational goals.

Source: Partially based on P. Nokache, "Cisco's Recruiting Edge," *Fortune* 136, no. 6 (September 29, 1997): 275–76.

text for the employees and managers to behave in a manner consistent with the mission and values of the organization.

The process of socialization is key to organizational performance. Hiring new employees, replacing those who leave, and training new recruits are costly endeavors. Effective organizations develop recruitment tools that allow them access to a large pool of interested candidates. Good selection processes focus on accurate consideration of a potential employee's technical job skills and that person's fit with the mission and culture of the organization. From hiring people who fit and can contribute to keeping the productive employees, the process of socialization allows the organization to maintain its culture.

An excellent example of a company that has strong selection processes is Cisco Systems, a San Jose networking company. Through extensive use of its Web page and relying on current employees to recruit people who will fit well, Cisco Systems has been able to attract the highly skilled employees it needs.[70]

The Strength of Culture, Subcultures, and Countercultures   The strength of the corporate culture depends on how strongly members share its values and basic assumptions. A classic example of a strong culture is that of IBM in the 1960s and 1970s. IBM's 450,000 employees worldwide looked and acted alike. They were known for conservative, blue suits (worn even by women); excellent, professional service; and a general middle-of-the-road, non-flashy style that reflected the company's cultural assumptions of hard and steady work. The IBM culture encouraged uniformity at the expense of creativity and innovation. Over time, the lack of innovation became a liability, IBM began to lose market share, and eventually laid off over 50 percent of its people.

Strong organizational culture
A culture that is well defined; members from different parts of the organization are aware of its components, most members accept its core values and assumptions, and most behave in ways that are consistent with it

Weak organizational culture
A culture that is not well defined, or one with which there is not much agreement or behavior consistent with what is defined

Subculture
A group in an organization that may agree with the organization's basic assumptions and core values but have many distinct values and behaviors

In an organization with a **strong culture**, members from different parts of the organization are aware of the well-defined culture, most accept its core values and assumptions, and their behavior is consistent with it. In organizations with a **weak culture**, there either is no well-defined culture, or not much agreement or behavior consistent with what is defined.[71] As a result, there may be many subcultures in the organization.

A **subculture** is a smaller group in the organization who may agree with the organization's basic assumptions and core values but whose values and behaviors differ from those of the general culture. Organizations with many subcultures are heterogeneous in the same way that national cultures are.

Almost all organizations include subcultures based on functional departments. The human resource group, for instance, may have different values from those of the manufacturing group. Similarly, the approach of salespeople to the product and to the customer may differ from that of the engineers in the same organization. The salespeople tend to be highly responsive to customer needs compared to engineers, who focus on the technical aspects of the product, sometimes without much regard for customer needs. Though these groups agree with the goals of the organization and share its basic assumptions and values, they have different ways of defining what is important.

The existence of subcultures is a normal part of any organization and can be either beneficial or detrimental, depending on what values are shared. On the one hand, if the subcultures generally agree on basic assumptions and core values but disagree on the behaviors needed to achieve them, the organization is likely to benefit from the creativity and diversity. If, on the other hand, subcultures disagree with the basic assumptions, then achieving the mission is unlikely because people will behave in manners inconsistent with it.

Although organizational culture provides stability, order, and guidance to managers in their decision making, it can also be a liability. For culture to be a benefit rather than an obstacle, it needs to be managed well.

Organizational Culture and Change   Is a strong culture always a positive factor in organizations? The answer depends on whether the culture supports overall effectiveness. Organizations with strong, well-established corporate cultures find them to be a barrier to successful change. Particularly, companies that face uncertain and changing environments and need to be flexible to adapt will find that their strong cultures resist change. For instance, in 1997, Apple Computers founder Steven Jobs asked Apple employees to stop competing with Microsoft and accept it as a partner. In the strong culture of Apple, Microsoft was the enemy. The culture, then, created a barrier to this change.

Managers face a difficult dilemma. To be successful, they need to encourage the development of a strong culture and socialize employees to share assumptions and core values. However, they also need to assure that the culture is not so entrenched as to prevent innovation and flexibility. To address this quandary, managers can allow subcultures to develop, or they can build a corporate culture that values change and flexibility.

The corporate culture provides a backdrop for all other business activities. In some cases the culture is obvious. In others it is barely noticeable. An effective culture can be either strong or weak, but most important, it must fit well with other contextual strategic forces and organizational elements. Furthermore, it helps guide the employees and managers to behave in a way consistent with the organization's mission.

Hot ▼ Link

We discuss organizational change and the role of culture in detail in chapter 14.

Integrating Culture with the Other Strategic Forces

We explained in the previous chapter how managers must integrate the forces of environment, technology, strategy, and structure. After reading this chapter, you should have a thorough understanding of how culture fits with the other four forces. The shared values and norms of

Summary Point 3.10   **How Does Culture Develop and How Is It Maintained?**

- Leaders influence the development of culture.
- The strength of culture is determined by how strongly members agree with basic assumptions.

- Subcultures are a normal part of any organization and should be actively managed.
- Strong cultures resist change unless the organization's core values include flexibility and change.

organizations provide the context in which the business develops the mission and strategy and designs the appropriate structure. For instance, Johnson & Johnson's corporate culture includes the belief that its prices must be reasonable, as shown by its mission statement: "We must constantly reduce our costs in order to maintain reasonable prices." The culture encourages managers to use strategies that reduce costs. Those strategies include using the latest production technology and designing structures that use corporate resources efficiently. Managers should combine the five contextual strategic forces so that the organization's culture, strategy, and structure allow its employees to behave in ways consistent with the organization's mission. When this happens, each individual's efforts will be directed toward organizational effectiveness.

Royal/Dutch Shell has become one of the most profitable companies in the world. Such was not always the case. The company was losing money in 1994 and could not respond to the uncertain environment of the changing oil business. It received bad publicity and many considered it an ineffective company. The new Shell Chairperson, Cornelius Herkstroter, decided to change the culture of the company. Shell director Sir John Jennings recalls: "We were bureaucratic, inward looking, complacent, self-satisfied, arrogant. We tolerated our own under-performance. We were technocentric and insufficiently entrepreneurial."[72]

After meeting with the top 50 managers, Herkstroter charted a new culture, mission, and strategy for the organization. Managers are now required to think about how everything they do contributes to the bottom line. The structure was completely redesigned with five committees and a flat matrix that now manages the decentralized structure of over 100 operating divisions around the globe. The company is attempting to become more organic, responding earlier to changes in the uncertain environment, and being more innovative in its products and technologies and more receptive to the national cultures in which it operates.[73] The changes at Royal/Dutch Shell involve consideration of the environment and the technology and a close fit among strategy, structure, and culture. The culture change focuses on how every Royal/Dutch Shell employee behaves to direct everyone's energy toward the new mission.

Hot ▼ Link

We cover organizational effectiveness in depth in chapter 15.

For updated information on the topics in this chapter, Web exercises, links to related Web sites, an on-line study guide, and more, visit our companion Web site at:
http://www.prenhall.com/nahavandi

A Look Back at the

MANAGERIAL CHALLENGE

Cirque du Soleil

Managing 1,200 employees representing 17 nationalities and 13 languages, working in four different cities, and performing simultaneously in several countries is no easy feat. The Cirque's mission includes "development of our human resources; a tangible and responsible presence in the community. Cirque is, first and foremost, an amazing team!"[74] Taking care that all employees focus on the company's mission is Marc Gagnon's major responsibility. "We feel that the quality of life of our company is good people, good tools, and good communication. So all this is part of my job," Gagnon says.[75] Gagnon used to know all the employees when the Cirque first started. With the continued growth—from 35 employees in Montreal and one tour bringing in $14 million in sales, to more than 200 employees in Montreal alone and several tours that made $150 million in 1997—Gagnon has given up on that task. Instead he focuses on knowing the tour managers and delegating to them the task of staying close to the employees.[76]

Another key aspect of the Cirque's culture is its dedication to community and social responsibility. It allocates 1 percent of its potential box office revenues to philanthropic endeavors for at-risk, disadvantaged youth.[77] Through workshops and other programs all over the world, the Cirque introduces young people living in the streets in dire conditions to the circus life and its requirements of determination, discipline, respect, and solidarity.[78] By taking care of its employees, integrating cultures, and giving back to the communities, the Cirque du Soleil has created a successful organization. The major challenge continues to be maintaining their culture and their success while growing at a dizzying pace.

■ Point of View Exercises

You're the Manager: You are one of the tour managers of the Cirque's many performances in charge of all aspects of the lives of your 120-plus cast and crew from different countries. What are the most important issues for you to take care of? How do you maintain close working relationships among your cast and crew?

You're a Crew Member: You are one of the crew members assigned to public relations working with people from 10 different nationalities in a Cirque tour in Singapore. What can you do to manage the inevitable cultural conflicts your coworkers will experience?

SUMMARY OF LEARNING OBJECTIVES

1. **Define culture and describe national culture, cultural diversity, and organizational culture.** Culture is a set of norms, customs, values, and assumptions that guides the behavior of a particular group of people. The three levels of culture are national, ethnic or other group cultures in a nation, and organizational. National culture is a set of values and beliefs shared by people within a nation. Ethnic and other cultural groups within each nation are the source of cultural diversity, the second level of culture. The third level of culture, organizational culture, is the set of values, norms, and beliefs shared by members of an organization. Given time, all organizations develop a unique culture or character.

2. **Outline four models that help managers classify national cultural values.** Four major models that business managers use to understand and classify national cultures are (1) Hall's high-low-context cultural framework, (2) Kluckhohn and Strodbeck's values orientation, (3) Hofstede's dimensions of cultural values, and (4) Trompenaars's cultural groupings. Each model provides general descriptions of different cultures' value systems but do not describe all individuals in a culture.

3. **Discuss the nature and role of cultural diversity in organizations and analyze approaches to managing diversity.** Cultural diversity refers not only to having people from different backgrounds in the organization but also to valuing and building on those differences to become more effective. The diversity of the United States means that the workforce is heterogeneous, consisting of men, women, ethnic minorities, and workers of all ages. Different cultures come together and manage to resolve their differences through acculturation. The four approaches to acculturation are assimilation, integration, separation, and deculturation. The most effective acculturation methods are assimilation and integration. To manage diversity successfully, managers must have strong support at the top, implement consistent reward and organizational policies, and act fairly to all.

4. **Describe the effect and development of organizational culture.** The culture of an organization has a substantial effect on people. It provides a sense of stability and order and helps its members maintain a sense of purpose in times of crisis. It provides a sense of direction and helps organize activities and set priorities. By helping the organization define itself, organizational culture helps the corporation adapt to its environment. Organizational culture has three major components. The most obvious component is observable aspects of culture, followed by shared values and beliefs, and finally basic assumptions.

KEY TERMS

acculturation, p. 87
assimilation, p. 87
cultural diversity, p. 84
deculturation, p. 88
diversity audits, p. 90
expatriates, p. 76
heterogeneous cultures, p. 75
high-context cultures, p. 77
homogeneous cultures, p. 75

individualism/collectivism, p. 81
integration, p. 87
low-context cultures, p. 77
management philosophy, p. 94
masculinity, p. 81
national culture, p. 75
organizational culture, p. 75

organizational socialization, p. 95
power distance, p. 81
separation, p. 87
strong organizational culture, p. 98
subculture, p. 98
uncertainty avoidance, p. 81
weak organizational culture, p. 98

REVIEW QUESTIONS

1. What are the three levels of culture and how are they connected?
2. Compare and contrast the four models of national culture.
3. Explain diversity and its effect on organizations.
4. What are the three components of organizational culture and how are they related?
5. How does culture affect the other contextual strategic factors and the behavior of people in organizations?

DISCUSSION QUESTIONS

1. In what types of national cultures would you feel comfortable as a manager, and which would pose a challenge to you? Why?
2. Is managing diversity by offering diversity training and mentoring programs a fad that will disappear soon, or do you think it is important to today's organizations?
3. How can the concept of acculturation be used to manage different people in organizations?
4. How can your knowledge of organizational culture and its three components help you in your daily job as a manager?
5. What is the effect of changing organizational culture on the other contextual strategic forces?

▶ SELF-ASSESSMENT 3
Are You Globally Aware?

The following questions allow you to assess the extent to which you are globally aware or globally competent as a manager. For each question, circle the number that best describes you. See Appendix 3 for a scoring key.

		STRONGLY DISAGREE				STRONGLY AGREE
1.	I have extensive knowledge of other cultures.	1	2	3	4	5
2.	I adapt easily to new situations.	1	2	3	4	5
3.	I have a good understanding of the global business environment.	1	2	3	4	5
4.	I believe that my culture and customs are generally superior to others.	1	2	3	4	5
5.	I can work well with people who are different from me.	1	2	3	4	5
6.	I have a lot of interest in having global experiences.	1	2	3	4	5
7.	New situations make me feel uncomfortable.	1	2	3	4	5
8.	I enjoy learning about other people and how they do things differently from me.	1	2	3	4	5
9.	I know very little about other countries' laws, customs, technologies, and so forth.	1	2	3	4	5
10.	I have traveled extensively outside of my own country.	1	2	3	4	5
11.	I have an interest in learning other languages.	1	2	3	4	5
12.	I believe that, for most things, there usually is one best way to get things done.	1	2	3	4	5

▶ TEAM EXERCISE 3
Narian Bridges

The following exercise is a cross-cultural role play designed to let you experience the challenges and opportunities of interacting with a different culture. The setting is the fictional country of Nari. You will be asked to play the role of either an American or a Narian. Read the exercise carefully; your instructor will provide you with further information.

BACKGROUND

Nari is a Middle-Eastern country with an ancient history and a rich cultural heritage. Through judicious excavation of a number of minerals, the country has obtained considerable wealth, and its stable political and social climate has attracted many foreign investors. As a result, Nari has launched a careful and well-planned development campaign. In the past 20 years, its economy has become the strongest in the region. The per capita income is the highest in the area, and the country's literacy rate is 80 percent for the population under 30 (which is 53 percent of the population).

The country has several ethnic and religious groups with no dominant majority. The largest religious groups are Moslems, Christians, Jews, and Zoroastrians. These four groups have shared social and political power for a number of years. The culture is warm and generally welcoming of outsiders, although criticism of the country and its culture is poorly accepted and not open for discussion. The extended family remains the core of society, with the father being the unquestioned head. Many younger Narians seek higher education in other parts of the world; however, almost all return eagerly to their country. Although there are some rumblings about opening up the political systems and allowing for more democratic participation, the authority of the family, of the community, and of the monarch are rarely, if ever, questioned.

The political system is an authoritarian monarchy. Although there is an elected parliament dominated by the major four religious groups, its powers are limited to being a consultative body for the king. This political system has been in place for over a thousand years. Compared to many of its unstable neighbors, Nari has enjoyed a very calm political climate. The current dynasty has been in power for over 400 years. Although the king himself is Zoroastrian, his wife is a Christian, a further indication of the pluralistic nature of the society. The Western press has been critical of the lack of democracy and the authoritarian nature of the government. The king has unceremoniously dismissed the charges as cultural colonialism and has emphasized the need to preserve the rich Narian culture while welcoming help in economic development from both the West and the East.

Following the strong family and monarchist traditions, Narian leaders are assigned total and absolute power. Leaders are assumed to be infallible. Narian leaders are confident in their complete knowledge of all they come to face. They do not ask questions and do not seek advice, even from equals. If leaders indicated such a potential of lack of knowledge or expertise, they would be considered incompetent. The Narian leader is expected to take care of loyal followers under any circumstance. As followers owe unquestioning obedience, leaders owe them total devotion. They are fully responsible for all that happens to their followers, in all aspects of their life. They are expected to help and guide them and come to their rescue when needed. Their primary duty is to take care of their followers.

In return, Narian followers are expected to be loyal, obedient, dutiful, and subservient. They accept their leader's orders willingly and wholeheartedly. All Narians are taught from the youngest age that leaders are infallible, as the proper functioning of the social order hinges on obedience and loyalty to leaders and elders and to others' fulfilling their responsibility as followers. Dissent and conflict are rarely displayed in public. If ever a mistake is made, regardless of where the fault lies, all individuals work on correcting it without assigning blame. If the leader has made a mistake, followers often quickly accept the blame to protect the leader's reputation and preserve social harmony. The person accepting that responsibility is always rewarded for his or her loyalty.

The role of women in Narian society has been very puzzling to Western observers. For more than 30 years, women have had practically equal rights with men. They can vote, conduct any kind of business transactions, take advantage of educational opportunities, file for divorce, obtain custody of their children, work in any organization, and so forth. The literacy rate for women is equal to that of men, and although fewer of them have pursued higher education, it appears that most women who are interested in working outside the home have found easy employment in the booming Narian economy. The interaction between men and women is not restricted and most Narian women, as well as Narian men, have adopted Western-style clothing.

ROLE-PLAY SITUATION

A U.S. engineering and construction company has won its first major governmental contract for construction of two bridges in Nari. The general terms have been agreed on. There still needs to be agreement on precise plans and timetables. The company is working closely with several U.S.-educated Narian engineers at the Narian ministry of urban development (UD). The minister of UD, Mr. Dafti, is a well-respected civil engineer, educated in Austria in the 1950s. In addition to Narian, he speaks fluent German, English, and French. He has been instrumental in the development of his country.

The role play is a meeting between Mr. Dafti and his Narian associates and the U.S. engineering team. The U.S. head engineer requested the meeting, which was granted quickly. The U.S. team is eager to get started on the project. The Narians are also ready to engage in their new business venture.

Please wait for further instructions.

Source: Adapted with permission from Afsaneh Nahavandi, "Narian Bridges," in *The Art and Science of Leadership* (Upper Saddle River, NJ: Prentice Hall, 1997): 21–23.

UP CLOSE

▶ Sexual Harassment or Cultural Misunderstanding?

Web Designs (WD) is a medium-size company that designs software for use on the Web; it has corporate clients all over the world. The company has headquarters in San Francisco and offices in Canada, England, Australia, France, and Italy. Due to considerable growth and many recent hirings, the top managers of WD have selected an outside consulting firm with an international training staff to provide formal management training to managers and supervisors through a series of seminars. The trainer/consultants also conduct managerial assessments to identify high-potential managers and supervisors who could then be targeted for further training and promotion. The training sessions are run on Friday afternoons from 3 P.M. to 5 P.M. for 10 weeks.

One training session is run by Jean-Marc Dufour, a 34-year-old French human resource (HR) specialist who is considered to be one of the best consultants in the company. The training is in San Francisco and attended by 20 WD managers and supervisors. One of these managers, Heidi Anderson, is a 25-year-old female supervisor with a degree in management information systems. Heidi started with the company immediately after her college graduation three years ago. She is ambitious and focused on her career. She wants to move up in management. Not only does she want to make a good impression, but she is also genuinely interested in the topic of Jean-Marc's seminar. Therefore, Heidi has been sitting in front of the class every day. She is extremely attentive, asks many interesting questions, and is obviously enjoying the class. She often stays when the session ends to ask Jean-Marc additional questions and to discuss employee problems with him.

Jean-Marc, who is an experienced trainer, finds the course at WD somewhat routine and boring. The participants have technical backgrounds, are very inexperienced in management, and by and large, do not appear very enthusiastic about the course. The one exception is Heidi. Jean-Marc enjoys her enthusiasm and her attention. In addition to being one of the best seminar participants, Heidi is also attractive. She often comes to class in shorts or short skirts with close fitting T-shirts. She is eager, smart, sexy, open, and approachable. He suspects that she has been flirting with him, maybe unconsciously. Although he is aware that she is technically his "student," and that he has to evaluate her at the end of the training, he sees no harm in enjoying her company.

One Friday afternoon after the session ends, Heidi comes up with a list of questions regarding a problem employee she is dealing with. As the session ended late and the office is closing, she invites Jean-Marc to have coffee so she can continue the discussion. Jean-Marc happily agrees. The coffee extends to dinner and the conversation turns to personal issues regarding significant others (both are unattached at the moment) and plans for the future. Jean-Marc extensively compliments Heidi for her intelligence and her looks. Heidi feels uncomfortable with the attention and the gradual turn to more personal issues, but she still enjoys Jean-Marc's company and continues to focus on all that she can learn from him.

The relationship between Heidi and Jean-Marc continues with several other dinners and meetings outside of class initiated by both of them. Heidi notices that Jean-Marc continues to be particularly attentive. She is increasingly confused about the meaning of his behavior and feels some pressure from him to make the relationship more personal. Last time they had dinner together, while dropping her home, he bent and kissed her on each cheek. She is still learning from him and does not want to make a bad impression, so she does not say anything that might offend him. However, she starts to look forward to the end of training class. To make matters more difficult, several class members tease Heidi about how good-looking Jean-Marc is

and what a cute couple they make. Heidi is surprised by the comments as she sees her interaction with him, while friendly, as strictly professional.

For his part, Jean-Marc sees his relationship with Heidi as simple fun and friendship. She is lots of fun, and although less mature than she appears in class, she is very smart and good company. Her obvious attraction to him does not hurt either. A little flirtation just makes life fun! Heidi is pleasantly different from most of the professional American women he has met who, in his opinion, have lost touch with their feminine side. They just want to talk about business. His friendship with Heidi has made his stay in the United States all the more pleasant, but he is looking forward to going back home.

At the end of the training, all participants take several paper-and-pencil assessments and participate in detailed role plays to help assess their learning and their potential for management. In spite of Heidi's enthusiasm, her scores on the written tests and her performance on role plays are disappointingly low. Jean-Marc agrees with the other trainers' assessment that, although Heidi has potential, she is still professionally too young and needs further experience before she is considered for further training and promotion.

When Heidi receives the news on her performance, she is devastated. She calls Jean-Marc who simply explains the evaluation process to her and tells her that she will do better next time. He tells her that she is young and that she has plenty of time. Getting no response, Jean-Marc wants to cheer Heidi up and asks her if she wants to go to dinner before he goes back to France. To Jean-Marc's surprise, Heidi yells "You bastard!" and hangs up. Jean-Marc tries to call back several times during that evening, but does not get an answer. He leaves the next morning for France.

While Jean-Marc is getting on his plane, Heidi walks into the HR office of Web Design and initiates the paperwork for filing sexual harassment charges against WD, the consulting firm, and Jean-Marc. You are one of the executives of WD. The HR director has just come to you with Heidi's complaints. The ball is in your court.

Questions

1. What is your analysis of the situation?
2. What role does culture play in the interaction between Heidi and Jean-Marc and the problems that ensue?
3. What responsibility did each person have? What responsibilities do WD and the consulting firm have?
4. How could the problems have been averted?
5. What will you do now?

NOTES

1. "The Quest," Cirque du Soleil Web site, accessed on-line at www.cirquedusoleil .com/en/odyss/quete, May 1998.
2. "Big Tent," *Fortune* 138, no. 8 (April 28, 1997): 367.
3. G. Flynn, "The Big Top Needs Big HR," *Workforce* (August 1997): 45.
4. Ibid., 40.
5. Ibid., 44.
6. E. T. Hall, *The Silent Language* (Garden City, NY: Anchor Press/Doubleday, 1973).
7. See C. A. Bartlett and S. Ghoshal, *Managing Across Borders, The Transnational Solution* (Boston, MA: Harvard Business School Press, 1989); C. A. Bartlett and S. Ghoshal, "Managing Across Borders: New Organizational Responses," *Sloan Management Review* no. 29, 9 (1992): 3–13; R. A. Bettis and C. K. Prahalad, "The Dominant Logic: Retrospective and Extension," *Strategic Management Journal*, 16 (1995): 5–14.
8. E. T. Hall, *Beyond Culture* (Garden City, NY: Anchor Press/Doubleday, 1976).
9. For a discussion of the concept of high and low context, see M. Munter, "Cross-Cultural Communication for Managers," *Business Horizons* (May–June 1993): 69–78.
10. F. Kluckhohn and F. L. Strodbeck, *Variations in Value Orientations* (Evanston, IL: Peterson, 1961).
11. F. Trompenaars, *Riding the Waves of Culture: Understanding Culture and Diversity in Business* (London: Nicholas Brealey, 1994).
12. G. Hofstede, *Culture's Consequences* (Thousand Oaks, CA: Sage, 1980); G. Hofstede, "Cultural Constraints in Management Theories," *Academy of Management Executive* 7, no. 1 (1993): 81–94; G. Hofstede, "An American in Paris: The Influence of Nationality on Organization Theories," *Organization Studies* 17, no. 3 (1996): 525–37; G. Hofstede and M. H. Bond, "The Confucian Connection: From Cultural Root to Economic Growth," *Organizational Dynamics* 16: 4–21.
13. Personal interview with Kristi Conlon, March 9, 1998.
14. A. Wooldrige, "From Multilocal to Multicultural," *Economist* 335, no. 792 (June 24, 1995): ss14–15.
15. *Fortune* (1997): 363.
16. A. Fisher, "The World's Most Admired Companies," *Fortune* 136, no. 8 (October 27, 1997): 232.
17. K. Labich, "Making Diversity Pay," *Fortune* 134, no. 5 (September 9, 1996): 177–78.
18. The Malaysia Yearbook (1996) http://www.jaring.my/msia/newhp.general/bumi.himt
19. http://www.trave.com.sg/sog/into/people/html
20. "Diversity: America's Strength," *Fortune* 135, no. 12 (June 23, 1997): 51–52.
21. D. Freedman, "Hispanic Birth Rates Up," *Arizona Republic*, February 13, 1998, p. A11.
22. M. Galen, "White, Male, and Worried," *Business Week* (January 31, 1994): 50–55; L. Himelstein and S. A. Forest, "Breaking Through," *Business Week* (February 17, 1997): 64–70. M. Johnson, "Still a Man's World at the Top, Survey Says," *Arizona Republic* October 18, 1996, E1–E2; L. Nathans-Spiro, "Is Wall Street Finally Starting to Get It?" *Business Week* (September 26, 1994): 54.
23. "Diversity: America's Strength."
24. H. Rheem, "Equal Opportunity for Women," *Harvard Business Review* 74, no. 4 (July/August 1996): 12–13; A. Bennett, "More Women Are Staying on the Job Later in Life Than Men," *Wall Street Journal* (Eastern ed.) September 1, 1994, B1–B2.
25. S. Poggioli, "Turkish Feminism," *Weekend Edition*, National Public Radio, March 7, 1998.
26. U.S. Bureau of Labor Statistics, "The Labor Force," *Monthly Labor Review*, November 1995, p. 30.
27. See A. P. Brief, R. T. Buttram, R. M. Reizenstein, S. D. Pugh, J. D. Callahan, R. L. McCline, and J. B. Vaslow, "Beyond Good Intentions: The Next Step Toward Racial Equality in the American Workplace," *Academy of Management Executive* 11, no. 4 (1997): 59–72; T. Cox, Jr., "The Multicultural Organization," *Academy of Management Executive*, 5, no. 2 (1991): 34–47.
28. K. Eichenwald, "Texaco to Pay Reward Payout in Bias Lawsuit," *New York Times*, November 16, 1996, 1, 23; M. Jackson, "Diversity Plans Stall at Firms, Survey Shows," *Arizona Republic*, December 6, 1996, E1.
29. S. E. Jackson and Associates, *Diversity in the Workplace: Human Resources Initiatives* (New York: Guilford Press, 1992); L. O. Graham, *The Best Companies for Minorities* (New York: Plume, 1993).
30. D. Moran, "Saving Money by Caring for Children," *Wall Street Journal* (Eastern ed.), August 1994, A10; J. J. Laabs, "Kinney Narrows the Gender Gap," *Personnel Journal* 73 (August 1994): 83–89; C. R. Schwenk, "Agreement and Thinking Alike: Ingredients for Poor Decisions," *Academy of Management Executive* 4, no. 1 (1990): 69–74; S. Feinstein, "Being the Best on Somebody's List Does Attract Talent," *Wall Street Journal*, October 10, 1989; J. Dreyfuss, "Get Ready for the New Work Force," *Fortune*, April 23, 1990, 165–81; L. Harrington, "Why Managing Diversity Is So Important," *Distribution* 92, no. 11 (November 1993): 88–92.
31. "Diversity: America's Strength," 58.
32. H. Lancaster, "Women at Kraft Tell How to Be Big Cheese While Handling Family," *Wall Street Journal*, April 23, 1996, B1.
33. M. Selz, "Small Company Goes Global with Diverse Workforce," *Wall Street Journal* (Eastern ed.), October 12, 1994, B2.
34. Himelstein and Forest, "Breaking Through," 64.
35. T. A. Stewart, "Get with the New Power Game," *Fortune* 135, no. 1 (January 13, 1997): 61.
36. J. Pfeffer, "People, Capability, and Competitive Success," *Management Development Review* 8, no. 5 (1995): 6–10; T. H. Cox and S. Blake, "Managing Cultural Diversity: Implications for Organizational Competitiveness," *Academy of Management Executive* (August 1991): 45–56.
37. For detailed presentations on the different ways in which different cultures interact, see J. Berry, "Acculturation: A Comparative Analysis," in R. J. Samuda and S. L. Woods (eds.), *Perspectives in Immigrant and Minority Education* (Lanham, MD: University Press of America, 1983): 66–77. For applications to organizational culture see A. Nahavandi and A. Malekzadeh, "Acculturation in Mergers and Acquisitions," *Academy of Management Review* 13, no. 1 (1988): 79–90; and A. A. Sales and P. H. Mirvis, "When Cultures Collide: Issues of Acquisitions," in J. R. Kimberly and R. E. Quinn (eds.), *Managing Organizational Transition* (Homewood, IL: Irwin, 1984), 107–33.
38. Himelstein and Forest, "Breaking Through," 68.
39. For an excellent analysis of the consequences of cultural diversity, see Cox and Blake, "Managing Cultural Diversity"; also see Moran, "Saving Money," and Laabs, "Kinney Narrows the Gender Gap."
40. For articles about generational differences, see D. Fenn, "Managing Generation X," *Inc* 18, no. 11 (August 1996): 91; D. B. Hogarty, "The Young and the Restless," *Working Woman* 21, no. 7/8 (July/August 1996); "No Cost Job Recognition That Works," *Human Resource Professional* 9, no. 2 (March/April 1996): 12; B. Nelson, "Give Generation X a Chance and a Challenge," *Human Resource Professional* 9, no. 2 (March/April 1996): 10–11; B. P. Sunoo, "How to Manage Generation X," *Personnel Journal* 74, no. 12 (December 1995): 118; C. Romano, "Generation X Horoscope," *HR Focus* 71, no. 9 (September 1994): 22; B. Tulgan, "Managing Generation X," *Executive Excellence* 12, no. 4 (April 1995): 6.
41. J. Martin, "So, You Want to Work for the Best," *Fortune* 137, no. 1 (January 12, 1998): 78.
42. K. Goldam, "Agency's Teams Leap the Generation Gap," *Wall Street Journal* (Eastern ed.), December 21, 1994, B2.
43. "Diversity: America's Strength."
44. Himelstein and Forest, "Breaking Through," 67.
45. Ibid., 68.
46. "Diversity: America's Strength," 56.
47. Himelstein and Forest, "Breaking Through," 70.
48. "Diversity: America's Strength," 54.
49. J. R. Houghton, "Unleashing the Power of People," *Executive Excellence* 13, no. 10 (1996): 10–14.
50. "Diversity: America's Strength," 54.
51. L. Smircich, "Concepts of Culture and Organizational Analysis," *Administrative Science Quarterly* (September 1983): 339–58.
52. See G. M. Walter, "Culture Collision in Mergers and Acquisitions," in P. J. Frost, L. F. Moore, M. R. Louis, C. C. Lundberg, and J. Martin (eds.), *Organizational Culture* (Beverly Hills, CA: Sage, 1985), 301–14; A. Nahavandi and A. R. Malekzadeh, *Organizational Culture in the Management of Mergers* (Westport, CT: Quorum, 1993).
53. Anonymous, "The Young CEOs," *USA Today*, November 11, 1996, 3B.
54. For an example, M. Kostera and M. Wicha, "The 'Divided Self' of Polish State-Owned Enterprises: The Culture of Organizing," *Organization Studies* 17, no. 1 (1996): 83–105; S. Baca, "Hungarian Culture and Management Issues

Within Foreign-Owned Hungarian Production Companies," presented at the International Conference on the Cultural Dimensions of International Mergers and Acquisitions, Copenhagen Business School, Denmark, August 1996.

55. H. Goldblatt, "AT&T Finally Has an Operator," *Fortune* 137, no. 3 (February 16, 1998): 79–82.

56. M. S. Schell and C. M. Solomon, "Global Culture: Who Is the Gatekeeper?" *Workforce* 76, no. 11 (1997): 35–39.

57. For a detailed discussion of the components and levels of organizational culture, see E. H. Schein, *Organization Culture and Leadership* (San Francisco, CA: Jossey-Bass, 1993).

58. J. C. Ramo, "A Survivor's Tale," *Time*, January 5, 1998, 66.

59. Ibid.

60. R. B. Lieber, "Why Employees Love These Companies," *Fortune* 137, no. 1 (January 12, 1998): 74.

61. C. Anderson, "Value-Based Management," *Academy of Management Executive* 11, no. 4 (1997): 25–46.

62. R. Levering and M. Moskowitz, "The 100 Best Companies to Work for in America," *Fortune* 13, no. 1 (January 12, 1998): 89.

63. Schein, *Organization Culture and Leadership*.

64. Anderson, "Value-Based Management," 41–45.

65. B. Morris, "If Women Ran the World, It Would Look a Lot Like Avon," *Fortune* 136, no. 2 (1997): 74.

66. A. Nahavandi and A. R. Malekzadeh, "Leader Style in Strategy and Organizational Performance: An Integrative Framework," *Journal of Management Studies* 30, no. 3 (193): 405–25; also see Schein, *Organization Culture and Leadership*.

67. T. E. Deal and A. A. Kennedy, *Corporate Cultures: The Rites and Ritual of Corporate Life* (Reading, MA: Addison-Wesley, 1982); Schein, *Organization Culture and Leadership*.

68. D. C. Feldman, "A Contingency Theory of Socialization," *Administrative Science Quarterly* (September, 1976): 434–35; Feldman, "The Multiple Socialization of Organization Members," *Academy of Management Review* (June 1981): 309–18.

69. Himelstein and Forest, "Breaking Through," 67.

70. P. Kakache, "Cisco's Recruiting Edge," *Fortune* 136, no. 6 (September 29, 1997): 275–76.

71. See Schein, *Organization Culture and Leadership*, and Nahavandi and Malekzadeh, "Acculturation in Mergers and Acquisitions."

72. J. Guyon, "Why Is the World's Most Profitable Company Turning Itself Inside Out?" *Fortune* 136, no. 3 (August 4, 1997): 122.

73. Ibid.

74. "A Word from the Presidents," Cirque du Soleil Web site, accessed on-line at www. cirquedusoleil.com/en/coulisse/presidents, February 11, 1998.

75. Flynn, "The Big Top," 41.

76. Ibid., 45.

77. "More Than a Circus," Cirque du Soleil Web site, accessed on-line at www.cirquedusoleil.com/en/coulisse/corpo/corpo, February 11, 1998.

78. "Cirque du Soleil's Outreach Activities," Cirque du Soleil Web site, accessed on-line at www.cirquedusoleil.com/en/coulisse/cirque_monde/monde, February 11, 1998.

▶ The Context at Jagged Edge

Jagged Edge Mountain Gear (JEMG) is a company that specializes in making, selling, and marketing climbing and cold weather outdoor gear. Its headquarters is located in Telluride, Colorado, a picturesque town nestled in the breathtaking San Juan Mountains. Walk into JEMG's original store on Main Street in Telluride and you have the feeling of entering an old mine. Rugged, fashionable clothing and mountaineering gear are displayed around a room that is filled with the faint smell of wood smoke. The floor is worn; the few pieces of furniture are rustic. Space is cramped and several people busily share computers in the small back office. There is constant interaction among the staff and customers.

After you enter the store you are likely to be greeted with a warm, friendly smile and questions about your stay in Telluride and your latest hiking, climbing, mountain biking, or skiing expedition. Several people typically join in to share stories of their mountain adventures. You may be making plans to join them later in the afternoon for a hike before you realize you are talking to Josh Bodine, the Telluride store manager, Tim O'Neill, JEMG's buyer, or even Margaret Quenemoen, JEMG's founder and one of the owners. They all have many stories to tell and plenty of ideas and advice about where to go and what to do. No one tries to sell you anything, but asking a simple question about any of the items results in an expert and professional answer. These are people who really know their sport.

A passion for mountain sports and making serious gear is the basis for the atmosphere at JEMG. That passion has led to a million-dollar business built on a headband. Founder Margaret Quenemoen started JEMG by selling headbands from a cart on the streets of Telluride in the winter of 1990. At the time she was broke, living in her car, and desperate for gas money. She has not stopped since that time, designing and manufacturing fashionable yet durable clothing for mountain sport enthusiasts. She opened the

first Jagged Edge Mountain Gear apparel store in 1993. After Margaret saw the potential of JEMG, she convinced her twin sister Paula to leave China and Tibet, where Paula was studying Chinese and trekking, to join her in Telluride.

The first store was soon followed by another, a wholesale division, and a catalog operation. The headband continues to be one of their best-selling product lines along with other popular items such as fleece outerwear made from recycled plastic containers. When describing how she started the company, Margaret says, "I had an idea. I was excited about creating something. I could make something I liked and create something that people would pay for. I have a vision and I see things through."[1]

JEMG has a strong foothold in the cold weather, extreme sports industry. Currently, it has 30 employees, 4 stores, a headquarters in Telluride, Colorado, and an office in Salt Lake City, Utah. Its merchandise is sold in 150 retail outlets. In addition, the company contracts with home sewing groups in several different states to manufacture its products and has established relationships with Chinese manufacturers to make its breathable mountain climbing shells and goose down jackets. The recent addition of a Web page and on-line catalog is bringing in new customers daily.

The JEMG reputation for hard-core, fashionable, and quality mountaineering clothing and gear has caught the eye of mountaineering enthusiasts from Japan to Chile with up to 25 percent of the wholesale business generated by international sales. Margaret Quenemoen says, "We want to become a nationally recognized competitor. We want to compete with the big boys."[2] JEMG is ready to take on large, entrenched companies such as North Face, Eddie Bauer, REI, and Patagonia. However, Margaret insists, "We are our own competition. We don't look at what everybody else is doing. We do what we think is right."[3]

An Asian philosophy that focuses on the journey and process is obvious in the company's catalog and its business plan. While many competitors emphasize the end goal of reaching the summit, the Quenemoens have built their business on the process of getting there. "The journey counts. We wanted to add a spiritual element to our clothes."[4]

Involvement in their community and being recognized as a "green" company are integral parts of JEMG's image. The company donates clothing domestically and internationally and is actively involved in the promotion and protection of mountain sports through cooperation with organizations such as the American Alpine Club and the Access Fund, an organization that promotes rock and ice climbing and protects mountain areas.[5] JEMG further demonstrates its environmental sensitivity by using fleece made from 100 percent recycled plastic soda bottles. Dyersburg of Tennessee and Malden Mills of Massachusetts, both with reputations for environmentally friendly policies, are JEMG's two fleece suppliers.

Everyone at JEMG lives and breathes mountain sports. Workdays are long but schedules are flexible. Paula Quenemoen heads the Salt Lake City office and leads the company's marketing efforts with Brad Barlage, her administrative assistant and the company's marketing director. She mentions, "If there is a really perfect powder day [a perfect ski day], I ask Brad, 'Why are you here? You need to go skiing.' I know he will be happier taking the day off; I will be happier, and he will come back and get his work done even better."[6]

In spite of the informal atmosphere, employees at JEMG have titles and formal responsibilities, as described in Table 1. However, few have seen or used the formal organizational chart. Margaret believes that the formal titles help people define their jobs and clarify their areas of responsibility. She states, "We have specific jobs, but everyone is expected to go outside their jobs. It's a group effort."[7]

Because nearly everyone starts working at JEMG by selling in one of the stores and then moves to different positions, they all know the different parts of the business well and can help one another at any time. They work hard together and play hard together. Rock and ice climbing, mountain biking, and skiing are part of regular off-work events during which a lot of decisions are made. "We not only work together, we play together," explains Margaret Quenemoen. "When we are out together, we are all at the same level."[8]

Questions

1. How would you evaluate the environment JEMG faces?
2. What is the company mission and structure? What is the company culture?
3. How well do the company's mission, structure, and culture fit together?

Notes

[1] Interview with Margaret Quenemoen, June 4, 1998.

[2] Ibid.

[3] Interview with Margaret Quenemoen, June 9, 1998.

[4] B. Vasquez, "Jagged Edge Nears $1M Climb to Top," *Denver Business Journal,* December 5–11, 1997, accessed on-line at http://www.jagged-edge.com/dbjpress.html.

[5] JEMG business plan.

[6] Interview with Paula Quenemoen, June 8, 1998.

[7] Interview with Margaret Quenemoen, June 4, 1998.

[8] Ibid.

Table 1 JEMG'S ORGANIZATIONAL JOB DESCRIPTIONS AND MANAGERS' BACKGROUNDS

Name	Job Title and Description	Background and Personal Information
Margaret Quenemoen	Founder, CEO, President, Chairman of the Board	B.A. in economics with business emphasis; experience as outerwear production manager, alpine and telemark skier, rock and ice climber
Paula Quenemoen	Executive Vice President, based in Salt Lake City, Utah; responsible for all JEMG marketing and catalog creation	B.A. in Asian studies and political science with minor in Chinese and international relations; experience as international offshore buyer in China, several governmental internships, winner of Matheson Leadership scholar award, skier, climber, and mountaineer
David Potter	Vice President; oversees all wholesale, mail, and retail operations	B.A. in history and education; registered NORBA bike racer, snowboarder, marathon runner, rock and ice climber, puppeteer and puppet maker, journalist, photographer, world traveler, and metalwork artist

(Table continued on next page)

Name	Job Title and Description	Background and Personal Information
Brad Barlage	Marketing Director and Paula's administrative assistant	Four years of outdoor industry experience, extreme skier, and ranked as a 5.14 climber, the highest possible ranking
Eric Gilmore	Designer and Production Manager	Experience in product development and design, ice and rock climber, mountain biker, kayaker, and telemark skier
Erlend Greulich	General Manager of retail stores and responsible for many human resource management functions such as benefits and employee handbook	17 years of outdoor industry experience, rock climber, mountain biker, kayaker, and telemark skier
Brian Tobia	Assistant Wholesale Manager and Warehouse Manager	Studies in criminal justice; rock and ice climber, mountain biker, and mountaineer
Josh Bodine	Telluride Store Manager	B.A. in psychology; nine years of retail experience; telemark skier, mountain biker, climber, kayaker, mountaineer
Cathy Bouton	Mountain Village Store Manager	Three years of retail experience; telemark skier, mountain biker, climber, kayaker, photographer, and writer
Michelle Ray	Mail Order Manager, public relations, and customer service	Education in creative writing and art; ice and rock climber, back country skier, runner, and landscape painter
Timothy O'Neill	Buyer	Education in liberal arts; ice and rock climber, white-water kayaker, actor, and percussionist
Josh Lear	Store Designer and Merchandiser	B.A. in liberal arts–film studies; rated number-two snowboard instructor in Telluride, hockey player, mountain biker, rock climber, backpacker, and mountaineer

Source: Information in Table 1 based on JEMG's business plan.

UNDERSTANDING AND MANAGING INDIVIDUAL DIFFERENCES

LEARNING OBJECTIVES

1. Define individual differences, identify their determinants, and explain their effect on behavior.
2. Describe the major personality dimensions and traits that influence work-related behaviors.
3. Distinguish between terminal and instrumental values, and explain how culture shapes values and how values affect ethics.
4. Identify the components of job satisfaction as a work-related attitude and discuss the link between job satisfaction and organizational behavior.
5. Describe the ways managers can use individual differences to manage their workforce.

CHAPTER OUTLINE

Elements of Individual Differences

Understanding Personality

Understanding Values

Understanding Work-Related Attitudes: Job Satisfaction

Using Individual Differences in Organizations

MANAGERIAL CHALLENGE

Differences Equal Success for the Chicago Bulls

From 1990 to 1998, the Chicago Bulls basketball team won six championships and had the best win-loss record in the National Basketball Association (NBA). Critics gave Phil Jackson, the Bulls' head coach, much of the credit for the Bulls' success even though he had some of the most talented players in professional basketball. Why give Jackson so much credit? He retained, coached, and helped to meld a team of individuals with vastly different personalities and styles.

As an example, compare Michael Jordan and Dennis Rodman, two of the team's superstars during this time period. Jordan, one of the most talented players in the NBA's history, is smart, supremely competitive without losing sight of the team's overall goal, and even-tempered. He represents the values of sportsmanship and dedication to the team. Rodman, also smart and highly competitive, is brash, overly aggressive, and at times out of control. He also savors attention. His stunts off the court as a female impersonator with ever-changing hair color and body tattoos and as a model resulted in unwanted publicity for the Bulls and the NBA. To many people, Rodman represents players who have little respect for their team or their fans.

As if two superstars were not enough, Phil Jackson also was blessed with other talented players such as Steve Kerr and Ron Harper who possessed poise under pressure, skills that complemented those of the superstars, and a willingness to let others take the spotlight. Many other players, such as Scottie Pippen, helped the team achieve its much-envied record. Phil Jackson successfully managed to integrate the styles and talents of these highly individualistic, skilled, and competitive players.

In spite of the team's success, the owners were unhappy with Jackson. They complained that Jackson sided with the players too often, spoiled the team, and kept the owners out of day-to-day decisions. The owners' dissatisfaction with the coach spilled onto the court, causing many players to talk of leaving and to worry that the owners were planning to trade them.[1] Jordan claimed that he wouldn't play for anyone but Jackson and threatened to retire.[2] "If I don't feel it's something I'm happy with, I certainly have alternatives," he stated.[3] Jackson acknowledged the discord with the Bulls' owners. "People come up to me all the time and say, 'I can't believe they won't bring you back.' I tell 'em, 'Believe it.'"[4] After the Bulls won their sixth championship in eight years, Jackson announced his resignation from the team. One angry fan stated: "[T]he Jerrys of the Chicago Bulls—owner Reinsdorf and general manager Krause—have succeeded in destroying one of the great sports dynasties. It seems unimaginable that these two would not offer a long-term contract to one of the National Basketball Association's greatest coaches, Phil Jackson."[5]

■ Questions

1. What role did individual differences play in the success of the Chicago Bulls?
2. How did Phil Jackson successfully manage the different players' personalities?
3. Why didn't the players' dissatisfaction with the owners affect their performance?

Managers everywhere face the challenge of understanding and managing individual differences. In this part of the text, we turn our attention to individuals, the smallest unit of analysis in organizational behavior. Hard-working employees who do their job well are essential to an organization's success. An organization cannot succeed in the long term without them. Effective managers need to analyze individual behavior in the context of the business setting to understand organizational behavior fully. In the next three chapters, we examine three key aspects of individual behavior in organizations: individual differences, perception, and motivation.

We are each unique in our views, reactions, and behaviors. You may be outgoing and seek the company of others whereas your brother or sister may be reserved and prefer quiet evenings at home. Some of us are intense and engage in a whirlwind of activities; others are relaxed and focus on a few specific tasks. The challenge of a new job that inspires one person may dishearten another. The skills that are easy for one employee to learn pose a challenge for another.

What makes us different from one another? In this chapter, we try to answer that question by investigating differences in individual characteristics in personality traits, values, and attitudes. We also link these individual differences to the organizational context we discussed in the previous chapters.

ELEMENTS OF INDIVIDUAL DIFFERENCES

Every person is unique because of a combination of many factors, including demographic, physical, psychological, and behavioral differences. These are at the core of who we are. In this chapter, we focus on understanding individual differences, personality traits, values, and attitudes that make each of us unique and affect our work-related behaviors. Figure 4.1 provides a framework for understanding individual differences and their complex components.

Determinants of Individual Differences

Heredity and environment are the two determinants of individual difference characteristics, as shown in Figure 4.1. The **interactionist view** of individual differences suggests that heredity and the environment interact to influence the development of individual differences. This view is widely accepted, though many experts debate the relative influence of each factor.

Heredity consists of an individual's gene pool, gender, race, and ethnic background. Heredity has an early, and some suggest indelible, influence on personality. For example, studies done with identical twins find that even when raised apart, the twins are more similar to each other than to their adoptive family members.[6]

Though genetic studies establish a link between heredity and some personality traits, research also shows that the environment strongly affects us. Influences include physical location, parents, culture, religion, education, and friends. A child born and raised in a poor, remote farm in Appalachia will think and behave differently from one born and raised in a wealthy suburb of Silicon Valley in Northern California. Similarly, a female child growing up in Japan is likely to differ from one raised in Sweden.

To understand individual differences, we must consider the interaction between heredity and the environment. Environmental and social conditions can reinforce genetic patterns to influence a person's personality, as can cultural factors, the educational system, and parental upbringing. For instance, in the United States the genetic traits typically associated with being male are further reinforced by social norms that encourage boys to be competitive and not show their emotions. Similarly, although female babies tend to develop language skills earlier than males, parents who speak more to their girls and schools that expect them to be proficient in language further reinforce their verbal skills.

Interactionist view
A view suggesting that heredity and the environment interact to influence the development of individual differences

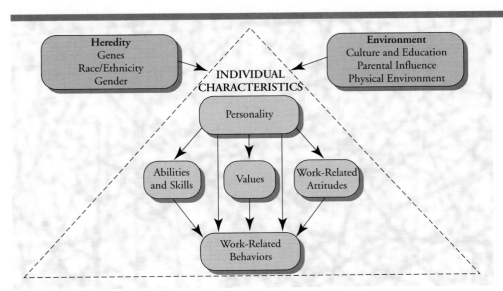

FIGURE 4.1
Individual Differences Framework

Although all individual characteristics are a result of genetic and environmental factors, one characteristic alone, be it a personality trait or a value, cannot predict how we behave. A complex blend of individual differences affects behavior. For example, knowing that a person is conscientious is not enough to understand what motivates that person to work harder. You also must understand many other traits and values.

Individual Characteristics

Figure 4.1 presents four major individual difference characteristics that affect work behaviors. These variables form a pyramid of sorts with personality at the top. In this section, we define each of the characteristics. We discuss each in depth in later sections.

Personality
A stable set of physical and psychological characteristics that makes each person unique

Personality **Personality** is a stable set of physical and psychological characteristics that makes each person unique. Personality is made up of a number of personality traits and is the product of interacting biological and environmental factors. It is the primary factor in individual differences and influences the other characteristics we discuss.

Let's examine the definition of personality closely. First, personality is *stable*. It tends to stay the same over time and across situations. It's not completely rigid, however, as personality can evolve gradually over the long run. Second, personality consists of a *set of characteristics* rather than one or two traits. This set develops over time and makes the individual unique.[7] Though most researchers agree that personality is a combination of an internal process and structure that affects behavior, not all agree on when and how personality develops, which traits are key, how easy it is to change, and to what extent personality influences organizational behavior.[8]

Consider the example of a shy and reserved person. His behavior will be stable across different situations and he is likely to be timid and reticent in most, although not all, social settings. The person may avoid large social gatherings where he does not know many people. He is likely to prefer working alone or in small groups and may avoid situations that require public speaking or being in the spotlight. Although this person's shyness may be a strong characteristic, it is not his only personality trait. He may also be conscientious, caring, concerned for others, creative, and artistic. The combination of these traits forms the personality; shyness is only one dominant trait.

Values
Stable, long-lasting beliefs and preferences about what is worthwhile and desirable

Values The next individual characteristic is values. **Values** are a person's stable, long-lasting beliefs and preferences about what is worthwhile and desirable.[9] Values are closely related to personality. Personality refers to a person's character and temperament whereas values are principles that a person believes. Like personality traits, values guide our behavior and are influenced by a combination of biological and environmental factors. For example, someone who holds the value that "honesty is the best policy" will attempt to behave fairly and honorably and show integrity in words and actions. Like personality, values are shaped early in life and are resistant to change. Values are also heavily influenced by a person's culture.

Attitudes
A stable pattern of response toward particular people, objects, or situations that a person has

Attitudes Next come **attitudes,** a consistent pattern of responses that individuals use when dealing with particular people, objects, or situations. Attitudes have an emotional, a cognitive, and a behavioral component.[10] The *emotional component* refers to how a person feels about the person, object, or situation. The *cognitive component* is what the person thinks, and the *behavioral component* is what the person does. Although all three components are part of attitudes, the emotional or *affective* component is the most important one. An example is an employee's attitude toward autocratic leadership. The emotional component of the attitude is "I don't like autocratic managers." The cognitive component is "Autocratic management leads to poor performance and dissatisfaction." Finally, the behavioral component would be: "I avoid working for autocratic managers."

As with the other two individual variables, attitudes affect behavior. However, the various components of attitudes are not always consistent. In other words, how you feel does not always predict what you think or how you will behave. You may not like working in a large organization but believe that doing so is beneficial to your career, so you accept a job with a multinational corporation. In spite of such potential inconsistencies, it is important for managers to understand their employees' work-related attitudes because they are a component of individual performance and effectiveness.

Abilities and Skills   Two other individual differences that affect behavior are ability and skill. **Ability**, or aptitude, is a natural talent to do something mental or physical. **Skill** is an acquired talent that a person develops related to a specific task. Whereas ability is somewhat stable over time, skills change with training and experience and from one task to another. You cannot train people to develop ability or aptitude, but you can train them to learn new skills. The goal in organizations is to recruit and hire employees who have certain abilities and aptitudes that fit the job requirements and then train them to acquire needed skills.

Overall, understanding individual differences is important in managing people and organizations better. Each individual difference provides some insight into the person, but relying on just one cannot explain a person's behavior. Furthermore, individual differences are not the only determinant of behavior. We consider the effect of individual differences in the next section.

Ability
A natural talent to do something mental or physical

Skill
An acquired talent that a person develops related to a specific task

---

Summary Point 4.1   **What Are the Characteristics of Individual Differences?**

- Heredity and the environment both contribute to create individual differences.
- Personality is a stable set of characteristics that makes each individual unique.
- Values are long-lasting beliefs about what is worthwhile and desirable.

- Attitudes are sets of beliefs and feelings toward people, objects, or situations.
- Ability refers to a natural talent to do something mental or physical whereas skills are acquired talents that can be developed and are related to a specific task.

The Effect of Individual Characteristics on Behavior

There are many measures of personality traits, values, and attitudes. No single measure of individual differences yields a complete understanding of an individual regardless of how detailed and well designed it is. Even the Minnesota Multiphasic Personality Inventory (MMPI), one of the most complete personality inventories available, cannot predict all behaviors of an individual.

A more useful approach is to consider a variety of individual difference factors that explain certain aspects of an employee's behavior. Ideally, to understand who a person is you would have to consider all possible aspects of his or her personality, the values and attitudes the person holds, his or her abilities and skills, and many demographic factors. These multiple perspectives can provide a broader insight into what makes a person unique.

Note that even with multiple perspectives, individual differences do not dictate our behaviors. When situations provide little guidance and are loosely structured, a person's individual characteristics can have a strong impact.[11] However, when the situation provides strong **behavioral cues**—cues that signal what behaviors and actions are expected and appropriate—most people behave according to those cues regardless of their personality traits. For example, a highly mechanistic organization with a strong culture that provides detailed, clear rules of behavior will

Hot ▼ Link

We described mechanistic and organic organizations in chapter 2, pp. 53–54.

Behavioral cues
Cues that signal what behaviors and actions are expected and appropriate

not encourage employees to express their individuality. In contrast, a loosely structured, organic organization that provides employees with autonomy will allow individual differences to surface.

Individual Characteristics Set the Limits

Personality traits and other stable individual characteristics determine and influence but do not dictate a range of work-related behaviors. For example, your personality traits determine to some extent whether you value hard work, set high goals for yourself, or have poor delegation skills. Particularly, they limit some of your behaviors and your choices. Although individual characteristics tend to be stable, that stability does not mean that people cannot behave in ways that are inconsistent with their personalities, values, and attitudes. Instead, each characteristic provides a behavioral zone of comfort. The **behavioral zone of comfort** includes a range of behaviors that are natural for the individual and feel comfortable to perform because they clearly reflect individual characteristics.

Behavioral zone of comfort
A range of behaviors that come naturally and easily and feel comfortable to perform because they reflect individual characteristics

Behaving outside that zone is difficult, takes practice, and in some cases, may not be possible. For example, expecting basketball player Dennis Rodman to act in a subdued and quiet manner may not be possible. However, while we are comfortable in our comfort behavioral zone, we learn and grow by moving to our zones of discomfort. The behaviors outside the comfort zone challenge us and push us to our limits. Therefore, although difficult, an effective learning method is to move outside the comfort zone.

For example, a person who values order and clarity is likely to select jobs and tasks that are familiar and well defined. She may hesitate to accept a position in an organization with an organic structure such as W. L. Gore. However, although well-defined jobs may be comfortable for this person, working as an associate in a team at Gore may teach her creative problem solving, mentoring others, and teamwork—all skills she had previously avoided learning.

A Word of Caution

A person's personality traits, values, attitudes, abilities, and skills interrelate in a complex way to influence, but not dictate, behaviors. Understanding personality traits can help you manage yourself and others better. Understanding people's values can determine how they can be motivated to perform most effectively. Being aware of attitudes may help predict an employee's actions. Knowing about an employee's abilities allows a manager to find the right job for that person. Having information about a person's skill level can help managers provide appropriate training and development.

Information about attitudes, abilities, and skills is often available to managers, but information about personality traits and values is not. Few managers have access to accurate personality information about their employees or the skills and training to guess a person's traits. Therefore, managers need to focus on work-related behaviors rather than on personality, values, and attitudes that are difficult to determine, measure, or change. Behaviors, in contrast, are easily observable, are measurable, and can be changed.

Individual differences can have a powerful impact on our behaviors. They limit some of our choices and create a behavioral range in which we are comfortable. Managers, then, should

---

Summary Point 4.2   **What Are Determinants and Limits of Individual Differences?**

- The combination and interaction of heredity and environmental factors determine individual differences.
- No single measure of individual differences provides a complete understanding of an individual.
- Individual differences do not dictate behaviors; they set limits for our behavioral ranges and guide our behavior.

- Although understanding personality and values can be helpful in self-awareness and in managing others, assessing personality and values is difficult. Managers, then, should focus on employees' work-related attitudes, abilities, skills, and behaviors.

Change Challenge

USE OF PERSONALITY IN MANAGEMENT DECISIONS

Twenty to thirty years ago, managers were allowed and encouraged to judge their employees based on their personal values, morals, traits, and other characteristics. It was common practice, even if not strictly legal, to reject job applicants because of their personal values, gender, religion, or race. For example, many businesses did not promote unmarried men until they "settled down," or they didn't hire or promote minorities because the firm's clientele was from the majority culture. Those with the right personality, values, and demographic characteristics were openly encouraged and rewarded. Those who did not fit a certain personality and demographic profile were rejected. Managers felt comfortable dealing with personal and private aspects of their employees' lives.

No more! Even though, unfortunately, many decisions are still made based on non-job-related characteristics, changes in U.S. labor laws and an increase in discrimination lawsuits have made all but impossible the use of personal characteristics as the articulated basis for a business decision.[a] Some of this change is clearly for the better. Personal characteristics that are not job related should not be used to make job-related decisions. As a result, managers must examine whether the individual differences they consider in hiring, evaluation, and promotion decisions are directly related to job performance.

For instance, Astra AB, a Swedish pharmaceutical company, agreed to pay a fine of $9.85 million to settle claims by its Westboro, Massachusetts, workers that they were being replaced based on their looks, not their job performance. Workers claimed that the company's former president, Lars Bildman, fired workers and replaced them with attractive, young, single women. After the settlement, Astra's new president, Ivan Rawley, stated: "As a company we are ashamed of the unacceptable behavior that took place. To each person who has been harmed and who has suffered because of that behavior, I offer our apologies."[b]

The flip side is that legal and risk-management criteria, rather than sound management criteria, can drive such decisions. Reliance on individual difference factors is not dead; managers are simply more cautious about using them.

> *a.* T. A. Stewart, "Escape from the Cult of Personality," *Fortune* 135, no. 5 (1998): 80.
>
> *b.* L. Miller, "Drugmaker to Settle Sex Suit for $9 Million," *Arizona Republic*, February 6, 1998, A11.

understand the interaction between individual differences—such as personal traits, values, and attitudes—and situational factors to help them match individual characteristics with organizational resources, opportunities, and goals. We examine personality traits and how they can affect work-related behavior in more detail next.

UNDERSTANDING PERSONALITY

Myriad personality traits affect work-related behavior. The wide range of employee traits adds to managerial challenges because every employee a manager supervises is unique, and each learns new behaviors at a different speed and with a varying amount of ease.

Managers often turn to personality research, which is meant to inform, develop self-awareness, and promote self-improvement. When accurate information about employee personality traits is available—for example, as part of questionnaires administered during interviews or in a training session—it can be used to match the individual to job situations to increase performance.

Despite the validity of the research on personality traits, its usefulness in a work setting is limited. Few traits are directly linked to job-related behaviors or performance. Most research indicates a correlation between traits and various behaviors but not a clear cause-and-effect relationship. As a result, many theorists believe that personality traits should not be used as tools for hiring, evaluation, promotion, or other job-related decisions. Until evidence proves a direct cause-and-effect relationship between traits and job performance, practitioners should avoid using traits as the basis for job-related decisions to avoid legal and ethical problems.

With that limitation in mind, in the following sections we examine a general personality-trait classification scheme—the Big Five personality dimensions. Then we explore four individual personality traits that affect job behavior: locus of control, Type A, self-monitoring, and Machiavellianism.

The Big Five Personality Dimensions

Conscientiousness
A personality dimension of reliability and dependability, being careful and organized, and being a person who plans

Extroversion/introversion
The degree to which people enjoy socializing, seek and enjoy the company of others, and express their feelings and emotions openly. Extroverts have strong tendencies toward socializing; introverts have weak tendencies

Over time, psychologists and human resource management researchers have condensed countless personality traits into a list of five major personality dimensions, known as the Big Five.[12] Researchers have found these five dimensions to be consistent components of personality. Table 4.1 describes the dimensions.

What Are the Five Dimensions? The first dimension of the Big Five is **conscientiousness**, which is defined as being reliable, dependable, careful, organized, and a planner. The dimension also includes being hard working, persevering, and achievement oriented.[13] As expected, research findings indicate that conscientiousness is related to work-related behaviors and performance.

The second dimension is **extroversion/introversion**. Being an extrovert means that you are sociable and that you seek and enjoy the company of others. Extroverts are talkative and express their feelings and emotions openly. A person's sociability, ambition, energy, and drive are other aspects of the extrovert dimension.

Table 4.1   BIG FIVE PERSONALITY DIMENSIONS

Personality Dimensions	Description
Conscientiousness	• Degree to which a person is dependable, responsible, organized, and forward looking (plans ahead)
Extroversion/introversion	• Degree to which a person is sociable, talkative, assertive, active, and ambitious
Openness to experience	• Degree to which a person is imaginative, broad-minded, curious, and seeks new experiences
Emotional stability	• Degree to which a person is anxious, depressed, angry, and insecure
Agreeableness	• Degree to which a person is courteous, likable, good-natured, and flexible

Sources: Based on descriptions provided by W. T. Norman, "Toward an Adequate Taxonomy of Personality Attributes: Replicated Factor Structure in Peer Nomination Personality Ratings," *Journal of Abnormal and Social Psychology* 66 (1963): 547–83; J. M. Digman, "Personality Structure: Emergence of the Five-Factor Model," *Annual Review of Psychology* 41 (1990): 417–40; Murray R. Barrick and Michael K. Mount, "The Five Big Personality Dimensions and Job Performance: A Meta-Analysis," *Personnel Psychology* 44, no. 1 (Spring 1991): 1–76.

The third dimension is **openness to experience**. It refers to being curious, creative, and broad-minded. Being open to new experiences includes being cultured and artistically sensitive. It also relates to general cognitive ability, motivation, and ability to learn.[14] The fourth dimension, **emotional stability,** refers to a person's level of anxiety, depression, and general emotional insecurity. This dimension has also been called neuroticism, indicating that at one extreme a person who is low on emotional stability may display neurotic behaviors.

The fifth dimension of the Big Five personality dimensions is **agreeableness**. It describes a person's general friendliness and courtesy as well as the degree to which she or he is trusting and liked by others. Agreeableness further includes flexibility and willingness to cooperate with others. Someone who is agreeable is sociable and friendly, generally easy to get along with, and willing to cooperate with others.

The Big Five dimensions allow many different traits to be grouped into a meaningful taxonomy for studying individual differences. The five dimensions are relatively independent and have several management implications.

Implications for Management   Several of the Big Five personality dimensions have links to work-related behaviors, although none is a strong predictor of performance. Of the five dimensions, conscientiousness is the most strongly correlated to job performance. This makes sense: Individuals who are dependable, organized, and hard-working tend to perform better in their jobs.[15] Most managers would agree that a good employee is dependable, shows up on time, finishes work by deadlines, and is willing to work hard. For instance, Andy Grove of Intel used to list which employees showed up on time. He believes that dependable employees perform better.

Extroversion is the Big Five dimension with the second highest correlation to job-related behaviors. Extroversion is particularly important in jobs that rely on social interaction, such as management or sales. It is less relevant for employees working on an assembly line or as computer programmers.[16] Unlike conscientiousness, which can apply to all job levels or occupations, extroversion is not an essential trait for all jobs and individuals can succeed without being extroverted. In fact, one of America's most admired leaders, the CEO of Hewlett-Packard (HP), is not an extrovert. "Lew Platt isn't a loud, extroverted guy, but he is . . . in his own quiet, blushing way getting his colleagues not only to understand but to agree [with his way]," says John Kotter, a Harvard business professor.[17]

Openness to experience can help performance in some instances but not others. For example, being open to new experiences can help employees or managers perform well in new training because they would be motivated to explore new ideas and to learn.[18] Bill Gates, the CEO of Microsoft, is legendary for being open to new ideas and opinions. After he traveled to India he observed: "Even though 80 percent of what you hear from customers is the same all over the world, you always learn something you can apply to our business."[19] But eagerness to explore new ways can be an impediment to performance on jobs that require careful attention to existing processes and procedures.

As one would expect, emotional stability relates to job behaviors and performance. At the extreme, individuals who are neurotic are not likely to be able to function in organizations. However, some degree of anxiety and worrying can help people do well because it spurs them to excel. Andy Grove's book, *Only the Paranoid Survive,* is an indication of the sense of anxiety that he instills at Intel to make sure employees perform and the organization excels. Finally, although agreeableness may be a highly desirable personality trait in social situations, it is generally not related to work-related behaviors or performance.

The most important managerial implication of the Big Five dimensions is that except for conscientiousness, no single trait is strongly linked to how well an employee will perform in all types and levels of jobs. Instead, managers need to consider many factors, especially the person-job fit. For example, a manager looking for a software salesperson might consider extroversion and openness to new experiences positive traits, whereas a manager looking for

Openness to experience
A tendency toward being curious, creative, and broad-minded

Emotional stability
A person's level of anxiety, depression, and general emotional insecurity

Agreeableness
A person's general friendliness, courtesy, and the degree to which she or he is trusting and liked by others

Hot ▼ Link

We described the contingency view of management in chapter 1, pp. 16–17.

an engineer to work on a team might consider emotional stability a more important trait. Measures of these traits or behavioral questions related to them may be included in the selection process to provide additional information. Consideration of fit with the situation is consistent with the contingency view of management.

Managers who try to understand employees by examining only one factor, such as how a person rates on one of the Big Five personality dimensions, risk labeling employees unfairly, oversimplifying their decisions, and engaging in discrimination. We continue to investigate these points in the following discussion of four individual personality traits that affect work behavior.

Summary Point 4.3   **What Are the Big Five Personality Dimensions?**

- The Big Five personality dimensions form the basis for a general classification of personality.
- The Big Five include the following dimensions: conscientiousness, extroversion, openness to experience, emotional stability, and agreeableness.

- Conscientiousness, extroversion, and openness to experience are related to various work-related behaviors.
- The relevance of any trait depends on the situation, the type of job, and the level at which a person is working.

Personality Traits

The Big Five provides a general classification of personality traits that have some effect on work-related behaviors. Researchers have also found several single personality traits that have been consistently related to work-related behavior. We analyze four of these traits: locus of control, Type A behavior pattern, self-monitoring, and Machiavellianism.

Locus of control
A personality trait that indicates an individual's sense of control over his or her life, the environment, and external events

Locus of Control   The **locus of control** concept indicates an individual's sense of control over his or her life, the environment, and external events.[20] People who have internal locus of control believe that what happens to them is a result of their actions. They feel a sense of control over and responsibility for their own lives. They tend to see their successes and failures as a reflection of their own efforts. People with an external locus of control feel that external factors control what happens to them. Take the locus of control test to see where you score.

General Description   If you scored on the internal side of the scale, chances are that you are less anxious, set higher goals, and conform less to authority than those who scored on the external side of the scale. Internals make greater efforts to achieve their goals and tend to be more task oriented than externals. People with high external locus of control believe external forces—such as luck, other powerful people, or divine powers—are the cause of many events in their lives. They rely on others' judgments and conform to authority more readily than internals.[21] Such individuals do not perceive that they have a great deal of control over their lives. As a result, they tend to be more reactive to events and less able to rebound from stressful situations.

Although locus of control is a stable personality trait, it can change with strong situational cues. For instance, studies of Poles compared locus-of-control scores before and after the fall of communism and found there was a significant increase toward internal locus of control after democratization.[22] When the political situation changed to give people more control, they felt they had more control over their lives. Socioeconomic factors and race also have an effect on locus of control. For example, some studies indicate that poor African-Americans tend to believe more strongly than middle-class Caucasians that powerful others and luck affect their fate.[23] The individuals' locus-of-control scores reflect actual limited control due to socioeconomic factors. As in the previous example, managers can create situations that either emphasize external or internal locus of control.

▶ SELF-ASSESSMENT 4.1
Locus of Control

Read the following statements and indicate whether you agree with Choice A or Choice B:

A	B
A	**B**
1. Making a lot of money is largely a matter of getting the right breaks.	1. Promotions are earned through hard work and persistence. _____
2. I have noticed a direct connection between how hard I study and the grade I get.	2. Many times the reactions of teachers seem haphazard to me. _____
3. The number of divorces indicates that more and more people are not trying to make their marriages work.	3. Marriage is largely a gamble. _____
4. It is silly to think that one can really change another person's basic attitudes.	4. When I am right I can convince others. _____
5. Getting promoted is really a matter of being a little luckier than the next person.	5. In our society, a person's future earning power depends on his or her ability. _____
6. If one knows how to deal with people, they are really quite easily led.	6. I have little influence over the way other people behave. _____
7. The grades I make are the results of my own efforts; luck has little or nothing to do with it.	7. Sometimes I feel I have little to do with the grades I get. _____
8. People like me can change the course of world affairs if we make ourselves heard.	8. It is only wishful thinking to believe that one can readily influence what happens in our society at large. _____
9. A great deal that happens to me is probably a matter of chance.	9. I am the master of my fate. _____
10. Getting along with people is a skill that must be practiced.	10. It is almost impossible to figure out how to please some people. _____

Scoring Key:

Give yourself 1 point for each of the following selections: 1B, 2A, 3A, 4B, 5B, 6A, 7A, 8A, 9B, and 10A. Scores are interpreted as follows:

    8–10 = High internal locus of control
     6–7 = Moderate internal locus of control
       5 = Mixed
     3–4 = Moderate external locus of control
     1–2 = High external locus of control

Source: Adapted with permission from Julian B. Rotter, "External Control and Internal Control," *Psychology Today* (June 1971): 42. Copyright 1971 by the American Psychological Association.

Implications for Management   Employees with an internal locus of control ("internals") are generally more satisfied with their work. Managers with an internal locus of control are more task oriented and more innovative in their decision making. They also tend to be more proactive.[24] Because of their tendency to be proactive, these managers demonstrate the motivation, energy, and self-confidence believed to be factors in effective leadership.[25] In contrast, managers with an external locus of control ("externals") do not feel they control events and tend to be reactive. They also tend to use more coercive power. One reason may be that they are not proactive, so they do not think that others will act on their own. Consequently, they tend to overcontrol their employees.[26] Bill Hoglund, a GM executive who worked as the head of the Saturn division, cautions against trying to control employees: "You don't try to control [the employees]; you provide the direction and let them work. And you don't set up systems and procedures for the 2 percent of the people . . . you shouldn't have hired in the first place."[27]

Managing employees with different levels of locus of control requires different approaches. An employee with an internal locus of control may need relatively little direction and feedback, whereas one with an external locus of control is likely to require closer supervision, more direction, and extensive feedback. When working with externally controlled individuals, managers need to set up situations with stronger behavioral cues. Similarly, those with an internal locus of control who tend to take credit and accept blame may be too hard on themselves, requiring a manager to remind them that not all mistakes and failures are caused by their actions.

Locus of control can also help explain some cross-cultural differences. In cultures with a strong fatalistic approach, people are more likely to believe that divine powers, karma, or natural forces determine individual behavior. In these types of cultures, employees and managers are less likely to be highly proactive or willing to accept responsibility for success and failure. For example, many Middle Eastern and African cultures have a more fatalistic culture than the United States. As a result, a Jordanian, Syrian, or Egyptian employee working in a U.S.-operated manufacturing facility may be more likely to refuse to accept responsibility for an error than the person's U.S. counterpart. Although the U.S. manager may see the employee's behavior as irresponsible, it may simply reflect a worldview in which control is outside an individual's hands.

Let's examine how locus of control provides insight into the personality of U.S. entrepreneurs. Most have an internal locus of control.[28] The drive, ambition, proactiveness, and self-starter attitude that defines entrepreneurs is closely related to this personality trait. A case in point is Herman Cain, the CEO and part owner of Godfather Pizza.[29] He grew up in a poor family in the racially segregated southern United States. Through an upbringing focused on self-reliance, encouragement, and ambition, Cain became the first person in his family to enter and finish college and earn a graduate degree. Cain always looks for new challenges and accomplishments. He attributes the success of his company to a willingness to risk everything, love what you do, and take control over events.

As with the Big Five personality dimensions, having information about your own or others' locus of control can help you understand areas of difficulty and resolve conflicts. Different employees will require different types of help, encouragement, and support to succeed. One size does not fit all. The next personality trait we consider, Type A, also deals with control but from a different point of view.

Type A
A personality trait evidenced when a person tries to do more in less and less time in an apparently tireless pursuit of everything

Type A   Since the late 1960s, the concept of the Type A behavior pattern has received considerable attention as a risk factor for coronary disease when researchers found that certain personality types, labeled Type A, had a higher occurrence and prognosis of coronary disease.[30] Currently only one Type A characteristic, hostility, continues to be linked to coronary problems. Other applications of the Type A concept are to social and work life. Are you a Type A? Take the test to find out.

▶ **SELF-ASSESSMENT 4.2**
Type A Behavior Pattern

Indicate whether each of the following items is true or false for you.
TRUE   FALSE

_____	_____	1.	I am always in a hurry
_____	_____	2.	I have list of things I have to achieve on a daily or weekly basis
_____	_____	3.	I tend to take one problem or task on at a time, finish, then move to the next one
_____	_____	4.	I tend to take a break or quit when I get tired
_____	_____	5.	I am always doing several things at once, both at work and in my personal life
_____	_____	6.	People who know me would describe my temper as hot and fiery
_____	_____	7.	I enjoy competitive activities
_____	_____	8.	I tend to be relaxed and easy going
_____	_____	9.	Many things are more important to me than my job
_____	_____	10.	I really enjoy winning both at work and at play
_____	_____	11.	I tend to rush people along or finish their sentences for them when they are taking too long
_____	_____	12.	I enjoy "doing nothing" and just hanging out

Scoring Key:

Type A individuals tend to indicate that questions 1, 2, 5, 6, 7, and 10 are true and questions 3, 4, 8, 9, and 12 are false. Type B individuals tend to answer in the reverse (1, 2, 5 as false and 3, 4 as true and so forth).

What Is a Type A Personality Trait?   Do you try to do more and more in less and less time? Do you work at a relentless pace on many different tasks without ever admitting that you are tired? These elements are two of four defining characteristics of a Type A personality trait. **Type A** is described as trying to do more in less and less time, in an apparently tireless pursuit of everything. Type As have an underlying *need for control* and strive to gain control over their environment.[31] The feeling of lack of control is particularly stressful for Type As. Contrary to Type As, Type Bs tend to have less need for control and do not work as hard to gain control over events.

Interestingly, although Type A and locus of control both have the construct of control as a key defining element, the two traits are not related. Individuals with an internal locus of control feel that they control their lives; Type As need an increasing amount of control over events. Some Type As have an internal locus of control and perceive that they control their own fate but still require more control and feel loss of control quickly. Others can have an external locus of control, perceive little control, and seek more. Similarly, those with a Type B personality can have either an internal or external locus of control.

The need for control manifests itself in the four general categories of behaviors that define the characteristics of Type A, as we see in Figure 4.2. The first Type A characteristic is *time urgency*, defined as having a concern about time and being in a hurry. Impatience with delays, worries about time, constantly checking a watch, getting upset when people are late, and rushing to get to places are all aspects of the Type A's time urgency. The time urgency leads people with a Type A personality to jump into action quickly, sometimes without careful planning. Other examples of time urgent behaviors include people who get to appointments either exactly

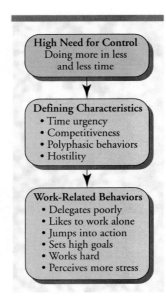

FIGURE 4.2
Type A Characteristics and Behaviors

on time, so as not to waste any time, or early so that there is no risk of being late. In all cases, there is concern and worry about time.

The second Type A characteristic is *competitiveness.* Type A individuals are generally highly competitive in work, social, and sport situations. They measure their performance by comparing themselves to others. They keep track of their performance. Coming ahead and winning are major concerns. An interesting example of competitiveness is Type As' belief that children need to learn about winning and losing but not allowing even young children to win at games unless they squarely deserve it! Another instance is the manager who feels competitive with top-performing employees. Her employees doing well may make her feel that she has lost control, so instead of encouraging and supporting them she may start competing with them.

The third Type A characteristic is *polyphasic behavior,* a type of behavior in which the person does several things at once, even when this is not required. Examples include dictating memos, reading reports, or altogether "doing something useful" when driving or in a meeting. A person with a Type A personality organizes his desk drawer while talking on the phone or makes sure to run several other errands on the way to dropping a package at the post office. Type As make a list of specific activities they have to undertake during a vacation and keep their companions moving at a frantic pace. Although all of us try to combine activities to save time in our busy lives, Type As demonstrate more polyphasic behaviors than Type Bs do. They are also more likely than Type Bs to feel that they should and can do many different things at once.

The last Type A characteristic is *hostility*, the only characteristic still linked to coronary problems. Type A hostility manifests itself in explosive speech, diffused anger, intolerance for delays or mistakes, and a generally fiery, aggressive, and a sometimes malicious style of interaction.[32] In the work environment, the hostility can be directed at co-workers, customers, or even bosses. Hostility is most likely manifested when Type As feel they are losing control. Missing a deadline may be just that for a Type B. In contrast, a Type A gets angry and lashes out at those who may have not cooperated or who interrupted and caused potential delays.

The four Type A characteristics of time urgency, competitiveness, polyphasic behavior, and hostility are a direct result of a need to control. A person with a strong Type A trait would show all four characteristics. Although Type A characteristics are neither uniformly bad nor good, being time urgent, competitive, hostile, and doing many things at once can have serious implications for managers.

Implications for Management   One of the first implications of Type A for management is that, compared to Type Bs, Type As tend to be poor delegators and generally prefer to work alone.[33] They like to maintain control over all aspects of their work. The inability to delegate can lead to inefficiency, a major pitfall for managers. Additionally, with the increasing focus on cooperation, use of teams, and empowerment style, Type A managers will find that their loner, "I'll do it myself" tendencies are drawbacks.

On the positive side, Type As set high performance goals and standards for both themselves and those around them. Some high-performing companies specifically hire employees with Type A tendencies. For example, at SunAmerica, a major Los Angeles-based insurance and annuity company, Chairman Eli Broad, favors hiring "A Types," and pushing them to achieve higher and higher goals. Most of his employees work 12-hour days and take home a lot of unfinished work. Such expectations may lead to high performance and high quality, but they can also cause overload and burnout when carried to an extreme. In addition, Type As also do not recognize or admit that they are tired and often do not understand other people's—maybe the Type Bs'—less intense approach to work.

The characteristics that define Type A are similar to the high energy and motivation that some consider to be key to successful leadership.[34] The Type A behavior pattern can easily be recognized in a number of business executives of small and large firms. Think about what you have read about Michael Eisner of Disney. Aside from Eisner's hospitalization for coronary

Student David Weekly sets high performance standards for himself as he juggles his activities. He runs two companies and one industry consortium—not to mention keeping up with his school work at Stanford. Does he seem to have a Type A or Type B personality trait?

problems, co-workers such as Michael Ovitz have complained or quit, claiming that Eisner couldn't relinquish control or share power.[35] Giovanni Agnelli, the young president of auto-maker Fiat, one of Italy's most powerful companies, works 12-hour days and has a reputation for dedication, seriousness, and high energy. Eli Broad himself appears to have a Type A personality trait. He is extremely demanding, tireless, sets higher and higher goals, and always seeks new challenges. A senior vice president at SunAmerica, Jim Rowan explains: "Eli's style is tough. Demanding doesn't even begin to describe it."[36]

It may appear that with so many executives having a Type A personality trait there may be a link between leadership and this trait, at least in the United States and other Western cultures. However, research suggests that Type Bs are actually the ones that make it to top of many organizations.[37] Those with a Type B personality trait tend to have the ability to analyze problems calmly and thoughtfully, to plan carefully, and to handle stressful situations without burning out. Therefore, although the Type As' tireless pursuit of goals may give them an advantage in today's competitive and fast-paced organizations, the Type Bs' ability to take things calmly and be more thoughtful provides them with an edge as well.

Ralph Larson, the laid-back CEO of Johnson & Johnson, is known for his reserved, thoughtful style of management. "Leadership to me is a question of substance, not style. I try to encourage, to give people a sense of self-worth and self-esteem, to instill confidence. I don't want people doing what I say; I want them to sort it out for themselves."[38] In 1998, under Larson's leadership, Johnson & Johnson again ranked as one of the top 10 most admired companies in the United States.

Self-Monitoring   When observing some people, we can easily identify their personality and style. They seem to be an open book. Their behavior is consistent over many different situations and follows from their attitudes. For example, Herb Kelleher, president of Southwest Airlines, is informal, intense, fun-loving, and exuberant no matter what the circumstances.

As compared to Kelleher, other people are harder to read. Their behaviors appear to change from one situation to another, and they do not reveal much about themselves. This difference may be due to a personality trait called self-monitoring. See how you score on the self-monitoring scale by taking Self-Assessment 4.3.

Self-monitoring
The degree to which people are capable of reading and using cues from the environment to determine their own behavior

What Is the Self-Monitoring Personality Trait?   The ability to read and use cues from the environment to determine behavior is the **self-monitoring** personality trait.[39] Individuals scoring high on the self-monitoring scale are able to read environmental and social cues and use them to adjust their behaviors. Those scoring lower on the scale either do not read the cues or do not use them to change their behavior.

The people who are high on the self-monitoring scale react to their perception of the environment, so their behavior is likely to change depending on the situation, not due to a change in values or attitudes. The behavior of those who are low on the scale tends to be more internally determined. Their attitudes and behaviors are likely to match. Low self-monitors, then, are likely to appear constant across different situations and are more predictable.

There are many interesting cultural differences in self-monitoring. People in the United States generally score in the middle of the scale. People in several other cultures, particularly those that are from high-context cultures, score higher on this scale. The high-context dimension alone, however, does not predict self-monitoring.

For instance, many of us would predict that the Japanese would score higher on the self-monitoring scale than the mainstream U.S. population. After all, the Japanese are known for paying attention to social situations and for behaving in socially appropriate ways in accordance with the many rules and regulations of society. Such an assumption is actually incorrect.

Because the Japanese learn the complex rules guiding various social situations early in life, they really do not need to read the environment for cues. The cues are in the rules; they are neither subtle to the Japanese nor changing. Behavioral guidelines depend on intricate social norms that are part of Japanese history, culture, and society. Given the relative cultural and ethnic homogeneity of Japan, these guidelines are likely to be consistent across situations. The low self-monitoring score of the Japanese may explain some of the difficulties they face when dealing with other cultures.

Implications for Management   Having a high score on the self-monitoring scale may indicate leadership skills.[40] Because managers must read environmental and individual cues quickly and accurately and adjust their behavior accordingly, there is some evidence to suggest that those with high self-monitor scores emerge as leaders more frequently than those with low scores.[41] Also, evidence suggests that those with high self-monitoring scores usually resolve conflicts cooperatively, in dealing with both their subordinates and their supervisors, another helpful managerial skill.

Self-monitoring has two other managerial implications. First, those with high scores are generally better able to cope with cross-cultural experiences that are ambiguous and require an ability to interpret environmental cues. Second, organizational changes are making leadership situations considerably less routine and more uncertain than they were 20 years ago, so strong self-monitoring skills may be an advantage.

Gender differences can play a role in self-monitoring as well. Some companies specifically train their women executives to be able to better read the all-male environment of the organization and adapt their styles accordingly. Cynthia Jones-Hundley of Anderson Consulting learned through one such training program that her style alienated her male associates. She notes that she has learned to read body language and monitor her actions more closely. "I don't get in people's faces as much anymore."[42]

▶ SELF-ASSESSMENT 4.3
Self-Monitoring

Indicate the degree to which you think the following statements are true or false by circling the appropriate number. For example, if a statement is always true, you should circle the 5 next to that statement.

5 = Certainly always true   2 = Somewhat false, but with exceptions
4 = Generally true   1 = Generally false
3 = Somewhat true, but with exceptions   0 = Certainly always false

1.	In social situations, I have the ability to alter my behavior if I feel that something else is called for.	5	4	3	2	1	0
2.	I am often able to read people's true emotions correctly through their eyes.	5	4	3	2	1	0
3.	I have the ability to control the way I come across to people, depending on the impression I wish to give them.	5	4	3	2	1	0
4.	In conversations, I am sensitive to even the slightest change in the facial expression of the person I'm conversing with.	5	4	3	2	1	0
5.	My powers of intuition are quite good when it comes to understanding others' emotions and motives.	5	4	3	2	1	0
6.	I can usually tell when others consider a joke in bad taste, even though they may laugh convincingly.	5	4	3	2	1	0
7.	When I feel that the image I am portraying isn't working, I can readily change it to something that does.	5	4	3	2	1	0
8.	I can usually tell when I've said something inappropriate by reading the listener's eyes.	5	4	3	2	1	0
9.	I have trouble changing my behavior to suit different people and different situations.	5	4	3	2	1	0
10.	I have found that I can adjust my behavior to meet the requirements of any situation I find myself in.	5	4	3	2	1	0
11.	If someone is lying to me, I usually know it at once from the person's manner of expression.	5	4	3	2	1	0
12.	Even when it might be to my advantage, I have difficulty putting up a good front.	5	4	3	2	1	0
13.	Once I know what the situation calls for, it's easy for me to regulate my actions accordingly.	5	4	3	2	1	0

Scoring Key:

To obtain your score, add up the numbers circled, except reverse the scores for questions 9 and 12. On those, a circled 5 becomes a 0, 4 becomes 1, and so forth. High self-monitors are defined as those with a score of approximately 53 or higher.

Source: R. D. Lennox and R. N. Wolfe, "Revision of the Self-Monitoring Scale," *Journal of Personality and Social Psychology* (June 1984): 1361. Copyright by the American Psychological Association. Reprinted with permission.

Machiavellian personality
An individual's willingness to manipulate others for personal gain and to put self-interest above the interest of the group

Machiavellian Personality   Do you believe that the ends justify the means? Are you skilled at manipulating others to get what you want? Are you a ruthless negotiator? If you have answered yes to all or some of these questions, chances are you have some elements of a **Machiavellian personality**. Self-Assessment 4.4 will help you see how Machiavellian you are.

What Is a Machiavellian Personality Trait?   The concept of the Machiavellian (Mach) personality is based loosely on Niccolo Machiavelli's *The Prince*.[43] The Mach scale measures an individual's willingness to put self-interest above the interests of the group and identifies a person's individual preference and ability to manipulate others for personal gain.[44]

Individuals with high scores on the scale are comfortable using various means to achieve their personal goals. They have few scruples and are willing to step outside the bounds of for-

---

▶ **SELF-ASSESSMENT 4.4**
Machiavellianism

For each statement, circle the number that most closely resembles your attitude.

	STRONGLY DISAGREE				STRONGLY AGREE
1. The best way to handle people is to tell them what they want to hear.	1	2	3	4	5
2. When you ask someone to do something for you, it is best to give the real reason for wanting it rather than giving reasons that might carry more weight.	1	2	3	4	5
3. Anyone who completely trusts anyone else is asking for trouble.	1	2	3	4	5
4. It is hard to get ahead without cutting corners here and there.	1	2	3	4	5
5. It is safest to assume that all people have a vicious streak, and it will come out when they are given a chance to show it.	1	2	3	4	5
6. One should take action only when it is morally right.	1	2	3	4	5
7. Most people are basically good and kind.	1	2	3	4	5
8. There is no excuse for lying to someone else.	1	2	3	4	5
9. Most people more easily forget the death of their father than the loss of their property.	1	2	3	4	5
10. Generally speaking, people won't work hard unless they're forced to do so.	1	2	3	4	5

Scoring Key:

To obtain your Mach score, add the number your have circled on questions 1, 3, 4, 5, 9, and 10. For the other four questions, reverse the numbers you have circled: 5 becomes 1, 4 is 2, and so forth. Total your 10 numbers to find your score. The higher your score, the more Machiavellian you are. Among a random sample of American adults, the average was 25.

Source: R. Christie and F. L. Geis, *Studies in Machiavellianism* (San Diego, CA: Academic Press, 1970). Copyright by the Academic Press, 1970. Reprinted with permission.

mal authority. These individuals may lack the honesty and integrity that are requirements for effective management. On the low end of the scale, individuals tend to be overly naive and trusting. Typically, those with scores in the middle of the scale have both the necessary political savvy and the integrity to be effective managers.

Some conditions allow people with high Mach scores to flourish. Particularly, uncertainty that results from a restructuring, change in leadership, or any organizational crisis provides settings that are ideal for those with Machiavellian personality traits because of their ability to manipulate others for their own advantage.[45] When there are clear rules and norms, as would be the case in an organization with a well-established, strong culture, those with high Mach scores cannot operate as effectively and are often less successful. The organization's culture and strong behavioral norms curtail their ability to manipulate and control events for personal gain.

Implications for Management   People with high Mach scores tend to have political and manipulation skills that allow them to move up quickly and appear highly successful in many organizations. However, they direct their attention and effort primarily to promote themselves. As a result, those with high Mach scores are often ineffective managers because they generally will support, motivate, and help employees only if doing so is to their own benefit.

Managers that have low Mach scores may also have disadvantages. They may not have enough political savvy and negotiation skills to provide their group with the necessary resources and visibility to succeed or to highlight their own accomplishments appropriately. Their open and trusting style also makes them easy targets for those with high Mach scores.

Neither the person with a very high nor one with a very low Mach score are likely to be effective managers. Generally, individuals who have mid-range Mach scores tend to be most effective. They have some political savvy and are good negotiators, but they also are able to resist manipulation from others. They are less likely to abuse power and more likely to focus on achieving organizational rather than personal goals.

A QUESTION OF ETHICS

Using Personality Tests	Are there any ways that managers could misuse or abuse personality trait measurement information? Explain. If yes, what ethical guidelines do you think a business should implement to safeguard against possible abuses?

Several cultural differences affect Mach scores. For example, managers from the People's Republic of China score higher on the Mach scale than their U.S. counterparts. It appears that the Chinese are more willing to use social power to accomplish their goals.[46] This finding is consistent with China's high-power distance culture where authority is broad and respected.

The U.S. press is full of examples of ruthless business leaders who wheel and deal their way to achieve their goals with considerable disregard for their employees. Herbert Haft, CEO of the Dart Group, is considered a ruthless negotiator who intimidates his way through disagreements and who is willing to break any relationship to win.[47]

Some leaders with high Mach scores are tolerated and successful because they obtain results in the highly competitive, complex business environment. Linda Wachner, CEO of the U.S. undergarment manufacturer Warnaco, is one of the few female chief executives of a Fortune 500 company. Her impressive financial results are as well known as her reputation as one of the toughest bosses in America. Former employees say that she will do anything to get what she wants and that she "demands absolute fealty." Wachner explains, "I've yelled at people, and I'm not ashamed of it. If you don't like it, leave. It's not a prison."[48]

Summary Point 4.4   **What Are Four Personality Traits That Affect Work Behavior?**

- Locus of control is an indicator of an individual's sense of control over the environment and external events.
- Type As try to do more in less and less time and tirelessly pursue their aims because of their need to control. Time urgency, competitiveness, polyphasic behavior, and hostility are the four behaviors associated with Type A.

- Self-monitoring refers to the degree to which people read and use cues from the environment to determine their behavior.
- Machiavellianism is defined as a willingness to put self-interest above the group's interests, and a preference and ability to manipulate others for personal gain.

Managers who are aware of their own personality traits and understand how those traits can affect their dealings with others can overcome some of the challenges they face. A manager who knows she has a high Type A score can focus on improving her delegation skills. A manager with a low Mach score should concentrate on improving his negotiation skills. The low self-monitor should pay more attention to others' reactions.

Knowledge of personality traits can also help a manager work with employees more effectively. For example, if a manager learns that one of his employees has high self-monitoring traits, all else being equal, that employee may be a good candidate for an assignment in a foreign country. Similarly, a person who is open to new experiences may be given new assignments more often than the one who is less broad-minded. Any project that needs considerable follow-through may be better handled by a worrier employee than by a relaxed, easy-going employee.

Appropriate and careful self-assessment of personality traits can help managers improve their performance. Managers who encourage employees to conduct self-assessment help those employees identify their strengths and weaknesses so they can achieve their potential more readily. The personality traits we investigated provide insight into the personality core. Other individual difference characteristics allow further understanding. We consider values next.

 UNDERSTANDING VALUES

Values are long-lasting beliefs about what is worthwhile and desirable. They are personal judgments about what is right and wrong, what is good and bad. As is the case with personality traits, values develop early in life and are based on culture, family, and our social and educational background. Just as with personality, values are influenced by heredity and environmental factors and are stable and resistant to change. Understanding values is important for managers because values affect work-related attitudes and behaviors. Furthermore, conflict between individual and organizational values can be a major source of frustration and problems.

We examine two types of values next. We also investigate how culture affects people's values, the interplay between values and ethics, and the challenge of managing value conflicts.

Value System and Culture

Value system
The way a person's values are organized and prioritized

The way in which a person's values are organized and prioritized is that person's **value system**. For instance, the value of family may be a top priority for one person in comparison to other issues such as faith, career, and social relationships. Other people may value their career more than their family, or put their faith and spirituality above all else. Each of us has a personal value system prioritized around what we value most. Some of us are aware of values and their priorities while others are unclear about their priorities and become aware of them only when conflict results. Helping employees, then, become more self-aware of their value system can

MANAGERIAL ADVICE
from the Experts

HANDLING PROBLEM EMPLOYEES

Whether it is a hostile, overly competitive person with a Type A trait, a manipulative person with a high Mach score, or an employee with extreme external locus of control who won't accept responsibility, managers have to deal with a range of personalities in the workplace. Here are some tips for handling problem employees:

- Openly and quickly talk to employees about their problem behaviors.
- Focus on the employee's specific behaviors and stick with verifiable facts. For example, say "You were yelling at Joe yesterday so loudly that I heard you all the way in the bathroom" rather than "You've been very hostile lately."
- Raise personality traits only if your group has used them in the past. Avoid saying, "I think your Machiavellian tendencies cause you to put your interests first."
- Keep your discussion separate from performance evaluation and other personnel-related decisions.
- Listen to the employee's version of events; be fair.
- Develop a common understanding about what is and is not appropriate behavior for your group and form a plan together for corrective action that has a timeline.
- When trying to change behavior, be supportive and provide frequent feedback, encouragement, and reminders (the good and the bad).
- Be patient; behaviors take time to change, which is partly why you need to address them as quickly as possible.

Source: Partially based on J. Viega, "Face Your Problem Subordinates Now," *Academy of Management Executive* 2, no. 2 (1988): 145–52. See also G. Alder, "When Your Star Performer Can't Manage," *Harvard Business Review*, July-August 1997: 22–36.

avoid value conflicts and the resulting problems. The first step, however, is for managers to understand their own values and priorities.

Types of Values   There are two types of values, terminal and instrumental.[49] **Terminal values** are goals for behavior or for a certain state of affairs that a person would like to achieve. For example, being happy is a goal that many people have. Other such values are peace, security, freedom, and salvation.[50] These are all states that people would like to achieve; they are terminal values.

    Instrumental values are the means, or instruments, that people believe they should use to reach the terminal values. Being honest and helpful are examples of instrumental values that many of us teach our children. Other instrumental values include ambition, courage, open-mindedness, obedience, logic, self-reliance, and forgiveness. Depending on your value system, you will rank certain terminal and instrumental values above others. Take Self-Assessment 4.5 to gain more information about your value system.

    Each individual's value system is unique, although much of it may be shared by members of the same culture. For example, the 1996 presidential elections in the United States revealed what some people called the "gender gap," a difference in the value system of men and women. Based on surveys done during the election, women placed a higher value on family and

Terminal values
Goals for behavior or for a certain state of affairs that a person would like to achieve

Instrumental values
The means, or instruments, that people believe they should use to reach the terminal values

▶ **SELF-ASSESSMENT 4.5**
Value Systems

Rank the values in each of the two categories from 1 (most important) to 5 (least important to you).

Rank	Instrumental Values	Rank	Terminal values
_____	Ambition and hard work	_____	Contribution and a sense of accomplishment
_____	Honesty and integrity		
_____	Love and affection	_____	Happiness
_____	Obedience and duty	_____	Leisurely life
_____	Independence and self-sufficiency	_____	Wisdom and maturity
_____	Humility	_____	Individual dignity
_____	Doing good to others (Golden Rule)	_____	Justice and fairness
		_____	Spiritual salvation

Scoring key:

The values that you rank highest in each group are the ones that are most important to you. Consider whether your actions, career choices, and so forth are consistent with your values.

Source: Based on C. Anderson, "Values-Based Management," *Academy of Management Executive* 11, no. 4 (1997): 25–46; M. Rokeach, *Beliefs, Attitudes, and Values* (San Francisco: Jossey Bass, 1968).

Hot ▼ Link

See chapter 3, pp. 75–76, for a discussion of the three levels of culture.

Cultural Values
- Individualism
- Masculinity
- Tolerance for ambiguity
- Power distance
- Time orientation

↓

Personal Value System
Terminal Values
Examples: happiness, individual dignity, wisdom, salvation
Instrumental Values
Examples: honesty, love, obedience, doing good

FIGURE 4.3
Cultural and Personal Values

---

social issues than did men, who focused more on economic problems. In addition to gender-based differences, many generational and culture-based value systems differences also exist.

Culture and Values Cultural values, also known as cultural dimensions, indicate what a cultural group considers to be important, worthwhile, and desirable. We share the values of our culture. The cultural values form the basis for our individual value system. For example, certain values—fairness, honesty, frugality, compassion, and humility—are universal. In contrast, the value of individual dignity is often present in individualistic, not collectivist, cultures.[51] Individual dignity refers to placing emphasis on the uniqueness, self-control, and self-governance of individuals. Those who are from individualistic cultures are more likely to hold individual dignity as a value than those who are from collectivistic cultures (see Figure 4.3).

In general, the Euro-American and U.S. cultures value individuality. As a result, many individuals in these cultures rate personal achievement and recognition highly. Organizations select individuals for rewards and recognition. Displays of individuality are welcomed, as evidenced by the respect many people have for entrepreneurs.

In a collectivist culture, society places a higher value on the community and a lower value on the individual. For instance, in Japan, conformity to the group is valued and rewarded. Parents teach children not to stand out or draw attention to themselves. A Japanese proverb states that "the nail that stands out will be hammered down." The proverb reflects the individual value system of many Japanese who believe they should sacrifice self for the good of the collective. Several Native American societies, such as the Navajos, have similar cultural values. Navajos devalue individualism and standing out in one's community and, in fact, consider such behavior inappropriate.

Hofstede's other cultural values of avoidance of uncertainty, power distance, and masculinity similarly affect individuals' value systems. When the culture values low-power distance, as in Sweden, individuals are likely to be cooperative and avoid status symbols and hierarchy. When the culture is masculine, individuals are likely to value honor and self-reliance.

The generational differences between Baby Boomers and Baby Busters depend in large part on conflicting values.

In addition to national cultural differences in value systems, theorists debate the effect of age, ethnic, and other group cultural differences on people's value systems. Research suggests that many people from the older generation in the United States believe the young do not value hard work and that they lack respect. It also indicates that the younger groups think the older generation's value system is stale and useless. Consultant Regan, who is part of the twenty-something generation, talks about what the younger generation wants: "Just tell me what you want me to do and leave me alone." However, he states, "Obviously the boss above them wants more direction and control."[52] Table 4.2 presents some value differences based on age.

Table 4.2 GENERATION-BASED VALUE DIFFERENCES IN THE UNITED STATES

Current Age Range	Defining Social and Historical Influences	Dominant Value System
55 +	Raised by Depression era parent in post-Depression period or around WWII	Hardwork; frugality; patriotism; Protestant work ethic
40–55	Baby boomers raised by WWII parents, grew up during Korean and Vietnam wars, Kennedy assassination and moon landing, rock & roll era, and Woodstock	Nonconformity; idealism; self-focus; distrust of establishment; happiness and peace
30–40	Raised by the early hippies; post-Vietnam era; Watergate	The "yuppies;" "me" generation; ambition; material comforts; success driven
up to 30	Peaceful era marked by few major events in the United States; recession and economic changes	Generation Xers; enjoyment of life; jaded; desire for autonomy and flexibility

Sources: M. E. Massey, "The Past: What You Are Is Where You Were When," videorecording (Video Publishing House); D. J. Cherrington, S. J. Condies, and J. L. England, "Age and Work Values," *Academy of Management Journal* (September 1979): 617–23; S. Ratan, "Generational Tensions in the Office: Why Busters Hate Boomers," *Fortune* (October 4, 1993): 56–70.

Each individual develops a different value system that shapes his or her attitudes and behaviors. Value systems affect ethical behavior in organizations, a critical implication for managers.

Ethics
A person's concept of right and wrong

Values and Ethics   One of the most important work-related values is **ethics**—a person's concept of right and wrong. Keep in mind the difference between legal and ethical standards. Many activities that are legal may not be ethical according to an individual's value system. For example, it's not illegal to ingratiate yourself with your boss by giving her false compliments or by telling her what she wants to hear about her management style. Depending on your value system, you may consider such behavior either unethical or a required ingredient for success.

Relativist ethical view
A belief that what is right or wrong depends on the situation or the culture

Two general views of ethics are the *relativist* and *universalist* views. Individuals with a **relativist ethical view** believe that what is right or wrong depends on the situation or the culture.[53] To illustrate, businesspeople in many places in the world consider gifts, bribes, or kickbacks acceptable behavior in contract negotiations, though these activities are both unethical and illegal based on U.S. values and laws.[54] A person with a relativist view of ethics would take a "When in Rome, do as the Romans do" approach. A U.S. manager who learns that it is generally accepted to bribe officials in Thailand to secure a contract would consider bribing a Thai official acceptable, ethical behavior. (Note that it is rarely possible for managers of U.S.-based companies to adopt a relativist view of ethics in business situations because U.S. laws forbid any form of bribery anywhere in the world.)

A QUESTION OF ETHICS

Value Differences?	Do you consider it ethical to influence your embassy to help a foreign business partner's son get a student visa to your country? Does your answer depend on what, if anything, you expect to gain from your action?

Universalist view of ethics
A belief that all activities should be judged by the same standards, regardless of the situation or culture

In contrast, a person with an **universalist view of ethics** believes that all activities should be judged by the same standards, regardless of the situation or culture. Many U.S. policies that regulate business conduct represent the universalist view. As a result, the government discourages or legally restricts U.S. companies and their managers from engaging in practices abroad that are considered unethical and illegal in the United States. For example, an oil company, based on U.S. laws of equal opportunity and the principles of cultural diversity, could appoint a female manager to its Saudi operations, in spite of the religious and cultural problems it might create. Figure 4.4 summarizes the difference between the relativist and universalist views of ethics.

The value and ethical issues facing managers are highly complex.[55] Global and cross-cultural issues further add to the complexity of the issues. There are no easy solutions, and ethical and value-driven issues will continue to be a major part of any manager's job.

Relativist View
- Different ethical standards apply in different places
- Culture is a major factor in ethical standards

Universalist View
- The same ethical standards apply everywhere
- Culture is not a factor in ethical standards

Value Conflict   Given that individual values are difficult to change, one issue that managers face is the conflict among values. **Value conflict** refers to disagreement among values that an individual holds or between individual and organizational values. Value conflict may occur in organizations in one of three ways:

- *Intrapersonal value conflict* occurs when a person holds two or more values that are inconsistent. A female manager who is ambitious and successful, who values her 50–70-hour-per-week career but still believes that she needs to be a traditional wife and mother, will experience intrapersonal conflict.
- *Interpersonal value conflict* occurs when two or more people hold opposing values. An older employee may value respect for authority and preservation of tra-

FIGURE 4.4
Contrasting Views of Ethics

ditions whereas his younger co-worker is rebellious and believes in radical change in organizations.

- *Person-organization value conflict* occurs when a person's values conflict with the organization's culture. An example is a person who values the environment, but finds that her employer caused environmental disasters in another part of the world.

Value conflict
Disagreement among values that an individual holds or between individual and organizational values

Although it is important to be aware of and to resolve any potential intrapersonal value conflicts, managers are more concerned with interpersonal and person-organization value conflicts. In many cases, interpersonal value conflict prevents co-workers from working together effectively and accomplishing the goals of the organization. Similarly, person-organization value conflicts are frustrating and, depending on the extent of conflict, can prevent individuals from fully committing to performance or cause them to quit their jobs.

Although it may appear easy and ideal simply to hire people whose values do not conflict with one another or with the organization's, such a solution is neither practical nor desirable; in many cases it is illegal. The challenge for managers is to help blend and integrate the various values and manage potential conflicts. It is also a manager's job to clarify the values of the organization to all employees. We examine these issues further in chapter 8 when we look at team effectiveness and in chapter 12, which examines conflict management.

Now that we have discussed personality traits and values, we examine attitudes with a special focus on job satisfaction.

Summary Point 4.5   **What Are Values?**

- A person's value system is the way that person's values are organized and prioritized.
- Terminal values are goals for behavior or for a certain state of affairs that a person would like to achieve. Instrumental values are the means, or instruments, that people believe they should use to attain their goals.
- A key work-related value is a person's ethics. Two contrasting views of ethics are the relativist or universalist

approaches. The relativist view of ethics depends on the situation or culture. The universalist view is consistent in all situations and cultures.
- A key challenge for managers is to integrate and blend and fit the values of different employees with those of the organization.

UNDERSTANDING WORK-RELATED ATTITUDES: JOB SATISFACTION

Attitudes are general feelings and beliefs about people and situations that can lead to behavior. You may believe that the organization you work for is a fair and socially responsible company. Because fairness and social responsibility are important terminal values for you, you feel happy about working there. As a result of your beliefs and feelings toward the organization, you are likely to continue to work hard and to stay in the firm. Attitudes are therefore made up of beliefs, feelings, and behaviors. Figure 4.5 presents examples of these three components of attitudes.

Although we often think that our feelings are consistent with our beliefs and behaviors, that is not always the case. For example, you may not like your job, but continue to do it well. You also may believe that the organization you work for is good and fair, but you don't like working there although you still work hard. The possible inconsistency between the three different components of attitudes explains the sometimes confusing findings related to job satisfaction and performance. One of the most important and most studied work-related attitudes is **job satisfaction**, which is defined as the general attitude that people have about their jobs.[56]

Job satisfaction
The general attitude that people have about their jobs

Feelings
- I like my boss
- I enjoy working with my assistant
- I dislike my co-workers; they make me angry
- I get irritated when I work with women

Beliefs
- I think my boss is decent
- My assistant is intelligent
- My co-workers are fools
- Women should stay at home

Behaviors
- I support my boss and help him or her
- I recommend my assistant for a raise
- I won't cooperate with my co-workers
- I ignore and discount the opinions of female co-workers

FIGURE 4.5
The Three Components of Attitudes

The five factors found to relate most closely to job satisfaction are listed in Table 4.3. Satisfaction with each factor affects the overall level of a person's job satisfaction. In spite of many changes in organizations, massive layoffs, and increasingly longer working hours, various surveys continue to indicate that U.S. workers are generally satisfied with their jobs. Surprisingly, what employees want from their jobs has also changed little. People continue to want good benefits and job security. Interesting and challenging work is an important factor in all survey results.[57]

Job Satisfaction and Performance

A logical assumption is that the attitude of job satisfaction is related to higher motivation and higher performance. Actually, as is the case with many other attitudes, how you feel about your job does not necessarily indicate how you will behave. The relationship between satisfaction and performance is far from clear and simple. Extensive research has not been able to establish clearly that satisfaction leads to higher performance.[58] A satisfied employee is less likely to leave the organization but not necessarily more likely to work harder and be more productive. Similarly, a dissatisfied employee may be more likely to quit the job but not necessarily be a poor performer. Consider the disputes among the Chicago Bulls players, coach, and owners. In spite of dissatisfaction with the owners—their bosses—both the coach and the players continued to perform. The relationship between satisfaction and performance is affected or moderated by many different factors (for a discussion of moderating variables, refer to Appendix 2). For example, the link is stronger when outside factors do not strongly affect the employee's performance. Additionally, the link between satisfaction and performance tends to be stronger for professionals and employees at higher levels of the organization. Finally, the rewards a person receives for good performance play a key role.

There is also the possibility that performance leads to higher satisfaction rather than the other way around.[59] As people do their jobs well, if the reward system is consistent and fair, they should receive better pay and promotions and should have a more positive relationship with their supervisor and their co-workers. As we see in Table 4.3, all these are elements of job satisfaction and may therefore increase job satisfaction.

Assume that you are generally satisfied with your job (remember that there are five components to overall job satisfaction). In spite of being satisfied, you do not perceive that the pay and benefits you receive are fair and equitable. You, therefore, think that your good job performance tends to go unrewarded. You may still be satisfied with your job, but your overall performance may suffer. The other possibility is that as you keep doing your job well, your salary increases so you start feeling more satisfied with your job. The opposite scenario would be the

Table 4.3   **FIVE FACTORS OF JOB SATISFACTION**

Job Factors	Description
The pay	The amount of wages, salary, and benefits and the individual's perception of their fairness
The job itself	How interesting and challenging a job is perceived to be
Promotion opportunities	Availability of opportunities for advancement
The supervisor	The boss's support and caring for employees
Co-workers and other people	Relationship with co-workers

Source: Based on P. C. Smith, L. M. Kendall, and C. L. Hulin, *The Measurement of Satisfaction in Work and Retirement* (Skokie, IL: Rand McNally, 1969).

CAREER ADVICE
from the Experts

WHAT TO DO IF YOU ARE
DISSATISFIED WITH YOUR JOB

Unfortunately, many of you are likely to be dissatisfied with your jobs at least at some point in your career. Here are some helpful steps you can take.

- Identify the aspect of the job that is causing your dissatisfaction. If all aspects are troublesome, you should seriously consider finding another job.
- Once you have isolated the aspects that are causing dissatisfaction, evaluate how important they are to you. For instance, pay may be bad, but the learning opportunities are great. Which one is more important?
- Discuss your areas of dissatisfaction with your boss. Present facts and propose solutions. Be constructive, receptive to ideas, and willing to negotiate.
- If the supervisor or co-workers are the problem, use your judgment about how receptive they may be to your feedback. If they are open, focus on facts and behaviors and discuss areas of conflict, seeking their help and suggestions in resolving them.
- If possible, ask for a transfer if you still like the organization but not your current job.
- Suffering in silence won't get you too far. Be proactive and constructive in changing your attitude, feelings, beliefs, or behavior.

Sources: Partially based on H. Lancaster, "You Have to Negotiate for Everything in Life, So Get Good at It," *Wall Street Journal,* January 27, 1998, B1; H. Lancaster, "In Today's Market, Don't Stick Around in a Dead-End Job," *Wall Street Journal,* March 10, 1998, B1.

case of someone who is highly dissatisfied with his job but desperately needs the pay and the benefits it brings. In spite of being dissatisfied, the person may continue to perform well.

More than any of the other individual difference characteristics discussed in this chapter, work satisfaction and its behavioral components are the domain of managers. It is the responsibility of a manager to be aware of potential problems with employee satisfaction and to take appropriate actions to help employees become more satisfied with various aspects of their jobs before their attitude leads to unproductive work behaviors. We focus next on how managers can use various individual difference variables, including personality traits, values, and attitudes, to be more effective.

 ## USING INDIVIDUAL
DIFFERENCES IN ORGANIZATIONS

Managers can use individual differences in two ways. First, they can test for various individual differences to help make human resource and personnel-related decisions such as selection and performance evaluation. Second, organizations are increasingly using tests of individual differences for self-awareness and development. This more recent use is beginning to gain wide acceptance in many organizations. We discuss both uses in the following sections.

Hot ▼ Link

We discuss reliability and validity
issues in Appendix 2, pp. 581–82.

Individual Difference Testing
in Human Resource Decisions

The major reasons for the decline in use of individual difference testing, particularly personality testing for HR decisions, are issues of reliability and validity. Even the best personality tests have some degree of subjectivity and their link to work-related behaviors and job performance is not well established or is established but it is not very strong.[60]

Some organizations use complex clinical tools such as the MMPI mentioned earlier in this chapter. These tests, designed for clinical use, are aimed at identifying psychological disorders rather than predicting work-related behaviors. However, in some work settings, such as in the nuclear industry, the use of the MMPI is justified to screen out disturbed employees who could be a threat to public safety. For most organizations, however, the cost and time involved in administering such tests are not worth their benefits. Instead, companies are more interested in simple, work-related individual differences. That is, employers may find that it is appropriate and relatively easy to use a series of personality tests to assess a potential employee's conscientiousness and dependability.

One type of personality assessment often used is integrity testing, designed to measure a potential employee's honesty. With the cost of employee theft and dishonesty increasing, companies such as Target, Home Depot, and many banks have employees take paper-and-pencil integrity tests. Although their use has been controversial and the research findings regarding their value contradictory, businesses continue to use them.[61] Some estimates indicate that millions of people take such tests every year and close to 50 percent fail them![62] The vagueness of the questions and their sometimes inaccurate scoring may be partly responsible for such a high failure rate for these tests. Tests of other individual differences, such as ability and skills, are considerably more legitimate, as they are more directly and reliably associated with work-related behaviors and job performance.

Legal, Ethical, and Managerial Issues The use of individual difference tests of various kinds is likely to continue. With computer technology, the scoring is faster and more accurate. When combined with a battery of other evaluation mechanisms, reliability and validity tend to increase. Legally and ethically, to be legitimate, an individual difference test used in a human resource decision must be clearly related to the behaviors, skills, and competencies needed for a job. Managers should conduct detailed job analyses—analyses that provide specific information about job requirements. In addition, a manager needs to assure that the tests used are well developed and well tested: They need to be reliable and valid.

Aside from the legal limits, there are other concerns about the use of personality traits as a management tool. The ability to identify the personality traits, values, and attitudes of your employees, team members, and co-workers is useful and can lead to better management and better interpersonal relationships. After all, the whole issue is to manage people better. Knowing that they are open to new experiences, have a high need for control, that they tend not to pay attention to others, or that they value social relationships above all else can be very useful in helping them do their job better.

The flip side, however, is first the danger of pigeonholing people (more on this issue in chapter 5). It is easy to start thinking of a certain co-worker as the "Type A," or the "low self-monitor" rather than as a whole person with a variety of skills, abilities, and interests that are not measured by any one personality trait. A second danger is that access to superficial personality data often leads managers to assume that one or two individual difference characteristics give them insight to a person's entire personality. Thinking that you really know a person when you actually know very little can lead to serious errors. As you will see in the next chapter, such assumptions can also lead to many perceptual problems.

Earlier in this chapter, we learned that managers typically do not have access to accurate information about their employees' individual differences such as personality traits, values, or attitudes. Few managers are trained to be able to make even an educated guess, so unless reliable personality test results are available, they should be very cautious when using their estimates of individual differences in managerial decisions. In spite of the potential usefulness of individual difference information, unless it is reliably obtained, the safer and more appropriate course is to focus on measurable job-related behaviors.

Self-Awareness

Organizations are spending considerable resources to help their managers and employees gain self-awareness through use of personality tests.[63] The search for self-understanding and self-improvement is becoming a major factor in organizational effectiveness. Through personality testing, feedback from different sources, Eastern style meditation, and self-discovery workshops, managers are learning more about themselves. Although not all tools are equally appropriate, the search for self-awareness is fast becoming a key to managerial and personal effectiveness. A successful search allows individuals to face their strengths and shortcomings and develop action plans for improvement before problems arise. Carla R. Alani, an associate director of finance at Colgate-Palmolive, for example, received advice from WOMEN Unlimited that made her more self-aware, allowing her to communicate better with her male colleagues. She received two promotions after seeking professional advice.[64]

In another instance, some health care executives found it difficult to identify and correct their own shortcomings because of the nature of their jobs, high performance expectations, and isolation from criticism. Many turned to consulting firms to devise tools, such as questionnaires or interviews, to assess their own profiles.[65] The goal was to provide feedback to the executives so they could become more self-aware and take appropriate corrective action for their own behavior.

Specific tools used in self-awareness include the use of **360-degree feedback**, a technique in which managers receive feedback about their behaviors, style, and performance from all levels including their bosses, peers, and subordinates.[66] Another tool that has gained popularity with companies such as AT&T and PepsiCo is meditation and self-reflection.[67] These individual tools are often combined with seminars such as Steven Covey's "Seven Habits of Highly Effective People" that focus on self-mastery and positive thinking.[68]

In times of change and increasing pressure on employees and managers to be flexible, creative, and to deliver high performance, the push toward better self-knowledge can help managers develop into more productive, successful employees. The various individual difference characteristics discussed in this chapter each represent one aspect of what makes a person unique. There may be some overlap as each trait provides information about one slice of an individual's personality. In other words, an individual may be conscientious and dependable, closed to new experiences, extraverted, have an internal locus of control, have a Type B personality trait, score in the mid-range of the Mach scale, and score high on the self-monitor scale. Although some combinations are intuitively more likely, the scales are not statistically correlated.

A reasonable assumption is that some combination of traits, values, beliefs, and attitudes makes certain behaviors more salient and dominant. For instance, a highly conscientious, low self-monitor Type A, with internal locus of control, from a culture where high power distance is valued is likely to have a highly proactive and aggressive style in many situations. Conversely, a high self-monitor, Type B who is agreeable and friendly and open to new experiences is likely to come across as a low-key, socially sensitive, and interpersonally oriented individual, especially if she feels that the situation requires such behavior.

360-degree feedback
A technique in which managers receive feedback about their behaviors, style, and performance from all organizational levels including bosses, peers, and subordinates

Assessing individual differences can help managers understand themselves and others and can spur self-improvement, which leads to greater productivity. Special care has to be taken, however, not to label people or to overgeneralize about their personalities, which are complex combinations of traits, values, and attitudes.

Individual Differences *in Context*

This chapter has focused on the individual, the smallest level of analysis in organizations. There are, however, many links between the individual and the organizational context we discussed in the first three chapters. We have already discussed the environment, particularly culture and social institutions that are part of the general environment, as one of the determinants of individual differences. In the case of individual differences, the more interesting issue is how personality influences the way managers define and manage the issues of the environment, technology, strategy, structure, and culture. For example, a manager's personality and values may affect the way she perceives certain opportunities and threats in the environment so that she enacts the environment of her organization in a particular way. Similarly, individual characteristics can strongly influence a manager's choice of organizational strategy, culture, and structure.

For example, research has shown that Type A managers engage in more risky strategies and find the environment to be more threatening.[69] Furthermore, Type A managers who need control are more likely to create centralized organizations and well-defined cultures. Other research findings on locus of control show a link between the personality of executives and how they manage the context of their organization.[70]

Douglas Ivester is the CEO of Coca-Cola who replaced the legendary Goizuetta. Ivester is described as an intensely competitive person with high expectations and an uncanny ability to work hard.[71] He spends most of his time on the road, constantly expects new ideas from his managers, and does not bother with formality. His go-getter style, focus on numbers, and competitiveness—all indicative of a Type A—are expected to push Coca-Cola to grow even more and to intensify its already fierce competition with PepsiCo.

For updated information on the topics in this chapter, Web exercises, links to related Web sites, an on-line study guide, and more, visit our companion Web site at:
http://www.prenhall.com/nahavandi

A L o o k   B a c k   a t   t h e

MANAGERIAL CHALLENGE

The Chicago Bulls

Phil Jackson was able to blend the styles and talents of Michael Jordan, Dennis Rodman, and the other players by making each player feel unique and valuing his contributions. Jackson had a good understanding of each player's individual differences, personality, values, and beliefs. He focused on intense physical and mental preparation before games, then let his players perform on the court with guidance as needed. He had few set plays and relied on his players' talent, creativity, and spontaneity to win games. He tried to avoid controversy by not getting involved with players' personal lives.

Jackson's respect for and understanding of each team member and his ability to combine the players' talents and styles to benefit the team inspired the deep sense of loyalty from his players that led to their unprecedented success despite the tension between Jackson and the Bulls' owners.[72]

■ Point of View Exercises

You're the Manager: Assume you were one of the owners of the Chicago Bulls during Phil Jackson's tenure. You wanted more involvement with and control over your team. Based on what you know of the coach, how could you have gotten involved without interfering with his success?

You're the Employee: As a member of the marketing group of the current Bulls organization, you work on promoting the team and its members. How can you use your knowledge of various personality traits and values to make it easier for you to work with the players to get their cooperation?

SUMMARY OF LEARNING OBJECTIVES

1. **Define individual differences, identify their determinants, and explain their effect on behavior.** Individual difference characteristics are what make people unique. They include personality traits, values, attitudes, abilities, and skills. Personality is a set of stable characteristics or traits that makes each individual unique. Values are long-lasting beliefs about what is worthwhile and desirable. Values, similar to personality traits, are stable and resistant to change. Attitudes are complex sets of beliefs and feelings that individuals have toward specific people, objects, or situations. Ability refers to a natural talent do something mental or physical. By contrast, skills are acquired talents that individuals can develop through training. A combination of heredity, or biological factors, and environmental, or situational, factors determines individual differences.

   Managers must realize that individual differences do not dictate people's behavior. Instead, they limit a person's behavioral range, making some behaviors easier and more comfortable than others.

2. **Describe the major personality dimensions and traits that influence work-related behaviors.** The Big Five are the major personality dimensions. They include conscientiousness, extroversion, openness to experience, emotional stability, and agreeableness. Although conscientiousness, extroversion, and openness to experience are linked to work-related behaviors in varying degrees, none of the five dimensions predict work behaviors.

   Four other personality traits affect behavior in organizations: locus of control, Type A, self-monitoring, and Machiavellianism. Locus of control is an indicator of an individual's sense of control. People with Type A characteristics typically indicate four major behaviors: a sense of urgency, polyphasic behavior, competitiveness, and hostility. Self-monitoring is the degree to which people are able to read and use cues from their environment to shape their own behavior. Machiavellianism indicates a person's willingness and ability to influence and manipulate others. These four traits affect how people work and how they manage others. Additionally, the cross-cultural differences in these traits make them important in cross-cultural situations.

3. **Distinguish between terminal and instrumental values and explain how culture shapes values and how values affect ethics.** Terminal values are goals for behaviors. Instrumental values are the means or instruments that are used to achieve goals. Ethics is one of the key work-related values. The relativistic view of ethics states that right and wrong depend on culture. The universalist view of ethics judges all situations by the same standards, regardless of culture or other situational factors.

4. **Identify the components of job satisfaction as a work-related attitude and discuss the link between job satisfaction and organizational behavior.** The factors that influence job satisfaction are pay, the job itself, promotions, supervisors, and co-workers. The link between job satisfaction and work performance is complex and moderated by many organizational and personal factors.

5. **Describe the ways managers can use individual differences to manage their workforce.** Individual differences are used in organizations to make human resource decisions such as hiring, evaluation, and promotion. Their proper use requires focus only on variables that have clear implications for work-related behaviors and performance. The second use of individual differences is to help employees become more aware of their strengths and weaknesses so they can use this knowledge for self-development.

KEY TERMS

ability, p. 115
agreeableness, p. 119
attitudes, p. 114
behavioral cues, p. 115
behavioral zone of comfort,
   p. 116
conscientiousness, p. 118
emotional stability, p. 119
ethics, p. 134
extroversion/introversion,
   p. 118

instrumental values, p. 131
interactionist view, p. 113
job satisfaction, p. 135
locus of control, p. 120
Machiavellian personality,
   p. 128
openness to experience,
   p. 119
personality, p. 114
relativist ethical view,
   p. 134

self-monitoring, p. 127
skill, p. 115
terminal values, p. 131
360-degree feedback,
   p. 139
Type A, p. 122
universalist view of ethics,
   p. 134
value conflict, p. 135
values, p. 114
value system, p. 130

REVIEW QUESTIONS

1. What are the determinants of individual differences?
2. Define each of the individual difference characteristics presented in the chapter. What are their similarities and differences?
3. Describe the Big Five personality dimensions. Which ones are linked to work-related behaviors?
4. Explain the characteristics of each of the personality traits presented in the chapter. How is each related to work behaviors?
5. How does culture affect values? What is the role of values in organizations?
6. Define the elements of job satisfaction and the link between job satisfaction and performance.

DISCUSSION QUESTIONS

1. As a manager should you change an employee's personality? Values? Attitudes? Behaviors?
2. If you had information about your employees' locus of control, Type A, self-monitoring, and Mach scores, how could you use that information ethically?
3. What can managers do to manage value conflicts in organizations?
4. As a manager, how can you help your employees increase their job satisfaction? What can you expect in return?
5. Now that you have increased self-awareness regarding some of your personality traits and values, how can you use the information?
6. How can managers use the information about their own personality in managing the five contextual strategic forces?

▶ **TEAM EXERCISE 4.1**
Your Ideal Organization

This exercise is designed to help you understand the way different individuals perceive and define organizations.

PART I: INDIVIDUAL DESCRIPTION

Think of working in the organization of your dreams. What would it look like? How would it be organized? How would people interact? Your assignment in this part of the exercise is to provide a description of your ideal organization. In doing so, consider the following organizational characteristics and elements.

What is your organization's name (no initials allowed)?

What industry is it in?

What is the mission of your ideal organization?

What is the culture? What are the basic assumptions? What are the behavioral norms? Who are the heroes? How do people interact?

How would people be organized? What is the structure? Consider issues of centralization, hierarchy, formalization, specialization, span of control, departmentation, and so forth.

What is the role of the manager? What is the role of followers?

Describe the physical location, office spaces, office décor, and other features.

Consider other issues such as dress code, work schedules, and others that you think are important in describing your ideal organization.

PART II: GROUP WORK

Your instructor will assign you to a group and provide you with further instructions.

▶ **TEAM EXERCISE 4.2**
Type A and Time Urgency

This exercise is designed to demonstrate the Type A's sense of time urgency and how it manifests itself in perception of time.

PART I: MEASURING TIME

- Students will be grouped in teams of three with one Type A, one Type B, and one observer (A or B) to keep time.
- The Type A and Type B are asked to close their eyes and raise their hands (without opening their eyes) when they estimate that *one minute* is up.
- The observer in each team will keep track of his or her two team members' time estimates and tell them to open their eyes when they have both finished.

PART II: REPORTS AND DISCUSSION

The times for each A and B person in the teams will be recorded on the board followed by a discussion of perception of time and its implication for managers.

UP CLOSE

▶ The Impossible Old-Timer at Super Soft

The software design team at Super Soft includes 14 members with computer science, education, and engineering backgrounds. The team is informally divided into the engineer and education groups with eight "techies" and six "eddies," as they call themselves. All but two members are male, with one woman in each of the groups. The atmosphere is generally relaxed and friendly with the various members talking to one another across their cubicles and spending a lot of time in one another's offices. In spite of the general goodwill and the need to interact extensively to design and test the software, there is tension among the members.

The eddies have problems with the senior engineer, Gary Rockwell, who is also the informal, de facto team leader because of his seniority. Without being able to pinpoint anything specific, they all feel uncomfortable around him. Many of the techies feel the same, although they tend to like Gary better.

The math education specialist describes his feeling: "I just can't trust him. I never know where he stands. He rarely says anything specific, but has a lot of war stories. When you ask him a question, he gives you a long history lesson and leaves you feeling stupid. I sometimes think he may be missing some screws!"

Chonda, the science specialist and the one woman in the eddies group says, "I just don't know what Gary does all day. He seems to spend more time with Jim the general manager than down here with his group. When he is here, he is typing away, but I don't quite know what he does. He obviously must be good at something because he makes more money than the rest of us and has been here for a long time—but he never really does anything for me."

Elizabeth, one of the software engineers, reports, "I disagreed with him once last year on a design issue and I was stupid enough to tell him, although I was right. He never said anything, just glared at me, and things have not been the same since. He did make the changes I recommended, though, and the product has been fine. He barely talks to me and I always worry about what he may be telling other people about me. You know, he just hangs out with the other two more senior members and with the managers. Those guys have power."

The arts specialist adds, "I have seen Gary with the managers and they seem to love him. They have lunch at the sandwich place across the street almost every day. Who knows what he tells them about us?" Another software engineer suggests: "Gary always gets what he wants. If you need anything for your work and you can't get it through regular channels, just get on Gary's good side and he'll get it for you. Just don't ask him for any real technical help. I am not sure he knows anything. But he sure can B.S. his way out of anything! You spend one hour with him and you have no idea what he said!"

One of Gary's team members provides this opinion of him: "You know, Gary seems to thrive whenever we are late in meeting our deadlines. He just jumps in and somehow gets a concession from our clients and from management. Last time he managed to do that, he saved us from losing our client and received a promotion. I don't know how he does it, but he never fails! But on a day-to-day basis, he seems bored and uninterested, yet I don't think we could do without him."

When the other two senior team members are asked about Gary, their view is quite different. One says "Gary is just a great guy. He has been here longer than anyone. He really knows his way around. The younger folks don't appreciate him or show him enough respect." The other adds: "Well, maybe Gary is not at the cutting edge of technical stuff, but his progress through the ranks is really impressive. Someone like him deserves respect."

The senior company manager provides an interesting view: "Gary has been here longer than almost anyone, which means a lot in our business. I have lunch with him almost every day. He always shows up at lunchtime and joins us, which is just fine. I have seen him work with clients. He is really good at working his way through the bureaucracy. I have a sense that his team may not be very fond of him, but he tells me they are fine. He has mentored quite a few of them, especially Elizabeth who needed a lot of help from what I understand. I have been thinking seriously about making him the manager and letting him supervise the team. That would really make things easier for me."

Questions

1. What is your analysis of Gary's behavior and style?
2. Is there a problem at the Super Soft design team?
3. If yes, what is it and what should be done about it?

THE BIG PICTURE

▶ The Business of Music at KnitMedia

Since his days as a college student in Madison, Wisconsin, Michael Dorf has been dealing with the challenges of managing individual differences. While still in school, he served as manager of the band Swamp Thing. Then he worked with the band to set up its own record label. Finally, he and a partner founded The Knitting Factory, a combination art gallery-performance space located in the heart of New York's trendy SoHo district. Dorf quickly expanded into a variety of related businesses, which he brought together under the corporate umbrella of KnitMedia.[73]

A handful of top executives now manages KnitMedia's global music empire from offices in New York and Amsterdam. In addition to the New York City club, the company manages worldwide tours for its musical artists, including Sonny Sharrock and Miracle Room; operates music festivals; and maintains a World Wide Web site. Given the company's international reach, it is not surprising that the management team is extremely diverse. Sascha von Oretzen, who manages the recording studio, hails from Germany; Ed Greer, who manages overall operations, comes from Scotland.[74]

Dorf's individual characteristics have strongly influenced the development and direction of KnitMedia. For example, unlike many Big Apple venues, his club requires no drink or food minimum—and business is booming. "Our Wisconsin approach seems to be working," Dorf comments. About values, he notes: "There's this whole honesty-and-integrity thing, and we work hard at that." From the start, Dorf's conscientiousness and openness to experience allowed him to solve problem after problem, paving the way for bringing new music to new audiences through KnitMedia.[75]

Despite differences in culture, personality, and skills, everyone on Dorf's team shares his enthusiasm for good music, his high standards, and his "work hard, play hard" approach. During the company's fast-growth mode, cash flow has been a problem—so Dorf motivates people with periodic bonuses, a great deal of responsibility, and the opportunity to work with wonderful musicians. Dorf consciously recruits "mature individuals looking to make a commitment." Because teamwork is critical to KnitMedia's success, he is less concerned with an employee's educational background than with the person's enthusiasm, intelligence, and flexibility.[76]

Dorf is determined to create "a big company with a small company feeling," even as he steps up the pace of club openings in the United States and Europe. But sustaining the small company feeling—and his employees' enthusiasm—may not be easy. One key element of Dorf's management style is not only to recognize but also to build on individual differences among employees. Mark Perlson, who manages the record label, observes that he is allowed the freedom to handle projects in his own way, with just a few guidelines provided by Dorf. Of course, not everyone works well in this kind of loosely structured business environment. This is only one of many issues Dorf will have to address if he is to keep everyone at KnitMedia focused on profitable expansion in the next decade.[77]

Questions

1. Based on the information provided, what is your analysis of Michael Dorf's major personality traits, values, and attitudes?
2. How do you think Dorf's personality and style reflect on the company's mission, structure, and culture?
3. Assume that you work at KnitMedia and you have been asked to use 360-degree feedback to provide input to Dorf about his style as a manager. What would you say? Would you want to continue working for him? Explain.

NOTES

1. R. Reilly, "Last Call?" *Sports Illustrated* (May 11, 1998): 40.
2. D. DuPree, "Jordan Vows He'll Retire," *USA Today*, February 5, 1998, 1C.
3. D. DuPree, "Will Michael Retire?" *USA Today*, April 23, 1998, 1A.
4. R. Reilly, "Last Call?" 40.
5. F. Pitts, "Bulls Management Destroys Sports Dynasty," *USA Today*, May 1, 1998, 12A.
6. L. M. Keller, T. J. Bouchard, Jr., R. D. Arvey, N. L. Segal, and R. V. Dawis, "Work Values: Genetic and Environmental Influences," *Journal of Applied Psychology* (February 1992): 79–88.
7. R. R. McCrae, "Moderated Analyses of Longitudinal Personality Stability," *Journal of Personality and Social Psychology* 65, no. 3 (1993): 577–85.
8. Another definition of personality is to consider it from an observer's point of view. In that case personality refers to an individual's public self and reputation. R. Hogan discusses the difference between the actor and the observer's points of view; see "Personality and Personality Measurement," in M. D. Dunnette and L. M. Hough (eds.), *Handbook of Industrial and Organizational Psychology* (Palo Alto, CA: Consulting Psychologists Press, 1991), 873–919.
9. M. Rokeach conducted extensive research about values; see *The Nature of Human Values* (New York: Free Press, 1973).
10. In spite of common use, there is little agreement over the definition of attitudes. W. J. McGuire reported more than 500 definitions of the term. "Attitudes and Attitude Change," in G. Lindzey and E. Aronson (eds.), *The Handbook of Social Psychology* 3d ed., vol. 2 (New York: Random House, 1985), 233–346. The original definition proposed by L. L. Thurstone focuses on the affective component ("Comment," *American Journal of Sociology* 52 (1946): 39–40). Many researchers, such as S. L. Crites, Jr., L. R. Fabrigar, and R. E. Petty have measured all three components ("Measuring the Affective and Cognitive Properties of Attitudes: Conceptual and Methodological Issues," *Personality and Social Psychology Bulletin* 20 (1994): 619–34).
11. Walter Mischel, "Toward a Cognitive Social Learning Reconceptualization of Personality," *Psychological Review* 80 (1973): 252–83; H. M. Weiss and S. Adler, "Personality in Organization Research," in B. Staw and L. Cummings (eds.), *Research in Organizational Behavior*, vol. 6 (Greenwich, CT: JAI Press, 1984); Murray Barrick and Michael Mount, "Autonomy as a Moderator of the Relationship Between the Big Five Personality Dimensions and Job Performance," *Journal of Applied Psychology* 78 (1993): 111–18.
12. W. T. Norman, "Toward an Adequate Taxonomy of Personality Attributes: Replicated Factor Structure in Peer Nomination Personality Ratings," *Journal of Abnormal and Social Psychology* 66 (1963): 547–83; J. M. Digman, "Personality Structure: Emergence of the Five-Factor Model," *Annual Review of Psychology* 41 (1990): 417–40; Murray R. Barrick and Michael K. Mount, "The Five Big Personality Dimensions and Job Performance: A Meta-Analysis," *Personnel Psychology* 44, no. 1 (Spring 1991): 1–76.
13. There are two interpretations of the conscientiousness dimension of the Big Five. Some researchers focus on dependability; see M. D. Botwin and D. M. Buss, "Structure of Act-Report Data: Is the Five-Factor Model of Personality Recaptured," *Journal of Personality and Social Psychology* 56 (1989): 988–1001; O. P. John, "Towards a Taxonomy of Personality Descriptors," in D. M. Buss and N. Cantor, *Personality Psychology: Recent Trends and Emerging Directions* (New York: Springer-Verlag, 1989). Others include the hard-working, achievement-oriented aspects; see Digman, "Personality Structure."
14. R. R. McCrae and P. J. Costa, Jr., "Validation of the Five-Factor Model of Personality Across Instruments and Observers," *Journal of Personality and Social Psychology* 56 (1987): 586–95.
15. Barrick and Mount, "The Five Big Personality Dimensions," Theodore Hayes, Harper Roehm, and Joseph Catellano, "Personality Correlated of Success in Total Quality Manufacturing," *Journal of Business and Psychology* 8, no. 4 (Summer 1994): 397–411.
16. Hayes, Roehm, and Castellano, "Personality Correlated."
17. T. A. Stewart, "Why Leadership Matters," *Fortune* 137, no. 4 (March 2, 1998): 82.
18. I. L. Goldstein, *Training in Organizations: Needs Assessment, Development, and Evaluation* (Monterey, CA: Brooks/Cole, 1986).
19. B. Schlender, "On the Road with Chairman Bill," *Fortune* 135, no. 10 (May 26, 1997): 81.
20. J. B. Rotter, "Generalized Expectancies for Internal Versus External Control of Reinforcement," *Psychological Monographs* 80, 1, whole no. 609 (1966); J. C. Chebat, C. Zucaro, and P. Filiatrault, "Locus of Control as a Moderator Variable for the Attribution and Learning Processes of Marketing Managers," *Journal of Social Psychology* 132, no. 5 (1992): 597–608.
21. P. E. Spector, "Behavior in Organizations as a Function of Employee's Locus of Control," *Psychological Bulletin* 91, no. 3 (1982): 482–97.
22. J. J. Tobacyk, "Changes in Locus of Control Beliefs in Polish University Students Before and After Democratization," *Journal of Social Psychology* 132, no. 2 (1992): 217–22.
23. S. L. Wenzel, "Gender, Ethnic Group, and Homelessness as Predictors of Locus of Control Among Job Training Participants," *Journal of Social Psychology* 133, no. 4 (1993): 495–505.
24. For studies about locus of control, see C. R. Anderson, D. Helreigel, and J. W. Slocum, "Managerial Response to Environmentally Induced Stress," *Academy of Management Journal* 20, no. 2 (1977): 260–72; Spector, "Behavior in Organizations."
25. S. A. Kirkpatrick and E. A. Locke, "Leadership: Do Traits Matter?" *Academy of Management Executive* 5, no. 2 (1991): 48–60.
26. C. R. Anderson and C. E. Schneier, "Locus of Control, Leader Behavior and Leader Performance Among Management Students," *Academy of Management Journal* 21 (1978): 690–98; N. M. Ashkanasy, "Supervisors' Responses to Subordinate Performance: Effect of Personal-Control Orientation and Situational Control," *Journal of Social Psychology* 131, no. 4 (1991): 525–44.
27. D. C. Smith, "Bill Hoglund Looks Back, Ahead," *Ward's Auto World* 30, no. 12 (December 1994): 40.
28. R. S. Brockhaus, "Internal External Locus of Control Scores as Predictors of Entrepreneurial Intentions," *Proceeding of the Academy of Management* (1975): 433–35; T. M. Begley and D. P. Boyd, "Psychological Characteristics Associated with Performance in Entrepreneurial Firms and Smaller Businesses," *Journal of Business Venturing* 2 (1987): 79–83.
29. W. Terry, "I Chose to Change My Life," *Parade Magazine* (October 13, 1996): 4–5.
30. For general information about Type A, see R. H. Rosenman and M. Friedman, "Neurogenic Factors in Pathogenesis of Coronary Heart Disease," *Medical Clinics of North America* 58 (1974): 269–79; D. C. Glass, "Behavioral, Cardiovascular, and Neuroendocrine Responses," *International Review of Applied Psychology* 32 (1983): 137–51; J. Schaubroeck, D. C. Ganster, and B. E. Kemmerer, "Job Complexity, Type A Behavior, and Cardiovascular Disorder: A Prospective Study," *Academy of Management Journal* 37, no. 2 (1994): 426–39.
31. For Type A and the need for control, see Michael J. Strube and Carol Werner, "Relinquishment of Control and the Type A Behavior Pattern," *Journal of Personality and Social Psychology* 48 (1985): 688–701; T. W. Smith and Frederick Rhodewalt, "On States, Traits, and Processes: A Transactional Alternative to the Individual Difference Assumption in Type A Behavior and Psychological Reactivity," *Journal of Research in Personality* 20 (1986): 229–51.
32. Michael Strube, Charles W. Turner, Dan Cerro, J. Stevens, and F. Hinchey, "Interpersonal Aggression and the Type A Coronary-Prone Behavior Pattern: A Theoretical Distinction and Practical Implications," *Journal of Personality and Social Psychology* 47 (1984): 839–47.
33. D. M. Miller, E. R. Lack, and S. Asroff, "Preferences for Control and the Coronary-Prone Behavior Pattern: 'I'd Rather Do It Myself,'" *Journal of Personality and Social Psychology* 49 (1985): 492–99.
34. Kirkpatrick and Locke, "Leadership."
35. "Disney's No. 2 Quits over Power Frustration," *The Arizona Republic*, December 13, 1996, A8.
36. J. Martin, "Eli Broad Runs Things His Way," *Fortune* 137, no. 7 (October 13, 1997): 177–78.
37. M. Friedman and R. H. Rosenman, *Type A Behavior and Your Heart* (New York: Knopf, 1974).
38. Stewart, "Why Leadership Matters," 82.
39. M. Snyder, "The Self-Monitoring of Expressive Behavior," *Journal of Personality and Social Psychology* 30 (1974): 526–37.
40. M. Kilduff and D. V. Day, "Do Chameleons Get Ahead? The Effects of Self-Monitoring on Managerial Careers," *Academy of Management Journal* 37, no. 4 (1994): 1047–060.
41. G. H. Dobbins, W. S. Long, E. J. Dedrick, and T. C. Clemons, "The Role of Self-Monitoring and Gender on Leader Emergence: A Laboratory and Field Study," *Journal of Management* 16, no. 3 (1990): 609–18.
42. L. Himelstein, "How Do You Get the Boys to Pass You the Ball," *Business Week* (February 17, 1997): 70.
43. R. Christie and F. L. Geis, *Studies in Machiavellianism* (San Diego, CA: Academic Press, 1970).
44. E. D. Jaffe, I. D. Nebensahl, and H. Gotesdyner, "Machiavellianism, Task Orientation, and Team Effectiveness Revisited," *Psychological Reports* 64, no. 3

(1989): 819–24; E. Panitz, "Psychometric Investigation of the MACH IV Scale Measuring Machiavellianism," *Psychological Reports* 63, no. 3 (1989): 963–68.

45. C. J. Shultz II, "Situational and Dispositional Predictors of Performance: A Test of the Hypothesized Machiavellianism X Structure Interaction Among Sales Persons," *Journal of Applied Social Psychology* 23 (1993): 478–98.

46. D. A. Ralston, D. J. Gustafson, F. M. Cheung, and R. H. Terpstra, "Differences in Managerial Values: A Study of U.S., Hong Kong, and PRC Managers," *Journal of International Business Studies* 2 (1993): 249–75; D. A. Ralston, D. J. Gustafson, R. H. Terpstra, D. H. Holt, F. M. Cheung, and B. A. Ribbens, "The Impact of Managerial Values on Decision-Making Behaviour: A Comparison of the United States and Hong Kong," *Asia Pacific Journal of Management* 10, no. 1 (1993): 21–37.

47. Brian Dumaine, "America's Toughest Bosses," *Fortune* 128, no. 9 (1993): 38–50.

48. B. Dumaine, "America's Toughest Bosses," *Fortune* 198, no. 9 (October 18, 1993): 141.

49. Rokeach, *The Nature of Human Values.*

50. Ibid.

51. C. Anderson, "Values-Based Management," *Academy of Management Executive* 11, no. 4 (1997): 25–46.

52. S. Ratan, "The Generation Tension in the Office: Why Busters Hate Boomers," *Fortune* 128, no. 8 (1993): 62.

53. T. Donaldson, "Global Business Must Mind Its Morals," *New York Times*, February 13, 1994, F11.

54. "Business Ethics: Hard Graft in Asia," *Economist* (May 27, 1995): 61; D. Milbank and M. M. Brauchli, "Greasing Wheels: How U.S. Concerns Compete in Countries Where Bribes Flourish," *Wall Street Journal*, September 29, 1995, A1–A4.

55. For an interesting discussion of global ethical issues, see B. Ettorre, "Why Overseas Bribery Won't Last," *Management Review* (June 1994): 21.

56. E. A. Locke, "The Nature and Causes of Job Satisfaction," in M. D. Dunnette (ed.), *Handbook of Industrial and Organizational Psychology* (Chicago: Rand McNally, 1976), 1297–1350; E. A. Locke, "Job Satisfaction," in M. Gruenberg and T. Wall (eds.), *Social Psychology and Organizational Behavior* (London: Wiley, 1984), 93–117.

57. For several reports of employee satisfaction, see Sheila Poole, "Worker Survey Uncovers Surprise: Most Are Satisfied with Their Job," *Atlanta Constitution*, May 8, 1996, E3; Michelle Martinez, "U.S. Workers Remain Upbeat," *HR Magazine* (May 1995): 14–16; Christopher Caggiano, "What Do Workers Want," *Inc* 14, no. 11 (November 1992): 101–2.

58. M. T. Iaffaldano and P. M. Muchinsky, "Job Satisfaction and Job Performance: A Meta Analysis," *Psychological Bulletin* (March 1985): 251–73; C. Ostroff,

"The Relationship Between Satisfaction, Attitudes and Performance: An Organizational Level Analysis," *Journal of Applied Psychology* (December 1992): 963–74.

59. M. M. Petty, G. W. McGee, and J. W. Cavander, "A Meta-Analysis of the Relationship Between Individual Job Satisfaction and Individual Performance," *Academy of Management Review* 9, no. 4 (1984): 712–21.

60. R. M. Guion and R. F. Gottier, "Validity of Personality Measures in Personnel Selection," *Personnel Psychology* 18 (1965): 135–63; F. J. Landy, *The Psychology of Work Behavior* (Pacific Grove, CA: Brooks/Cole, 1989).

61. H. J. Bernardin and D. K. Cooke, "Validity of an Honesty Test in Predicting Theft Among Convenience Store Employees," *Academy of Management Journal* 36 (1993): 1097–1108; D. S. Ones, C. Viswesvaran, and F. L. Schmidt, "Integrity Tests: Overlooked Facts, Resolved Issues, and Remaining Questions," *American Psychologist* 50, no. 6 (1995): 456–57; M. L. Rieke and S. J. Guastello, "Unresolved Issues in Honesty and Integrity Testing," *American Psychologist* 50, no. 6 (1995): 458–59; D. S. Ones, F. L. Schmidt, and C. Viswesvaran, "Controversies Over Integrity Testing: Two Viewpoints," *Journal of Business and Psychology* 10 (1995): 487–501.

62. M. Budman, "The Honesty Business," *Across the Board* (November–December 1993): 34–37.

63. B. O'Reilly, "360 Degree Feedback Can Change Your Life," *Fortune* 130, no. 8 (1994): 93–100.

64. Himelstein, "How Do You Get."

65. D. L. Nowlin and C. Hickok, "Executives Look in the Mirror," *Healthcare Forum Journal* 35, no. 4 (1992): 64–69.

66. O'Reilley, "360 Degree Feedback."

67. S. Sherman, "Leaders Learn to Heed the Voice Within," *Fortune* (August 22, 1994).

68. S. R. Covey, *Seven Habits of Highly Effective People* (New York: Fireside Books, 1989).

69. A. Nahavandi, P. J. Mizzi, and A. R. Malekzadeh, "Executives' Type A Personality as a Determinant of Environmental Perception and Firm Strategy," *Journal of Social Psychology* 132, no. 1 (1992): 59–67.

70. See D. Miller and C. Droge, "Psychological and Traditional Determinants of Structure," *Administrative Science Quarterly* 31 (1986): 539–60.

71. B. Morris, "Doug Is It," *Fortune* 137, no. 10 (May 25, 1998): 70–84.

72. Reilly, "Last Call?" 41.

73. Gary Dessler, *Management* (Upper Saddle River, NJ: Prentice Hall, 1998), 30.

74. Ibid., 30, 73, 208, 209, 327.

75. Michael Dorf, *Knitting Music* (New York: Knitting Factory Works, 1992).

76. Dessler, *Management*, 326–27, 524.

77. Ibid., 524, 209, 363, 490, 644–45.

UNDERSTANDING PEOPLE: SOCIAL PERCEPTION

LEARNING OBJECTIVES

1. Describe the physical and social perception processes and explain how culture affects them.
2. Present a three-stage model for understanding social perception and highlight the factors that affect each stage.
3. Discuss the biases that affect perception, the difficulties of overcoming them, and ways to manage them.
4. Describe the process and elements of self-presentation and impression management.
5. Explain how managers can reduce the effect of perceptual biases in performance evaluations.

MANAGERIAL CHALLENGE

Pearson PLC, Fighting Stereotypes

When Marjorie Morris Scardino cracked the glass ceiling at Pearson PLC, she shattered perceptions on both sides of the Atlantic. Texas-born Scardino took over as CEO of the $3.6 billion media and entertainment conglomerate in January 1997 with a mandate to revitalize one of the United Kingdom's 100 leading companies. She is the first woman ever to achieve such a high position.[1] Pearson owned the *Financial Times* newspaper, Penguin Books, Madame Tussaud's wax museums, and half of *The Economist* weekly magazine. But its return on equity lagged behind that of its British counterparts—not the best situation for a publicly traded concern.[2]

How did a former rodeo-barrel racer rise to the top at a conservative corporation based on another continent? After law school, Scardino joined the Associated Press in West Virginia. She then teamed with her husband to start a Pulitzer Prize-winning newspaper in Georgia. When the newspaper failed, the couple came to New York, where Scardino became CEO of *The Economist*'s North American operations. As a result of her marketing acumen, the magazine more than doubled its circulation within seven years.[3]

Next, Scardino was summoned to London as CEO of the magazine's global operations, where she boosted earnings by 130 percent in just four years. Then she was named CEO of Pearson, a company roughly ten times the size of *The Economist*. During her first week, she sent an e-mail of self-introduction to all 17,000 employees. "I do my best in an atmosphere of energy, some urgency, and a good amount of humor," she wrote. "I do not want to be associated with an organization that's not decent and fair."[4]

She sports a baseball cap at meetings and sprinkles colorful American slang throughout her communications. Pearson's chairperson called her "an enthusiast and an enthuser."[5] Her egalitarian attitude, in contrast to traditional British reserve, makes her decidedly approachable. Her style has been described as "a mixture of Boston bluestocking, Southern good ol' girl, and dock-worker."[6] Now employees, stockholders, competitors, and industry analysts are watching as Scardino sets a new course for Pearson.

■ **Questions**

1. How do you think the British public and businesspeople view this Texan woman?
2. What effect does her image have on the people she works with and on her company?

Scardino's career and challenges illustrate how perceptions affect organizations. She has to cope with cultural and gender stereotypes and manage people's perceptions to operate effectively in her organization. A key part of her success is understanding others, herself, and the world around her. Managers must observe people and situations, gather information, interpret that information, and make decisions based on some facts and many subjective interpretations. To be effective, they must also manage how others view them.

These decisions involve a complex process of gathering, selecting, and interpreting social information and cues. Very little of that information is objective. Most of the people-related information that managers deal with is open to interpretation. The mental process of gathering, selecting, and organizing the information we receive, interpreting the data, and making judgments based on our interpretation is the focus of this chapter. We explore the process of social perception, the factors that affect how we view ourselves and others, the biases that affect our perception, and their managerial implications, particularly in image management and performance evaluation.

■ THE PERCEPTION PROCESS

We are constantly bombarded with so many cues from our environment that we cannot pay attention to them all. For instance, you may receive clear cues from the physical environment but not pay attention to them. It may be pleasantly cool in the room where you are now sitting. You may have some music in the background and hear the hum of the air conditioner. The chair you are sitting on may be comfortable but your reading light insufficient. You will pay attention to some of these cues and ignore others.

Perception
The mental process of selecting those cues and stimuli that we pay attention to

Perception is the mental process we use to pay attention selectively to some stimuli and cues and not to others. Before discussing the three stages of the perception process, we contrast physical and social perception and consider the effect of culture on our perception of others.

Physical and Social Perception

Physical perception is the process of gathering and interpreting information about physical objects. This process is relatively objective because the physical environment is stable. For example, you know that you will not be able to go through a wall; the presence of the wall is objective and easily testable. The way we perceive others and ourselves functions in much the same way as our perception of the physical environment. When we interact with others, there are many cues and signals that beg for our attention. The way people dress; their facial and other physical characteristics; their tone of voice, accent, nonverbal behaviors; their eye contact with others; how often they smile; and the message they communicate are but a few of the many cues that people consciously or unconsciously send in social interaction. We pay attention to some but not all cues, depending on how important they seem to us.

Physical perception
The process of gathering and interpreting information about physical objects

     Social perception is the process of gathering, selecting, and interpreting information about how we view ourselves and others. Because information about people is often subjective and open to interpretation and because people change in response to many different situations, social perception is a subjective rather than objective process.[7] Organizational behavior focuses on the social perception process because social perceptions affect how managers make decisions about people and organizations.

Social perception
The process of gathering, selecting, and interpreting information about how we view ourselves and others

Basic Perception Processes

Because the perception process requires us to select, interpret, and use stimuli and cues, the process is subject to considerable error, a serious drawback. Take a few minutes to examine the images in Figures 5.1 and 5.2. These figures are classical tests of physical perception. Did you make the same errors as most people? Even though we can measure the images objectively, and we know we are making errors in our perception, we are still not able to perceive the images accurately. Our interpretation of the images is based on our assumptions, which in turn lead to the perceptual errors.

     Another example that highlights the limits of perception is shown in Figure 5.3. The figure demonstrates **closure,** which refers to how we fill in missing information to understand a stimulus. Closure is a crucial part of the perception process. When we do not have all the facts—which is most of the time when we interact with the social environment—we rely on assumptions to fill in missing information. Closure, then, allows us to finish an unfinished picture or to interpret an unclear situation by completing it with our personal, previous experiences and assumptions.

Closure
The process of filling in missing information to understand a stimulus

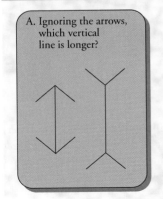 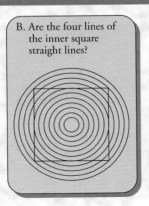 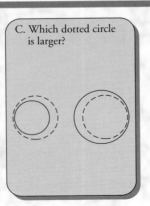

A. Ignoring the arrows, which vertical line is longer?

B. Are the four lines of the inner square straight lines?

C. Which dotted circle is larger?

FIGURE 5.1
Common Perceptual Illusions

Use a ruler to answer these questions. The answers may surprise you.

FIGURE 5.2
Perceptual Illusion Based on Faulty Assumptions

The assumption that the floor is level exaggerates the perception of height differences.

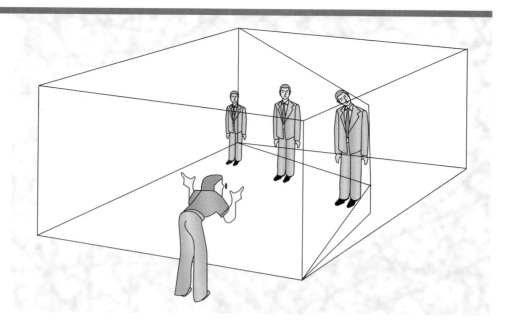

Hot ▼ Link

See chapter 2, p. 50, to review the span of control concept.

The figures illustrate physical perception. However, similar processes affect social perception. Consider how closure can affect a manager's evaluation of an employee. The manager who has a large span of control over 25 people has limited contact with each employee. Over the past six months, however, he has received one customer complaint about a particular employee and has personally observed a loud argument between the same employee and a supervisor from another department. When compared to everything else the employee may have done, these two samples of behaviors are indeed limited, but they are the most direct information the manager has. Based on these two samples, and having little time to gather more information, the manager may use closure to fill in the picture and decide that the employee has a short fuse and the potential for being a troublemaker. We see then that the social perception process is subject to many errors.

Culture and Perception

Culture greatly affects how we perceive our world and others around us. Recall that culture includes the behaviors, norms, values, and assumptions associated with a certain group. Culture, then, affects how we view the world and interpret events.

All work-related behaviors—from your method of greeting others and style of work dress to how you resolve conflict and provide feedback to your employees—depend on your culture.[8] Behaviors have meaning only within a certain cultural context. Once outside a familiar cultural context, people can interpret what we say and do in unexpected ways.

For example, an Australian or American employee interprets a manager's admission that she does not know the answer to a question as an indication that the manager hasn't run across the situation before. In contrast, a French or Brazilian employee is likely to interpret the manager's admitted lack of knowledge as incompetence. The interpretations differ because France and Brazil are cultures with a higher power distance than Australia or the United States, where people with power are supposed to have considerable knowledge. People see and interpret the situation from their own cultural perspectives.

Misperceptions are at the core of many cross-cultural communication problems. The simple behaviors that are perceived and interpreted one way in one culture are interpreted differently in another culture.[9] If managers lack information or are unfamiliar with cross-cultural situations, they are likely to provide closure by relying on information from their own culture.

Consider the example of a U.S. employee, Ms. Thompson, who starts working for a large firm in Spain. The boss, Mr. Rodrigues, meets with her on the first day. After lengthy greetings, Mr. Rodrigues inquires about Ms. Thompson's family, her father's and grandfather's professions, her mother's family, and her siblings. He spends a considerable amount of time making what appears to Ms. Thompson to be irrelevant and inappropriate small talk about her family and personal background, travels, personal interests, and impressions of Spain. Ms. Thompson carefully sidesteps all the personal questions.

The meeting lasts almost one hour without Ms. Thompson having been told much about her assignments or Mr. Rodrigues's expectations. Ms. Thompson is baffled and Mr. Rodrigues is irritated. Both players in this case perceive and interpret the situation from their own cultural perspective. Social and family ties are key to the fabric of Spanish society.[10] You are who your family is. Most employers do not believe they can know and trust you without assessing your lineage. In that context, Mr. Rodrigues is simply trying to establish that his new employee has the essential and necessary family ties to be trustworthy. He is using family ties as the means to provide closure to the situation. He considers Ms. Thompson's unwillingness to discuss her family background as evasive.

Conversely, in U.S. organizations, social and family relationships are not considered relevant to an employee's ability to do the job. Ms. Thompson is therefore understandably upset by the personal questions. Because she lacks information about the Spanish culture, Ms. Thompson fills in the missing, confusing information incorrectly. She applies her knowledge of the U.S. culture and determines that Mr. Rodrigues's behavior is inappropriate and overly personal. Ms. Thompson's and Mr. Rodrigues's misperceptions of the other's behavior are due to a closure process in which differing cultural perspectives cause the misunderstanding.

FIGURE 5.3
Closure

Our tendency to assume these four lines form a box illustrates closure.

Hot ▼ Link

We discussed high power distance in chapter 3, pp. 81–84.

Summary Point 5.1   **Can You Describe the Perception Process?**

- Perception is the mental process we use to pay attention selectively to some stimuli and cues and not to others.
- The process of sifting through all the information we gather and receive from our social environment, of interpreting all the data, and of making decisions based on our interpretation is called the social perception process.

- Closure allows us to interpret an unclear situation by completing it with our personal, previous experiences and assumptions.
- Culture influences how we see the world and provides us with the tools to interpret a situation, but it can lead to misunderstanding in a situation that requires closure.

THE THREE STAGES OF PERCEPTION

Social perception is a multistage process, as depicted in Figure 5.4. The figure identifies the three stages of perception and the factors that affect each stage. In the following sections, we examine each of the three stages: attention, organization, and interpretation and judgment.

Attention Stage

Attention stage of perception
The selection of stimuli, cues, and signals to which we will pay attention

The first stage of the social perception process involves paying attention to signals from the environment. Who do we notice? What grabs our attention? The **attention stage** involves selection of stimuli, cues, and signals to which we will pay attention. For example, as your professor stops to read his notes for a moment in class, you suddenly may pay attention to the keys he is jiggling in his pocket. That noise may then lead you to pay attention to his particularly baggy pants. If you live in New England, your new boss's Southern accent may capture your attention. An older manager may first notice her new employee's hand tattoo and multiple earrings.

Perceptual filter
The process of letting some information in while keeping out the rest

It is in the attention stage of perception that we consciously and unconsciously select various social cues to which we pay attention. We filter out some information and allow other cues to enter the perceptual process. The process of letting some information in while keeping out the rest is called the **perceptual filter**. At the core of the perceptual filter process is **selective attention**—that is, we pay attention to some, but not all, physical and social cues. We choose among different signals as a result of selective attention.

Selective attention
The process of paying attention to some, but not all, physical and social cues

Salient cues
Those cues that are somehow so striking that they stand out

Many factors determine what makes it through our perceptual filter during the attention stage. Culture is one factor; another is salience.[11] **Salient cues** are those that are in some way so striking that they stand out. We use salient elements and cues more heavily than other cues in our perceptual process.

FIGURE 5.4
The Three Stages of Social Perception

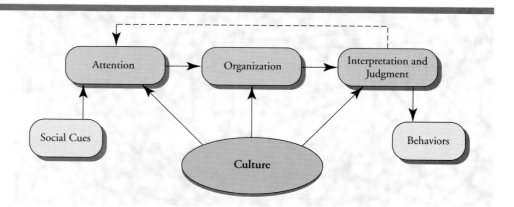

What determines the salience of one cue as opposed to others? All else being equal, we will pay attention to cues that are novel, unusual, brighter, more dynamic, or noisier than others. Marjorie Scardino's Texan accent and the fact that she is one of the few women in a top managerial position in Great Britain both make her salient. People notice her and remember her. Similarly, a tattoo and earrings that may appear mundane for an 18-year-old may be unusual and therefore salient for the older manager.

A new employee is novel by definition, particularly in a department that may not hire many new employees. The other employees' attention will be focused on that new employee. For a while, everyone will remember what he wore, how he talked, what he said, and how he reacted. If he is pleasant, his co-workers will remember it well. If he appears even slightly unfriendly, they quickly label him as such. Being the salient element in the environment, the new employee passes through everybody's perceptual filter. Similar behaviors from other employees are likely to go unnoticed. In such a case, the simplest little slipup or mistake may damage the new person's future in the organization.

Intensity of stimuli is another factor that affects salience. You are likely to pay attention to a loud voice, a brightly colored shirt, or someone's strong perfume. For example, research in perception has shown that those who wear brightly colored clothes are remembered better in meetings. Others pay attention to what they say.[12]

Cultural differences may also make events stand out in our minds. For instance, standing close to others during conversation and touching people you do not know intimately is considered normal in Middle Eastern and Mediterranean cultures. This behavior goes unnoticed in those regions. However, the same behavior is for the most part unusual in the United States where people feel uneasy if a co-worker stands too close while talking to them. The co-worker's behavior is salient—that is, it is something that you are likely to pay attention to and to remember. Her behavior, then, makes it through your perceptual filter.

Salience becomes important during speeches or presentations, when the audience makes a decision about whether to listen to the speaker. Cecilia MacDonald, a public speaking expert who teaches corporate executives to make effective speeches, states: "People make a decision in the first 30 seconds about whether they are going to listen to you."[13] To make her point, she once purposely appeared to be disorganized in making a speech. The audience lost interest in her presentation. "It destroyed my credibility," she noted.[14] The salient point for her audience was her disorganization.

In all these examples, we remember people and make decisions about them because they stand out. Their salience allows them to make it through our perceptual filter. This does not mean that you should necessarily work at making yourself salient so others can remember you better. People may remember you better, but they may also evaluate you in more extreme ways.[15]

Once information breaks through the perceptual filter to grab our attention, we need to organize the cues and information in meaningful sets that we can use later.

Organization Stage

The second stage of the social perception process is **organization.** During this stage we organize the information that the perceptual filter allowed through during the attention stage. We group the information into an orderly and useful whole. We assign the new information to categories that are familiar to us. We create relationships among the various parts and put them in bundles and chunks that we can remember.

The major process at work in this stage is the use of schemas.[16] **Schemas** are mental or cognitive models or patterns that people apply to understand certain situations and events. They are frameworks that allow us to fill in information in social settings. For instance, people use schemas in the closure process to help complete incomplete pictures. Although we may be aware of some of the schemas we hold, they usually operate at a subconscious level.

*Organization stage
of perception*
The organization of information that the perceptual filter allowed through during the attention stage

Schemas
Mental patterns that people apply to explain certain situations and events

Here's an illustration of the schema process. We all have schemas about what happens the first day on a new job. We'll meet with our new boss and co-workers, get a tour of the department or building, be introduced to others, and be told about the job and our assignments. The schemas about "the first day at a new job" tell us what is "normal" and what is not. Based on these schemas, you can determine whether anything unusually positive or negative took place. Not meeting with the boss (who sat in her office all day talking on the phone) would suggest a negative occurrence because it violates the expectations set by the first-day schema.

Schemas in the Balance   Schemas are useful in that they allow us to process information quickly. They help us remember details and complete gaps in information. Using schemas makes us very efficient information organizers. Because they help us organize information, schemas also allow us to remember people and events better. The advantages and disadvantages of schemas are summarized in Figure 5.5.

On the negative side, schemas can lead to error: We use closure too quickly and accept information that seems to fit too readily. Think back to the first-day-on-the-job example. Schemas may prompt us immediately to interpret the boss's failure to greet us as a negative event, even though she simply might have been dealing with a crisis.

Another disadvantage of schemas is their resistance to change. This resistance is due in part to our lack of awareness of the schemas we hold. Another reason is that even when we are aware of schemas, we are not willing to abandon them easily. If you have several years of successful work experience in traditional organizations, you have already formed schemas of an appropriate boss-employee relationship, the way co-workers are supposed to behave, and the role of managers. It's taken time to develop these schemas and you consider them effective. Your schemas might make it difficult for you to accept a team-based, boundaryless structure of a new employer, as this structure is likely to violate your schema in such instances as employees proposing new procedures and work rules without seeking your approval first.

Facing situations that do not fit into our schemas often creates some stress and requires us to pay close attention so that we interpret the new behavior or event correctly.

Hot ▼ Link

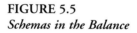

We described boundaryless organizations in chapter 2, pp. 60–62.

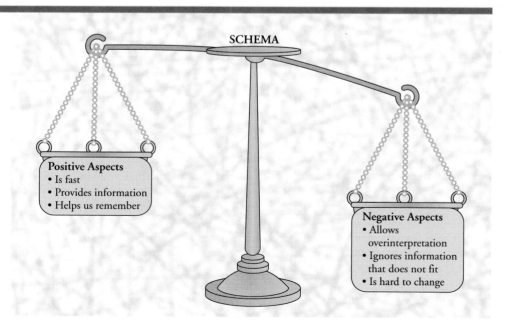

FIGURE 5.5
Schemas in the Balance

SCHEMA

Positive Aspects
• Is fast
• Provides information
• Helps us remember

Negative Aspects
• Allows overinterpretation
• Ignores information that does not fit
• Is hard to change

Schemas and Culture   Our schemas for various situations and events are greatly influenced by our cultural background. In the northeastern part of the United States, interaction among people tends to be more formal and businesslike. In southern states, informality, social hospitality, and politeness are the norm. Crossing borders leads to further changes in our schemas for various situations, as we saw in the example of Ms. Thompson in Spain.

In many parts of the world, formal interaction, respect for authority, and the presence of clear status symbols characterize the boss/employee schema. An employee in India calls his boss by the boss's last name and shows many signs of respect and deference. Because typical U.S. schemas are based on more informal work relationships, the U.S. employee working in India who does not defer to the boss and uses first names is likely to appear rude. His behavior will not fit the Indian schema for boss-employee relationships.

Similarly, the U.S. schema about smiling differs from those of other cultures. In the United States, smiling is a sign of friendship and indicates a person's degree of niceness and happiness. In many Asian cultures, smiling can indicate a lack of seriousness or respect. Particularly, men in many Asian cultures do not smile as much as men in the United States and other Western cultures.[17] The Korean proverb "The man who smiles a lot is not a real man" spotlights how the Korean smiling schemas contrast with beliefs in some Western cultures.

Recently, BankBoston successfully changed the U.S. business and cultural schema associated with loans to inner-city, minority-owned businesses. Gail Snowden, a Radcliffe graduate, is the group executive at BankBoston who convinced the bank to start investing in the poor neighborhoods.[18] Of African-American descent, she had grown up in the Grove Hill area of Boston. She knew that all banks, including hers, ignored the low-income urban neighborhoods. Banking in inner cities was considered too risky. Snowden changed the schema by working with a team to survey the local population about their needs and creating a tailor-made program for the urban dwellers of Boston. Business is so good that the program has been expanded to other New England cities and has won three national ratings for excellence. Michael Porter, a Harvard Business School professor, explains the success of BankBoston's decision: "They've seen beyond the misconceptions and silly assumptions about the inner city."[19]

When interacting with others, we need to be aware that our schemas affect our perceptions. Some information fits into existing schemas and is quickly organized and stored away.

Gail Snowden did not share the commonly held schema regarding banking in inner cities. She therefore implemented a highly successful program that profited both BankBoston and the community.

Other stimuli may not fit any existing schema, however. This new information may lead to the creation of a new schema, or may be forgotten because it contradicts what we already know and we have no ready-made category to help us store it. Once information is organized and stored, we use it to interpret events and people and to make judgments.

Interpretation and Judgment Stage

Interpretation and judgment stage of perception
The clarification and translation of organized information to allow for the attribution of meaning

In the third part of social perception, the **interpretation and judgment stage,** we clarify and translate the information we have organized so we can decide on its meaning, as shown in Figure 5.6. Through interpretation, we also make a judgment or form an opinion about the event or the person. Through judgment, we decide the cause of the behavior.

For instance, you observe that your new employee is being polite and friendly to the people she meets. You wonder whether she is simply behaving as most people would when they start a new job or whether she is a particularly nice person. To decide, you need to assign a cause to her behavior, a process we discuss next.

Attribution process
The process of assigning a cause to a behavior

Internal or personal attributions
The process of assigning a cause to the behavior that is related to internal factors within a person

External or situational attributions
The process of assigning a cause to the behavior that is related to factors external to the person

The Attribution Process   The process of assigning a cause to a behavior is called the **attribution process.**[20] One of the first steps in the attribution process involves deciding whether the cause of a behavior is internal or external. If you make an **internal attribution**, you attribute the cause of behavior to factors within the control of or "inside" the person. These are factors that are permanent or stable (such as personality, values, or natural ability) or less permanent (such as effort or motivation). Because internal attributions refer to the person, they are also called personal attributions.

We make **external attributions** when we think that factors "outside" the person are the cause of behavior. These are factors such as the physical setting, task difficulty, the organizational culture, the presence and behavior of other people, or luck. Because external attributions refer to the situation as the cause of behavior, they are also called situational attributions.

Attributions are a central factor in any social perception process. In managerial situations, most decisions regarding people require managers to make attributions about the cause of behavior, as Figure 5.7 shows. For example, when interviewing a potential employee, managers need to decide whether the person has real talent and potential or whether he is simply well prepared for interviewing but has little real talent.

The same attribution process operates in performance reviews. As we'll see in chapter 6, although some performance data may be objective, managers still need to interpret each employee's performance. Is the best performer bright and hardworking (internal attributions) or just lucky to have landed a big client through pure coincidence (an external attribution)? What about the employee who had a bad year? Was it for lack of effort, lack of ability, a tough territory, or bad luck?

Deciding the cause of behavior—making attributions—is essential in the manager's decision about what to do about an employee's good or bad performance.[21] A manager might

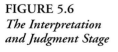

FIGURE 5.6
The Interpretation and Judgment Stage

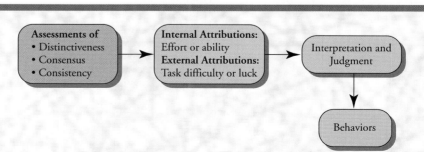

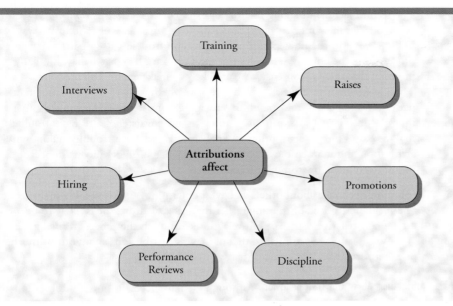

FIGURE 5.7
Attributions in Managerial Decisions

not rank a performer who had top results in an easy territory as high as a person whose performance results were slightly lower but who worked very hard and had a tougher territory. The poor performer who did not try will be rated more harshly than the equally poor performer who tried hard but lacked the necessary training to do the job well. All other personnel decisions regarding raises, training, promotion, discipline, and so forth similarly require managers to make attributions.

As demonstrated by the examples, *effort* and *ability* are used in internal attributions, while *task difficulty* and *luck* are the major factors used in external attributions.[22] When making internal attributions, the cause of behavior can be either how hard the person tried or how capable he or she is. Similarly, external attributions involve assessing the situation in terms of the degree of difficulty of the job performed and uncontrollable factors that affected behavior.

Managers, just like all of us, are likely to overuse internal attributions and underutilize external ones.[23] This means that managers are likely to see their employees' internal characteristics as the cause of their behavior and overlook the power of situations. For example, managers evaluating employees are more likely to assume that lack of ability or lack of effort and motivation are the cause of poor performance. They are much less likely to attribute poor performance to situational factors, such as lack of training, poor support from other employees, poor equipment, or even their own poor leadership.

Information We Use to Make Attributions   When making either internal or external attributions, we use three types of information: distinctiveness, consensus, and consistency.[24]

- First, we consider whether the behavior we are considering is unique or *distinctive* to a particular task or situation. Does the person behave like this in all situations? If yes, then we are likely to attribute the cause of the behavior to the person. If not, then we may consider environmental factors. To show how this factor applies in an organizational setting, a manager evaluating his employees would look at the distinctiveness of employees' performance histories. Do they perform as well at all tasks or is the good performance unique and specific to computer-related tasks? If the performance is a one-shot behavior, and distinctive to a situation, an external attribution is more likely.

- The second factor in making internal or external attributions is *consensus*. Does everybody act the same way or is the person acting in a particularly unusual way? Did everyone in the poor performer's team have trouble with a particular new process or is the employee in question the only one? If others behave similarly, meaning that there is consensus, we are likely to make external attributions.
- The last factor is *consistency*, which refers to whether there is some consistent pattern in the behavior. Depending on what is consistent, we may make either internal or external attributions. If there is no consistency, we have trouble making any kind of attribution. A manager would have trouble making an attribution about an employee whose performance is highly inconsistent from month to month, or from task to task.

Attributions we make about others' behavior determine our actions. If a manager attributes poor performance to lack of training rather than lack of effort, she is likely to be less critical and offer a constructive course of future action. Although the process of making attributions about others is somewhat similar to that of making attributions about our own behaviors and actions, there are several differences that we describe next.

Making Attributions About Our Own Behavior   Although we have access to more information about ourselves than we do about others, researchers have found that we tend to follow the same patterns to decide the cause of our own behavior as we do to decide why others behave as they do.[25] We consider our actions and behaviors and deduce our intentions and attitudes from them. This concept, known as the **self-perception theory,** refers to people's tendency to look for internal and external factors when asked to explain the cause of their own actions.[26]

The self-perception theory of attribution leads to some interesting results. Consider how we explain our actions when we're rewarded for them. Say a highly creative designer just received a high bonus for her creativity. How would she explain the reason for her actions? Would she say she really loves her job or attribute her behavior to the high bonus? How would the employee who often helps other co-workers without getting any tangible reward explain his behavior?

Interestingly, when we receive high tangible external rewards for our actions, such as money or public recognition, we are more likely to see the external reward as the cause of our behavior. Conversely, when there are no clear external rewards, we tend to attribute our behavior to internal causes. The top designer is more likely to tell you that she worked hard because of the bonus rather than for love of her job. The helpful employee who gets no obvious reward will tell you that he really enjoys helping others. The tendency to make external attributions about our own behaviors when an external reward is given is called **overjustification.**[27]

Overjustification has many implications for managers. It suggests that giving people external rewards for doing tasks they enjoy may reduce their internal motivation to do the task. If the reward is large and important enough, people tend to make an external attribution—that is, they see the reward rather than their internal motivation as the cause of their actions.

The implications of overjustification are that, whenever possible, managers should emphasize internal factors and make them salient to maintain employees' internal interest and motivation. Highly public recognition and rewards can provide short-term results, but they may backfire in the long run.

Because we act on the basis of our attributions about others and ourselves, it is essential that our attributions be as correct and objective as possible. Misjudging an employee may have serious legal, ethical, and performance-related consequences. It is important that managers hire, promote, demote, and fire the right person for the right reasons. In the next section, we consider several biases that affect our perception of ourselves and others.

Self-perception theory
A theory suggesting that people make attributions about themselves by looking at their own behavior

Overjustification
The tendency to make external attributions about our own behaviors when an external reward is given

---

Summary Point 5.2   **What Are the Three Stages of the Perception Process?**

- In the first stage of perception, known as the attention stage, we select signals, cues, and stimuli that are salient and ignore the rest through the use of a perceptual filter.
- In the second stage we organize the information that has focused our attention. We often rely on schemas to organize incomplete information.

- The third stage is interpretation and judgment. In that stage, we clarify and translate the information we have organized and decide on its meaning.
- The process of assigning a cause to a behavior is the attribution process. In this stage, we judge whether a behavior is caused by internal or external factors.

■ PERCEPTUAL BIASES

As we saw in Figures 5.1 through 5.3, our perceptual process is far from accurate. At every stage of the perception process, we selectively pay attention to some but not all information, use schemas to organize the data, and make interpretations and judgments about the data that are subject to error. These errors are to a large extent a normal part of the physical and social perceptual processes. However, through identification and awareness, we can manage specific perception errors. In the following sections, we identify several common perception biases, difficulties in overcoming them, and ways to manage them.

Biases

Our perceptual abilities allow us to process a vast amount of information quickly and efficiently. However, this efficiency often leads to ineffective decisions because we do not process the information thoroughly or correctly. Instead we often take cognitive shortcuts, such as ignoring information that does not fit our expectations or making assumptions based on perceptions rather than objective facts. The shortcuts we use to be efficient and that can cause perceptual distortions are known as **perceptual biases.** The biases in turn lead to mistakes in judgment.

> *Perceptual biases*
> *Perceptual distortions, often caused by cognitive shortcuts, that lead to mistakes*

When these biases operate, we stop gathering information and instead rely on our assumptions to fill in the missing information. We explore five perceptual biases that affect organizational behavior: the halo effect, stereotyping, primacy and recency effects, fundamental attribution error, and the self-serving bias.

Halo and Similarity Effects

A bias that usually affects perception during the attention and organization stages is the halo effect.[28] The **halo effect** occurs when a general impression or evaluation of one characteristic of a person or situation creates a halo—a positive impression that becomes the central factor around which all other information is selected, organized, and interpreted. The horn effect is just the opposite. A single trait or occurrence creates a negative impression that colors and influences all other events.

> *Halo effect*
> *A perceptual bias in which one characteristic creates a positive impression that becomes the central factor around which all other information is selected, organized, and interpreted*

A recent study in the United Kingdom indicates that a person's first name, for example, can have a significant impact on how the person is perceived.[29] Another example is someone who is introduced as an "Intel" or "IBM" employee. If Intel or IBM is doing well, a positive halo is created for that person, giving instant credibility. If Intel or IBM is not doing well, however, the introduction creates a negative halo.

A powerful factor that can create a halo is the "similar to me" effect.[30] The **similar-to-me effect** occurs when we develop a liking for a person we perceive to be similar to us or dislike those who are different from us. A lack of similarity can be very serious in cross-cultural situations where the other person is bound to be different.

> *Similar-to-me effect*
> *A perceptual bias that leads us to develop a liking for a person that we perceive is similar to us or to quickly dislike those who are different*

TLC Beatrice CEO Loida Lewis used her creativity and acumen to overcome the "similar to me" effect.

A case in point is the example of Loida Lewis, CEO of TLC Beatrice International Holdings, a major food manufacturer and retailer. Lewis took over the company shortly after her husband died. As a Philippine-born U.S. citizen without much business experience at the head of the largest black-owned firm in the United States, she was different from the other top-level managers based on her gender and ethnicity. As a result, she faced strong negative reactions on many fronts. It took considerable effort for her creativity and outstanding performance to overcome the negative impressions. Her perseverance paid off. The organization is doing well under her stewardship and she was named *Working Woman* magazine's top female CEO.[31]

Halos and horns are triggered automatically as we interact with people. As with other biases, they are not easy to avoid. Being aware of how halos and horns operate and understanding their effect on our perception is one of the best defenses. If we allow them to operate, we will fail to see individual differences in people with whom we work, thereby clouding our judgment about others' behavior.

Stereotype
A generalization about an individual based on one's perception of the group of which the person is a member

Stereotypes   Stereotypes act in much the same way as a halo, but rely on a person's judgment of group characteristics rather than on a single trait. A **stereotype** is a generalization about an individual based on one's perception of the group in which the person is a member. Such groups may include race, gender, sexual orientation, functional area, and so forth. We decide who a person is based on the group to which we think he or she belongs. Stereotypes are so powerful that they can prevent managers from recognizing an employee's individual differences.

Why do stereotypes operate? The main reason is that they allow us to become efficient information processors. Based on our stereotypes, we can quickly select the information we will pay attention to, organize it, and make an interpretation and judgment. We therefore do not have to continue gathering information and can concentrate on other cues.

How do stereotypes operate? If a stereotype is activated in the attention stage, we use it as the basis of our perception and stop gathering information. Because we stop paying attention, we fail to notice information that contradicts the stereotype. Stereotypes also influence the way we interpret and judge a person. For instance, a commonly held stereotype of the Japanese is that they are good at imitation and bad at innovation. If you rely on this stereotype, you are likely to stop collecting information about the creativity of your new Japanese employee. Instead, you may start searching for information that would confirm her inability to innovate.

Consider the challenges that Marjorie Scardino of Pearson PLC faced. As we discussed in the Managerial Challenge, she started as a rodeo barrel racer then moved to newspaper publisher to the *Economist* publisher to CEO of a media conglomerate. Since her first day, the British newspapers have questioned her credentials and her fitness for the job. Some questioned how a mother of three had time to run a multibillion-dollar British conglomerate. Others poked fun at her spouse, calling him "househusband." People even attributed the successful acquisition of All American Communications, Inc., a producer of TV shows such as "Baywatch," to Pearson TV director Greg Dyke rather than to Scardino's strategic and management skills. Scardino has fought back with disarming humor and excellent people-management skills.[32]

Although stereotypes help us process information quickly, they compromise effectiveness and accuracy, often for a long time. Once formed, stereotypes are resistant to change.[33] Recent research indicates that racial and gender stereotypes about African-Americans and women, for instance, continue to be held widely.[34] The comments made about Pearson CEO Scardino illustrate that many people continue to see women as primarily family focused, uninterested in careers, and nonaggressive.[35] Such stereotypes survive in spite of considerable evidence that shows they are inaccurate.[36]

Think back to the example of BankBoston's Gail Snowden. Stereotypes of minorities in inner cities prevented banks from taking advantage of a good business opportunity. Snowden did not rely on such stereotypes. Instead she collected accurate information and designed banking programs that fit the needs of the inner-city customers. Donna Wilson, a member of Snowden's original team, states: "She told us we had a responsibility to the people we serve and said, 'We do not have the luxury of failure.'"[37] Snowden's success depended on her personal knowledge of the poor neighborhoods and her savvy in overcoming the misperceptions of her peers at BankBoston. She decided to downplay the social cues of poverty and bad loan risks, and instead "went out and quickly proved that we could do well by doing good," says Chad Gifford, BankBoston's CEO.[38]

A QUESTION OF ETHICS

Whistle Blowing or Political Correctness?

You are aware that a manager in your department holds strong negative stereotypes about African-Americans. The manager makes numerous jokes and other derogatory comments in private conversations. Although you cannot point to specific instances where his bias has affected his business decisions, you are uncomfortable with his behavior and worried about its implications for your organization. What should you do? Explain your answer.

Primacy and Recency Primacy and recency are two other perceptual biases.[39] The **primacy effect** is a perceptual bias that leads people to overemphasize early information. For instance, we remember our first impressions of others and they color our later perceptions. The early information, then, provides an organizing structure that influences other perceptual stages. In some sense, the first impression becomes a halo or horn that affects later information gathering and interpretation of a person's behavior.

The primacy effect suggests that the new employee who makes a bad impression on the first day of work will have a hard time overcoming the early mistakes. As a matter of fact, research indicates that most of us form a strong and long-lasting impression in the first few minutes after we meet someone. Cecilia MacDonald, the public speaking expert who pretended to be unprepared, felt the impact of primacy effect. Many people who saw her perform that skit couldn't alter their first impression. "Some people thought it was funny, but most thought I was disorganized." To avoid the negative impact of the primacy effect, she's never done a similar skit.[40]

The flip side of the primacy effect is the **recency effect**, whereby we pay attention to the most recent information at the expense of earlier data. The recency effect takes place most

Primacy effect
A tendency to overemphasize early information

Recency effect
A tendency to overemphasize the most recent information rather than earlier data

often when there is a time lag between the early and later information. For instance, say a manager has not had much contact with an employee during recent months. The manager is likely to base her performance evaluation on the employee's activities on the latest project, without giving enough weight to earlier examples of work and performance.

Similar to halos and stereotypes, primacy and recency effects bias our perception mostly at the attention and organization stages. They provide organizing structures that influence the other information that is gathered and how it is organized. Although these effects have a strong influence on our interpretation and judgment and our attributions about people, the attribution process itself is subject to specific biases that we consider next.

Fundamental Attribution Error We mentioned earlier our tendency to underestimate situational factors and overestimate personal factors when making attributions about others' actions. This tendency is called the **fundamental attribution error**.[41] For example, if your boss is unresponsive, you are more likely to blame the behavior on his lack of interpersonal skills than the organizational pressures and deadlines he faces. Similarly, you are more likely to attribute the uncooperative behavior of a fellow manager to her personality rather than to a lack of time. We tend not to give people the benefit of the doubt.

Fundamental attribution error
The tendency to underestimate situational factors and overestimate personal factors when making attributions about others' actions

An interesting research finding is that the fundamental attribution error works in reverse when we are looking for causes of our own behavior. When we explain our own actions, we rely more on external attributions. This process is called the **actor-observer difference**.[42] Observers, those who perceive others, tend to make internal attributions about the cause for the behavior of those they observe. However, actors make external attributions about their own behavior. The reason for the different attributions is that access to different types of information leads to different perspectives.[43] In contrast to observers, actors have information about their own history and how they behave in different situations. As a result, they have views of the distinctiveness and consistency of their behavior that are likely to differ from observers' views. Because of the different perspectives, environmental factors are more salient to the actor than to the observer, so an actor is more likely to make external attributions.

Actor-observer difference
The tendency to rely more on external attributions when explaining our own actions

Consider the case of a relatively new employee who has just had a run-in with a client. The employee knows from his prior encounters with other clients in previous jobs that this particular client is rude, difficult, and overly demanding. The employee has been in sales for many years and has rarely run into this type of trouble. He also knows that the recent illness of his father has created a lot of stress for him and contributed to his uncharacteristic temper flare-up. The employee knows that his behavior is distinctive and has low consistency. From his point of view, the client's rudeness is the focus. These factors all lead the employee to decide that the cause of the problem is the client, an external attribution, not himself.

The situation looks different to the boss. She does not yet have extensive information about her new employee's style or performance. Because the client may have called and complained about the employee's lack of responsiveness, her attention will be focused on the complaint and the employee. Another factor that could affect her perception is that reports of conflicts with clients are uncommon. The manager who observes the situation makes an internal attribution about the cause of the employee's behavior. She may decide that he is inexperienced and needs training or that he is impatient and not well suited for this type of job (both internal attributions). Because she has little to no information about the employee's prior behavior, the employee is salient in the situation, and his behavior has low consensus.

The example illustrates how the actor-observer difference and the fundamental attribution error can lead to poor judgment, disagreement, and misunderstanding. Awareness of the bias can help managers avoid these pitfalls. Managers can also take extra steps to overcome the bias. In our case, for instance, the employee and the manager could resolve their differences with an exchange of information, more objective data collection, good listening, and more experience working together.

Self-Serving Bias   Although actors are quick to make external attributions about their own short-comings, they are also quick to accept credit—an internal attribution—when they succeed. The tendency to accept credit for success and reject blame for failures is called the **self-serving bias**.[44]

On the one hand, when we do poorly on a test, mess up a presentation, lose a client, or fail to achieve our goals on the job, we blame situational factors rather than make an internal attribution about our own lack of effort or ability. We perceive the unfair professor, the inattentive audience, the demanding client, or the unreasonable company goals as the cause of our poor performance. On the other hand, we tend to believe we are successful because we are smart and work hard. Few of us give credit readily or completely to our boss's coaching and motivational skills or to simply having been lucky when we perform well.

You can see many examples of the self-serving bias operating in the business press. Have you noticed how often business executives take credit for the success of their firms, but blame the economy, the competitors, the global market, the value of the dollar, the government, or some other external factors for poor performance and failure?

The upheaval at Apple Computer is a prime example. Three CEOs made serious errors in judgment about the future of personal computing. First, Apple's co-founder and CEO, Steven Jobs, adamantly refused to allow outside suppliers access to the Apple operating system so that they could build programs for the Macintosh. Then, executives who followed Jobs made other marketing and pricing errors that led to the firing of the third CEO in late January 1996. In 1997 Apple's board of directors asked Steven Jobs to return and "reinvent" the company.

Each of the CEOs blamed the competition for their failures on the job rather than admit that they misjudged the situation or made bad decisions. Jobs, for example, stated that "IBM is going to take over—it'll be the greatest monopoly of all time, like owning every oil company and car company."[45] In 1988 John Sculley, then CEO of Apple, decided that Microsoft was a competitor that could not be trusted. He refused to cooperate with Microsoft and instead filed a lawsuit against that company, claiming copyright infringement. In 1997, however, Apple reversed its position, announcing a major cooperative effort between Apple and Microsoft.[46] In all instances, Apple CEOs found external factors to blame for their mistakes.

The combination of the fundamental attribution error, the actor-observer difference, and the self-serving bias makes for interesting interaction between managers and their employees. On the one hand, managers blame poor performance on their employees' lack of skills and effort whereas the employees blame it on poor leadership skills. On the other hand, both will tend to believe that their own ability and hard work led to success and forget to give the other side much credit.

Given the amount of information we have to process, being efficient is necessary and desirable. Perceptual and attribution biases allow us to be efficient and quick in our social perception, but they can also cause errors. In the following sections, we investigate the reasons that overcoming biases is so difficult.

Self-serving bias
A person's tendency to accept credit for success and reject blame for failures

---

Summary Point 5.3   **Can You Identify Key Perceptual Biases?**

- The halo (horn) effect occurs when a positive (negative) impression colors all other perceptions.
- Stereotypes are broad generalizations about a person based on perceptions of the group in which the person is a member.
- Primacy occurs when we give early information too much weight; recency occurs when we overemphasize more recent information.

- Fundamental attribution error refers to the overuse of internal attributions.
- Actors tend to overuse external attributions about their behavior; observers rely more on internal attributions about actors.
- Taking credit for personal successes and blaming failure on external causes is called the self-serving bias.

Change Challenge

PERCEIVING OTHERS
THROUGH ELECTRONIC VIBES . . .

Ten years ago, few organizations required employees to use e-mail. Today, e-mail and electronic chatrooms are commonplace. This change poses challenges in how we perceive and interact with others. Does the use of e-mail mean that we'll have fewer perceptual biases? The answers are mixed. On one hand, the absence of facial expressions and tone of voice can lead to serious error. On the other hand, instead of reacting to a person, workers react to the person's ideas. If we cannot see the person we're dealing with, we aren't prone to stereotypes that are triggered by sight. There may also be fewer opportunities to form a halo or horn. Additionally, e-mail provides more time for people to react to one another, cool down if upset, and write a response when ready.

The use of technology creates its own perceptual challenges. Some biases might be eliminated, but others increase. Use of certain fonts and bolding has special meanings for Internet enthusiasts. Capital letters can suggest that the party is angry and shouting. A black background on the screen means "mourning."

Issues of who gets what message are also confusing and give way to more rather than fewer misperceptions. A private e-mail intended for one person may be forwarded to hundreds of others. Now try to explain that you didn't mean what you wrote. For technology to help us be objective and reduce biases, the rules of interaction and etiquette must be well defined. We also can't make assumptions about this communication medium. It still requires that we use selective attention, organization, and interpretation. E-mail, then, is still subject to perceptual biases.

E-mail requires a new etiquette (known as netiquette) that is not fully developed and is often unknown to various users.[a] Therefore, organizations that use e-mail should provide their employees with training to help them understand the rules, benefits, and pitfalls of this new communication medium.

a. H. Row, "It's (Real) Time to Talk," *Fast Company* (June–July 1998): 218.

Difficulty in Overcoming Biases

Now that we are aware of the potential biases in perception, why can't we simply avoid them? As we see in Figure 5.8, four factors make this task harder than it looks. In addition, once biases affect perception, recognizing them and preventing their negative effect can be difficult.

First, people have a *need for consistency* that pushes them to look for information that supports their assumptions and beliefs.[47] As a result, they either avoid looking for or ignore information that disproves their perceptual biases because it does not fit their existing views. These avoidance techniques give people a greater sense of control over events. For instance, managers who have already decided to open an international branch office may look only for positive information that confirms their decision and ignore any contradictory input.

Phenomenal absolutism
Believing that what you perceive is objective reality

Second, **phenomenal absolutism,** defined as believing that what you perceive is objective reality rather than your interpretation of reality, makes it hard to recognize the impact of biases in social perception. Research indicates that phenomenal absolutism influences many behaviors and social interactions. For instance, people tend to look for support for their inter-

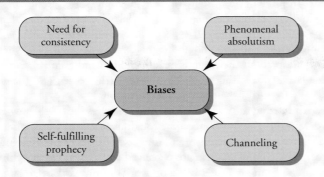

FIGURE 5.8
Difficulties in Overcoming Biases

pretation of events rather than seeking other points of view. Most of us are skilled at looking for and gathering information that supports our perception. Our need for consistency, phenomenal absolutism, and pressures for efficiency contribute to this type of information search. Too many stimuli beg for our attention. The sooner we can organize and interpret one issue, the sooner we can tackle another.

Third, *channeling* reinforces our biases.[48] **Channeling** is the process of limiting our interaction with another so that we avoid receiving information that contradicts our judgment. Channeling is also called confirmatory hypothesis testing because we set up the situation to confirm our hypotheses about others.

For example, if you dislike someone, you may not interact with or may be aloof toward her. Because of your actions, the other person is likely to behave in cold and unfriendly ways, thereby providing you with further confirmation of your perception. In another instance, a manager's perception that a Japanese subordinate lacks creativity may lead her to assign the employee routine tasks. The employee, then, does not have the chance to demonstrate his creativity. The manager has channeled the employee's behavior to confirm her perceptions.

Channeling can have a profound effect on organizational behavior. For example, research indicates that women are generally perceived by both male and female managers to be less competent, less capable of leading, and more likely to quit because of family pressures. In response, many managers behave in ways that confirm these perceptions. They provide women with fewer training opportunities, limited exposure to diverse experiences, and more routine, less challenging assignments. In many professions, women are bypassed for key promotions because the position requires that they supervise men. Is it any surprise that many women quit their less-challenging, less-upwardly mobile jobs? Organizations that channel women's behavior because of gender stereotypes assure that the stereotypes become reality. The serious legal implications aside, the potential missed opportunities are costly and the organization is the ultimate loser.[49]

To prevent channeling and its negative effects, Coopers & Lybrand, a major accounting firm, instituted specific programs to encourage women to receive promotions to top positions. The company established a mentoring program for women and sensitivity training for all employees to ensure its goals were met. Linda A. Hoffman, a managing partner, states: "Many of the things you must do to succeed are more comfortable for men than women."[50]

Perceptual biases can cause serious errors in judging others. The fourth reason it is difficult to overcome our biases is one of the most powerful effects of perceptual biases. The **Pygmalion effect** or **self-fulfilling prophecy** refers to one's expectations and perceptions becoming reality because of the strength of the original expectation. Pygmalion is a Greek mythological sculptor who fell madly in love with the beautiful female statue he had carved and named Galatea. The strength of his love and his prayers to the goddess Aphrodite brought

Channeling, or confirmatory hypothesis testing
The process by which we limit people's interactions with us so their behaviors support our expectations

Pygmalion effect, or self-fulfilling prophecy
The process by which one's expectations and perceptions become reality because of the strength of the original expectations

his creation to life. In modern life, the myth of Pygmalion is used to describe the process by which our beliefs and expectations influence others' behaviors to the point that they behave as we originally expected. Our prophecy or expectations fulfill themselves.[51]

Early demonstration and research about this process showed that when teachers were given bogus information about their pupils' reading ability and even IQ scores, their expectations matched the false scores rather than the children's true scores, and the children's performance began actually to mirror their teachers' expectations.

Other research relating the concept to management has shown the power of a manager's expectations in determining performance.[52] Through a variety of verbal and nonverbal messages and behaviors, managers consciously and unconsciously communicate their expectations to their employees. The employees who are perceived to have potential, who have a positive halo, or who are similar to the manager based on work or non-work-related factors are treated differently from those who are not on the "A list." Those who are expected to succeed are assigned more challenging tasks; benefit from clearer communication and more frequent, more positive feedback; and are coached more actively. Those who are not expected to succeed typically do not receive any of these benefits. Both groups are rewarded further for confirming the original stereotypes (channeling) and any actions and behaviors that do not fit expectations are ignored, forgotten, or explained away. Eventually, employees in both groups confirm the manager's expectations.

The self-fulfilling prophecy can have positive effects as well. Consider the example of AES, an independent producer of electrical power based in Arlington, Virginia. Dennis Bakke, the co-founder of the company, sets extremely high expectations for his employees and they always meet those goals. AES employees are trusted to make multimillion-dollar decisions on their own. In turn, AES managers have high employee expectations. One employee, Carlos Baldi, explains his relationship with his director, Oscar Prieto: "[Freedom] was very scary at the beginning. Every time I had to make a decision, I thought, 'Should I call Oscar?' But he just said, 'You know better than I do—you decide.'"

Pietro decided that AES employees in Argentina should be empowered to help meet his high expectations. "We broke all the rules. No overtime. No bosses. No time records. No shift schedules. No assigned responsibilities. No administration. And guess what? It worked! It's a matter of believing in people."[53] AES is growing rapidly and profitably partly because of its managers' high expectations of performance and trust in their employees. Their expectations create a positive self-fulfilling prophecy.

Self-fulfilling prophecies can have positive effects. Management at AES trusts its employees such as Allessandra Marinheiro. Employees in turn have the freedom to make fast, effective decisions.

Perceptual biases in organizational settings have serious repercussions. The organization may not treat individuals fairly and may be held legally accountable as a consequence. Additionally, the organization may be deprived of potentially high performers and saddled with poor performers. For example, if several top managers' negative stereotypes of workers 55 and older result in older workers being passed over for promotions or being fired, the organization may never be able to take advantage of marketing to and developing products for the older large market segment.

Allstate Insurance works hard to make sure biases do not affect its hiring and promotion decisions. It surveys its 50,000 employees quarterly on how its managers are meeting the organization's goal of developing and promoting employees regardless of race and gender. Chuck Martin, an African-American, holds the company's top sales position. How do efforts to eliminate bias and increase diversity benefit the business? Allstate has become the nation's top property insurer for Hispanics and African-Americans.[54]

The social perception process is by nature subjective, so it is bound to have some biases and errors. Although biases cannot be avoided entirely, awareness of potential pitfalls of the social perception process can help managers minimize errors and help turn potential problems into advantages. In addition, managers and employees must learn to actively manage the perceptual process.

Summary Point 5.4   **Why Do People Have Difficulty Overcoming Biases?**

- People have a need for consistency that leads to a sense of control when their expectations are supported.
- Phenomenal absolutism is believing that what you perceive is objective reality.

- Channeling, or confirmatory hypothesis testing, is the process by which we limit people's interactions with us so their behaviors support our expectations.
- Self-fulfilling prophecy refers to the process by which a person's expectations and perceptions of others become reality.

Managing Biases

Individuals and organizations can take four key steps to reduce the negative effects of perceptual biases and to improve decision making.

1. *Recognize the biases.* In this first step, managers teach people to recognize biases through informal or formal training. For instance, this chapter should help you identify situations in which your decisions were or might be affected by perceptual biases. Cross-cultural and diversity training is a specialized type of training that can help manage cultural stereotypes and attribution biases. For instance, diversity training encourages participants to identify and express their stereotypes and work on developing alternative views.

2. *Develop awareness of the areas and situations in which biases are most likely to operate.* Training helps to develop this awareness. Training and awareness alone are usually insufficient, however. You may be quite sensitive to perceptual biases immediately after reading this chapter but may find that in a few weeks or months you've forgotten about them.

3. *Offer constant reminders and support.* Colleagues and leaders in organizations need to offer reminders and support to prevent managers and employees from reverting to biases. Repeatedly and consistently, leaders need to discourage negative biases and reinforce the positive aspects of any stereotyped

MANAGERIAL ADVICE
from the Experts

MANAGING PERCEPTIONS

Managing the perceptual process is essential for managers. Some practical advice follows:

- Be aware that perceptions are by definition selective and biased. They provide only part of the picture.
- Increase your contact and opportunities to observe your employees so that you will develop a more complete picture of them.
- Collect objective data whenever possible. Facts and figures are less subject to biases than impressions.
- Seek additional information from many different sources including customers, co-workers, and other managers.
- Obtain training in interviewing and performance appraisal through your organization, workshops, personal research, and reading.

groups. Consider the case of Denny's restaurants, where the top management failed to convey a message of nondiscrimination. As a result, the company received bad publicity and faced many lawsuits when patrons perceived that Denny's employees acted in a discriminatory manner.

4. *Provide opportunities for frequent contact.* The organization should offer frequent contact with members of stereotyped groups as well as training to further minimize biases.[55]

Perception is the way we gather information about the world around us. Every day managers rely on their perceptions to make decisions about hiring, training, promotion, raises, discipline, and so forth. Because perception is inherently biased and subject to error, managers must understand the perception process, be aware of the potential pitfalls and problem areas, and actively manage the process. With recognition, awareness, constant reminders, and frequent contact with others, managers can make better decisions about employees' behavior. Now we turn our attention to two managerial applications of the perceptual process: managing the image we project to others and evaluating performance.

Summary Point 5.5 How Can We Overcome Biases?

- Recognizing biases is the first method anyone can use to limit the use and the impact of biases.
- People should be made aware of the effect of biases and how they use them.
- Following initial training and awareness, there must be constant reminders.
- Another way to overcome biases is by frequent contact with members of groups being stereotyped.

IMAGE MANAGEMENT: HYPOCRISY OR WISE MANAGEMENT?

Most of us can remember a co-worker who received kudos despite poor performance or another who didn't get any credit in spite of excellent work. We may also know of managers who get promoted without fully deserving it and others who are highly effective but go unnoticed. We often attribute such situations to politics: "Who you know is more important than what you know." However, the cause may not be so simple. Most of these situations present complex challenges in managing social perception.

Impression management is the act of consciously, carefully monitoring and managing the impression we make on others. A key aspect of impression management is **self-presentation,** which refers to the actions we take to control the impressions we present. Being effective is one thing. Having others, particularly your supervisors, recognize that you are a good performer, is another. If all this sounds like something you consider somehow "shady," downright unethical, or manipulative, consider the legitimate corporate public relations efforts aimed at managing the impression we have of organizations.

Almost all major companies in the United States have public relations departments that actively manage their public image. For example, Salt River Project (SRP), a major utility company in the southwestern United States, has implemented a number of family-friendly human resource policies that give flexibility to working parents. The company's policies benefit employees, their families, and the company. How does SRP benefit? Aside from attracting top-notch employees, SRP can tout its community spirit in a well-managed corporate public relations campaign.[56]

Impression management is about self-presentation and the roles we play in our professional life.[57] Behave like a confident, fair professional and others are likely to treat you that way. If, however, you appear unsure or biased, those around you will treat you accordingly, eventually creating a self-fulfilling prophecy. Scardino, profiled in the Managerial Challenge, uses her stereotypical image as an easygoing Southern woman to charm the British company she leads and the press. She also consciously cultivates the stereotypes of Americans as relaxed and informal to further reinforce her image as an approachable manager.

Impression management
The act of consciously, carefully monitoring and managing the impression we make on others

Self-presentation
The actions we take to control the impressions we present

Managing Impressions Through Self-Presentation

Social scientists frequently compare self-presentation to theatrical appearances.[58] Just as with a play, many of us prepare thoroughly for our role in an important social interaction. We consider what to wear, the setting, some conversation topics, and so forth. We should also consider who our audience is. For instance, when preparing for a job interview, you gather information about the company's products and reputation, learn more about the interviewer, and have information about the company's mission and organizational culture. This audience information allows you to tailor your presentation to make a good impression. Few of us would consider this careful preparation unethical or shady.

The goal of impression management is to appear in the most positive light so that we can better achieve our goals. Impression management does not mean that people lie about themselves or present an exaggerated image of who they are. It simply means that they make an effort to present themselves well. In a work setting, the three critical components in impression management are the person's *competence*, *role*, and *verbal and nonverbal messages*, as we see in Figure 5.9.

- *Competence* is the most important aspect of impression management.[59] Credible past and current performance signals competence to others. To make a good impression, we must first perform well. There must be substance to back up the

FIGURE 5.9
Components of Impression Management

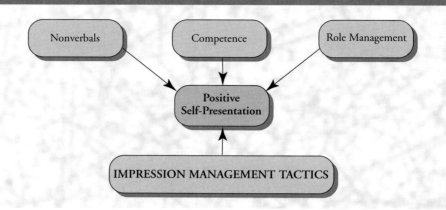

image. Without competent behavior to support our self-presentation, impression management borders on unethical conduct.

- *Clarifying roles* is the second aspect of managing impressions. You must let others know your role—that is, let them know the characteristics of your expected behavior in the organization. Your boss, co-workers, and employees should know what you are expected to do and what the boundaries of your job and responsibilities are.

- *Clear and consistent messages,* verbal and nonverbal, must accompany self-presentation. Verbal messages include the content and tone of what we say and how we say it. **Nonverbal messages** are communications we make without using language. We send them through our demeanor, facial expressions, and body posture. What do I say? How do I say it? How do I carry myself? Is my office organized or messy? Am I dressed appropriately? Do I maintain eye contact? These verbal and nonverbal messages must fit the role.

Nonverbal messages
Communications sent without using language

Tactics of Impression Management

Once we establish competence, clarify our roles, and send clear and consistent messages, we can further manage impressions by using four general tactics as outlined in Table 5.1.[60] The first tactic is to emphasize similarities. The goal of this tactic is to encourage others to like us. For example, we can stress similar interests. That is, a salesperson might talk with a client

T a b l e   5 . 1   **IMPRESSION MANAGEMENT TACTICS**

Tactic	Description	Goal
• Emphasizing similarity	Highlight similarity in goals, interests, hobbies, and so forth and behave in style and manner similar to those of the person with whom you are ineracting.	Encourage others to like you because of your similarity to them.
• Conforming to situation	Behave in ways the situation requires.	Appear appropriate.
• Self-promotion	Present yourself in a positive light.	Appear competent.
• Ingratiation	Flatter the other person by presenting him or her in a positive light.	Be liked.

about the common interest they have in golf. An employee could highlight how much he likes the outdoor activities his boss enjoys. We can also emphasize similar styles by matching our style with that of the other person. If the person is outgoing and loud, we draw on our most extroverted self; if she is quiet and reserved, we accentuate the introverted aspects of our own personality.

A second method of impression management is to conform to the requirements of the situation. The goal of conforming is to appear appropriate. In a business meeting, we conduct ourselves in a professional manner similar to the style and actions of those in charge of the meeting. During a job interview, the interviewee pays attention to cues from the interviewer about how formal to be and what type of behavior is suitable.

Note that for the first two tactics in impression management a critical skill is the ability to read cues from others and the situation. Careful observation with a keen eye for reading situations—such as those with high self-monitoring tendencies—can be very helpful in self-presentation and impression management.

The third tactic for impression management is **self-promotion,** which refers to a person's presenting positive information about himself or herself to appear competent. Too much self-promotion can make a person appear egotistical and vain; too little can lead to lack of recognition. The key to successful self-promotion is to select the right context, make sure that one's accomplishments support the claim of competence, and use modesty wisely. Boasting is most effective when done in response to questions or requests and with some level of self-deprecation.

Research suggests that many women aren't effective at self-promotion, which may be due to their socialization as young girls. Traditionally, girls are taught to be quiet, smile, avoid conflict, build consensus, and make sure their physical appearance is feminine. As a result, female managers and employees often do not speak their minds. They make self-deprecating statements such as "I am not the expert" or "I may be wrong" before they state their opinions. In the business world, many feminine traits that young girls learn to exhibit early in life are perceived as signs of incompetence and lack of confidence.[61]

Colgate-Palmolive executive Carla Alani did not like to promote herself. She often sat quietly in meetings and folded her arms. "That sends the message, 'Why should you listen to little ol' me?'"[62] Her competent performance went unnoticed because of perceptual biases and poor impression management. With training, however, she learned how to create a more positive, strong impression.

The last tactic for impression management is **ingratiation,** the process of presenting another person in a positive light. The goal of ingratiation, like that of emphasizing similarities, is to be liked by the other person. However, it can easily backfire when exaggerated or used out of context. Ingratiation must be sincere or it is likely to fail.

Given the power of impressions and phenomenal absolutism (believing what you perceive to be reality), active management of the impressions others have of you is an essential part of being effective. A person who plans to use impression management tactics must also anticipate the consequences of his or her actions. If used to deceive and develop inaccurate impressions, the tactics of impression management are not only unethical but also likely to backfire. If they are used to assure that reality and perception match, their use is both legitimate and helpful.

Job seekers and businesses rely on impression management skills to gain a competitive advantage. Many business schools provide their graduates with interview training programs that teach them how to present themselves effectively and convey a positive impression to the interviewer. All else being equal, those who make a better impression have a greater chance of being hired. Continental Airlines and uniform manufacturer UniFirst Corporation of Boston send their employees to courses on etiquette, including conversation skills, so they can provide better services to and make more positive impressions on customers.[63] Polaroid, Pruden-

Hot ▼ Link

We discussed self-monitoring in chapter 4, pp. 125–27.

Self-promotion
An impression management tactic in which one presents positive information about oneself to appear competent

Ingratiation
The process of presenting another person in a positive light

tial Insurance, and Novell send their high-potential female managers to an outside company that teaches women how to adjust their behavior and better manage their self-presentation in the business world.[64]

Poor impression management can have dire consequences for managers. Consider the case of Phoenix-based America West Airlines' executives who in the early 1990s guided their company out of bankruptcy after financial restructuring and employee layoffs. In 1995, these executives asked the bankruptcy court in Arizona to grant them a considerable pay raise. The executives claimed the bankruptcy made it harder to manage the organization so their jobs were more demanding. At the same time, other employees were asked to make wage concessions. Employees were outraged and the press had a field day. One other detail: These were the same managers who, through their own questionable expansion decisions, had driven the firm into bankruptcy. What kind of impression do you think these executives made on the firm's stakeholders?

Summary Point 5.6   What Is Impression Management?

- Impression management is the conscious and careful monitoring and management of the impression we make on others.
- The three factors of impression management in a work setting are establishing credibility through competence,

understanding your role, and monitoring verbal and nonverbal communication.
- The four tactics of impression management are establishing similarity, conforming to situations, self-promotion, and ingratiation.

A QUESTION OF ETHICS

| *Exaggeration or a Lie?* | You are interested in working for a company that does extensive business in Central and South American countries. You know that being fluent in Spanish will give you an edge. You are currently taking a Spanish course that will improve your basic knowledge of the language. Since you expect to be fluent by the time you actually get the job, you decide to write in your resume that you are fluent in Spanish. Is this legitimate positive self-presentation or is it unethical? |

The issues of how we perceive others and how we manage the impressions we project intersect in the area of performance evaluation. Managers perceive others and evaluate employees based on those perceptions. Those who are evaluated must manage impressions to obtain a good evaluation. Next we discuss the impact of social perception in the performance evaluation process.

 EVALUATING PERFORMANCE

Social perception in general and attribution in particular affect many managerial decisions, as we saw in Figure 5.7. For example, our perceptions are a critical part of the interview and hiring process. Another managerial decision-making area that perception affects directly is performance evaluation. That area includes decisions about items such as compensation, promotions, or disciplinary actions.

To evaluate employees fairly, managers must recognize that performance evaluation depends to a great extent on how they perceive others and themselves, and how their employees manage impressions. In the upcoming sections, we review the impact of perception on the evaluation process, the three methods used to evaluate employees, and ways to reduce perceptual biases in performance reviews.

Performance Evaluation Methods

Performance evaluation has two goals. The first is employee *evaluation*; the second, employee *development*.[65] Evaluation allows a manager to assess an employee's past performance and predict future performance. Results are used to allocate raises, decide on promotions, and identify high- and low-potential employees.

Development guides future performance. Unfortunately, development is often given short shrift because it requires managers to assess employee and organizational needs; assist with career planning; and have a strategic, long-term view of the organization. These activities take time and training that few managers have. As a result, managers may miss opportunities to motivate employees and improve their performance.

The three methods of performance evaluation are traits, behaviors, and outcomes. Because of the emphasis in industry practice, our discussion of these three methods concentrates on the evaluative, rather than the development, component.

Three General Approaches   The first performance evaluation method is the **trait method** in which managers rate employees on individual personality traits. Though personality assessment was once a major part of employee evaluation, it is now usually combined with evaluation of objective data concerning work-related behaviors and outcomes to reduce the effect of perceptual biases.

Trait method
A performance evaluation method in which managers rate employees on individual personality traits

The three individual traits most often used in employee performance appraisal are reliability, loyalty, and general motivation and energy. Although traits continue to be part of many performance evaluations, such methods have been criticized for being subjective and ambiguous. As our discussion of perceptual biases shows, halos, stereotypes, self-serving biases, and so forth can all affect managers' views of an employee's reliability or loyalty. For example, a manager is more likely to consider an employee to be reliable and loyal if the employee is similar to the manager. Racial and gender stereotypes can further affect whether women and minorities are considered loyal and reliable.

The **behavioral method** of performance evaluation focuses on work-related behaviors rather than personality traits. For example, instead of rating an employee's reliability (a personal trait), the behavioral method would ask specific questions about work behavior that relates to reliability, such as these:

Behavioral method
A performance evaluation method that focuses on work-related behaviors

- Does the employee come to work on time?
- Does he or she complete work by deadlines?
- Does the person provide assistance and guidance to co-workers?

The behavioral approach has two main advantages. First, it is more objective and precise than the trait method because managers can measure behaviors objectively. Rather than rating an employee low on reliability and loyalty because of tardiness, for instance, a manager using the behavioral approach would state that the employee was late 15 days last month. Second, the behavioral approach is more legally defensible than the trait approach because behaviors can be tied clearly to performance.

In spite of clear advantages, the behavioral method also has several disadvantages. First among them is the difficulty and cost of developing a precise and accurate list of relevant work-related behaviors. Every job may require a separate set of behavioral ratings that is likely to change over time. The organization must then review and revise the evaluation form continually. Additionally, behaviors alone may not accurately measure performance in complex jobs. For example, the social skills and personal relationships that many experienced salespeople use cannot be broken down easily into a set of behaviors. Similarly, the intuition that many effective internal auditors use to investigate potential accounting problems cannot be described behaviorally.

Outcome approach
A performance evaluation method that considers the results employees achieve

Focus on outcome helps overcome some of the problems with both the trait and the behavioral approaches of performance evaluation. The **outcome approach** considers the results employees achieve. Such results include amount of sales, number of products made, number of clients processed, number of errors, and so on. One advantage of the outcome approach is that it can provide clear criteria for performance of simple and complex jobs. Second, because results are generally measured objectively—for instance, number of units sold or amount of revenue generated—the potential for perceptual errors is greatly reduced.

As with the other two methods, the outcome method has disadvantages. The outcome method is difficult to apply to jobs that do not have easy-to-measure outcomes. Delivering quality service has become a motto for many service organizations. However, even with constant customer survey and feedback, establishing whether quality service has been achieved is a subjective, not an objective, determination. Another disadvantage of an outcome-oriented performance evaluation is that it ignores the long-term job process. Although reliance on outcomes clarifies the link between performance and outcome, the outcomes tend to be short-term ones (what did the employee achieve in three, six, or 12 months?). This short-term focus discourages employees from developing work processes that are beneficial in the long term.

For instance, individual salespeople may be highly successful in an outcome-oriented system that rewards quarterly sales. But such a system may not reward employees who cooperate with other salespeople, share information, or obtain training in new sales methods and technology. All these factors may not have an immediate effect on quarterly sales but can benefit the organization in the long run. The organization, then, creates a culture that discourages employees from planning and thinking about long-term effects.

Which System Should Managers Use? Each of the three major approaches—traits, behaviors, and outcomes—has clear advantages and disadvantages, so which method is preferable? The answer is, managers should understand the three methods in enough depth to combine them in a manner that suits the job.

A helpful way for managers to think about combining the three approaches is to visualize the evaluation process. Recall the open systems concept discussed in chapter 1. The three performance evaluation methods mirror the open systems framework. Traits are what an individual brings into the job; they are the input. Behaviors are actions that get the job done; they are the process. Outcomes are the output of the work. Just as understanding an organization requires consideration of the whole system, evaluating performance requires consideration of the input, process, and output factors. The weight that a manager places on each factor depends on the specific job.

Hot ▼ Link

We discussed open systems in chapter 1, pp. 15–17.

Honeywell's performance evaluation system demonstrates how managers can blend the three evaluation approaches. In the division that makes various industrial control mechanisms, managers are rated first on their performance on maintaining product quality, cost, and inventory levels. These are all measurable outcomes. Next, they are rated on general behaviors that include teamwork, selection, training, and motivation of other employees, attendance, availability, and punctuality. In addition, managers consider some trait-oriented questions such as initiative, judgment, and openness to feedback. The form ends with an assessment of general strengths and weaknesses and future development areas.

The Honeywell evaluation process has taken time and money to develop. Because of the size of the company, there is a wide range of jobs. Honeywell must therefore develop numerous performance evaluation tools suitable for each type of job at great cost. Although smaller organizations also need to evaluate their employees fairly and accurately, they often do not have

CAREER ADVICE
from the Experts

MAKING THE BEST OF A BAD REVIEW

Even the best and brightest performers receive below average reviews from time to time. If it happens to you, your goal should be to learn as much as you can from the review and move forward.

- Try to stay objective, even if the review is unfair and inaccurate.
- Review the evaluation for possible factual errors and inaccuracies.
- Ask factual questions to help clarify the review. Focus on process issues. For example, ask what was used to determine performance, how the data were gathered, what criteria were used, and so on.
- Do not argue, even if you are convinced you are correct. Take a cooling-off period and schedule another meeting.
- Avoid making sarcastic or defensive comments. They are not constructive and add to the potential for biases and misinterpretation.
- Ask what you should and can do to improve in the future. Focus your questions on specific behaviors and outcomes.
- If you feel you have been unfairly treated, follow your company's appeal process calmly and professionally.

Source: Based on S. P. Robbins and P. L. Hunsaker, *Training in Interpersonal Skills,* 2d ed. (Upper Saddle River, NJ: Prentice Hall, 1996): 70–75, 266–69.

the resources available to companies such as Honeywell. However, smaller organizations often have fewer job classifications, so they do not need to develop as many different evaluation tools.

A well-designed performance evaluation has five key elements that can reduce the potential for perceptual biases. Any organization can implement these elements, no matter what the size or resources of the company.

Elements of a Well-Designed Performance Evaluation System

Managers need to be aware of whether the evaluation process they are using is flawed. Here are some indicators of poorly designed and implemented performance evaluation systems:

- The same performance standard is used for all employees regardless of job level, skills, and experience.
- All employees receive similar ratings that are in the same range.
- The reviews are similar from year to year.
- There is no clear documentation available to document either good or poor performance.
- Performance evaluation methods and criteria change every year and are unrelated to organizational mission and goals.
- Good performers are not rewarded; poor performers are.

Table 5.2   ELEMENTS OF A WELL-DESIGNED
                PERFORMANCE EVALUATION SYSTEM

Element	Description
Clear criteria	Organizations should provide clear, written performance criteria to all managers and employees. These criteria have to be based on a detailed job analysis that identifies the job's tasks, skills, and responsibilities.
Training	Managers must be fully familiar with the criteria and methods used to evaluate employees and the effects of perceptual biases on the evaluation process. Many large organizations provide formal training in evaluation. Smaller organizations often rely on informal training and experience.
Objective data	Performance evaluation must be supported by objective data such as behavioral examples or measurable work outcomes, instead of opinions.
Opportunity to change	Employees must have reasonable opportunities to change and improve their behavior. Training is one such opportunity.
Appeal mechanisms	Organizations should provide formal appeal mechanisms that allow employees a second chance for a review before the business makes final decisions.

A good performance evaluation system must support the mission and goals of the organization and provide managers with clear means of evaluating progress toward the goals. Five elements must be present in a well-designed performance evaluation system: clear criteria, training for evaluators, objective data, opportunity to change, and appeal processes. Table 5.2 describes these five elements.

Because these five elements take much of the guesswork out of the evaluation process, they can sharply reduce problems arising from perceptual biases. As an added benefit, these elements can safeguard against lawsuits arising from the performance evaluation process.

The social perception process is an integral part of our everyday life. As individuals and managers, interpreting behavior and judging the causes of others' actions is at the core of all social interactions. The social perception process influences the decisions that managers make regarding people. Although the process is inevitably biased, managers can take many steps to recognize and reduce the potential for biases.

Summary Point 5.6   **How Can Managers Evaluate Performance Effectively?**

- Performance evaluation includes the two components of employee evaluation and development.
- Combining these three methods to suit the job allows an organization to reduce the negative effects of perceptual biases on performance evaluation.

- The three main methods of evaluation are the trait, behavioral, and outcome methods.
- The five key elements of a well-designed performance evaluation system are clear criteria, training, objective data, opportunity to change, and an appeal process.

Perception *in Context*

Perception is an individual process. However, how each of us sees and interprets events affects larger organizational factors. Particularly, perception affects how managers deal with contextual strategic factors. Here, we analyze three of those factors: the environment, strategy, and culture. First, enacting the environment of an organization involves perception. Managers must accurately evaluate their environment and decide which elements are relevant for their organization. Selective attention and various biases affect this process. For example, BankBoston managers broke the cycle of stereotypes of inner cities by including small inner-city businesses as part of their environment. As the head of BankBoston's community programs, Gail Snowden included people of color in the bank's advertisements in the local Vietnamese, Chinese, and Spanish newspapers. Perceiving the inner-city residents as part of the bank's customer environment opened up opportunities the bank had previously ignored.

Second, formulating the strategy of an organization is also dependent on perception. Which strategies are selected and which ones discarded depend to a large extent on the perceptual biases of the managers of the organization. As managers collect information about their organization's strengths and weaknesses, they are making judgments at every step that are colored by their personal biases and stereotypes. Similarly, as managers design and adjust the structure of their organization, their decisions about who should be promoted, who should receive what title, and who should report to whom are all dependent on the managers' perceptions.

Finally, culture has a strong influence on managers' perceptions. What is acceptable in one national or organizational culture may be perceived as inappropriate in another. In one organization, providing direct, immediate, and thorough feedback may be the norm; in another, managers may offer feedback only occasionally.

Perception further influences the development of certain cultures in organizations. Managers who use stereotypes in hiring, for example, may signal that such an action is sanctioned by the organization. If used repeatedly, stereotyping becomes a shared value and part of the culture of the organization.

For updated information on the topics in this chapter, Web exercises, links to related Web sites, an on-line study guide, and more, visit our companion Web site at:
http://www.prenhall.com/nahavandi

A Look Back at the

MANAGERIAL CHALLENGE

Pearson PLC

Marjorie Morris Scardino's appointment as CEO of Pearson PLC provoked considerable comment, in part because she is the first woman to head a top 100 U.K. company. Another reason is her background as a Texas-born, rodeo-rider, lawyer, and journalist—not the usual credentials for the top executive of a British conglomerate. Clearly, Scardino does not fit many people's expectations for a top executive of a British publishing empire.

But then, Pearson needs some serious renovations, and Scardino has made a good impression from the very beginning of her career at the firm. The fact that she does not fit stereotypes makes her stand out. She is able to get the attention she needs to implement change. Her employees expect her to be different. They are therefore more likely to accept her ideas.

When she moved up to become Pearson's CEO, Scardino's subtle self-promotion not only reinforced her competence—it also further set the stage for the business changes she inevitably has to make. Her American slang, her relatively informal management style, even her baseball cap signal the start of a new era. After just seven months on the job, Scardino publicly announced her intention to double Pearson's market capitalization within five years, which sent the company's stock soaring. Scardino said, "There will be more changes. But for now our aim is to get every business to perform better."[66] In the coming years, Scardino will remain very much in the public eye as she pursues her goal of remaking Pearson.

■ Point of View Exercises

You're the Manager: As the managing editor at *The Economist,* you supervise levels of editors and writers working on the weekly magazine. How can you structure a performance evaluation system for your staff to assure a fair and accurate review? How can you prevent biases from affecting the process?

You're the Employee: As a columnist at *The Economist,* your managing editor will soon evaluate your performance. What perceptual biases do you think are most likely to influence your editor's evaluation of your behavior? How can you manage his or her impression of you?

SUMMARY OF LEARNING OBJECTIVES

1. **Describe the physical and social perception processes and how culture affects them.**
    Perception is a mental process that we use to pay attention selectively to some stimuli and cues. Social perception refers to our understanding of the social environment. The perception process is inherently flawed and subject to many biases. Culture and cultural values strongly influence how individuals perceive and interpret the social environment. The effect of culture on perception can result in misinterpretation and misunderstanding. The same behavior may have different meanings in different cultures. Without an understanding of the cultural differences, managers may misunderstand the meaning of their own or others' behavior.

2. **Present a three-stage model for understanding social perception and highlight the factors that affect the attention, organization, interpretation, and judgment stages.**
    The social perception process takes place in the three stages of attention, organization, and interpretation. At the attention stage, we let in some but not all information by using a perceptual filter and selective attention. At the organization stage our schemas of events and people guide how we organize and remember information. Schemas are mental models that are resistant to change and strongly influenced by culture. The attribution process comes into play in the interpretation stage. Through attribution we assign the cause of behavior to either the person (internal) or the situation (external). We also consider the distinctiveness, consensus, and consistency of behavior when making attributions.

3. **Discuss the biases that affect perception, the difficulties in overcoming them, and ways to manage them.** Several biases affect the perceptual process. The halo/horn and similar-to-me biases cause us to base our impression of people on one positive or negative factor. Stereotypes based on group membership are another bias. Primacy and recency are two other perceptual biases, which are the tendencies to put too much weight on either early or late information. The fundamental attribution error leads us to underestimate the strength of the situation and overuse internal attributions about others. We also fall prey to self-serving bias by accepting credit for success but rejecting blame for failures. All the biases make us more efficient information processers but less effective if they lead to errors in judgment.

    Overcoming biases is difficult because we seek consistency to gain the illusion of control. Phenomenal absolutism—that is, believing that what you perceive is objective reality rather than your interpretation of reality—makes it even harder to recognize the effect of biases in social perception. Channeling and self-fulfilling prophecy are two other processes that encourage biases. In channeling, we limit our interaction with someone so that we never have the opportunity to receive information that may disconfirm our judgment. Through channeling, our behavior causes people to behave the way we expect, thereby forming a self-fulfilling prophecy. By learning to recognize their biases through training, including cross-cultural training, awareness, constant reminders, and frequent contact and interaction, managers can reduce the negative effect of biases.

4. **Describe the process and elements of self-presentation and impression management.**
    Impression management is the conscious and careful monitoring and management of the impression we make on others. Self-presentation, credibility built on competence, role management, and consistent verbal and nonverbal messages are the key aspects of impression management. The four tactics for impression management are to emphasize similarities between you and the other person, to conform to the requirements of the situation, to self-promote to highlight your competence, and to engage in ingratiation.

5. **Explain how managers can reduce the effect of perceptual biases in performance evaluations.** The goal of performance evaluation is to evaluate and develop employees. Both

goals are strongly influenced by how we perceive others and ourselves. Among the three methods of evaluating employees, the behavior and goals approaches are less subject to biases as compared to the trait approach. A well-designed evaluation system is one that relies on clear criteria, training for evaluators, and objective data; it has an appeal process.

KEY TERMS

actor-observer difference, p. 164
attention stage of perception, p. 154
attribution process, p. 158
behavioral method, p. 175
channeling, or confirmatory hypothesis testing, p. 167
closure, p. 151
external or situational attributions, p. 158
fundamental attribution error, p. 164
halo effect, p. 161
impression management, p. 171

ingratiation, p. 173
internal or personal attributions, p. 158
interpretation and judgment stage of perception, p. 158
nonverbal messages, p. 172
organization stage of perception, p. 155
outcome approach, p. 176
overjustification, p. 160
perception, p. 150
perceptual biases, p. 161
perceptual filter, p. 154
phenomenal absolutism, p. 166

physical perception, p. 151
primacy effect, p. 163
Pygmalion effect, or self-fulfilling prophecy, p. 167
recency effect, p. 163
salient cues, p. 154
schemas, p. 155
selective attention, p. 154
self-perception theory, p.160
self-presentation, p. 171
self-promotion, p. 173
self-serving bias, p. 165
similar-to-me effect, p. 161
social perception, p. 151
stereotype, p. 162
trait method, p. 175

REVIEW QUESTIONS

1. Compare and contrast physical and social perception.
2. How does culture affect how we perceive others?
3. List the three stages of social perception and the major elements that affect each stage.
4. Define each of the perceptual biases and provide an example of how they affect decision making.
5. What are the elements of impression management?
6. Describe the methods of performance evaluation and discuss how each method addresses the problems of our perceptual process.

DISCUSSION QUESTIONS

1. How can managers use the information regarding the effect of culture on perception to make better decisions?
2. In your opinion, which of the biases described in this chapter would be the hardest to overcome? Why?
3. Think of a situation when biases affected your decision or judgment. What could you have done to prevent their impact?
4. How comfortable do you feel using impression management tactics to improve your chances of getting a promotion? Why?
5. How can managers use the information about biases and different methods of performance evaluation to evaluate their employees better?

▶ SELF-ASSESSMENT 5
What Stereotypes Do You Hold?

All of us have stereotypes of various groups. The stereotypes we hold depend on our culture, where and when we grew up, and many other factors such as our family, friends, and personal experiences. This self-assessment is designed to help you explore your stereotypes, their sources, and their consequences.

1. IDENTIFY YOUR STEREOTYPES

Using the following table, identify several stereotypes that you hold about different groups; for each one, tell what you believe to be its source and any possible personal experience you have had that you think directly supports the stereotype. You should target stereotypes that you would like to change. One example is provided. Remember that this is a self-assessment, not to be shared with the class or your group. The more honest you are, the more you will bene-fit from the exercise.

Stereotype	Source	Personal Experience
• The Japanese are team members, not leaders.	• My father always said that. • Business press says they work in groups.	• A Japanese team member last semester was very quiet. • Asian students rarely talk in class.
•	•	•
•	•	•
•	•	•

2. LOOKING FOR DISCONFIRMATION

For each of the stereotypes you listed in step 1, consider events or evidence that you have directly or indirectly experienced that contradicts your stereotype. You may have to work hard at this step, as you will not remember contradictory examples easily. An example is again provided.

Stereotype	Disconfirmation
• Japanese are not leaders.	• The Japanese lead the world in many areas of business. • The Japanese are courageous military leaders.
•	•
•	•
•	•

How easy was it for you to remember your stereotypes and the disconfirming evidence? Did you remember the source of your stereotypes? Chances are, most of you do not really remem-ber where they came from. Why is it so hard to remember disconfirming evidence and infor-mation? What can you do to start changing the stereotypes you hold?

▶ TEAM EXERCISE 5
The Case of the College Teacher

1. INDIVIDUAL WORK:

Read the following case carefully as often as you think is necessary for full understanding. You will not be able to read it again until the end of the exercise as instructed by your professor.

A well-liked college teacher had just completed making up the final examination and had turned off the lights in the office. Just then a tall, dark, broad figure appeared and demanded the examination. The professor opened the drawer. Everything in the drawer was picked up and the individual ran down the corridor. The dean was notified immediately.

Source: Joseph A. Devito, *General Semantics: Guide and Workbook,* rev. ed. (Deland, FL: Everet/Edwards, 1974), p. 55.

Answer the following questions individually about the case you have just read *without* referring to the case. Circle *T* if the statement is true or correct, *F* if it false, and *?* if you are not sure or cannot tell.

1.	The thief was tall, dark, and broad.	T	F	?
2.	The professor turned off the lights.	T	F	?
3.	A tall figure demanded the examination.	T	F	?
4.	The examination was picked up by someone.	T	F	?
5.	The examination was picked up by the professor.	T	F	?
6.	A tall dark figure appeared after the professor turned off the lights.	T	F	?
7.	The man who opened the drawer was the professor.	T	F	?
8.	The professor ran down the corridor.	T	F	?
9.	The drawer was never actually opened.	T	F	?
10.	Three people are referred to in this case.	T	F	?

2.   GROUP WORK: COMPARE AND DISCUSS

Without turning to the case or changing any of your answers, compare your answers with those of your team members. Discuss any discrepancies. The goal is not to come to an agreement and a common group answer but to explore areas of differences and their causes.

3.   SCORING AND DISCUSSION

Your instructor will provide you with the scoring key for the questions. What explains your score? What processes are operating? What are the implications?

UP CLOSE

▶ A Smile Is Just a Smile, or Is It?

After obtaining a business and engineering degree in South Korea, Hun Lee Kim spent six months in a management training program at a prestigious U.S. university. He has three years of work experience in Korea and Singapore and he was hoping to get a one- or two-year internship in a large U.S. high-tech firm before he returns home. All his efforts for the past three months have failed and Kim is very discouraged.

Kim had prepared a detailed resume and attached a picture of himself in which he was careful to project a solemn expression that would show potential employers his respect for them and the seriousness with which he takes this activity. Out of twenty letters and resumes he sent out, he received only three interviews. All his other classmates had eight to ten interviews and all had at least two offers.

For all three interviews, Kim gathered considerable information about the company and was extremely well prepared. During the interviews, he was careful to show respect, not to interrupt the managers talking to him, and to answer their questions very clearly. In all three cases, Kim found the interviewers to be silly and even childish. He thought that they joked around too much and did not appear to be taking the interviews seriously. Kim, however, made sure that he demonstrated his commitment and avoided conveying a frivolous attitude.

Jerri Hirsch, the internship director, is puzzled by Kim's lack of success. He is one of their best students and has much to offer as an intern. She decides to call the HR directors of the companies that interviewed him to find out what is going on. The first one said, "The guy was really unfriendly. He looks good on paper, but he is just too uptight for a job that requires openness and flexibility. We did not think he could fit well in our company." The response from the second HR director was similar. "Kim did not appear to have much initiative. This is just an internship, but we always look for people who have the potential to contribute long term. He knew the facts, but not much more." The third HR manager was kinder. She stated, "Maybe Kim was intimidated by our relaxed style; we are very informal around here. I am sure he is very nice and he obviously has the technical competence, but he is too serious and somber for our organizational culture. We need real go-getters."[67]

Questions

1. What are the causes of Kim's lack of success?
2. What role do cultural stereotypes play?
3. What attributional processes are operating?
4. If you were Jerri Hirsch, how would you explain the situation to Kim and what advice would you give him?

THE BIG PICTURE

▶ Rebuilding Morrison Knudsen

Morrison Knudsen, the company that built the venerable Hoover Dam and the Trans-Alaska pipeline, was facing the biggest construction project of its corporate life. After coming to the very brink of financial disaster in 1995, the company had to rebuild itself almost from the ground up, with new management, new strategy and—ultimately—new ownership.[68] What happened to Morrison Knudsen? And would it survive?

Morrison Knudsen lost $60 million in 1987 on $1.9 billion in revenues from constructing bridges, factories, and power plants. Looking for a turnaround in 1988, the company named William Agee as CEO. A Harvard MBA, Agee had served as CFO of Boise Cascade, a paper manufacturer and then as CEO of Bendix, an auto-parts manufacturer. But when Agee's plans for a high-tech remake of Bendix went awry, and he tried—and failed—to take over Martin Marietta, Bendix was sold. Soon afterward, Morrison Knudsen hired Agee.[69]

Despite his impressive management background, Agee was no stranger to controversy. During his time at Bendix, he publicly denied rumors about an affair with his vice president for strategic planning, Mary Cunningham, whom he later married. He was also criticized for his role in the Martin Marietta takeover bid. Still, the early days at Morrison Knudsen showed Agee at his best. He energized demoralized employees with his charismatic speeches and his relaxed style; he hired talented managers; and he sold off unprofitable divisions to shore up finances.

Yet on a personal level, Agee and Cunningham never fit well with others inside Morrison Knudsen and its Boise, Idaho, community. Some people said the Agees were distant; some were put off by the personal scandal surrounding Agee's annulment and divorce from his first wife, who was well liked when she lived in Boise. And Agee didn't fit in the firm's tough corporate culture; in his words, "I wasn't one of the boys."[70]

Agee was demanding, firing managers without warning and surrounding himself with managers who agreed with him. Even worse, his vision of Morrison Knudsen as a maker of train and locomotive equipment was not working. Although the company was winning contracts, it had major problems with product design and manufacturing. In the middle of these business problems, Agee underwent major surgery and, citing a hostile environment in Boise, he moved his family to California, where he summoned company executives for meetings.[71]

In 1994, the board of directors received an anonymous letter detailing the company's financial woes and Agee's inappropriate management actions. Agee ignored the letter, but board members investigated and several months later they fired the CEO. Company employees in Boise cheered when they heard the news. But Morrison Knudsen was not yet out of danger. With Robert Tinstman as CEO, the company cobbled together financing to stay afloat. In 1996, it was acquired by Washington Construction Group, and Tinstman was named CEO of the combined company.[72] By 1998, the company was profitable, with nearly $2 billion in annual revenues.[73]

Questions

1. How did perceptions of Agee's behavior affect the situation at Morrison Knudsen?
2. If you were CEO Tinstman, what would you do to boost job satisfaction among managers and employees at Morrison Knudsen? Explain your answer.

NOTES

1. B. Angelo, "Marjorie Scardino Yanks Their Chain," *Columbia Journalism Review* (May–June 1997), accessed on-line at http://cjr.org/html/97-05-06-scardino.
2. L. Colby, "Yankee Expansionist Builds British Empire," *Fortune* 137, no. 5 (1998): 102–4.
3. Angelo, "Marjorie Scardino."
4. Ibid.
5. Colby, "Yankee Expansionist."
6. Ibid.
7. For a review of the research on social perception, see H. R. Schiffmann, *Sensation and Perception: An Integrated Approach* (New York: Wiley, 1990); S. T. Fiske and S. E. Taylor, *Social Cognition* (Reading, MA: Addison-Wesley, 1991); S. T. Fiske, "Social Cognition and Social Perception," in E. W. Porter and M. R. Rosenzweig (eds.), *Annual Review of Psychology*, vol. 44 (Palo Alto, CA: Annual Reviews, 1993), 155–94; and S. Plous, *The Psychology of Judgment and Decision Making* (Philadelphia: Temple University Press, 1993).
8. G. Hofstede, "Cultural Constraints in Management Theories," *Academy of Management Review* 7, no. 1 (1993): 81–94; and A. Laurent, "The Cultural Diversity of Western Conceptions of Management," *International Studies of Management and Organization* 8, no. 1 (1983): 75–96.
9. For recent studies about difference in interpretation of behavior based on culture, see F. Trompenaars, *Riding the Wave* (Avon, UK: The Economist Books, 1993); M. W. Morris and K. Peng, "Culture and Cause: American and Chinese Attributions for Social and Physical Events," *Journal of Personality and Social Psychology* 67, no. 6 (1994): 949–71; and F. Lee, M. Hallahan, and T. Herzog, "Explaining Real-Life Events: How Culture and Domain Shape Attributions," *Personality and Social Psychology Bulletin* 22, no. 7 (1996): 732–41.
10. See Carl Rodrigues, *International Management: A Cultural Approach* (St. Paul, MN: West, 1996): 337.
11. For a discussion of the concept of salience, see Fiske and Taylor, *Social Cognition*; for a recent study of the effect of salience, see A. R. McConnell, S. J. Sherman, and D. L. Hamilton, "Illusory Correlation in the Perception of Groups: An Extension of the Distinctiveness-Based Account," *Journal of Personality and Social Psychology* 67, no. 3 (1994): 414–29.
12. See Fiske and Taylor, *Social Cognition*.
13. E. Matson, "Now That We Have Your Complete Attention," *Fast Company* (March 1997): 127.
14. Ibid.
15. S. Taylor, "A Categorization Approach to Stereotyping," in D. L. Hamilton (ed.), *Cognitive Processes in Stereotyping and Intergroup Behavior* (Hillsdale, NJ: Erlbaum, 1981): 83–114.
16. Review of the concept of schemas can be found in S. T. Fiske and S. L. Neuberg, "A Continuum of Impression Formation from Category-Based to Individuating Processes: Influences of Information and Motivation on Attention and Interpretation," in M. P. Zanna (ed.), *Advances in Experimental Social Psychology*, vol. 23 (New York: Academic Press, 1990): 1–74.
17. N. Dresser, "Even Smiling Can Have a Serious Side," *Los Angeles Times*, May 9, 1994, 1–5.
18. R. S. Johnson, "Banking on Urban America," *Fortune* 137, no. 4 (1998): 128–32.
19. Ibid., 129–30.
20. H. H. Kelley, "The Process of Causal Attribution," *American Psychologist* (February 1973): 107–28.
21. W. A. Trahan and D. D. Steiner, "Factors Affecting Supervisors' Use of Disciplinary Actions Following Poor Performance," *Journal of Organizational Behavior* 15, no. 2 (1994): 129–39.
22. B. Weiner, "An Attributional Theory of Achievement Motivation and Emotion," *Psychological Review* (October 1985): 548–73.
23. L. Ross, "The Intuitive Psychologist and His Shortcomings: Distortions in the Attribution Process," in L. Berkowitz (ed.), *Advances in Experimental Social Psychology*, vol. 10 (New York: Academic Press, 1977): 174–221.
24. See Kelley, "The Process of Causal Attribution."
25. R. E. Nisbett and T. D. Wilson, "Telling More Than We Can Know: Verbal Reports on Mental Processes," *Psychological Review* 84 (1977): 231–59.
26. S. Bem, "Self-Perception Theory," in L. Berkowitz (ed.), *Advances in Experimental Social Psychology*, vol. 6 (New York: Academic Press, 1972): 1–62.
27. For the original study of overjustification, see M. Lepper, D. Greene, and R. Nisbett, "Undermining Children's Interest with Extrinsic Rewards: A Test of the 'Overjustification Hypothesis,'" *Journal of Personality and Social Psychology* 28 (1973): 129–37. For more recent applications, see E. L. Deci and R. M. Ryan, "Intrinsic Motivation and Self-Determination in Human Behavior (New York: Plenum, 1985).

28. J. M. Feldman, "A Note on the Statistical Correction of Halo Error," *Journal of Applied Psychology* (1986): 71, 173–76.
29. G. P. Erwin, "First Names and Perceptions of Physical Attractiveness," *Journal of Psychology* 127, no. 6 (1993): 625–31.
30. E. D. Pulakos and K. N. Wexley, "Relationship Among Perceptual Similarity, Sex, Performance, and Ratings in Manager-Subordinate Dyads," *Academy of Management Journal* 26 (1983): 129–39.
31. *The Economist* (August 26, 1995): 59.
32. L. Colby, "Yankee Expansionist Builds British Empire," *Fortune* 137, no. 5 (1998): 102–104, 106, 108.
33. C. N. Macrae, G. V. Boendenhausen, A. B. Milne, and J. Jetten, "Out of Mind and Back in Sight: Stereotypes on the Rebound," *Journal of Personality and Social Psychology* 67, no. 5 (1994): 808–17; and Z. Kunda and K. C. Oleson, "Maintaining Stereotypes in the Face of Disconfirmation: Constructing Grounds for Subtyping Deviants," *Journal of Personality and Social Psychology* 68, no. 4 (1995): 565–79.
34. B. P. Allen, "African Americans' and European Americans' Mutual Attribution: Adjective Generation Technique (AGT) Stereotyping," *Journal of Applied Social Psychology* 26, no. 10 (1996): 884–912.
35. V. Valian, *Why So Slow?: The Advancement of Women* (Boston, MA: MIT Press, 1998).
36. Allen, "African Americans'."
37. Johnson, "Banking on Urban America," 130.
38. Ibid.
39. Pious, *The Psychology of Judgment*.
40. Matson, "Now That We Have," 127.
41. See Ross, "The Intuitive Psychologist"; J. W. McHoskey and A. G. Miller, "Effects of Constraint Identification, Processing Mode, Expectancies, and Intragroup Variability on Attributions Toward Group Members," *Personality and Social Psychology Bulletin* 20 (1994): 266–76; J. L. Hilton, S. Fein, and D. T. Miller, "Suspicion and Dispositional Inference," *Personality and Social Psychology Bulletin* 19 (1993): 501–12.
42. E. E. Jones and R. E. Nisbett, "The Actor and the Observer: Divergent Perceptions of the Causes of Behavior," in E. E. Jones et al. (eds.), *Attribution: Perceiving the Causes of Behavior* (Morristown, NJ: General Learning Press, 1972): 79–94; K. Karasawa, "An Attributional Analysis of Reactions to Negative Emotions," *Personality and Social Psychology Bulletin* 21 (1995): 456–67.
43. J. T. Johnson and K. R. Boyd, "Dispositional Traits Versus the Content of Experience: Actor/Observer Differences in Judgments of the 'Authentic Self,'" *Personality and Social Psychology Bulletin* 21 (1995): 375–83.
44. D. J. Miller and M. Ross, "Self-Serving Bias in Attribution of Causality: Fact or Fiction?" *Psychological Bulletin* 82 (1975): 213–25; K. Tandon, M. A. Ansari, and A. Kapoor, "Attributing Upward Influence Attempts in Organizations," *Journal of Psychology* 125, no. 1 (1991): 59–63.
45. S. Levy, "A Big Brother?" *Time* (August 18, 1997): 25.
46. Ibid., 29.
47. Research about the need for consistency dates back to L. Festinger's *A Theory of Cognitive Dissonance* (Evanston, IL: Row Peterson, 1957) and later interpretations by D. Bem's "Self-Perception Theory," in L. Berkowitz (ed.), *Advances in Experimental Social Psychology*, vol. 6 (New York: Academic Press, 1972).
48. M. Snyder and W. B. Swann, Jr., "Hypothesis-Testing Processes in Social Interaction," *Journal of Personality and Social Psychology* 36 (1978): 1202–12; S. Gangestad and M. Snyder, "Hypothesis-Testing Processes," in J. H. Harvey, W. Ickes, and R. F. Kidd (eds.), *New Directions in Attribution Research*, vol. 3 (Hillsdale, NJ: Erlbaum, 1981): 171–98.
49. A. B. Fisher, "When Will Women Get to the Top?" *Fortune* (September 21, 1992): 44–56; and J. K. Swim and L. T. Sanna, "He's Skilled, She's Lucky: A Meta-analysis of Observers' Attributions for Women's and Men's Successes and Failures," *Personality and Social Psychology Bulletin* 22, no. 5 (May 1996): 507–19.
50. L. Himelstein and A. S. Forest, "Breaking Through," *Business Week* (February 17, 1997): 68.
51. The original research on the self-fulfilling prophecy was done by R. Rosenthal and L. Jacobson, *Pygmalion in the Classroom: Teacher Expectation and Pupils' Intellectual Development* (New York: Holt, Rinehart & Winston, 1968). Recent work relating the concept to management is reviewed in D. Eden, *Pygmalion in Management: Productivity as a Self-Fulfilling Prophecy* (Lexington, MA: Lexington Books, 1990), and S. L. Neuberg, T. C. Judice, L. M. Virdin, and M. A. Carrillo, "Perceiver Self-Presentational Goals as Moderators of Expectancy Influences: Ingratiation and Disconfirmation of Negative Expectancies," *Journal of Personality and Social Psychology* 64 (1993): 409–20.
52. Eden, *Pygmalion in Management*.

53. A. Markels, "Power to the People," *Fast Company* (February/March 1998): 165.

54. L. E. Wynter, "Allstate Rates Managers on Handling Diversity," *Wall Street Journal*, October 1, 1997, B1.

55. For a discussion, see D. A. Harrrison, "Beyond Relational Demography: Time and the Effects of Surface- and Deep-Level Diversity on Work Group Cohesion," *Academy of Management Journal* 41, no. 1 (1998): 96–107.

56. "Family Friendly SRP: Flexibility Is Company Watchword," *Arizona Republic*, September 17, 1996, A1, A10; for other examples, see *The Economist* (December 17, 1994): 58.

57. B. R. Schlenker, *Impression Management: The Self-Concept, Social Identity, and Interpersonal Relations* (Monterey, CA: Brooks/Cole, 1980); M. R. Leery and R. M. Kowalski, "Impression Management: A Literature Review and Two-Component Model," *Psychological Bulletin* 107 (1990): 34–47.

58. E. Goffman, *The Presentation of Self in Everyday Life* (Garden City, NY: Doubleday, 1959).

59. Eden, *Pygmalion in Management.*

60. Fiske and Taylor, *Social Cognition.*

61. D. Tannen, *That's Not What I Meant* (New York: Ballantine, 1986), and *You Just Don't Understand* (New York: Ballantine, 1990).

62. L. Himelstein, "How Do You Get the Boys to Pass You the Ball," *Business Week* (February 17, 1997): 70.

63. Carl Quintanilla, "Creative Classes: Employee Training Adopts Some Unconventional Methods," *Wall Street Journal*, June 24, 1997, A1.

64. Himelstein, "How Do You Get."

65. J. N. Cleaveland, K. R. Murphy, and R. E. Williams, "Multiple Uses of Performance Appraisals: Prevalence and Correlates," *Journal of Applied Psychology* 74 (1989): 130–35.

66. Colby, "Yankee Expansionist," 103.

67. For more detailed information about the cultural differences in the meaning of smiling see N. Dresser, "Even Smiling Can Have a Serious Side," *Los Angeles Times*, May 9, 1994, 1–5.

68. John Greenwald, "The Wreck of Morrison Knudsen," *Time* (April 3, 1995), accessed on-line at www. pathfinder.com.

69. Brian O'Reilly, "Ages in Exile," *Fortune* 131, no. 10 (May 29, 1995): 51–74.

70. Ibid., 60.

71. Ibid., 60–65.

72. "Troubled Morrison Knudsen Agrees to Sale," *Seattle Times*, May 17, 1996, accessed on-line at www.seattletimes.com/extra/browse/html/altmorr_051796.html.

73. "Morrison Knudsen Reports $32 Million Profit for 1997," press release, *PR Newswire*, January 26, 1998, accessed on-line at www.yahoo.com/prnews/981026/id_morriso_1.html.

MANAGING PERFORMANCE THROUGH MOTIVATION AND OUTCOMES

LEARNING OBJECTIVES

1. Define motivation, explain its importance, and review its three components.
2. Describe how and why the expectancy framework helps managers understand motivation.
3. Identify the individual, job-related, and organizational factors that affect motivation.
4. Discuss the importance of behaviors, learning, and consequences in managing performance.

MANAGERIAL CHALLENGE

Rebuilding at Malden Mills

Compared to the hundreds of businesses that have laid off employees—even during profitable years—Malden Mills, maker of the popular Polartec fabric, is a remarkable exception. Malden Mills is a 130-year-old textile manufacturer in Lawrence, Massachusetts. Its CEO, Aaron Feuerstein, was celebrating his birthday when word came that three of his factory buildings were on fire. Feuerstein rushed to the site and watched as flames gutted the buildings.[1] Feuerstein faced a daunting challenge: What to do with the business and its employees in the aftermath of the fire?

The simplest option was to take the fire insurance money and close down. Another solution—one that many local manufacturers had already chosen—was to relocate to an area where labor costs were lower. Either way, the city would lose one of its last remaining large employers. Family pride also figured in Feuerstein's decision: His grandfather had founded the mill, and the grandson now had to decide the fate of the business and its 3,200 employees.[2]

Standing at the fire scene, the CEO suddenly noticed that a key production building had not yet burned. If that building was spared, Feuerstein told his engi-

neering director, the business could be saved.[3] When the building did not burn, the CEO announced his decision to begin rebuilding Malden Mills immediately.[4] He also announced his decision to keep all employees on the payroll during the reconstruction, up to 90 days, at a weekly cost of $1.5 million.[5] Malden Mills was known for paying above-average wages, one of the ways Feuerstein showed appreciation for his employees' hard work. Now the CEO decided to continue paying thousands of employees—even though many could not return to work for weeks or months.[6] Would this decision pay off?

■ Questions

1. How would employees' motivation be affected by Feuerstein's decision to keep paying the workforce?
2. Would their motivation be affected by his leadership? In what ways?

Malden Mills values its employees and their contributions, and rewards them with high salaries and continued job security. One of the major roles of managers is to motivate employees to do their jobs well so that the organization can achieve its goals. But what motivates job performance? Think back to times when you were excited and energized about doing a task. How did it feel? How did your enthusiasm affect your performance? This chapter examines answers to these questions. We explore the individual, job-related, and organizational factors that contribute to motivation. We look at all these factors because motivation depends as much on the individual as it does on co-workers, managers, and the organization.

First, we define and describe the motivation process, including key components of that process. Then we examine a framework, known as the expectancy model, that allows us to consider the individual, work, and organizational influences on motivation. Finally, we investigate how to manage performance through opportunities and outcomes.

WHAT IS MOTIVATION?

Motivation
A state of mind, desire, energy, or interest that translates into action

The word *motivation* comes from the Latin verb "to move." **Motivation** is a state of mind, desire, energy, or interest that translates into action. You are motivated when you are interested in doing something. Motivation has a strong behavioral component. It is important to managers for three reasons. First, motivation, by definition, leads to action. Second, it is one of three major factors in work performance. Third, managers can influence employee motivation because it is not a stable state of mind.

Importance of Motivation

Motivation is one of the three key performance elements. As the following formula shows, performance is a function of ability, motivation, and opportunity.

$$\text{Performance} = f\{\text{Ability} \times \text{Motivation} \times \text{Opportunity}\}$$

Ability refers to a natural talent to do something mental or physical. It tends to be stable over time, so managers have relatively little influence over a person's ability. Organizations take advantage of and manage different levels of ability by recruiting, selecting, and hiring people with the right type and level of ability and placing them in jobs that fit their capabilities.

Motivation is the second element of performance. In contrast to ability, motivation is not a stable individual characteristic. Although there may be a relationship between some per-

Hot ▼ Link

In chapter 4 we defined ability on p. 115 and discussed the relationship between personality traits and motivation on pp. 120–30.

sonality traits and level of motivation, motivation is not a trait. A person's motivation changes from situation to situation and over time. Because motivation is not permanent, managers can influence employees' motivation levels through various actions.

The third component of the performance formula is opportunity. Just as with motivation, performance opportunities vary in different situations and over time. Managers can strongly influence performance opportunities. As a matter of fact, one of the methods managers use to motivate employees is to provide the right performance opportunities.

Before we continue, it is important to differentiate between job satisfaction and motivation. As you may remember from chapter 4, job satisfaction is an attitude or feeling about one's job. It includes satisfaction with pay, co-workers, supervision, promotion, and the organization. Motivation has deeper roots. It includes not only attitudes about the job but also factors such as individual needs. **Needs** are based on personality and values and are related to things that are lacking and are desired. Individual needs relate to work motivation and are therefore an important issue in managing people and organizations. Early approaches to motivation focused primarily on needs. The needs views proposed by Maslow, Herzberg, and McClelland continue to be highly popular with managers even though current research offers more complex explanations.

In addition to needs, motivation has a strong behavioral aspect—that is, the drive to act—that is not necessarily present in job satisfaction. In spite of the differences, motivation and satisfaction are closely linked. Being motivated to do a job well is difficult when you are dissatisfied with it. Similarly, a highly satisfying job is also likely to motivate. Being dissatisfied with your job may motivate you to search for another job or quit. Also, you can be satisfied with the job, but not be motivated to work hard because of dissatisfaction with the pay, your manager, or other factors.

Current Trends and Limitations of Motivation Research

Jobs and organizations have altered drastically over the past 20 years. Consequently, one would expect the factors that motivate people on the job would also have changed greatly. Surprisingly, research findings suggest that they haven't.[7]

What the Research Findings Tell Us   Studies indicate that from the early 1970s to the mid-1980s, about an equal number of people were dissatisfied as were satisfied with their jobs. An interesting finding was that the older the person was, the higher the job satisfaction. For example, close to 60 percent of those over 57 said they were satisfied, compared to only 33 percent of the 18- to 26-year-old group.[8]

Survey research also suggests that the ranking of factors that motivate people on the job has also remained stable over time. First, people ranked a sense of accomplishment as one of the most important motivating factors.[9] High income and financial rewards are also ranked high, though financial rewards for work are a more central issue for individuals with lower incomes and for those from poorer countries.[10]

Much has remained the same over time, but some changes that affect motivation have occurred. First, loyalty to the company is no longer a strong motivational factor. People feel less loyal to employers because of decreased job security, in part due to global competition and new technologies that trigger layoffs and outsourcing. This trend is not limited to the United States. It is also apparent in countries such as the United Kingdom, France, Germany, Japan, and Korea.[11] Employers in these countries are decreasing their commitment to lifelong employment in search of more efficiency and higher profits.[12] Aiwa, the Japanese low-price electronic equipment maker, slashed 1,300 of its 3,600 jobs in Japan, breaking the tradition

Hot ▼ Link

We described the concept of job satisfaction in chapter 4, pp. 135–37.

Needs
Related to things that are lacking and are desired

Hot ▼ Link

We discuss needs theories of motivation in Appendix 1 on p. 576.

in that country of lifetime employment. Furthermore, it has shifted 90 percent of its production capacity to cheaper overseas markets.[13]

As a result of diminished job security, employees are more willing to "job hop," and they do not expect to spend their careers in one organization. Rather, employees seem to prepare themselves for a **portfolio career**—a career in which people develop a portfolio of their accomplishments in different companies that keeps them employable. Those who are laid off or want to change jobs can rely on their portfolio to secure a new job more easily.[14]

Portfolio career
A career in which employees develop a portfolio of accomplishments in different companies that keeps them employable

The lack of loyalty to a company and the portfolio approach result in high turnover, a significant cost to organizations. Recruitment and training expenses increase; remaining employees have to work harder until the company finds and trains a new person; and customers experience a drop in quality of products and services, no matter how temporary. By some estimates, U.S. firms on average lose half their employees in four years and half their customers in five.[15]

Given the decrease in job security and loyalty, how should managers keep employees motivated to work hard and stay with the organization? We examine motivational factors that may help managers meet this challenge.

What Motivates People Depends on the Culture   The desire to work hard and feel excited and energetic about doing a job is probably a universal state. All cultures include the idea of motivation. However, the factors that motivate people vary among cultures. Motivational factors

---

CAREER ADVICE
from the Experts

MANAGING A PORTFOLIO CAREER

Keeping motivated and interested when you are worried about the next wave of layoffs is no easy feat. Viewing your career as a portfolio that includes many different companies is one way to stay focused. What follows are some additional pointers:

- Put together and regularly update a performance portfolio that highlights your accomplishments, similar to the portfolio a performer, artist, or architect would compile.
- Look for risky but interesting career opportunities that force you to stretch your abilities and skills.
- Be willing to compromise and adapt to the organization in which you want to succeed.
- Find mentors who can teach you skills and look out for you.
- Surround yourself with people who have different abilities and skills so that you can learn from one another.
- Look at your career from a long-term perspective and accept temporary inconveniences as challenges that can help you in the long run.

Sources: Hal Lancaster, "Life Lesson: Walk on the Wild Side along Path to the Top," *Wall Street Journal*, March 12, 1996, B1; also see Hal Lancaster, "Two Executives Tell How They Thrived in Non-traditional Jobs," *Wall Street Journal*, May 14, 1996, B1; Hal Lancaster, "You Might Need a Guide to Lead You Around Pitfalls," *Wall Street Journal*, July 30, 1996, B1.

depend on cultural values and individual needs. Because the values can differ from culture to culture, people from different cultures will have diverse reasons for being excited and energetic about doing their jobs.

The concept of self-actualization proposed by Maslow states that the individual strives to achieve his or her personal best during a lifetime. This theory makes sense only in the context of a Western culture in which individualism is prized and time is perceived as linear. In a collectivist culture, the group or community is central to motivation and the self is often subjugated. Self-actualization, then, would not motivate. Additionally, in a culture for which time is perceived as circular and which has deep-rooted beliefs in reincarnation and karma, the idea of achieving self-actualization in a lifetime takes on a different meaning. In such cultures self-actualization is long term and can occur over several lives.

A recent study highlights another example of motivational differences related to culture. The study showed that Japanese-owned maquiladoras (foreign-owned businesses in Mexican border towns) were better able to motivate and retain employees than the U.S.-owned maquiladoras. The researchers attributed the Japanese success to the similarity between the Japanese and Mexican cultures. Both countries' national cultures tend toward high power distance, strong uncertainty avoidance, and collectivism.[16] As a result, workers were easier to train in the structured Japanese ways of performing the work. Mexicans readily accepted the instructions and followed them. American firms, however, had different expectations of their Mexican workers—expectations that the workers would take the initiative and be motivated to get the job done at all costs. These values did not fit the cultural values of the Mexican workforce.[17]

Motivational factors can differ among cultures within the same country, as well. Kingston Technology, based in Orange County, California, has become the world's largest maker of add-on memory technologies for PCs.[18] Its two owners, John Tu and David Sun, imported "Asian family values" when they founded the business 10 years ago. The company's mission and culture focus on treating everyone as a family member. The style of the two founders and the way they motivate their employees are partially determined by their culture. The company does deals on a handshake, trusts suppliers and customers without a contract, always delivers on time, and takes care of employees. In fact, Kingston's 800 employees are promised one to two years of pay if any layoffs occur. They receive above-market wages, and in some cases the company has even paid the employees' home mortgages. As a result, employees are motivated to work hard and stay with the firm. The rate of employee turnover has averaged 2 percent in the last 10 years.

These examples illustrate that culture can determine what motivates people. Managers from a collectivist Asian culture will use the group and a sense of community as the focus of motivation. U.S. and Australian managers are more likely to focus on individual rewards and

The cultural heritage that Kingston owners John Tu and David Sun bring to the business creates a work environment that motivates employees to work hard and remain with this high-tech firm. Do you think the culture of family values could work in other firms? Why?

achievements. When working across cultures, managers need to be aware of how their own cultural values and the values of their employees affect how they view their jobs and what motivates them.

As future managers, you should also be aware that the concepts of motivation and performance management that we discuss in the remainder of this chapter have limited application in cultures other than that of the United States. Most motivational studies we present have been conducted on U.S. workers by U.S. researchers. Until the body of research from other cultures grows, managers will need to rely on their grasp of cultural differences and their own common sense.

We have described motivation, examined its importance in performance, and reviewed the trends and limits of motivation research findings. Now we explore three components of the motivation process.

Components of Motivation

To understand the motivation process, we explore three components of motivation—individual differences, job factors, and organizational factors. The first component of motivation is *individual differences,* which we discussed in chapter 4. For example, people with an internal locus of control may have more motivation and show more initiative than those with an external locus of control. Similarly, those with Type A characteristics may appear to be more "go-getters" than those with Type B characteristics. Values are another individual difference that influences motivation. For instance, people with a Protestant work ethic are perceived to be highly motivated, hard workers.

Many of these differences in motivation are superficial. The issue is not that those with Type A characteristics or those with the Protestant work ethic are more motivated. Rather, they are motivated by different things and in different ways. For example, Generation Xers may not be motivated by the traditional factors of loyalty, security, and a stable career. Instead, they seek challenging, flexible work.

Gender differences may also affect work motivation. Typically, women rate job security and personal fulfillment as more important than status and wealth, which are ranked higher by men.[19] Other studies show that having meaningful work is a more important motivational factor for women than for men.[20]

The second component of motivation is the *actual job* that people do. Since the time of the industrial revolution and with the ideas proposed by Herzberg (see Appendix 1), researchers have viewed the job factor as the key to motivation and performance. If the job offers workers interesting tasks, challenging work, a sense of achievement, and an opportunity to use and develop skills, they are more likely to be motivated. Though people's individual differences determine what they consider to be interesting and challenging, managers who wish to motivate need to keep in mind that the job has to be interesting to the person doing it.

The third component of motivation is the *organization.* To motivate employees to do their job, the organization must provide the right climate and opportunities. The organizational component includes corporate culture, structure, strategies, mission, norms, policies, and practices. These factors provide the setting in which the individual performs a job. An enthusiastic person performing a highly interesting, challenging job is likely to lack motivation if the organization has a hostile, harsh, culture; a structure that inhibits progress; or a strategy that seems unethical. Similarly, a highly supportive culture, a structure that offers workers flexibility, and a strategic mission that workers believe in may lessen the negative effects of dull, routine jobs.

To understand motivation fully, managers must consider the individual, the job, and the organizational setting in which the job is performed. Not all three elements are relevant in every case, but all three contribute to motivation. The expectancy framework, discussed next, allows managers to examine these three components.

Summary Point 6.1   **What Is Motivation?**

- Motivation is an internal energy and desire to act.
- Motivation is important to managers for three reasons:
  1. It leads to action.
  2. It is one of the three factors in performance.
  3. It is variable so managers can influence motivation levels.

- Findings show that a sense of accomplishment and financial rewards have consistently motivated people over time.
- Culture has a strong effect on the factors that motivate, so research findings in one culture often have limited applicability to another culture.
- The three components of motivation are individual differences, the job, and the organization.

MANAGING PERFORMANCE THROUGH MOTIVATION: THE EXPECTANCY FRAMEWORK

To consider the individual, work, and organizational components of motivation, we focus on a motivation model, proposed by Victor Vroom, called the *expectancy model.*[21] The model assumes that motivation is a cognitive or mental process, as we see in Figure 6.1. It considers how people feel their efforts are linked to performance and outcomes. Because the model is cognitive, the individual's perception of events is equally important as and in some cases more important than the objective or actual state of affairs. That is, an employee's belief about a motivational factor is more important than the reality of the situation.

The framework's focus on perception rather than reality is a crucial factor for managers because people often believe perception is reality, even though perceptions are biased. Managers should understand how their employees view a situation to understand how to motivate them.

The expectancy model outlines three major beliefs that people must have to be motivated to work. First, they must perceive that their *efforts* (E) are likely to lead to good *performance* (P). In other words, effort has to be *instrumental* to good performance. Second, people must *expect* that their performance is clearly linked to certain *outcomes* (O). And finally, they have to *value* (V) the outcomes of their performance.

In summary, the model assumes that an individual is likely to be motivated if the following occurs:

- Clear E–P linkage
- Clear P–O linkage
- Having a valued outcome (V)

However, if any one of these linkages does not occur, the person will lose his or her motivation to perform. For example, if a worker feels that he lacks the training or expertise to perform well—no matter how hard he tries—he is unlikely to be motivated to work (a weak E–P link). If an employee receives a raise for her top performance that is better than the industry

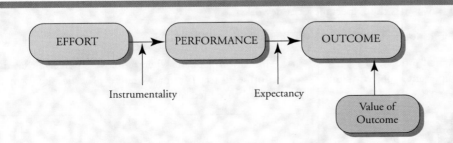

FIGURE 6.1
The Expectancy Process

In spite of high salaries, many professional athletes do not feel that their efforts lead to high performance or that their salaries are determined by their performance. As a result, they may lose their motivation to play well.

average, she may still feel cheated (weak P–O linkage) if the raise does not live up to her expectations or she suspects that others have received more. Finally, if an employee is rewarded by a raise that he does not value because he would rather have more time off instead of the money (a weak O–V link), the worker may lack motivation.

Consider the example of highly paid professional athletes. Fans often are bewildered when some basketball or baseball players who earn several million dollars a year do not put in total effort or perform to their potential. In spite of the high salaries (valued outcomes), they may not perceive that their performance is linked to those outcomes (weak P–O). Instead, the negotiation skills of agents, the player's free agency status, and the bidding for the player by other teams strongly determine the salary. Similarly, because of the presence of many talented athletes on any given team and intense competition, working hard and playing well alone do not guarantee performance and recognition (weak E–P).

Managers need to understand their employees' perceptions about themselves, their jobs, and the organization to influence those perceptions and strengthen motivation. The expectancy framework allows managers to consider individual, job, and organizational motivation factors for a complete view of individual motivation.

Summary Point 6.2   What Is the Expectancy Framework?

The Expectancy Framework is a model for understanding motivation. It assumes the following:

- Motivation is a cognitive or mental process.
- Employees' perceptions are as important as objective reality.

- Motivation happens when employees perceive that their effort leads to performance and expect their performance to lead to valued outcomes.

FACTORS THAT AFFECT MOTIVATION

Using the expectancy model as our general framework, we consider the individual, work, and organizational factors that affect work motivation. Figure 6.2 provides an overview of factors that may affect each link in the expectancy model.

The Individual Component

Individual differences and needs affect motivation in two ways. First, an individual's personality can affect that person's perception of how effort leads to performance (E–P). Second, a person's needs and cultural values determine what she values and how she expects to be rewarded for her work efforts.

Individual Personality Differences A person's personality affects motivation because different personality traits influence how events are viewed, perceived, and interpreted. Two personality differences are particularly important: locus of control and self-esteem. First, individuals with an internal locus of control are more likely to feel that performance is the result of their own efforts. Those with an external locus of control are less likely to do so. Second, individuals with a high degree of self-esteem feel that their performance is linked to their own efforts and, as a result, have a strong sense of instrumentality. The opposite is true of those with a low sense of self-esteem.[22]

Managers can either build on individual differences or compensate for them by actively managing the E–P linkage. For example, managers need to make the E–P link clear through regular feedback and encouragement for individuals with an external locus of control or a low sense of self-esteem. Pointing out good performance and the behaviors that caused it helps employees see that their effort is what leads to good performance.

Needs In addition to personality differences, individual needs also affect the motivation process. Focusing on needs is one of the oldest approaches to understanding motivation, as described in Appendix 1. In spite of the intuitive appeal of this approach, there is little evidence that needs are the primary determinants of a person's motivation.[23] However, needs have a role in motivation. They determine what outcomes an individual values in an organizational setting. For example, a person who has considerable material wealth and status is less likely to need financial rewards than someone who does not have them.

People with a high need for achievement want a high degree of recognition through rewards such as designation as employee-of-the-month or top performer, other public recog-

Hot ▼ Link

We discussed locus of control in chapter 4, pp. 120–22.

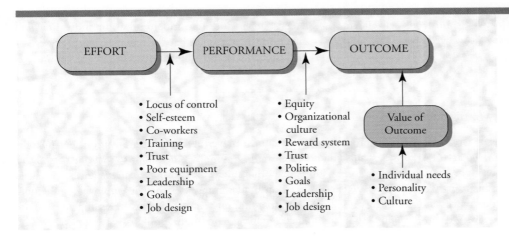

FIGURE 6.2
Factors Affecting Each Link in the Expectancy Process

Hot ▼ Link

We discuss needs theories, including achievement and affiliation needs, in Appendix 1, p. 576.

nition, and so forth. Surveys show that many employees rank immediate recognition as their most highly preferred method of motivation.[24] Other employees with a high need for affiliation would value the interaction with co-workers and customers. If the outcome for their good performance is getting a promotion that will isolate them from others, the value of the promotion will be small.

Younger workers tend to have a need for independence and control over their work environment. Some break rules by walking down the hallways in their socks, drinking beer on the job, and even bringing their pets to work. Yet, they are willing to work extremely hard, if work is fun. "Work is not work. It's a hobby that you happen to get paid for," says Richard Barton, the 30-year-old leader of Microsoft's Expedia travel Web site.[25]

The key to using needs and other individual differences in understanding motivation is to recognize that each individual is unique. Every employee will value outcomes and will perceive work events differently. Both managers and employees should discuss and understand these individual preferences. In addition to individual differences such as personality and needs, a person's culture also affects motivation.

Culture   A person's cultural values, based on nationality or other group culture, influence the motivation process in the same way that individual differences do. Particularly, culture will influence the outcomes an employee values. In the Euro-American culture, public recognition for good performance is generally appreciated.

In contrast, many people from Native American cultures dislike public recognition. Being singled out, even for good deeds, not only is a source of embarrassment but also indicates that the individual considers herself superior to others. Such perception is not desirable in a community-oriented culture because it may negatively affect the sense of harmony of the tribe. A manager who wants to encourage her Pima employee by asking co-workers to give him a round of applause is creating an outcome that is not valued by that employee and that is, consequently, unlikely to motivate him. However, if the manager were to mention to the employee's tribe members that he had made the tribe proud by his hard work, the praise becomes a community outcome and would be more likely to motivate this Native American employee.

Individual differences, including personality, needs, and culture, all affect our perception and interpretation of events. Understanding these differences allows managers to tailor motivation to each employee.

Summary Point 6.3   **What Individual Factors Affect Motivation?**

- Personality traits such as locus of control and self-esteem influence how work events are viewed, perceived, and interpreted.

- Needs determine how much value an individual will place on the outcome that the organization provides.
- Culture affects the value individuals place on various outcomes.

The Work

The work that we do is probably the single most powerful source of motivation. Fortunately, what each of us considers challenging, interesting, and motivating differs so that one person can be highly motivated to perform a job that another might find boring. In all instances, managers can strongly and positively affect motivation by designing jobs that fit employees' individual differences and needs, by providing appropriate training and tools, and by setting appropriate goals. We consider job design, training and working conditions, and goal setting next.

Job Design Job design includes many elements—the amount of challenge and autonomy a worker has, how many skills the job requires, how significant the job is to the organization, and so forth. Having an interesting job creates positive internal feelings that are independent from outside rewards. This type of motivation is called **intrinsic** (or internal) **motivation**.[26]

Job design affects both the effort-to-performance and the performance-to-outcome linkages of the expectancy model. For instance, feeling that your job has a direct impact on the overall performance of the organization strengthens the effort-to-performance and the performance-to-outcome linkages. The "open book management" techniques discussed in chapter 2 demonstrate the positive benefits of linking individual effort and job performance to organizational outcomes. When employees have access to financial performance indication, they see how their efforts contribute to overall organizational performance. Jack Stack, president and CEO of SRC Holding Corporation of Springfield, Missouri, has implemented open book management in his company. He states: "The more people understand what's really going on in their company, the more eager they are to help solve its problems."[27]

Similarly, when employees share in company profits, they see how their efforts and performance translate into actual financial outcomes. Many products now list the names of the individuals who produced them. This practice allows the employees to take pride in their work and to receive direct customer feedback. Lincoln Electric, the Cincinnati-based manufacturer of welding machines, traces defective products to the employees who worked on them. The number of defects partially determines employee bonuses.[28]

Theorists have debated ways to design jobs that result in high performance. Early scientific management theorists proposed making jobs simpler. Later theorists, such as Herzberg, suggested that organizations make jobs more challenging and interesting. Both approaches failed to take a contingency view because they did not consider how individual factors might influence whether the job design would motivate the person.

Such a contingency view is at the heart of the modern job design approach proposed by management professors Richard Hackman and Gary Oldham.[29] They suggest that to motivate an employee, managers must consider the job and the person's individual needs. Then managers should tailor the job to meet that employee's individual needs. We present the Hackman-Oldham Job Design model in Figure 6.3.

As we see in Figure 6.3, the model has three parts: job characteristics, critical psychological states, and outcomes. Hackman and Oldman believe that job characteristics determine

Intrinsic motivation
Motivation resulting from factors that are not affected by external rewards

Hot ▼ Link

We discuss scientific management and Herzberg's motivation theories in Appendix 1, p. 576, and open book management and the contingency view in chapter 2, p. 60.

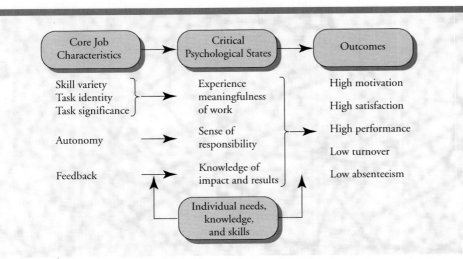

FIGURE 6.3
The Hackman-Oldham Job Design Model

Source: J. R. Hackman and G. R. Oldham, *Work Redesign* (Reading, MA: Addison-Wesley, 1980), p. 90. © 1990 by Addison-Wesley Publishing Co., Inc. Reprinted by permission of Addison Wesley Longman.

critical psychological states that in turn lead to specific outcomes. We examine the three parts of the Hackman-Oldman model next, beginning with job characteristics.

Job Characteristics and Motivation   Hackman and Oldham have designed the Job Diagnostic Survey (JDS) to measure various job characteristics.[30] One of the major goals of the JDS is to measure the **motivating potential score** (MPS) of a job. The formula for MPS follows:

Motivating potential score (MPS)
Indicator of the challenge level of a job, made up of skills variety, task identity, task significance, autonomy, and feedback

$$\text{MPS} = \frac{(\text{skill variety} + \text{task identity} + \text{task significance})}{3} \times \text{autonomy} \times \text{feedback}$$

How much MPS does your job have? Is your job routine or is it challenging, with sufficient potential to motivate you? Take the self-assessment to find out. Notice that your score indicates the job's *potential* to motivate, not the actual level of motivation. Whether a job's potential to motivate leads to actual motivation depends on the issue of fit that we discuss later in this section.

As the formula indicates, to determine a job's motivating potential we first consider the number of skills, or *skill variety*, needed to perform that job. **Skill variety** refers to the number of different skills used to do a job. Examples of jobs that use relatively few skills would be traditional assembly line or receptionist's jobs. Examples of jobs that require many skills are nursing, teaching, or running a business. The traditional assembly-line worker is assigned one task and needs few skills to perform it. The nurse has to use technical, administrative, management, and people skills to perform the job.

Skill variety
Refers to the number of different skills used to do a job

The second element in determining the motivation potential of a job is **task identity**, which is defined as the extent to which the job allows a person to identify with it or to feel that he or she controls or "owns" the outcome. The assembly-line jobs anchor the low task identity side of the scale and most nursing and teaching jobs are at the high end. The traditional assembly-line worker, for instance, has no idea which car she worked on and cannot

Task identity
The extent to which the job allows a person to identify with it or feel that he or she owns the outcome

▶ **SELF-ASSESSMENT 6.1**
How Much MPS Does Your Job Have?

	STRONGLY DISAGREE				STRONGLY AGREE
1. To do my job, I use many different skills.	0	1	2	3	4
2. I feel a strong sense of ownership toward the product/service I make/deliver.	0	1	2	3	4
3. I feel that what I do is important to the organization.	0	1	2	3	4
4. I can make many decisions regarding how to do my job without checking with my boss.	0	1	2	3	4
5. I get direct information and quick feedback regarding my performance as I do my job.	0	1	2	3	4

Scoring key:

Add your scores for questions 1, 2, and 3 and divide by 3. Multiply that number by your score on question 4, then multiply the result by your score on question 5. The minimum MPS is 0; the maximum is 64. Scores below 10 indicate a job with low MPS. Scores between 11 and 30 indicate moderate MPS. Scores above 31 indicate a job that is challenging.

identify with the task or the outcome. In contrast, nurses and teachers can identify the patients or students with whom they have worked and therefore they feel a sense of ownership about how well or poorly the patients or students do.

The third MPS factor is the significance of the person's task to the organization and its overall performance. **Task significance** refers to the importance of a job to the organization or to the wider community. Jobs and tasks that are essential to the organization, especially if they cannot be performed by someone else easily, have strong significance. Jobs that are inessential or can be performed by substitute workers easily have low significance. The job of a teacher has high significance to the school and to the community at large, whereas a clerical worker's job tends to have less significance.

Task significance
The importance of a job to the organization or to the wider community

Having to use many skills, identifying with the job, and feeling that the job has impact and significance for the organization are the basic elements of a motivating, challenging job. In addition to those three job characteristics, we must also consider the level of autonomy and feedback that a job provides. As you can see from the MPS formula, these two factors are critical to the determination of a job's motivating potential. Without autonomy or feedback, the MPS will be zero.

Autonomy refers to the degree to which a person can make independent decisions and act without having to check with a supervisor. Having autonomy provides a sense of responsibility and ownership that is essential to a challenging job. To illustrate, the job of sales representatives who travel to customers has a high degree of autonomy. The representatives receive training and goals and are trusted to make the sale. Most clerical jobs, however, have low autonomy because the workers handle records and process paper but can make few significant decisions on their own.

Autonomy
The degree to which a person can make independent decisions and act without having to check with a supervisor

The last factor in MPS is the degree of feedback the job provides. **Feedback** refers to information about performance. Some jobs provide immediate and direct feedback to employees regarding their performance. Other jobs do not; they require lengthy data collection or interpretation by another person such as a manager or supervisor. For example, customer service jobs usually offer immediate feedback. The customer either is or is not satisfied with the employee's actions and responses. On the other end of the spectrum are data entry jobs where mistakes can go unnoticed for long periods of time. Feedback is not immediate and comes in the form of a manager's evaluation.

Feedback
Information about performance

Consider Paul Rogers, a star software engineer who works for Trilogy Development Group, in Austin, Texas. The 29-year-old has a huge corner office with a beautiful view of the surrounding hills, a large aquarium with exotic fish, and a full-size keyboard for times when he needs to relax. His work is significant to the survival of Trilogy, he uses a variety of skills to get his work done, he knows which parts of the developed software are his, and he has significant autonomy and feedback. "It's all about keeping top performers happy," states Joe Liemandt, the 29-year-old co-founder and CEO of Trilogy.[31] Interestingly, whereas Rogers has the corner office, CEO Liemandt works in a small, five-by-five-foot cubicle. Before you feel sorry for him, consider that as the founder of Trilogy, his stake is worth over $500 million.

Although there is some room for perceptual differences, the MPS is a relatively objective measure. Employees and managers can determine the motivating potential of a job. Once this is determined, the next step is to design jobs that match the person's individual differences and needs.

Matching the Person and the Job   As we see in Figure 6.4, the key to designing a job that motivates people to perform well is matching the person and the job. One of the major strengths of the Hackman-Oldman job design approach is that jobs and people are described rather than judged. In other words, there are no "bad" jobs or unmotivated people. Managers need to know both the needs of their employees and the various jobs that need to be performed in the organization. If there is a match between the job and the person, there will be high per-

FIGURE 6.4
Matching the Job to the Person

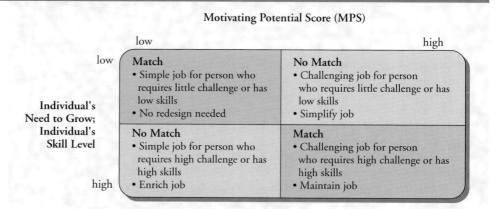

formance, job satisfaction, and strong motivation. If there is mismatch, the employee will lack motivation, experience job dissatisfaction, and probably perform poorly.

Examine the four boxes in Figure 6.4. The upper left and lower right boxes show a match between the person's needs and the job's characteristics. Although the job described in the upper left corner is routine and the person performing that job does not need challenge, positive outcomes are likely to result because of the match between the person and job. The box in the lower right corner shows a situation that some would consider ideal: a motivating job for a person who seeks challenge. Again, high motivation and performance are likely because of the match.

The remaining two boxes in the lower left and the upper right describe mismatches between the person and the job. Such situations create motivation and performance problems. In one instance, the job is too simple; in the other case, it is too complex.

Younger workers are willing to walk away from jobs that do not provide them with the right level of motivation or for which they feel poorly suited. Paul is a 29-year-old financial expert who quit his job trading fixed-income derivatives for a major Wall Street firm to start his own business. He states: "It got to the point where I'd look up at the clock and it was two o'clock, and I'd wish it was five o'clock. The minute that started to happen I said, 'Life's too short to put up with this, man. I'm outta here.' I'm a big believer in doing exactly what you want to do."[32]

Given that organizations include jobs with different levels of challenge and people with different levels of needs, the job design focus on a match allows for a contingency approach that can lead to high motivation and high performance. Instead of suggesting that all jobs need to be enriched, as proposed by Herzberg and other human relations movement theorists in the 1950s and 1960, the focus on a match recognizes the diversity of organizational and individual needs.

Having a good match between the person and the job helps ensure that the person's effort leads to high performance, thereby clearing the path between E and P. Similarly, effective job design can strengthen the link between performance and outcome (P–O), further increasing the potential for motivation.

Now that we have examined job design, we turn next to training and working conditions, the second element of the work factor in motivation.

Training and Working Conditions Managers can improve employee motivation through training and better working conditions. Consider the case of an employee who puts in long hours and a lot of effort but who, because of lack of training, wastes time reinventing the wheel or performing many activities the wrong way. Similarly, equipment breakdowns, inappropriate

MANAGERIAL ADVICE
from the Experts

TIPS FOR REDESIGNING JOBS

Changing the MPS of a job to match the needs of employees requires creativity, especially because every job and every organization will be different. The following tips can help managers redesign jobs to make them more challenging for those employees seeking more challenge.

- Combine several tasks and rotate employees among jobs to increase skills variety.
- Make sure employees can identify the products or processes on which they have worked. For instance, managers can implement a system in which employees who contributed to a product have their names on it.
- Have individuals or teams work on a complete process or product from beginning to end to increase both task identity and task significance.
- To increase task significance, involve employees in strategic issues by providing them information about the overall company.
- Put your employees in touch with their customers by offering direct customer contact and feedback.
- Train employees to make job decisions as appropriate and gradually increase their level of responsibility and autonomy.

Source: J. R. Hackman and G. R. Oldham, *Work Redesign* (Reading, MA: Addison-Wesley, 1980).

tools, and poor working conditions waste effort, leading to a poor linkage between the amount of effort the employee puts in and the performance he sees from his effort. Lack of training and poor working conditions and tools therefore affect the effort-to-performance linkage.

Think about how you feel when a software failure causes a loss of work or a poor Internet connection thwarts your online research capability. If these problems occur occasionally, you may ignore them and plug along; but if the problems persist and you have to start over constantly, you are likely to become frustrated and unmotivated. Eventually you will stop trying. Providing training that allows employees to focus their efforts appropriately and providing equipment, tools, and working conditions that support rather than hinder efforts are key to building employees' perceptions that their efforts lead to good performance.

We have seen that job design, training, and working conditions affect motivation. Managers can also use goal setting to increase employees' motivation and performance.

Goal Setting   Working toward clear goals is an essential factor in the effort-to-performance linkage. Because of the importance of goal setting in directing and motivating employees, considerable research examines the goal-setting process.[33] Early work on goal setting focused on the concept of **management by objectives (MBO)**. MBO details precise steps in setting objectives with employees, monitoring progress, and providing feedback and correction.[34] In general, MBO and many other goal-setting methods assume that an employee must have clear, challenging, measurable, and specific goals to be motivated and to perform well.[35]

Management by objectives (MBO)
Focuses on setting goals, monitoring progress, and giving feedback and correction

What Are Appropriate Goals? Goals should focus attention and direct employee efforts, resulting in increased motivation. Appropriate goals need to be **SMART**—that is, they need to be (1) *s*pecific, (2) *m*easurable, (3) *a*chievable but challenging, (4) *r*easonable, and (5) *t*imely. Figure 6.5 summarizes the five elements of SMART goals.

SMART goals
Specific, measurable, achievable, reasonable, and have a time frame

Let's examine in more detail the five elements of SMART goals. First, goals must be *specific*. Telling an employee that she needs to do a better job is not a helpful comment because it is too general. Telling her that her sales need to improve by 5 percent provides a specific target. Second, goals should be *measurable*. Setting a goal of 10 percent fewer errors on insurance claims is a measurable goal. Setting a goal for your insurance representatives that they need to make fewer mistakes cannot be measured easily because what is considered "fewer" is a matter of interpretation. The representative who catches one of her mistakes in a given week can legitimately claim that she has made fewer mistakes. However, the manager can also assert that catching one error is not enough. The fact that "fewer" is not precise leads to confusion.

Third and fourth, goals should be *achievable* and *reasonable*. If goals are set so high that they are impossible to reach, they likely will decrease motivation. If you know you can't achieve a goal, you aren't likely to try. A reasonable goal is not only achievable but should also be set at the appropriate level of difficulty, being neither too easy nor too hard.[36] For example, it is reasonable to expect an experienced salesperson to increase his sales by 5 to 10 percent every year. The same goal would not be reasonable for a new salesperson.

Fifth, SMART goals should have an *appropriate time frame*. Employees must have a reasonable deadline for achieving the targeted goals. For example, a manager may urge her assistant to broaden her education and skills by taking college courses. In spite of regular encouragement, the employee may not take the courses unless the two agree on some time frame, say "in the next year I will take two college courses."

To see how the five elements of SMART goal setting work together, consider academic performance goals. Many students mistakenly set goals that are too high, given their current level of performance. The student who is close to failing might set a goal of getting all As in her classes after the first round of Ds on her three midterms. Such a goal is neither achievable nor timely. As soon as she receives a grade lower than A (a likely prospect given her past performance with Ds), she will be discouraged and her motivation will drop.

A more appropriate goal for the D student might be to earn all Cs in the next term and at least one B in the term after that. For a student earning mostly Bs and As, an appropriate goal might be to achieve As in three out of four classes taken next term. In both cases, the goals are specific, measurable, achievable, reasonable, and timely (have a workable time frame), given the needs of each student and past performance.

FIGURE 6.5
SMART Goals

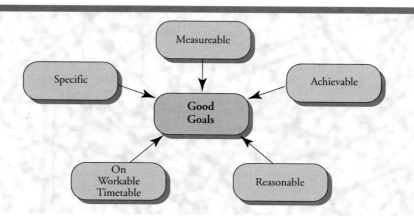

Organizational goals need to follow a similar pattern. They have to be clear, specific, appropriately challenging, and reasonable in terms of time. Ideally, all goals should be measurable. However, not all goals can be measured precisely, a factor that limits the applicability of goal setting. For instance, consulting firms face the challenge of trying to satisfy their clients' needs. Consultants have to be creative because each client seeks solutions to novel problems.

Now imagine that a consulting firm decides to set goals for its consultants to make them more productive. Setting limits for the number of hours each consultant can spend with a client or asking that each consultant service two additional clients per month is a counterproductive efficiency goal. After all, the only reason for a client to pay the high fees of a consulting firm is to receive personal attention and help with unique problems.

Trying to set measurable goals for jobs that do not have measurable outcomes is often counterproductive because the goals rarely relate directly to the outcome. In the consulting example, the only goal is client satisfaction, which is a subjective outcome and tough to measure. The firm will be not be served well by giving its consultants efficiency goals that are not related to this desired outcome.

For jobs that have clearly measurable goals, such as sales ("sales representatives should increase sales in their region by 5 percent this year"), SMART goal setting can help link efforts to performance more clearly. The result is likely to be increased motivation. On the other hand, for workers in jobs where outcomes are not easily measured, SMART goal setting is likely to be counterproductive and may reduce rather than increase motivation. Let's explore how managers set goals for jobs that have measurable outcomes.

The SMART Goal-Setting Process   As Figure 6.6 indicates, the SMART goal-setting process involves three steps: (1) set goals by applying the SMART rules, (2) involve employees in goal setting, and (3) support employees through monitoring and feedback as they work on achieving the goals.

Employee involvement in specific goal setting leads to higher performance because it strengthens the effort-to-performance and the performance-to-outcome linkages. For instance, understanding how goals link to various positive outcomes helps increase employees' motivation to work toward the goals.

Involvement in the goal-setting process is crucial for two additional reasons. First, employee feedback helps managers set SMART goals. Second, employee participation leads to commitment and acceptance of the goals.[37] The buy-in and commitment further motivate employees to perform their jobs well.

Involving the employee should take into account both the employee's and the organization's needs. Employees may set low goals; the organization may demand too much. The needs of the two must be balanced. The skillful manager negotiates goals to assure a fit between the two.

FIGURE 6.6
The Three SMART Goal-Setting Steps

Summary Point 6.5   **What Job Factors Affect Motivation?**

- The job itself is the single most important component of motivation.
- To help motivate an employee, the manager should match the job to the employee's needs.
- Skill variety, task identity, task significance, autonomy, and feedback are key factors in designing jobs that motivate.
- Training and job tools influence motivation.

- SMART goals are specific, measurable, achievable, reasonable, and timely.
- SMART goal setting has limited application to jobs that have hard-to-measure outcomes.
- The goal-setting process involves three steps: (1) setting goals according to SMART rules, (2) involving employees in goal setting, and (3) supporting employees as they strive to reach goals.

The final step in goal setting is monitoring and providing feedback and support after the goals are set. Monitoring allows the manager to see whether the employee is progressing well. The manager needs to stay in touch through regular formal and informal meetings to allow the employee to provide feedback; to request assistance, training, or resources; or to renegotiate deadlines or goals.

We have so far considered two factors—the role of individual differences and the job situation—that can be used to motivate employees. Next, we investigate the third and final factor: the organization.

The Organization

Organizational elements that affect employee motivation include organizational culture, leadership, co-workers, and the concept of *equity*. Some researchers argue that although these elements cannot motivate employees by themselves, they can enhance motivation if they work to support individual and job-related factors.[38]

Organizational Culture, Politics, and Trust   Even a highly motivated individual doing the most challenging job will have trouble maintaining consistently high motivation and performance if the organization does not have a supportive, trusting culture. An organization that has a culture in which negative political game playing, gossiping, in-fighting, abuse, and general hostility are prevalent will have difficulty keeping employees motivated, regardless of how well jobs are designed and goals are set. In a distrustful climate, employees are likely to feel that factors other than performance determine outcomes. The result will be a reduction in employee work motivation because of a weaker performance-to-outcome linkage.

Conversely, a climate of support, openness, trust, and collegiality can help compensate for other problems. Think back to Malden Mills, the company profiled in the Managerial Challenge. Its organizational culture of concern for employees, trust, and loyalty contributed to employee motivation and continued performance, especially after the fire. Employees without state-of-the-art equipment or formal training may still be motivated and perform well if they feel supported and valued by the organization. Although by itself a healthy and supportive culture is not sufficient to motivate employees, it provides the background that allows the individual and job factors to work. Leadership and co-workers operate in a similar manner.

Leadership and Co-Workers   Leaders and co-workers can have a positive or negative effect on motivation and performance. Managers and co-workers who support an employee's work efforts help strengthen the E–P linkage. If the people you work with do not help you, your efforts are likely to be wasted. For example, they may not provide the technical assistance you need or may forget to mention key information you need in your report or proposal. The outcome is poor performance.

In the worst case, co-workers and poor leadership can sabotage a person's efforts, preventing her from performing well. Even though you may be doing an excellent job, colleagues and managers may denigrate your efforts and accomplishments to the point that you lose your motivation to work. If co-workers and leaders are supportive, however, employees thrive.

Leadership influences employees' perception that their good performance will lead to positive outcomes (P–O linkage). At Malden Mills, for example, Feuerstein's leadership inspires trust and loyalty. An employee must trust his boss to evaluate him fairly; recognize his work; and recommend him for a raise, a bonus, or a promotion when appropriate. Few of us expect immediate rewards for our good performance. However, if the organization consistently ignores good performance and does not relate it to positive outcomes, the P–O linkage will weaken and motivation will be adversely affected.

Equity   Probably the most important organizational factor linking performance to outcome is the individual's perception of equity. **Equity** is a sense that something is fair, just, and impartial. Employees will perceive that an organization is acting equitably if they are receiving the outcomes they feel they deserve.[39] Equity differs from equality in that equality refers to having the same outcomes or rewards as someone else. An employee may receive a grade or raise equal to someone else's, but still feel that it is inequitable because she worked harder and performed better. At the heart of the sense of equity is the concept of what a person puts into a certain situation and what he gets in return.

Equity in motivation theory is defined as the employee's perception of the fairness of and balance of the ratio of inputs to outputs. To feel that an organization is equitable, people must feel that their effort, time, education, previous experience, and whatever else they bring to their work are roughly matched by the salary, recognition, promotion, and other outputs they get for their work. Malden Mills created a sense of equity by taking care of employees even when they could not produce because of the fire. Figure 6.7 depicts the state of equity.

Scenarios for Inequity   A sense of inequity results when you perceive that your inputs do not match your outputs. Figure 6.8 on page 209 shows three different states of inequity. The first state is a common one: "What I put in is more than what I get. That is, my salary, title, bonus, and so forth are not enough compared to my hard work." The second scenario, known as over-equity, is less harmful to motivation than the first one. In the case of over-equity you receive more output than you deserve, given the input. Our ego and various perceptual biases make us less likely to notice this type of inequity compared to the first situation. Have you ever felt that you were paid too much, that you didn't deserve your latest promotion, or that you didn't earn the good grades that you received in your classes last semester?

The third situation shows that in determining equity, we not only look at our inputs and outputs but we almost always compare them to other people's.[40] As a point of comparison, you may pick one or more people at work or in your classes who you believe give inputs similar to yours. When comparing your input-to-output (I/O) ratio to these people, even

Equity
A sense that something is fair, just, and impartial. In motivation equity refers to perceiving that your inputs and outputs are balanced

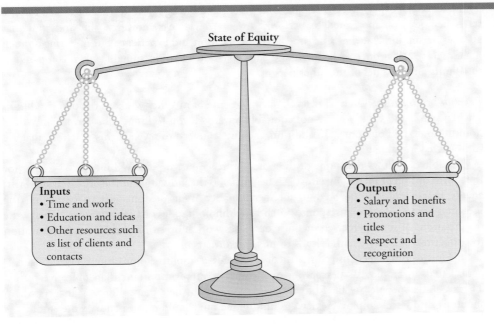

FIGURE 6.7
State of Equity

Team Challenge

MOTIVATING TEAM MEMBERS

Teams have worked wonders in many organizations. They can achieve many feats that individuals alone cannot. However, teams pose a motivational challenge, especially in individualistic cultures in which personal achievement and recognition motivate people. Clearly, a team is not for everyone. For some, working in teams is an uplifting, highly motivating experience. For others, it is limiting and frustrating.[a] Are you willing to motivate your teammates and in turn be motivated by them? Is peer pressure enough to motivate you, or do you have be individually recognized to feel successful?

If you are motivated by how quickly you climb the corporate ladder because of your personal accomplishments, you should think twice before you consider working for team-oriented companies such as Boeing, Intel, industrial design firm Ideo Product Development, and the Medium Engine Product Division of Caterpillar Inc. All these firms want employees who are willing to give up their personal agenda in exchange for the pleasures of teamwork. However, they are all willing to tie your reward to the success of your team.[b]

a. T. A. Stewart, "The Great Conundrum: You vs. the Team," *Fortune* 134, no. 10 (1996): 165–66.

b. R. Y. Bergstrom, "Teams: Dedicated Players," *Production* 106, no. 2 (1994): 58.

though your own I/O ratio is balanced, you will still perceive inequity if you think someone else with similar input receives greater output than you do.

Suppose a new employee negotiated long and hard to get the salary and title that she felt matched her experience, education, and potential. Having received what she asked for, she starts her new job motivated to perform. After a few weeks, however, she finds out that another person hired at the same time has less education and experience but is getting a much higher salary. What once seemed fair and equitable now seems inequitable when compared to the inputs and outputs of the other person.

Reactions to Inequity   On a basic level, having a sense of inequity weakens the perceived linkage between P and O. If you are not equitably rewarded, you feel that your performance does not lead to desired outcomes. In addition, inequity can lead to several other reactions that are summarized in Table 6.1.

Table 6.1 shows that none of the potential reactions to perceived inequity—except for the fourth option of increasing effort—is beneficial to the individual or the organization. First, energy that should be devoted to job performance is devoted instead to correcting the inequity. Second, potential responses such as withholding ideas or sabotage can damage the organization. In sum, perceived inequity decreases work motivation and increases motivation to correct the inequity. Neither leads to high performance.[41]

How can managers use equity theory to increase employee motivation? They must recognize that an employee's perception of inequity is more important than objective reality. That's because people are likely to behave according to their perceptions. Managers, then, shouldn't dismiss an employee's views as unfounded but should instead address the employee's perceptions and provide hard facts and data to change inaccurate perceptions. The employee who inaccurately perceives her salary to be too low is likely to be convinced with specific data

FIGURE 6.8   *Examples of Inequity*

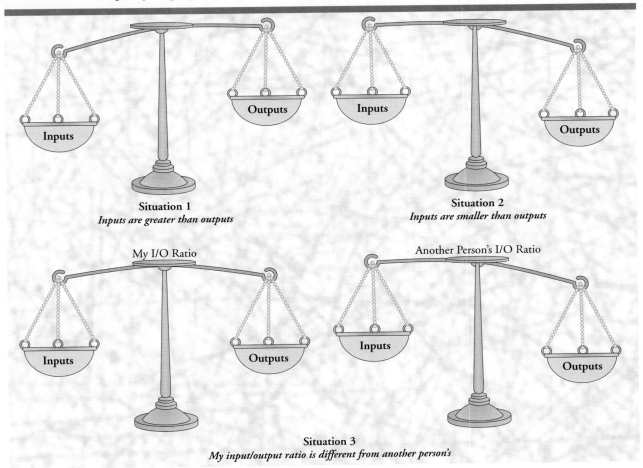

Situation 1
Inputs are greater than outputs

Situation 2
Inputs are smaller than outputs

Situation 3
My input/output ratio is different from another person's

Table 6.1   POTENTIAL REACTIONS TO INEQUITY

Reaction	Example
1. Increase outputs	Employee asks for a raise or promotion.
2. Decrease inputs	Employee works fewer hours or holds back ideas from the organization.
3. Decrease output	Worker refuses promotion or raise.
4. Increase inputs	Employee works harder or gets a college degree.
5. Pick a different comparison person	Employee finds someone who, in his or her estimation, is more similar to him or her.
6. Increase the comparison person's input	Employee sabotages or refuses to cooperate with the comparison person, which makes comparison person's job harder.
7. Decrease other person's output	Employee's complaints about comparison person's output prevents comparison person from receiving a raise or promotion.
8. Quit or transfer	Employee leaves to avoid feeling of inequity.

about salaries in her department. If, as in many cases, the organization keeps such data confidential, the manager may have a difficult time changing the employee's perceptions.

Consider the case of an organization that conducted a study of salaries as a result of long-standing accusations and complaints of gender bias. The results of the study were then used to increase all female employees' salary by 10 percent to 20 percent. One may expect that the female employees were satisfied with the outcome. However, given that salaries in the company were secret, many female employees continued to suspect that the problem was worse than originally thought. In addition, male employees who were previously satisfied with their salaries started complaining about inequitable treatment.

This example points out the challenge of working with people's perceptions of inequity. As mentioned in chapter 5, perceptions are powerful and difficult to change. The role and power of perceptions in motivation increase the difficulty of keeping employees motivated.

We have explored the three major motivation factors: the person, the job, and the organization. Managers are typically responsible for influencing motivation. In traditional organizations, for instance, the manager would be entirely responsible for assigning, creating, or designing jobs. In less traditional organizations, a team or an individual employee may be involved in such decisions, as we'll see in the next two chapters. In both cases, however, the manager can have a strong effect on employees' job performance. Based on the role of organizational factors in motivation, managers must be watchful of the organizational culture, monitor interpersonal relations, and attempt to correct real or perceived inequities through actions or discussion with their employees.

Our discussion of motivation as a component of performance focused on the expectancy approach, a cognitive model that considers the individual's perceptions and expectations of outcomes. Another approach to managing performance is to concentrate on observable behaviors and to control the situation in which they occur and the consequences of those behaviors. We explore the latter performance management approach in the rest of the chapter.

A QUESTION OF ETHICS

Secret Salaries   In some cases, accurate knowledge of other employees' salaries can help motivate employees who have misperceptions about such information. However, in most organizations, salary structures are secret. Do you think it's fair for a company to keep salaries confidential? Is it more fair to provide full salary information? Is there a way to maintain employee privacy and still allow information in special circumstances? Do you think it is ethical for employees who work in a company that keeps salaries confidential to exchange salary information with other employees? Explain.

Summary Point 6.6   What Organizational Factors Affect Motivation?

- An organizational culture of trust, openness, and collegiality is key to motivation because it clears the path from performance to outcome.
- Supportive and positive relations with co-workers and managers can help strengthen the effort–performance and performance–outcome linkages.
- Equity, defined as the perception of justice and fairness, affects the performance-to-outcome linkage.
- Individuals assess equity by looking at the balance of their inputs and outputs and by comparing themselves to others.
- Perceptions of inequity motivate individuals to take actions which, except for increasing one's effort, often have negative consequences for organizations.

■ MANAGING PERFORMANCE BY PROVIDING OPPORTUNITIES AND MANAGING OUTCOMES

Recall that performance is a function of ability, motivation, and opportunities. Motivation is a cognitive process, so managers focus on employees' *perceptions* to increase their motivation and improve performance. We now examine how managers can improve performance by focusing on employees' behavior and the situation in which the behavior occurs. First, we investigate *learning theory.* Then we examine how that theory can help managers improve employee performance.

Focusing on Behaviors and Learning

Why do some theorists advocate managing performance through behavioral learning as opposed to motivation? They argue that—compared to mental processes—behaviors are easier for managers to observe and control and for individuals to change.

The focus on learning rather than on individual personality and perception dates back to the turn of the twentieth century with the behaviorist approach in psychology. This approach, associated primarily with psychologist B. F. Skinner, is generally known as **learning theory** because of its focus on learning behaviors.[42] According to learning theorists, managers can influence employee performance by providing the environment and opportunities that encourage appropriate performance-related behaviors and discourage performance-hindering behaviors.[43]

Learning theory
An approach to understanding and predicting human behavior that focuses on learning behaviors

Learning in Organizations   Learning theory has influenced most modern organizations, as demonstrated by their reliance on training and development programs to enhance employee productivity and effectiveness. Xerox Corporation offers its employees extensive training through simulations and seminars to support the company's considerable growth. The goal is to reinforce the company mission of continuous learning. Chris Turner, the leader of Xerox's XBS division, says the goal is "creating a community of inquirers and learners." She further states: "We've got to create an organization where everyone has lot of knowledge of the business."[44]

Internationally, companies that succeed are often known for their well-trained workforce. The German apprenticeship system assures German organizations of a supply of highly skilled employees. Japanese companies use long and extensive on-the-job training as a learning tool in their organizations. In China, Xian-Janssen Pharmaceuticals, Ltd., is rated as one of the top Chinese joint ventures, mainly because of its extensive training program in which new employees spend three to six months learning the company's methods before joining the regular work staff.[45]

In South Korea, one of the leading industrial organizations, the Samsung Group, has instituted a new training program that leads to increased productivity and better employee participation.[46] Similarly, the multinational firm of Colgate-Palmolive has been successful in its manufacturing operations in Eastern Europe mainly because of its thorough training program.[47]

Another factor that affects learning and performance in organizations is the organization's culture. One of the most important concepts to emerge from recent research in this area is the *learning organization.*[48] **Learning organizations** are systems that over time enhance their ability and capacity to innovate and create. Proponents of this concept argue that organizations, just like individuals, need to focus on developing new skills, competencies, and strategies and must ensure that all the members of the organization learn them, too. To do this, the business must create a culture and structure that support learning and information exchange. Those businesses that cannot adapt and innovate because of their culture and structure are bound to be ineffective and perform poorly in today's environment. We explore the concept of learning organizations further in chapter 15.

Learning organizations
Systems that over time enhance their ability and capacity to innovate and create

Organizations all over the world require their employees to continue to learn new skills to broaden their knowledge base. For example, Samsung of South Korea relies on educational programs to help increase productivity. Increasingly, the emphasis on continuous learning is a key to success.

Elements of Learning Successful learning in organizations depends on managers' understanding of the *principles of learning* and their application to management situations. The principles of learning are based on a simple model called the Antecedent-Behavior-Consequence (ABC) model.

As an illustration of learning principles, consider this example. A busy manager has finally finished the yearly performance evaluations and ranking of her employees. She now needs to decide on several actions based on her evaluations. Although decisions regarding the top performers may appear easier than those relating to the bottom performers, they are equally difficult. In the first case, our manager needs to assure that the top performers continue to do well. Each needs to be groomed for potential promotions. What training should they get? Which projects should they be assigned to provide challenge and growth? Should she leave them alone or work closely with them? Should she create nonmonetary programs to provide them with recognition or rely on the raise and bonus that headquarters has assigned?

The manager must also decide what to do with the poor performers. Which one is performing poorly because of a lack of training and knowledge? How should she discipline those who are lazy and need a good wake-up call? When should she reward them if their performance starts improving?

On a more general level, what messages is the organization sending about performance? How are people rewarded? What are the expectations? What are the structural and managerial obstacles to change and to learning? These and many other decisions challenge managers who try to provide learning opportunities for employees. In the next section, we examine the ABC learning principles and their applications to organizations and performance management.

Summary Point 6.7   How Does Learning Theory Help Manage Performance?

- Learning theory focuses on behavior.
- The principles of learning are based on the assumption that individual behaviors need to be clearly tied to their consequences.

- Managers need to focus on encouraging performance-enhancing behavior and discouraging performance-hindering behavior.

Learning Principles

The traditional approach to learning is to focus on the individual and the immediate environment that he or she faces. At the heart of learning theory is the assumption that behaviors are learned and influenced by managing the consequences of those behaviors. People repeat behaviors that bring them satisfaction and pleasure, and stop those that bring them dissatisfaction and pain. This principle is known as the **law of effect**.[49]

Reinforcement theory recommends providing an organizational environment and response patterns that reward and encourage desirable behaviors while punishing and discouraging undesirable ones. Reinforcement theory is based on the idea that external factors such as rewards and punishments determine a person's behavior. Put another way, the consequences of a person's behavior determine that person's future action. According to reinforcement theory, a manager's reaction to an employee's poor performance will determine whether the employee will continue to perform poorly or decide to work harder.

Consequences of Behavior To control behaviors through consequences, managers can use positive reinforcement, negative reinforcement, and punishment, as summarized in Table 6.2. We review each type of action next.

Reinforcers A **reinforcer** is an outcome or event that increases the likelihood that a behavior will occur again. It is easy to confuse reinforcers with rewards. **Organizational rewards** are positive outcomes that organizations provide to individuals. Examples of organizational rewards include promotions, raises, bonuses, public recognition such as employee-of-the-month awards, and letters of commendation. As discussed in the motivation section, whether an organizational reward encourages the desired behavior depends on the needs of the individual. Therefore, not all organizational rewards act as reinforcers for all individuals. Additionally, not all reinforcers are positive and pleasant.

A **positive reinforcer** is a pleasant outcome that follows a desired behavior and is aimed at encouraging the behavior. A manager publicly recognizing her best salesperson at the end of each month is trying to create positive reinforcement. Like a positive reinforcer, a **negative reinforcer** is also aimed at encouraging a certain behavior. However, it is unpleasant and comes before the behavior occurs. The supervisor who threatens a regularly tardy employee with a reprimand or a reduction in pay is using negative reinforcement. The goal is to encourage the employee to be on time. The threat, a negative event, takes place before the behavior occurs and stops when the employee comes in on time.

Those of us who nag our friends, spouses, roommates, and children to get them to do what we want are using negative reinforcement. The appreciation we express—the hugs and kisses and other positive events we deliver after they do what we asked—are positive reinforcement. Although one reinforcer is positive and the other one negative, they are both called reinforcers because they aim at increasing a desired behavior. The focus on increasing the rate of a behavior distinguishes reinforcement, especially negative reinforcement, from punishment.

Law of effect
People repeat behaviors that bring them satisfaction and pleasure, and stop those that bring them dissatisfaction and pain

Reinforcement theory
Theory that recommends rewarding and encouraging desirable behaviors, and punishing and discouraging undesirable ones by providing an organizational environment and response pattern that will guide proper behavior

Reinforcer
An outcome or event that increases the likelihood of a behavior occurring again

Organizational rewards
Positive outcomes that organizations provide individuals

Positive reinforcer
A pleasant outcome that follows a desired behavior and is aimed at encouraging the behavior

Negative reinforcer
An unpleasant outcome preceding a behavior aimed at encouraging a certain behavior

T a b l e   6 . 2   CONSEQUENCES OF BEHAVIOR

Type	Nature	Goal	Timing
Positive reinforcement	Pleasant event or outcome	Increase a certain behavior	After behavior takes place
Negative reinforcement	Unpleasant event or outcome	Increase a certain behavior	Before behavior takes place
Punishment	Unpleasant event or outcome	Decrease a certain behavior	After behavior takes place

Punishment
A negative event that occurs after an undesirable behavior and is aimed at stopping that behavior

Punishment The third option for a manager to manage behavior through consequences is the use of punishment. **Punishment** is a negative event that occurs after an undesirable behavior and is aimed at stopping that behavior. The typical punishments in organizations are oral and written reprimands, docking of pay, demotions, and firing. All these negative actions are aimed at getting employees to stop something they are not supposed to do. The consistently tardy employee who does not respond to the threat (negative reinforcement) may receive a formal reprimand and have his paycheck docked; eventually, he may even be fired (punishments).

Using Consequences to Manage Behavior Organizations can use a combination of positive and negative reinforcers and punishment to manage employee learning and performance. To use such a combination well, managers must recognize several rules and processes that we investigate next.

Golden Rules Reinforcements and punishments are effective only if used in combination and with care. As shown in Table 6.3, two key factors for effective use are the timing and amount of reinforcement and punishment.

The rules for using reinforcement and punishment focus on clearly linking behaviors and their consequences. First, whether you use reinforcement or punishment, the key is to focus on *work-related behaviors*. The goal should not be to change an employee's personality or non-work-related behaviors. The target should be, at all times, behaviors that contribute to or detract from performance and productivity.

Second, it is important that managers provide a *quick response* to either positive or negative behaviors. If an employee is late or makes too many personal phone calls, his manager should discuss the problems as soon as possible rather than wait for the regularly scheduled evaluation several months later. Third, managers must be consistent with different employees and across situations to encourage desired behaviors. The fourth rule in Table 6.3 urges managers to provide meaningful reinforcers for desired behaviors. Consider an organization that offers movie tickets or a complimentary dinner for two to employees who share ideas that save the organization millions of dollars. Is the reward meaningful? Will it encourage sharing of ideas? Such rewards are not large enough to encourage the desired behavior. A percentage of the cost saving or a share in the business generated by the new idea is more likely to reinforce

Table 6.3   RULES FOR USING REINFORCEMENT AND PUNISHMENT

Rule	Description
• Focus on specific, job-related behaviors.	Identify specific behaviors rather than general attitudes; stay away from issues and behaviors that are not directly related to job performance.
• Respond quickly.	Provide reinforcement or punishment as soon as possible to make the connection between behavior and consequence clear.
• Be consistent (the "hot stove" rule).	The same behavior, good or bad, should lead to the same consequence every time and for everybody (the "hot stove" should burn everyone every time).
• Remember that the larger the positive reinforcer, the better.	Generally, provide as large a positive reinforcer as possible.
• Use punishment sparingly.	Although punishment is sometimes necessary, it can have negative consequences; therefore, it should be used sparingly and as a last resort.
• Give praise in public; punish in private.	With the exception of some cultures, public praise is more effective than private praise; punishment, however, should be private.
• Provide alternative behaviors after punishing.	Because punishment is aimed at stopping undesirable behaviors, follow up with examples of alternative positive behaviors.

innovation. One manager, for example, decided that the best way to reinforce the right level of productivity for his employees was to give them a substantial share of each client's fees, resulting in a 60 percent raise for each employee.[50]

The last three rules address the use of punishment in organizations. Punishment requires careful application because it has many negative consequences. Managers should use punishment sparingly and as a last resort. Relying on punishment as the primary method of managing employee behavior can lead to fear, resentment, lack of productivity, and potentially damaging behaviors. Another very important point is that employees should be punished in private. Public reprimands humiliate the employee and increase the negative effects of punishment. In one organization we visited, a manager openly berated a telephone sales agent in front of 50 other employees. A few minutes later, he asked why his business had almost a 100 percent yearly turnover. The answer of course was that his almost exclusive reliance on punishment created an intolerable climate, causing most of the turnover. Finally, if managers use punishment, they should clearly point out alternative behaviors that they consider desirable. That way, employees know how to replace unacceptable behavior with acceptable behavior for which they will not be punished.

Applying learning principles to organizations takes careful thought and planning. The process of setting up appropriate reinforcement systems is lengthy and complex. Organization Behavior Modification models try to simplify this process.

Organization Behavior Modification The application of learning principles to manage organizational behavior is often referred to as **organization behavior modification (OB Mod)**.[51] OB Mod proposes a five-step process that identifies and encourages appropriate employee behaviors. We present the OB Mod steps in Figure 6.9.

The first and most important step in OB Mod is for managers to *identify specific desirable and undesirable behaviors*. They must answer the question: "What must employees do and not do to perform well?" Be on time, respond quickly to customer and co-worker requests, fill out paperwork by deadline, and so forth are obvious examples. However, it is not always easy

Organizational behavior modification (OB Mod)
The application of learning principles to manage organizational behavior

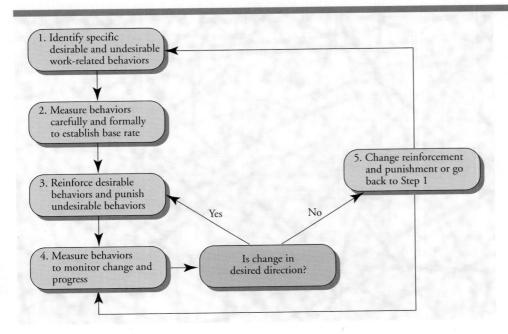

FIGURE 6.9
The Organization Behavior Modification Process

for managers to define clearly what they want. For example, do employees need to be at work from 9 to 5 to get their jobs done? In traditional organizations, the answer is yes. However, in many organizations, employees can do their job off site at all hours of the day or night. Being present during the traditional work day, then, is not always a required behavior.

Merrill Lynch has redefined what behaviors are required for its telecommuting employees to perform their jobs. The company provides each employee who telecommutes with about $7,000 of state-of-the-art technology that includes a laptop computer, a fax machine, and a printer to allow telecommuters to link with co-workers and customers. They also make sure that employees have proper office space and ergonomic equipment, and they provide training for employees to learn to stay organized and set up a routine for work at home.[52] The company has identified these behaviors as key to performance for telecommuting employees.

The second step in OB Mod is to measure the frequency of identified behaviors to establish a baseline. The baseline helps managers apply the model in an objective, realistic manner. The third step is to apply reinforcement and punishment to encourage desirable behaviors and discourage undesirable ones. To use reinforcement and punishment effectively, managers should be mindful of the rules set forth in Table 6.3. Fourth, after a given period of time under the new reinforcement, managers need once again to measure the frequency of the behaviors and compare this assessment to their earlier baseline.

Fifth, if change has occurred in the right direction—meaning desirable behaviors have increased and undesirable ones decreased—managers must focus on maintaining the reinforcement and punishment they used. If change has not occurred in the right direction, they must either reconsider the behaviors they identified in step one or change the consequences in step three.

The OB Mod process has several distinguishing characteristics. First, it focuses entirely on specific, work-related behaviors. Second, it emphasizes careful measurement of all target behaviors at three key times: before anything is done so as to establish a base rate, during the intervention, and after intervention. These measurements monitor changes systematically. Third, OB Mod recommends an ongoing process to reassess the target behavior choices and the use of various reinforcers and punishment.

A crucial step for organizations is to analyze carefully what they actually reward. Many unproductive behaviors go unnoticed or are even rewarded by organizations. In a classic article entitled, "On the Folly of Rewarding A While Hoping for B," Professor Steven Kerr provides several examples of how organizations reward behaviors they say they do not want.[53] He discusses universities' statements about the importance of teaching while rewarding only research, and other organizations' setting goals of quality while encouraging efficiency through the reward system, often at the expense of quality.

A QUESTION OF ETHICS

Attending Social Hours?	Is it desirable for employees to attend the informal social hour after work? If it helps employees' careers, should the manager reward such behaviors formally or informally? How should managers handle fairly and ethically those employees who do not attend after-work social hours? Does it make a difference if the employees don't attend because they have family responsibilities? Does it matter that alcohol is consumed at the social hour and the employees have religious and moral objections to the sale and consumption of alcohol?

Organizations often say they'll reward one type of behavior but instead reward another. For instance, organizations may say they value creativity and innovation but punish those who try to be creative and fail. Those who play it safe are rewarded instead. If creativity and innovation are desired outcomes, then the consequences for creativity and experimentation, which in some cases are failure, need to be positive rather than negative.

Motivating employees to perform well is a complex task that involves interaction among the individual, the job, and the organization. The right person has to be selected, the job has to match the person's needs, and the organization has to provide the right opportunities for performance, including support, leadership, training, and reward systems to encourage performance. To motivate employees and manage performance, managers need to have a good understanding of each employee's individual differences—personality traits, needs, and values—and match those to the job the person does. The jobs have to be regularly evaluated and redesigned when necessary. In addition, managers must analyze the organizational policies, culture, and structure. Once managers understand what motivates employees, they then need to manage their employees' performance by providing the right learning and performance opportunities and by managing the consequences of employee actions.

Summary Point 6.8   **How Can Managers Apply Learning Principles?**

- Assume that people will repeat behaviors that bring them satisfaction and pleasure and stop those that bring them dissatisfaction and pain.
- Use positive and negative reinforcers to increase desirable behaviors.

- Recognize that organizational rewards are not always reinforcers for all individuals.
- Use punishment to decrease undesirable behaviors.
- Apply OB Mod, a formal process for identifying performance-related behaviors and managing those behaviors by managing their consequences.

Motivation *in Context*

As you have read in this chapter, motivation is a highly individual process. Motivating employees depends on managing the individual, job-related, and organizational factors that affect how each person perceives his or her work and the outcomes he or she gets. However, the organizational context is crucial. Particularly, strategy, structure, technology, and culture are key contextual factors that affect employee motivation.

On a general level, an employee's motivation and interest to work in an organization starts with a fit between what the person values and is looking for and what the organization has to offer. The mission and goals of the organization must therefore generally fit with the goals, values, and aspirations of employees. Managers face the challenge of creating that fit through work assignment, training, goal setting, career planning, and so forth.

A second contextual force that affects motivation is the structure of the organization. How people are organized to work impacts the work itself, an employee's relationships with co-workers, the level of autonomy and feedback, interaction with supervisors, and the opportunity to learn and be challenged. Managers need to create the right structure so that employees have the autonomy and the skill variety they need to perform their tasks. Debbie Herd, a recruiter for J.C. Penney, explains: "It occurred to us that Gen Xers will work 90 hours a week if they have their own business. So we decided we needed to make them *think* they are entrepreneurs."[54] "Freedom and responsibility are the very best golden handcuffs there are," explains David Witte, CEO of Ward Howell International executive search firm.[55] These managers have used the structure to motivate their employees.

We have already discussed how poor equipment and inappropriate tools can impede motivation by weakening the E–P linkage. Managers therefore must be mindful of how technology affects their employees. Having the right tools and training motivates people to perform their jobs well. Conversely, poor training and insufficient technology tools lead to frustration and decreased motivation.

Using technology in creative ways can be a powerful motivating factor. For example, Boeing relies on technology to allow its production workers fast access to the tools they need. The company uses tool vending machines developed by Vortex Technologies, a high-tech company based in Cincinnati, Ohio, to dispense power tools on the shop floor. Not only do workers have quick access to the right tools, the system also allows managers to monitor when and where tools are used so they can keep a sufficient supply on hand.[56] The appropriate use of technology removes obstacles to getting the job done and increases motivation.

Finally, culture at the national, ethnic or group, and organizational levels is key to motivation. As we discussed earlier, people from different cultures have different needs and values. Therefore, different factors motivate them. Managers must understand the impact of national and ethnic culture on motivation to be able to manage people in a global environment. Additionally, managers must be aware how their organizational culture supports or blocks motivation. At one level, as is the case with strategy, the organizational culture must fit with individual employee values. At another level, the culture must provide a context that supports employees' efforts, allows them to do their jobs, and rewards them fairly and equitably.

For updated information on the topics in this chapter, Web exercises, links to related Web sites, an on-line study guide, and more, visit our companion Web site at:
http://www.prenhall.com/nahavandi

A L o o k B a c k a t t h e

MANAGERIAL CHALLENGE

Rebuilding at Malden Mills

Aaron Feuerstein's focus on employees is rare in today's business world. His decision to continue paying the entire workforce while rebuilding after a devastating fire definitely helped his employees, their families, and the community. It also brought Malden Mills considerable media attention and earned the CEO a meeting with President Clinton.[57] But Feuerstein demonstrated more than social responsibility: He demonstrated good business sense. "I make it my personal business to see to it that I have loyalty and goodwill [among] my people," he later explained. "They're the valued asset, they're not just a cuttable expense. They're the people who make the quality for us and our products."[58]

In all, the company paid out $10 million in wages and benefits—but the investment quickly paid off. Within three months, two of the company's three divisions were operating at near-capacity; within 21 months, nearly all the employees were back at work.[59] Just as important, Malden Mills employees were showing even more motivation than before. In the past, up to 7 percent of the company's Polartec fabric failed to meet top-quality standards. After the fire, that figure dropped to just 2 percent. "This is a direct result of the goodwill and determination of our people to show their gratitude to Malden Mills," Feuerstein says.[60]

By showing loyalty to the workforce, Malden Mills increased the employees' motivation and loyalty, which in turn led to higher performance. The employees felt that their efforts were appreciated (E–P); their long-term loyalty and performance led to the desired equitable outcomes (P–O); and they were rewarded by keeping their jobs (V). Employee Idalinda Henriquez sums up the situation: "I wanted to show appreciation to Aaron Feuerstein. He's a good man. I'm a good worker. He needed our help."[61]

■ Point of View Exercises

You're the Manager: As a production manager at Malden Mills, how could you use positive or negative reinforcers to encourage employee behaviors that contribute to overall performance, such as increased attention to quality?

You're the Employee: As a production employee at Malden Mills, what positive reinforcers would you value—and what negative reinforcers would be meaningful to you?

SUMMARY OF LEARNING OBJECTIVES

1. **Define motivation, explain its importance, and review its three components.** Motivation is to the desire, the energy, and the interest to act. Along with ability and opportunity, motivation is one of the three factors in performance. However, employee motivation is, to a great extent, under the control of managers. The three components of motivation are individual differences, the work itself, and organizational factors.

2. **Describe how and why the expectancy framework helps managers understand motivation.** The expectancy model of motivation proposes that motivation is a cognitive or mental process in which individuals are motivated if they feel that their efforts (E) are likely to lead to performance (P), that performance will get them outcomes (O), and finally that they value (V) the outcomes offered. The expectancy model helps managers understand motivation because it considers the individual, work, and organizational factors of motivation.

3. **Identify the individual, job-related, and organizational factors that affect motivation.** Individual differences affect motivation by impacting each of the linkages in the expectancy model. Personality differences such as locus of control and self-esteem affect the extent to which an individual feels his or her efforts are linked to performance. Individual needs and culture are important when determining which outcomes individuals will value.

   The work itself is one of the key factors in motivation. For employees to be motivated, their need for challenge has to match the work's potential for motivation or motivating potential score (MPS). Task variety, task significance, task identity, autonomy, and feedback determine the MPS of a job. Jobs can be designed or redesigned to achieve fit with the employee. In addition, goal setting is another work factor in motivation. Setting goals that are specific, measurable, achievable, reasonable, and timely help motivation. Goals have to be at the appropriate level of difficulty to motivate employees. Furthermore, involving employees in goal setting gains commitment and further supports motivation.

   A positive organizational culture, appropriate leadership, and supportive co-workers are organizational factors in motivation. In addition, another key organizational factor is the sense of equity. A sense of equity occurs when a person believes that his or her inputs match the outputs obtained from work, especially when compared to the inputs and outputs of others. A sense of inequity leads to lack of motivation and a variety of corrective actions that detract from performance.

4. **Discuss the importance of behaviors, learning, and consequences in managing performance.** An alternative approach to performance management is to focus primarily on people's behavior rather than on their cognition. As opposed to mental processes, behaviors are easier for managers to control and for individuals to change. The behavior approach relies on learning principles that are based on a simple model called the Antecedent-Behavior-Consequence (ABC) model. Individuals will change their behavior based on the consequences. Behaviors that bring pleasure are repeated; those that bring pain or no consequence are stopped.

   Learning principles rely on reinforcement and punishment to manage behavior and create learning. A reinforcer is an outcome or event that increases the likelihood that a behavior will occurr again. It can be either positive or negative. Punishment is always negative and aimed at stopping a behavior. By focusing on work-related behaviors, providing immediate and consistent consequences, and combining positive and negative reinforcement and punishment, an organizational behavior modification (OB Mod) program can be set in place to manage employee performance.

KEY TERMS

autonomy, p. 201
equity, p. 207
feedback, p. 201
intrinsic motivation, p. 199
law of effect, p. 213
learning organizations,
    p. 211
learning theory, p. 211
management by objectives
    (MBO), p. 203

motivating potential score,
    p. 200
motivation, p. 190
needs, p. 191
negative reinforcer, p. 213
organizational rewards,
    p. 213
organization behavior
    modification (OB Mod),
    p. 215

positive reinforcer, p. 213
portfolio career, p. 192
punishment, p. 214
reinforcer, p. 213
reinforcement theory,
    p. 213
skill variety, p. 200
SMART, p. 204
task identity, p. 200
task significance, p. 201

REVIEW QUESTIONS

1. What role does motivation play in performance?
2. Describe the expectancy model of motivation and explain how it addresses the three major components of motivation.
3. How do individual differences affect motivation?
4. Describe the elements and implications of the job design model.
5. Compare and contrast positive and negative reinforcement and punishment.
6. How can managers use reinforcers and punishment to manage performance?

DISCUSSION QUESTIONS

1. What are the areas of a manager's and an employee's responsibility in motivation?
2. To what extent should a manager consider the national culture of each employee in motivation?
3. What are the implications of the job design model for how we recruit, manage, and evaluate employees?
4. How can managers use organizational culture as a motivational factor?
5. What are the ethical considerations of using OB Mod to manage employee behaviors?

▶ SELF-ASSESSMENT 6
Goal Setting

Select one area in your personal or professional life in which you would like to set some goals.

1. GOALS
Write up to three goals you would like to accomplish:

1. _____

2. _____

3. _____

2. EVALUATE THE GOALS

Evaluate your goals on each of the following dimensions using the 1 to 5 scale (1 = not at all; 5 = to a great extent). See Appendix 3 for a scoring key.

	Goal #1	Goal #2	Goal #3
1. Is the goal specific?	1 2 3 4 5	1 2 3 4 5	1 2 3 4 5
2. Is the goal clear?	1 2 3 4 5	1 2 3 4 5	1 2 3 4 5
3. Can you achieve the goal given your resources?	1 2 3 4 5	1 2 3 4 5	1 2 3 4 5
4. Is the goal doable given your skills and abilities?	1 2 3 4 5	1 2 3 4 5	1 2 3 4 5
5. Is there a specific time frame for achieving the goal?	1 2 3 4 5	1 2 3 4 5	1 2 3 4 5
6. Is there some flexibility in your time frame?	1 2 3 4 5	1 2 3 4 5	1 2 3 4 5
7. Can the goal be measured quantitatively?	1 2 3 4 5	1 2 3 4 5	1 2 3 4 5
8. Can you think of specific ways you could measure progress?	1 2 3 4 5	1 2 3 4 5	1 2 3 4 5
9. Is the goal challenging (neither too easy nor too hard)?	1 2 3 4 5	1 2 3 4 5	1 2 3 4 5
10. Will accomplishing the goal provide a learning opportunity?	1 2 3 4 5	1 2 3 4 5	1 2 3 4 5

3. REFINE YOUR GOALS

For each of the goals you have set, consider areas of improvement. Do they need to be more specific, measurable, achievable, and/or reasonable? Do you need a time frame? Refine and rewrite your goals based on the evaluation.

1. _____
2. _____
3. _____

▶ TEAM EXERCISE 6
OB Mod In Action

1. SELECT TARGET

Each group must select specific target behaviors to be changed and managed. Examples are changing the arrival habits of a habitually late employee, improving a receptionist's interaction with clients, improving sales skills, assuring that paperwork is completed, and so forth. The behaviors can also be related to a personal aspect such as getting one's roommate to pick up his or her messes, improving family members' message-taking skills, getting children to do homework on time, and so forth. The behaviors selected must be related to a team member's actual current or past experiences.

2.   DESIGN OB MOD PROGRAM

Following the OB Mod model in Figure 6.9, design a modification program to manage target behavior. The steps to include are these:

a.   Identify and list specific desirable and undesirable behaviors related to selected target.
b.   Identify possible baseline measures for those behaviors.
c.   Describe specific reinforcement and punishments to be used.
d.   Prepare brief contingency plan if behaviors are not managed as desired.

3.   PRESENT PLAN

Each group presents their plan to the class with clear justification for each step. The plans will be evaluated on how clearly and specifically behaviors are identified, the appropriateness of the behaviors selected, the measures, the reinforcement and punishment, and the contingency plan proposed.

UP CLOSE

▶ Too Much of a Good Thing

Paul Sutton had been working for the student life department of Southern University (SU) for almost two years. He started as a student adviser in general advising, working with freshmen and transfer students. He worked his way up to a graduate program coordinator position. During the two years at SU, he was promoted three times and received a nearly 50 percent raise in salary. His promotions and raises were unprecedented in the typically stodgy university system. Paul's boss, however, knew a top performer when she saw one and wanted to keep encouraging him for his work performance and creativity.

Paul came to SU with experience from both private industry and the public sector. After getting a B.S. in international business and marketing with honors, he had worked for a major high-technology company in strategic planning and corporate public relations for two years. He was consistently ranked as a high performer and was rated as a high-potential employee. His three bosses noted his strongest feature as "being an exceptionally quick learner with high energy." Paul had also worked for the city government in community relations. He left that job after six months in spite of high ratings and the promise of a good raise. His boss at the city offered him new responsibilities and new positions, to no avail.

Paul came to SU looking for a challenging position. He wanted to do something he had never done before and universities looked like a place where he could do his own thing and learn something new. The best part of his job was his boss who trusted him and left him alone. He also loved working with students and had developed an exceptional reputation as a highly effective adviser and recruiter. His regular job duties were simple. They included advising prospective graduate students and handing them off to specific program advisers once they selected an area as well as assisting the graduate dean with recruitment efforts. In addition, Paul was involved in a large number of activities ranging from SU's development campaign, to the design of databases for undergraduate admission, to cooperating with the public relations office on the design of brochures.

Paul's students and people outside his office loved him. His boss could not stop singing his praises. She sincerely believed that Paul was invaluable to her office and often worried about his being bored. Just like Paul's previous boss in the city, she was willing to do anything to keep Paul at SU.

Paul's immediate co-workers, who included several other advisers and the clerical staff working in admissions and registration, were less enthusiastic. Hard-driving, unforgiving, perfectionist, and unreasonable were the adjectives they used to describe Paul. Two of the department's secretaries had threatened to quit because of Paul's work demands. The situation was tense enough that they were reassigned. Paul's fast promotion and raises had also created considerable resentment among his peers. The dislike was mutual. Paul found most of his immediate co-workers to be only mildly competent, generally lazy, and lacking any initiative or serious dedication. He thought they just did their jobs, but not much more.

In spite of Paul's fast promotions and other successes, he was not happy. The job at SU was beginning to look a lot like the one at the high-tech firm. The first year was great, but things were just not very interesting from then on. He knew he was valued and was contributing, but he felt underutilized. He also knew that he was close to reaching the organization's limit on promotion and raises. There simply was not enough room to move up in the system. To keep himself busy, Paul had started his own small public relations business on the side, working with small day-care centers and private schools. Although the business was very small, he really enjoyed the time he spent on it. He felt challenged and often stayed up late to work on his own business. He had been thinking about simply quitting SU. He had enough money saved to carry himself for a while but did not want to let his boss down and felt guilty about leaving his students.

Questions

1. What is your analysis of the situation?
2. If you were Paul's boss, what would you do?
3. If you were Paul, what would you do?

THE BIG PICTURE

▶ Can AT&T Simultaneously Cut and Motivate?

By the time C. Michael Armstrong was named CEO in late 1997, AT&T was ready for a wake-up call. The telecommunications giant was still losing ground in the U.S. long-distance telephone market; its overhead costs were higher than those of its competitors despite layoff announcements, and it had lost $4 billion before spinning NCR off after an ill-fated foray into computers. Now Armstrong, the first outsider to hold AT&T's top position in nearly eight decades, faced the daunting task of preparing the company for the marketplace realities of the new millennium.[62]

Before joining AT&T, Armstrong had engineered a successful turnaround at Hughes Electronics by drastically cutting costs, realigning management, entering new markets, and instituting new pay-for-performance programs. To attack AT&T's large bureaucracy, slow decision-making process, and burdensome overhead expenses, Armstrong decided on a strategy using some of the same tactics.[63]

One of his top priorities was chopping AT&T's overhead costs from 29 percent of revenues to a more competitive 22 percent within two years. Although this meant cutting $3 billion annually from the overall budget, the CEO stressed that deep cuts were absolutely necessary. He reined in the budget for buying consulting services, put a moratorium on hiring for new jobs, and announced that more than 10 percent of the workforce would be laid off.[64]

Nearly a year before, AT&T had been rocked by the announcement that some 40,000 employees would be laid off. Nonetheless, the total number of employees had remained unchanged until Armstrong's layoff plans were set in motion. As many as 11,000 managers received early retirement packages, and up to 7,000 nonmanagement positions were to be cut through layoffs and attrition.[65]

Although Armstrong's ambitious cost-cutting plans were aimed at bettering AT&T's financial performance, layoffs are rarely painless. Those who retain their jobs often face new obstacles and a difficult adjustment. They have to take over the work of colleagues who are now gone—even though there are many fewer people to do the same amount of work (or more). Survivors may lose trust in the company and experience "survivor guilt" over being allowed to keep their jobs while colleagues were forced to leave. Any rumors of additional layoffs only add to the stress, making employees more fearful and interfering with their ability to focus on their work. In the wake of Armstrong's layoff decision, AT&T must face the immense challenge of keeping the workforce motivated while creating a firmer foundation for profitable operation in the years ahead.

Questions

1. Use the expectancy model to discuss how AT&T's layoffs, unrelated to individual performance, affect the survivors' motivation.
2. With CEO Armstrong continuing to put his mark on AT&T, how will changes in organizational culture and leadership be likely to affect individual motivation?
3. If you were a marketing manager for AT&T's long-distance telephone service, what could you do to motivate your remaining employees after layoffs have been completed? Identify two specific strategies you might apply.

NOTES

1. Richard Lorant, "Rebuilding Corporate Compassion," *Seattle Times,* December 11, 1996, accessed on-line at http://www.seattletimes.com/extra/browse/html/mald_121196.html.
2. Kenneth D. Campbell, "Malden Mills Owner Applies Religious Ethics to Busienss," *MIT Tech Talk* (April 16, 1997): accessed on-line at http://web.mit.edu/newsoffice/tt/1997/apr16/43530.html.
3. Lorant, "Rebuilding Corporate Compassion."
4. Thomas Teal, "Not a Fool, Not a Saint," *Fortune* 134, no. 9 (November 11, 1996): 201–4.
5. Shelly Donald Coolidge, "Corporate Decency Prevails at Malden Mills," *Christian Science Monitor* (March 28, 1996), accessed on-line at http://www.nl.org/anr/stories/maiden.
6. Eric Convey, "Malden Mills Celebrates a Special Day," *Business Today.com* (September 15, 1997): accessed on-line at http://www.businesstoday.com/archive/topstories/mm15.
7. For detailed information about statistics on work satisfaction, see D. A. Gilbert, *Facts on File Publications* (New York: Facts on File, 1988), and L. Harris, *Inside America* (New York: Vintage, 1987).
8. Gilbert, *Facts on File*, and Harris, *Inside America.*
9. Gilbert, *Facts on File.*
10. E. Diener and M. Diener, "Cross-Cultural Correlates of Life Satisfaction and Self-Esteem," *Journal of Personality and Social Psychology* 68, no. 4 (1995): 653–63.
11. S. Strom, "Pitfall of Cutting Korea's Lifetime Work Force," *New York Times*, February 24, 1998, C4.
12. "Real People, Real Issues," *Business Europe* 35, no. 41 (1995): 4–5.
13. J. Rohwer, "Japan's Quiet Corporate Revolution," *Fortune* 137, no. 6 (March 30, 1998): 84.
14. T. A. Stewart, "Gray Flannel Suit?" *Fortune* 137, no. 5 (March 16, 1998): 76–82; S. L. Robinson and D. M. Rousseau, "Violating the Psychological Contract: Not the Exception but the Norm," *Journal of Organization Behavior* 15, no. 3 (1994): 245–59; and B. O'Reilley, "The New Deal: What Companies and Employees Owe One Another," *Fortune* (June 13, 1994): 44–52.
15. R. Donkin, "Loyalty Bonus Should Not Be Devalued," *Financial Times*, November 1, 1995, 15.
16. T. McDermott, "TQM: The Total Quality Maquiladora," *Business Mexico* 4, no. 11 (1994): 42–45.
17. Ibid.
18. "Doing the Right Thing," *The Economist* (May 20, 1995): 84.
19. L. H. Chusmir and B. Parker, "Success Strivings and Their Relationship to Affective Work Behaviors: Gender Differences," *Journal of Social Psychology* 132, no. 1 (February 1992): 87–99.
20. J. G. Miller and K. G. Wheeler, "Unraveling the Mysteries of Gender Differences in Intention to Leave to Organization," *Journal of Organizational Behavior* 13, no. 5 (1992): 465–78.
21. V. H. Vroom, *Work and Motivation* (New York: Wiley, 1964).
22. For an example, see T. L. Thomas and L. Sarsfield-Baldwin, "The Effects of Self-Esteem, Task Label, and Performance Feedback on Task Liking and Intrinsic Motivation," *Journal of Social Psychology* 131, no. 4 (1991): 567–72.
23. R. Kanfer, "Motivation Theory and Industrial and Organizational Psychology," in M. D. Dunnette and L. M. Hough (eds.), *Handbook of Industrial and Organizational Psychology*, vol. 1 (Palo Alto, CA: Consulting Psychologists Press, 1990), 75–170; D. T. Hall and K. E. Nougaim, "An Examination of Maslow's Need Hierarchy in an Organizational Setting," *Organizational Behavior and Human Performance* (February 1968): 12–35.
24. For a discussion, see B. Nelson, "Dump the Cash, Load on the Praise," *Personnel Journal* 75, no. 7 (1996): 65–70.
25. N. Munk, "The New Organization Man," *Fortune* 137, no. 5 (March 16, 1998): 65.
26. A. P. Brief and R. J. Aldag, "The Intrinsic-Extrinsic Dichotomy: Toward Conceptual Clarity," *Academy of Management Review* 2 (1997): 496–99.
27. A. Muoio (ed.), "The Truth Is, the Truth Hurts," *Fast Company* (April–May 1998): 100.
28. A. Sharplin and J. A. Seeger, "The Lincoln Electric Company, 1996," in A. A. Thompson and A. J. Strickland, *Strategic Management* (Boston, MA: Irwin–McGraw-Hill, 1998): 896–922.
29. J. R. Hackman and G. R. Oldham, *Work Redesign* (Reading, MA: Addison-Wesley, 1980).
30. Ibid.
31. Munk, "The New Organization Man," 74.
32. Ibid., 68.
33. E. A. Locke and G. P. Latham, *A Theory of Goal Setting and Task Performance* (Englewood Cliffs, NJ: Prentice Hall, 1990); M. E. Tubbs, "Goal Setting: A Meta-Analytic Examination of the Empirical Evidence," *Journal of Applied Psychology* 71 (1986): 474–83.
34. P. F. Drucker, *The Practice of Management* (New York: Harper & Row, 1954); R. Rodgers and J. E. Hunter, "Impact of Management by Objectives on Organizational Productivity," *Journal of Applied Psychology* 76 (1991): 322–36.
35. Locke and Latham, *A Theory of Goal Setting.*
36. E. A. Locke, K. N. Shaw, L. M. Saari, and G. P. Latham, "Goal Setting and Task Performance: 1969–1980," *Psychological Bulletin* (July 1981): 123–33.
37. Ibid.
38. In addition to reviewing Appendix 1 for a detailed discussion of the motivation-hygiene theory proposed by Herzberg, see F. Herzberg, B. Mausner, and B. Snyderman, *The Motivation to Work* (New York: Wiley, 1959).
39. Equity theory was first developed by J. S. Adams, "Toward an Understanding of Inequity," *Journal of Abnormal and Social Psychology* 67 (1963): 422–36.
40. For an example, see P. Singh, "Perception and Reaction to Inequality as a Function of Social Comparison Referents and Hierarchical Levels," *Journal of Applied Social Psychology* 24, no. 6 (1994): 557–65.
41. For a study on the impact of inequity, see S. A. Geurts, B. P. Buunk, and W. B. Schaufeli, "Social Comparison and Absenteeism," *Journal of Applied Social Psychology* 24, no. 21 (1994): 1871–90.
42. B. F. Skinner, *The Behavior of Organisms* (New York: Appleton-Century-Crofts, 1938).
43. For discussion of use of learning theory in management, see F. Luthans and R. Kreitner, *Organizational Behavior Modification and Beyond: An Operant and Social Learning Approach* (Glenview, IL: Scott, Foresman, 1985).
44. A. M. Webber, "XBS Learns to Grow," *Fast Company* (October–November 1996): 114, 115.
45. A. Stevenson-Yang, "Putting the Corps into Corporate," *China Business Review* 21, no. 6 (November/December 1994): 50–51.
46. "New Asian Values," *Business Asia* 27, no. 5 (March 1995): 3–4.
47. S. Caudron, "Create an Empowering Environment," *Personnel Journal* 74, no. 9 (September 1995): 28–36.
48. The concept of learning organizations was proposed by P. Senge, *The Fifth Discipline: The Art and Practice of the Learning Organization* (New York: Doubleday, 1990).
49. The law of effect was first proposed by E. L. Thorndike, *Educational Psychology: The Psychology of Learning* (New York: Columbia University Press, 1913).
50. Munk, "The New Organization Man," 74.
51. Luthans and Kreitner, *Organizational Behavior Modification*; L. W. Frederiksen, ed., *Handbook of Organizational Behavior Management* (New York: Wiley, 1982).
52. L. Chadderdon, "Merrill Lynch Works—at Home," *Fast Company* (April–May, 1998): 70–72.
53. S. Kerr, "On the Folly of Rewarding A While Hoping for B," *Academy of Management Executive* 9, no. 1 (1995): 7–14; originally published in the *Academy of Management Journal* 18 (1975): 769–83.
54. Munk, "The New Organization Man," 74.
55. Stewart, "Gray Flannel Suit," 82.
56. S. Shafer, "Peanuts, Popcorn, or Power Tool?" *Inc. Technology*, no. 3 (September 15, 1997): 24.
57. Teal, "Not a Fool, Not a Saint," 201.
58. Paul Solman, "Bridging the Gap," *Public Broadcasting System* (March 20, 1996), accessed on-line at http://www.pbs.org/newshour/bb/economy/corporate_responsibility_3-20.
59. J. Amparano, "Taking Good Care of Workers Pays Off," *Arizona Republic*, January 23, 1998, E1, E3; Convey, "Malden Mills Celebrates a Special Day."
60. Coolidge, "Corporate Decency Prevails at Malden Mills."
61. Lorant, "Rebuilding Corporate Compassion."
62. Peter Elstrom, "New Boss, New Plan," *Business Week* (February 2, 1998): 122–26, 128, 133.
63. Steve Rosenbush, "AT&T Begins Corporate Reorganization," *USA Today*, January 23, 1998, accessed on-line at www.usatoday.com/life/cyber/tech/ctc003.
64. Elstrom, "New Boss, New Plan."
65. Peter Elstrom, "AT&T's Cup of Tea?" *Business Week* (February 9, 1998): 48.

VIDEO CASE 2

ON LOCATION!

▶ The Individual at Jagged Edge

It takes a special person to work at Jagged Edge. The Quenemoens have a clear idea of what they want in their employees. Margaret Quenemoen says her employees "have to have an excellent work ethic. They have to be self-starters and be able to think. They must be energetic and interested in mountain sports."[1] Paula adds, "We are not corporate. Work is simply an extension of who we are."[2] With those clear criteria in mind, JEMG has had no trouble attracting the type of employees it wants. It seems that the right people have walked in the door and asked to work there. "We use a formal application and résumé, but then we just talk. The right person becomes obvious."[3]

Consider Tim O'Neill, JEMG's buyer. As he tells his own story, Tim lived in the dirt in a tent he called the "O'Neill Sphere" for many years. "I didn't have a goal. I was looking for the meaning of life."[4] One of his friends knew Margaret and arranged for an interview. Tim met with David Potter, JEMG's vice president, and he was hired. He has been committed to the company ever since. O'Neill first worked in the store and became a store manager. He liked being store manager and working with customers directly and felt he had a lot of freedom. Now as a buyer, he has more stress, but he enjoys being responsible and involved: "Jagged Edge has allowed me to broaden my view."[5]

Others, like Josh Bodine, the Telluride store manager, enjoy not only the company but also the location. Josh likes working in a small town where everybody is relaxed and people smile on the job. He also likes being close to the sports he loves so much.[6] Tim O'Neill agrees: "I would never [live or work] in the city. Location is key for me. I get to be here in a playground like the San Juans."[7]

Motivating people like O'Neill and Bodine is not a major challenge. They all share a passion for the mountains. Additionally, the company is growing and there is plenty of opportunity to learn new things. The Quenemoens work on keeping things exciting. Margaret states: "We expect a lot, but there are always opportunities." For example, when Josh Lear joined JEMG it was obvious that he was very excited about the company. An avid snowboarder rated as one of the best instructors in Telluride, he fit right in. He was made store manager, work that involved lots of numbers. "It was awful; he wasn't happy; he really looked so depressed." Margaret was convinced he was the right fit for JEMG, so she moved him to store design and merchandising. Lear has flourished. Paula and Margaret credit part of their success to Lear's creative ideas. "Everybody has their forte," says Margaret.[8]

Erlend Greulich manages all the retail stores and performs the human resource functions for the company. He came to Jagged Edge with 17 years of retail experience. He sees another challenge. He put in place the human resource policies and procedures, the employee handbook, and the professional benefit package that bring consistency and continuity to the operations. He believes these are essential because high turnover is a major problem in the industry. The way he views it, for JEMG to succeed, its employees must harness their considerable sport expertise. "A company like McDonald's spends several thousand dollars to teach employees how to make a hamburger. I can't even begin to imagine the cost of our training." However, the retail salaries rarely reflect the high level of expertise and experience that the jobs at JEMG require. "It is really hard to pay people what they are worth."[9] So they leave after a few months or a few years and are hard and costly to replace.

Greulich and other managers at JEMG compensate for this problem by providing many tangible and intangible rewards. JEMG offers higher than average pay and a generous benefits package that includes housing allowances for some employees and accident insurance, an essential factor

227

for people involved in such extreme sports. In addition, Greulich sends personal thank-you notes and takes time to provide one-on-one attention and detailed feedback to his employees. He also insists on involving them in decision making and keeping them informed. "Personal loyalty has to be developed through personal relationships. We have to earn our employees' respect on a personal level. It is the glue that helps us go through difficult times."[10]

Being small makes evaluating employees both easy and challenging. Everyone knows everyone else. The owners believe that they have a good feel for their employees. Margaret says, "We promote from within. We get a strong feel about a person. You get to know them and see their work ethic." There is no formal evaluation process. Margaret simply lays it all out on the table. "I like to let people know where they stand. I give them both the good and the bad. There is no misunderstanding."[11] Paula works hard on building a casual atmosphere. "I am not really comfortable with hierarchy," she explains.[12] However, she believes that she has to remain aloof enough to be able to confront her employees when needed.

Questions

1. What is the typical profile of JEMG employees? How well does that profile fit the company mission and culture?
2. How does JEMG motivate its employees?
3. What challenges do small size and informality present in the evaluation process?

Notes

[1] Interview with Margaret Quenemoen, June 4, 1998.

[2] Interview with Paula Quenemoen, June 8, 1998.

[3] Interview with Margaret Quenemoen, June 4, 1998.

[4] Interview with Tim O'Neill.

[5] Ibid.

[6] Interview with Josh Bodine, June 9, 1998.

[7] Interview with Tim O'Neill.

[8] Interview with Margaret Quenemoen, June 4, 1998.

[9] Interview with Erlend Greulich, June 9, 1998.

[10] Ibid.

[11] Interview with Margaret Quenemoen.

[12] Interview with Paula Quenemoen.

THE BUILDING BLOCKS OF GROUP BEHAVIOR

LEARNING OBJECTIVES

1. Outline the elements and types of groups, reasons for joining groups, and the effect of national and organizational culture on groups.
2. Explain when groups should be used and identify their potential advantages and disadvantages.
3. Discuss the effects of group size and composition and the importance of roles and norms in group behavior.
4. Explain the role and effects of cohesion, conformity, and deviance in groups.
5. Describe the stages of group development and the challenges members face at each stage.

CHAPTER OUTLINE

Basic Elements

When to Use Groups

Internal Group Structure

Cohesion, Conformity, and Deviance

Stages of Group Development

Groups in Context

MANAGERIAL CHALLENGE

James Cameron's Titanic

The R.M.S. *Titanic* sank nearly 90 years ago, but James Cameron's movie *Titanic* enjoyed smooth sailing after its premiere in December 1997. The movie quickly became the biggest box-office draw of all time and captured 11 Academy Awards (including cinematography, sound, art direction, and visual effects), thanks to the romantic appeal of Leonardo DeCaprio and Kate Winslet—and the dramatically realistic scenes of the luxury liner sinking.[1] Behind the scenes, *Titanic* presented a complex management challenge—in part because of the various groups that created the intricate special effects, and producer-director-writer Cameron's penchant for realism.

Generally, producers like James Cameron bring together a new combination of cast, crew, and outside technical experts for every film. Some group members may have worked together on previous projects; others are hired to handle specific tasks for the current project. Adding to the pressure is the requirement of completing the work within a set time frame. For the *Titanic*, the original shooting schedule of 138 days stretched to 160 days, causing the budget to swell to $200 million.[2]

Cinematographer Russell Carpenter, who filmed *True Lies* with Cameron, was hired a few weeks before shooting began. He had only a short time to meld the photography crew hired by Cameron with the additional crew members he planned to hire.[3] On the technical side, when filming began at Fox Studios Baja in Mexico, the head electrician hired local lighting experts to work with the U.S. team. This diverse group initially grappled with both language and attitude differences.[4]

Detailed digital effects were critical to *Titanic*. Cameron's own company, Digital Domain, handled most of these effects, although another firm was hired for selected tasks such as adding icy breath mists for the ocean scenes.[5] With so much riding on the outcome, the ability of the various groups to work well together was essential to the success of this epic.

■ Questions

1. Why did Cameron use various groups to perform the tasks he needed?
2. What challenges did the group members face?

The making of *Titanic* required the coordinated efforts of many different people. Similarly, organizations consist of people performing various tasks that help achieve the organization's goals. Although lone individuals perform some activities, groups perform the majority of work in organizations. Groups, then, are a permanent part of organizational life.

Chapters 4–6 of this text examined individual behavior in organizations, its sources, and its effects. Understanding individual behavior is a key aspect of managing people in organizations. However, managers must also understand group interaction, group processes, and the effects of groups on individual behavior. A group is more than a collection of individuals. It is a system in which the whole is greater than the sum of the parts. Chapters 7–9 will help you understand groups as systems.

In this chapter we explore the building blocks of groups. First, we examine the nature and types of groups and why we form them. Then we consider when to use groups and how to structure them. We also investigate three key factors related to group behavior: *cohesion*, *conformity*, and *deviance*. We close by looking at how groups develop and explore how contextual forces affect group behavior in organizations.

Hot ▼ Link

We discussed the concept of systems in chapter 1, pp. 15–17.

■ BASIC ELEMENTS

Group
Two or more people who interact in an organized manner to perform a task or activity to achieve a common goal

A **group** is two or more people who interact in some organized manner to perform a task or activity to achieve a common goal.[6] This definition has several elements, as illustrated in Figure 7.1. First, a group involves more than one person. Second, group members must have interaction. This interaction can be face-to-face or through other means such as e-mail or interactive computer software. Third, members have different roles and assignments so groups have some formal or informal hierarchy. Fourth, groups must have a purpose, a goal, and some reason for being. The reason may be social or work related. Fifth, members must perceive that they are a group. Finally, group members must have some degree of interdependence and draw satisfaction from group interaction.

These six elements distinguish collections of people that form groups and those that do not. Departments in an organization—for example, accounting, marketing, human resources, and so forth—have all the elements of groups. So do various subunits within these departments. For instance, people in the creative division at advertising and marketing communica-

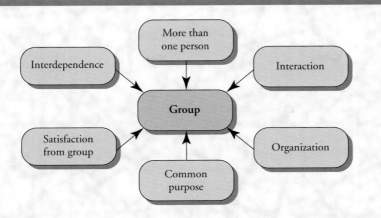

FIGURE 7.1
Elements of Groups

tions firm Saatchi & Saatchi interact formally at meetings and informally via telephone, e-mail, and face-to-face on a daily basis as they plan for and develop ways to market products.

In contrast, the students in your university are not really a group. There is no organized interaction and no common goal that requires some degree of cooperation among all students. However, if students organize around a common cause, say opposition to a tuition increase, where they have a unified purpose and organization, then they become a group. Having defined groups, we next consider the different types of groups and reasons people join groups.

Types of Groups

There are two general types of groups. **Formal groups** have required, prescribed goals and form to satisfy an organizational need. The different departments in an organization are examples of formal groups. The different groups that worked on the production of *Titanic* described in the Managerial Challenge are formal groups. **Informal groups** are not required by an organization. They exist because of the members' common interests, social ties, or friendship. While formal groups are generally related to work, informal groups typically focus on social interaction.

The distinction between formal and informal groups is not always clear. Many formal groups have informal functions and many informal groups become formal. Say that a group of people who work together start to play golf on weekends. That formal work group then becomes an informal group, too. Conversely, a group of friends may discover that they share a common interest in protecting a wilderness area that their state wants to sell to developers. The group can formalize their informal interactions through a charter and bylaws that would help them achieve their new goal of blocking the sale of public lands.

Formal and informal groups follow similar patterns of interaction. Their nature may affect the extent or intensity of the use of group processes. For instance, *roles* and *norms* exist in both formal and informal groups. In formal groups, roles are clearly defined and accompanied by formal titles. Informal groups assign roles less strictly.

Formal groups
Groups that have prescribed goals that satisfy organizational needs

Informal groups
Groups that exist because of members' common interests, social ties, or friendship

---

Summary Point 7.1   **What Is a Group and What Types of Groups Exist?**

- A group is two or more people who interact through various means in some organized manner to perform a task or activity to achieve a common goal.

- Formal groups are based on organizational needs.
- Informal groups are based on social needs.

Why We Join Groups and the Role of Culture

Hot ▼ Link

To review need theories, see pp. 197–98, and Appendix 1, p. 576.

We join groups for two main reasons. First, we join groups to help *satisfy individual needs* and reinforce our sense of identity.[7] People need others to help meet their own needs. Joining groups partially satisfies security and social needs. Groups also provide physical and psychological protection and opportunities to interact with others with similar views or interests. For instance, you may join a fraternity, a sorority, or a social club to feel supported by others who have similar interests in social activities.

Group membership helps satisfy other individual needs such as self-esteem needs. Think about the pride we feel when a group of people values and appreciates us. We can also satisfy our affiliation needs through membership in a group of people for whom we feel kinship. None of these needs could be satisfied without the presence of and interaction with others in an organized manner.

The second reason we join groups is to achieve goals that are too complex or time-consuming for an individual to achieve. As discussed in chapter 2, one of the major reasons organizations create departments is to handle complex, time-consuming tasks. For example, no person alone could market a new product nationwide. Having an organized marketing department means that many people can work together to accomplish this goal. Together, the member groups that worked on *Titanic* achieved goals that would be impossible for one person. The accomplishment of goals further helps satisfy our need for achievement or provides us with self-esteem and status.[8]

National and Organizational Culture Although groups exist in all organizations and in all cultures, they are not equally prevalent or equally valued in all parts of the world and in all organizations. National and organizational cultures have a profound effect on the extent to which groups are used and valued. In highly collectivistic cultures, such as Malaysia and several Latin American countries, people generally define themselves in terms of the group rather than in terms of individuals.[9] They draw their self-esteem and sense of self from belonging to a group. The person's family, clan, or the organization in which he or she works plays a central role in the person's identity.

For instance, Japanese employees closely identify with their organization because they perceive it to be an extension of their family. Employees ask their manager's permission before they get married, and managers in traditional Japanese companies consider matchmaking of

The strong sense of group at Celcom, a Malaysian company, is partly related to the collectivistic values of the national culture.

employees to be part of their duty. Similarly, the tradition of taking care of employees is very strong in Mexican organizations. PIPSA, one of the largest producers of paper in Mexico, pays the private school tuition of the 6-year-old son of Virgilio Molino, the company's 30-year-old electrician. Molino himself is not able to afford the $900 per year tuition. If his son maintains a minimum grade point average and finishes his schooling successfully, PIPSA will hire him when he turns 18, the age at which his father was hired.[10] PIPSA's benefits and hiring policies support the family- and group-oriented culture of Mexico.

In individualistic cultures, such as those of the United States or Australia, individuals may join groups to satisfy their needs and accomplish goals, but groups are used more for task accomplishment and less for establishing personal identity. People primarily draw their sense of self and their self-esteem from their own accomplishments rather than from their clan or organization.

We see then that cultural factors greatly influence the predominance and roles of groups in individuals' lives, society, and organizations. The less community oriented the culture, the more individual rights and differences are essential. In collectivist cultures, groups—both small and large—are central to people's lives.

The business implication for managers dealing with collectivist cultures is that groups are the center of performance for organizations. Individuals are likely to be comfortable with group bonuses and the group (at all levels) will take responsibility for its individual members. For example, training a new employee is everyone's responsibility. The lackluster performance of another is everyone's problem.

In individualistic cultures, managers must focus primarily on individual performance and individual rewards. They can rely on the various groups only for a specific, clearly assigned task. The training of a new employee is assigned to a particular person or small group and more often is simply the problem of the manager or the human resource department. Poor performance is an individual problem and is remedied on an individual basis.

Organizational culture also affects how groups are used and perceived. Some organizations stress individual performance almost exclusively; in others, groups play a central role. In some cases, the industry determines the organizational culture and the degree of group orientation. For instance, investment banking and brokers tend to be individualistic. They compete with each other and focus on personal rewards. At Smith-Barney, individual brokers are rewarded for the value of their clients' portfolio.

In contrast with investment banking, advertising and marketing activities typically require extensive collaboration and interaction, so the organizational culture of such companies tends to be more group oriented. For example, employees at the Abelson Company, an advertising agency based in New York and London, rely extensively on one another to take care of their clients. A team of a creative person and an account manager handle most client accounts. The teams then work with freelancers to take care of their clients' needs. Neda Neghabat, Abelson's co-creative director, states: "There just never seems to be enough people. The visual metaphor for our company is the atom molecule, or ripples on a lake. We are the nucleus and the outside people and teams are around us."[11]

It is interesting that many organizations with an individualistic culture are moving toward more cooperation and interaction. The assembly line in car manufacturing traditionally has focused on each person doing his or her job. After seeing the success of the Japanese and Swedes in producing high-quality cars using effective work groups, U.S. auto manufacturers started using work groups also. A case in point is the Saturn product line of GM cars. Saturn used work groups instead of a traditional assembly line to manufacture its products with great success. Because Saturn was concerned about cooperation between management and unions, empowerment, and teams when it was created, the company's culture supported the use of work groups.

Although Saturn's success encouraged the use of groups in other GM divisions, the overall culture of GM does not support groups as readily. GM's strong culture emphasizes control,

Hot ▼ Link

We discussed mechanistic organizations in chapter 2, pp. 53–54.

status, and following rules. Its culture reflects its mechanistic, hierarchical structure and presents an obstacle to innovation and change.[12] As a matter of fact, recent union-management negotiations at GM threatened to force Saturn to adopt more GM practices, such as switching to bonuses that reward individuals rather than work groups. Saturn employees soundly defeated the proposals. Their vote signaled that the employees wanted to maintain their group-oriented culture.[13]

As you read on, consider how both national and organizational culture affect the various aspects of groups, from size and composition to roles, cohesion, and conformity. Now let's explore when to use and when not to use groups.

Summary Point 7.2   **Why Do We Join Groups and How Do National and Organizational Cultures Affect That Decision?**

- People join groups for two main reasons:
  1. To satisfy individual needs
  2. To perform complex or time-consuming tasks

- The degree to which a national culture is collectivist or individualistic affects the use and function of groups in an organization.
- Organizational culture can also affect people's decision to join groups.

CAREER ADVICE
from the Experts

LEARN TO WORK IN GROUPS

Working in a group is often a challenge for those from individualistic cultures, but more organizations are looking for people with effective group skills. Here are some quick tips that can help you prepare to work in groups:

- Add group management to your portfolio of skills; take college and training courses in this area.
- Be familiar with group and team trends. Read the latest books and articles on these trends and be able to discuss their implications for management.
- Develop listening skills and learn how to offer constructive feedback to group members. For instance, practice critiquing others' work without getting personal.
- Gain experience in working in many different types of groups. Volunteer for groups whenever you get a chance.
- Consider the long-term benefits of forgoing some immediate individual recognition to work in groups.

Your ability to demonstrate these skills may help you succeed in today's changing organizations.

Source: Based on A. Fisher, "Starting Anew," *Fortune* 137, no. 6 (March 30, 1998): 167.

■ WHEN TO USE GROUPS

As with all other organizational behavior topics we've analyzed, the use of groups is based on various contingency factors. Groups are not a cure-all. People working together do not always outperform people working alone.[14] As a matter of fact, groups can waste a lot of time and resources trying to coordinate activities. However, they also can, if managed well, be highly productive in organizations. The key is learning when and when not to use groups to accomplish tasks. First, we explore three key factors that help managers decide when to use groups: task complexity, timing, and commitment. Then we assess the advantages and disadvantages of groups.

Factors in the Use of Groups

Three main factors determine whether the use of groups is appropriate and desirable, as shown in Figure 7.2: task complexity, time, and commitment. The first issue to consider is the complexity of the task. A **complex task** has many different elements and potential solutions. One individual cannot easily manage a complex task that requires highly diverse opinions and skills. However, one person can efficiently accomplish a simple task. Using groups for complex tasks, then, is appropriate. For example, designing and implementing a marketing campaign for a new product requires creative and artistic talents as well as design, organizational, and financial skills. One person is unlikely to have all these skills. A group of carefully selected individuals can have the right combination of skills to accomplish such a complex task.

Complex task
One that has many different elements and potential solutions

Consider the example of the Pathfinder mission to Mars. On July 4, 1997, NASA's Pathfinder landed on Mars, sending back astonishing pictures of the surface of that planet.[15] The success of this mission was a tribute to NASA's engineers, administrators, computer programmers, and thousands of other individuals who worked on the project for many years. The building of the spacecraft was a highly complex task. Numerous organizations all over the world designed different pieces of equipment for the craft. One person or one company could not have accomplished this feat.

The Pathfinder mission also exemplifies the second factor in the use of teams: the issue of *time*. Groups are inherently wasteful and inefficient; they take longer to do most tasks.[16] Individuals are considerably more efficient than groups. If finishing a job quickly is essential and time is the main concern, the manager should assign the task to one person. However, if finishing quickly is not the primary concern, the manager may want to use a group. The main objective of the

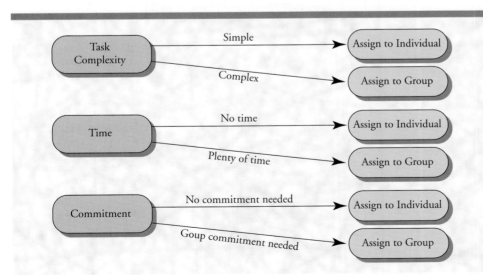

FIGURE 7.2
Factors in the Use of Groups

Pathfinder mission was to reach the surface of Mars successfully. Although time was important and everyone worked under a deadline, time was not the main concern. It made sense, then, to rely on groups to develop solutions and design equipment that could carry out the mission.

The last factor to consider when selecting between individuals or groups is the issue of *commitment*. People who are involved in decision making will have a stronger commitment to the decision, more motivation to execute the decision, and higher performance.[17] Therefore, using a group of people rather than one person to complete a task will lead to a higher level of commitment to that task. The scientists and engineers working on the Pathfinder spacecraft made numerous decisions about what experiments to conduct, which backup systems and pieces of equipment to include, and how to analyze incoming data. As each decision was made, the group members' commitment level increased as did their performance level.[18]

The three factors of task complexity, time, and commitment are not sequential, meaning that a manager does not need to consider them one at a time. They all play a role in the decision to use individuals rather than groups. In making such a decision, a manager needs to consider which of the three factors is most important. In many situations, time is short and quick action is needed, but the task is complex and employee commitment is essential. Managers need to weigh the various factors to decide which one dominates, given the situation.

Returning to the Pathfinder example, NASA's managers' experience in launching space shuttles and similar projects had shown them that people working on this complex project had to be committed to deliver high-quality results. Given this need for commitment and the complexity of the task, the use of groups was appropriate.

Advantages and Disadvantages of Groups

Recall that groups can satisfy individual needs and help complete complex tasks. These two factors are among the first benefits of groups. However, the use of groups has other positive and negative consequences, as outlined in Figure 7.3.

Advantages   One of the major advantages of using groups is the *potential for creativity*. An individual, no matter how intelligent and creative, cannot match the creativity of a group of equally

FIGURE 7.3
Groups in the Balance

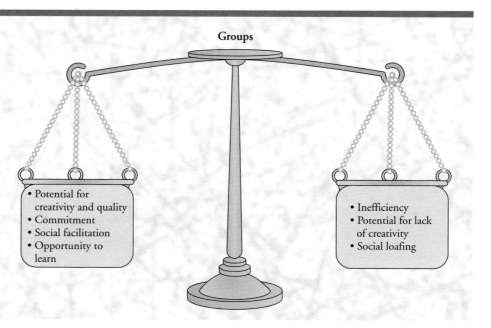

bright individuals set on solving a problem. People working together bring different perspectives, viewpoints, ideas, and solutions. The more diverse the group, the more diverse the alternatives and solutions. However, simply putting a group of different people together does not guarantee a creative solution. To succeed, the group must have clear goals, the right balance of complementary skills, and the right environment to maximize its creative potential.

A second benefit of a group is the potential for *higher-quality decisions and performance* than can often be achieved by an individual. Because of the potential creativity and the diversity of the group members' input, the quality of the decision or the task completed by the group is generally higher than that of individuals, especially when the task is complex. Groups can rely on different skills and divide the task to take advantage of each member's unique contribution. Such a division of labor and responsibilities leads to higher-quality performance.

One of the key decisions for each group working on the Pathfinder mission was which equipment to include and exclude on the spacecraft. Many decisions were tough but necessary because of limited resources and space. For instance, one group decided that they could not afford to include certain seismology readers to record the seismic activity of Mars. As it turned out, this was a good decision, but it required the collective input of the group.

Working in groups can have two other benefits for members. First, people who contribute to the task are more likely to develop a higher level of commitment to task. Recall from the discussion of goal-setting in chapter 6 that participation leads to heightened commitment. Second, working in groups can result in **social facilitation**—the tendency of individuals to work harder in the presence of others.[19] We become self-conscious and self-aware in groups and want to maintain a positive self-image.[20] We also develop concern and worry about being evaluated, known as evaluation apprehension.[21] Because we want to present ourselves positively and worry about how we may be evaluated, we work harder. Social facilitation is most likely to happen when a person is experienced at and comfortable with the task.[22]

The final major benefit of using groups in organizations is that groups provide an excellent environment and opportunity for employees to learn new skills and new behaviors. The group can formally and informally train its members to perform their jobs better. It can provide a safe, comfortable environment for practicing new behaviors and skills. Once again, taking advantage of this benefit depends on the right environment and on how well a group is managed and used. Particularly, as we discuss in the next chapter, groups do better when they have clear goals and specific performance expectations.[23]

Consider the following example. Hal Rosenbluth, the 44-year-old CEO of Rosenbluth International, reorganized the travel agency around groups in 1993.[24] By 1996, the travel agency had grown to $2.5 billion in sales with over 3,500 employees in 1,000 locations in 41 countries around the world. Rosenbluth's group idea was very simple. Standing in the middle of "cow pie" in a farm in North Dakota one day, he realized that "the family farm is the most efficient type of unit I have ever run across, because everybody on the farm has to be fully functional and multifaceted."[25] So he created an organization grouped like a family farm.

Instead of having hundreds of managers and layer-on-layer of employees, he designed 100 "family units or farms." Just like any small farm, members of Hal's family farms rely on one another for creativity to solve their daily problems. They meet and discuss before making important decisions. Everyone is committed to making the farm a success, every member's work is always under scrutiny from the peers, and everyone needs to learn and improve all the time. Rosenbluth is known for its mantra that employees, referred to as associates, are the most important assets of an organization. Just as on a family farm, each member is regarded as valuable and needs to learn and develop continuously or the farm will not produce. He explains: "At the end of the day, our only sustainable competitive advantage are the associates, and the environment in which we work."[26]

The potential benefits of groups explains why organizations are using teams more readily, as we discuss in chapter 8. However, groups present a number of disadvantages that managers need to recognize.

Hot ▼ Link

We discussed participation in goal setting in chapter 6, pp. 203–5, and self-presentation in chapter 5, pp. 171–72.

Social facilitation
Occurs when individuals work harder in the presence of others

Hal Rosenbluth of Rosenbluth International uses the model of a family farm as the basis for groups in his travel business. Everyone on the farm helps everyone else learn so that the job gets done well.

Disadvantages The first disadvantage of groups is that they are *inefficient* and take longer to perform tasks than individuals would. The issue of efficiency needs to be balanced against the need for creativity and quality. Arriving at a creative, high-quality decision quickly is often difficult, if not impossible.

The second disadvantage of groups is their *potential lack of creativity*. This may sound contradictory, given that one benefit of groups is greater potential creativity, but note that we said potential, not guaranteed, creativity. Groups can easily lose their creative potential if members refuse to share ideas, are scared to voice different viewpoints, are pressured into agreeing with one another, or are simply too comfortable to want to change things.

Social loafing
People work less hard when their individual contribution to a task cannot be measured

The final disadvantage of groups is their tendency to lead to social loafing.[27] **Social loafing** refers to the tendency of members to work less hard when their individual contribution to a task cannot be measured. It can be a serious obstacle to group productivity. If group members feel that their efforts are lost in the group and that they will get neither credit nor blame for their performance, they are less likely to work hard. As can be expected, the tendency toward social loafing increases in larger groups and in groups whose members do not know one another well. The tendency decreases when a group works on a challenging task and is rewarded for high productivity.

Interestingly, social loafing tends to be higher in individualistic as opposed to collectivist cultures.[28] When the group is important, individuals work hard to achieve group goals.[29] Social loafing occurs less frequently in China and in Israel, both collectivist cultures, than in the United States or Great Britain. However, if managers in individualistic cultures can convince group members of the importance of the task they are performing, they may be able to decrease social loafing.

Managers can take a number of steps to increase the benefits and reduce the disadvantages of groups, including these:

- Controlling the size and composition of the group
- Considering the group's stage of development
- Monitoring norms
- Managing conformity and deviance and their role in the group's internal processes

We turn to these issues next, beginning with how to structure groups effectively.

Summary Point 7.3   **What Are the Advantages and Disadvantages of Groups?**

Advantages	Disadvantages
• Potential increase in creativity and quality	• Inefficiency
• Commitment	• Potential loss of creativity
• Social facilitation	• Social loafing
• Opportunities for individual learning and growth	

INTERNAL GROUP STRUCTURE

Long before groups became a structural option in organizations, social scientists studied group processes and dynamics and identified a number of factors in the performance of groups.[30] These factors include group size and composition, roles and norms, cohesion and conformity, deviance, and stages of group development.

Group Size and Composition

Determining the size and composition of a group is one of the first decisions managers make when forming a group. How many people should be included and what should members' background and skills be? Should there be an even or odd number of members? These are important factors as they can determine whether a group functions effectively and is productive or whether its members fall into social loafing and lose creativity.

Group Size Although there is no ideal size of a group, groups that are larger than eight to twelve members are less likely to function smoothly as groups. Additionally, having an odd number protects against deadlocks in case of disagreement. Generally, as size increases, individuals do not have the opportunity to participate and are less likely to take responsibility for their own actions and for the outcome. Smaller groups provide the opportunity for extensive interaction among members and a chance for all members to have input. Member satisfaction and learning also drop as size increases.[31]

Additionally, as groups get larger, subgroups form to deal with different issues or to take on different parts of the task. The formation of subgroups is not, in and of itself, a negative factor. Subgroups allow large groups to function better by forming smaller clusters. However, as is the case with departments that specialize in different tasks and activities, subgroups can lose touch with one another and the result can be poor integration.

Hot ▼ Link

We discussed integration in chapter 3, p. 87.

Consider the example of the boards of directors of major U.S. corporations. Many large corporations such as GM, IBM, and Exxon have boards of 35 to 40 members who represent many different organizational stakeholders. The entire board meets only occasionally. Instead, the boards divide into several subgroups or committees of six to ten members assigned to various tasks.[32] Examples of these committees include a compensation committee that decides the pay and benefits for the CEO and other top managers and an audit committee that reviews and assures the accuracy of the company's financial statements. By dividing tasks among smaller groups, the boards of directors can accomplish their mission efficiently while allowing the directors to debate and resolve issues. The board of Levi Strauss breaks into groups so often that the company's boardroom has not one but four tables to facilitate teamwork.[33]

However, the work of these subgroups needs to be coordinated well. For instance, the compensation subcommittee of a board may decide that the CEO should receive a raise for

Organizations such as Levi Strauss recognize the need for small groups and support them by providing a physical environment that encourages group work.

her excellent performance. At the same time, the audit subcommittee may decide for financial reasons that no one should receive any raises. These two decisions are contradictory and require the two subcommittees to interact and coordinate their decisions. To make large groups effective, managers can help members form subgroups and devise procedures for integration such as sharing meeting notes, exchanging members, and holding regular common meetings.

Group Composition   In addition to size, managers must also pay close attention to the group's composition. Many factors affect how group members are selected. Managers often base their selection on the requirements of the task. A job may require technical expertise, so technical experience determines who becomes a group member. However, there are additional considerations. Generally groups that have **homogeneous** membership, meaning members who are similar to one another in a number of different ways, are able to get along better.[34] People who are similar tend to like each other and have easier interaction. **Heterogeneous** group membership, with members of different backgrounds, styles, and so forth, are more likely to face conflict and disagreement.

Homogeneous groups
Groups with members who
have a number of similarities

Heterogeneous groups
Groups with members who
have many differences

Before you decide that group members should be similar, consider three issues that affect creative decision making. First, the more similar the group members, the less creative they are likely to be. People who are similar tend to think the same way. Accordingly, they will not look at issues from different points of view. Second, some conflict is necessary for good decision making. If everyone always agreed, few new ideas would be considered.[35]

The third issue is related to diversity. If managers chose group members on their ability to get along and have few conflicts, they would most likely exclude any diversity from their group. The diversity can take many forms. A group could include a male member in an all

A QUESTION OF ETHICS

How Homogeneous Should a Group Be?

Do you think it's ethical for a manager to select only women and minorities to join a high-profile group charged with reviewing the diversity practices of the organization? Does your opinion change if you learn that the most highly qualified candidate(s) were included? What if the manager insisted on creating a diverse group to tackle this high-profile issue, but because of the diversity requirement the manager excluded two of the most highly qualified candidates?

female group, a marketer in a group of engineers, an Asian in a predominantly Hispanic group, or a Southern European in a Scandinavian group. Note, though, that the goal of the diversity is not diversity for its own sake. Rather, it is to bring in new points of view and ideas to the group when the task could benefit from it. For instance, a culturally diverse group that designs a marketing campaign for a new product can help develop better plans for reaching different cultural market segments.

To reap the benefits of groups, the group composition should not be homogeneous. For example, Chase Manhattan Bank brought diversity to its board of directors by including Theodore M. Hesburgh, a Catholic priest and president of the University of Notre Dame. David Rockefeller, Chase's president, said that Hesburgh was there to "represent the conscience of the board." Rockefeller further stated, "We have a lot of moral, ethical problems in banking today. . . . We're doing about $43 billion worth of business a year, so maybe there's some good to be done in that, as well as some evil to be avoided."[36]

Managers need to balance the need for easy, comfortable interaction with the importance of creative, productive group processes and decision making. Next we discuss how groups manage their internal processes through roles and norms.

Summary Point 7.4   **How Do Size and Composition Affect Groups?**

- Large groups are more inefficient than small groups but get their task done by forming subgroups.
- Although homogeneity leads to easier interaction, heterogeneity helps creativity and better decision making.

- Homogeneous groups are those with members from similar backgrounds; heterogeneous groups have members from different backgrounds.

Roles and Norms

One of the defining elements of a group is the presence of hierarchy or structure. All groups develop some type of structure. Different members take on different tasks and fulfill different functions. Some members become leaders; others are followers. Similarly, groups quickly establish rules regarding how members should behave and how they get activities done.

Roles in Groups   As people take on different aspects of the group's activities and perform different functions, members adopt or are assigned different roles. **Roles** in groups are specific formal or informal sets of behaviors and activities that each person performs. Formal roles include titles and other status symbols. Groups have leaders, treasurers, secretaries, and so forth. Informal roles are not as clearly defined but nonetheless are known to group members. For example, one member may take on the role of arranging locations for the meetings; another may act as devil's advocate.

Roles
Specific formal or informal activities that each person performs in the group

The types of roles in groups fall into the three general categories of task, relationship, and self-oriented roles, as shown in Figure 7.4.[37] **Task roles** relate to the job or task that the group is doing. **Relationship roles**, also called maintenance roles, relate to the social interaction among group members. **Self-oriented roles** are roles that exist to satisfy the individual member's needs. The first two types of roles are necessary for the group's effectiveness. The third type often detracts from group performance.

Task roles
Roles that relate to the task the group is performing

Relationship roles
(maintenance roles)
Roles that aid the social interaction among group members

Task Roles   The task roles include seeking and providing information, elaborating on issues and topics of discussion to ensure that the group understands the issues, evaluating information and group activities, monitoring information and group performance to assure that all is going well, and coordinating various activities related to the task at hand. One or more mem-

Self-oriented roles
Roles focused on satisfying the individual member's needs

FIGURE 7.4
Roles in Groups

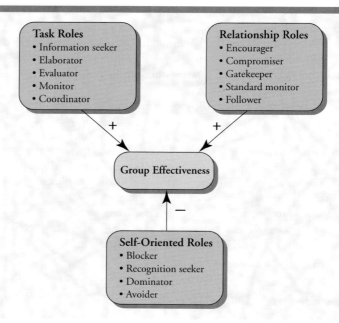

bers can perform these roles simultaneously. Several members, for instance, can do research and provide information to the group. Similarly, several members can monitor the quality of the group's work or keep track of progress to assure that the group is meeting deadlines.

Task roles help the group perform its job and achieve its goals. When looking at groups as a system, task roles are focused on the outcome. At Rosenbluth International, family group managers (referred to as leaders) and associates together decide who performs the coordinating, information-gathering, and information-monitoring tasks of groups.

Relationship Roles Relationship roles include encouraging or motivating group members, proposing compromises when conflict arises, gatekeeping so the group is protected from inappropriate internal and external interference, monitoring the group for proper behaviors, and finally being a follower who supports the group in achieving its goals. As with task roles, one or more members can perform relationship roles.

In contrast to task roles that focus on the specific goal of the group, relationship roles assure smooth internal functioning and focus on the group process. These roles are necessary to maintain appropriate civil social interaction needed to complete the task. Rosenbluth explains that all members first need to become friends in his family group before the work can get done. He argues that "if your co-workers become your friends, you'll never let each other down. You can accomplish anything."[38]

In groups that do not appoint or select a leader, individuals who effectively perform numerous task and relationship roles are likely to become group leaders. Groups that formally appoint or select a leader typically assign many of the task and relationship roles to that leader. Formal and informal leaders are expected both to help the group achieve its goals and to maintain internal processes.

Self-Oriented Roles The self-oriented roles include blocking the group's progress or activities, engaging in activities to get personal recognition, dominating the group, and as a last resort avoiding participation in the group. As opposed to task and relationship roles that are necessary for successful group functioning, self-oriented roles satisfy an individual's needs at the expense of the group. Typically, individuals who perform these roles have little concern for the group or its goals.

A self-oriented person who dominates the conversation and blocks others from contributing their ideas is a case in point. That person turns all activities to enhance or highlight personal accomplishments, further derailing the group from performing its task. Another method used is avoiding participation, thereby depriving the group of input or withholding information from other group members. If not managed well, self-oriented roles can damage the group's performance seriously.

At Rosenbluth International, one group leader's self-orientation clashed with her group. This specific group leader wouldn't develop her associates, an important task that all leaders must perform. Her failure to train associates harmed her group. "After a while, she realized that she couldn't go that route. So she left the company. I know it was because of the pressure of the team," explains Bobbee Rose, a reservation associate manager.[39] As this example shows, self-oriented roles are unnecessary and often harmful for group functioning.

Norms   As groups develop and members take on different roles, they develop rules regarding how the group should function. **Norms** are shared rules and expectations about group members' behaviors. They develop early and continue evolving as group members interact. Many group norms are not formally stated, but members still clearly understand and share them.

Norms become obvious when a group member or an outsider violates them. For example, a group norm about avoiding sexual jokes can be implicit and not discussed but may become a topic of discussion when a new member tells a sexual joke. At that point, the group verbalizes its norm to educate the new member.

Purpose of Norms   Having norms allows a group to bring order and control to the members' interactions. Norms regulate group social interactions and the way a group achieves its tasks. These regulations ensure smooth group processes. Norms also set the group apart from other groups, thus helping provide the group with its identity. One group may have a norm about meeting deadlines; another may be more relaxed about deadlines and instead focuses on quality. One group may have formal interactions and tolerate little humor during group meetings whereas another is relaxed and accepts social bantering. The collection of a group's norms eventually becomes part of its culture, just as the collection of an organization's norms is part of its culture (see Table 7.1).

For groups to work well, one expert suggests that managers let everyone develop some norms and stick to them while working on a project. Tami Urban, a consultant who works at Cambridge Technology Partners, suggests agreeing on the following three norms: respecting others' working hours, not being late for meetings, and listening to and respecting others' opinions.[40] Although simple, these norms allow the group to move quickly to accomplishing the task.

Group norms are important to group functioning. They develop early, take time and resources to maintain, and can affect group members acutely if violated.

Development of Norms   Group norms usually develop in one of four ways: through leaders, critical incidents, specific member requests, and historical responses to issues (see Table 7.2). The earlier a group establishes several basic norms, the more quickly it can start functioning effectively. Leaders and critical incidents in the group can help establish group norms. The first time two members get into an argument, for example, the group will establish rules of conduct such as "no yelling; no swearing; no personal attacks." U.S. congressional norms, for instance, regulate personal attacks on other congressional members. Representative J. D. Hayworth (R-Arizona) received strong rebukes from the other members when he frequently broke the norm of civil discourse during his freshman term of office. During debates, he was

Norms
Shared rules and expectations about group members' behaviors

T a b l e 7 . 1
THE PURPOSE OF NORMS

- Provide a sense of order and control
- Regulate social interaction and work performance
- Allow for smooth internal functioning
- Help establish the group's culture and identity

Table 7.2   DEVELOPMENT OF NORMS

Events	Examples
• Leaders establish norms	The group leader states that she is a stickler for punctuality; the group therefore agrees that being on time is a key norm.
• Critical incidents in the group	Heated arguments between two members lead to the development of norms regarding arguing
• Specific requests from group members	One member who is offended by another's racial jokes specifically requests that group members agree not to use them
• History of interaction	If the first meeting starts with brief social interaction before the group gets down to the task, all other meetings follow the same pattern and a norm develops for brief social interaction before work.

asked to tone down his personal attacks on the opposition, to stop questioning the motives of his opponents, and to stick to the issues.

Another way norms get established is through a specific request from one or more of the group members. One member may state that he gets irritated with others when they are late and then suggest that members agree on a norm about being on time. Finally, norms develop through time as the group members work together. The behaviors and interactions selected from the beginning set the stage for the norms and become part of the group's history.

Once norms are established, they are difficult to change. In many ways, norms are the groups' schemas for various behaviors and situations. As is the case with any schema, once formed, they are resistant to change. You may have noticed that group members in your class groups or at work stick to simple and often insignificant norms by saying, "This is the way we have always done things." Changing norms requires a change in the order of things and a reconsideration of how things should be done. As you will learn in chapter 14, change always creates some stress and resistance. The resistance to change is particularly strong for the central norms of the group.

Central and Peripheral Norms   Recall that organizational culture has three levels. The deepest level involves basic assumptions about the nature of people. These assumptions are difficult to change as they are the basis for values and behaviors. The other two levels, especially the first level of behaviors and symbols, are more superficial and thus easier to change.

Norms follow a similar pattern, as depicted in Figure 7.5. **Central norms** are basic rules of behavior that are key to the group's identity, goals, and survival.[41] Other norms are **peripheral norms** that support the central norms but are not central to the group's identity or task. Doing quality work and respecting others are examples of central norms, whereas being on time and friendly are peripheral. The central norms are equivalent to the third, deep level of culture. The peripheral norms are closer to the first and second levels.

One of the central norms of behavior at Procter & Gamble (P&G), the Cincinnati-based manufacturer and marketer of major brands of household products such as Tide detergent and Crest toothpaste, is that managers must be promoted from within the organization. Individuals who have worked their way up the organization ladder now occupy 31 of the top 32 positions in the company. This central norm leads to peripheral norms, such as cross-training future managers and making sure that employees are so satisfied they do not leave. For example, Carol Tuttle, P&G's vice president of human resources, has held several positions in the organization that include brand management, advertising, and recruiting. She spent six years in Venezuela and has received seven promotions in her 22-year career in the company.

Hot ▽ Link

We discussed organizational culture in chapter 3, pp. 90–99.

Central norms
Rules of behavior that are essential to the group's identity, goals, and survival

Peripheral norms
Rules of behavior that support central norms but aren't central to the group's identity or task

She states: "It's always challenging, always exciting. I don't think I've ever been bored for five minutes."[42] The central norm of promoting from within has led to the peripheral norm of cross-training.

While central norms are resistant to change, peripheral norms can change as different behaviors are needed to support the goal achievement at different points in time. Groups can afford to be lenient in the enforcement of their peripheral norms. However, not enforcing central norms threatens the group's existence and reason for being, and therefore, cannot be tolerated. For instance, at P&G if cross-training in multiple divisions becomes too expensive, the organization may abandon it for another creative way of training its future leaders. The commitment to internal promotions will continue.

Groups that are inflexible in changing their peripheral norms may become overly rigid and as a result lose some creativity. Next, we consider the issue of how groups enforce their norms in our discussion of conformity, cohesion, and deviance. Although these topics are part of the internal structure and processes of groups, their importance to group functioning deserves separate attention.

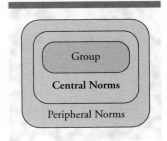

FIGURE 7.5
Central and Peripheral Group Norms

Summary Point 7.5   What Are Roles and Norms?

- Roles are specific formal or informal activities that each person does in a group.
- Task roles focus on the task; relationship roles maintain internal functioning; groups need both. Self-oriented roles are focused on the individual and can be damaging to the group.
- Norms are shared rules and expectations about group members' behaviors.

- The purpose of norms is to provide guidelines for action, an identity to the group, and a sense of order and control.
- Norms develop through critical incidents, specific requests, and group history of interaction.
- Central norms are basic rules of behavior that are key to the group's identity and goals; peripheral norms support the central norms but are not central to the group's identity or task.

COHESION, CONFORMITY, AND DEVIANCE

One of the most desirable qualities of a group is cohesion. **Cohesion** (also called cohesiveness) is the degree to which members of the group are attracted to the group and to one another. Cohesive groups are tight and supportive. Members of a cohesive group perceive less intergroup conflict.[43] They share deeply the central and peripheral norms of the group. They want to be in the group and work at supporting group goals and one another.

One of the main factors in cohesive groups is that no one has to enforce norms. Members of cohesive groups voluntarily conform to the group. **Conformity** refers to the extent to which people adhere to group norms. For instance, among the employees of Harley-Davidson, manufacturer of the famous motorcycles in Milwaukee, Wisconsin, many tattoo the company name on their bodies with pride as a way to conform to this group norm.[44]

Although cohesive groups have many benefits, managers must watch for some potential drawbacks. In the sections that follow we consider factors that lead to cohesion, its advantages and disadvantages, and the issue of deviance.

Cohesion (also called cohesiveness)
The degree to which group members are attracted to the group and to one another

Conformity
The process of abiding by the group norms

Building Cohesive Groups

How can managers build cohesive groups? The answer is within a manager's reach, as summarized in Figure 7.6. Managers can increase cohesion by taking seven steps to enhance the value that individual members place on belonging to the group.[45] The first step is to keep the

FIGURE 7.6
Building Cohesive Groups

group relatively small to allow all members to participate and interact fully.[46] The next step is to manage group composition. Because people who are similar tend to get along better, managers should pick group members who have some common bonds, such as social interests, hobbies, educational background, or work expertise.

The third step that managers can take to build group cohesion is to provide members with ample opportunity for work and social interaction. The interaction builds the group members' friendship and trust. Howard Stevenson, Harvard Business School professor, believes that successful groups need to be familiar with each other. "We have to know each other, know how we work together, so that when a crisis comes we don't have to spend a long time coordinating."[47]

The fourth step in building cohesiveness is to provide the group with sufficient resources to do its task and to avoid infighting and competition over resources. Having to compete internally for various resources is a quick way of destroying a group's cohesiveness. Along with resources, managers must reward cooperation among group members. Although in the United States organizations typically reward individual work, building group cohesion requires that some group rewards also be provided. Sixth, groups that avoid formal, rigid hierarchies and status differences among members tend to be more cohesive.[48]

Competition with an external group can also increase cohesion. This group can be in another organization, such as a competitor, or inside the organization, such as another department. Providing the group with some isolation from the outside can further help boost the group's sense of identity and its cohesion. Finally, groups that are successful are more cohesive than those that are not.[49] Managers need to take special care to provide the group with opportunities for success early to help build the group's sense of accomplishment. Early failures can easily demoralize a group that has not yet built a history of success.

If managers help build a cohesive group, they are likely to see many advantages and several potential disadvantages. We discuss these next.

Advantages and Disadvantages of Cohesion

People who are part of a cohesive group enjoy several benefits. Members of cohesive groups are generally more satisfied and happier because they feel supported and valued.[50] Practitioners

Change Challenge

INTRODUCING CONFLICT IN GROUPS

Increasingly, the pendulum is swinging back—organizations that trained employees and managers to avoid conflict are now looking for positive ways to cope with conflict. In the past, many practitioners assumed that conflict was destructive and the result of poor communication and misunderstanding. Now many see that conflict caused by genuine differences of opinions, values, and approaches can be a source of creativity. Conflict in work groups can benefit the organization if managed well.

Bill Gates, the CEO of Microsoft, asks top managers to debate issues in what he calls his "kitchen cabinet." The idea is to have an open, honest, and emotional discussion in an informal setting that leads to creative solutions for the organization's important problems. Stephen Case, the CEO of Internet provider America Online, selected a group of executives who are dissimilar to him so they will question and challenge each other and everything.

The key to managing conflict successfully in groups is to recognize individual differences, respect members' feelings, create a supportive environment, and focus on finding solutions while avoiding blame.

believe group cohesion strengthens commitment to the organization.[51] In addition, members tend to be more motivated to achieve the group's goal.

Is better performance a benefit of cohesive groups? Not necessarily. As we learned in chapter 6, increased satisfaction and motivation do not always lead to better performance. If group norms include high productivity and performance, then members of cohesive groups are likely to be productive. If, however, the norms of the group aren't based on high productivity, then performance is not likely to be high.

Consider the example of a cohesive group of computer programmers. They interact extensively at work and outside of work and consider one another friends and co-workers. Through the years, the group has developed a norm for doing its job well, but not too well. That way, the group can avoid increases in quotas or higher demands from management. Members of this group, in spite of being cohesive and satisfied, are not likely to be high performers. They follow their group norm for good average performance rather than organizational requirements for excellence.

Although cohesive groups may work against organizational goals and norms, they do provide a supportive environment for learning, a key benefit. Such an environment allows members to experiment, make mistakes, and learn new skills and new behaviors without fear of ridicule or negative organizational consequences. It is a lot easier to try out a new skill with supportive group members encouraging you and without your manager looking over your shoulder. In addition, the cost of failure is bearable. Many police organizations, for instance, make sure that new officers are in groups with veterans. This simple technique provides an excellent learning environment for the new officers; it allows them to gain self-confidence and experience and to make mistakes without major career consequences.

Another advantage of cohesive groups is the creation of strong norms and a strong culture. As long as the group norms do not work against the organizational goals and culture, cohesive groups can be a considerable benefit to organizations. Managers do not have to monitor employees in cohesive groups closely because they willingly abide by the norms and the culture of their

Table 7.3   ADVANTAGES AND DISADVANTAGES OF COHESION

Advantages	Disadvantages
• Increased satisfaction and motivation	• Focus on group norms at the expense of the organization
• Increased learning due to supportive environment	• Loss of creativity
• Creation of strong norms and strong culture	• Groupthink

group. Although the strong culture can be a benefit, it can also lead to a loss of creativity, as members do not want to rock the boat by disagreeing with one another. Their attraction to the group leads them to avoid controversial issues that may jeopardize the group's cohesion.

Overall, managers should encourage group cohesion because of its advantages. The major disadvantages are the potential loss of creativity, possibility of poor decision making, and the unwillingness to deal with difficult issues, as Table 7.3 shows. We explore the disadvantage of *groupthink* in detail next.

Special Problem of Cohesive Groups: Groupthink

Groupthink
Poor decision making that results from group cohesion

The biggest danger of cohesive groups is a process called *groupthink*. **Groupthink** refers to poor decision making that results from group cohesion.[52] Social psychologist Irving Janis first introduced the concept. It has since then been applied to many organizational events and situations.[53]

Consider the events surrounding the Space Shuttle *Challenger* disaster of 1986. The engineers at Morton Thiokol had information about the lack of reliability of the shuttle's O-rings below certain temperatures. The information was discussed and eventually suppressed internally. As a result, it was not used when the decision to launch *Challenger* on January 28, 1986, was finally made. The space shuttle had been sitting on the launch pad at subfreezing temperatures for hours. Seventy-two seconds after launch, *Challenger* exploded, killing all passengers aboard. The failure of the O-rings to seal at cold temperatures was the cause. These events demonstrate the disastrous effect of groupthink.[54]

Elements of Groupthink   Groupthink occurs in highly cohesive groups that isolate themselves from outside influences and must address a complex problem that has many possible solutions. These groups also have a well-liked, powerful leader who voices opinions strongly. The groups lack formal procedures for examining alternative solutions. Because of the attraction to the group and to the leader, members who have disconfirming information or contrary opinions do not state them publicly. Those who do are pressured to be silent by other members. The antecedents, symptoms, and consequences of groupthink are presented in Figure 7.7.

The high cohesion, the complexity of the situation, the presence of a strong, directive leader, the insulation from the outside, and the lack of formal established procedures to consider alternatives all lead to the eight groupthink symptoms. These symptoms first cause the group to overestimate its capabilities through the illusion of invulnerability and a sense of morality. They encourage the group members to believe they have the one correct path and answer. The second step is the closing of the mind to alternatives and external information. This is achieved by rationalizing the group's positions and decisions and using negative stereotypes to describe outsiders who criticize the group or who simply provide a different opinion. The final step is the pressure for unanimity that develops through self-censorship and the illusion that the group members all agree. If these fail, various individuals guard the group from dissenting information and apply direct pressure on dissenters to fall back in line.

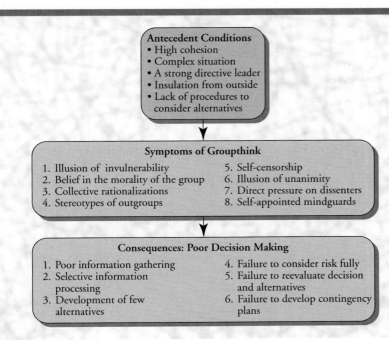

FIGURE 7.7
Groupthink

Sources: Based on I. Janis and L. Mann, *Decision Making: A Psychological Analysis of Conflict, Choice, and Commitment* (New York: Free Press, 1977); I. L. Janis, *Groupthink*, 2d ed. (Boston: Houghton Mifflin, 1982); G. Moorehead, "Groupthink: Hypothesis in Need of Testing," *Group & Organization Studies*, December 1982.

If you think groupthink operates only in isolated situations, think again. A large number of political, social, and business mistakes can be attributed to executives falling prey to groupthink. Examples range from President Johnson's decision to escalate the Vietnam War, to Coke's failed move to retire its classic formula, to numerous mergers and acquisitions that take companies outside their areas of expertise, to Union Carbide's board of directors' decision not to upgrade its plant in Bhopal, India, leading to more than 2,000 deaths in the late 1980s.

Every day, cohesive and well-meaning groups of political leaders and their advisers, and business leaders and their boards of directors make decisions without fully considering available data and without evaluating all the alternatives. The pressure to make a decision that maintains the group's internal cohesion results in groupthink. The desire to be liked by and belong to the group and the presence of a strong leader induce group members to suppress their doubts and go along with poor decisions. Surprisingly, preventing groupthink is a relatively simple process.

Preventing Groupthink   To prevent groupthink, managers must encourage members to consider alternative decisions through formal, agreed-on processes. This process includes introduction of new ideas to the group, either through group members or external experts. To ensure the success of the process, managers must help members develop a group norm that values debate and disagreement as a positive group element, not a negative one. To encourage such a norm, leaders must stay away from the group while members debate alternatives. The absence of the leader encourages creativity, development and evaluation of alternatives, and reconsideration of old ideas. Managers can take six specific steps to prevent groupthink:

- Assign group members the role of critical evaluator.
- Bring in outsiders with differing opinions.
- Create subgroups and rotate membership among them.
- Assign several devil's advocates.
- Provide clear rules to encourage disagreement and constructive conflict.
- Encourage an open climate through nondirective leadership.

By instituting preventive measures, organizations can reap the motivational and learning benefits of cohesive groups without falling victim to groupthink.

Deviance in Groups

Cohesive groups are cohesive because members are attracted to the group and willingly conform to its norms. We considered the benefits and disadvantages of such willing conformity. If everyone always conformed to the group, how would new ideas ever come forth? Furthermore, what happens when a group member is not willing to conform to the norms? Individuals who do not conform to the group and deviate from the norms are called **deviants**. In spite of the negative connotation of the term *deviant*, deviants can play an important role in group creativity and effectiveness.

Deviants
Individuals who do not conform to the group and deviate from the norms

A QUESTION OF ETHICS

How Far Should Groups Go to Enforce Norms? One of your employees does not follow the department's well-established informal norms about proper business attire. Instead of conservative suits, the employee wears outfits the group considers more suitable for an evening at a nightclub. That same employee takes the informal Friday dress code too far. How far should you, as a manager, go to enforce those norms? What is and is not acceptable behavior on your part, and on the part of other group and department members?

Positive and Negative Deviance   Whether a deviant is tolerated or treated harshly, meaning rejected or ostracized, depends on the norms the deviant is rejecting.[55] The reaction of the group will differ greatly based on whether the deviant rejects central or peripheral norms. The four options for accepting or rejecting group norms are presented in Figure 7.8.

The first two cases involve acceptance of central norms. In the first instance, *conformity*, the individual fully conforms to the peripheral norms and the central norms. The person is a happy, well-accepted member of the group. The second option, *creative individualism*, involves rejecting the peripheral norms while accepting the central ones. Individuals who are in this situation usually are well tolerated by the group because rejection of peripheral norms does not threaten the group. They are not really deviants and are often called eccentrics, or creative individuals. How well the group accepts and tolerates them depends on their value and contribution to the group's goals.

FIGURE 7.8
Types of Deviance

Source: Based on F. Schein, *Organization Psychology*, 3d ed. (Upper Saddle River, NJ: Prentice Hall, 1980), Table 6.1, p. 100. Adapted with permission of Prentice Hall.

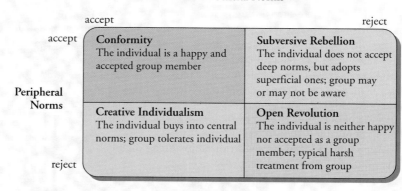

	Central Norms	
	accept	reject
Peripheral Norms accept	**Conformity** The individual is a happy and accepted group member	**Subversive Rebellion** The individual does not accept deep norms, but adopts superficial ones; group may or may not be aware
Peripheral Norms reject	**Creative Individualism** The individual buys into central norms; group tolerates individual	**Open Revolution** The individual is neither happy nor accepted as a group member; typical harsh treatment from group

To illustrate, consider the case of a well-respected scientist who, while agreeing with the goals of the research laboratory's creativity and safety, does not join in the political lobbying activities in which many group members engage. Although other group members tease the scientist about being antisocial, they continue to tolerate the violation because the scientist conforms to the central norms.

The other two options presented in Figure 7.8 are threatening to the group because they both involve rejection of the central norms of the group. In the case of *subversive rebellion*, the group may not recognize the individual as deviant because he accepts peripheral norms while rejecting central ones. The person may appear, on the surface, to conform to the group. The individual who is in *open revolution* is the one groups label as deviant. Few if any groups have much tolerance for such members because they do not accept either central or peripheral norms.

Typically, group members put direct pressure on deviants and increase interaction with them for a while.[56] Various group members will talk to the deviant and argue and reason with this person to try to bring him or her back into the group. If coaxing does not work, group members may threaten various punishments. The increased interaction with the deviant will go on for a while. If no change occurs, the group will start isolating the deviant, eventually ostracizing and even expelling the person from the group. It is interesting that groups pressure members engaged in open revolution while ignoring those engaged in subversive rebellion, although both can be equally destructive to the group.

One of the benefits of deviants is to help the group be creative. No group can tolerate a total rejection of its central norms without some action, but encouraging creative individualism is a way for group members in cohesive groups to move the group forward.

Deviance as a Creative Process: Idiosyncrasy Credit   As individuals conform to central and peripheral norms of the group, they earn credit with other members. These credits are like funds that accumulate for future spending. Because they demonstrate their loyalty to the group, its values, norms, and goals, members can then spend their credit by deviating even from central norms occasionally without fear of punishment. These credits are called **idiosyncrasy credits**.[57] In some cases, mistakes and missteps use up the credits. In other cases, members use them consciously to move the group forward. They provide conforming members with latitude to behave outside the group norms. As we see in chapter 9, idiosyncrasy credit is a major factor in leadership.

Idiosyncrasy credit
A process that allows cohesive groups to be creative by giving credit to conforming members who can then use the accumulated credits to deviate from the group

Imagine what happens when a long-time, well-respected, well-mannered member of a group suddenly starts screaming at another member during a meeting. The others know this is deviant behavior, but because it's never happened before members attribute it to a one-time loss of control and let it go. This deviant member simply uses some of his idiosyncrasy credits. If the behavior occurs in several other meetings, the member will not have any credits left and will be pressured to correct his behavior and abide by the group norms of civility and respect.

In many cases, conforming to the norms of groups earns members idiosyncrasy credits. In other cases, a group gives a person with established expertise from the outside credit for past accomplishments.

Idiosyncrasy credit provides the means for *legitimate deviance* within a group. Without allowing some deviation from norms, groups stagnate and are unable to survive in the long run. Allowing members in good standing, those who have proven themselves to the group, to deviate encourages creativity in conforming and cohesive groups.

In this section we investigated cohesion, its advantages and disadvantages, and focused on groupthink as the strongest potential danger of cohesive groups. We also explored solutions to groupthink and considered the role and management of deviants in groups. In the following section we examine the stages of group development.

Summary Point 7.6 **What Are Cohesion, Conformity, and Deviance?**

- Cohesion is the degree to which group members are attracted to the group and to one another.
- Conformity is the extent to which group members adhere to group norms.
- Cohesion provides satisfaction, learning, and a strong group culture. It may also lead to groups that are internally focused, lose creativity, and engage in groupthink.
- High cohesion, a complex situation, a strong leader, the absence of formal procedures for considering alterna-

tives, and insulation from outsiders are the conditions that lead to groupthink.
- Individuals who do not conform to the group and do not follow its norms are called deviants.
- Depending on whether deviants accept or reject the central and/or the peripheral norms of the group, their act can be classified as conformity, creative individualism, subversive rebellion, or open revolution.
- Individuals earn idiosyncrasy credit by being a valued member of the group.

STAGES OF GROUP DEVELOPMENT

It takes time for any group to become cohesive and effective.[58] As most of you have experienced in class or work groups, when people first form a group, they spend much of their time on what some of you—particularly those of you who have Type A tendencies—label as useless chitchat and irrelevant small talk. You may also have noticed that groups almost always run into conflict within a few days or a few weeks after forming. Some groups never resolve their problems. Others manage to overcome them and move on to perform their job.

This progression in the life of groups—from a collection of individuals to a group with well-established processes, roles, norms, and goals—involves different stages of group development. We examine six major stages of group development and consider the challenges of each stage. Figure 7.9 summarizes these stages.

Stages and Challenges

The stages shown in Figure 7.9 suggest that groups go through a number of stages before they become mature and fully functioning. Although all groups go through a developmental process, not all spend an equal amount of time in each stage. Various factors, such as new members, new leadership, or a new task, can also reverse the development process. We describe each stage in Table 7.4 and list the challenges groups typically face at each stage.

FIGURE 7.9
Stages of Group Development

Source: Based on stages of group development presented by L. N. Jewell and H. J. Reitz, *Group Effectiveness in Organizations* (Glenview, IL: Scott, Foresman, 1981).

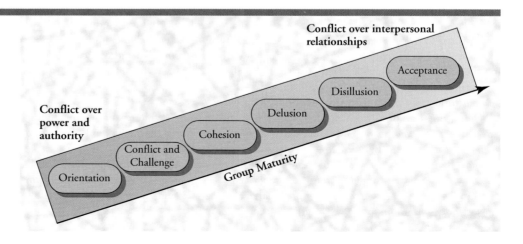

Table 7.4   THE SIX STAGES OF GROUP DEVELOPMENT

Stage	Description	Major Challenges
1. Orientation	Group members are tentative in getting to know one another, in establishing their roles, and in determining leadership. No norms are yet established.	• Find leader for group • Establish roles • Create group norms
2. Conflict and challenge	Power struggles start over norms and leadership. Subgroups form with varying degrees of conflict.	• Resolve power struggles • Establish clear rules • Learn to manage conflict
3. Cohesion	Subgroups resolve their differences and attraction to group is established. Leadership is established; norms develop.	
4. Delusion	The group develops a sense of harmony and agreement; norms and leadership are well accepted; members seek agreement and avoid conflict; the group has a sense of false security.	• Avoid complacency • Avoid groupthink • Develop unvoiced resentment
5. Disillusion	Conflict erupts over interpersonal issues and unresolved problems; the group becomes fragmented, with subgroups fighting over power; there is a sense of disappointment and disillusionment.	• Experience intense interpersonal conflict • Overcome disappointment with group • Maintain interest in group
6. Acceptance	Norms and roles are adjusted; new leadership evolves; members accept individual and subgroup differences.	

Each of the stages of development presents special challenges. During the early stages of development the major challenges and obstacles are establishment of norms, roles, and leadership. The group's initial assigned leader may or may not emerge as the actual leader by stage 3. Various members will challenge the authority of the leader and fight to establish their own roles and norms. These processes are an inherent part of the development of the group. If members manage the conflicts and struggles well and openly, the group has a chance of moving to the next stage. Unfortunately, many members become stressed and leaders become offended about the conflicts and either ignore them or deal with them too harshly. As a result, the group does not resolve the conflict completely and has trouble moving to the next stage. Each of the challenges must be dealt with before the group can move forward.

In the later stages, leadership struggles are generally resolved. The group is in the cohesion and delusion stages, enjoying a period of peace and harmony. Rules and norms are well established and leadership is well accepted. Many groups reach stages 3 and 4 without having faced any major external challenges. These are the stages in which groupthink is most likely to happen. Not being fully comfortable yet with one another but wanting to keep the group intact, members are unwilling to challenge one another. As the group moves toward the last stages, interpersonal conflicts are likely to be the major focus because of disappointment over the group's performance.

If a group manages to overcome the various challenges and reach the acceptance stage, it is mature enough to handle differences, disagreements, and conflicts. Processes are well in place and members are willing to be flexible. This final stage of development is where groups aspire to be.

Using Stages to Manage Groups

Having knowledge of the stages and the challenges groups face can help managers move the group to maturity.

- The first implication for managers is that no group can become cohesive and effective immediately. All groups need time to work through obstacles and challenges. Although managers can help by clarifying goals, suggesting norms

MANAGERIAL ADVICE
from the Experts

LEADERSHIP IN GROUPS

Groups need different types of leadership at different stages. Being an effective manager of groups requires careful monitoring of the group and the flexibility to play different roles at different times.

- In early stages, a manager needs to provide clear direction regarding the group's goals. The focus should be on task roles and the leader should demonstrate personal commitment to the goals.
- Early help in setting norms and deciding on roles avoids confusion and unnecessary delays.
- When conflict erupts, be willing to confront and resolve issues related to both task and relationship conflicts.
- As the group moves to a more mature stage, the leader needs to step back and let the group function on its own as much as possible to develop the flexibility needed for creativity.
- Too much interference from the leader defeats the purpose of having a group.
- At late stages, the leader needs to be ready to jump back in when conflict increases at the same time he or she plays maintenance roles.

Sources: Based on B. Barthelemy, *The Sky Is Not the Limit: Breakthrough Leadership* (Boca Raton, FL: St. Lucie Press, 1997): 135–77; also see C. E. Larson and F. M. LaFasto, *Teamwork: What Must Go Right/What Can Go Wrong* (Newbury Park, CA: Sage, 1989): 118–28.

and rules, and appointing leaders, members need to manage their own challenges as a way to grow.

- The second implication of stages and challenges for managers is that conflict is an integral part of group interaction. Although there are clear cultural differences regarding how much conflict is acceptable and comfortable for individuals, in most Western countries, and particularly in the United States, managing conflict openly and constructively is necessary for groups to develop. You will learn more about how to help groups manage conflict in chapters 8 and 13.
- The last managerial implication of the six stages is that groups do not move through these stages in only one direction. Some groups never resolve challenges and may need to be disbanded and reformed. Other groups reach a certain stage but are set back because of a new task, changes in membership, changes in organizational factors, or new leadership. Moving down the maturity scale may be distressing to both managers and group members, but it can also provide an opportunity for renewal and greater creativity. Think back for a moment to the Managerial Challenge on *Titanic*. Because of time pressure and frequent changes in membership dictated by the movie's technical requirements, many of the groups that worked on *Titanic* did not become fully mature and reported conflict and frustration as a result.

Summary Point 7.7   **What Are the Stages of Group Development?**

- Groups go through six developmental stages that influence their effectiveness and performance.
- The six stages are orientation, conflict and challenge, cohesion, delusion, disillusion, and acceptance.

- Each stage presents a challenge that needs to be resolved before the group can move to the next stage.
- Groups can move back and forth among stages depending on their composition and other situational factors.

The role of managers in helping their groups mature and become effective is essential. In traditional organizations, managers are assigned as group leaders automatically and are expected to control the group tightly. Although such an approach is often efficient, many organizations find that it stifles creativity and flexibility, the core contributions that groups provide organizations. Increasingly, organizations rely on mature, cohesive, and flexible groups to be the cornerstone of the organization's decision making, production, and management systems. These mature groups are the teams in today's organizations, the topic of our next chapter.

Groups *in Context*

Groups function within larger organizational contexts and are themselves a contextual factor for individuals. The dynamic, complex environment that many organizations face today spurs managers to use groups more frequently. Complex problems require creative solutions that well-managed groups can provide. As a result, groups have become an integral part of many organizations' strategy and structure. Managers are also finding that they must understand national, ethnic, and organizational culture to manage groups successfully.

Let's return to the Rosenbluth example to see how its use of groups in response to the environment affects its strategy, structure, and culture. The company president's decision to change strategy to become better run and more competitive led to the use of groups as the center of the new structure. The mission of having a travel agency that operated like a family farm sent the message that the culture of the units needed to be tight-knit and supportive. Furthermore, the new strategy meant that all group members had to be treated as friends and as family members to create a supportive work environment.

Technology further affects groups and their productiveness. Groups can become more cohesive through the use of technology or they can become distant and less productive if technology is not used wisely. Hal Rosenbluth supports his new group-based family farm strategy with a state-of-the-art computer information system that allows group members to accomplish their tasks better and stay in touch with one another. Rosenbluth's Global Distribution Network links all the organization's units and provides vital information instantly to its travel agents about its hundreds of thousands of clients. Although the organization operates as 100 small family units, it uses the technology to act like a large business and be successful in a highly competitive travel environment.

Managers can use technology, strategy, and structure to support groups and help them become more effective. For groups to succeed, the organizational context must support and encourage them.

For updated information on the topics in this chapter, Web exercises, links to related Web sites, an on-line study guide, and more, visit our companion Web site at:
http://www.prenhall.com/nahavandi

A Look Back at the

MANAGERIAL CHALLENGE

James Cameron's **Titanic**

Making *Titanic* was truly a titanic project. Filming took longer than planned, and then the movie's summer debut had to be postponed until December to allow time for the final editing and postproduction work. In all, James Cameron—as producer, writer, and director—needed more than two years to bring this story to the big screen.

Cameron used a combination of group members (who had worked together on previous projects) with part-time members (who were needed for specific locations or tasks) and outside specialists (who handled digital effects on a subcontracting basis). Although this combination provided maximum flexibility and promoted creativity, the groups struggled to achieve maturity.

Even though the project faced time constraints, group members pitched in because of the bonds of cohesion they had forged during previous projects. Cinematographer Russell Carpenter noted, "If a crew works with a director of photography for any length of time, they're going to know what his favorite solutions are for any given problem. Also . . . most of the people I brought to the shoot had worked with Jim [Cameron] before, so they knew the kinds of physical and spiritual demands that would be made on them."[59]

Gaffer John Buckley, the head electrician, faced barriers in building a well-performing group from a diverse crew of U.S. and Mexican lighting experts. "In the beginning," says Buckley, "it was hard because some of the [American] crew seemed elitist. Part of that was due to the language barrier."[60] For example, after crew members disagreed about who should set up equipment, Buckley established a new rule: The person who brought a light onto the set would also hang and focus it. Clarifying duties and showing respect for the expertise of all crew members helped the group resolve conflicts.

Despite all the complications, managers and crew members alike found *Titanic* a rewarding project. "This picture was a mammoth undertaking," Buckley said later, "and I'm really proud of it because I gave it everything I had, as did everybody else on the crew." Cinematographer Russell Carpenter agreed. "I'll remember *Titanic* as a challenge and a testament to Jim's visionary gifts and drive," he said, "but perhaps more importantly, I'll recall that I was supported through it all by a group of talented and committed crew members. That's the bottom line for me."[61]

■ Point of View Exercises

You're the Manager: As John Buckley's assistant, you manage a crew of lighting experts working on the oceanfront sets. You and your crew face many conflicts. What can you do to make your crew more cohesive?

You're the Employee: As a lighting expert on Buckley's team, you are generally open to all kinds of ideas and interested in forging closer relationships with co-workers. You provide a lot of support for others and care about the group running well. What type of team role are you playing? What are the potential drawbacks of this role?

SUMMARY OF LEARNING OBJECTIVES

1. **Outline the elements and types of groups, the reasons for joining groups, and the impact of national and organizational culture on groups.** A group is two or more people who interact in an organized manner to perform a certain task or activity to achieve a common goal. Formal groups are based on organizational needs with required and prescribed goals. Informal groups exist because of the members' common interests, social ties, or friendship. We join groups to help satisfy individual needs and to achieve goals that are too complex or too time consuming for any one individual to achieve. National as well as organizational cultures have a profound effect on the extent to which groups are used and valued.

2. **Explain when groups should be used and identify their potential benefits and disadvantages.** Groups should be used when the task is complex, time is sufficient to allow for group processes, and commitment of group members to the decision is essential to its implementation. The benefits of groups include potential creativity, higher-quality decisions, and a supportive environment in which employees can learn new skills and new behaviors. The disadvantages of groups include inefficiency, a potential lack of creativity, and social loafing.

3. **Discuss the effect of group size and composition and the importance of roles and norms in group behavior.** Groups that are larger than eight to twelve members are less likely to be able to function smoothly as groups. As groups get larger, subgroups are likely to form and require increased coordination. Groups that have homogeneous membership are able to get along better. Heterogeneous group members are more likely to face conflict and disagreement. The composition of the groups needs to be determined primarily by the task the group is performing.

   Roles are specific formal or informal activities that each person performs in a group. Group roles include task, relationship, and self-oriented roles. Norms are shared rules and expectations about group members' behaviors. The purpose of norms is to regulate social interactions and to provide the group with a unique identity. Central norms define the group whereas peripheral norms support the central norms.

4. **Explain the role and effects of *cohesion, conformity,* and *deviance* in groups.** Cohesion is the degree to which members of the groups are attracted to the group and to one another. Conformity is the extent to which members adhere to group norms. Benefits of cohesion are increased satisfaction and motivation, increased learning due to a supportive environment, and creation of strong norms and a strong group culture. Disadvantages of cohesion may include adherence to group norms at the expense of the organization, loss of creativity, and groupthink. Groupthink is a process of poor decision making due to group cohesion. Creating norms for disagreement and debate and encouraging evaluation of alternatives can prevent groupthink.

   Deviants are individuals who do not conform to group norms. Those who violate central norms are treated more harshly than those who violate peripheral norms. Although groups cannot tolerate a total rejection of central norms, encouraging creative individualism is one of the ways cohesive and conforming group members can help move the group forward. As individuals conform to central and peripheral norms of the group, they earn idiosyncrasy credit, which they can then use to move the group forward.

5. **Describe the stages of group development and the challenges members face at each stage.** The six stages of group development are orientation, conflict and challenge, cohe-

sion, delusion, disillusion, and acceptance. Groups can move back and forth among stages depending on their composition and other situational factors. In the early stages, conflict over power and authority threatens the group. In later stages, conflict is over interpersonal issues. Groups have to resolve their conflicts before they can perform well.

KEY TERMS

central norms, p. 244
cohesion, p. 245
complex task, p. 235
conformity, p. 245
deviants, p. 250
formal groups, p. 231
group, p. 230
groupthink, p. 248

heterogeneous groups, p. 240
homogeneous groups, p. 240
idiosyncrasy credit, p. 251
informal groups, p. 231
norms, p. 243
peripheral norms, p. 244

relationship roles, p. 241
roles, p. 241
self-oriented roles, p. 241
social facilitation, p. 237
social loafing, p. 236
task roles, p. 241

REVIEW QUESTIONS

1. What are the defining characteristics of groups and why do people join them?
2. List the situations in which groups should be used in organizations and the potential benefits and disadvantages of using groups.
3. How can managers increase group cohesion? What are the benefits and disadvantages of group cohesion?
4. Describe the symptoms, consequences, and solutions to groupthink.
5. Describe the stages of group development and the challenges that members face at each stage.

DISCUSSION QUESTIONS

1. How would you deal differently with groups from an individualistic culture versus groups from a collectivist culture?
2. Consider a group you have worked with in the past. What were some of the group's central and peripheral norms? To what extent were the norms functional or dysfunctional?
3. How can individuals with self-oriented roles be managed to become productive group members?
4. What are managers' responsibilities in avoiding groupthink?
5. What are the implications of deviance and idiosyncrasy credit for groups? How can you use these concepts to improve your management of the groups you work with?

▶ SELF-ASSESSMENT 7
Assertiveness

Being an effective group member requires the ability to be open and honest with other members without being aggressive. Excessive aggression or passivity can prevent the open exchange needed to build cohesive groups. Assertiveness is key.

INTERPERSONAL RESPONSE INVENTORY

How true are the following statements as descriptions of your behavior? Enter the number that represents your answer in the space provided at the beginning of each statement.

4 = Always true   3 = Often true   2 = Sometimes true   1 = Never true

Please respond to every statement. See Appendix 3 for the scoring key.

Your response   **Statement**

_____   1. I respond with more modesty than I really feel when my work is complimented.

_____   2. If people are rude, I will be rude right back.

_____   3. Other people find me interesting.

_____   4. I find it difficult to speak up in a group of strangers.

_____   5. I don't mind using sarcasm if it helps me make a point.

_____   6. I ask for a raise when I feel I really deserve it.

_____   7. If others interrupt me when I am talking, I suffer in silence.

_____   8. If people criticize my work, I find a way to make them back down.

_____   9. I can express pride in my accomplishments without being boastful.

_____   10. People take advantage of me.

_____   11. I tell people what they want to hear if it helps me get what I want.

_____   12. I find it easy to ask for help.

_____   13. I lend things to others even when I don't want to.

_____   14. I win arguments by dominating the discussion.

_____   15. I can express my true feelings to someone I really care for.

_____   16. When I feel angry with other people, I bottle it up rather than express it.

_____   17. When I criticize other people's work, they get mad.

_____   18. I feel confident in my ability to stand up for my rights.

Source: D. D. Bowen, R. J. Lewicki, D. T. Hall, and F. S. Hall, *Experiences in Management and Organizational Behavior*, 4th ed. (New York: Wiley, 1997): 87–88. Adapted by permission of John Wiley & Sons, Inc.

▶ **TEAM EXERCISE 7**
Group Problem Solving

Your instructor will assign you to groups that represent the departments in an organization. At the company president's request, each department needs to solve the following five puzzles.

MEMO FROM YOUR COMPANY PRESIDENT

Our major competitor has already found the answers to the problems I am asking you to solve. They therefore have a competitive advantage over us. We have a chance to catch up with them if we solve these problems within the next six months (15 minutes).

THE BUSINESS PROBLEMS

1. Create four equilateral triangles with the six toothpicks you have in front of you.

2. All members of the group should be able to perform this task.
   Take hold of each end of the rope. Once you have hold of the ends of the rope, you can't let go. Now make a knot in the rope.

3. Solve the "T" puzzle by forming the four pieces of cardboard into the letter "T."

4. An odd story: Three men went into a diner and each had a single cup of cof-
    fee. Each put an odd number of lumps of sugar into his coffee. In total they
    put 12 lumps of sugar into their cups. How many lumps did each consume?
5. Connect these dots without lifting your pen and without going over the
    same line more than once.

```
·     ·     ·

·     ·     ·

·     ·     ·
```

Source: This exercise is partially based on E. Rose, "It's Those Little Problems That Are Hard to Figure Out," in G. M. Parker (ed.),
The Handbook of Best Practices for Teams (Amherst, MA: HRD Press, 1996): 33–41.

The instructor will provide you with solutions.
Total Number of Problems Solved: _____

GROUP DISCUSSION
1. How would you rate the quality of cooperation in your group?
2. How was your group organized?
3. Did all members participate equally? Was everyone given time to provide input?
4. How did the time pressure affect group processes and outcome?
5. Which task, relationship, and self-oriented roles did members play?
6. What norms did your group develop?
7. What could be improved?

UP CLOSE

▶ The Lucky Dozen

Manuel Bermudez was furious. This was the Lucky Dozen's fourth meeting, and for the fourth time David Stevenson, his co-leader, used the term *qualified minority*. "Why don't you ever say 'qualified majority,' or 'qualified white?'" Bermudez exploded. This type of interaction had become the norm in the group.

Bermudez, Stevenson, and ten other co-workers were members of a prestigious, high-profile group formed to evaluate and upgrade the services that the organization provides to its customers. The Lucky Dozen, as they were nicknamed, represented each of the company's 12 divisions. They were chosen because of their leadership potential. They knew they were being watched closely by employees as well as upper management.

In spite of the talent and the pressure to succeed, problems began the first day. During their first meeting, the company president gave them their charge to upgrade the quality of services, delivered a pep talk, and told them they had a great deal of autonomy and power to do what they thought was best. As soon as the president left, bickering started over who should be the group leader. After much debate and three rounds of secret ballots, Bermudez and Stevenson were tied. When neither was willing to yield, the other members convinced them to be co-chairs. They reluctantly accepted. Soon debate arose concerning who should set the agenda, call the meetings, take notes, and many other details. In addition, two camps quickly emerged regarding how to define a customer and quality and how the group should operate.

To make matters worse, David suggested that because Manuel was a Mexican-American, he should focus on representing the views of the minorities in the organization and let David represent the majority view. Manuel responded by saying that he represented everyone in his division, *everyone!* David also suggested that Manuel was selected for this group because he was one of the few "qualified minorities." Manuel had a few choice words for David on these occasions and jokingly kept referring to him as "Your Majesty!" Continuing to compete for leadership, David and Manuel, in a game of one-upmanship, incessantly reminded others of their accomplishments in the company.

The other ten members could only agree that they were losing their patience with their two leaders. Jackie Lee, the HR representative, had brought piles of customer satisfaction surveys and kept insisting that the group should just get to work. The interpersonal problems, she said, would go away if they ignored them. John Young, another group member, suggested: "If we don't show some results soon, we will be disbanded and really lose face with our colleagues." Two other group members spent most of their time talking to others trying to make peace and to see whether they could find a compromise. Almost no one had noticed that Jerry Mitchell and Anna Lucinda had not said a word since the second meeting and that Adam Kline had left early during the last three meetings.

By their sixth meeting, the group as a whole still had not agreed on anything. The leaders continued to bicker. However, within each of the two subgroups, some work was getting done. One group was reviewing customer data; the other was starting some benchmarking based on what other similar companies had done. Only two weeks were left before the group had to report back to management.

Questions

1. What are the causes of the group's problems?
2. What is your prediction for the future of the Lucky Dozen? Explain.
3. If you were the manager who created the team, could you have averted the problems that arose in the group? Explain.
4. As a member of the team, what can you do to help?

THE BIG PICTURE

▶ Powering Up for Green Energy

Nothing turns an industry upside down quite so quickly as deregulation, as Doug Hyde was well aware. After 20 years in the utility business, Hyde was ready for formidable challenges—and exciting opportunities—when California opened its $23 billion electricity market to competition in 1998.[62] Hyde gave up his post as CEO of Vermont's Green Mountain Power to become president of Green Mountain Energy Resources (GMER), a start-up partially owned by Green Mountain Power.[63] Now his little-known firm is promoting energy from environmentally sound sources, competing against the significant resources of established giants such as Enron and Pacific Gas & Electric.

Change was everywhere. Where Green Mountain Power was slow moving, GMER was "like a rocket with a lit fuse," in Hyde's words. Where the regulated environment had been fairly formal and orderly, deregulation was anything but. "It's not entirely clear what a day in my new life is," Hyde commented. "We've gone from planning to doing in three months, and the job changes every minute."[64]

Hyde's staff consisted of 40 employees and more than 40 skilled subcontractors. With the deadline for California's deregulation only months away, they were under pressure to create a complete business infrastructure from scratch. Individual groups attacked specific tasks such as building a data warehouse of customers and prospects. Speed was critical. Instead of printed memos and scheduled meetings—trappings of traditional utilities—Hyde encouraged communication via e-mail and informal interaction. An area between office cubicles was set aside for employees to gather, talk, even play basketball.

Over time, GMER has developed a unique culture far removed from the sedate climate of Green Mountain Power. Instead of formal business attire, employees are beginning to wear more casual clothing to the office. After an employee threatened to cut a chunk out of Hyde's tie, he gave up his suits and switched to khakis.

Still, Hyde resisted the urge to tighten control and take command. Allowing groups to retain responsibility for their projects fostered "creative interactivity," he believed.[65] It also nurtured the all-important group spirit that GMER would need to become a serious contender in a highly competitive market. Working together to plan future operations contributed to this team spirit.

For example, Hyde and his staff recently went away for a two-day planning meeting, leaving one employee behind to solve an urgent systems problem. When the staff returned to the office, everybody joined in a group hug to comfort the lone employee. "I would, and did, trade a lot to be part of that kind of spirit," observed Hyde.[66] Clearly, nothing would ever be the same in the energy industry.

Questions

1. What advantages of groups was Doug Hyde relying on to support GMER's goals?
2. What contributed to the cohesiveness of the groups at GMER?
3. If you were Doug Hyde, what steps would you take to avoid groupthink at GMER?

NOTES

1. B. Weintraub, "After 'Titanic,' an Omen of Big Power for Big-Cost Directors," *New York Times*, March 25, 1998, B1, B6.
2. Susan Stark, "James Cameron Steered 'The Titanic' and Still Loves the War of Making Big-Budget Movies," *Detroit News*, December 13, 1997, accessed on-line at www.detnews.com/1997/accent/9712/14/12130024.
3. David E. Williams, "All Hands on Deck," *American Cinematographer* (December 1997), accessed on-line at www.cinematographer.com/magazine/dec97/ahod/index.
4. Ibid.
5. Ron Magid, "After Depth and Breath to the Titanic," *Cinematographer* (December 1997), accessed on-line at www.cinematographer.com/magazine/dec97/titanic/adabt/index.
6. For other definitions of groups, see J. W. McDavid and M. Harari, *Social Psychology: Individuals, Groups, Societies* (New York: Harper & Row, 1968); M. E. Shaw, *Group Dynamics: The Psychology of Small Group Behavior* (New York: McGraw-Hill, 1976).
7. E. R. Smith and S. Henry, "An In-Group Becomes Part of the Self: Response Time Evidence," *Journal of Personality and Social Psychology* 22, no. 6 (1996): 635–42.
8. T. L. Robbins and L. D. Fredendall, "The Empowering Role of Self-Directed Work Teams in the Quality Focused Organization," *Organization Development Journal* 13, no. 1 (1995): 33–42.
9. H. Triandis, *Individualism and Collectivism* (Boulder, CO: Westview, 1995).
10. E. Matson, "You Can Teach This Old Company New Tricks," *Fast Company* (October/November 1997): 46.
11. Interview with Neda Neghabat, co–creative director and account executive, The Abelson Company, March 26, 1998.
12. A. Taylor III, "GM: Time to Get in Gear," *Fortune* 135, no. 8 (1997): 96.
13. A. J. Cummins, "Saturn Workers Vote to Retain Innovative Labor Past with GM," *Wall Street Journal*, March 2, 1998, B10.
14. W. K. Gabrenya, Jr., B. Latane, and Y. Wang, "Social Loafing in Cross-Cultural Perspective," *Journal of Cross-Cultural Psychology* 69 (1983): 69–78.
15. Interview with Brian Muirhead, project engineer for Pathfinder, "All Things Considered," National Public Radio, July 8, 1997.
16. V. H. Vroom and P. W. Yetton, *Leadership and Decision Making* (Pittsburgh, PA: University of Pittsburgh Press, 1973).
17. D. Collins, R. A. Ross, and T. L. Ross, "Who Wants Participative Management?" *Group and Organization Studies* (December 1989): 422–45.
18. Interview with Muirhead.
19. M. Erez and A. Somech, "Is Group Productivity Loss the Rule or the Exception? Effect of Culture and Group-Based Motivation," *Academy of Management Journal* 39, no. 6 (1996): 1513–37; J. A. Wagner, III, "Studies in Individualsim-Collectivsim: Effects on Cooperation in Groups," *Academy of Management Journal* 38 (1995): 152–72.
20. R. A. Wicklund, "Objective Self-Awareness," in J. C. Naylor (ed.) and D. Ilgen (assoc. ed.), *Advances in Experimental Social Psychology*, vol 8 (Orlando, FL: Academic Press, 1975): 233–75.
21. S. G. Harkins, "Social Loafing and Social Facilitation," *Journal of Experimental and Social Psychology* 23 (1987): 1–18; E. Weldon and L. R. Weingar, "Group Goals and Group Performance," *British Journal of Social Psychology* 32 (1993): 307–34.
22. R. Kanfer and P. L. Ackerman, "Motivation and Cognitive Abilities: An Integrative/Aptitude-Treatment Interaction Approach to Skill Acquisition," *Journal of Applied Psychology* 74 (1989): 657–90.
23. Erez and Somech, "Is Group Productivity Loss."
24. R. Walker, "Back to the Farm," *Fast Company* (February/March 1997): 122.
25. Ibid., 112.
26. Ibid., 118.
27. The concept of social loafing was originally proposed by B. Latane, K. Williams, and S. Harkens, "Many Hands Make Light the Work: The Causes and Consequences of Social Loafing," *Journal of Personality and Social Psychology* 37 (1979): 822–32. For an example of more recent research, see S. J. Karau and K. D. Williams, "Social Loafing: A Meta-Analytic Review and Theoretical Integration," *Journal of Personality and Social Psychology* 65 (1993): 681–706.
28. W. K. Gabrenya, Y. Wang, and B. Latane, "Social Loafing and an Optimizing Task: Cross-Cultural Differences Among Chinese and Americans," *Journal of Cross-Cultural Psychology* 16 (1985): 223–42.

29. P. C. Earley, "East Meets West Meets Mideast: Further Exploration of Collectivistic and Individualistic Work Groups," *Academy of Management Journal* 36 (1993): 319–48.
30. For a classic study of groups, see D. Cartright and A. Zander, *Group Dynamics: Research and Theory* (Evanston, IL: Row, Peterson, 1953).
31. P. Oliver and G. Marwell, "The Paradox of Group Size and Collective Action: A Theory of the Critical Mass," *American Sociological Review* (February 1988): 1–8.
32. For example, see the annual report of any Fortune 500 company, including GM, IBM, and Exxon.
33. J. Hassink, "Boardrooms of the Fortune 500: Tables of Power," *Fortune* 135, no. 8 (1997): 153.
34. S. E. Jackson, J. F. Brett, V. I. Sessa, D. M. Cooper, J. A. Julin, and K. Peyronnin, "Some Differences Make a Difference: Individual Dissimilarity and Group Heterogeneity as Correlates of Recruitment, Promotion, and Turnover," *Journal of Applied Psychology* 76 (1991): 675–89; for a review, see F. Milliken and L. L. Martins, "Searching for Common Threads: Understanding the Multiple Effects of Diversity in Organizational Groups," *Academy of Management Review* 21 (1996): 402–33.
35. R. L. McLeod and S. A. Lobel, "The Effects of Ethnic Diversity on Idea Generation in Small Groups," *Academy of Management Best Paper Proceedings* (1992): 227–31; W. E. Watson, K. Kumar, and L. K. Michaelsen, "Cultural Diversity's Impact on Interaction Process and Performance: Comparing Homogeneous and Diverse Task Groups," *Academy of Management Journal* 36, 590–602.
36. A. R. Horton, *What Works for Me: 16 CEO's Talk About Their Careers and Commitments* (New York: Random House, 1986): 170.
37. The issue of roles in groups was first discussed by K. D. Benne and P. Sheats, "Functional Roles of Group Members," *Journal of Social Issues* (1948): 41–49.
38. R. Walker, "Back to the Farm," 120.
39. Ibid.
40. M. Fischetti, "Team Doctors, Report to ER!" *Fast Company* (February–March 1998): 176.
41. The central norms have also been called pivotal norms in a model proposed by E. H. Schein in his book *Organizational Psychology*, 3d ed. (Englewood Cliffs, NJ: Prentice Hall, 1980).
42. A. Fisher, "The 100 Best Companies to Work for in America," *Fortune* 137, no. 1 (January 12, 1998): 70.
43. G. Labiance, D. J. Brass, and B. Gray, "Social Networks and Perception of Intergroup Conflict: The Role of Negative Relationships and Third Parties," *Academy of Management Journal* 41, no. 1 (1998): 55–67.
44. R. Levering and M. Moskowitz, "The 100 Best Companies to Work for in America," *Fortune* 137, no. 1 (January 12, 1998): 86.
45. L. Festinger, "Informal Communication in Small Groups," in H. Guetskw (ed.), *Groups, Leadership and Men: Research in Human Relations* (Pittsburgh: Carnegie Press, 1951).
46. Industry experts also recommend that the size of groups needs to be kept small to facilitate communication. See R. Y. Bergstrom, "When the Blackboard Isn't Big Enough," *Production* 106, no. 3 (March 1994): 61.
47. T. A. Stewart, "Gray Flannel Suit?" *Fortune* 137, no. 5 (1998): 82.
48. A. Zander, *Motives and Goals in Groups* (New York: Academic Press, 1971); A. Zander, *Groups at Work* (San Francisco: Jossey-Bass, 1977).
49. L. W. Porter and E. E. Lawler, *Managerial Attitudes and Performances* (Chicago: Dorsey, 1968).
50. Research by Alvin Zander supports the common belief that members of cohesive groups are generally more satisfied and happier; see A. Zander, *Making Groups Effective* (San Francisco: Jossey-Bass, 1982).
51. See research by J. Yoon, J. W. Ko, and M. R. Baker, "Interpersonal Attachment and Organizational Commitment: Subgroup Hypothesis Revisited," *Human Relations* 47, no. 3 (March 1994): 329–52.
52. M. E. Turner, A. R. Pratkanis, P. Probasco, and C. Leve, "Threat, Cohesion, and Group Effectiveness: Testing a Social Identity Maintenance Perspective of Groupthink," *Journal of Personality and Social Psychology* 63, no. 5 (1992): 781–96.
53. I. Janis, *Groupthink*, 2d ed. (Boston: Houghton Mifflin, 1982).
54. G. Moorhead, R. Ference, and C. P. Neck, "Group Decision Fiascoes Continue: Space Shuttle Challenger and a Revised Groupthink Framework," *Human Relations* 44 (1991): 539–50.

55. E. H. Schein, *Organization Psychology*, 3d ed. (Upper Saddle River, NJ: Prentice Hall, 1980).

56. P. Lauderdale, "Deviance and Moral Boundaries," *American Sociological Review* 41 (1976): 660–76.

57. E. P. Hollander, "Competence, Status, and Idiosyncrasy Credit," *Psychological Review* 65 (1958): 117–27; E. P. Hollander, "Leadership and Social Exchange Processes," in K. J. Gergen, M. Greenberg, and R. Willis (eds.), *Social Exchange: Advances in Theory and Research* (New York: Plenum, 1980).

58. R. D. Banker, J. M. Field, R. G. Schroeder, and K. K. Sinha, "Impact of Work Teams on Manufacturing Performance: A Longitudinal Study," *Academy of Management Journal* 39 (1996): 867–90.

59. Williams, "All Hands on Deck."

60. Ibid.

61. Ibid.

62. Kristen Bole, "Power Firms Heading West with Visions of Striking Gold," *San Francisco Business Times*, March 30, 1998, accessed on-line at www.amcity.com/sanfrancisco/stories/current/focus1.html.

63. Emily Esteron, "A Shock to the System," *Inc. Tech 1998*, no. 1 (1998): 50.

64. Ibid., 53.

65. Ibid., 58.

66. Ibid.

TURNING GROUPS INTO TEAMS

LEARNING OBJECTIVES

1. Explain what a team is, its five characteristic elements, its role in organizations, and the effect of culture on teams.
2. Identify the four different types of teams used in organizations.
3. Discuss the characteristics of self-managed teams.
4. Describe how managers can make teams effective through internal team building.

MANAGERIAL CHALLENGE

The Tokyo String Quartet

Changing first violinists can pose a major challenge, even for a highly proficient musical group like the Tokyo String Quartet. This chamber music group maintains a rigorous annual schedule of more than 100 concerts, captivating audiences from Naples to New Haven. When the quartet's members are not on stage, they are in RCA Victor's recording studio, perfecting their performances of the quartet's repertoire. For these dedicated musicians, classical music has become big business indeed.

Cellist Sadao Harada and violist Kazuhide Isomura are two of the founding members of the quartet, officially formed at New York's Julliard School in 1969.[1] Second violinist Kikuei Ikeda became a member in 1974. Then, in 1981, Toronto-born Peter Oundjian joined as first violinist—disturbing the quartet's comfortable routine.[2]

After decades of playing together, the three Japanese members know one another extremely well. Although each is an accomplished musician in his own right, all have learned to work together as a team, fusing their skills and talents to form the quartet's unique musical sound. In a profession where innovation and creativity are heralded, the Tokyo String Quartet's familiar routine could have led to a deadening complacency.[3]

But Peter Oundjian did not fit into the routine. He was different. He questioned everything, from the musical compositions to the concert bookings. A less cohesive team would have imploded under the added pressure. Yet what could have been a scenario for disaster turned into triumph as the other members joined Oundjian in examining the quartet's cherished traditions—enriching an already successful group. "We began to question everything along with him, and it's been continually challenging," noted Ikeda. "This is what people should want in their work lives."[4]

When Oundjian suffered a hand injury in 1996, the Tokyo String Quartet faced the prospect of recruiting another first violinist. Could this team of musicians triumph again?

■ **Questions**

1. What makes the Tokyo String Quartet such a high-performing team?
2. Why would a new member of this team face challenges?

In spite of changing membership, the Tokyo String Quartet functions as a team. Organizations realize that to be successful in today's fast-paced world they must rely on more than individual effort and expertise. They must achieve the coordination and integration that makes the Tokyo String Quartet effective. Few of us have the skills, knowledge, and creativity needed to address all business challenges. Businesses face many complicated problems that are complex and multifaceted. How can an organization solve such problems? The answer for many is to turn to teams. If one person cannot know everything and do everything, a team may be able to. The use of teams can increase productivity, especially on complex tasks, improve integration among groups and departments, cut down the time required for new product development, and increase employee satisfaction.[5] Teams have become the business trend of the 1990s and experts expect their use to grow in the next few decades.

Organizations of all sizes and types are including teams in their production, sales, marketing, financial, or management structures. Despite the increased use of teams, many do not perform well because organizations do not know how to build or support effective teams.[6] Managers and team members are often frustrated by the conflict and lack of performance. However, managers can and must learn team-development tools to succeed in their organizations.

In this chapter, we examine ways that managers can help teams become an asset to the organization. First, we explore the differences between groups and teams and examine the main types of teams that business organizations use. In that section, we place a special emphasis on *self-managed teams*. Then we consider ways managers can help build teams and make them more effective.

WHAT'S A TEAM?

Teams
Mature groups with highly interdependent members who are fully committed to a common goal

The distinction between groups and teams is a matter of degree. A group is two or more people who interact with one another through various means in some organized manner to perform a task or activity to achieve a common goal. **Teams** are mature groups with highly interdependent members who are fully committed to a common goal. Though all teams start out as groups, not all groups become teams.

Key Characteristics of Teams

Teams and groups have many common characteristics: a number of people who interact, an internal structure, team members with roles, and a common purpose. For example, although the crews who worked on *Titanic* were effective, few achieved the degree of harmony and integration of the Tokyo String Quartet. Teams and groups differ in several significant ways, as shown in Table 8.1.

The first distinguishing characteristic of a team is its members' full *commitment to a common goal and approach*, often one they have developed themselves. Members must agree that the team goal is worthwhile and agree on a general approach to that goal. Such agreement provides the vision and motivation for team members to perform. Second is *mutual accountability*. To succeed as a team, members must feel and be accountable to one another and to the organization for the process and the outcome of their work. Although group members report to a leader or manager and are accountable to them, team members take on responsibility and perform because of their commitment to the team.

The third characteristic of a team is a team *culture based on trust and collaboration*. Whereas group members share norms, team members have a shared culture. Team members are willing to compromise, cooperate, and collaborate to reach their common purpose. A collaborative climate does not mean the absence of conflict, however. Conflict enhances team creativity and performance if handled constructively. Related to the team culture is *shared leadership*. Whereas groups have one assigned leader, teams differ by sharing leadership among all members.

Finally, teams develop *synergy*. In organizational behavior, we use the term **synergy** to mean the process of combining two or more actions that results in an effect that differs from the total of the individual actions. Put another way, the whole is greater than the sum of the parts. Synergy in teams means that team members working together achieve more than members working individually would.

Consider an example of an effective team. Say you have a car accident in Boston on a winter evening. If you're lucky (given your unfortunate circumstances), you will be one of the 200 people who are taken each night to the Emergency Room (ER) of Mass General Hospital, one of the finest teaching hospitals in the world.[7] ER nurses, doctors, and technicians constantly tackle life and death issues. In severe trauma cases, these professionals work in teams. Trauma teams consist of a range of highly trained medical experts who know how to work with others in a crisis. The team has a clear goal: Keep patients alive. Generally, each member

Synergy
The process of combining two or more actions that results in an effect that differs from the total of the individual actions

Table 8.1 GROUPS AND TEAMS

From Group . . .	. . . to Team
Members work on a common goal.	Members are fully committed to a common goal and mission that they have developed.
Members are accountable to manager.	Members are mutually accountable to one another.
Members do not have clear, stable culture and conflict is frequent.	Members trust one another and the team has a collaborative culture.
Leadership is assigned to a single person.	Members all share in leadership.
Members may accomplish their goals.	Team achieves synergy: 2 + 2 = 5

Sources: J. R. Hackman, *Groups That Work (and Those That Don't)* (San Francisco: Jossey-Bass, 1990); J. R. Katzenbach and D. K. Smith, *The Wisdom of Teams: Creating the High Performance Organization* (New York: Harper Business, 1993).

understands exactly what task to perform without confusion. There is no time for bickering, disagreements, or power struggles. Instead, each member trusts that the others will do their jobs competently and quickly.

Alasdair Conn, Chief of Emergency Services at Mass General, says: "Making a decision, even a wrong decision, is better than not making one at all."[8] Accordingly, all members of the ER team need to be able to make critical split-second decisions that often mean the difference between life and death for the patients. Each member—the attending physician, an intern, or a nurse—trusts that their fellow team members can provide direction to the team when needed.

As opposed to the typical hierarchical medical profession, the ER team at Mass General is flat. There are no all-powerful bosses and all ideas are welcomed and considered. Maryfran Hughes, who manages the 60 nurses of the emergency services of Mass General, looks for nurses who are able to adapt to the incredible demands of this job and who are team players. Being adaptable and flexible are keys to doing the job well and helping a patient survive the trauma.[9]

The potential for teams, such as the Mass General ER team, to be productive, creative, solve complex problems, and deliver high performance has led many organizations to incorporate them into their structures.

How Do Teams Fit in Today's Organizations?

As we discussed in chapters 1 and 2, many organizations are changing from hierarchical to team-based structures. The move from traditional hierarchies to teams can be seen as a continuum, depicted in Figure 8.1. On one end are organizations with traditional structures and departments that use groups to perform various tasks under management control. On the other end are organizations that are fully based on teams that have considerable autonomy and control. For instance, Corning Inc. uses teams with a high degree of success. Top managers of Corning give teams considerable autonomy to perform their tasks.[10] The teams' design and delivery of such intricate products as fiber-optic cables and their focus on quality and customer service are partly responsible for Corning's ranking as the most admired company in its industry.

Many of today's organizations fall in the middle of the continuum presented in Figure 8.1. They have kept some of their traditional departments and management control while using teams for specific purposes. For instance, at Goldman Sachs, a highly profitable Wall Street investment firm, individual financial advisers still manage the portfolios of customers. At the same time, teams of experts work on specific tasks. One employee stated, "Teamwork here is better than on any professional sports team I've ever seen."[11]

As organizations move to team-based structures, the control shifts from management to employees. Team-based structures do not mean that teams do as they please. Upper management still sets the general direction, vision, mission, and goals. However, employees at all levels make decisions and control their own activities. For example, at SEI Investments, a

FIGURE 8.1
From Traditional Hierarchies to Team-Based Organizations

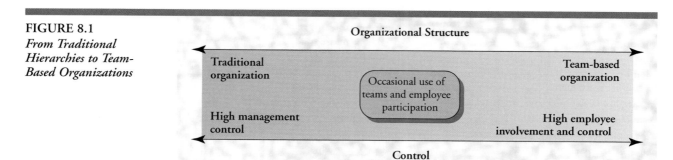

Organizational Structure

Traditional organization

Occasional use of teams and employee participation

Team-based organization

High management control

High employee involvement and control

Control

medium-size financial-services organization based in Oaks, Pennsylvania, top leaders set the general direction. They decide what projects the organization undertakes. To tackle the projects, the employees decide which teams are needed, for what purpose, and for how long. They disband the teams when the task is complete.[12]

Regardless of the extent to which teams are used, to help them succeed organizations must do the following:

- *Provide a clear standard of high performance expectations.* The team's common goal and approach has to be based on strong expectations for excellent performance. Such expectations for high performance set the tone for team members' behaviors and activities. At SEI Investments, for instance, top managers set the targets for performance for each team. The teams then decide how to achieve those targets. Henry Greer, president and CEO of SEI, adds: "Since they're closest to the client, the teams know what they can do to move the ball forward."[13]

- *Provide organizational support.* Teams cannot exist and function in a vacuum. The organizational structure and culture must provide teams with the necessary resources, time, training, and rewards or risk poor performance. At SEI Investments, the structure is flat with no assigned offices, no walls, and fully moveable furniture and computers. Teams move their workstations around at will. "We wanted to throw away any structure that would impede us from doing what was right for the business," says Greer. The culture is based on innovation, flexibility, and speed of service for the clients. "The biggest hiring criterion is cultural fit," states Dave McLaughlin, a team leader.[14]

- *Adjust internal and external leadership.* Team leaders must guide the group and remove obstacles rather than command, control, or dictate action. Leaders of the organization must encourage teams or run the risk that team members will become frustrated and unmotivated or that they will lack resources to accomplish goals. SEI Investments has a concept that it calls fluid leadership. "People figure out what they are good at, and that shapes what their roles are. There's not just one leader," notes CEO Al West.[15] Senior Executive Richard Lieb explains: "I won't send out a memo declaring that someone is the go-to person on a project. You've got to show leadership ability through your knowledge, initiative, and energy."[16] Finally, West explains his leadership style: "I lead where I figure it really matters, and I let the other people lead where it matters to them. The result is that my top managers are 10 times better as businesspeople than they were a few years ago. And my job is a lot more fun."[17]

Despite many success stories, many organizations have struggled or failed to implement teams. One possible reason for the difficulty in implementing teams is culture.

Effect of National Culture and Diversity on Teams

Team success is harder to achieve in individualistic cultures such as the United States, Australia, or France. In cultures with strong collectivist values such as Japan, individuals give up their personal goals for the good of the team more easily, seek approval from and are accountable to teams more readily, and are more willing to cooperate and compromise because they value team relationships. For instance, as we discussed in chapter 7, social loafing is less likely to occur in collectivist cultures.

Additionally, in culturally heterogeneous countries such as the United States, teams within organizations have diverse membership. As a result, the individualistic culture of some team members clashes with the collectivist culture of others. This clash makes it harder to achieve commitment to a common goal, mutual accountability, and a collaborative climate.

Hot ▼ Link

We discussed social loafing in chapter 7, p. 238.

Being able to manage cultural diversity to their advantage allows organizations such as the Dodgers to reap the benefits of teams.

When all members of a team are from the same cultural background, especially if they all value collectivism, consensus is easier to achieve.

The Los Angeles Dodgers faced many challenges related to managing a team with diverse cultures in the 1997 baseball season.[18] The team included players from the United States, the Dominican Republic, Mexico, Japan, and Korea. Dodgers' management cited cultural differences as a factor that contributed to the team's lackluster performance, frequent disagreements, and dugout fights. Players tended to hang out with others from their home country instead of interacting with all their teammates. Mike Piazza, one of the team's stars, questioned whether everyone was on the same page: "You would like to think everybody has that same common goal to win, but there may be guys just interested in staying here. . . . Everybody has personal goals, but it seems like the championship teams find a way to combine their personal goals with an underlying desire to win [for the organization]."[19]

Other major and minor league baseball teams face similar cultural challenges. As a result, some have made culture the focus of their training. For example, the White Sox hired Sal Artigia as coordinator of cultural development to work with Latin players as soon as they join the minor leagues. Other teams like the Mets have done little to integrate the non-U.S. players, in spite of having the largest percentage of players from Latin American countries.

A QUESTION OF ETHICS

Equal Work   What are the ethical implications of working on a team in which you do less than your share of the work but get rewarded as an equal member of the team? Is it fair to take the full reward? Does it depend on your cultural orientation?

The success of Asian team-based management techniques has greatly influenced the use of teams in Western countries. However, some team failures in the West should be blamed on lack of fit between teams and a culture in which the individual is the primary focus. As a result, Western management experts have suggested that teams need to be combined with attention to the individual. Team members from highly individualistic cultures must be rewarded and recognized for their individual contributions to the team. For teams to work well in individualistic cultures, managers must take the following steps:

- Encourage individuals to be cooperative and share in the team's commitment and approach.
- Hold individuals accountable to the team while still maintaining their value in individual performance.
- Encourage individuals to empathize with others.
- Learn to manage conflict.

Teams are the focus, but the organization also encourages and recognizes individuals for their individual contributions and performance.[20]

Although culture can present a challenge to team implementation, it is not an insurmountable barrier. As we've just seen, managers can balance cultural values and team requirements.

Summary Point 8.1   What's a Team?

- Five key elements of teams are commitment to a common goal, mutual accountability, a collaborative climate, shared leadership, and synergy.
- Today's organizations are moving from high management control to team-based structures in which employees have considerable input and control.

- These team-based organizations require high performance expectations, organizational support, and appropriate leadership to succeed.
- The degree to which a culture is collectivist or individualistic affects the ease of implementation of teams.

We have defined teams, analyzed how they differ from groups and how they fit in today's organizations, and considered the effect of culture on the use of teams. Next we discuss the different types of teams that are used in today's organizations.

TEAMS AND EXISTING ORGANIZATIONAL CULTURES

Traditional organizations often have a difficult time converting to team-based structures. A major factor is an existing organizational culture that resists changes that threaten the balance of power in the corporation. Titles, hierarchies, organization charts, corner offices, perks, and other indicators of power must be discarded, or at least reduced, before an organization can move to a team-based structure. Managers who may have vied for a special title or a higher status must learn to live with no title and less status under the new structure.

Teams with or without the approval of managers make many decisions reserved for executives. In effect, everything has to change for the organization to succeed in implementing teams. Typically, however, companies that are successful do not attempt to convert to team-based organizations. The change process is at times so arduous that organizations turn to teams only when crisis looms on the horizon. Interestingly, modern organizations such as H-P, GE, Volvo, Intel, and SEI changed to a team-based structure to prepare themselves for the challenges of the twenty-first century rather than in reaction to a crisis.

TYPES OF TEAMS

Organizations use different types of teams to accomplish their goals. Some teams are simple and have a specific focus. Others are complex and focus on broad problems with organizationwide implications. We consider the factors that differentiate teams and the different types of teams next.

From Work Teams to Process Teams

Teams differ on two major dimensions: (1) the *complexity of their task*, and (2) the *fluidity of their membership*. **Task complexity** refers to the extent to which a task is intricate and consists of many different interrelated parts. **Membership fluidity** refers to the extent to which the team membership is stable. Membership in fluid teams changes often based on task requirements. Figure 8.2 depicts the combination of these two dimensions and how managers can use them to define different types of teams.

Type I teams are simple work groups that in many cases have not fully become teams yet. They have common goals but still report to a manager to whom members are accountable. Their task is simple and their membership stable. Their focus is on internal organizational issues such as how to make production more efficient. Their goal is simple problem solving. The biggest obstacle these types of teams face is the lack of training to do their job well.

Blue Cross/Blue Shield of Maine designed a Type I work team for its accounting department to reduce employees' stress and increase their productivity. The work team created a flexible work schedule that was then approved by management and immediately put into effect. It also created documentation policies for the department, easing everyone's work. The existing level of trust between the department manager and the employees allowed the work team to succeed. The results of this team's hard work were then passed on to the corporate management as an example of how the organization could design effective teams that deal with internal company issues.[21]

Like Type I teams, Type II administrative teams have stable membership, but their tasks are more complex and they tend to focus on external and internal issues. Members have a common goal focused on coordinating organizational efforts, but each member still has indi-

Task complexity
The extent to which the team's task is intricate and consists of different interrelated parts

Membership fluidity
The extent to which the team membership is stable

FIGURE 8.2
Types of Teams

Source: A. Nahavandi and E. Aranda, "Restructuring Teams for the Re-Engineered Organization," *Academy of Management Executive* 8, no. 4 (1994): 58–68. Reprinted with permission of the Academy of Management, P.O. Box 3020, Briar Cliff Manor, NY 10510-8020, via Copyright Clearance Center, Inc.

Team Membership Fluidity

	Team Membership Fluidity: low		high
Task Complexity: low	**Type I: Simple work teams** Goal: Simple problem solving Focus: Internal and specific Blocks: Lack of training Levels: First-level work teams *Example: Quality circles*		**Type III: Cross-departmental teams** Goal: Intergration in structure and setting ground rules Focus: Internal and specific Blocks: Organizational structure Levels: First and middle levels *Example: Cross-functional teams*
Task Complexity: high	**Type II: Administrative teams** Goal: Problem solving and selling ideas Focus: Internal, external, and broad Blocks: Lack of empowerment Levels: Management *Example: Management teams*		**Type IV: Process teams** Goal: Creative problem solving and implementation Focus: Strategic and broad Blocks: Preparedness Levels: All levels *Example: Self-managed teams*

vidual goals. The major challenge of these teams is often a lack of power to implement their decisions fully.

Type III and IV teams have changing or fluid membership. Different people enter and leave the team depending on task and situational requirements. The Type III simple teams have an internal focus on organizational issues. The typical obstacle these teams face is the functional or other traditional organizational structures. These structures impede interaction and integration of the functions. Type IV process teams are creative, problem-solving teams with a broad focus on the whole organization. These are the ideal teams that are the basis for team-based organizations. Their biggest challenge is preparing their members and the organization to accept and use teams.

Many organizations move from the simple Type I to Types II, III, and eventually Type IV teams. As organizations move from work teams that function parallel to existing structures to process teams that may disband existing structures, they move from traditional organizations to becoming team-based organizations.

We consider typical examples of each of the four types of teams next. Because of the importance of process teams in today's organization, we describe them in more detail in the next section.

Simple Work Teams Example: Quality Circles

The simplest and most basic types of teams are those formed inside existing work units to support day-to-day work and activities. These **work teams** are created either to deal with issues that require input from more than one person or to generate commitment from employees. Work teams do not require considerable organizational or managerial change nor do they require much organizational commitment to function well. Their scope is limited to individual work units. Because members of work teams are from the same department or work unit, they generally have similar focus and tend to work together relatively easily. One example of work teams is quality circles.

Quality circles (QCs) are small work groups of eight to ten volunteers from a common work area who meet to find solutions to specific problems about the quality of work processes, products, or services. Their goal is to allow those most familiar with particular work problems to propose solutions to them. There are four characteristics of quality circles:

- Clear and specific focus on one work unit
- Focus on quality improvement
- Limited power of implementation
- Regular meetings

Because their mutual accountability, shared leadership, and strength of culture are limited, QCs do not fully qualify as teams. However, we discuss them here because they represent some of the earlier forms of teams used in organizations.

The Japanese first used quality circles as part of their quality improvement programs. After observing Japan's success in the 1970s and 1980s, many U.S. organizations experimented with quality circles as a means of introducing teams into organizations, in part because QCs are relatively easy to integrate into existing structures. As a work team, quality circles do not require any structural changes in the organization. They can function alongside other management and decision-making structures to provide another point of input and ideas for management to consider.[22]

Many organizations implement quality circles as an employee involvement tool. In many cases, they are the only teams in an organization, a situation that can lead to ineffectiveness. For instance, the Wallace Company Inc., a Houston-based oil pipeline distribution firm, had many problems with its quality circles, including the employees' fear to discuss

Work teams
Groups created either to deal with issues that require input from more than one person or to generate commitment from employees

Quality circles
Small work groups of eight to ten volunteers from a common work area who meet to find solutions to specific problems about the quality of work processes, products, or services

changes with management. After hiring a consultant, the company expanded the use of quality circles to the entire organization with the idea that they all be allowed to evolve into quality improvement process teams, eventually making most of the decisions related to how the organization operates.[23]

Quality circles have several additional benefits besides encouraging employee involvement. They can help train employees to take on decision-making responsibilities and train managers to allow and encourage employee participation. Quality circles, however, face considerable obstacles that can block success:[24]

- They rely on employee volunteers, so generating enough interest can be hard because employees lack either interest or time.
- Lack of knowledge of the work processes or poor training in group communication and conflict creates impediments to success.
- Management often resists the use of quality circles.
- The simplicity of quality circles and the relatively little time it takes to create them is also an obstacle. Few changes can be expected as a result of a volunteer activity that takes relatively little of employees' time.

Summary Point 8.2   **How Do Teams Develop and What Are Quality Circles?**

- Teams differ in how complex their task is and how fluid their membership is.
- The four types of teams are simple work teams, administrative teams, cross-departmental teams, and process teams.
- Examples of simple work teams are quality circles formed by groups of eight to ten people from a common work

area who come together to find solutions to specific quality problems.
- Quality circles function parallel to existing organizational structures and have limited implementation power. They allow for introduction of teams in organizations without major organizational change.

The use of quality circles has decreased because organizations are replacing them with more complex types of teams. However, work groups such as quality circles are an easy way for managers to introduce teams to an organization.

Administrative Team Example: Management Teams

The second type of teams presented in Figure 8.2 are administrative teams. The typical example is a **management team** made up of managers and supervisors from different work units. Numerous organizations have long used management teams for various purposes. The main purpose of these teams is coordination of administrative and managerial tasks to achieve organizational goals.[25] Also, these teams are often responsible for strategic planning and strategic change.

For instance, the managers of the Baltimore Syrup Operations of Coca-Cola USA designed such a team to deal with the closure of its plant and reorientation of its workforce for a new environment. Senior managers of each unit of the plant joined a management team that had the goals of making sure the plant runs efficiently before it closes in a few years and of preparing the organization for strategic change. Although managers still ran their units, a significant part of their time was spent on coordinating activities related to the plant closure.[26]

The specific goals of management teams tend to be more vague than those of either work teams or task forces because their focus is both departmental and organizational. Management teams consist of managers with different goals and focus, so their mutual goals are not always clear. As a result, these teams require considerable coordination and effort. To succeed, management teams must develop goals, responsibilities, and areas of accountability

Management team (administrative team) Team of managers and supervisors from different work units with the goal of coordination of administrative and managerial tasks to achieve organizational goals so that they can decide what goals and responsibilities they will and will not undertake.[27] Management team goals may include improved communication, increased coordination, and the integration of goals and functions on an organization- or departmentwide basis.

Cross-Departmental Team Examples: Cross-Functional Teams and Task Forces

The third type of team is the **cross-departmental team**. These teams are made up of members from different departments and are formed to address a specific problem either within a particular work unit or within the whole organization. The scope of a cross-departmental team can be narrow—a specific work unit problem, for instance—or broad enough to deal with an organizationwide problem. Examples include task forces and work teams. Work teams are a permanent feature of a work unit whereas task forces are temporary. Because task forces are temporary, they have a limited effect on overall organizational structure and culture.

> **Cross-departmental teams** *Teams of members from different departments that are formed to address a specific problem either within a particular work unit or within the whole organization*

Cindy Casselman of Xerox heads a task force created to deal with an organizational issue. She spearheaded the formation of the Xerox Intranet (a network that connects members of an organization) so that its 85,000 employees could access unedited news about their company. "Employees were telling us they wanted timely, relevant, honest information," Casselman states.[28] After getting the approval of her boss in Stamford, Connecticut, she recruited Rick Beach, the head of advanced technology business services in Palo Alto, California, and Malcolm Kirby of the Xerox information management division in Rochester, New York. The task force was able to cut through the Xerox bureaucracy and gain the approval and resources to start WebBoard, the internal communication system for the entire company.[29]

A common type of task force is a **cross-functional task force** or **cross-functional team**. These teams consist of members from different functional areas with different expertise. The use of cross-functional task forces allows managers to gain a diverse perspective on issues and problems they face. In spite of specialization in most organizations, the problems businesses face are rarely limited to one department. For example, a sales decline has financial implications and may also have an effect on future design, production, and marketing of products.

> **Cross-functional task forces** *Teams whose members are from different functional areas with different expertise designed to provide broad perspective*

Similarly, staffing is a multidimensional issue that impacts many different functional areas. A proposed change in staffing policy requires input from different functional areas. Cross-functional teams or task forces can handle such broad issues.

Kodak uses cross-functional teams oriented toward customers' needs. They identify best business practices that can then be implemented in other parts of the organization. Kodak's experience with these teams has shown that having a supportive culture and a customer focus make these cross-functional teams successful.[30]

Because of the increased use of process teams in today's organizations, we examine process teams separately in the next section.

Summary Point 8.3   What Are Management Teams and Cross-Departmental Teams?

- Management teams consist of managers and supervisors from different work units. Their goal is coordination of administrative and managerial tasks to achieve organizational goals.
- The goals of management teams tend to be more vague than those of either work teams or task forces because their focus is both departmental and organizational.

- Cross-functional teams or task forces are made up of members from different departments and are formed to address a specific problem either within a particular work unit or within the whole organization.
- The use of cross-functional task forces allows managers to gain a diverse perspective on issues and problems they face.

MANAGERIAL ADVICE
from the Experts

MANAGING CROSS-FUNCTIONAL TASK FORCES

Today's managers must be able to use cross-functional task forces and teams well. In designing and managing such teams, managers need to consider several issues:

- If the task force is designed to implement ideas, include members from various levels of the organizations. Creating a team with members from different levels can also help foster cooperation and reduce the barriers between employees and managers.
- Monitor the team to ensure that the free exchange of ideas and creativity is not stifled if managers and employees are on the same team.
- Select members for their expertise and diverse perspectives but also for their ability to compromise and solve problems collaboratively.
- Allow the team enough time to complete its task. The more complex the problem, and the more creative the solution needs to be, the more large blocks of time the members will need.
- Coordinate with other managers to free up time for the members.
- Provide clear goals and guidelines on what you expect the team to do. Tell them what they can and cannot address.
- Don't hover, but check with the team regularly to address questions and remove obstacles.

Source: Based on information in E. K. Aranda, L. Aranda, and K. Conlon, *Teams: Structure, Process, Culture, and Politics* (Upper Saddle River, NJ: Prentice Hall, 1998).

PROCESS TEAMS

Process teams
Teams that do not have departmental affiliation and that function independently to undertake broad organizational-level process improvements

Hot ▼ Link

We discussed reengineering in chapter 1, p. 24.

Process teams, the basis for today's team-based organization, do not have departmental affiliation and function independently to undertake broad organizational process improvement.[31] Process teams look at any and all organizational work processes, recommend, and implement change with the goal of higher effectiveness and efficiency. Their scope is the whole organization, they are complex, and they can have considerable organizational impact. To some extent, process teams have goals that are similar to those of task forces. However, as compared to task forces, they are permanent and have very broad powers to change the organization and its practices. Reengineering efforts that have led to many structural changes in organizations are often the result of the recommendations of process teams. The use of such teams often leads to partial or total disbanding of traditional departments.

Zeneca Ag Products, an agricultural products company, reengineered its North American division by disbanding its traditional structure and instituting a team-based process strategy that focuses on customers. The company was losing money to lower-cost competitors and therefore had to make radical changes in its method of operations. The new teams not only redesigned the business strategy of the organization but also completely revamped every business process from the appraisal system to training and development to the compensation system.[32]

Another use of process teams is the SWAT team at Mervyn's, the department store chain with 270 stores in 14 states with 32,000 employees. Just like its police force namesake, the SWAT team at Mervyn's rushes into the stores that need to resolve a critical problem quickly. It is a team "of highly trained people who can be deployed anywhere in the company's buying division, at any time, wherever they are needed," reports Michael Shank, the co-leader of the SWAT team. The team attempts to solve any problem that may affect the organization, such as flextime and parental leave. "SWAT-team members are some of the most valued employees in the organization," according to Bruce Tulgan, a consultant familiar with Mervyn's.[33]

Self-Managed Teams

A commonly used process team in organizations is the self-managed team. **Self-managed teams (SMTs)** are teams of employees who have full managerial control over their own work.[34] This level of employee control requires organizational structure and culture that differ from those of a traditional firm with a hierarchical organization. Self-managed teams implement many of the job design concepts we discussed in chapter 6. Because they are responsible for the whole task, members use many different skills, identify with the task, and have a sense that their contribution is significant. By definition, members of SMTs have considerable autonomy and feedback. The Tokyo String Quartet functions like a self-managed team.

Numerous organizations such as Toyota, General Foods, and Procter & Gamble have used self-managed teams successfully for decades. In fact, Procter & Gamble claimed its self-managed teams were one of the company's trade secrets.[35] A classic illustration of a company that used self-managed teams successfully is Volvo, the Swedish car manufacturer. Volvo jettisoned the typical assembly-line structure in favor of self-managed teams. Each team was responsible for manufacturing a large section of a car. The teams could decide how to organize its workers to accomplish its task. The result was significant improvements in product quality and greater employee satisfaction.

Self-managed teams (SMTs) Process teams of employees who have full managerial control over their own work

Hot ▼ Link

We discussed job design concepts in chapter 6, pp. 199–200.

Characteristics of SMTs

Self-managed teams have the following six characteristics:

1. *The power to manage their work.* Self-managed teams can set goals, plan, staff, schedule, monitor quality, and implement decisions.
2. *Members with different expertise and functional experience.* Some members may be from marketing, finance, production, design, and so on. Without a broad range of experience, the team could not manage all aspects of its work.
3. *No outside manager.* The team does not report to an outside manager. Team members manage themselves, their budget, and their task through shared leadership.
4. *The power to implement decisions.* Unlike employee participation teams, these teams can take action without management approval of their ideas. Stanley Gault, chairman of Goodyear, the largest tire manufacturer in the United States, says that "the teams at Goodyear are now telling the boss how to run things. And I must say, I'm not doing half-bad because of it."[36]
5. *Coordination and cooperation with other teams and individuals affected by the teams' decisions.* Because each team is independent and does not formally report to a manager, the teams themselves rather than managers must coordinate their tasks and activities to achieve integration.

6. *Internal leadership based on facilitation.* Leadership often rotates among members depending on each member's expertise in handling a specific situation. Instead of a leader who tells others what to do, sets goals, or monitors achievement, team leaders remove obstacles for the team and make sure that the team has the resources it needs. The primary role of the team leader is to facilitate rather than control. **Facilitation** means that the leader focuses on freeing the team from obstacles, allowing it to reach the goals it has set.

Facilitation
The leader focuses on freeing the team from obstacles to allow the team to reach the goals it has set

Pharmacia & Upjohn, the newly merged pharmaceutical giant, revamped its organizational structure to establish self-managed teams. Pharmacia & Upjohn includes experts from different parts of the organization as team members and gives them wide latitude to make decisions about how to provide service. The objective is to allow those closest to the customer to make decisions that affect customer service.[37]

USAir, the sixth largest carrier in the United States, used a self-managed team to design a new low-fare airline, initially called US2.[38] President of USAir, Rakesh Gangwal, asked two dozen of its employees who had no startup experience to find the best way to compete with Southwest Airlines. A catering truck driver and baggage handler in Baltimore and an aircraft cleaner in Pittsburgh were among the two dozen airline employees who joined the design team that spent four months investigating the competition.

The team traveled extensively on Southwest, Shuttle by United, Alaska Airlines, and Delta Express to learn what makes each competitor efficient and effective. The team members then assembled in the Doubletree Hotel in Arlington, Virginia, and worked on their startup idea. Every team member had an equal vote and the power to implement the team's plans.

After four months of intensive work, MetroJet was selected as the startup's name. President Gangwal announced the MetroJet takeoff date of June 1, 1998. After the announcement, the team was disbanded and members were sent back, reluctantly, to their regular jobs. "It's kind of like letting your child be married off," claimed ramp supervisor Greg Solek.[39] Bill Freiberger, head of the machinists union at USAir, reflected that before this experience he thought teams were all "smoke and mirrors." Now he believes in them.[40]

A QUESTION OF ETHICS

Unions and Teams

Some union leaders are leery of the use of teams. One of their major concerns is that teams take on increased workloads and do many traditional management functions without a commensurate increase in salary or benefits. They claim that the use of teams often results in exploitation of employees who end up working longer hours and increase productivity but are not fully rewarded for their work. Do you agree with the unions' position? Are there ethical problems with using teams?

Because self-managed teams require a change in management structure and culture, their adoption and successful implementation require extensive organizational commitment.

The *lack of commitment* is the most common reason for failure of SMTs in today's organizations.[41] SMTs can be successful if the organization and its employees are patient, receive extensive training, and learn to function without traditional supervisors.

Lynn Mercer, a Lucent Technologies cellular phone factory manager, is dedicated to the concept of self-managed teams and has made it a success. The teams in her operation decide how the work should be done, what improvements are needed, and who should perform them. She says that she just sets the mission of the factory and leaves the rest up to the teams: "If I give you an endgame you can find your way there." Lucent's teams elect their own leaders. The teams are successful becaue they are exceptionally flexible; this freedom allows them to adapt to

Summary Point 8.4   **What Are Process Teams?**

- Process teams consist of employees who have full managerial control over their own work.
- Self-managed teams (SMTs)
  1. Have the power to implement their own decisions
  2. Function without outside management
  3. Rely on internal facilitation by a team leader

4. Often need extensive cooperation and coordination with other teams and individuals
5. Require complete change in organizational structure and culture
- SMTs are an example of process teams.

---

the ever-changing needs of the cellular phone industry, and members truly understand their customers' needs. The results have been remarkable: Mercer's factory has not missed a deadline in over two years and labor costs remain a very low percentage of total costs.[42]

In addition to overall commitment from the organization, the success of self-managed teams requires a number of other specific factors. We next consider the factors that make teams effective.

 ## MAKING TEAMS EFFECTIVE THROUGH TEAM BUILDING

From the Tokyo String Quartet to Mass General's trauma team, we have seen that organizations use teams to handle complex problems that one person could not solve working alone. However, a significant number of teams do not perform well for numerous reasons.[43] Their internal processes are ineffective or they are not well integrated into existing structures. If not

CAREER ADVICE
from the Experts

HOW TO BUILD YOUR TEAMING SKILLS

These days, managers are looking for employees who already have teaming skills when they join their organization. So how do you build such skills in your current job?

1. Look for any assignment that requires you to be in a team, even a team of two.
2. Build credibility with your teammates by doing extra work.
3. Give everyone credit for his or her ideas.
4. Spread the wealth. If rewards are given, make sure everyone gets something.
5. Think long term. For example, you may want to deemphasize your current pay if the skills you gain will get you a raise in the future.
6. Remember that your market value depends on your specialization and your teaming skills.

Sources: Based on J. Martin, "So, You Want to Work for the Best," *Fortune* 137, no. 1 (1998): 77–78; see also R. Henkoff, "Are You (More Than) Ready for a Pay Raise?" *Fortune* 136, no. 11 (December 8, 1997): 233–38; A. Fisher, "Starting Anew," *Fortune* 137, no. 6 (March 30, 1998): 165–67.

well managed, employees may feel that teams are a waste of time. In organizations that do not fully commit to teams, frustration, conflict, and bitterness rather than performance result.[44]

The less-than-perfect record of teams in U.S. organizations has not slowed their use. Organizations are relying on teams more than ever, particularly as layoffs reduce the number of employees and managers look for ways of maintaining and improving performance.[45] In this section, we present the internal team and organizational factors that help make teams effective.

The first set of factors that help teams become effective relates to internal functioning. **Team building** is defined as activities aimed at improving the internal work and relationship processes of teams. Team building requires attention to both task and interpersonal relationships.

Team Cohesion, Maturity, and Composition

Helping a group become mature and cohesive is the first step toward team success. That means that managers must select members with care and provide them with opportunities for interaction and in some cases competition with outside groups. Groups also need the time to develop their norms and decide what they consider deviant and creative behavior. Additionally, managers must give the members sufficient time to develop into a mature group. Once a group reaches maturity, managers need to take additional steps to develop a high-performance team.

Another factor that managers and teams members must pay attention to is the composition of the team. Membership in effective teams is based on expertise in various areas that are necessary for task accomplishment. Teams that face diverse and complex tasks can be more effective if they maintain a flexible, fluid membership. Fluid membership can be achieved through the shamrock team structure. The **shamrock team** combines a small group of core permanent members, part-time members, and outside subcontractors or consultants.[46] The shamrock team is similar to the model that virtual organizations adopt as described in chapter 2. It allows for flexibility, quick action, and change, while it avoids groupthink, one of the major problems of mature and cohesive teams. Because of frequent change, the shamrock team creates a dynamic environment that may be more appropriate for cultures such as that in the United States that are present and action oriented.[47]

Handling Diversity

One of the major challenges for teams in U.S. organizations and other heterogeneous cultures is handling the diversity of team members. Researchers have found that without a conscious effort and active management, teams drive out individuals who are different from other team members.[48] In Japan, where many of the team concepts were first implemented, the collectivistic and high power distance values and long-term orientation emphasize the search for group harmony, respect for those with higher status, avoidance of open conflict, and slow progress because of the need to build consensus. The same approach to team building does not work well in more diverse and individualistic cultures.

Today U.S. and Western businesses understand that they must preserve an individual focus yet still encourage collaboration and cooperation. To be successful, U.S. teams need to value individual differences and capitalize on the benefit of diverse members who have different values, goals, and skills. Steps to handle diversity in U.S. teams include these:

- *Preserving and rewarding individual contributions.* This means combining team and individual rewards. Besides giving each member the appropriate pay, Jerry McAdams, team-reward specialist at the consulting firm of Watson Wyatt Worldwide, suggests that if the team's project is completed satisfactorily, the members should be given a large sum of money to divide among themselves. He suggests the bonus should average about $10,000 per team member.[49]

Team building
Activities aimed at improving the internal work and relationship processes of teams

Hot ▼ Link

We discussed stages of group development, cohesion, and norms in chapter 7, pp. 229–55.

Shamrock team
Team that combines a small group of core permanent members, part-time members, and outside subcontractors or consultants

Hot ▼ Link

We discussed groupthink in chapter 7, pp. 248–50.

Hot ▼ Link

We discussed cultural values in chapter 3, pp. 93–94.

- *Encouraging and managing positive and constructive conflict.* Rather than aiming for harmony and quick consensus, diverse teams should focus on capitalizing on the conflict that results from diversity. Members should then be trained to manage conflict well. Tom Ruddy, who designs high-performance work systems for Xerox's 2000 teams, suggests that teams agree on some basic rules of behavior as the way to manage their conflict. For example, he has developed a card that says: "In meetings everyone's opinion will be heard." If one member cuts off another, others will lift the card and remind the person about the rule. "After a while, team members internalize the proper behavior," he maintains.[50]
- *Focus on short-term as well as long-term results.* Given the U.S. short-term and proactive orientations, teams must focus on both short- and long-term goals to avoid losing member interest and motivation. Tami Urban, a consultant for Cambridge Technology Partners, a systems-integration company based outside Boston, suggests that teams agree on some "norms" quickly as a way of seeing immediate success, and then tackling the bigger problems. Agreeing on these norms "is a low-key way for people who have never worked with each other to learn how to make group decisions and resolve conflict."[51]

The goal of diverse teams should be to capitalize on the different perspectives that individual members bring. Another factor that further supports such actions is developing team trust.

Developing Trust

Teams must commit to a common goal, develop mutual accountability, and learn to collaborate. These actions cannot occur without trust. Trust is defined as each team member's faith in the others' intentions and actions. Having gone through the various stages of development together, team members should, if the challenges are well managed, have developed some trust in one another. The members of the Tokyo String Quartet implicitly trust one another based on their excellent skills and common dedication to quality and innovation. In addition, members can further build trust through five other means, highlighted in Figure 8.3.

The first way to build trust is through open communication, in which all team members are informed of activities and decisions in a timely fashion and have the opportunity to provide input. Providing and receiving timely and honest feedback is essential to open communication. Another requirement for open communication is the second element in building trust: integrity. You cannot trust a person who is not truthful and does not have integrity. Team members need to be particularly watchful to maintain their integrity and credibility.

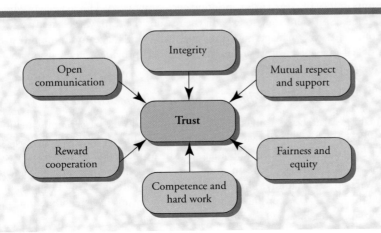

FIGURE 8.3
Building Trust

The open communication and integrity lead to mutual respect and support, which further build trust. Respect involves genuine acceptance of team members and their differences. Support requires being available to help, coach, and advise others. In addition to building trust, respect and support create a climate where learning and experimentation are encouraged.

The last three factors in building trust are fairness and equity in what members do and how they are rewarded, being competent, and rewarding cooperation and teamwork. Team members need to learn to give each other credit for ideas and accomplishments. They also must do their fair share of the work and focus on maintaining their competence. Finally, trust comes from cooperation. Team members cannot be expected to trust those with whom they are competing for status or resources.

Christopher Barnes, a consultant for Price Waterhouse in Atlanta, explains how a team he led in his previous job failed to accomplish its mission.[52] At the time, he was an industrial engineer for Challenger Electrical Distribution, a subsidiary of Westinghouse, at a plant in Jackson, Mississippi, that made electrical boxes. From the beginning, there was a lack of communication: "Other people in the company weren't told why this team was important. So no one supported us." Another reason for the failure of the team, he thinks, was that managers did not trust the team so they did not give it the autonomy it needed. "Managers didn't give up their control over team members. As a result, they undermined the team's work," Barnes states.[53] One year after conception, the team was disbanded.

The six factors that build team trust are all interdependent and necessary. There cannot be fairness, respect, or support without integrity. Team members cannot support one another unless they have open communication and are cooperating. They cannot be fair if they do not do their best, and so forth. All of these factors take time to develop. In addition to using group dynamics and developing trust, team building also requires clear goals.

Setting Clear Goals

Hot ▼ Link

See the expectancy model and goal setting in chapter 6, pp. 195–96.

Effective teams are committed to common goals. Unless the team sets clear, well-developed goals accepted by all team members, goal commitment and achievement are not possible. We described the elements of good goals in chapter 6. They include specific goals that are measurable, achievable, and reasonable; they also have a time frame. These elements are essential to teams. Without a clear sense of direction, team members flounder. Their efforts do not lead to clear performance and they are bound to lose their motivation.

In the Challenger Electrical Distribution example, Christopher Barnes's team was given the goal, "Make things better." Barnes believes that with such a vague goal, it was inevitable that the team would fail.[54]

The importance of clear goals cannot be overemphasized. The managers who create the teams have to take sufficient time to explain the reasons the team was created and clarify their vision. In some cases, the manager sets team goals, allowing for team input and participation. In the case of self-managed teams, organizational leaders provide general vision and direction. The team themselves then set their goals.

Selecting Team Members Who Complement One Another

Hot ▼ Link

We discussed the Big Five personality traits in chapter 4, pp. 118–30.

No individual is perfect, but a team can be. This statement is the basic premise behind a model of team building developed by R. Meredith Belbin of the Industrial Training Research Unit in Cambridge, England.[55] Belbin suggests that each of us plays one or more team roles in our work groups. He identified eight team roles based on the four factors of intelligence, dominance, extroversion, and stability. The last two factors are part of the Big Five personality traits we discussed in chapter 4. According to Belbin, effective teams have team members with complementary roles. Table 8.2 presents these eight team roles.

Table 8.2   TEAM ROLES

Team Roles	Traits	Strength	Challenge
Coordinator	Stable, trusting, dominant, calm, extrovert	Coordinates the efforts of others; welcomes others' ideas; takes care of relationships; is disciplined	Can be too laid back and disinterested and a weak communicator
Shaper	Anxious, dominant, extrovert, highly motivated	Task focused; intense; often the team leader; integrates ideas; challenges others; does not tolerate poor performance	Impatient, demanding, and headstrong
Plant	Dominant, very intelligent, introvert, imaginative	Name comes from the fact that "planting" this person can energize the group with new ideas; source of new ideas; creative; focused on the "big picture;" bored with details	Impractical and harsh with others, a weak communicator
Monitor-Evaluator	Intelligent, stable, introvert, objective	Serious; dependable; analytical; critical; careful and thorough; excellent evaluator	Lacks inspiration and has trouble with others, dry and boring
Implementor	Stable, controlled, reliable, organized	Practical organizer; disciplined; sincere; hard working; builder	Lacks flexibility and has trouble adjusting to change
Resource Investigator	Stable, dominant, extrovert, curious	Relaxed; sociable and enthusiastic; focused on external relationships; responds well to challenge and change	Loses interest with routine and does not work well alone
Team worker	Stable, extrovert, low in dominance, perceptive	Sensitive; focused on others; likable; unassertive; loyal to others; responds well to people; builds team cohesion	Indecisive and cannot manage conflict
Finisher	Anxious, introvert, has high standards	Worrier; unassertive; focused on deadlines and task completion; good at follow-through	Compulsive and gets bogged down in irrelevant details, poor delegator

Sources: Based on information in R. M. Belbin, *Management Teams: Why They Succeed or Fail* (Oxford, UK: Heinemann, 1981), and G. Wilson, *Problem Solving and Decision Making* (London: Kogan Page, 1993).

All eight roles are necessary for a complete team. All teams need shapers and coordinators to lead the task and relationship processes. Plants bring creativity. Resource investigators establish the external linkages whereas implementors bring practicality to the team. Monitors, evaluators, and finishers assure quality and completion whereas the team workers maintain team spirit. Each role has both strengths and weaknesses.

Having eight people, one from each type, would create a complete team with a high potential for success. Although this can be achieved through selection when a team is created, it is rarely possible to balance team roles in addition to expertise, department affiliation, or other task-related factors. Instead, Belbin suggests that although each of us has a dominant team role, we also have one or more less dominant team roles that we can rely on, if needed. For example, a person may be primarily a shaper but also have some characteristics of a plant. Similarly, a team worker may have elements of a coordinator and resource investigator. If the team is lacking some of the eight types, members should rely on their less dominant team role styles to help complete the team.

Belbin proposes that teams use the roles as a starting point to identify the team's strengths and weaknesses and to make decisions about which roles members can play to help the team achieve its goals. Other tools such as the Myers Briggs Type Inventory, which you will read about in chapter 10, are also used to help team members become aware of their strengths and weaknesses and compensate for the latter.

Appropriate Leadership

We have already discussed the need to change from a command-and-control leadership role to a facilitator role in managing teams. Team leaders, whether appointed by the organization or chosen by team members, must be aware of their role as facilitators and avoid overcontrolling and overdirecting their teams.[56] As facilitators, their role is to help define goals, provide assistance and support, and remove internal and organizational obstacles for the team members to perform their task. Additionally, as opposed to traditional models of management, in which managers' only role is to supervise others, team leaders themselves continue to contribute to the team as members.

Ruth Wageman, a professor at Columbia University's Graduate School of Business who studies self-managed teams in numerous corporations, defines the critical role of leaders in team design. She explains, "The most critical role of leadership is to get the team set up right."[57] From then on, leaders should coach the team sparingly.

Charles Manz and Henry Sims proposed a model for team leadership that involves self-leadership or superleadership of each team member.[58] **Superleadership** is the process of leading people to lead themselves. As a result, team members are taught and encouraged to make their own decisions and accept responsibility to the point that they no longer need leaders. Superleadership within teams means that all team members set goals, observe, evaluate, critique, reinforce, and reward one another and themselves. In such an environment, the need for one leader is reduced. Team members themselves decide what they need and how to achieve it. Superleadership includes the following three elements:

- *Personal goal setting:* Individuals and teams set their own performance goals and performance expectations.
- *Observation and self-evaluation:* Team members observe their own and other team members' behaviors and provide feedback, critique, and evaluate one another's performance.
- *Self-reinforcement:* Team members provide feedback and support to one another.

One of the decisions that teams need to help them become more effective is the type and amount of training the members need.

Superleadership
A process of leading people to lead themselves

Providing Training

Organizations that implement teams typically provide a variety of training for them beyond the technical training needed to accomplish the task. The team's training may include conflict management, managing interpersonal skills, time management, facilitation training, and so forth. The focus is to help members manage interpersonal relationships better so they can create a collaborative climate in which commitment to a common goal is possible.

Many organizations have a series of courses for their team members. For instance, Honeywell Corporation uses a training program that helps team members identify their interpersonal style and encourages them to use knowledge of themselves and others in resolving conflicts and working together. Similarly, Corning Inc. contracted with Marietta College to develop customized team-training programs for Corning teams in the company's Parkersburg, West Virginia, plant. Team members learn to improve their interpersonal and team facilitation skills.[59] In another type of training, Joe Bonito of Pfizer Pharmaceuticals trains teams to get the right type of support from their organization by recruiting their bosses. "If you can show the boss that your team is doing something unique, something that will create a competitive advantage, the boss will want to become the de facto sponsor," Bonito says.[60]

Training teams in process and interpersonal skills is essential to team building. The traditional training that managers receive to supervise employees does not translate well to a team environment, so organizations need to adjust their training based on the types and numbers of teams they are using.

In addition to standard training on group processes and communication, managers should allow team members to select the type of training they need. This choice is part of enabling the team to make its own decisions and allows teams to focus on their own needs. For example, one team may need more help in basic communication, listening, and providing feedback; another may need training in time management and running meetings. Imposing standardized training, beyond some basics, on all teams works against the empowerment of teams and is a waste of organizational and team resources.

Rewarding the Team

A tough obstacle to successful team performance is how to reward teams in cultures that tend to reward only individual performance. At SEI Investments, the Pennsylvania-based investment firm referred to earlier, the 140 self-managed teams are rewarded by incentive compensation that ranges from 10 percent to sometimes more than 100 percent of base pay. Some teams decide themselves how to divide the pot of money they receive; other teams appoint a neutral facilitator to distribute the sum among the members of the team.[61] Jerry McAdams, a compensation expert, suggests that teams should be rewarded immediately with bonuses and then receive deferred awards later if their work shows long-term benefits to the company. The later reward shows teams that "the key mark of success was a result that would hold up."[62]

We discussed earlier how the Dodgers manage diversity. They and other sports teams also struggle with how to reward team members' individual performance and teamwork. The Dodgers address the issue by providing incentive clauses in players' contracts for team-based achievements, hoping to encourage more cooperation in an individualistic culture. Many other organizations have started to do so as well.

A recent survey of successful companies showed that most are now relying on team incentives to supplement salaries of employees.[63] For example, Hallmark Cards moved aggressively to implement team-based incentives for its numerous teams.[64] Behlen Manufacturing, a steel manufacturer, is another company that adjusted its compensation plan to the reality of team structures. Under Tony Raimondo's leadership, Behlen created permanent teams that dramatically improved customer satisfaction. Along with the new structure, the company has put together a pay plan that blends the needs of the individuals with the goals of the organization. The plan includes some base pay augmented with gain-sharing bonuses, profit sharing, and stock options.[65]

Summary Point 8.5   **How Can Managers Help Build Effective Teams?**

- Team building is defined as any number of activities that are aimed at improving the internal work and relationship processes inside teams.
- Basic group dynamics can be used to increase cohesion, manage stages of group development, and set up norms.
- Building trust requires integrity, open communication, mutual respect and support, fairness and equity, competence and hard work, and cooperation.
- Teams can capitalize on diversity of their members by encouraging and managing conflict.

- Clear goals are essential to team building.
- The team roles approach suggests that each individual can play a different role in teams and that their combination creates team synergy.
- Appropriate team leadership is focused on facilitation and eventually on developing self-leadership skills within each team member.
- Teams need to receive training in team process and interpersonal skills.

We have identified various ways teams can strengthen their internal processes through using group dynamics concepts, building trust, setting clear goals, understanding team roles, developing appropriate leadership, and receiving training. Managers must also understand the context of organizations to support their teams' performance effectively. Next we examine how teams affect and are affected by the contextual factors of environment, technology, strategy, structure, and culture.

Teams *in Context*

Successful implementation of teams depends on appropriate and effective internal team processes. Smooth internal processes alone are not enough. In addition, managers must consider the organizational context in which teams are operating. Organizations implementing work teams or simple management teams need to make minor organizational and structural adjustments to make those teams effective. Strong team building along with some organizational support is often sufficient. However, if an organization is moving toward a team-based structure with self-managed teams, the organizational context must change to support and integrate teams.[66]

In chapters 2 and 3, we identified the five contextual strategic forces of environment, technology, strategy, structure, and culture. The last four of these forces can be used to strengthen teams and make them part of the organization. We've already discussed the implications of national culture and diversity on teams, so we turn to organizational culture.

Creating an Organizational Culture That Supports Teams

Organizational experts consistently agree that teams cannot be effective unless the organizational culture accepts their value. Managers cannot create a team to reengineer basic work processes if the organization maintains a highly mechanistic, inflexible, and traditional culture. Similarly, managers cannot expect a climate of cooperation and mutual accountability to develop if employees are rewarded solely on their individual achievement. The culture of the organization must recognize or, better yet, embrace the importance of teams. Without such a culture, teams cannot achieve their full potential.

Hot ▼ Link

We discussed the three levels of organizational culture in chapter 3, pp. 95–96.

An organizational culture that encourages individual achievement, competition, status, and hierarchy does not dovetail with a team-based organization. Change must occur at all levels of organizational culture. Obvious behaviors such as focusing on individual achievement, reward systems, and open competition have to be addressed first. The next step is to change values and norms. Finally, basic assumptions about the role of individuals in performance have to change.[67]

CEO Al West of SEI Investments realized that his organization was stagnating under its existing culture and he needed to revamp the business completely. Before creating teams, he eliminated everyone's administrative staff and instructed managers to do their own faxing, typing, and travel planning. "That really broke the back of the old culture," he stated. Then he moved the company to new headquarters with a completely flexible design. According to West, "The buildings are the capstone of the cultural change."[68]

Now the 140 self-managed teams create their own workspace. West supplemented the new culture with an incentive reward system that supports a culture of cooperation. In addition, members of any new team have to convince other members of the organization to join their team so that it can accomplish its goals. The power of persuasion is the only power that individuals have to gain the support of the organization's members. Bob Aller, a team leader for SEI's investor-strategy team and a former Procter & Gamble employee, observed that "at P&G, the hard part was getting an idea approved. But once you got approval, the resources of the company fell behind you. Here, getting approval is the easy part. The hard part is mar-

The openness and flexibility of SEI's organizational culture is demonstrated by its flexible office design. All the office equipment is moveable. Teams connect instantly to the rest of the organization through the ceiling hanging "pythons," cables that carry electricity, Internet access, and a dial tone.

shalling the resources. You have to convince people to get involved."[69] The new culture of SEI is based on innovation, flexibility, and customer responsiveness.

Figure 8.4 summarizes the changes that businesses must make in organizational culture to support teams fully. Along with cultural changes, teams need to be well integrated into the organization's structure.

Adjusting the Structure to Support Teams

When managers use quality circles to improve customer service or create a task force to recommend purchase of a database, they change the way people organize to work. The result is a change in their organization's structure. Teams are one way to organize the human resources of an organization. A team-based structure focuses on groups of people rather than individuals.

Work or administrative teams can work parallel to traditional functional structures. However, implementing a team-based organization involves a wholesale change in the structure of the organization. The hierarchy, the span of control, how people are grouped to do their work, allocation of responsibilities, and finally how activities are coordinated and integrated are significantly different in a traditional compared to a team-based organization. SEI underwent such a change. SEI President Greer remembers that the company had to "throw away any structure that would impede us from doing what was right for the business."[70]

Table 8.3 compares the elements of structure for a traditional and a team-based organization. In chapter 2, we identified formalization, specialization, standardization, hierarchy, centralization, differentiation, and integration as the elements of structure. Their combination makes each orga-

From	To
• "I" thinking prevails.	• "We" thinking prevails.
• Success is based on individuals.	• Success is based on teams.
• Competition between individuals leads to creativity.	• Cooperation between individuals leads to creativity.
• Managers are in charge and are responsible and accountable for others' work.	• Managers' role is to provide resources and remove obstacles.
• Information is power and should be kept to oneself.	• Individuals are responsible for their own and their teams' work.
• Individuals should specialize in a clear task or function.	• Information should be widely shared.
	• Individuals should learn many skills.

FIGURE 8.4
Cultural Changes Needed to Support Teams

Table 8.3 STRUCTURAL ELEMENTS IN TRADITIONAL
AND TEAM-BASED ORGANIZATIONS

Structural Element	Traditional Organization	Team-Based Organization
Formalization	All activities and procedures are clearly described in formal written documents.	Activities and procedures depend on each team's goals and are not necessarily formally stated.
Specialization	Individuals and departments specialize in a particular task or function.	Individuals and teams learn as many tasks and functions as they need to perform their job.
Standardization	Activities are standardized across individuals and departments; the same procedures and rules apply to all.	Activities and procedures change from group to group; focus is on local solutions developed by each team to fit its goals and needs.
Hierarchy	There are clear lines of reporting up the organization and many levels with each manager having few reports.	The organization is flat, horizontal; it has lateral rather than hierarchical relationships and only a few levels.
Centralization	Decisions are made by managers at each level and passed down to employees; the structure is centralized.	Decisions are made by teams with coordination and integration among teams; the structure is decentralized.
Differentiation	Departments and functions are clearly differentiated.	Differentiation is based on teams working on projects or processes.
Integration	Activities are coordinated by managers of different departments or through individuals or departments charged with integration.	Each team is responsible for coordinating with other teams.

nization unique. Overall, as compared to traditional organizations, team-based organizations have lateral and horizontal structures rather than hierarchical and vertical ones. Activities and procedures are based on solutions that each team develops rather than on formalized, standardized processes that apply to the entire organization. Decision making is shared and decentralized to the lowest possible levels rather than handed down the hierarchy by a few top executives.

Lynn Mercer from Lucent Technologies explains that although all instructions are still written down in her team-managed factory, every individual can make online changes to a procedure if the individual's team agrees. Not only do teams have the power to change procedures, but others can learn from them and do not have to reinvent the wheel. Teams decide on local solutions to problems, and as one manager mentioned: "We solve problems in hallways rather than conference rooms."[71] Lucent's structure is flat, and decision making is highly decentralized and localized.

The organizational chart of a true team-based organization, shown in Figure 8.5, does not include vertical lines or boxes that include one person's name and title. Instead, circles identify teams of individuals who must cooperate extensively so that their activities complement and do not conflict with those of all other teams.[72] The teams in Figure 8.5 can be work or task teams, or more complex process teams.

Not all organizations need to or should aim to adopt a complete team-based structure. Many organizations such as Kellogg's, American Airlines, and Citicorp function effectively with traditional structures that include some team-based elements. One expert, Jon Katzenbach, a director at McKinsey & Co. consulting firm, advocates that organizations think hard before jumping into the teaming structure. Even after teams are formed, "team members should ask if the work could be done more effectively if the team were disbanded," Katzenbach suggests.[73]

Even with some but not all elements of a team-based structure, organizations must make the necessary cultural and structural changes to allow the teams to function well and reach their potential. In addition to cultural and structural changes, successful teams need to play a meaningful role in the strategy of the organization.

The flat structure at Lucent supports teams that make decisions in a highly decentralized, collaborative manner.

Teams as a Competitive Strategic Advantage

There needs to be a compelling business reason to create and use teams in an organization. Otherwise, the business should not undergo the often painful, wholesale changes needed to become team based. When teams are essential to implementing the strategy of an organization, there is then a strategic imperative for their use. Consider, for instance, the case of 3M Company. Its managers must show that 25 percent of their division's annual revenue comes from new products. This mandate requires a strategy of constant, quick innovation and renewal. 3M relies on its product innovation teams to carry out this aggressive strategy so that the company can stay ahead of its global competition.

Let's revisit SEI Investments and consider its strategy. CEO West realized that the organization was stagnating because it lacked a competitive advantage. The company developed a new strategy to regain an advantage: Become more responsive to customers than other firms in the industry. The decision to restructure as a team-based organization occurred because of the new strategy. Under the teaming design, teams form to solve a client's problem and then disband. With no organization chart, no offices, and no hierarchies, the new strategy, culture, and structure all fit together. The results have been positive. SEI employees are satisfied with their work and the organization is more profitable. Three years after the self-managed teams were implemented, company revenues shot up 30 percent. The company's market value is now close to $1 billion.[74]

Teams that work on activities and tasks that are not directly tied to the strategic focus of the organization will feel that their efforts are inconsequential. As a result, their members lose inter-

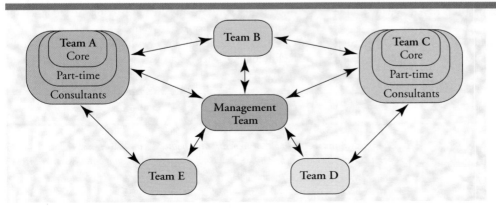

FIGURE 8.5
Team-Based Organizational Chart

est and lack motivation. In such cases, the team does not live up to expectations.[75] For example, a team at Texas Commerce Bank was asked to reduce overhead by $50 million. The team failed because its members could not see the link between this goal and the bank's overall customer-orientation and service strategy. After management let the team set its own goal, team members decided to try to bring employees closer to customers, a goal directly tied to the strategy of the bank. After the team set its own strategic goal, it saved the business nearly $100 million.[76]

Team expert Katzenbach explains the logic of linking team activities to company strategy. "Teams aren't motivated by numbers—not even big numbers. They're motivated by something to do in the marketplace, like beating a competitor."[77] Organizations that link their teams' activities to their core business strategy are more likely to witness highly motivated members who do top quality work.

Using Technology to Support Teams

Information technology is key to effective teamwork. Without extensive access to and sharing of information, a team simply cannot function in today's organizations.[78] Teams need access to information from inside and outside the organization to set and adjust their goals, change their internal processes, and complete their tasks. Teams also provide information to the organization, such as ideas, proposals, competitive analyses, and recommendations. Indeed, organizations often measure team effectiveness by placing a value on the usefulness of that information.

Organizations can enhance team processes and support them with the use of various information technologies. For instance, technology helps teams coordinate activities with other teams; plan and manage complex projects; allow many to work on a project at the same time; and do a better job of identifying tasks, sequences, milestones, and cost estimates.[79]

Let's take a final look at SEI. Recall that it uses cable "pythons" to allow teams to stay connected with other teams, with clients, and with the outside world. The company even uses software to track the location and composition of its teams. Having immediate access to information about clients and markets is directly tied to the strategy and structure of SEI. Teams have to know instantly what the clients need and then provide those services quickly. The information technology fully supports this strategy.

Teams can have a positive impact on organizations if they are effective. Their effectiveness depends on smooth internal processes and genuine organizational support. The internal team factors and organizational contextual factors have to fit to address both organizational and individual needs.

Hot ▼ Link

We discussed the elements of information technology in chapter 2, p. 44.

Summary Point 8.6   How Do Contextual Factors Influence Team Effectiveness?

- For teams to succeed, organizations have to change some or all of their cultural elements.
- Organizations have to make the necessary structural changes to allow the teams to function well and reach their potential.

- Successful teams are an integral part of the strategy and competitive advantage of organizations.
- Organizational technology with focus on information technology has to be adjusted to support team-based structures.

For updated information on the topics in this chapter, Web exercises, links to related Web sites, an on-line study guide, and more, visit our companion Web site at:
http://www.prenhall.com/nahavandi

A   L o o k   B a c k   a t   t h e

MANAGERIAL CHALLENGE

The Tokyo String Quartet

When Peter Oundjian became a member, the Tokyo String Quartet was already a highly cohesive group. The group was small; members shared a common interest in chamber music; and in the endless round of rehearsals and performances, all had ample opportunity to work and socialize together. Their diverse musical talents provided sufficient resources for the group's work and cooperation was rewarded by fame and fortune.

Oundjian accepted the group's central norms of exceptional performance, a key element in its long-term success. However, he questioned the peripheral norms that had been established over the years as the group reached maturity. His questioning returned the group to earlier stages of development, causing its members to rethink their roles and interaction. But instead of viewing Oundjian as a deviant in open revolution, the other members chose to view him as a creative individual who could rejuvenate the group.[80] The first violinist's talent and previous accomplishments provided him with the idiosyncrasy credit to deviate from the quartet's norms.

Then, 15 years after joining the group, Oundjian injured his hand. Unable to continue performing, he left the quartet and shifted his focus to conducting, becoming artistic director of Caramoor in New York.[81] Now the Tokyo String Quartet had to enlist a new first violinist. After a thorough search, the group selected Ukranian-born Mikhail Kopelman, formerly a member of the Moscow Philharmonic Orchestra and the Borodin Quartet. And once again, the Tokyo String Quartet triumphed, effectively leveraging the skills of their new first violinist to forge an even more dynamic and sensitive sound.[82]

■ Point of View Exercises

You're the Manager: The first violinist serves as the leader of the quartet. If you were Mikhail Kopelman, how vigorously would you question the group's musical selections for an upcoming concert? Do you think the other members would be open to your questioning if you cited musical concerns? If you cited personal preferences?

You're the Employee: You're the second violinist with the Tokyo String Quartet and you have perfected the musical selections for the upcoming concert. Would you be open to the new first violinist's objections regarding musical selections? What could Kopelman say that would convince you to change the selections?

SUMMARY OF LEARNING OBJECTIVES

1. **Explain what a team is, its five characteristic elements, its role in organizations, and the effect of culture on teams.** Teams are mature groups with highly interdependent members who are fully committed to the common goal. Commitment to a common goal and common approach, mutual accountability, shared leadership, a collaborative culture, and synergy are the defining characteristics of teams. National, ethnic, and organizational cultures affect the ease of implementation and the success of teams in organization.

2. **Identify the four different types of teams used in organizations.** Organizations use four main types of teams: simple work teams, administrative teams, cross-departmental teams, and process teams. The two characteristics that differentiate types of teams are the complexity of the task they accomplish and the fluidity of their membership. Work teams have simple tasks and stable membership. Administrative teams also have stable membership but deal with more complex tasks. Cross-departmental teams have relatively simple tasks with fluid membership. Process teams have both complex tasks and fluid membership.

3. **Discuss the characteristics of self-managed teams.** Self-managed teams are process teams of employees from different work areas who have full managerial control over their own work without having to report to an outside manager. Self-managed teams are a structural element of an organization. They have the power to set goals, plan, staff, schedule, monitor quality, and implement their decisions. Extensive coordination with others outside the team is necessary for success.

4. **Describe how managers can make teams effective through internal team building.** Team building includes activities aimed at improving the internal work and relationship processes inside teams to create commitment, task focus, mutual accountability, and an open climate. Team building requires developing mature teams, monitoring team composition, developing trust, clarifying goals, selecting complementary members, rewarding members fairly, and providing team training.

KEY TERMS

cross-departmental team, p. 275
cross-functional task force or cross-functional team, p. 275
facilitation, p. 278
management team, p. 274

membership fluidity, p. 272
process teams, p. 276
quality circles (QCs), p. 273
self-managed teams (SMTs), p. 277
shamrock team, p. 280
superleadership, p. 284

synergy, p. 267
task complexity, p. 272
team building, p. 280
teams, p. 266
work teams, p. 273

REVIEW QUESTIONS

1. List the defining characteristics of teams.
2. How does national culture affect the level of difficulty in implementing teams in organizations?
3. Track the evolution of teams in organizations and describe the two factors that identify the different types of teams.
4. Describe the defining elements of a self-managed team.

5. Identify the factors that managers can use to build teams.
6. Review contextual organizational factors that are needed to support teams.

DISCUSSION QUESTIONS

1. Consider a group you belong to at work or in your personal life. Which elements of a team does the group have? What is missing? How can you help your group become a team?
2. To what extent should managers consider culture before they implement teams in their organization?
3. Are some types of teams better than others? What factors should managers consider before they select the type of team to use?
4. What are the implications of using shamrock teams for the ways we manage people in organizations?
5. Are any of the contextual factors (environment, technology, strategy, structure, and culture) more important than others in managing teams? Justify your answer.

▶ SELF-ASSESSMENT 8
Individual Responsibility in Developing Trust

Consider the latest team experience you have had. This could be in a class group project or at work in a work team or task force. Evaluate your own behavior by circling the most appropriate number on the 1 to 5 scale for each statement. See Appendix 3 for a scoring key.

STATEMENTS	NEVER				ALL THE TIME
1. I come to meetings fully prepared and share my work with others.	1	2	3	4	5
2. I do my fair share of the work in the team.	1	2	3	4	5
3. I seek opportunities to learn new skills that my team needs (for example, through training or personal work).	1	2	3	4	5
4. I voice my disagreement with other team members openly and honestly.	1	2	3	4	5
5. I recognize others' accomplishments and give them fair credit for their work.	1	2	3	4	5
6. I take special care to be accurate and honest in my actions and words.	1	2	3	4	5
7. I provide help and assistance to other team members.	1	2	3	4	5
8. My team members are aware of where I stand on issues and what they can expect of me.	1	2	3	4	5
9. I encourage other team members and support their efforts through my words and actions.	1	2	3	4	5
10. I provide team members with open feedback regarding their actions and performance.	1	2	3	4	5
11. I am fully accountable for my words and actions.	1	2	3	4	5
12. I share all relevant information I have with my team members.	1	2	3	4	5

STATEMENTS	NEVER				ALL THE TIME
13. I treat all team members the same and do not expect special treatment for myself.	1	2	3	4	5
14. I accept other team members' ideas and approaches and consider them openly.	1	2	3	4	5
15. I volunteer to do work that is needed.	1	2	3	4	5

▶ **TEAM EXERCISE 8**
Developing a Team Charter

Developing a team contract or charter is a key step in getting a team organized to become effective. After being assigned to a group (or using existing teams in class), draft a team charter for a hypothetical or actual project that the team members must work on.

PART I: TEAM CHARTER

The following are elements that need to be included in a team charter. Each team should take time to discuss the following items openly and reach agreement on them. Each team should then add appropriate items depending on the issues it faces.

1. Team Mission

Clearly state the team's mission: the reason it was created.

2. Membership

Evaluate each team member's skills, strengths, and weaknesses as they relate to team tasks and activities.

Members	Skills	Strengths	Weaknesses
•	•	•	•
•	•	•	•
•	•	•	•

3. Specific Goals

State specific goals, deadlines, and milestones (various points that indicate progress).

Goals	Milestone 1	Milestone 2	Milestone 3	Milestone 4
•	•	•	•	•
•	•	•	•	•
•	•	•	•	•

4. Challenges and Solutions

Identify the key challenges that your team faces and list ideas for overcoming each.

Key Challenges	How We Can Overcome
•	•
•	•
•	•

5. Available Resources

What additional resources beyond team members do you have to help accomplish your goals? You have already reviewed your team strengths and weaknesses. Now list additional resources that are available to you inside and outside the organization.

Internally in the organization (consider people, technology, facilities, and so forth):
Externally:

6. Team Norms and Rules

List the norms and rules of your team. Focus on the key central and peripheral ones. This is a good time to reconsider the ways each norm affects the team's purpose.

Norm or rule (indicate whether central or peripheral)	Who can enforce?	What is the penalty?
•	•	•
•	•	•
•	•	•

7. Other Special Issues Our Team Needs to Consider

List any other issues your team has to consider to function well and accomplish its task.

PART II: TEAM PRESENTATIONS

Each team should present its charter to the class and explain the logic underlying their decisions.

UP CLOSE

▶ Building Cross-National Teams

Hans Gunter feels up to the challenge that he has set for himself. As the manager of the biggest division of a German office furniture manufacturing company with factories and distribution all over Europe, he knows he can create true multinational teams that are needed to make his division effective.

For years, experts have urged European business and political leaders to prepare for the inevitable forces of change that have transformed the way organizations are managed in Asia, the United States, and Canada.[83] Self-managed teams are taking root in North American and Asian countries, and European leaders need to meet that challenge.[84] Gunter does not want his group to fall into the stereotypical patterns of European teams—bickering over subsidies and turfs, nationalism, and isolationist tactics such as closing markets to firms in countries that are not European Union members.

Gunter wants to create self-managed teams that can be nimble, flexible, and highly competitive. He needs them to compete with the U.S. multinational companies such as Haworth and Herman Miller. His division operates manufacturing plants in Germany, France, Norway, Portugal, and Italy. Gunter has to deal with a range of ingrained cultural stereotypes, such as the belief that Northern Europeans are superior to Southern Europeans,

that the French are too nationalistic, the Italians and the Portuguese are unruly, the Norwegians are cold, and the Germans are too controlling. Italians claim to have the best design skills, Portuguese say they can produce the most efficient products, Germans claim to have the best trained workforce, Norwegians point to the worldwide appeal of Scandinavian design, and the French argue that they are the world center of style.

Gunter wants to harness the skills and perspectives that workers from each country offer and create cross-national teams. He needs his design, marketing, and manufacturing people to be able to move from one location and one country to another easily and effectively. He also wants to prove that Europeans can overcome their national differences and function as a team.

Questions

1. As a consultant hired to help Hans Gunter implement teams in his division, what are the actions you recommend that he take?
2. Propose short-term and long-term plans for reorganization and ideas to support teams by focusing on internal team and organizational factors.

THE BIG PICTURE

▶ Virtual Teamwork at IBM

Virtual teamwork is all in a day's work for John Patrick, who has organized a number of such initiatives at IBM since 1993. Back then, the Internet made barely a blip on corporate radar screens. As one of IBM's senior strategists, Patrick had been experimenting with programs for browsing files on computer systems connected around the world. IBM was then a large, lumbering company in trouble, and Lou Gerstner had been brought in as CEO to reinvigorate the venerable computer firm.

Skipping from file to file on the Internet, Patrick became convinced that IBM needed to get involved with this emerging phenomenon. So he drafted a "Get Connected" memo about new ways to communicate in the digital world—including now-commonplace techniques such as assigning each employee an e-mail address and creating a corporate Web site. Patrick's ideas resonated with employees all over IBM. "People didn't know where I reported in the company, and they didn't care," remembers Patrick. "We shared a common vision that the Internet was going to change everything and that IBM should be a leader."[85]

A grass-roots group of IBMers from a wide variety of functions, units, and locations flocked to Patrick's e-mail discussion list to join the Get Connected team. They had "no budget, no head count, no authority," he says. "Everything we did was informal."[86] In just six months, this virtual team designed IBM's corporate Web site, which went live in May 1994. Later that year, a team of volunteers from 12 different IBM businesses worked with Patrick to create the company's first exhibit at Internet World, a major industry trade show.

Not long afterward, IBM developed an official Internet strategy and created a task force for implementation. When the company established an Internet division, Patrick was named vice president of Internet technology. Since then, his Get Connected virtual team has branched out to help more than 10,000 IBM business customers harness the power of the Internet to communicate with *their* customers. Patrick's newest project, WebAhead, is a virtual team effort to develop innovative cutting-edge Internet applications.[87]

How does Patrick describe his role at IBM? "Some people call me the strategist, some call me a visionary, and some call me chief dreamer," he says. "I feel like a very lucky person to get to work with advanced Internet technology as my full-time job."[88]

Questions

1. Which of the four characteristics of teams can be applied to the Get Connected virtual team?
2. What team role(s) does John Patrick appear to have played in the Get Connected virtual team?
3. If you were a member of IBM's Get Connected team, which of the team roles would you assume? Why?

NOTES

1. "Tokyo String Quartet," *Classics World Biography*, accessed on-line at www.caramoor.com/focus_oundjian.com, February 17, 1998.
2. K. Labich, "Elites Teams Get the Job Done," *Fortune* (February 19, 1998): 94–96.
3. Ibid.
4. Ibid.
5. D. R. Denison, S. L. Hart, and J. A. Kahn, "From Chimneys to Cross-Functional Teams: Developing and Validating a Diagnostic Model," *Academy of Management Journal* 39 (1996): 1005–23.
6. R. T. King, Jr., "Levi's Factory Workers Are Assigned to Teams, and Morale Takes a Hit," *Wall Street Journal*, May 20, 1998, A1, A6.
7. K. Labich, "Elite Teams," *Fortune* 133, no. 3 (February 19, 1996): 97–99.
8. Ibid., 97.
9. Ibid., 98.
10. E. A. Robinson, "The Ups and Downs of the Industry Leaders," *Fortune* 137, no. 4 (1998): F4; S. J. Liebowitz and K. T. Holden, "Are Self-Managing Teams Worthwhile? A Tale of Two Companies," *SAM Advanced Management Journal* 60, no. 2 (1995): 11–18.
11. R. Levering and M. Moskowitz, "The 100 Best Companies to Work for in America," *Fortune* 137, no. 1 (1998): 85.
12. S. Kirsner, "Every Day It's a New Place," *Fast Company* (April/May 1998): 132.
13. Ibid., 134.
14. Ibid.
15. Ibid., 132.
16. Ibid.,
17. Ibid., 134.

18. R. Newhan, "Diversity Divides Dodgers, Hampers Play, Piazza Says," *Los Angeles Times*, reprinted in *Arizona Republic*, June 27, 1997, pp. C1, C8.

19. Ibid., C1.

20. P. C. Early and M. Erez, *Managing Across Cultures and Countries: Inside Understanding* (New York: Oxford University Press, 1996); D. C. Limirick, "Managers of Meaning: From Bob Geldof's Band Aid to Australian CEOs," *Organizational Dynamics* (Spring 1990): 22–23; A. Nahavandi and E. Aranda, "Restructuring Teams for the Re-Engineered Organization," *Academy of Management Executive* 8, no. 4 (1994): 58–68.

21. S. Ayotte, "Team Building in an Accounting Department," *Management Accounting* 75, no. 9 (1994): 54–56.

22. For discussion about quality circles, see E. E. Lawler, III and S. A. Mohrman, "Quality Circles: After the Honeymoon," *Organizational Dynamics* (Spring 1987): 42–54; J. L. Cotton, D. A. Vollrath, K. L. Froggatt, M. L. Lengnick-Hall, and K. R. Jennings, "Employee Participation: Diverse Forms and Different Outcomes," *Academy of Management Review* 13, no. 1 (1988): 8–22.

23. S. Overman, "Teamwork Boosts Quality at Wallace," *HR Magazine* (May 1991): 30–34.

24. G. E. Ledford, E. E. Lawler, III, and S. A. Mohrman, "Quality Circle and Its Variations," in J. P. Campbell, R. J. Campbell, and Associates (eds.), *Productivity in Organizations* (San Francisco: Jossey-Bass, 1988): 255–94; J. L. Cotton, *Employee Involvement* (Newbury Park, CA: Sage, 1993).

25. E. Aranda, *Teams* (Upper Saddle River, NJ: Prentice Hall, 1998).

26. S. Phillips, "Team Facilitates Change at Turbulent Plant," *Personnel Journal* 73, no. 10 (1994): 110–17.

27. Aranda, *Teams.*

28. M. Warshaw, "The Good Guy's Guide to Office Politics," *Fast Company* (April/May 1998): 168.

29. Ibid., 157–78.

30. "Kodak's Picture Is Changing," *Management Decision* 34, no. 5 (September 1996): 3–5.

31. Aranda, *Teams.*

32. W. J. Timms, "Team-Based Compensation at Recently Reengineered Zeneca Ag Products," *Employment Relations Today* 22, no. 2 (1995): 43–52.

33. P. Carbonara, "Mervyn's Calls in the SWAT Team," *Fast Company* (April–May 1998): 54.

34. For discussion and examples of self-managed teams, see B. Dumaine, "Who Needs a Boss?" *Fortune* (May 7, 1990): 52; D. Barry, "Managing the Bossless Team," *Organizational Dynamics* (Summer 1991): 31–47; S. Crum and H. France, "Teamwork Brings Breakthrough Improvements in Quality and Climate," *Quality Progress* 29, no. 3 (1996): 39–43; R. J. Spencer, "Success with Self-Managed Teams and Partnering," *The Journal for Quality and Participation* 18, no. 4 (1995): 48–54; D. R. Beal, "Teaming to Win," *Chief Executive* no. 4 (May 1994): 22–26.

35. K. Fisher, *Leading Self-Directed Work Teams* (New York: McGraw-Hill, 1993), 5.

36. J. Greenwald, "Is Mr. Nice Guy Back?" *Time* (January 27, 1992): 43.

37. R. Smith, "Pharmacia Upjohn Forms New 'Teams' for Animal Health," *Feedstuffs* 68, no. 10 (1996): 10–11.

38. S. Carey, "USAir 'Peon' Team Pilots Start-Up of Low-Fare Airline," *Wall Street Journal*, March 24, 1998, B1, B2.

39. Ibid., B2.

40. Ibid.

41. See T. Petzinger, Jr., "How Lynn Mercer Manages a Factory That Manages Itself," *Wall Street Journal*, March 7, 1997, B1.

42. Ibid.

43. See the results of a survey about the success of teams, "The Downfall of Teams," *Training and Development Journal* (February 1993): 9–10; "Why Teams Don't Work," *Sales and Marketing Management* (April 1993): 12.

44. For some examples, see D. D. O'Connor, "Trouble in the American Workplace: The Team Player Concept Strikes Out," *ARMA Record Management Quarterly* 24, no. 2 (1990): 12–15.

45. Nahavandi and Aranda, "Restructuring Teams."

46. For a detailed discussion of shamrock teams, see Nahavandi and Aranda, "Restructuring Teams."

47. See C. C. Manz and C. P. Neck, "Teamthink: Beyond the Groupthink Syndrome in Self-Managing Work Teams," *Journal of Managerial Psychology* 10, no. 1 (1995): 7–16.

48. F. J. Milliken and L. Martins, "Searching for Common Threads: Understanding the Multiple Effects of Diversity in Organizational Groups," *Academy of Management Review* 21, no. 2 (1996): 402–33.

49. J. McAdams, "Prescription for Pay," *Fast Company* (February–March 1998): 177.

50. M. Fischetti, "Team Doctors, Report to ER," *Fast Company* (February–March 1998): 176.

51. Ibid.

52. Ibid., 173.

53. Ibid.

54. Ibid.

55. Meredith Belbin's work on team roles is based on a small group research laboratory set up at the Administrative Staff College at Henley, Oxon, which runs an internationally famous 10-week course for high-potential middle managers. R. M. Belbin, *Management Teams: Why They Succeed or Fail* (Oxford, UK: Heinemann, 1981); for further discussion of his work, see G. Wilson, *Problem Solving and Decision Making* (London: Kogan Page, 1993): 104–9.

56. J. R. Katzenbach and D. K. Smith, *The Wisdom of Teams: Creating the High Performance Organization* (New York: Harper Business, 1993).

57. Fischetti, "Team Doctors," 174.

58. C. C. Manz and H. P. Sims, Jr., "Leading Workers to Lead Themselves: The External Leadership of Self-Managing Work Teams," *Administrative Science Quarterly* 32 (1987): 106–29; C. C. Manz and H. P. Sims, Jr., "Superleadership: Beyond the Myth of Heroic Leadership," *Organizational Dynamics* 19, no. 4 (1991): 18–35; C. C. Manz, "Self-Leading Work Teams: Moving Beyond Self-Management Myths," *Human Relations* 11 (1992): 1119–40.

59. G. R. Ray, J. Hines, and D. Wilcox, "Training Internal Facilitators," *Training and Development* 48, no. 11 (1994): 45–49.

60. Fischetti, "Team Doctors," 177.

61. Kirsner, "Every Day It's a New Place," 132.

62. Fischetti, "Team Doctors," 177.

63. "Team Incentives Prominent Among 'Best Practice' Companies," *Quality* 35, no. 4 (April 1996): 20.

64. S. E. Gross and J. Blair, "Reinforcing Team Effectiveness Through Pay," *Compensation and Benefits Review* 27, no. 5 (September–October 1995): 34–39. For a description of the team-based pays of several companies, see B. Geber, "The Bugaboo of Team Pay," *Training* 32, no. 8 (1995): 25–32.

65. D. J. McNerney, "Team Compensation: Simple, Variable, and Profitable," *HR Focus* 71, no. 9 (September 1994): 9–11.

66. For information about teams and their role in the overall organization, see A. S. Mohrman and A. M. Mohrman, Jr., *Designing and Leading Team-Based Organizations* (San Francisco: Jossey-Bass, 1997); D. W. Jamieson, "Aligning the Organization for a Team-Based Strategy," in G. M. Parker (ed.), *The Handbook of Best Practices for Teams* (Amherst, MA: HRD Press, 1996): 299–312; D. A. Roming, *Breakthrough Teamwork: Outstanding Results Using Structured Teamwork* (Chicago, IL: Irwin, 1996): 231–45.

67. For the three-level model of culture, see E. H. Schein, *Organizational Culture and Leadership* (San Francisco, CA: Jossey-Bass, 1995).

68. Kirsner, "Every Day It's a New Place," 133.

69. Ibid., 134.

70. Ibid.

71. Petzinger, "How Lynn Mercer Manages."

72. For information on linkages used by teams, see Mohrman amd Mohrman, *Designing and Leading*, 22–23.

73. Fischetti, "Team Doctors," 172.

74. Kirsner, "Every Day It's a New Place," 132.

75. R. T. Pascale, "Perspectives on Strategy," *California Management Review* (Spring 1984): 47–72.

76. Fischetti, "Team Doctors."

77. Ibid., 173.

78. For an excellent analysis of the importance of technology for teams, see D. Mankin, S. G. Cohen, and T. K. Bikson, *Teams and Technology: Fulfilling the Promise of the New Organization* (Boston: Harvard Business School Press, 1996).

79. P. R. Harris, "Team Development for European Organizations," *European Business Review* 93, no. 4 (1993): 3–11; see also P. Lloyd, "*L'etat, c'est nous!* Technology Shifts Power Towards Teams," *European Business Review* 95, no. 1 (1995): ii–v.

80. Labich, "Elite Teams."

81. "Peter Oundjian, Man with a Vision," *In Focus* (February 17, 1998), accessed on-line at www.caramoor.com/focus_coundjian.com.

82. Richard Nilsen, "A Feast for the Ears," *Arizona Republic*, January 19, 1998, accessed on-line at http://newslibrary.krmedia-stream.com.

83. P. R. Harris, "Team Development for European Organizations," *European Business Review* 93, no. 4 (1993): 3–11; P. Lloyd, "*L'etat, c'est nous!* Technology Shifts Power Toward Teams," *European Business Review* 95, no. 1 (1995): ii–v.

84. A. Myers, A. Kakabadse, T. McMahon, and G. Spony, "Top Management Styles in Europe: Implications for Business and Cross-National Teams," *European Business Journal* 7, no. 1 (1995): 17–27.

85. Eric Ransdell, "IBM Grassroots Revival," *Fast Company* (October–November 1997): 188.

86. Amy Oringel, "John Patrick: Reinventing Big Blue," *Developer.com* (March 2, 1998), accessed on-line at www.developer.com/news/profiles/022598_patrick.

87. Ibid.

88. John Patrick, "Welcome," IBM Web site, accessed on-line at http://adtech.internet.ibm.com/patrick/welcome, March 2, 1998.

LEADING PEOPLE

LEARNING OBJECTIVES

1. Identify the elements of leadership, highlight the three major approaches to leadership, and explain the role of leadership across cultures.
2. Compare and contrast the elements and predictions of the five major contingency approaches to leadership.
3. Discuss the change-oriented models of leadership including charismatic, transformational, visionary, and exemplary leadership.
4. Highlight the link between leaders and the contextual factors in organizations.

MANAGERIAL CHALLENGE

Samsung

"Our dream and Korea's future" reads the billboard near the Samsung Group engine plant in Pusan, South Korea.[1] Those five words sum up the ambition of Lee Kun Hee, Samsung's chair, to steer a course into the jam-packed global automotive industry. Taking over from his father, who founded the country's second-largest *chaebol* (conglomerate), Lee heads a tightly knit group of 28 companies, employing 260,000 employees in such industries as computer memory chips, consumer electronics, shipbuilding, aircraft parts, and the media.[2]

In announcing Samsung's entrance into the competitive auto industry, Lee set the formidable goal of becoming one of the world's top ten automakers by 2010. The road ahead would be anything but smooth, given deteriorating regional economic conditions, industrywide excess capacity, and Samsung's lack of experience in automotive manufacturing. Still, Lee had triumphed over seemingly impossible odds in the past. Facing crushing competition from Japanese chip-makers, he had set up two research teams to race against each other in the search for new technology. That race yielded the "stack" technology that allowed Samsung to overtake its chip-making rivals.[3]

Lee champions decentralized management and delegation, allowing each company's managers to handle their own affairs. Educated in the United States and in Japan, he encourages creativity by loosening the hierarchical structure and promoting individual decision making, unusual moves for a Korean *chaebol*. His rallying cry, "Best in quality, no matter what," has led Samsung to make world-class products in every category.[4] But can his leadership bring Samsung success in the global automotive industry?

■ **Questions**

1. What effect did Lee's ambitious goals have on Samsung's employees and managers?
2. How could Lee leverage his leadership position to pursue his new vision?

Lee Kun Hee is a modern leader guiding his organization through major change. However, the subject of leadership is neither new nor exclusively the domain of business. As long as people have organized into groups to accomplish a task, there have been leaders and followers. Philosophers and historians from all civilizations have written about leaders and leadership. Lao Tzu, the 500 B.C. Chinese philosopher and reputed founder of Taoism, was anticipating current views of leadership when he wrote, "A leader is best when people barely know he exists. . . . When his work is done, his aim fulfilled, they will say: We did it ourselves."

Some leaders seem larger than life. They motivate, create, destroy, and rebuild through what seems to be sheer strength of their will. Although we may be dazzled, we often forget that their achievements depended on others. Leadership is a group process. It is the hard work of employees that turns a faltering company into a profitable one. It is the initiative of volunteers that achieves a nonprofit institution's goals. It is the team, not the coach, who wins the game.

In this chapter, we examine the different approaches to leadership. First, we explore the current research and practice of leadership to discover how to improve our leadership skills. We investigate leadership basics, review major leadership theories, and examine the ways that leaders use to implement change. Throughout the chapter we also provide you with practical guidelines on how to become a better leader.

LEADERSHIP BASICS

Leaders guide, direct, and help others achieve goals. They have commanding authority or influence. Researchers have developed many different definitions of leadership. It has been defined as an integral part of the group process,[5] as an influence process,[6] as the initiation of structure,[7] and as the instrument of goal achievement. The various definitions of leadership have several common themes. First, leadership is a *group phenomenon*; there are no leaders without followers. Leadership always involves interpersonal interaction. Second, leaders use their *influence* to guide groups through a certain course of action or toward the achievement of certain goals. Leadership, then, requires influence or persuasion. The third theme follows from the second. Leadership is *goal directed*. Fourth, the presence of a leader often assumes some form of *hierarchy* in a group. The leaders are at the top of that hierarchy, even when the hierarchy is very flat. Lee Kun Hee of Samsung demonstrates all these leadership elements. He is at the top of his company, guiding and influencing all employees to achieve the goals. In this section, we define leadership, present the three general approaches to understanding the leadership process, and consider cross-cultural differences in leadership.

What Is Leadership?

Once we combine the four themes of group phenomenon, influence, goal orientation, and hierarchy, we can define a **leader** as any person who influences individuals and groups in an organization, helps them establish goals, guides them toward achievement of those goals, and allows them to be effective as a result. Dee Hock, the founder and CEO emeritus of Visa, Inc., states: "Given the right circumstances, from no more than dreams, determination, and liberty to try, ordinary people consistently do extraordinary things. To lead is to create those circumstances, then go before and show the way."[8]

The two general requirements of leadership are *competence* and some degree of conformity to the group or organization. **Competence** is the ability and expertise to perform one or more tasks well. Although as we will see later in this chapter, leaders do not need to have a particular set of traits, they must demonstrate competence in one or more areas that relate to the group they are leading.

Conformity, as discussed in chapter 7, refers to the acceptance of group norms. Potential leaders must show that they are loyal to the group and its central norms through conformity. Deviants are rarely, if ever, selected to be group leaders. Leaders must conform to group norms to develop the idiosyncrasy credit that they need to move the group forward. They can then use the credit to propose novel ideas and to deviate from the group's accepted norms and goals when needed. Linda Chavez-Thompson, the executive vice president of AFL-CIO, in Washington, D.C., and the highest-ranking woman in the U.S. labor movement, has fought hard to gain her position on the leadership team of this labor union. "In my 30 years in the labor movement, 'pushy broad' is one of the nicer names that I've been called. If I really believe in something, and others don't, I don't just let it go—I'm tenacious," she claims.[9]

Before we present the current models of leadership and their applications, we provide an overview of the history of the field and how researchers and practitioners have struggled to explain the leadership process. Understanding the history of leadership is valuable in two ways. First, it helps us understand current theories better because many borrow from previous concepts. Second, it teaches us what does not work so that we do not repeat mistakes made earlier.

The Three Approaches to Understanding Leadership

The formal scientific study of leadership dates back to the beginning of management as a science during the turn of the twentieth century. Three general approaches have been used to understand leadership: the *trait*, *behavior*, and *contingency* approaches.

Early Trait Approach Are leaders born, not made? Are there some traits that differentiate leaders from their followers? These questions guided the early approach to leadership. From the 1900s to 1940s, most leadership studies focused on identifying leadership traits that distinguished leaders from followers.[10] This **trait approach** aimed at identifying individual characteristics such as demographic factors or personality traits that distinguished leaders from followers.

The results failed to support the common belief that some people have certain traits that make them better leaders. Although researchers found that some individual differences and traits—such as originality, popularity, sociability, and aggressiveness—related to leadership, they could not establish strong and reliable relationships. As a result, individual differences could be not be used reliably to predict who would become a leader—let alone which leader would be effective.

These early findings indicate that leadership requires more than a combination of personality traits. A leader's personality can limit that person's behavioral range and make it more or less difficult for him or her to learn certain behaviors or undertake some actions. Overall, however, traits alone cannot predict leadership.

Leader
Person who influences individuals and groups in an organization, helps them establish goals, guides them toward achievement of those goals, and allows them to be effective as a result

Competence
The ability and expertise to perform one or more tasks well

Hot ▼ Link

We discussed conformity, norms, deviance, and idiosyncrasy credit in chapter 7, pp. 229–64.

Trait approach
Aimed at identifying individual characteristics such as demographic factors or personality traits that distinguished leaders from followers

Hot ▼ Link

See chapter 4, p. 116, for a discussion of the role of personality and the behavioral zone.

Current Views of Traits in Leadership   In spite of weak early research support, many of us continue to believe that personality and other individual differences are related to leadership. If asked to describe leaders we admire, we are likely to use words such as *confident, decisive, caring*, and so forth.

Using contemporary statistical methods, several researchers have taken a new look at old research and showed that traits such as intelligence and dominance are associated with leadership.[11] Others have proposed that although several traits alone are not enough to make a leader, their presence is a precondition for effective leadership.[12] Specifically, business leaders must have high energy, integrity, and self-confidence, be intelligent and motivated to lead, and have knowledge of their business.

These traits describe Bill Bartmann, one of the richest men in the United States.[13] When his Pipe Service Inc. business fell victim to the sharp drop in oil prices in 1985, Bartmann said a teary-eyed goodbye to this 70 employees but refused to declare bankruptcy. He stated "I owe this money, I'm not bankrupt, I'm broke."[14] In spite of owing $1 million to the American Bank of Muskogee in Oklahoma, he convinced the bank president to lend him another $13,000. Bartmann used the loan to start a business of buying bad loans. Bartmann describes his new business: "We want to take people who are in debt by the hand, and show them the ladder to recovery."[15] His energy, expertise, integrity, and self-confidence have helped make him one of the richest people in the United States.

Recent studies of leadership in other cultures have further supported the importance of traits. For example, key traits for Russian business leaders are ambition, energy, and competence whereas the Chinese value hard work and integrity in their leaders.[16] Based on the early and current research on the role of individual differences and particularly traits in leadership, it is important for organizations to consider some traits when selecting leaders. However, they need to remember not to rely on traits alone as the sole predictor of leadership. A leader's effectiveness depends on many other factors that we consider in this chapter.

Behavior Approach   Because early research on traits failed to explain why some leaders are more effective than others, researchers turned their attention to *what leaders do* rather than *who leaders are*. The **behavioral approach** to leadership considers behaviors that leaders undertake to be effective. Extensive research about leadership behavior in the past 50 years has shown that there are two major sets of behaviors associated with leadership: those that relate to the task, and those that relate to taking care of people.[17]

Behavioral approach
Considers behaviors that leaders undertake to be effective

Task behaviors are generally called **initiation of structure**. They are concerned with defining and organizing the task to help followers achieve goals. For example, Lakshmi Mittel, the founder and owner of Rotterdam-based Ispat International NV, a steel conglomerate, is known for his emphasis on task and his obsession with detail.[18] After he acquires a new steel mill, his team of managers enters the new mill and starts managing the way Mittel directs. "They come in and run the operations very well. They control costs very, very closely," explains the chairman of Nucor steel company, Kenneth Iverson. An Indian expatriate living in London, Mittel states: "If I've decided something, I get it done. I have an aggressive approach, but I believe I'm a reasonable negotiator." Mittel is now one of the richest people in the world.[19]

Initiation of structure
Leadership behaviors concerned with defining and organizing the task to help followers achieve the goals

Relationship behaviors are called **consideration.** They include behaviors aimed at creating mutual trust and respect with followers. For instance, Wind Eagle and Rainbow Hawk, co-founders of Ehama Institute in Los Gatos, California, explain that leaders need to act the same way as the Native American chiefs used to act in the old days. "Leaders today, like the Old Chiefs, need to teach by example, get all the people involved, gather all perspectives, and create an organic whole. People don't want autocratic regimes. They want wholeness, participation, balance."[20] Table 9.1 summarizes typical behaviors associated with initiation of structure and consideration.

Consideration
Leadership behaviors that aim at creating mutual trust and respect with followers

Wind Eagle and Rainbow Hawk have built a business based on teaching leaders to share their gifts and listen to those around them. These consultants recommend sincerity, benevolence, and courage.

In contrast to the trait approach, the behavior approach offers objective, measurable results that managers can translate into practice. Because behaviors can be learned, organizations can train a leader to perform specific behaviors. The behavior approach to leadership does not suggest that one set of behaviors is more important than another set. Leaders who show both structuring and consideration behaviors tend to be effective, but the research results are not always consistent. There is strong research support that consideration leads to higher employee satisfaction. However, the same behavior sometimes leads to low performance ratings by the leader's supervisor.[22] Additionally, high initiation of structure leads to high performance in some studies and high turnover and grievances in others.

Leaders' initiation of structure and their consideration behaviors continue to be crucial to many current views of leadership that we consider later in this chapter. However, similar to the trait approach, the research results are inconsistent. Additionally, the behavior approach alone cannot fully explain the leadership process because it fails to consider both individual traits and situational characteristics. As a result, leadership research and practice have turned to a contingency approach.

Contingency Approach Is a leader who is strong-willed and domineering more effective than one who is soft-spoken and allows participation? Should a leader be controlling and impose struc-

Table 9.1   LEADERSHIP BEHAVIORS

Initiation of Structure	Consideration
• Leader lets members know what is expected of them	• Leader treats all members as his or her equal
• Leader schedules all work to be done	• Leader is friendly and approachable
• Leader encourages use of uniform procedures	• Leader does little things that make work pleasant
• Leader assigns task to each member	• Leader looks out for members

Source: These samples are based on questions in the Leader Behavior Description Questionnaire (LBDQ).

Hot ▼ Link

See chapter 1, pp. 16–17, for a discussion of contingency concepts.

ture? Should she show empathy and consideration for her followers? Should he provide clear directions or let the group come up with its own solutions? The answers to these questions depend on which leadership traits or behaviors work. This view is the basis for the contingency approach to leadership. Since the 1960s, the assumption that what makes a leader effective depends on the situation has guided leadership research and practice.

Case studies support the validity of the contingency view. As circumstances have changed, many extraordinary business, religious, and political leaders have been shunned and rejected by the people who once admired them. For instance, Ronald Allen, who as the CEO of Delta Airlines saved the company from possible bankruptcy, was fired by Delta's board of directors for being too hard-nosed and causing low morale in the organization.[23] Similarly, George Watson Jr. was booted out of office after successfully leading IBM for many years. Bill Bartmann, discussed earlier, has also seen his share of both success and failures.

Why do leaders' powers wax and wane? Why aren't leaders effective all the time? Research helps us answer these questions. Effective, appropriate leadership depends on the task, the followers, and other elements in the leadership situation.

Before we discuss current contingency approaches to leadership in detail you need to be aware that most leadership theories we discuss have been developed and tested in the United States and in some cases other Western countries. As a result, they do not always apply to other cultures.

Be Mindful of Cross-Cultural Differences

Hot ▼ Link

See the discussion of national culture and power distance in chapter 3, pp. 73–110.

National culture influences perceptions and expectations of effective leadership and how leaders are chosen. In countries with relatively low power distance, such as the United States, employees do not expect leaders to be failure proof. In high power-distance cultures, leaders who make and admit mistakes deal a deadly blow to their credibility and authority.

For instance, a CEO from the United States can make a mistake, admit it, apologize, and remain on the job. A Japanese CEO, however, typically resigns after admission of a serious error, knowing that his followers have lost confidence in his ability to lead. This contrast can be seen vividly in airline crashes. When a Japanese airliner crashes, the CEO, after providing ceremonial condolences to the family of the deceased, resigns, accepting personal responsibility for the tragic event. In a similar situation, the CEO of a U.S. airline admits that some mistakes have been made and retains his position. The followers do not lose confidence in him because they accept the idea that everyone makes mistakes.

Hot ▼ Link

To review cultural values that affect leadership selection, see chapter 3, the groupings by Trompenaars, pp. 79–80.

National cultural also affects how one becomes a leader. In many Western cultures, individual achievement and performance determine who become leaders. In other cultures, such as many Middle Eastern countries, leadership is ascribed based on family and clan. The achievement/ascriptive dimension strongly influences what is expected of leaders and how others view their performance.

Now that we have defined leadership and identified the three major approaches to leadership, we next examine the contingency theories that dominate contemporary views of leadership.

A QUESTION OF ETHICS

| *How Much Is a Leader Worth?* | U.S. business leaders sometimes earn 10 to 20 times as much as their counterparts in other industrialized nations in salary, bonuses, and other benefits.[24] Are such salaries justified? Are they ethical? Explain. |

Summary Point 9.1   **What Is Leadership and What Theories Help Explain It?**

- The four major elements of leadership are group processes, influence, goal orientation, and hierarchy.
- Early leadership research and practice focused unsuccessfully on identifying leadership traits that distinguish leaders from followers. Although some traits are central to leadership, traits alone cannot fully predict effectiveness.
- The behavior approach to leadership identified initiation of structure and consideration as the basic leadership

behaviors, although those behaviors alone cannot explain the leadership process fully.
- Current views of leadership focus on a contingency view that claims that effective leadership depends on the situation.
- Cross-cultural differences related to power distance and how leaders are selected affect views of leadership. Accordingly, U.S. leadership theories do not always apply to other cultures.

 ## CONTINGENCY LEADERSHIP

For the past 35 years the contingency view has dominated modern leadership theory. The five contingency theories that we investigate in the following sections share the idea that effective leadership is a function of both the leader and the situation.[25] They differ in the leadership characteristic they use and in how they measure effectiveness. We consider Fiedler's Contingency model, the Normative Decision model, Path-Goal theory, Leader-Member Exchange, and substitutes for leadership.

Fiedler's Contingency Model

Fred Fiedler developed the first comprehensive leadership contingency model in the 1960s.[26] That model is the most researched of all leadership contingency theories. Fiedler's basic premise is that the match between the leader's style and the leadership situation determines the leader's effectiveness. If the leader's style matches the situation, the leader will be effective. If it does not, the leader will be ineffective. We examine the leadership style part of the model first, the situational analysis (known as the amount of situational control) second, and then consider the evaluation and practical applications of the model.

Leader's Style   To determine a leader's style, Fiedler uses a measurement tool, called the **least preferred co-worker (LPC) scale**, to determine whether the leader has a *task* or *relationship* orientation. Fiedler's research shows that people's perception and description of their least preferred co-worker indicate their basic goals and priorities toward either accomplishing a task or maintaining relationships. Before you read further, take a minute to complete the LPC scale in Self-Assessment Exercise 9.1.

According to Fiedler, people with low LPC scores—those who give a low rating to their least preferred co-worker (describing the person as incompetent, cold, untrustworthy, and quarrelsome)—are task motivated. **Task motivation** means the person is primarily motivated by task accomplishment. Task-motivated individuals draw their self-esteem primarily from accomplishing their task well.[27]

People who have high LPC scores and rate their least preferred co-worker relatively positively (describing that person as loyal, sincere, warm, and accepting) are relationship motivated. **Relationship motivation** means that the person is motivated primarily by interpersonal relations. Relationship-motivated individuals draw their self-esteem primarily from having good relationships with others. Table 9.2 summarizes the differences between task- and relationship-motivated individuals.

Least Preferred Co-worker (LPC) scale
Scale used in Fiedler's Contingency model to determine whether the leader has a task *or* relationship *orientation*

Task motivation (or low LPC)
The person is primarily motivated by task accomplishment

Relationship motivation (or high LPC)
The person is primarily motivated by interpersonal relations

▶ SELF-ASSESSMENT 9.1
Least Preferred Coworker Scale (LPC)

To fill out this scale, think of a person with whom you have had difficulty working. That person may be someone you work with now or someone you knew in the past. He or she does not have to be the person you like the least, but should be the person with whom you have had the most difficulty working. Rate this person on the following scale.

										SCORE
Pleasant	8	7	6	5	4	3	2	1	Unpleasant	___
Friendly	8	7	6	5	4	3	2	1	Unfriendly	___
Rejecting	1	2	3	4	5	6	7	8	Accepting	___
Tense	1	2	3	4	5	6	7	8	Relaxed	___
Distant	1	2	3	4	5	6	7	8	Close	___
Cold	1	2	3	4	5	6	7	8	Warm	___
Supportive	8	7	6	5	4	3	2	1	Hostile	___
Boring	1	2	3	4	5	6	7	8	Interesting	___
Quarrelsome	1	2	3	4	5	6	7	8	Harmonious	___
Gloomy	1	2	3	4	5	6	7	8	Cheerful	___
Open	8	7	6	5	4	3	2	1	Guarded	___
Backbiting	1	2	3	4	5	6	7	8	Loyal	___
Untrustworthy	1	2	3	4	5	6	7	8	Trustworthy	___
Considerate	8	7	6	5	4	3	2	1	Inconsiderate	___
Nasty	1	2	3	4	5	6	7	8	Nice	___
Agreeable	8	7	6	5	4	3	2	1	Disagreeable	___
Insincere	1	2	3	4	5	6	7	8	Sincere	___
Kind	8	7	6	5	4	3	2	1	Unkind	___
									TOTAL	___

Scoring Key

A score of 57 or below indicates that you are task motivated or low LPC. A score of 64 or higher indicates that you are relationship motivated or high LPC. If your score falls between 58 and 63, you will need to determine for yourself in which category you belong.

Source: F. E. Fiedler and M. M. Chemers, *Improving Leadership Effectiveness: The Leaders Match Concept*, 2d ed. (New York: Wiley, 1984). Adapted by permission of John Wiley & Sons, Inc.

Table 9.2 DIFFERENCES BETWEEN TASK- AND RELATIONSHIP-MOTIVATED INDIVIDUALS

Task Motivated (Low LPC)	Relationship Motivated (High LPC)
• Draws self-esteem from completion of task	• Draws self-esteem from interpersonal relationships
• Focuses on the task first	• Focuses on people first
• Can be harsh with failing employees	• Likes to please others
• Considers competence of co-workers to be key trait	• Considers loyalty of co-workers to be key trait
• Enjoys details	• Gets bored with details

In spite of some problems with the validity of the LPC scale, it has received strong support from theorists and practitioners. It has even translated well to other cultures for use in leadership research and training.[28] One central premise of the LPC concept is Fiedler's assumption that *leadership style is stable* and not easily changed. Leaders, then, cannot change their style to match the situation.

Situational Control (Sit Con) Fiedler uses three factors to describe the situation. In order of importance, the factors are (1) the relationship between the leader and the followers, (2) the amount of structure of the task, and (3) the position power of the leader. Fiedler combines the three elements to define the amount of control the leader has over the situation.

According to the model, the most important element of any leadership situation is the quality of the relationship and the cohesion between the leader and the followers and among the followers. Good **leader-member relations (LMR)** means that the group is cohesive and supportive. In such a case, the leader has a high degree of control for implementing what he or she wants. When the group is divided and has little respect or support for the leader, the leader's control is low.

Task structure is the second element of a leadership situation. **Task structure (TS)** refers to the degree of clarity a task has. A highly structured task has clear goals, procedures, one or a few correct solutions, and can be easily evaluated. For instance, making a blueprint based on specifications is a highly structured task. An unstructured task is one for which the goals are not clear; there are no or few procedures on how to do the task; there are many different ways to do it, many possible solutions, and no easy way to check results. Developing a public relations campaign is unstructured.

Whereas the leader has a lot of control over a structured task, an unstructured task provides little sense of control. One factor that moderates task structure is the leader's experience level. On the one hand, if the leader has experience with a task, he or she will perceive it as more structured. On the other hand, not having experience will make any task appear unstructured.

The third and least influential element of the leadership situation is the leader's position power. **Position power (PP)** refers to the leader's official power and influence over subordinates to hire, fire, reward, or punish. The leader who has a lot of formal power feels more in control than the one who has little power. For example, typical managers have considerable position power whereas a coordinator in charge of volunteers has little.

The combination of LMR, TS, and PP yields the amount of **situational control (sit con)** the leader has over the situation. A good relationship between leader and followers, a highly structured task, and high position power for the leader form one end of the control continuum, providing the leader with high control over the leadership situation. This high control makes for a comfortable and easy leadership environment. In the middle of the continuum are situations where either the leader and the followers do not get along or the task is unstructured. In such situations, the leader does not have full control over the situation and the leadership environment is more difficult.

At the other end of the situational control continuum, the leader-member relations are poor, the task is unstructured, and the leader has little power. Such a situation is chaotic and unlikely to continue for a long period of time in an organization. Clearly, this crisis environment does not provide the leader with a sense of control or any ease of leadership.

Predictions of the Model At the core of the Contingency model is the concept of match. If the leader's style matches the situation, the leader will be effective. The Contingency model predicts that low-LPC, task-motivated leaders will be effective in high and low situational control whereas high-LPC, relationship-motivated leaders will be effective in moderate situational control. In other words, because the leader's style is constant, a leader's effectiveness changes as the situation changes. Figure 9.1 presents the predictions of the model.

Leader-member relations (LMR)
In Fiedler's Contingency model, refers to cohesion of the group and the quality of interaction between the leader and follower and among group members

Task structure (TS)
In Fiedler's Contingency model, refers to the degree of clarity a task has

Position power (PP)
In Fiedler's Contingency model, refers to the leader's official power and influence over subordinates to hire, fire, reward, or punish

Situational control (sit con)
In Fiedler's Contingency model, the combination of LMR, TS, and PP that indicates the amount of control the leader has over the situation

FIGURE 9.1
Fiedler's Contingency Model

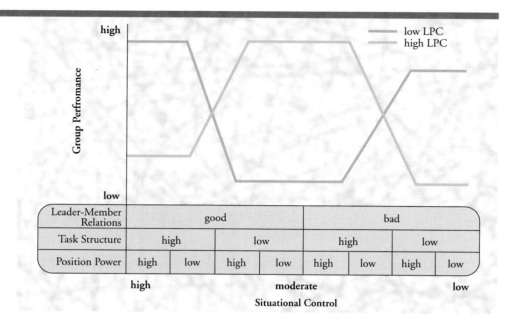

In high-control situations (the left side of the graph in Figure 9.1), the task-motivated, low-LPC leader feels at ease. Her basic source of self-esteem is not threatened, so she can relax, take care of details, and help the group perform. The same high-control situation has a different effect on the relationship-motivated, high-LPC leader. He is likely to be bored, may feel that there is nothing to do, and have the sense that nobody needs him. Because the group is cohesive and the task is clear, the leader mainly needs to take care of details and to remove obstacles. Neither of these activities is appealing to the high-LPC, so he is not effective in high-control situations.

Moderate situational control (the middle of graph in Figure 9.1) stems from either lack of cohesiveness or lack of task structure. In either case, the situation is ambiguous and uncertain, and task completion is in jeopardy. The relationship-motivated, high-LPC leader's skills at interpersonal relations and participation are well suited for the situation. She draws followers' participation and focuses on resolving task and relationship conflicts. The same elements that make moderate control attractive to relationship-motivated leaders make the situation threatening to the task-motivated, low-LPC leader. The lack of group support, the ambiguity of the task, or both make the low-LPC leader feel that the task may not be completed. The task-motivated leader becomes autocratic, ignores the task and relationship conflicts, and tries simply to complete the task. As a result, groups led by a low-LPC person perform poorly in moderate control.

As the situation becomes chaotic and reaches a crisis point with no group cohesion, no task structure, and no strong position power (the right side of the graph in Figure 9.1), the task-motivated, low-LPC leader's need to complete the task pushes him to take over and make autocratic decisions without worrying about the group. As a result, although performance is not very high, in chaotic, crisis situations, groups led by a low-LPC leader get some work done.

For the relationship-motivated, high-LPC leader, the low situational control environment is a nightmare. The group's lack of cohesion is further fueled by its inability to perform the task and makes efforts at reconciliation close to impossible. The high-LPC leader's efforts to gain support from the group are, therefore, useless. In an attempt to protect her self-esteem, the high-LPC leader withdraws, leaving the group to fend for itself, which usually results in low performance.

Marilyn Moats Kennedy, managing partner of Career Strategies, a consulting firm based in Wilmette, Illinois, is a task-motivated, low-LPC leader. She describes her leadership style this way: "Leaders can't succeed if they care more about how people feel than how they perform. So focus on output, not on attitude. Sincerity and competence rarely share a soul. Reward the latter and forget the former."[29] Contrast her views with those of Mort Meyerson, chairperson of Perot Systems, a computer firm based in Dallas, Texas. His leadership style tends toward a relationship-motivated high LPC. "Most companies are still dominated by numbers, information, and analysis. That makes it much harder to tap into intuition, feelings, and nonlinear thinking—the skills that leaders will need to succeed in the future. If you work with the whole person, and their whole mind, you will reach a better place—for them and the company."[30]

Evaluation and Application In spite of the large number of studies supporting Fiedler's Contingency model that have been done over the past 30 years, the model has also come under considerable attack, particularly for the validity of the LPC scale.[31] The majority of the concerns have been addressed with further research during the past 30 years.[32] As a result, the contingency model emerges as one of the most reliable and predictive models of leadership.

MANAGERIAL ADVICE
from the Experts

HOW TO CHANGE
YOUR LEADERSHIP SITUATION

Effective leaders manage their leadership situation to create an environment in which they can function comfortably. How to change your leadership situation depends on your style of leadership. Here are some suggestions on how to manage the leadership situation:

- To increase group cohesion and improve your relationship with followers,
  1. Spend more time with followers
  2. Organize social activities outside work
  3. Transfer troublesome followers out of your team
  4. Raise morale by obtaining more rewards for your followers
- To change the degree of task structure,
  1. Request tasks with which you are familiar so you will have more structure or reduce structure by asking for novel tasks
  2. Ask for clear instructions or get training to learn the task better
  3. Develop your own step-by-step procedures and records to increase structure
  4. Include more followers in the discussion
- To change your power,
  1. Gain more power by improving your relationship with your followers
  2. Develop expertise in your job
  3. Request increases in authority from your boss
  4. Gain access to resources to use as rewards

Source: F. E. Fiedler and M. M. Chemers, *Improving Leadership Effectiveness: The Leaders Match Concept,* 2d ed. (New York: Wiley, 1984). Adapted by permission of John Wiley & Sons, Inc.

The Fiedler model has several practical implications for managers:

1. Leaders must *understand their style and the situation* to predict how effective they will be.
2. Leaders should focus on *changing the situation* to match their style instead of trying to change how they act.
3. *Good relationship with followers* is very important to a leader's ability to lead and can compensate for lack of power.
4. Leaders can compensate for ambiguity of a task by getting *training* and experience.

Fiedler's focus on changing the situation rather than the leader is unique to his model. The normative decision model that we consider next assumes that the leader can change styles depending on the situation.

Summary Point 9.2   What Is Fiedler's Contingency Model?

- Leadership effectiveness is contingent on the match between the leader's style and the requirements of situation.
- Leader style is determined by the LPC as being either task or relationship motivated.
- The situation is defined in terms of the control it provides the leader through leader-member relations, task structure, and position power.

- Task-motivated leaders are most effective in high- and low-control situations; relationship-motivated leaders are most effective in moderate-control situations.
- The focus of leadership training should be for the leader to learn to change the situation to fit his or her style.

The Normative Decision Model

Should a leader make decisions alone or involve followers? What factors do leaders need to consider to determine how to make decisions? The Normative Decision model, developed by leadership researchers Victor Vroom, Philip Yetton, and Arthur Jago, answers these questions.[33] Vroom's model is a contingency approach to leadership that focuses on leadership decision making rather than general leadership style. It is called "Normative" because it recommends that leaders adopt certain leader styles based on the prescriptions of the model.

Like Fiedler, Vroom recommends matching the leader and the situational requirements. However, the two differ on several points. First, the Normative model is limited to decision making rather than general leadership. Second, contrary to the Fiedler model, it assumes that leaders can adopt different decision-making styles as needed. Finally, the model is concerned mostly with quality of the decision rather than group performance.

The Normative Decision model relies on two basic group dynamic principles: (1) groups are wasteful and inefficient, and (2) participation in decision making leads to commitment. The model proposes that the leader needs to adjust his or her decision style depending on the importance that the decision be high quality and the likelihood that employees will accept the decision.

First, we explore the decision styles of the Normative Decision model. Second, we look at the contingency factors of the model. Then we see how the combination of decision-making style and contingency factors applies to the model. Finally, we explore the model's practical implications.

Leader's Decision Styles   The Normative Decision model identifies three general decision methods that are available to leaders. The first method is **autocratic (A),** in which the leader makes a deci-

Hot ▼ Link

For a discussion of when groups should be used, see chapter 7, pp. 235–39.

Autocratic decision style
A decision style whereby the leader makes a decision with little or no involvement from followers

Table 9.3   DECISION STYLES UNDER
THE NORMATIVE DECISION MODEL OF LEADERSHIP

Decision Style	AI	AII	CI	CII	G
Description	Make unassisted decision	Ask for specific information but make decisions alone	Ask for specific information and ideas from each group member	Ask for information and ideas from whole group	Share information and ideas with group and reach consensus
Who makes the decision	Leader	Leader	Leader	Leader and group	Group

Key: A = Autocratic, C = Consultative, G = Group

Sources: V. H. Vroom and A. G. Jago, *The New Leadership: Managing Participation in Organizations* (Englewood Cliffs, NJ: Prentice Hall, 1988); V. H. Vroom and P. W. Yetton, *Leadership and Decision-Making* (Pittsburgh: University of Pittsburgh Press, 1973).

sion with very little or no involvement from followers. The second decision method is **consultation (C),** in which the leader consults with followers yet retains the final decision-making authority. The third decision method is **group (G).** Here the leader relies on consensus building to solve a problem. The decision styles and their subcategories are summarized in Table 9.3. The leader needs to decide which style to use depending on the situation that the leader and the group face.

Contingency Variables: Defining the Problem   The Normative Decision model focuses on the *quality of the decision* and the *need for acceptance and commitment by followers* as the two central contingency factors. Six additional contingency factors to consider are these: (1) whether the leader has enough relevant information to make a sound decision, (2) whether the problem is structured and clear, (3) the likelihood that followers will accept the leader's decision, (4) whether the employees agree with the organizational goals, (5) whether employees are cohesive, and (6) whether they have enough information to make a decision alone. We describe these eight contingency factors in Table 9.4.

Consultation (C)
A decision style whereby the leader consults with followers but makes the final decision

Group (G)
A decision style whereby the leader relies on group consensus to make the decision

Table 9.4   CONTINGENCY FACTORS
IN THE NORMATIVE DECISION MODEL

Contingency Factor	Question to Ask
Quality requirement (QR)	How important is the quality of the decision?
Commitment requirement (CR)	How important is employee commitment to the implementation of the decision?
Leader information (LI)	Does the leader have enough information to make a high-quality decision?
Structure of the problem (ST)	Is the problem clear and well structured?
Commitment probability (CP)	How likely is employee commitment to the solution if the leader makes the decision alone?
Goal congruence (GC)	Do employees agree with and support organizational goals?
Employee conflict (CO)	Is there conflict among employees over solution?
Subordinate information (SI)	Do employees have enough information to make a high-quality decision?

Sources: V. H. Vroom and A. G. Jago, *The New Leadership: Managing Participation in Organizations* (Englewood Cliffs, NJ: Prentice Hall, 1988); V. H. Vroom and P. W. Yetton, *Leadership and Decision-Making* (Pittsburgh: University of Pittsburgh Press, 1973).

The combination of the eight contingency factors creates different leadership situations. Each situation requires a different decision-making style to ensure that a quality decision is made and implemented by followers within the required time frame.

The Model's Predictions   The Normative Decision model is a decision tree, as shown in Figure 9.2. Leaders ask the series of questions listed in Table 9.4. The questions relate to the contingency factors and should be asked sequentially. By responding "yes" or "no" to each question, managers can determine which decision style(s) are most appropriate for the problem they face.

An autocratic decision-making style is appropriate in the following situations:

- *When the leader has sufficient information to make a decision.* If the leader has sufficient information, use of an autocratic style is usually more efficient. This is especially true in cases where subordinates are cohesive, they agree with the organization's goals, and they are are likely to implement decisions despite a lack of involvement in decision making.
- *When the quality of the decision is not essential.* Generally, it's more efficient to allow the leader to make a decision that does not need to be high quality. No one would want to involve a group to decide where to buy a pack of pencils to restock the office cabinet, for example.
- *When employees do not agree with each other.* If employees cannot agree, a decision might never be made unless the leader takes charge.

FIGURE 9.2
Normative Decision Model

Source: Reprinted from Victor H. Vroom and Philip W. Yetton, *Leadership and Decision Making* (Pittsburgh: University of Pittsburgh Press, 1973), © 1973 by University of Pittsburgh Press.

QR	Quality requirement:	How important is the technical quality of this decision?
CR	Commitment requirement:	How important is subordinate commitment to the decision?
LI	Leader's information:	Do you have sufficient information to make a high-quality decision?
ST	Problem structure:	Is the problem well structured?
CP	Commitment probability:	If you were to make the decision by yourself, is it reasonably certain that your subordinate(s) would be committed to the decision?
GC	Goal congruence:	Do subordinates share the organizational goals to be attained in solving this problem?
CO	Subordinate conflict:	Is conflict among subordinates over preferred solutions likely?
SI	Subordinate information:	Do subordinates have sufficient information to make a high-quality decision?

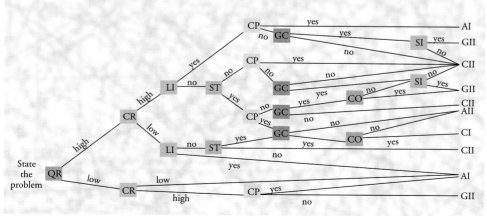

- *When employees do not agree with the goals of the organization.* Even when the leader does not have all the information, he or she needs to make the decision alone when employees are not supportive of organization goals; otherwise, the employees' decision might not benefit the organization.

A consultative style of decision making is appropriate in the following situations:

- When the leader has sufficient information, but the employees demand participation to implement the decision.
- When the leader has insufficient information; employee consultation will help the leader gather more information and also develop employee commitment.
- When the followers generally agree with the goals of the organization.

A group-oriented decision style should be used when the leader does not have all the information, quality is important, and employee commitment is essential.

Evaluation and Application   Research studies have provided support for the Normative Decision model.[34] Managers can become more effective when they follow the model's recommendations regarding which decision style to use. The decision methods are clearly defined and its contingency factors are based on extensive research about group dynamics and participative management.

Some practitioners and theorists contend, however, that the model has two main weaknesses. First, it is too complex to have practical value. Few managers have the time to work their way through the decision tree to conclude which style to use given the situation. Second, the assumption that leaders have the ability to use any of the decision approaches equally well may be flawed. Not all leaders can be autocratic for one decision, consultative for another, and group oriented for still others. Although this mix may constitute an ideal for leadership effectiveness, it may not be possible, given differences in personality and personal style preferences and each person's behavioral range.

The Normative Decision model, when compared to Fiedler's Contingency model, has a narrower focus on leadership decision making. Within that limited focus, the model works well and can be a very helpful tool for leaders. The model offers several practical implications:

- Leaders must *understand the situation* and understand how and when to use the different decision methods.
- *Participation is not always a desirable* leadership style.
- Leaders must pay particular attention to their *followers' needs and reactions* when making a decision.

Summary Point 9.3   **What Is the Normative Decision Model?**

- The model assumes that the most effective leadership decision style depends on the requirements of the situation. Decision style options include autocratic, consultative, and group decision making.
- The situation is defined primarily in terms of the quality requirements and the need for employee acceptance of the decision.

- An autocratic style is most efficient and should be used when the quality requirements are low and acceptance from followers is likely.
- Consensus and group-oriented decision styles should be used when the quality needs are high and employee acceptance is essential.
- The focus of leadership training is to teach the leader to use the different styles and to recognize various situations where they apply.

The Normative Model offers practical and useful recommendations regarding which situational factors leaders must consider while assuming that the leader can learn to change styles based on those factors.

We have so far discussed two of the major contingency views of leadership. Both Fiedler's theory and the Normative model focus on the match between a leader's style and the situation. Although both theories consider many contingency factors, neither considers the leader-follower relationship to be critical. In contrast, the two contingency models we discuss next focus on the relationship between the leaders and the followers as a key contingency factor.[35] Those models are the Path-Goal and the Leader-Member Exchange theories.

Path-Goal Theory

The Path-Goal theory of leadership proposes that the key role of the leader is to clear the paths so that employees can accomplish goals.[36] By doing so, the leader allows employees to fulfill their needs, and as a result, reaches his goals as well. The conceptual bases for Path-Goal theory are the expectancy model of motivation and the research on leader behavior. The expectancy theory suggests that to motivate employees, managers must remove obstacles that weaken the linkages between effort and performance, and performance and outcomes. In Path-Goal theory, the role of the leader is to engage in either initiation of structure or consideration to help strengthen linkages among effort, performance, and outcome, and help motivate and satisfy followers.

The model makes three assumptions. It assumes that the leader can (1) correctly analyze the situation, (2) decide which behaviors are required, and (3) change his or her behavior to match the situation.

Elements and Predictions Two contingency factors used to evaluate the situation are the nature of the task and the characteristics of followers.

- *Nature of the task.* Leaders must consider the degree of structure and clarity of the task. This concept is akin to task structure in Fiedler's model. If the task is new and lacks structure, followers are likely to waste their efforts trying to perform the task because of inexperience and a lack of knowledge. They will feel frustrated and unmotivated. If a task has structure and is familiar, followers may suffer from boredom performing the task.
- *Characteristics of followers.* Leaders must take into account the needs of their followers to be able to remove obstacles. One variable that research identifies as important in Path-Goal theory is the follower's need for challenge. For instance, some employees may need guidance and clear instructions; others like to be challenged and given more autonomy to do their own problem solving. A leader must consider followers' characteristics before choosing the appropriate behavior in a given situation.

Once the leader identifies the situational factors, she must change her leadership behaviors of initiation of structure and consideration to fit the situation. Figure 9.3 presents a general model for the Path-Goal approach.

Path-Goal proposes two general hypotheses. First, when the task is highly structured, unambiguous, or boring, the leader needs to be supportive and considerate to increase employee satisfaction. The leader's consideration and supportive behaviors remove the blocks to employee satisfaction. Second, in an unstructured, ambiguous, or novel task, the leader's structuring behaviors are key. In such situations, the followers need instructions and direction. By providing direction, the leader removes major obstacles to employee motivation and satisfaction.

Hot ▼ Link

For a review of the expectancy model, see chapter 6, pp. 195–96.

Situational Contingencies
• Task structure
• Employee need for autonomy

↓

Leader Behaviors
• Initiation of structure
• Consideration

↓

Leadership Effectiveness
• Employee satisfaction and motivation

FIGURE 9.3
Path-Goal Theory of Leadership

The theory suggests that a leader must assess follower characteristics—such as desire to learn and to be autonomous—and adjust his behavior accordingly.[37] A follower who likes challenges and needs autonomy will not want the leader to be directive, even if the task is unstructured. For that employee, leader structuring may be either irrelevant or detrimental because it may reduce satisfaction.

Limitations and Practical Applications   In spite of several supportive research studies, the research support for Path-Goal theory has been mixed.[38] However, because this theory views the leader as an obstacle remover and motivator, and provides guidelines about when task or relationship behaviors should be used, it can enrich a leader's approach to managing others. Certainly, recognizing the importance of the relationship between leaders and followers will help leaders using a contingency approach. Brian Hall, CEO of Santa Cruz, a California-based financial services company, thinks there has been a major shift in organizations from "task first" to "relationship first." He believes that in the modern work environment, managers and employees need to establish relationships first before getting down to the task.[39]

Some practical implications of Path-Goal theory are these:

- Managers and leaders must primarily play the role of obstacle remover.
- They must pay attention to the needs of followers before they decide whether they need to remove obstacles.
- They must provide minimum guidance to followers who seek challenge.
- They must be supportive and understanding to help motivate those who are working on routine tasks.

Summary Point 9.4   **What Is Path-Goal Theory?**

- The primary role of the leader is to remove the obstacles that are in the followers' path.
- When the task is ambiguous, novel, or unstructured, the leader needs to impose structure.

- When the situation and task are routine and followers are bored, the leader needs to provide consideration and support.

Leader-Member Exchange

Many of us experience leadership, either as leaders or followers, as a personal relationship between a leader and a follower rather than as a group phenomenon. We interact daily with our bosses and forge an individual relationship with them. Similarly, leaders and managers do not have the same relationship with all their followers and employees. Each pair, or dyadic relationship, is different.

Elements and Predictions   This idea is at the core of the Leader-Member Exchange (LMX) theory, also called the Vertical Dyad Linkage model of leadership.[40] The model, presented in Figure 9.4, suggests that leaders establish a one-on-one relationship with each employee. Each relationship varies greatly in terms of the quality of the exchange. In each exchange, the leader and follower establish a role for the follower. Those followers who have a high-quality relationship—the **in-group**—have a rich exchange with mutual trust, liking, and respect. They enjoy the confidence of their leader, who provides them with challenging and interesting assignments. They have a positive halo. Consequently, their errors may be overlooked or attributed to factors outside their control.[41]

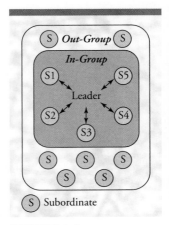

FIGURE 9.4
Leader-Member Exchange Model

In-group
Followers who have a high-quality relationship with the leader

Out-group
Followers who do not have a quality relationship with the leader

Hot ▼ Link

See chapter 5, pp. 161, 167, for a definition of halo effect and self-fulfilling prophecy.

In exchange for the in-group status, that group's role is to work hard, to be loyal, and to support the leader. For the members of the in-group, high-quality exchange is likely to become a self-fulfilling prophecy and lead to high performance and high satisfaction.[42]

The other group of followers—the **out-group**—does not have the same quality relationship with the leader. The leader may perceive its members as less motivated or less competent, interact with them less, and provide them with few opportunities to perform. Their role tends to be limited to that defined by formal job descriptions and there may be little or no expectation of high performance, commitment, or loyalty from them. Regardless of whether the leader's perception is accurate or not, there is a good chance that members of the out-group will live up, or down, to the leader's expectations.

As an example of an out-group management team, consider the case of John R. Walter, who was the president of AT&T and in line to succeed its CEO, Robert Allen. Apparently Walter became so popular with the employees that Robert Allen changed his mind and decided not to support him for the CEO position. He even convinced the AT&T board to withdraw its support of Walter.[43]

According to the LMX model, the relationship between the leader and each follower is formed early and has several stages. Development of the leader-follower relationship starts with an initial stage of testing and assessment for both the leader and the subordinate.[44] In some cases, the initial assessment will earn the subordinate a chance to be in the in-group. In some instances, it will not.

The second stage of the relationship exists only for those selected to be in the in-group. In this stage the leader and subordinates develop mutual trust and respect and work toward a third stage of mutual commitment. This third stage involves an exchange in which there is an intense emotional bond between the leader and the followers and a total commitment to the leader's vision. Given that LMX addresses interpersonal relationships between the leader and followers, it is not surprising that cultural differences affect those relationships.

Effects of National and Ethnic Culture on Leader-Member Exchange   Culture can have a profound effect on who is and who is not part of the leader's in-group. In the United States and other individualist, ascriptive cultures such as Australia, the focus is first on individual competence and performance. As a result, formal human resource policies, procedures, and day-to-day personnel practices focus on fairness, on equal opportunity, and on hiring those who are most qualified for the jobs based on their personal competence. Similarly, in an individualistic culture, people believe that it is fair and appropriate for a leader to pick his in-group members based on their competence and contribution to the organization. Anything else would be deemed favoritism, nepotism, or in some cases illegal discrimination.

The concepts of nepotism and favoritism are unusual and irrelevant in collectivist cultures where loyalty to one's village, clan, or family is the primary concern. Managers hire people they know or those who are recommended by others they know. Skills and competence are secondary to such personal recommendations. In Hong Kong and Malaysia, a leader is obligated to take care of his own people first. In many Middle Eastern countries, including various Arab countries and non-Arab ones such as Afghanistan and Iran, a leader surrounds himself with family and clan members who are loyal and who can be trusted. Doing otherwise would be disloyal to one's community and considered foolish. A wise leader would not allow strangers into the in-group, no matter how competent and qualified they were. Outsiders are hired to help the organization, but access to the in-group is based on community factors.

Limitations and Applications of the Leader-Member Exchange Model   In spite of its strong intuitive appeal, the LMX model needs clarification on a number of points. For instance, the factors that lead to the development of an in-group or an out-group relationship need more attention. There is little information regarding the desirability of having the two groups, or the conditions under which followers move from one group to the other. There are also many cultural factors that are likely to determine who belongs to the in-group; these have not been fully explored. Furthermore, the impact of the leader's perceptual biases has also not been fully clarified.[45]

Overall, LMX has not yet enjoyed extensive empirical research, although there appears to be a renewed interest in the model. However, practitioners appreciate its intuitive appeal—most if not all have experienced the feeling of being part of either the in-group or the out-group. Leaders who take the time to identify their in-group and out-group can focus on the different relationships and membership selection. By examining these relationships, leaders may be better able to assess accurately the contribution each individual makes to the organization.

The development of an individual exchange with each employee is a natural part of any interaction. Such a situation can be highly positive for an organization, allowing for the identification of competent individuals and assuring that they achieve organizational goals. However, the creation of in-groups and out-groups can also be highly detrimental. The key issue is the basis used to form such relationships. Although LMX research suggests that personal compatibility and employee ability are the basis for selection, organizational reality does not always match theory.[46] Leaders have excluded many highly competent and able employees from their in-group based on personal dislike or organizational politics. After all, leaders are subject to human error just like the rest of us.

Managers can apply the LMX model in five ways:

- Pick in-group members based on competence and contribution to the organization.
- Regularly evaluate the criteria for in- and out-group membership.
- Assign tasks to followers who have the most applicable skills, regardless of group membership.
- Maintain fluid groups in which movement in and out is possible.
- Whenever possible, avoid highly differentiated in- and out-groups.

We have explored four contingency models of leadership that assume leaders are important to group and organizational effectiveness. But are leaders always necessary? This is the question addressed by the substitutes for leadership that we address next.

Summary Point 9.5   **What Is Leader-Member Exchange?**

- Leadership is considered a personal relationship and exchange between the leader and each follower.
- Some followers who are in the leader's in-group and enjoy the leader's attention are expected and likely to perform well.

- Some followers who are in the leader's out-group are ignored and are expected and likely to perform poorly.
- In- and out-groups can be useful and productive when they are based on performance rather than personal factors.
- Cultural differences affect the criteria for being in the in- or out-group.

Substitutes for Leadership

In some situations, a relationship with a leader is not required to satisfy followers' needs. Self-managed teams, for instance, work independently and lead themselves. In addition, there are various aspects of the work environment, such as a well-designed job or a cohesive team, that allow employees to achieve their goals without having to interact with their leader.

The model of substitutes for leadership identifies situations that substitute for or neutralize leader behavior. The theory relies on initiation of structure and consideration as the major leader behaviors.[47]

Team Challenge

WHAT IS THE BEST WAY TO LEAD TEAMS?

The majority of the leadership models currently in use apply to relatively traditional organizational structures, so they do not apply well to the flat structure of team-based organizations. However, the concept of leadership is changing because the use of teams is on the rise. The biggest change? The leader's role is shifting from providing structure, command, and control to facilitating. Two examples of the leader-as-facilitator approach are proposed by P. Block in his book *Stewardship* and by J. Belasco and R. C. Stayer in their book *Flight of the Buffalo.*[a] These authors suggest that the primary role of leaders in a team environment is to get out of the way. Leaders should encourage followers to develop their own solutions, provide followers with resources and assistance as needed, and allow them to implement solutions.

One of the biggest challenges leaders face in team-based organizations is being able to let go. Having been trained in traditional leadership models and methods, many leaders feel useless and irrelevant in the team structure. The ability to redefine and adjust to the team leadership environment is one of the major tasks of today's leaders and managers. Sara Levinson, president of NFL Properties, explains how her management style fits well with what her management team needs. "They agree that my emphasis on group communication, soliciting their ideas and opinions, is a major characteristic of my management style. They also say it's why they think I'm a good leader."[b]

a. P. Block, *Stewardship: Choosing Service over Self-Interest* (San Francisco: Berret-Koehler, 1993); J. Belasco and R. C. Stayer, *Flight of the Buffalo: Soaring to Excellence, Learning to Let Employees Lead* (New York: Warner Books, 1993).

b. A. Muoio, "Women and Men, Work and Power," *Fast Company* (February–March 1998): 80.

Substitutes *Situational or individual factors that replace the leader's actions*

Neutralizers *Situations and factors that make the leader's actions irrelevant*

Substitutes and Neutralizers   The substitutes-for-leadership theory proposes that various organizational, task, and employee characteristics can act as *substitutes* or *neutralizers* for traditional leadership behaviors. **Substitutes** are situational or individual factors that replace the leader's actions. **Neutralizers** are situations and factors that make the leader's actions irrelevant. Generally, if followers have access to clear information about the task and its requirements because of their own experience or that of their co-workers, or through information available in manuals and training, they will not need the leader to structure the task. Similarly, when support and empathy are not needed or are available through other sources such as co-workers, the employees will not seek or need the leader's consideration behaviors. The other sources act as substitutes for the leader's actions.

Consider the case of computer programmers who often change jobs by doing the same type of programming for different employers. These programmers know their trade and once a leader explains what needs to be programmed, they require no other direction. As two respected experts on the future of organizations, Stan Davis and Christopher Meyer, explain, "Programmers in Silicon Valley identify much more strongly with what they do than with their employers, just as doctors and lawyers make their chief allegiance to their profession."[48] They depend on their teams or their profession to provide them with direction. As a result, these programmers are loyal to their profession and not to the organization where they work or its leaders. Their profession substitutes for leadership.

Neutralizers can include a leader's lack of power or a corporate culture that prevents leader and employee interaction. If a leader lacks the power to deliver outcomes to followers, the employees will disregard the leader's actions. Similarly, a leader will have no effect on followers if he or she tries to but cannot engage in consideration or structuring behaviors because of a rigid organizational culture. Other neutralizers include the geographic distance between leaders and followers or an indifference to the rewards the organization offers. Table 9.5 identifies situations where substitutes and neutralizers may work.

For instance, MBA students from some of the most prestigious business schools such as Harvard and Wharton used to accept positions in the major consulting firms like McKinsey long before they graduated. However, the long hours required to serve the firm's clients, the amount of travel, and no prospect of stock ownership have taken their toll. Many high-powered MBAs are leaving their high-paying consulting jobs.

The new crop of MBAs is shunning consulting jobs, no matter how well they pay, and accepting positions in technology companies instead. Andrew Adams, the director of career development at Wharton School of the University of Pennsylvania, explains: "For a 30-year-old who has lived through a pretty robust economy, that offer from McKinsey wasn't the hardest thing in the world to get, compared with an offer from Silicon Valley. And he could get a piece of a company that will be worth hundreds of millions of dollars."[49]

The indifference to the reward the consulting firms provide is neutralizing the actions of the leaders who want to keep the best and the brightest MBAs in their companies. "Firms want people of a certain pedigree so they can bill the rates they do," explains Karen Dowd, of Brecker & Merryman, a New York career consulting organization.[50]

Limitations and Applications of the Substitutes-for-Leadership Model   The leadership substitute model has not been extensively tested so its validity and applicability are still in question. Also, the nature

Table 9.5   LEADERSHIP SUBSTITUTES AND NEUTRALIZERS

Substitutes or Neutralizers	Consideration	Structuring
Follower Characteristics		
1. Experience and training		Substitute
2. Professionalism	Substitute	Substitute
3. Lack of value for goals	Neutralizer	Neutralizer
Task Characteristics		
1. Unambiguous tasks		Substitute
2. Direct feedback from task		Substitute
3. Challenging task	Substitute	
Organizational Characteristics		
1. Cohesive team	Substitute	Substitute
2. Leader's lack of power	Neutralizer	Neutralizer
3. Standardization and formalization		Subsitute
4. Organizational rigidity		Neutralizer
5. Physical distance between leaders and followers	Neutralizer	Neutralizer

Source: S. Kerr and J. M. Jermier, "Substitutes for Leadership: Their Meaning and Measurement," *Organizational Behavior and Human Performance* 22 (1978): 375–403.

of various substitutes and neutralizers and the situations to which they apply need further clarification because they are not well defined. Finally, the few studies of the model conducted in non-U.S. cultures have not supported the model's conclusions.[51]

However, like the LMX, the leadership substitutes model is intuitively appealing and addresses processes not considered by other models. Namely, it questions the need for leadership in some situations and points out the difficulty of providing effective leadership when many substitutes and neutralizers exist. In addition, leaders should consider using substitutes if they help the organization achieve its goals more effectively.

Whether substitutes will be beneficial or detrimental depends on the culture, strategy, and goals of an organization and on a specific leader's personality. Some control-oriented leaders, or leaders in organizations with traditional structures and hierarchies, may perceive substitutes as a loss of control and authority. For organizations with a relatively flat structure and those that rely on teams, substitutes can be beneficial. A self-managed team is one substitute for leadership. If the team is designed correctly and receives the support it needs from the organization, it can succeed.[52]

Leaders who use substitutes judiciously can free their time for other activities, such as strategic planning or relationship building with outside stakeholders while still allowing the organization to achieve its objectives. Third, the model suggests that leaders must learn to change the situation by setting up or removing substitutes and avoiding neutralizers. The focus on the leadership situation is similar to Fiedler's Contingency model.

Some practical applications of the substitutes-for-leadership model follow:

- Leaders must learn to recognize the presence of substitutes and neutralizers.
- They must encourage the development of substitutes and avoid neutralizers whenever possible to encourage employees to take responsibility and free their time for more strategic activities.
- To be able to develop substitutes, leaders must learn to change the situation.

Summary Point 9.6   **What Is the Substitutes-for-Leadership Theory?**

- Factors such as training, experience, and clear tasks act as a substitute for the leader's task-oriented behaviors.
- Factors such as a cohesive work team, professionalism of employees, and a challenging task can substitute for relationship-oriented behavior.

- Factors such as the leader's lack of power can make leadership irrelevant.
- Leaders and organizations can use knowledge of substitutes and neutralizers to reduce the need for leadership or strengthen the role of the leader.

Contingency-based models have dominated OB leadership research for nearly 40 years. These models all suggest that there is no one best way to lead. What works depends on the situation. Each of the models we explored defines the situational factors differently, although task structure and group cohesion appear in all of them. Table 9.6 summarizes the similarities and differences among the contingency models. Most models focus on the match between leadership styles and the situation. Fiedler considers the leader's style relatively stable and recommends that leaders work to change their situation. The other models recommend that leaders change their styles to match the situation.

In the past few years, OB researchers have developed new approaches to leadership that are based on the role of leaders in changing organizations. We investigate three of those theories next.

Table 9.6   COMPARISON OF CONTINGENCY MODELS OF LEADERSHIP

	Leader Characteristic	Follower Characteristic	Task	Other Factors	Effectiveness Criteria
Fiedler's Contingency model	LPC based on motivation; not changeable	Group cohesion	Task structure	Position power	Group performance
Normative Decision model	Decision-making style; can be changed	Group cohesion	Available information	Agreement with goals Time	Quality of the decision
Path-Goal theory	Leader behavior; can be changed	Individual followers need to grow	Clarity and routineness of task		Follower satisfaction and motivation
Leader-Member Exchange					Quality of relationship with followers
Substitutes	Leader behavior; can be changed	Group cohesion	Clarity of task; availability of information	Organization culture, structure, and processes	Need for leader

 CHANGE-ORIENTED LEADERSHIP

For some, the concept of leadership conjures up images of political and organizational leaders who accomplish impossible feats. When people are asked to name leaders, Mahatma Ghandi, John F. Kennedy, Martin Luther King, and Margaret Thatcher are often mentioned. These leaders and others like them exude confidence and engender extreme emotional responses in their followers. These charismatic leaders convince followers to undertake major changes that are sometimes revolutionary. Similarly, in business organizations some leaders energize employees. Remember John R. Walter, the former president of AT&T? He was very popular in the company, especially when compared to Robert Allen, the CEO. "He is energetic, he has charisma; he takes charge," said an AT&T executive about Walter. "People here loved John and hated Allen," explained an executive recruiter close to the company.[53]

As we know, many businesses have perceived a need for dramatic change in the way they function because of factors such as global competition and technology. Because the rate of organizational change has skyrocketed, leadership scholars have begun to research the role of the leader in creating and sustaining major organizational change. Although the contingency concept still applies, the models we examine concentrate on how leaders manage change. We explore three change-oriented theories: charismatic leadership, transformational and transactional leadership, and exemplary leadership.

Charismatic Leadership: A Relationship Between Leaders and Followers

In the early 1920s, philosopher and sociologist Max Weber introduced the concept of charisma in leadership theory. **Charisma** is the ability to appeal to others' emotions and form profound and powerful bonds.[54] Only recently have OB researchers considered charisma in the scientific study of leadership.[55] One reason for examining charisma in leadership research is the assumption that leadership involves a relationship between the leader and the followers,

Charisma
The ability to appeal to others' emotions and form profound and powerful bonds

not just an analysis of the leader's traits and personal characteristics. Charismatic leaders forge a strong relationship with followers, acting as role models and heroes. Let's examine the characteristics of charismatic leaders, their followers, and the situational requirements for charismatic leadership, including cultural factors.

Charismatic Leaders and Their Followers   As we have defined it, charisma is a leader's ability to relate to others. However, this ability depends in large part on the followers. Consider that not all of us agree on who is charismatic. To cult followers, their leader has tremendous charisma. Those of us outside the cult wonder where the magic is. Hitler had a charismatic hold on millions of Germans in the 1930s and 1940s. In spite of the impact of his power, he appears hideous to many of us. To understand charisma, one must understand the leader, the followers, and the leadership situation.

The Leader   Leaders identified as charismatic have the following common personality and behavioral characteristics:

- High degree of confidence
- Strong conviction in the correctness of ideas
- High energy, enthusiasm, and expressiveness
- Excellent communication skills
- Role-modeling and image-building skills

Although many of the characteristics—such as self-confidence, energy, and communication—are generally related to all leaders, the combination of the previous characteristics is what defines the charismatic leader.

Two dominant characteristics of charismatic leaders are self-confidence in their own abilities and a strong conviction in the correctness of their beliefs and actions.[56] Steve Case, the 39-year-old CEO of America Online (AOL), shows both self-confidence and strong conviction in his beliefs. He has the vision that everyone likes to sit at home and be connected to

AnSan su Kyi, leader of the political resistance in Myanmar, has left an indelible mark on her followers. Her charismatic leadership energizes thousands. Although business leaders rarely wield such power, they are also able to accomplish considerable change in their organizations and industries.

the world through a computer. He made others believe in his vision and the result is a cyber-space company that dominates the airwaves. Even when the company had just started, Case believed that he would succeed. "In a little company everybody's got to believe. But there needs to be somebody who believes no matter what. That was Steve. Steve believed from the first day that this was going to be a big deal," explained Marc Seriff, MIT graduate and AOL's first head of technology.[57]

Other examples include GE's president Jack Welch's insistence on overhauling his well-established and sometimes stodgy corporation by keeping only those units that were number one or two in their industries as part of the GE family. The self-confidence is further associ-ated with lack of internal conflict. Where noncharismatic leaders doubt themselves in the face of failure and criticism, the charismatic leaders know that they are right and project that confidence.

The third characteristic of charismatic leaders is high energy. Their enthusiasm about their ideas and actions, their expressiveness, along with their use of nonverbal cues lend dra-matic support to the verbal message, which they deliver with considerable skill. Additionally, charismatic leaders have exceptional articulation and communication skills that allow them to communicate both the content of their ideas and their excitement about them to subordi-nates. Steve Case is both extremely energetic and skilled in communicating his ideas to the members of his organization.[58]

Finally, charismatic leaders carefully craft their message and present themselves as role models to their followers. They "walk their talk," whether it is through the self-sacrifice they demand of their followers (such as Nelson Mandela, who spent many years in jail, or Su Kyi, who has been under house arrest), or the self-control they demonstrate (for example, the peaceful civil disobedience modeled by Martin Luther King). The fact that Andy Grove, the chairman of Intel, works in a very small cubicle is an example of role modeling for employees of that firm. Hatim Tyabji, president and CEO of Verifone Inc. of Redwood City, California, states: "The first principle of leadership is authenticity: 'Watch what I do, not what I say.' Leadership requires moral authority. You can't have moral authority if you behave differently from your people. If you want your people to be frugal, then don't spend money on perks designed to make your life more comfortable."[59]

The process of role modeling can also be symbolic. PepsiCo's CEO, Roger A. Enrico, decided to forgo his $900,000 salary in 1998 and asked PepsiCo's board to spend the money on scholarships for employees' children. He stated in a memo to the employees: "At a com-pany like PepsiCo, everyone can make a difference, but in my opinion nobody is more impor-tant than the thousands of men and women who make, move and sell our products. So I decided to do something personal as a way to say thanks to our often unsung heroes."[60] Whether actual or symbolic, the role modeling and the powerful verbal message contribute to the enhanced image of the leader. Many cult leaders make use of all these behaviors to create a powerful and self-perpetuating mystique that strengthens their relationship with and their hold on followers.

Charismatic leaders are masterful impression managers.[61] They surround themselves with dramatic and mystical symbols to enhance further the mystique of the leader as a larger-than-life figure. John F. Kennedy developed the image of Camelot.[62] Business leaders use equally effective symbols to get closer to their followers. Steve Case wears khaki pants and polo shirts and is known by his first name throughout AOL, for instance. "Nothing about him says media Mogul—he . . . lunches on turkey sandwiches and Sun Chips, and has the boyish good looks of an aging fraternity brother."[63]

The Followers Without both the leader and the follower characteristics, there cannot be a charismatic leader. Without the frenzied followers, Hitler would not be considered charismatic. The same is true of cult leaders. Even for positive and constructive charismatic leaders such as

Steve Case, the leader of AOL, has many of the characteristics of charismatic leaders, which he uses to inspire his followers to do their best.

Ghandi, followers demonstrate particular characteristics and behaviors. The followers of these leaders have five characteristics:

- High degree of respect and esteem for the leader
- Loyalty and devotion to the leader
- Affection for the leader
- High expectations for success
- Unquestioning obedience

The relationship between charismatic leaders and their followers is highly emotional. First, followers have a high degree of respect and esteem for the charismatic leader. They are devoted and loyal, and they have considerable affection for their leader. The emotional bond leads to the last two characteristics of followers. First, they have high expectations for success that mirror the leader's strong conviction of the correctness of his or her action. Second, because of their affection, respect, and loyalty, followers *obey* the leader without question. They have total confidence in their leader's vision and direction and often follow blindly. These follower characteristics typically develop in certain situations that we consider next.

The Charismatic Situation For charismatic leadership to make an impact, the right situation needs to exist. The four situational requirements that foster the bonding between leader and follower are presented in Table 9.7. The key component is a *crisis situation* in which followers are distressed.[64] The crisis can either be real, as was the case with the pre-war German economic crisis of the 1930s, or the leader may create it, as is the case with many cult leaders who predict Armageddon and the end of the world. Although less dramatic, intense competition, dire financial situations, and the risk of plant closing are examples of crisis in business organizations.

Because of the sense of crisis, followers perceive a need for change. This perception is the second situational requirement. Third, because the followers have accepted the need for

Table 9.7   SITUATIONAL REQUIREMENTS
OF CHARISMATIC LEADERSHIP

Situation	Description and Example
• Sense of distress or crisis	A feeling that survival is threatened. For example, in case of intense competition, threat of bankruptcy or layoffs, or risk of plant closing.
• Perceived need for change	Realization that existing state of affairs is not effective. For example, accepting the need for layoffs to keep business afloat.
• Opportunity to propose new goals and ideas	Because the need for change is accepted, leader has a chance to propose change—for example, proposing a new vision for the enterprise.
• Availability of dramatic symbols	Using symbolic actions to describe situation. For example, top leader and managers accept a salary cut.

change, the charismatic leader has the opportunity to propose new goals and ideas. The leader promises a new vision, radical solutions, and a break from the unwanted values of the past.[65] These goals may have been previously unacceptable but are now agreed to because of the sense of crisis. Finally, the development of charismatic leadership requires the availability of dramatic symbols. The business leader may announce that she will not be getting a raise, or that she is investing her own money in the company. The luxurious executive office may be closed and managers moved to the shop floor.

In the crisis situation, the leader's high confidence in her actions motivates the followers and creates a self-fulfilling prophecy. The more confident the leader, the more motivated the followers will be. The followers, then, carry out the leader's wishes with conviction. Such motivation and hard work increase the chances of success, which provides further proof of the leader's vision for the future.

Consider the case of Howard Charney, the charismatic 47-year-old CEO of Grand Junction Networks, a fast-growing producer of digital switches in Fremont, California. By selling the company to Cisco Systems in 1995, he made himself and about half his employees millionaires. Debra Pelsma, the company's senior parts buyer and planner, met Charney in the summer of 1993 when he was at 3Com. "He was so optimistic, so sincere, so genuine. I decided I'd follow him anywhere."[66] "He is the kind of guy people walk through walls for," says Kathryn Gould, a venture capitalist and the lead investor in Grand Junction Networks.[67]

Charney built the company by putting together a talented team and energizing its members to work hard and believe in the vision. For instance, Charney asked Margot Gangola to quit her job, join the company, and be on the engineering team. She states: "Howard had a great reputation, but the company seemed too small, too high risk." Eventually, she agreed to join the organization. "I knew I'd live through long days and nights for at least 18 months, just to get up and running. But we had an amazing team."[68] The vision that Charney had for Grand Junction was accomplished through the hard work of these talented individuals. And more than 40 of them became millionaires when the company was purchased by Cisco Systems.

Cultural Factors Culture is a situational variable that affects the emergence of charismatic leaders, but it has received little attention. Some evidence suggests, however, that certain cultural traditions make it more likely for charismatic leadership to occur.[69] Specifically, the research suggests that cultures with a strong tradition of prophetic salvation are more amenable to charismatic leadership. For instance, the Judeo-Christian and Islamic beliefs in the coming of a savior create fertile grounds for charismatic leaders. Prophets, by definition, are charismatic saviors.

Consider the recent rise of Islamic fundamentalism, which is typically tied to a prophetic spiritual leader. The rise of Khomeini in Iran, for instance, has all the elements of a typical charismatic relationship, including leader and follower characteristics, the intense and calculated image management on the part of the leader, and the sense of crisis due to the political climate of Iran in the late 1970s.

Other cultures do not have such prophetic traditions. Chinese history, for example, has few strong charismatic figures with Mao Zedung being one of the exceptions. Periods of crisis and change have certainly occurred. However, it appears that the relationship between leaders and followers is based more on the social hierarchy and need for order, as is prescribed in the Confucian tradition, than on the intense emotional charismatic bonds that exist in Judeo-Christian and Islamic religions.

Limitations and Applications   The study of charismatic leadership is interesting and exciting. It is often difficult, however, to study the processes associated with charismatic leadership as they occur and many of our more detailed case studies continue to focus on political and historical figures. We therefore continue to rely on anecdotal rather than rigorous scientific analysis. In spite of the limited amount of scientific study, theories of charismatic leadership have several practical applications for today's business leaders:

- Leaders must have passion for their beliefs and actions.
- Developing a close bond with followers can be a strong motivating factor.
- Leaders must develop their articulation skills to be able to communicate their message clearly and passionately.

As in the social and political arenas, charismatic leadership in business organizations emerges in times of crisis. It is no coincidence that the concept of charismatic leadership has dominated U.S. academic and popular views of leadership for the past decade. The need to revitalize industrial, educational, health, and governmental institutions has created two of the essential elements for charismatic leadership: a sense of crisis and a perceived need for change. The concept of charisma and its emergence in crisis is the basis for the transformational leadership model, which we discuss next.

A QUESTION OF ETHICS

| *Unethical Charismatic Leadership* | The ability to influence followers strongly and to convince them to perform tasks that they never before thought possible is the basic element of charismatic leadership. In your opinion, what factors should guide a charismatic leader who wants to lead in an ethical manner? |

Summary Point 9.7   **What Is Charismatic Leadership?**

- Charismatic leadership is a relationship and a strong emotional bond between leaders and followers.
- Charismatic leaders display self-confidence, strong convictions, high energy, excellent communication skills, and active role modeling and image building.
- Followers of charismatic leaders have high respect, esteem, loyalty, devotion, and affection for the leader.

They also have high expectations of success and display unquestioning obedience.
- Charismatic leadership most often develops in situations of real or perceived crisis when there is perceived need for change and opportunity to propose new ideas; dramatic symbols are also frequently available.

Transformational Leadership

Transformational leadership theory suggests that leaders engage in two general sets of activities. One set includes **transactional leadership**, the day-to-day leadership activities of taking care of tasks and motivating followers. These activities are transactional because they focus on a contract, exchange, or transaction between the leaders and followers. Followers perform in exchange for the direction, support, rewards, and other activities the leaders provide.

The second set of leadership activities deals with planning and implementing major changes in organizations. These activities are **transformational leadership** because their goal is to transform organizations. Transformational leadership explains how some leaders succeed in achieving large-scale change in organizations, thereby allowing others to learn how to manage change successfully.[70] We next contrast transactional and transformational leadership and consider the elements of transformational leadership.

Transactional Leadership Transactional leadership deals with routine activities necessary to get the job done. These include the initiation of structure and consideration behaviors we presented earlier. The majority of the models we discussed in this chapter, such as Fiedler's Contingency model, the Normative Decision model, and the Path-Goal model fall in this category.

Transactional leadership is based on the concept of exchange between leaders and followers. The leader provides followers with direction, resources, rewards, and so forth in exchange for motivation, productivity, and effective task accomplishment. This exchange involves providing the **contingency rewards**—rewards based on or contingent on performance—that are a major component of motivation and performance. We teach leaders to provide contingent rewards to reinforce appropriate behaviors and discourage inappropriate ones. When well managed, contingent rewards can be highly satisfying and beneficial to the leader, his followers, and the organization.

Another type of transactional relationship is *management by exception* (MBE), which is popular with many managers. Leaders using **management by exception** interact with followers and intervene in their work only when things go wrong. There is little goal setting, positive reinforcement, or encouragement; the leader relies almost exclusively on discipline and punishment. Unfortunately, some managers confuse this "I only interfere when employees make a mistake" style with empowerment. After all, followers have the freedom to do as they please—until they make a mistake. However, while empowerment requires a supportive, positive environment in which risk taking is encouraged, MBE does not create this type of environment because the focus is on correction and punishment rather than positive performance management and motivation. As a result, MBE leads to employee dissatisfaction and low performance.

In times of change, transactional leadership is ineffective. Transactional relationships can lead to high performance, but transactional contracts do not inspire followers to aim for excellence, nor do they energize people to take on challenging tasks.[71] Rather, they focus on short-term immediate outcomes. How then are major organizational changes achieved? The answer is through transformational leadership.

Transformational Leadership Many current leadership scholars and practitioners have proposed that what U.S. organizations need is not only basic transactional leadership but also leadership that inspires followers and enables them to enact revolutionary change.[72] The three factors of transformational leadership presented in Figure 9.5 are charisma and inspiration, intellectual stimulation, and individual consideration.

Charisma and Inspiration.   Charisma, one of the three central factors of transformational leadership, leads to an intense emotional bond between leaders and followers. The result is loyalty and trust in the leader and emulation of the leader. Followers then are inspired to implement the leader's vision. The followers' strong loyalty, respect, and inspiration pave the way for major orga-

Transactional leadership
Leadership activities that involve an exchange between leader and follower and deal with day-to-day leadership activities of taking care of task and motivating followers

Transformational leadership
Leadership activities that deal with planning and implementing major changes in organizations and aim to transform organizations

Hot ▼ Link

For a discussion of rewards, motivation, and performance, see chapter 6, pp. 189–227.

Contingency rewards
Rewards contingent upon performance

Management by exception
Leadership style whereby the leader only interacts with followers or intervenes when things go wrong

Hot ▼ Link

See the consequences of punishment in chapter 6, p. 214.

FIGURE 9.5
Transformational Leadership Factors

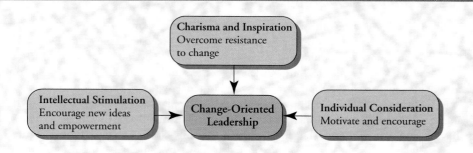

nizational change. The earlier example of Howard Charney, the CEO of Grand Junction Networks, illustrates how the leader's charisma inspires followers to accomplish visionary goals.

Intellectual Stimulation.   The second factor in transformational leadership is the leader's ability to challenge followers to solve problems. The leader and followers question and examine old values and assumptions in search of new answers. By encouraging followers to look at problems and solutions in new ways the leader pushes followers to perform beyond what they previously considered possible. The charismatic bond provides support and encouragement in this endeavor and prevents followers from feeling isolated. Intellectual stimulation has a strong empowering component that reassures followers of their abilities and capabilities, enabling them to search out new solutions.

Individual Consideration.   The last factor of transformational leadership is closely related to the LMX model described earlier. It involves the development of a personal relationship with each follower. Each is treated differently, but equitably; followers receive individual attention that leaves them feeling special, encouraged, and motivated. The leader's individual consideration allows each follower's skills and abilities to be matched to the needs of the organization.

Charisma and inspiration, intellectual stimulation, and individual consideration allow the leader to undertake the necessary transformational changes in an organization. The charismatic emotional bond overcomes psychological and emotional resistance to change. The intellectual stimulation provides new solutions and innovation and empowers followers. The individual relationship between leader and follower encourages followers and provides them with additional motivation (see Figure 9.5).

The transformational leadership model shifts our attention away from small group leadership and from daily leadership activities aimed at group performance and employee satisfaction to large-scale organizational change and performance.

Another key factor in large-scale organizational change and the creation of an organizational vision is exemplary leadership.

Visionary and Exemplary Leadership

Visionary leadership
Leadership theory that emphasizes the leader's role in creating and articulating an inspiring vision for followers

Leadership researchers and practitioners have proposed theories in recent years that center on how the leader's vision and confidence in the followers' abilities can transform organizations.[73] **Visionary leadership** emphasizes the leader's role in creating and articulating an inspiring vision for followers.[74] Having a clear and well-articulated vision is essential in today's dynamic environment. It provides focus and direction that can motivate followers to implement necessary changes.

Lee Kun Hee of Samsung has been able to provide such a vision for his company. His simple vision of "Our dream and Korea's future" energizes and inspires employees at Samsung. His motto of "Best in quality, no matter what" further focuses their attention and motivates them to do their best.

Chris Hassett and his brother are a team of visionary leaders who built Pointcast Inc. in the Silicon Valley. They wanted it to be a state-of-the-art media company, delivering time-sensitive information to specific clients. The entrepreneurs attracted venture capital and succeeded in forming a team of talented individuals to pursue their dream. Jaleh Bisharat, Pointcast's marketing vice president, states the mission of the company this way: "What you know defines how you succeed. That creates pressure on people. We offer tools to relieve that pressure. We help people cope."[75] Pointcast has become one of the major success stories of Silicon Valley in the late 1990s. For visionary leadership to be effective, leaders must not only be able to express and explain their vision clearly; they also must demonstrate it through their actions.

Exemplary leadership underscores the importance of the leader's setting an example for followers. Figure 9.6 outlines the factors in exemplary leadership.[76] Changing organizations requires leaders to be role models for their followers. Leaders have to commit themselves to questioning old beliefs and assumptions if they are to create a new common vision. Through empowerment, encouragement, and proper role modeling, leaders can motivate followers to implement the newly developed vision. The driving force behind a leader's ability to fulfill this commitment is credibility. Earlier we mentioned how Howard Charney's vision and commitment and his credibility empowered his followers to achieve the mission of Grand Junction Networks. Charney states: "What do people come to work for? To be successful. To be appreciated."[77]

Surveys of followers that asked which characteristics they admire and expect most from their leader indicate that honesty, the ability to be forward looking, the capacity to be inspiring, and basic competence are key factors in a leader's credibility.

Like the transformational leadership approach, visionary and exemplary leadership allows us to explain one of the most interesting and visible sides of leadership. Both models let us talk about the interesting leaders—those whom everyone agrees are the "real" leaders. These theories satisfy our need to find and explain heroes. This search—maybe this wish—for heroic leadership seems to be part of the fabric of many cultures. The intuitive appeal of the change-oriented concepts is undeniable. However, many questions remain unanswered.

Limitations and Applications of Change-Oriented Leadership Transformational leadership theory and other change-oriented models have three main limitations. First, measuring the behaviors of transformational leadership or the ability to inspire and enable continues to be a challenge. We rely on anecdotes and case studies that provide rich data but are limited in the reliability or validity necessary for rigorous scientific study. Second, in spite of the theories' emphasis on leader behaviors, it is difficult to see how leaders could learn to be charismatic and inspiring. These qualities seem to be related to personality traits that develop early in life. It may be easy to teach a leader how to provide contingent rewards, but can we teach leaders how to inspire

Exemplary leadership
Leadership theory that underscores the importance of the leader setting an example for followers

Hot ▼ Link

For a discussion of the limits of personality and its behavioral range, see chapter 4, p. 116.

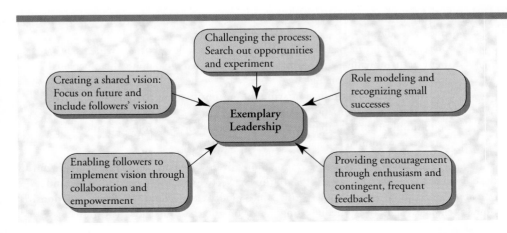

FIGURE 9.6
Exemplary Leadership Factors

Based on J. M. Kouzes and B. Z. Posner, *The Leadership Challenge* (San Francisco: Jossey-Bass, 1995).

CAREER ADVICE
From the Experts

BUILDING CREDIBILITY

Having credibility is essential to being an effective leader. If followers do not believe in your integrity and honesty, you will lose the power to influence them. Here are some tips on building and maintaining your credibility:

- State your position on issues clearly and let people know where you stand.
- Listen to others and respect disagreement and differing opinions.
- Focus on integrating your views with those of your followers.
- Concentrate on building consensus rather than win-lose, even when you are on the winning side.
- Provide frequent honest feedback, both positive and negative.
- Develop your followers and encourage their success.
- Hold yourself and others accountable by practicing what you preach.

Sources: J. M. Kouzes and B. Posner, *Credibility: How Leaders Gain and Lose It, Why People Demand It* (San Francisco: Jossey-Bass, 1993); J. M. Kouzes and B. Posner, *The Leadership Challenge* (San Francisco: Jossey-Bass, 1995).

and challenge followers? The ability to learn such behaviors is probably related to the leader's behavioral range.

The third limitation of transformational leadership and other change-oriented leadership models is their apparent suggestion that there is one best way to lead. None of the theories proposes a contingency view that considers task, organizational, and follower characteristics. Clearly, change-oriented and visionary leadership is needed in times of crisis. However, the same style is likely to be ineffective when an organization needs to stabilize its internal structure and culture. Change-oriented leadership, by definition, fits in times of change, not in all situations.

The major application of change-oriented leadership occurs when leaders provide a challenging vision for their organization. Compared with the contingency theories that deal with day-to-day leadership activities, change-oriented leadership theories address the need for change. Specifically, based on change-oriented theories, business leaders must:

- Keep in mind the importance of providing an overall vision that can inspire followers.
- Understand and manage their relationship with followers to provide each of them with individual attention and guide them in matching their personal needs with organizational goals.
- Be aware of the importance of symbols and positive impression management in creating inspiration and change.
- Be mindful of the fact that they are role models for their followers and maintain their credibility.

Our views of leadership are becoming more diverse and complex. These changes mirror the complexity and diversity of our organizations. Effective leadership depends more and more on the organizational and cultural setting. One model clearly does not fit all situations. In times of change, the leader's role in setting the vision and the course for the future is essential.

Summary Point 9.8   **How Do Leaders Implement Change?**

- Transformational leadership addresses large-scale change in organizations.
- Transactional leadership deals with day-to-day goal setting and exchanges and can be very successful.
- Transformational leadership includes intellectual stimulation of followers, displays of charisma, and individual consideration of followers from the leader.

- Exemplary leadership requires the leader to question old assumptions and practices to develop a new vision.
- Credibility is the basis for a leader's ability to enact major changes.

Meanwhile, leaders must be able to motivate employees on a day-to-day basis to perform in a way that moves the organization toward its goals.

Leadership *in Context*

Leadership is an individual and group phenomenon. We have been considering the role of leaders in clarifying the task for their followers, supporting them, and creating change in organizations. Although these activities are essential to effectiveness, leaders play many other roles. First, top leaders are the ones who define and enact the environment for the organization. They decide which elements are important and which are not. Chris and Greg Hassett defined the specific environment of Pointcast as being in the information delivery media business and not any other business. Their decision is the basis for the organization's mission and strategy and influences all other contextual factors of technology, culture, and structure.

Hot ▼ Link

See the definition of *enactment* in chapter 2, p. 39.

In addition to enacting the environment, the top leaders have responsibility for the initial design and implementation of the mission, goals, and strategy for an organization. We discussed earlier the importance of providing a clear and inspiring vision. It is the leader who must then translate the vision to mission, goals, and eventually strategy and guide the organization in their implementation. At Grand Junction Networks, Charney turned the vision into a specific strategy that his team of engineers and other experts turned into reality.

Perhaps the most central impact of leaders is on the culture of an organization. Organizations come to closely mirror their founders' personality and style. Both Pointcast and Grand Junction Networks' cultures reflect the personality of their leaders. Chris and Greg Hassett are hard driving, innovation driven, and informal. Charney is entrepreneurial, fast changing, and flexible.[78] Founders and other powerful leaders decide what the basic assumptions are and what is valued and what is not. They continue to influence the culture by role modeling desired behaviors, deciding what gets rewarded, selecting other top leaders who fit their vision, and so forth.

Finally, the strategy and culture that the leaders select and encourage are often implemented through the structure of the organization. Much like culture, organizational structure comes to reflect the top leader's style. The control-oriented executive encourages a hierarchical structure; the leader who is more participative develops a flatter organization.[79] Both Pointcast and Grand Junction Networks have flat structures with teams driving their strategy and implementing it.

Although we have focused on the importance of leaders in this chapter, you need to keep in mind that leadership is a group process. There are no leaders without followers. The need for flexibility and responsiveness to the environment suggests that followers are equally as important as leaders to the organization and its goals—if not more so. Leadership is often more diffuse and shared in team-based organizations. Therefore, today's organizations need all their employees to think like leaders. On the one hand, they must understand the business environment, interpret the organization's mission, and implement the goals and strategies. They also must decipher the culture and structure and use them to become more effective. On the other hand, team members must devise their own goals and create and manage their own culture and structure. These activities, traditionally assigned to top leaders and middle managers, are now the responsibility of all employees.

For updated information on the topics in this chapter, Web exercises, links to related Web sites, an on-line study guide, and more, visit our companion Web site at:
http://www.prenhall.com/nahavandi

A Look Back at the

MANAGERIAL CHALLENGE

Samsung

Of his role as chair of Samsung, Lee Kun Hee has said, "I am here to lead our people."[80] Relaxing the hierarchical traditions of chaebol management is only one sign of his visionary and exemplary leadership. He regularly challenges the status quo and has considerable experience in creating a shared vision of the future. For example, the company has instituted a new policy of basing salary increases on merit rather than seniority, another break from chaebol tradition.[81] At a time when Japanese chip-makers dominate the electronics industry, he has aggressively pursued new technology to even the odds. Instead of holding tight to the management reins, he has empowered managers in each company to make their own decisions while following the shared vision of world-class quality.

Lee's leadership has spurred great achievements—but can it catapult Samsung into a market-leading position in the automotive market? The chaebol's unswerving commitment to quality is a distinct advantage, as is its licensing of production technology from Nissan. Another edge is Samsung's electronics know-how, which is important because some 30 percent of automotive parts now involve electronics. Still, Samsung will need to invest an estimated $13 billion in its quest to join the ranks of the world's best automakers.[82] Lee continues to reaffirm his commitment to the automotive strategy. But the next few years will be crucial—and success is far from assured.

■ Point of View Exercises

You're the Manager: As a manager in Samsung's U.S. subsidiary, you know that the engineers you supervise are highly skilled, independent, and competitive. In this situation, how would you apply the contingency factors in the Normative Decision model to a new product decision?

You're the Employee: As an engineer in Samsung's U.S. subsidiary, you know that your manager lacks an engineering background. Under Path-Goal theory, how might your manager's leadership behaviors influence your effectiveness when the task is structured and unambiguous?

SUMMARY OF LEARNING OBJECTIVES

1. **Identify the elements of leadership, highlight the three major approaches to leadership, and explain the role of leadership across cultures.** A leader is a person who influences individuals and groups within an organization, helps them in the establishment of goals, and guides them toward achievement of those goals, thereby allowing them to be effective. The two general requirements of leadership are competence and conformity. Three general approaches to leadership are the trait, behavior, and contingency approaches. What is considered good leadership is strongly determined by cultural factors. Power distance and relationship with others are two of the central cultural values that influence leadership. The achievement/ascriptive dimension of culture also strongly influences what is expected of the leader and how his or her performance is viewed.

2. **Compare and contrast the elements and predictions of the five major contingency approaches to leadership.** The five major contingency approaches to leadership are Fiedler's Contingency model, the Normative Decision model, Path-Goal theory, Leader-Member Exchange, and substitutes for leadership. Fiedler's basic premise is that leadership effectiveness is a function of the match between the leader's style and the leadership situation. The leader's style is determined in terms of task or relationship orientation using the Least Preferred Coworker (LPC) scale. The situation is defined in terms of situational control, which includes leader-member relations, task structure, and position power. The Contingency model focuses on changing the situation rather than the leader's style to maintain their match. The Normative Decision model proposes that the leader needs to adjust his or her decision style depending on the importance of the decision and the likelihood of employee acceptance of that decision.

   When the leader has information and support from the group, the leader can make decisions alone. When employee commitment is needed or the task is complex, the group has to be involved in the decision.

   The Path-Goal theory of leadership proposes that the key role of the leader is to clear the paths for employees so they can accomplish goals. The Leader-Member Exchange (LMX) model suggests that leaders establish a one-on-one relationship with each employee. Those followers who have a high-quality relationship—the in-group—have a rich exchange, with mutual trust, liking, and respect. The other group of followers—the out-group—does not have the same quality of relationship with the leader.

   Substitutes for leadership propose that various organizational, task, and employee characteristics can provide substitutes for the traditional leadership behaviors of consideration and initiation of structure.

3. **Discuss the change-oriented models of leadership including *charismatic, transformational, visionary*, and *exemplary* leadership.** Charismatic leadership involves a relationship and a strong emotional bond between leaders and followers. Charismatic leaders display self-confidence, excellent communication skills, and active impression management, and their followers display devotion, obedience, and high expectations for success. Charismatic leadership most often develops in situations of real or perceived crisis. Transformational leadership is focused on large-scale change in organizations; transactional leadership focuses on day-to-day goal setting and exchanges. Visionary leaders set clear and inspiring visions for their followers. Exemplary leadership requires the leader to question old assumptions and practices to develop a new vision.

KEY TERMS

autocratic (A), p. 310
behavioral approach, p. 302
charisma, p. 321
competence, p. 301
consideration, p. 302
consultation (C), p. 311
contingency rewards, p. 327
exemplary leadership,
   p. 329
group (G), p. 311
in-group, p. 316
initiation of structure, p. 302

leader, p. 301
leader-member relations
   (LMR), p. 307
least preferred co-worker
   (LPC) scale, p. 305
management by exception,
   p. 327
neutralizers, p. 318
out-group, p. 316
position power (PP), p. 307
relationship motivation,
   p. 305

situational control (sit
   con), p. 307
substitutes, p. 318
task motivation, p. 305
task structure (TS), p. 307
trait approach, p. 301
transactional leadership,
   p. 327
transformational leader-
   ship, p. 327
visionary leadership, p. 328

REVIEW QUESTIONS

1. Compare and contrast the three major approaches to leadership. What does each con-tribute to our understanding of leadership?
2. Compare and contrast the contingency models presented in this chapter.
3. Describe the elements of charismatic leadership.
4. Compare and contrast transformational and transactional leadership.
5. List the key elements in change-oriented models of leadership.

DISCUSSION QUESTIONS

1. What role does personality play in leadership? How can the concept be used to increase leadership effectiveness?
2. What are the major strengths and weaknesses of the contingency approaches to leader-ship? Why do they continue to dominate our views of leadership?
3. How can you use each of the contingency models to improve your leadership effectiveness?
4. What explains the appeal of change-oriented leadership? What do these reasons add to our knowledge of leadership?
5. Which of the leadership models presented in the chapter appeals most to you? Why?

▶ SELF-ASSESSMENT 9
Are You a Team Leader?

Rate yourself on each of the following items using the following scale:

1	2	3	4	5
Strongly disagree	Somewhat disagree	Neither agree nor disagree	Somewhat agree	Strongly agree

_____   1. I enjoy helping others get their job done.
_____   2. Managing others is a full-time job in and of itself.
_____   3. I am good at negotiating for resources.

_____   4. People often come to me to help them with interpersonal conflicts.
_____   5. I tend to be uncomfortable when I am not fully involved in the task
           that my group is doing.
_____   6. It is hard for me to provide people with positive feedback.
_____   7. I understand organizational politics well.
_____   8. I get nervous when I do not have expertise at a task that my group
           is performing.
_____   9. An effective leader needs to have full involvement with his or her
           team's activities.
_____   10. I am skilled at goal setting.
_____   **Total**

See Appendix 3 for a scoring key.

Source: A. Nahavandi, *The Art and Science of Leadership* (Upper Saddle River, NJ: Prentice Hall, 1997). Used with permission.

▶ TEAM EXERCISE 9
When Are You Most Effective?

STEP 1: INDIVIDUAL DESCRIPTIONS

Individually, think of one leadership situation in which you were highly effective and one situation in which you were not.

Describe each situation in terms of

- The characteristics of the group and individuals you were leading; the amount of cohesion and support inside the group

- The type of task your group was doing

- Your role as a leader

- Your own actions and behaviors

STEP 2:   GROUP DISCUSSION

Your instructor will assign you to groups. Within your group, discuss the following:
- What was the situational control for every member's individual leadership situation?
- To what extent did the members' effectiveness match the predictions of Fiedler's contingency model?
- How useful were the contingency model's elements in helping you understand the factors that affect your leadership effectiveness? What was helpful? What was missing?

STEP 3: GROUP PRESENTATIONS

Each group makes a five-minute presentation of their observations, conclusions, and recommendations.

Source: A. Nahavandi, *The Art and Science of Leadership* (Upper Saddle River, NJ: Prentice Hall, 1997). Used with permission.

UP CLOSE

▶ Centralizing Purchasing

E. T. Pasco is the western regional manager in charge of purchasing for Health Associates (HA) for western states. She joined HA a month ago with almost ten years of experience in purchasing with one of HA's major competitors. HA hired Pasco in large part to create a centralized companywide purchasing system similar to the one she developed in her previous job.

HA has more than 30 associated health clinics and hospitals in Pasco's region alone. Each of the centers has been operating somewhat independently, without much control from the regional purchasing manager. Several clinics are cooperating with one another and have informal arrangements that allow them to get better prices from suppliers than any one could buying alone. However, the purchasing managers from the larger hospitals in Pasco's region have almost no contact with one another. As a result, they often compete for suppliers and fail to achieve economies of scale that would allow them to save considerable money. In some cases, the purchasing managers rely on totally different suppliers and have managed to obtain advantageous contracts.

In spite of the inefficient system, the local managers, many of whom have been with the company for a long time, are satisfied with their autonomy and have indicated that they do not see the need for a change. However, with the pressure to cut health care costs, the HA board of directors and the group's president have identified purchasing as one area in which savings need to be achieved.

Pasco's appointment was announced through a memo from HA's president. The memo mentioned the need to cut costs in all areas and indicated the need to focus on purchasing as a first step. Pasco has been charged with centralizing purchasing and she is expected to reduce purchasing costs by at least 15 percent within a year.

Pasco has not had time to meet the local purchasing managers who report to her. She has heard from only a few of them, and though they were civil, they were not overly friendly. Having only six months to show the first results, Pasco feels that she needs to start planning and implementing changes as soon as possible. She spends the next few weeks developing a plan for centralizing her region's purchasing. She relies heavily on her previous experience which applies well, given the similarity of the situations. In preparing her plan, she also requests company-specific data from several of the HA managers and includes those in her plan. Once her plan is complete, she forwards it to her boss for feedback. His response is highly enthusiastic and he gives her the go-ahead to continue planning and to start the implementation.

With her boss's support locked up, Pasco prepares a detailed memo for the local purchasing managers and attaches her plan. Although Pasco expects some complaints from the managers, she does not get any. Very encouraged, she assumes that they all liked the plan and have started its first implementation phase, which involves extensive data collection. Two months later, Pasco visits three of the local offices to check on progress. To her surprise, nothing has been done. She calls the other five offices and finds similar situations.

Questions

1. Using concepts of the Normative Decision model, analyze the problem Pasco is facing.
2. If you were Pasco, how would you change your approach now to get results?

THE BIG PICTURE

▶ The Brains and Heart of Southwest Airlines

An unconventional management style and unyielding competitive zeal helped Herb Kelleher build Southwest Airlines from a tiny, cash-strapped start-up in 1971 to a $3.8 billion national airline today. The hard-charging co-founder and CEO became known for his cross-country jaunts to motivate employees with his upbeat humor and good-natured antics. His charisma was so inspirational—and so critical to the airline's success—that Southwest decided to create a culture committee of more than 100 corporate missionaries to keep that spirit burning brightly in every corner of the company.[83]

The CEO's well-honed people skills and keen business sense have certainly kept Southwest soaring since its takeoff in 1971. But if Kelleher is considered the brains of Southwest Airlines, Colleen C. Barrett is clearly the heart. The highest-ranking female airline executive in the United States, she has long been Kelleher's second in command. In addition to supervising marketing, human resources, and eight other divisions, she created the culture committee, dispatching members as needed to help address morale and productivity problems in far-flung locations around the country.[84]

Like Kelleher, Barrett wanted to keep employees motivated and satisfied because she believed that higher workforce loyalty translates into higher performance. To build team spirit and entrepreneurialism—and ward off numbing bureaucracy—Barrett used many simple but effective gestures, including birthday cards, picnics, and ceremonies. But even as she empowered the airline's employees and celebrated their successes, she also managed with a firm hand, firing new recruits when their attitude and behavior did not measure up. "People get this image—fun, different, party place, Herb's half nuts," she explained. "We have to remind them first and foremost, you have to work."[85]

Through the years of working closely together, Kelleher and Barrett have become good complements for the other's leadership styles. Mark Boyer, one of Southwest's pilots, summed up his view of the top managers this way: "I love and adore Herb Kelleher, but when it comes to the daily preservation of who we are, she's the one."[86] And as the airline with the ticker symbol LUV continues to expand beyond 2,200 daily flights, 50 destinations, and 24,000 employees, Barrett and Kelleher will be using both brains and heart to keep the entire workforce loyal and motivated.

Questions

1. In terms of the leadership theories presented in this chapter, how would you describe Herb Kelleher?
2. In terms of the leadership theories presented in this chapter, how would you describe Colleen Barrett?
3. If you worked for Southwest Airlines, how would you react to Kelleher and Barrett as leaders?

NOTES

1. L. Kraar, "Behind Samsung's High-Stakes Push into Cars," *Fortune* (May 12, 1997): 119.
2. Ibid.
3. L. Nakami, "Father Figure," *Asiaweek* (December 12, 1997): 77.
4. Ibid.
5. D. Krech and R. S. Crutchfield, *Theory and Problems of Social Psychology* (New York: McGraw-Hill, 1948).
6. B. M. Bass, *Leadership and Performance Beyond Expectations* (New York: Free Press, 1985); D. C. Cartwright, "Influence, Leadership, Control," in J. G. March (ed.), *Handbook of Organizations* (Skokie, IL: Rand McNally, 1965); D. Katz and R. L. Kahn, *The Social Psychology of Organization* (New York: Wiley, 1966).
7. G. C. Homans, *The Human Group* (New York: Harcourt, Brace, 1950).
8. D. Hock, "What It Means to Lead," *Fast Company* (February–March 1997): 98.
9. A. Muoio, "Women and Men, Work and Power," *Fast Company* (February–March 1998): 71–72.
10. For an extensive review of the history of leadership, see B. M. Bass, *The Handbook of Leadership* (New York: Free Press, 1991).
11. R. G. Lord, C. L. De Vader, and G. M. Alliger, "A Meta-Analysis of the Relation Between Personality Traits and Leadership Perception: An Application of Validity Generalization Procedures," *Journal of Applied Psychology* 8 (1986): 407.
12. S. A. Kirkpatrick and E. A. Locke, "Leadership: Do Traits Matter?" *Academy of Management Executive* 5, no. 2 (1991): 48–60.
13. J. Useem, "The Richest Man You've Never Heard Of," *Inc* 19, no. 12 (September 1997): 42–59.
14. Ibid., 45.
15. Ibid., 58.
16. S. M. Puffer, "Understanding the Bear: A Portrait of Russian Business Leaders," *Academy of Management Executive* 8, no. 1 (1994): 41–54.
17. For research on initiation of structure and consideration, see D. G. Bowers and S. E. Seashores, "Predicting Organizational Effectiveness with a Four-Factor Theory of Leadership," *Administrative Science Quarterly* 11 (1966): 238–63.
18. C. Adams, J. Karp, and L. Ingrassia, "How Calcutta Business Became a Global Player in the Steel Industry," *Wall Street Journal*, March 18, 1998, A1, A8.
19. Ibid.
20. Wind Eagle and Rainbow Hawk, "What It Means to Lead," *Fast Company* (February–March 1997): 99.
21. The LBDQ was developed from a list of nearly 2,000 leadership behaviors. Subsequent analyses narrowed the list to the current LBDQ. See E. A. Fleishman, "The Measurement of Leadership Attitudes in Industry," *Journal of Applied Psychology* 37 (1953): 153–58; A. W. Halpin, "A Factorial Study of the Leader Behavior Descriptions," in R. M. Stogdill and A. E. Coons (eds.), *Leader Behavior: Its Description and Measurement* (Columbus, OH: Ohio State University, Bureau of Business Research, 1957).
22. M. Castaneda and A. Nahavandi, "Link of Manager Behavior to Supervisor Performance Rating and Subordinate Satisfaction," *Group and Organizational Studies* 16, no. 4 (1991): 357–66.
23. J. S. Lublin, "Top Executives' Departure Put Heat on Boards," *Wall Street Journal*, July 18, 1997, B1, B2.
24. See a discussion of executive pay by J. Abramson and C. J. Chipello, "High Pay of CEOs Traveling with Bush Touches a Nerve in Asia," *Wall Street Journal*, December 30, 1991, A8.
25. M. M. Chemers, "An Integrative Theory of Leadership," in M. M. Chemers and R. Ayman (eds.), *Leadership Theory and Research: Perspectives and Directions* (New York: Academic Press, 1993): 293–320.
26. F. E. Fiedler, *A Theory of Leadership Effectiveness* (New York: McGraw-Hill, 1967).
27. For more detailed information on task and relationship motivated styles, see Fiedler, "A Theory of Leadership Effectiveness"; F. E. Fiedler and M. M. Chemers, *Improving Leadership Effectiveness: The Leaders Match Concept*, 2d ed. (New York: Wiley, 1984); M. M. Chemers and G. J. Skrzypek, "An Experimental Test of the Contingency Model of Leadership Effectiveness," *Journal of Personality and Social Psychology* 24 (1972): 172–77; R. Rice, "Psychometric Properties of the Esteem for Least Preferred Coworker (LPC) Scale," *Academy of Management Review* 3 (1978): 106–18; R. Rice, "Construct Validity of the Least Preferred Coworker," *Psychological Bulletin* 85 (1978): 1199–1237.
28. For critiques of the LPC scale, see R. Ayman and M. M. Chemers, "Relationship of Supervisor Behavior Ratings to Work Group Effectiveness and Subordinate Satisfaction Among Iranian Managers," *Journal of Applied Psychology* 68, no. 2 (1983): 338–41; R. Ayman and M. M. Chemers, "The Effect of Leadership Match on Subordinate Satisfaction in Mexican Organizations: Some Moderating Influences of Self-Monitoring," *International Review of Applied Psychology* 40 (1991): 299–314.
29. "What It Means to Lead," *Fast Company* (February–March 1997): 98.
30. Ibid., 99.
31. See C. A. Schreisheim and S. Kerr, "R.I.P. LPC: A Response to Fiedler," in J. G. Hunt and L. L. Larson (eds.), *Leadership: The Cutting Edge* (Carbondale: Southern Illinois University Press, 1977); R. P. Vecchio, "Assessing the Validity of Fiedler's Contingency Model of Leadership Effectiveness: A Closer Look at Strube and Garcia," *Psychological Bulletin* 93 (1983): 404–8; J. R. Kennedy, Jr., "Middle LPC Leaders and the Contingency Model of Leadership Effectiveness," *Organizational Behavior and Human Performance* 30 (1982): 1–14.
32. R. Ayman, M. M. Chemers, and F. E. Fiedler, "The Contingency Model of Leadership Effectiveness: Its Levels of Analysis," *Leadership Quarterly* 6, no. 2 (1995): 147–67; L. H. Peters, D. D. Hartke, and J. T. Pohlmann, "Fiedler's Contingency Theory of Leadership: An Application of the Meta-Analysis Procedure of Schmitt and Hunter," *Psychological Bulletin* 97 (1985): 274–85; M. J. Strube and J. E. Garcia, "A Meta-Analytical Investigation of Fiedler's Contingency Model of Leadership Effectiveness," *Psychological Bulletin* 90 (1981): 307–21.
33. V. H. Vroom and A. G. Jago, *The New Leadership: Managing Participation in Organizations* (Englewood Cliffs, NJ: Prentice Hall, 1988); V. H. Vroom and P. W. Yetton, *Leadership and Decision-Making* (Pittsburgh, PA: University of Pittsburgh Press, 1973).
34. For examples of studies supporting the normative decision model, see A. Crouch and P. Yetton, "Manager Behavior, Leadership Style, and Subordinate Performance: An Empirical Extension of Vroom-Yetton Conflict Rule," *Organizational Behavior and Human Decision Processes* 39 (1987): 384–96; A. G. Jago and V. H. Vroom, "An Evaluation of Two Alternatives to Vroom/Yetton Normative Model," *Academy of Management Journal* 23 (1980): 347–55; D. Tjosvold, W. C. Wedley, and R. H. G. Field, "Constructive Controversy: The Vroom-Yetton Model and Managerial Decision-Making," *Journal of Occupational Behavior* 7 (1986): 125–38.
35. For a comparison of the different contingency views of leadership, see M. M. Chemers, "An Integrative Theory of Leadership," in M. M. Chemers and R. Ayman (eds.), *Leadership Theory and Research: Perspectives and Directions* (New York: Academic Press, 1993): 293–320.
36. R. J. House, "A Path-Goal Theory of Leader Effectiveness," *Administrative Science Quarterly* 16 (1971): 321–39; R. J. House and G. Dessler, "The Path-Goal Theory of Leadership: Some Post Hoc and A Priori Tests," in J. G. Hunt and L. L. Larson (eds.), *Contingency Approaches to Leadership* (Carbondale, IL: Southern Illinois Press, 1974); R. J. House and T. R. Mitchell, "Path-Goal Theory of Leadership," *Contemporary Business* 3 (Fall 1974): 81–98.
37. R. W. Griffin, "Task Design Determinants of Effective Leader Behavior," *Academy of Management Review* 4 (1979): 215–24; J. E. Stinson and T. W. Johnson, "The Path-Goal Theory of Leadership: A Partial Test and Suggested Refinement," *Academy of Management Journal* 18 (1975): 242–52.
38. For some critiques of path-goal, see H. K. Downey, J. E. Sheridan, and J. W. Slocum, Jr., "Analysis of Relationships Among Leader Behavior, Subordinate Job Performance and Satisfaction: A Path-Goal Approach," *Academy of Management Journal* 18 (1975): 253–62; A. D. Szilagyi and H. P. Sims, "An Exploration of the Path-Goal Theory of Leadership in a Health Care Environment," *Academy of Management Journal* 17 (1994): 622–34.
39. T. A. Stewart, "Gray Flannel Suit?" *Fortune* 137, no. 5 (March 16, 1998): 82.
40. F. Dansereau, Jr., G. B. Graen, and W. J. Haga, "A Vertical Dyad Linkage Approach to Leadership Within Formal Organizations: A Longitudinal Investigation of the Role Making Process," *Organizational Behavior and Human Performance* 13 (1975): 46–78; G. B. Graen and J. F. Cashman, "A Role Making Model of Leadership in Formal Organizations: A Developmental Approach," in J. G. Hunt and L. L. Larson (eds.), *Leadership Frontiers* (Kent, OH: Kent State University Press, 1975): 143–65; G. B. Graen and W. Shiemann, "Leader-Member Agreement: A Vertical Dyad Linkage Approach," *Journal of Applied Psychology* 63 (1978): 206–12.
41. For some examples, see "The Significance of Socializing," *Harvard Business Review* 72, no. 1 (1994): 8; C. C. Wilhelm, A. M. Herd, and D. D. Steiner, "Attributional Conflict Between Managers and Subordinates: An Investigation of Leader-Member Exchange Effects," *Journal of Organizational Behavior* 14, no. 6 (1993): 531–44.
42. T. N. Bauer and S. G. Green, "Development of Leader-Member Exchange: A Longitudinal Test," *Academy of Management Journal* 39, no. 6 (1996): 1538–67; H. Klein and J. Sim, "A Field Study of the Influence of Situational Constraints, Leader-Member Exchange, and Goal Commitment on Performance," *Academy of Management Journal* 41, no. 1 (1998): 88–95.
43. J. J. Keller, "AT&T's Walter Quits After Boardroom Rebuff," *Wall Street Journal*, July 17, 1997, B1.

44. G. B. Graen and M. Uhl-Bien, "The Transformation of Work Group Professional into Self-Managing and Partially Self-Designing Contributors: Toward a Theory of Leadership-Making," *Journal of Management Systems* 3, no. 3 (1991): 33–48.

45. For a recent study of the effect of cognitive factors in LMX, see E. M. Engle and R. G. Lord, "Implicit Theories, Self-Schemas, and Leader-Member Exchange," *Academy of Management Journal* 40, no. 4 (1997): 988–1010.

46. G. B. Graen and J. F. Cashman, "A Role Making Model of Leadership in Formal Organizations: A Developmental Approach," in J. G. Hunt and L. L. Larson (eds.), *Leadership Frontiers* (Kent, OH: Kent State University Press, 1975): 143–65.

47. S. Kerr and J. M. Jermier, "Substitutes for Leadership: Their Meaning and Measurement," *Organizational Behavior and Human Performance* 22 (1978): 375–403.

48. D. H. Pink, "One Thing's for Sure—the World's a Blur," *Fast Company* (April–May 1998): 88–89.

49. A. Taylor, "Consultants Have a Big People Problem," *Fortune* 137, no. 7 (April 13, 1998): 164.

50. Ibid., 163.

51. J. L. Farh, P. M. Podsakoff, and B. S. Cheng, "Culture Free Leadership Effectiveness versus Moderators of Leadership Behavior: An Extension and Test of Kerr & Jermier's 'Substitutes for Leadership' Model in Taiwan," *Journal of International Business Studies* (Fall 1987): 43–60.

52. M. Fischetti, "Team Doctors, Report to ER!" *Fast Company* (February–March 1998): 176.

53. Keller, "AT&T's Walter Quits."

54. R. J. House, "A 1976 Theory of Charismatic Leadership," in J. G. Hunt and L. L. Larson (eds.), *Leadership: The Cutting Edge* (Carbondale, IL: Southern Illinois University Press, 1977).

55. J. A. Conger, *The Charismatic Leader: Behind the Mystique of Exceptional Leadership* (San Francisco, CA: Jossey-Bass, 1989); J. A. Conger and R. N. Kanungo, *Charismatic Leadership: The Elusive Factor in Organizational Effectiveness* (San Francisco, CA: Jossey-Bass, 1988); House, "A 1976 Theory."

56. M. F. R. Kets De Vries and D. Miller, "Personality, Culture, and Organizations," *Academy of Management Review* 11 (1986): 266–79; B. M. Bass, *Leadership and Performance Beyond Expectations* (New York: Free Press, 1985).

57. M. Gunther, "The Internet Is Mr. Case's Neighborhood," *Fortune* 137, no. 6 (March 30, 1998): 71.

58. Ibid., 68–80.

59. H. Tyabji, "What It Means to Lead," *Fast Company* (February–March 1997): 98.

60. N. Deogun and J. S. Lublin, "PepsiCo's Enrico Forgoes 1998 Salary, Asks Firm's Board to Fund Scholarship," *Wall Street Journal*, March 25, 1998, A1.

61. Conger, *Charismatic Leader*; House, "A 1976 Theory."

62. See Bass, *Leadership and Performance*.

63. Gunther, "The Internet," 71–72.

64. Bass, *Leadership and Performance*; P. E. Spector, "Behavior in Organizations as a Function of Employee's Locus of Control," *Psychological Bulletin* 91, no. 3 (1982): 482–97.

65. K. B. Boal and J. M. Byron, "Charismatic Leadership: A Phenomenological and Structural Approach," in J. G. Hunt, B. R. Baliga, H. P. Dachler, and C. A. Schriesheim (eds.), *Emerging Leadership Vistas* (Lexington, MA: D. C. Heath, 1987).

66. P. Dillion, "Is Selling Out 'Selling Out'?" *Fast Company* (February–March 1998): 92.

67. Ibid.

68. Ibid.

69. B. Bass, *The Handbook of Leadership* (New York: Free Press, 1990); R. H. Dekmejian and M. J. Wyszomirski, "Charismatic Leadership in Islam: The Mahdi of the Sudan," *Comparative Studies in Society and History* 14 (1972): 193–214; P. Singer, "Toward a Re-Evaluation of the Concept of Charisma with Reference to India," *Journal of Social Research* 12, no. 2 (1969): 13–25; R. Tsurumi, "American Origins of Japanese Productivity: The Hawthorne Experiment Rejected," *Pacific Basin Quarterly* 7 (Spring/Summer 1982): 14–15.

70. Transformational leadership was first proposed by J. M. Burns, *Leadership* (New York: Harper & Row, 1978), and later refined by Bass and his associates.

71. For a discussion of the negative effects of management and contingent reward, see A. Zaleznik, "The Leadership Gap," *Academy of Management Executive* 4, no. 1 (1990): 7–22.

72. Bass, *Leadership and Performance*; Bass, *Handbook of Leadership*; W. Bennis and B. Nanus, *Leaders: The Strategies for Taking Charge* (New York: Harper & Row, 1985); Conger and Kanungo, *Charismatic Leadership*.

73. Bennis and Nanus, *Leaders*, emphasizes the need for the leader to demonstrate exceptional behaviors. Conger and Kanungo, *Charismatic Leadership*, stresses the importance of empowerment, and the setting of personal examples of risk taking and competence. B. Shamir, "The Charismatic Relationship: Alternative Explanations and Predictions," *Leadership Quarterly* 2 (1991): 81–104, adds the need to set challenging goals and showing personal consideration.

74. See M. Saskin, "The Visionary Leader," in J. A. Conger and R. N. Kanungo (eds.), *Charismatic Leadership* (San Francisco: Jossey-Bass, 1988): 124–25; B. Nanus, *Visionary Leadership* (New York: Free Press, 1996), 8.

75. Dillion, "Selling Out," 104.

76. J. M. Kouzes and B. Z. Posner, *Credibility: How Leaders Gain and Lose It, Why People Demand It* (San Francisco: Jossey-Bass, 1995); J. M. Kouzes and B. Z. Posner, *The Leadership Challenge* (San Francisco: Jossey-Bass, 1995).

77. Dillion, "Selling Out," 94.

78. Ibid.

79. A. Nahavandi and A. R. Malekzadeh, "Leadership Style in Strategy and Organizational Performance: An Integrative Framework," *Journal of Management Studies* 30, no. 3 (1997): 405–25.

80. Nokoni, "Father Figure," 77.

81. "Samsung Cuts Jobs and Pay as Koreans Brace for Pain," *New York Times*, November 27, 1997, D1.

82. Kraar, "Behind Samsung's High-Stakes Push into Cars."

83. Allen R. Myerson, "Air Herb," *New York Times Magazine* (November 9, 1997): 36.

84. Scott McCartney, "Airline Industry's Top Ranked Woman Keeps Southwest's Small-Fry Spirit Alive," *Wall Street Journal*, November 30, 1997, B1, B11.

85. Myerson, "Air Herb," B1.

86. Ibid.

The Group at Jagged Edge

To describe how Jagged Edge Mountain Gear relies on teams, vice president David Potter states: "If we didn't have teamwork, we couldn't get the job done. There's always a backup."[1] JEMG does not have a formal team structure. If anything, the formal organizational chart is clearly traditional and functional. However, the reality of work does not always mirror the formal organizational structure.

A strong sense of camaraderie permeates the organization. The Quenemoens work hard at developing this sense of cohesion in their company. Their task is made easy because their employees all share a passion for mountains and winter sports. They spend time together at work, then spend time together scaling the mountains. Margaret Quenemoen observes that "we not only work together, we play together."[2] Many at JEMG have friendships with one another formed on expeditions they took before joining JEMG.

The sense of camaraderie and trust that develops while doing mountain sports translates into an ability to cooperate and work together. The employees at JEMG know that they can rely on one another for help and support. David Potter explains: "I can jump into any of the jobs here." The bond between employees is further reinforced by a sense of being the "little guy" in a tough corporate world and a strong desire not to become corporate. Potter states, "We are in a struggle. We see ourselves as the underdog."[3] Tim O'Neill, JEMG's buyer, has the same view. "We're all invested in this equally."[4] What distinguishes the corporate world and JEMG's culture? According to Paula Quenemoen, "Corporate means that you are in it for the money. They don't do the sports. They cut corners. Our products evolved through our own use."[5]

Few important decisions at JEMG are made without some degree of involvement from various employees and managers. Margaret Quenemoen says that in most cases, all employees get together and "tear things apart."[6] For example, in designing a piece of equipment or clothing, the whole group will have input. The decision to relocate provides a more dramatic example. Recently, Margaret Quenemoen considered moving the central office away from Telluride. In spite of being a mecca for ice climbing and mountain sports, the town, she believes, lacks the business infrastructure needed to support a growing business. She suggested the move to her employees. After some discussion, they soundly rejected it. As a result, JEMG has now moved to a new location in Telluride and is planning to stay in town for a long while.

In spite of the use of groups to make many of the decisions and a strong sense of camaraderie, the Quenemoens remain firmly in charge of the business. Margaret describes herself as "honest and blunt. I have no secrets and I can be abrasive. But there is no misunderstanding."[7] She likes to interact closely with all aspects of her company. "I am in the trenches with them, and I think people respect me for the hard work I do."[8] People who work closely with Margaret look up to her. Potter, who has been with JEMG longer than any other employee, remembers having trouble finding a job because he lacked experience. Margaret hired him, he believes, because "she doesn't look at your past, she looks at your potential." He adds: "She lets you climb, but she is there for you. You're never told you can't do something."[9]

Developing employees' potential appears to be a theme with many other managers at JEMG. Paula Quenemoen considers her assistant, Brad Barlage, to be her partner. Potter, using a climbing analogy, states: "You take care of the other person, but they are doing the climbing themselves."[10] Erlend Greulich, retail store manager in charge of human resource management, is eloquent about the leadership at JEMG. He believes that managers must develop a personal relationship of trust and loyalty. He states, "My job is to look at the person and the position. I look and I observe. I then suggest changes that are easy to make. When they work, people trust me and are ready to do more. I become a catalyst. My role is to empower and enable. The leaders have to let people do their job."[11] He likes to involve people in early stages and get their input, then make the final decision alone.

Questions

1. How is group cohesion achieved at JEMG? How are groups used?
2. What styles of leadership do you observe at JEMG?
3. How does the use of teams and the leadership style fit with the organization's mission and culture?

Notes

[1] Interview with David Potter, June 8, 1998.
[2] Interview with Margaret Quenemoen, June 4, 1998.
[3] Interview with D. Potter.
[4] Interview with Timothy O'Neill, June 8, 1998.
[5] Interview with Paula Quenemoen, June 8, 1998.
[6] Interview with M. Quenemoen.
[7] Ibid.
[8] Interview with Margaret Quenemoen, June 4, 1998.
[9] Interview with D. Potter.
[10] Ibid.
[11] Interview with Erlend Greulich, June 8, 1998.

MAKING DECISIONS

LEARNING OBJECTIVES

1. Describe the rational, bounded rationality, linear, intuitive, and garbage can models of decision making.
2. Highlight the role of culture in decision making.
3. Explain the effect of *heuristics* and biases in managerial decision making.
4. Define creativity and specify ways managers can encourage it.
5. Review the special characteristics and tools of group decision making.

MANAGERIAL CHALLENGE

Philips Electronics

Big, cutting-edge firms do not necessarily hold an edge in profitability or productivity. Consider the situation at Philips Electronics N.V., the Netherlands-based global maker of audio and video equipment, telecommunications gear, semiconductor chips, and personal care products. Despite its reputation for innovation—Philips recently shared a Grammy Award with Sony for developing the compact disc—and its $39 billion in worldwide sales, the company's bottom-line results often lag behind those of top competitors.[1] Over a 20-year period, top management implemented three major restructuring initiatives of the company's many business divisions and still failed to completely reverse the company's course.[2]

The company's latest turnaround effort began in late 1996, when Philips hired Cor Boonstra away from Sara Lee to become CEO. Boonstra is a talented marketer and experienced cost-cutter who pledged to generate strong cash flow, boost profit growth to double-digit levels, and increase the company's stock price. But remaking Philips entailed many tough decisions. For example, some financial analysts urged significant, across-the-board workforce cuts. Boonstra disagreed, preferring to evaluate each part of the company methodically and then prune business divisions that did not support the company's mission or performed poorly. Using this approach, he completed the sale of 18 businesses and arranged the sale of another 13 within his first five months.[3]

Boonstra is also weighing other major actions.[4] Should Philips outsource some of its manufacturing operations to Asia, a move some competitors made more than 10 years ago? Given the intense competition from Motorola, Nokia, Ericsson, and other global rivals, how far should Philips go to become a market leader in digital cellular telephones—on top of its investment of $500 million to build new factories in California, France, and Singapore? Boonstra is allowing plenty of time for consideration: He would not announce his new strategy for more than a year after his appointment as CEO.

■ **Questions**

1. What factors influence Cor Boonstra's decisions about the future of Philips?
2. What problems might he face in making these decisions?

Cor Boonstra of Philips has to make many difficult decisions. Managers in organizations make individual and group decisions daily: How can I finish this job on time? Whom should I hire? How should we reward employees? Which products should we make? Every aspect of organizational life involves making choices. In every case, people make decisions with less-than-perfect information. Because of uncertainty in decision making and potential perceptual biases, organizations establish procedures to ensure that the information gathered is as accurate as possible. They also use information technology and organizational structure to improve decision making.

In this chapter, we explore five decision-making approaches, the effects of culture and perceptual processes on decision making, and the ways creativity can influence decisions. Then we examine groups as decisoin makers and look at the tools that can improve their decision-making process.

FIVE DECISION-MAKING MODELS

To improve managerial decision making, researchers and practitioners have developed numerous decision-making theories. In this section we investigate five of the best-known decision-making models: rational decision making, bounded rationality, linear, intuitive, and garbage can models. Each makes different assumptions, so managers should have a working knowledge of all because one may be more applicable than another in a specific situation. We start with the model of orderly, rational decisions.

Rational Decision Making: The Ideal

Decision makers who want to find an ideal solution should follow a rational decision-making process. The **rational decision-making model** proposes objective, orderly, structured information gathering and analysis to reach an optimally informed decision. Figure 10.1 shows the eight steps of this model. Note how similar this process is to the social perception process. Both involve understanding the situation, organizing and interpreting information, and taking action.

The rational decision-making model gives managers a blueprint for reasoned, careful decision analysis. The goal of the model is to eliminate potential sources of biases, misperceptions, and error. It has five general assumptions:

Rational decision-making model
A decision-making model that assumes decisions are based on objective, orderly, structured information gathering and analysis

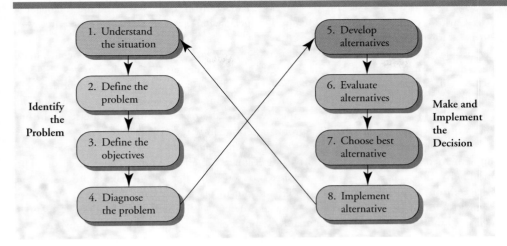

FIGURE 10.1
Rational Decision Making

- Managers have access to all information about the situation.
- Managers are aware of all alternatives and their consequences and can evaluate them properly.
- Managers' goal is to make the best decision possible (optimize).
- The organization can eliminate interpersonal conflicts, personal biases, and power struggles.
- There are no cost or time restrictions.

Let's examine the steps in rational decision making in more detail.

The Eight Steps of Rational Decision Making   The first four steps in the rational decision-making model help managers identify a problem through systematic information gathering. A systematic process reduces biases and ensures that managers consider all relevant information. First, managers must *understand the situation* that requires their attention. What are the issues involved? Who is affected? What are the implications? Although some degree of selective attention will occur, decision makers should actively seek and gather objective information about the situation rather than rely on random data and selective perception.

The second step in rational decision making is to use objective information to *define the problem*. Alan Leibman, the general manager of the Ritz-Carlton Hotel in Sydney, Australia, used customer feedback that was gathered systematically to define his problem. He thought customers were dissatisfied with the hotel services but he did not know why. The data revealed that customers did not feel the hotel offered sufficient quality given the price they paid for services.[5]

The third step in rational decision making is to *define the objectives*. What does the manager want to achieve by making a decision? What is the expected performance outcome? Leibman's objective was to ensure that the Ritz-Carlton hotel received the highest possible rating from all its customers. In effect, he wanted zero defects.[6]

Determining the desired outcome of the decision helps *diagnose the problem,* the fourth step in the decision-making process. This step requires managers to understand the problem and its root causes. Often they need more data to assure that the problem is properly identified. Leibman, for instance, asked hotel employees to file daily defect reports in which they reported any problems that customers or employees identified. These reports were then routed to managers. Managers used the data, along with information from other sources, to complete a Daily Quality Production Report that outlined the extent of any quality problems.

The last four steps of the rational decision process focus on making and implementing the decision. Managers *generate a series of alternative solutions* to the problem. The goal is to seek many ideas without settling on one early. Kim Dutton, quality and training manager at Ritz-Carlton, collected the Daily Quality Production Reports and evaluated each employee's proposal for resolving each problem.[7]

The sixth step in rational decision making is *evaluating each alternative*. Generally, managers list, compare, and analyze the strengths and weaknesses of each alternative. This step helps them *select one of the alternatives*—the seventh step and core of the rational decision-making process. Steps one through six involve gathering objective data to develop a solution. Managers at the Ritz-Carlton, for example, evaluated alternative solutions and selected the one that would be most likely to solve a problem permanently rather than temporarily.

The last step is *implementing the selected alternative* with sufficient resources. Once implemented, managers must monitor and evaluate the effectiveness of their decision. This means that they start again with the first step of the rational decision-making process. At the Ritz-Carlton, once a solution was chosen and put in place, managers checked in 30 days to review the decision implementation. The zero defects policy and employee involvement in decisions that supported the policy made the hotel one of the most successful in Sydney.[8]

In reality, the assumptions of the rational decision-making model rarely exist. In most situations, managers do not have complete access to information. The bounded rationality model, discussed next, describes a decision-making process that occurs more often in organizations.

Summary Point 10.1   **What Are the Steps of Rational Decision Making?**

- The rational decision-making process encourages objective, thorough gathering and use of information to make rational decisions.
- The model assumes that managers have complete information about the situation, the alternatives, and their consequences; that managers want to make the best decision; that decisions are made without interference from biases or interpersonal conflicts; and that decision makers do not have time or cost constraints.

- To identify a problem, managers must move through the first four steps of the decision-making process: understand the situation, define the problem, define objectives, and diagnose the problem.
- To make and implement a decision, managers must move through the last four steps of the decision-making process: develop alternatives, evaluate alternatives, choose an alternative, and implement a solution.

Bounded Rationality: The Reality

Because the assumptions of the rational decision-making model seldom exist, researchers have used other models to describe the way managers usually make decisions in organizations. Managers who understand the decision process can inject more accuracy into their own decision-making procedures. The **bounded rationality model** acknowledges the organizational and individual factors that constrain decision making, as shown in Figure 10.2.[9] These constraints limit or "bound" managers' ability to make rational decisions.

The following assumptions guide the bounded rationality model:[10]

Bounded rationality model
Decision-making model that assumes numerous organizational and individual factors restrict rational decision making

- Early alternatives and solutions are quickly adopted because of perceptual limitations.
- Managers rarely have access to all the information they need.
- Managers are not aware of all possible alternatives and cannot fully predict the consequences of each one.
- Organizational goals constrain decisions.
- Conflicting goals of multiple stakeholders can restrict decisions, forcing a compromise solution.

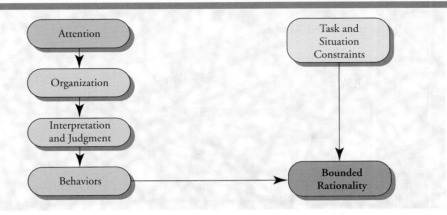

FIGURE 10.2
Bounded Rationality

As the assumptions indicate, the perceptual process is an individual factor that constrains rational decision making. First, as we learned in chapter 5, people have limited information processing abilities so they cannot process all available information. Second, perceptual biases affect decision making. Third, the complexity of the environment and the task affect how objectively managers make decisions.

Because an individual's perceptual process is limited, when a complex decision looms, most decision makers reduce the problem to a manageable size. They limit the number of choices and the amount of information they gather. As a result, they may not find the ideal solution, but instead find one that is acceptable and satisfactory.

To illustrate the constraints of the decision-making process, let's examine the case of Chris Moreno, the office manager of a law firm in charge of computerizing the office. Her employers, the partners at the firm, have given her a budget and a deadline of three months to select a system and another three months to get everyone up and running.

She must find a computer system that can accommodate the needs of the lawyers and their support staff, including the payroll supervisor and the administrative assistants. She may have detailed, accessible information about the performance advantages, disadvantages, and costs of various computer manufacturers and models. However, she has little objective information available to make more complex decisions, such as how best to train the lawyers and their support staff in computer skills, which computer system can support the needs of everyone at the firm, or how to meet her deadline and stay within budget.

The computer system decision depends on many factors—the lawyers' goals, monetary and time constraints, the computer skills of each person, and the amount of time each can spend on learning a new system, just to name a few. Given the lack of information, her schedule, and the complexity of the situation, Chris won't be able to review every possible decision alternative and select the perfect solution. Rather, she compromises by finding the first solution that is good enough, given her ability to process information, her perceptual biases, the deadline, and a number of other environmental constraints.

Just like Chris Moreno, most of us make decisions that are not ideal. Instead, we satisfice.[11] **Satisficing** is the process of making a decision that is satisfactory and acceptable but not necessarily optimal. As part of the satisficing process, we search for alternatives until we find one that is acceptable. When we find that alternative, our search stops. The order in which we consider alternatives, then, biases the final decision.

Most of our personal and business decisions are based on satisficing rather than optimizing. For example, few of us find ideal jobs. We tend to take the first acceptable offer. The company and salary may be excellent, but the location is not. Or the job is less than ideal but the location is near family and friends.

Hot ▼ Link

Review the perception process in chapter 5, pp. 150–54.

Satisficing
The process of making a decision that is satisfactory but not necessarily optimal

---

Summary Point 10.2   **What Is Bounded Rationality?**

- The bounded rationality decision-making model accepts the reality that numerous organizational and individual factors restrict rational decision making.

- Instead of optimizing, individuals often satisfice, which means they make satisfactory and acceptable, but not necessarily ideal, decisions.

Linear Models versus Intuition

Benjamin Franklin wrote in 1772 that he often made decisions by listing his personal pros and cons for each choice and giving each item a subjective numerical weight. Does Franklin's method lead to better decisions than those based on intuition? The answer is yes.[12]

Linear model
A model in which the decision maker lists positive and negative factors of each decision alternative and assigns each factor a numerical weight

Franklin advocated the use of what is now known as the *linear model of decision making*.[13] With the **linear model**, managers list all the positive and negative factors of a decision and assign each factor a numerical weight. Table 10.1 provides an example of this decision-making process.

Research evidence suggests that use of linear models leads to better decisions than those based on intuition or hunches.[14] Although both the selection of pros and cons and the weights assigned to each decision factor are subjective, considering each item's relative importance leads to a more thoughtful analysis and evaluation of priorities. For example, one study showed that experienced bank loan officers were about 75 percent correct (based on default rates) when they used intuition and judgment based on a number of financial data about giving business loans. However, their accuracy rates increased to 82 percent when they used formal linear models with the same data.[15]

Several other studies and mathematical experiments demonstrate the effectiveness of linear models. Some theorists believe that the linear process partially corrects for various perceptual biases, such as halo and primacy effects, by forcing decision makers to consider all factors at the same time. In addition, the process of the linear model provides order and systematic analysis to an otherwise subjective evaluation of alternatives. The systematic process helps correct for biases.

Table 10.1   **EXAMPLE OF THE LINEAR MODEL OF DECISION MAKING**

Gary has to decide whether to accept a job offer with a company in Seattle. Gary is a mountain climber and skier who was born and raised in Phoenix. Most of his family and friends are still in Arizona. He lists the pros and cons of the new position using a linear model, and considers the importance of each item by assigning it an importance weight ranging from −3 to 0 to 3. Three means the item is important and positive; −3 means it is important and negative.

Reasons for Moving	**Weight**	**Reasons Against Moving**	**Weight**
• More pay	2	• Large, stable company with moderate growth	−1
• Challenging job	3	• Stress of more challenging job	−1
• Advancement opportunities	1	• Leave friends and family	−2
• Excitement of new city	1	• Warm weather	−1
• Better schools	3	• Lose money on house	0
• Rock climbing, skiing, and other outdoor mountain sports	3	• Lose current company pension	−1
Total Score	14	**Total Score**	−6

Based on the linear model, Gary decides to accept the job in Seattle.

Just as the rational model prescribes an ideal decision-making process and bounded rationality describes reality, the linear model prescribes a sound decision-making process and intuitive decision making describes reality. In spite of strong research support for formal decision-making processes, such as the rational and linear models, managers at all levels often continue to rely on past experience and their general sense of the situation to make decisions. This process, called **intuitive decision making,** is widely used because of several factors:[16]

- High levels of uncertainty about the problem, the decision criteria, and the goals of the decision
- Decisions that are novel that managers have no past experience from which to draw
- Limited information and facts about the problems, possible alternatives, and their consequences
- Many possible alternatives that are difficult to analyze objectively
- Time pressure to make a decision

These factors suggest two common themes—uncertainty and complexity. When managers face such complex decisions that they cannot get accurate information fast, they tend to rely on their hunches, intuition, and general experiences either to generate alternative solutions or to make a final decision. Given the choice between intuition or the linear model, however, managers should opt for the linear model to make more accurate, less-biased decisions.

Another model that describes organizational decision making is the garbage can model, so called because decision makers lack information and do not make orderly, rational decisions based on facts or experience. We analyze this model next.

Intuitive decision-making model
Decision-making model that assumes managers make decisions by relying on past experience and their personal assessment of a situation

---

Summary Point 10.3   **How Does the Linear Model Compare to Intuitive Decision Making?**

- Similar to intuitive decision making, the linear model relies on subjective judgment. However, decision makers who use the linear model list the pros and cons of each decision alternative and assign each point a numerical weight to signify its importance.

- The linear model improves decision-making accuracy by forcing managers to evaluate all factors at the same time in a systematic way.
- Despite the research support for using formal decision-making processes, managers tend to rely on intuition, especially when they face complex decisions, time pressure, and uncertainty.

The Garbage Can Model

The *garbage can model* of decision making acknowledges that some decisions are made in an irrational, disorderly fashion. In the **garbage can model**, managers use information about events, people, alternatives, and opportunities in a haphazard way to generate ideas and potential solutions that may apply to the problem.[17] Table 10.2 describes the four factors that affect the decision.

Contrary to assumptions of the rational decision-making model, the four factors described in Table 10.2 do not occur in a sequential or orderly fashion, meaning the problem does not always precede alternatives and solutions.[18] For example, a decision to keep up with the industry trend of using teams may cause managers to view their current operation as a problem because it is not team based. In reality, the operation may be highly efficient and effective. Unlike the rational decision-making, bounded rationality, or linear models, the garbage can model may or may not lead to satisfactory solutions.

Garbage can model
Decision-making model that assumes managers use information about events, people, alternatives, and opportunities haphazardly to generate ideas and potential solutions to problems

Table 10.2 FACTORS IN THE GARBAGE CAN MODEL

Factors	Description and Examples
The problems	A gap exists between actual and desired outcomes. *Employee performance or production levels are lower than expected; customer complaints are higher than normal.*
The solutions	Answers are not always tied to problems; sometimes they precede or define problems. *The solution is to jump on the team bandwagon to implement new technology that will improve efficiency—even though the business is already highly efficient.*
The participants	Employees are involved in the problems and solutions. *Dissatisfied employees are included; managers may do a satisfaction survey.*
The opportunities	Managers have opportunities to make a decision, whether a problem exists or not. *Opportunities could include restructuring; introducing new technology; hiring new employees.*

Consider railroad giant Union Pacific's (UP) acquisition of Southern Pacific (SP). The merger gave Union Pacific managers plenty of opportunity to make decisions and identify solutions to problems that didn't exist. For instance, a haphazard decision led to a problem with SP's main switching station in Houston. The station became so jammed that traffic could not enter or exit. "Customers started complaining when their cargo was not picked up or delivered on time," explained a company spokesperson.[19]

What happened? After the merger, UP managers implemented a solution to a non-existent problem. They decided the Houston yard operation needed modernization, so UP sent a large quantity of fast-moving locomotives to Houston. But the Houston yard, SP's nerve center, ran efficiently in large part because its experienced managers visually inspected the yard and used their experience to prevent logjams. SP managers even drove to customers' plants before dawn to inspect their railcars to ensure that nothing could delay operations. The addi-

This massive logjam at the Houston yard of Southern Pacific occurred because managers failed to gather and evaluate information in a systematic way. The result of the poor decision making? Customer complaints, delays, and a public relations nightmare.

tion of the fast-moving locomotives threw off the engineers' traffic-flow time estimates, creating numerous problems.

The ripple effects of the decision led to clogged railways in Texas and in other southern states. The company spokesperson admitted: "We had westbound trains lined up all the way to Phoenix and Tucson, waiting to get into southern California."[20] In the middle of the mess, UP managers ignored customers' suggestions and solutions. "They accused customers of lying. They were arrogant. When we tried to make suggestions, they said, 'Leave us alone,'" reported a frustrated customer.[21]

As this example of the garbage can model illustrates, managers do not always behave in an orderly, logical fashion. It also suggests that managers pay attention to issues that stand out and are salient and may ignore others.

In this section, we examined the five different types of decision-making models: rational, bounded rationality, linear, intuitive, and garbage can. Each model offers managers different insight into the steps, processes, and biases in decision making. In the next section, we discuss the effect of culture on decision making.

Summary Point 10.4   **What Is the Garbage Can Model?**

- The garbage can model is a decision-making process suggesting that managers use information in a haphazard way to generate ideas and potential solutions that may apply to the problem.

- According to the model, four factors affect a decision: problems, solutions, participants, and opportunities.

 ## CULTURE IN DECISION MAKING

How managers perceive a situation, define a problem and goals, select a solution, whether long- or short-term, and so forth depend on national and ethnic cultural values. In addition, culture can affect how well employees implement and abide by managers' decisions. We investigate the six key questions, summarized in Table 10.3, that managers should ask to ascertain how culture affects the decision-making process. We discuss each question in detail next.

Table 10.3   CULTURAL FACTORS THAT AFFECT DECISION MAKING

Factor	Description
• Group or individual goals	Does society place primary value on individual rights or group and social harmony? In individualistic cultures, the rights of the individual take precedence over the group.
• Individual or group decision making	Do individuals or groups make decisions? In individualistic cultures, individuals rather than groups make decisions.
• Tolerance for ambiguity	Does the culture tolerate ambiguity and uncertainty or avoid them? In cultures that tolerate ambiguity, individuals are comfortable with unclear solutions.
• Time orientation	Is the culture short- or long-term oriented? Are people focused on past, present, or future? Is time viewed as linear or holistic and circular?
• Proactive or fatalistic approach	Does the culture value being proactive over accepting fate? In proactive cultures, individuals take on issues and attempt to change them rather than passively accepting events.
• Objectivity or subjectivity	Does the culture rely on objective or subjective information? In objective cultures, individuals rely on facts and figures rather than intuition and feeling to make decisions.

1. Does the culture promote group or individual goals? Decision makers from collectivist cultures value group harmony and cohesion, so their goals emphasize what is best for the community or the group.[22] For instance, say a business needs to make a decision about how to cut costs. A company in a country that has a collectivist culture, such as Thailand or Costa Rica, will tend to be reluctant to lay off employees because layoffs harm society at large and negatively influence group harmony.

In contrast, decision makers from individualistic cultures place a higher value on individual rights and goals. Their decisions are more likely to focus on what is best for individuals, such as those who own the business, rather than the effect of the decision on employees or society at large.

2. Does the culture support individual or group decision making? Certain cultures more than others support individual decision making. In high power distance cultures, such as Singapore and South Korea, loyalty and obedience drive decision making. The Confucian influence makes it acceptable for managers to make decisions alone, without consulting followers.[23] Managers are assumed to have the necessary knowledge and power to make decisions alone.

Furthermore, masculine cultures tend to value independence and autonomy, so decision makers will be more likely to make decisions alone. In more feminine cultures, such as that of Sweden, decision makers will be more likely to consult with followers when making a decision. Such cultures do not assume that managers have broad power or knowledge. Because of egalitarian views, followers expect to contribute their input and expertise in decisions.

Note that masculinity, power distance, and individualism may provide contradictions. Consider U.S. cultural values. On the one hand, the mainstream culture values individualism highly and has a moderate degree of masculinity that encourages independence and self-sufficiency. These two factors point to individual rather than group decision making. On the other hand, U.S. power distance tends to be low. This leads to followers' expectation to participate in decisions.

3. How does the culture tolerate uncertainty? The goal of decision making in cultures that do not tolerate uncertainty well is to reduce uncertainty as much as possible. The Japanese tendency to make long-term plans stems partially from the need to reduce uncertainty. For instance, Seiko, the giant multinational Japanese watchmaker, urges its managers to develop

Canon's deliberate business decisions are driven partially by a national cultural value of low tolerance for risk.

250-year plans. Although developing such plans may seem ridiculous to Westerners, it provides Seiko managers with a comfortable level of certainty about the future of their business.

Low tolerance for ambiguity further influences the willingness to take risks. Risky decisions, by definition, have uncertain outcomes. The outcome of less risky decisions is more predictable. Canon, the famous Japanese manufacturer of cameras and printers, has been reluctant to enter the digital age. When Canon chairperson Ryuzaburo Kaku decided to invest in laser printers, the company did so by forging an alliance with Hewlett-Packard, thereby reducing Canon's risk exposure.[24]

4. What time orientation does the culture have? Some cultures emphasize making long-term rather than short-term decisions. In cultures with a linear and short-term time focus, such as the United States or Germany, the effect of decisions is considered in a linear fashion. In other words, decision makers ask how their decision affects this or that person in the short term. In less linear cultures such as India, decision makers solve problems in a more circular and holistic manner, considering broad consequences for now and for the distant future.

5. Does the culture value proactivity or fatalism? Cultural values of fatalism and proactivity also affect decision making. In fatalistic cultures, such as those of Mexico and many Middle Eastern countries, managers tend not to approach problems proactively. In some cases, managers may not even acknowledge or recognize that a problem exists. The cultural values encourage the belief that individuals do not have a great deal of control over events. Decision making, then, may be slow or decision makers may decide that the best course of action is to do nothing.

Consider the frustration of many Western managers who hear expressions such as "Inshaalla" (God willing) or "Allah O Akbar" (God is great) when negotiating with Middle Eastern managers who will not finalize a decision. The Middle Easterners do not believe they have control over events and feel comfortable letting things be, insisting that in due time the Almighty will decide on the right course of action.

A recent camel race in the heart of the German capital illustrates this point further. Several German businesses, in association with Arab partners, decided to set up a camel race in the famous, tradition-bound Berlin racetrack. The goal of the venture was to show German business's goodwill and cultural sensitivity in the hope of gaining favorable consideration in future contracts from Arab nations. The majority of the spectators were Germans. The race started an hour late, thoroughly irritating the orderly, time-conscious Germans. To make matters worse, many camels simply refused to race or would stop half-way in the race to graze, oblivious to their jockey's commands. German spectators said that Germans could have run the race better; it was a matter of control and organization, both of which they thought were lacking. To the Arab partners and spectators, the fuss was ridiculous. After all, camels are notoriously temperamental and there was no reason to try to manage something that is unmanageable.[25]

6. Does the culture tend toward objective or subjective decision making? In many Western cultures, managers prefer to rely on objective, measurable facts and figures to make their decisions. These cultures believe rational decisions based on objective facts are better than decisions based on hunches and intuition. As a result, managers who may make a subjective decision will go to great pains to find objective data to support and justify them.

In contrast, the use of intuition is fully accepted in several Asian and Middle Eastern cultures. Managers may rely on their feelings, past experiences, or even on interpretations of dream and astrological indicators to make a decision.

Knowledge of how culture affects decision making helps managers identify problems, set goals, and find better solutions. For instance, a U.S. executive planning to change the structure of its French subsidiary from a traditional, hierarchical structure to a self-managed team structure needs to consider the role of high power distance. Because the French have high power distance, they value hierarchy and status. Therefore, employees and managers may not easily accept a structure based on diffused and egalitarian power. In other respects, the two cul-

---

Summary Point 10.5   How Does Culture Affect Decision Making?

- Managers should assess the effects of culture on decision making. Not only does culture affect the way managers make decisions, it also affects how effectively employees will implement and abide by decisions. To determine the cultural effects, managers should ask six questions:
  1. Does the culture focus on individual or group goals?
  2. Does the culture value individual or group decision making?

  3. How does the culture tolerate uncertainty?
  4. What time orientation does the culture have? (Short term or long term? Linear or circular?)
  5. Does the culture value proactivity or fatalism?
  6. Does the culture prefer objective or subjective information?

---

tures are more similar. Both focus on individual goals and tolerate individual decision making. Time orientation is generally linear in France and the United States and both cultures are proactive and rely on objective data. However, the French have less tolerance for ambiguity than U.S. managers.

We reviewed the cultural factors that affect how managers make decisions. Next we consider various decision-making rules and biases.

 RULES AND BIASES IN DECISION MAKING

No decision can ever be free of bias. Selective attention, personal judgment and interpretation, and other subjective processes affect decision making at various points. The more complex the decision, the more likely it is to have bias.

Programmed decisions
Routine decisions that have clearly outlined procedures

Simple, routine decisions that have clearly outlined procedures are **programmed decisions**. Most organizations have standard policies and procedures that direct programmed decisions. Because they are simple and have clear guidelines, programmed decisions are less likely to be subject to error and biases. **Nonprogrammed decisions** are novel and made infrequently.[26] Because these decisions are novel, organizations lack clear standards and procedures as a guide in making them. Typically, managers cannot rely on historical information to make nonprogrammed decisions because no two decisions are alike. As a result, they are more likely to be subject to biases.

Nonprogrammed decisions
Novel, nonroutine decisions that are made infrequently

For instance, one group of developers plans to offer tourist trips to outer space. Because this unusual service has never been offered, no formal procedures govern the pricing and promotion decisions. Some of the decisions the developers will make may be arbitrary or even inaccurate. These decisions, then, are nonprogrammed. The challenges of a global business environment, rapid change, and customer demands for quality mean that managers face more nonprogrammed than programmed decisions.

In the following sections, we investigate decision-making rules—known as heuristics—and biases that affect managerial decisions, especially nonprogrammed decisions.

Decision-Making Rules: Heuristics

Decision heuristics
The tendency to make mental shortcuts while making decisions

Managers, like all people, simplify the decision-making process. This tendency to make mental shortcuts is called **decision heuristics**.[27] The first decision heuristic is **availability**, a tendency to pay attention to events we remember, often at the expense of other more relevant information. For example, a manager who has recently observed several legal battles over hiring processes is likely to overestimate how common such lawsuits are. The easy recollection does not necessarily represent the actual percentage of lawsuits. However, it does influence her decision-making process in how to document and manage hiring in her department. Similarly, if

Availability
A tendency to pay attention to information we remember because it is so accessible

Change Challenge

HOW MANAGERS USE INFORMATION ABOUT A CHANGING ENVIRONMENT

Analyze the situation. Evaluate new competitors. Expand into Malaysia. Find a solution to lagging sales. Managers have so many decisions to make in a rapidly changing business environment that the amount of information needed to make accurate, timely decisions is overwhelming. As a result, managers must rely on information gathered by others. Information technology and various management information systems (MIS) can help managers access better information. However, several factors reduce the usefulness of such systems.[a]

First, formal information systems are too limited in the type of information they include. Much of the information is not rich or detailed enough to be helpful to managers. For instance, most MIS systems include summary data about people, markets, and competitors, such as the total number of employees, the number of people in a particular market segment, or the total number of units sold by competitors. The summary statistics omit qualitative details.

Second, the time lag between gathering, entering, and making information available to managers tends to be large. As a result, managers may hesitate to rely on information they suspect is dated. They rely on their own judgment instead. Finally, managers can process only limited information at any one time. MIS often provides more information than managers can handle, so they tend to use a few comfortable sources of data rather than all that is available to make decisions.

The use of technology to provide information to various levels of the organization can help improve decision making. However, the usefulness of MIS is still limited by the type of information it offers, the speed of entering the information, and managers' information-processing capabilities.

a. M. Browne, *Organizational Decision-Making and Information* (Norwood, NJ: Ablex, 1993).

---

you had several recent negative experiences with salespeople in your organization, that information is likely to influence your decision to join the sales department.

Another heuristic that leads to errors in decision making is **representation,** the process of evaluating an event without comparing it to others or without putting it in proper context.[28] For instance, people may point to recent frequent hiring of women and minorities in their organization as proof that there is a bias against white males. They may consider the recent hiring to be representative of their organization's policy. What they fail to consider is the overall hiring pattern for the past five to ten years, which demonstrates that women and minorities are still only a small percentage of all hires.

Another heuristic is **anchoring and adjustment,** whereby we select a starting point for a decision and adjust our thinking based on our first anchor or starting point.[29] For instance, graduate students who look for their first job often develop an idea about a minimum acceptable salary based on what their friends tell them or general information they read in newspapers. They use this minimum pay anchor to judge the job offers they receive. If the anchor is based on accurate and objective data, the decision process is likely to start well. However, if the initial anchor is inappropriate, it will bias the rest of the decision process.

Representation
The process of evaluating an event without comparing it to others or comparing situations that are not similar

Anchoring and adjustment
The process whereby we select a starting point for a decision and adjust our thinking based on our first anchor or starting point

Framing
The process of placing a situation in context before making a decision

The last decision heuristic is **framing**—the process of placing a situation in context before making a decision. When managers frame the situation in positive terms, they take fewer risks because they perceive chances of success to be high. They therefore become conservative and are not willing to take unnecessary risks.[30] In contrast, when managers frame the situation in negative terms, they take more risks because they perceive that there is little to lose. As a result, they become bolder in their decisions.

An excellent example of the effect of framing is Kraft Foods' decision to sell Log Cabin Maple syrup to Aurora Foods Inc. Kraft's managers did not see how the famous maple syrup line fit with Kraft's pastas, meats, and cheeses. From their perspective, Log Cabin was a distraction. To Aurora CEO Ian Wilson, the syrup fit well with the company's recent purchase of Duncan Hines' brand foods from Procter & Gamble, Mrs. Butterworth's syrup from Unilever, and Mrs. Paul's frozen seafood products from Campbell Soup Co. Because major companies act conservatively and discard products that do not fit with their core businesses, Aurora can buy these established "orphans" and make them a success. "The best thing that's happened to us is that it's fashionable [for them] to be a core business," states Wilson.[31] He frames these well-known brands as opportunities. For instance, within one year of buying Aunt Jemima frozen breakfasts from Quaker Oats Co., Aurora's managers have been able to increase its sales by 14 percent.[32]

Summary Point 10.6   What Are Decision Heuristics?

- Decision heuristics are mental shortcuts in the decision process.
- Availability is the tendency to pay attention to events we remember.
- Representation is the process of evaluating events without comparing them to others or putting them in the proper context.

- Anchoring and adjustment occur when managers select a starting point for a decision and adjust their thinking based on their first anchor or starting point.
- Framing is the process of placing a situation in context before making a decision.

Decision heuristics are simplification patterns that managers use in making decisions. The overall effect of using heuristics is that managers do not gather accurate and appropriate information before making their decisions. They therefore increase the likelihood of making mistakes. In addition to such oversimplifications, managers must also watch for biases that affect the accuracy of their decision making.

Decision-Making Biases

Numerous biases prevent managers from making objective and rational decisions. In this section, we highlight four decision-making biases: escalation of commitment, cognitive dissonance, propensity for risk, and reliance on past experience.

Escalation of commitment
Continuing a course of action in the face of negative information

Escalation of Commitment   Decision makers' tendency to continue a course of action in the face of negative information is known as **escalation of commitment**.[33] This tendency is also referred to as "throwing good money after bad." Many managers have trouble admitting that they have made a mistake, especially if they have invested substantial resources in the decision. Escalation of commitment can lead to poor decision making, especially when managers fail to consider objective factors.

For instance, Apple Computer refused to open its computer's internal system to outsiders and allow cloning, in spite of all objective data to the contrary. For over a decade, Apple's

CEOs insisted they had made the right decision, even as the company lost market share to Windows-based systems. In 1996, the CEO of Apple, Gilbert Amelio, reversed this decision and licensed the operating system of Macintosh computers to outside vendors and clones. The decision was too little, too late and only made matters worse. The new Mac clones cut deeply into Mac sales, and the company's market share declined even further—from 11 percent to just 4 percent in 1997. When Apple founder, Steve Jobs, returned as Apple CEO, the company reverted to its closed system.[34] The *Wall Street Journal* then ranked Apple the worst company for investors among the 1,000 largest U.S. companies in the past five years.[35]

Figure 10.3 presents the factors that contribute to escalation of commitment.[36] First, organizational factors such as poor communication, unclear goals, the reward system, and politics and culture play a major role. When managers do not clearly know what is expected of them or have not defined what success and failure are on a project, they are not likely to recognize the point at which they need to change their course of action. Additionally, if a company has a history of firing its managers when a project fails, then managers and employees are not likely to admit failure. Instead, they will escalate their commitment to a failing project rather than admit failure. The cost of failure is simply too high. Finally, a negative political climate and a culture of distrust both will encourage escalation of commitment.

Advanced Micro Devices (AMD), for example, has had an unenviable record of pouring good money after bad. CEO Jerry Sanders has repeatedly failed to live up to expectations, consistently choosing wrong strategies for the company in its competition with Intel. However, AMD's board of directors has continued to give him stock options. *Fortune* rated AMD as one of its six worst performing enterprises.[37] Escalation of commitment helps explain why AMD's board of directors continues to support and reward a CEO when he has not performed well.

Other factors that contribute to escalation of commitment are external pressures on managers. Consumers may demand performance and stockholders want financial accountability for spent resources. There also may be threat of legislation. All these factors encourage managers to stick to the course of action, as the cost of failure appears to be high.

The third set of factors that contributes to escalation of commitment relates to individual managers.[38] Particularly, fear of losing face and protecting their ego are likely to cause managers to deny failure. Managers may also feel peer pressure to stick to their course and not admit a mistake. The individual factors in escalation of commitment relate to the preservation of self-esteem.

Finally, the type of task may be one of the most important contributors to escalation of commitment.[39] When managers do not get clear feedback from the task as to how well they

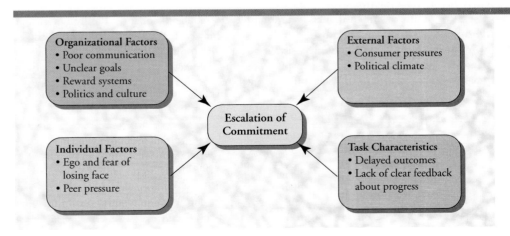

FIGURE 10.3
Factors That Contribute to Escalation of Commitment

are doing or when they do not receive quick financial returns, they continue on their course of action pouring more resources and hoping to reap the expected benefits.

Monitoring the factors presented in Figure 10.3 can help managers prevent escalation of commitment. More specifically, managers should do the following:[40]

- Provide clear outcomes.
- Define failure clearly so that employees and managers know when to change course.
- Bring in outside evaluators to review progress.
- Be tolerant of mistakes and failures.

Cognitive dissonance
The result of holding inconsistent or conflicting beliefs and attitudes

Cognitive Dissonance The second bias that affects decision making is cognitive dissonance. **Cognitive dissonance** occurs when people hold inconsistent or conflicting beliefs and attitudes.[41] It tends to be uncomfortable because we cannot reconcile the differences easily. Figure 10.4 outlines the factors in cognitive dissonance.

Consider the example of Randy Dizan, a manager at Insurance Data. Randy has to select between two assistants he has groomed for a promotion. He has invested time and resources in both people and cares about them. Although one assistant is somewhat better qualified, the other is a favorite with upper management. Randy's decision is, therefore, important to his own career, as he may be blamed for selecting the "wrong" person. No matter whom he promotes, there will be both positive and negative consequences. After he picks the less-qualified but better-connected person, in spite of his personal preference for the other, he experiences cognitive dissonance. His behavior—the decision he just made—does not match what he knows is right. Cognitive dissonance is a typical reaction after having made a difficult decision and this example demonstrates three of its major elements:

- The decision maker considers the decision important.
- There are a number of mutually exclusive alternatives.
- All alternatives have advantages that are forgone when not selected.

Experiencing dissonance leads to poor decision making. Once managers make a decision they are not comfortable with, they are likely to escalate their commitment to it, selectively pay attention only to information that supports it, disregard other disconfirming information, and distort information to fit their decision. In some cases, managers may even change the way they previously viewed other positive alternatives. All these actions reduce dissonance by making the selected alternative look more attractive and those that were not selected look less attractive.

Let's return to our Insurance Data example. To reduce dissonance, Randy Dizan may try to reconcile his actions and beliefs and convince himself that he made the correct choice by finding fault with the work of the assistant he did not promote. He may even give him poor ratings to support his decision not to promote him. The actions associated with post-decisional dissonance can lead to a self-fulfilling prophecy, further reinforcing a bad decision.

FIGURE 10.4
Antecedents and Consequences of Cognitive Dissonance

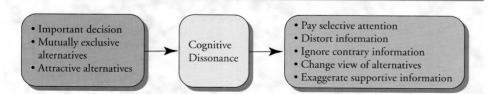

A QUESTION OF ETHICS

Dealing with Dissonance

Your company's culture is one in which salaried employees work hard and receive many informal benefits. For example, almost all employees log some personal travel expenses as business expenses reimbursable by the company. All employees and managers take advantage of this benefit.

Recently, after working numerous 65- to 70-hour weeks, you rewarded yourself by taking a four-day trip to a luxurious resort with your spouse. Although you met with a potential client for several hours over lunch one day, the rest of the trip was for pleasure. The formal policy suggests that you should pay for most of the trip and you pride yourself on your integrity. Your boss and other employees suggest that you shouldn't worry about it and claim the whole trip as a business expense. How would you handle this situation?

Propensity for Risk   Another bias in decision making is an individual's **propensity for risk**.[42] Risk propensity refers to an individual's risk tolerance. Some people have a high tolerance for risk and are willing to try out new, often risky solutions, whereas others are *risk averse*. **Risk averse** people avoid risk and lean toward conservative solutions. People's risk-taking tendency influences how they view a situation, what elements they consider, and how much attention they pay to positive and negative factors. The risk takers are more likely to disregard the potential problems or to find them challenging. Risk-averse people will focus more on the potential problems and see them as obstacles.

Propensity for risk
An individual's tolerance for risk

Risk averse
Tending to avoid risk

Consider the CEOs of two major U.S. corporations. Roger Smith, General Motor's CEO, ran the giant company using a conservative strategy. His tendency was not to take risks that might jeopardize the future of the company. During his tenure, GM grew moderately, but slowly returned to profitability. Contrast that with the risk-taking tendencies of Ted Turner, CEO of Turner Broadcasting System. He often took great risks that reshaped his broadcasting and news organizations. During his tenure, TBS and its many subsidiaries grew to become a formidable force in the industry, culminating in its acquisition by Time Warner Inc. in 1995.[43] CEOs Smith and Turner have different risk propensities; Smith is risk averse whereas Turner is a risk taker.

Relying on Past Experience   A final bias in decision making occurs when managers rely on past experience. Managers rely on their past successful patterns of decision making rather than on hard facts and data to make a decision. Successful managers simply repeat their previously successful patterns rather than fully analyze each situation they face. They rely on their own rules of thumb. This tendency can lead to poor decision making.

A well-known manager who uses the same rule of thumb in many different companies is Al Dunlap. Nicknamed "Chainsaw Al" and "Rambo in Pinstripes" by his employees, he buys a company, becomes the CEO, lays off scores of its employees, and sells pieces of the organization for profit. During Dunlap's brief tenure at Scott Paper, he laid off 11,000 people. His reward? He earned about $100 million in salary, perks, and stock options.

Dunlap then became the CEO of Sunbeam in 1996, where he trimmed the size of the workforce by half, from 12,000 to 6,000, and sold many parts of the company. Dunlap strongly defends his decision to lay off employees in the eight companies he headed before taking over Scott Paper and Sunbeam. However, only two still exist as independent companies. Now, experts question Dunlap's managerial decisions, partly because many of Sunbeam's top managers have quit. Scott Graham, an analyst for CIBC Oppenheimer in New York, states: "Right now this company needs stability . . . and right now one has to question whether that is the case."[44] The layoffs and piece-by-piece sales of Sunbeam's businesses led to tremendous instability, and no real improvement.[45] Dunlap was finally ousted by the Sunbeam board of directors in June 1998.

Summary Point 10.7   **What Are the Decision-Making Biases?**

- Escalation of commitment is the decision makers' tendency to continue a course of action in spite of negative information. Organizational factors, external pressures, preservation of self-esteem, and task characteristics contribute to escalation of commitment.

- Cognitive dissonance occurs when a person holds inconsistent beliefs or attitudes.
- Propensity for risk refers to the amount of risk an individual is willing to accept.
- Reliance on past experience instead of hard facts and data can bias decision making.

The focus of decision making in organizations is to gather and assess accurate information and eliminate biases to make the best decisions. In programmed decisions, managers can achieve these goals by applying the models we presented. However, managers who face nonprogrammed decisions can use rational models only as a starting point. Finding novel solutions to the novel problems further requires that managers exercise creativity in decision making. We review the elements of creative decision making next.

 CREATIVITY IN DECISION MAKING

Creativity (also divergent thinking or lateral thinking) The ability to link or combine ideas in novel ways

Given the uncertainty that many businesses face, organizations often grapple with unusual problems that require novel solutions. **Creativity**—also known as divergent or lateral thinking—is the ability to combine and link ideas in novel ways to generate novel and useful alternatives.[46] Lateral thinking focuses on moving away from the linear approach advocated by rational decision making.[47] In addition, the novel ideas have to be accepted and recognized as useful or of some value by others.[48] Some management theorists and practitioners believe that employee creativity and innovation are the core of an organization's success.[49] For instance, research indicates that a manager's ability to redefine old problems in new ways is essential to organizational effectiveness, given the uncertainty that many businesses face.[50]

Costa Rican president Jose Maria Figueres thought creatively when he broke with tradition to steer his country toward high-tech business and away from further development of the coffee, banana, and tourism industries.[51] Based on advice from Harvard strategy professor Michael Porter, President Figueres devoted resources to attracting high-tech companies such as Taiwan's Acer Group, Microsoft, Motorola, Intel, and Lucent. Because of the president's creativity, San Jose, the Costa Rican capital, is fast becoming Latin America's high-tech capital. Michael Ward, a Latin America director at Microsoft, says that Costa Rica's approach should be "a blueprint for what other nations, not only in Latin America but all around the world, are starting to talk to us about."[52] Figueres's creativity paid off. The high-tech industry now employs thousands of Costa Ricans. The country's deal with Intel alone is expected to bring in $1 billion, 30 percent more than Costa Rica earns from its tourism industry.

Meditrust is a development company specializing in housing for the elderly. Under the leadership of CEO Abraham D. Gosman, Meditrust is providing a novel solution to an old problem: The U.S. population is aging, two-earner families cannot take care of their elderly, and nursing homes are the answer in only some cases.[53] Meditrust develops various types of housing in a campus setting that offers assisted living and medical facilities. If offers a range of options to accommodate the changing needs of the elderly. Residents can choose from a menu of services, ranging from minimal assistance to a high level of assisted living. Living in these one-stop units costs 40 percent less than living in a nursing home. Meditrust's facilities increase the seniors' sense of control and reduce the family members' guilt.

Elderly-housing developer Meditrust has been successful in serving its elderly customers by thinking creatively about ways to address their complex and multiple needs.

Characteristics of Creative People

Some executives, such as President Figueres and Abraham Gosman, seem to have an uncanny ability to sift through massive amounts of information and select what is and is not relevant; many others, however, have limited information-processing and decision-making skills. The successful managers listen intently to all sources, especially to bad news, to know where the next problem is emerging. They value subjective as well as objective information. They turn facts, perceptions, gut feelings, and intuitions into reality by making bold and informed decisions. These executives do not rely solely on the rational decision-making models. Their reliance on creativity is key to their success.

In addition to his risk-taking propensity, Ted Turner is known for his creativity. He pioneered the all-news network with the creation of CNN and made the venture commercially viable. He also developed the practice of starting his network's programming five minutes past the hour to catch the attention of people flipping through different channels. He is further credited with the "colorization" of old movies that has attracted younger viewers to classic pictures. All these ideas were novel and their success far from guaranteed.

What do creative executives have in common? They share four characteristics:[54]

- *Perseverance in the face of obstacles and self-confidence:* Creative individuals persevere longer than others in the face of problems and have strong beliefs in the correctness of their ideas.
- *Willingness to take risks:* Creative individuals take moderate to high risks rather than extreme risks that have strong chances of failure.
- *Willingness to grow and openness to experience:* Creative individuals are open to experiences and are willing to try new methods.
- *Tolerance of ambiguity:* Creative individuals tolerate lack of structure and not having clear answers.

As this list suggests, creative people tend to be confident in the paths they select and are willing to take risks when others give up. They focus on learning and are willing to live with uncertainty to reach their goals. Michael Moschen, perhaps the world's greatest juggler, is also a management consultant who has built a successful career on teaching managers how to be creative. A recipient of the McArthur "genius" award, he prepares carefully for each task. Part of his preparation is to consider fully the possibility of failure. "The only way to learn is to recognize, in the little failures, how to avoid the big ones. To learn how to be successful, *to learn how to learn*, you have to be willing to accept failing 99 times out of 100. And through this familiarity with failure, you'll gain the humility required for any task." He advocates learning

Juggler Michael Moschen uses his experience to teach managers how to be creative. His clients may not learn how to juggle like he does, but they learn the importance of thinking outside the box.

and mastering the task, breaking it down to pieces and then putting it back together "to create something magical."[55]

Next, we highlight individual and organizational factors that increase and encourage creativity in decision making, and we identify several tools that can be used to increase creativity.

Factors in Creativity

Few business students describe themselves as creative. Creativity is typically associated with artistic professions. However, regardless of how creative you think you are, there is no reason that any one of us cannot be more creative in the way we approach issues and generate alternative solutions to problems.

Hot ▼ Link

We discussed norms and creative individualism in chapter 7, pp. 243–45.

Questioning Attitude   An essential factor for creative problem solving is developing a *questioning attitude* that allows consideration of various alternatives. Individuals or organizations that do not allow or tolerate questioning of values, assumptions, and norms cannot be highly creative. For example, teams must encourage their members to question their peripheral norms regularly if they are to foster creative individualism. Similarly, organizations need to question the long-held beliefs in their industry and evaluate whether they still fit today's business environment.

Cunningham Communication Inc. has developed a strong culture based on questioning the norms of its industry. This public relations (PR) firm, located in Palo Alto, Phoenix, Austin, and Cambridge, is reinventing PR. Founded by Andrea Cunningham, the organization has a creative flair in its approach to PR. "Ten years ago our job was to manipulate the press. It wasn't that hard to do. . . . If you had enough charisma and made relationships with them, it was fairly easy. Today you have to communicate with 300 people about every client. It's just not possible [to manipulate them]," she states. Her managers pride themselves in always telling the truth to the clients. "If the shareholders aren't buying the stock because they don't like the new CEO, or if the products are really good but the service sucks, we're the people that bring that information to the table. I pride our senior consultants on having the ability and the guts to tell CEOs the truth."[56]

Culture, Structure, and Leadership   Three other interrelated factors affect creativity: national, ethnic, or organizational *culture; organizational structure;* and *leadership.* First, the traditions and values that we each hold are deeply rooted and often prevent us from considering ideas that conflict with our cultural values. For instance, the cultural values of each generation relating to respect for authority and hierarchy may prevent many middle managers in the 50 to 60 age range from exploring team structures. Similarly, if the national culture does not value individualism and standing out, creativity is likely to be reduced.[57]

Organizational culture acts in much the same way. It is very difficult for individual employees to be creative and seek novel solutions if the organizational culture values tradition and conformity. A judgmental, critical culture prevents managers and employees from taking risks. If obedience to authority and respect for the past are at the core of an organization's culture, expecting employees to be highly creative is unreasonable. An organizational culture that rewards people who question everything is more likely to foster creativity.

For instance, IBM, always known for its strict culture of conformity, had to develop a creative subculture to succeed in building a Web site for the Atlanta Olympics in just 90 days. "But to get the Web site done, we had to break practically every rule in the IBM handbook," mentions John Patrick, IBM's chief Internet technology officer. "We got together a team of about 50 people. These were just kids—and they had Nerf guns and radio-controlled cars that they'd drive around in the parking lot at night. We ended up having a catering service come in. We established visiting hours for wives and children. It was almost like a prison," Patrick explains. "You can achieve amazing things and have highly motivated, incredibly loyal people—if they think management is willing to ignore the rules to get things done."[58] The result was a successful Web site that handled 100 million hits during the Atlanta Olympics.

Closely linked with organizational culture are leadership and structure. As we discussed in chapters 3 and 9, leadership and culture are closely linked. Leaders foster credibility when they are able to inspire followers and encourage and empower them to take risks and make their own decisions. Autocratic leaders who demand obedience impede the creative process. Similarly, rigid, mechanistic structures that impose rules and regulations and restrict free interaction and exchange of ideas hinder creativity.[59]

Fear of Risk A final factor in creativity is the *fear of taking risks*. This factor is partially related to individuals' risk-taking propensity. Risk takers are less likely to fear failure and therefore are more likely to implement novel ideas.[60] Another issue in fear is an organization's lack of tolerance of mistakes. If managers punish experimentation, mistakes, and failure, their employees will quickly stop proposing novel ideas. Although most organizations need and say that they want creative solutions to old problems, those who take risks and fail are treated harshly. Managers and employees focus on finding the "right" answers, on being practical and logical rather than on exploring all possibilities and solutions. The search for the right answer is most likely to happen when poor decisions can directly affect the decision maker.[61]

To encourage risk taking, United Technologies circulated a memo that pointed out the number of successes and failures of famous people such as Babe Ruth (he struck out 1,330 times and hit 714 home runs) and highlighted the sentence "Don't worry about failure. Worry about chances you miss when you don't even try."[62]

Overall, creativity is likely to flourish in an open environment that encourages participation. Autocratic leadership and obvious status differences and status symbols stifle even the most creative employees. Having special benefits for some but not all employees sends a message about who is valuable and who is not. Benefits such as first-class travel, separate dining areas, and so forth separate people who need to interact and work together. Reducing the "us against them" feeling allows for a free flow of ideas, encourages risk taking, and reduces fear. Renn Zaphiropulos, a Xerox plant manager, had just such a plan in mind when he put on work overalls and personally painted over the reserved parking signs in the parking lot.[63] An organization that wants to encourage creativity has to provide its employees with proper tools and training, autonomy to make decisions, and rewards for novel solutions.[64] We review next the ways that managers can encourage creativity.

Tools for Encouraging Individual Creativity

Some tools to encourage and enhance creativity are sophisticated and complex; others are as simple as the old idea of suggestion boxes. Dana Corp., a Toledo-based auto parts manufacturer with over 45,000 employees, has used suggestion boxes to tap into the creativity of its employees. Dana CEO, Woody Morcott, has made suggestions from employees part of the culture of the organization. In 1996 alone, Dana employees averaged 122 suggestions per month on how to improve productivity, save resources, and improve morale. The company implements over 70 percent of employees' suggestions. The result? Dana Corp. has saved millions of dollars through the years. Morcott explains that when managers implement employees' creative ideas, the number of complaints decreases dramatically.[65]

There are two major tools for enhancing individual creativity. Both focus on thinking in a nonlinear manner outside the confines of the standard process, otherwise known as thinking "outside the box." The most popular creative problem-solving technique is *brainstorming* (or brainsailing, as some prefer to call it). In **brainstorming**, individuals focus on generating a large number of possible ideas without initially judging or evaluating them. A helpful tool of brainstorming is building on each other's ideas when working in a group.

The second tool that managers can use to encourage creativity is *cooperative exploration*. **Cooperative exploration** requires individuals to consider a problem by taking different positions.[66] The typical approach that many of us take is to consider the positive and negative sides of issues and debate them. Although this method can be effective, it oversimplifies and polarizes issues and encourages arguments rather than creative thinking. Instead, cooperative exploration forces managers to look at issues from various viewpoints, thereby encouraging lateral and divergent thinking (see Figure 10.5). Table 10.4 describes the six viewpoints in creative exploration using the example of a decision to close a plant.

Decision-making skills are essential for organizational and personal effectiveness. On an organizational level, managers' decisions affect employees, shareholders, community members, and other organizational stakeholders. On a personal level, many decisions have a long-term effect on your career and future. In either case, the use of rational decision making and creativity tools can help improve the chances that decisions are not subject to undue bias.

We so far have considered several decision-making models and the importance of creativity in organizations. In the last part of the chapter, we identify the special features of team decision making and describe tools that can help teams make better decisions.

Brainstorming
A creative process in which individuals generate a large number of ideas without censorship

Cooperative exploration
Creativity tool that requires individuals to consider a problem by taking different positions

FIGURE 10.5
Cooperative Exploration and Linear Models

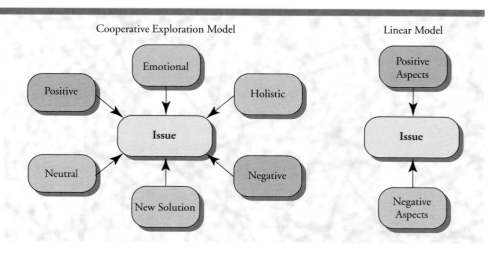

Table 10.4 VIEWPOINTS IN COOPERATIVE EXPLORATION

Viewpoint	Description and Examples
Neutral	Person does not take a side for or against the issues. What are the facts?
	Examples: The organization's financial situation, the economic impact on the community if the plant closes, analysis of competitors
Emotional	Person considers only the emotional aspects of the issue. Who gets hurt? What emotions may be triggered?
	Examples: Effect on employees and their families, the destruction of the community, the burden on the company's stakeholders if the plant stays open
Negative	Person considers only the negative aspects of the issue. What may go wrong? What if it does not work?
	Examples: Negative effect on the company's financial health, loss of clients, reduced production capacity, inability to compete
Positive	Person considers only the positive aspects of the issue. What are the benefits?
	Examples: Positive benefits of becoming more efficient, reduced overhead, positive market response, benefit to shareholders
New Solutions	Person considers only the new creative possibilities. What if . . . ?
	Examples: Allowing employees or the community to buy the plant, find a buyer, close only part of the plant
Holistic	Person takes a bird's-eye view of the issue. What is the big picture? What are the long-term implications? How does everything fit together?
	Examples: The strategic and social implications, whether the solution supports the company's strategy; long-term effect on the community and the firm's finances

Source: Based on information in E. DeBono, *Serious Creativity: Using the Power of Lateral Thinking to Create New Ideas* (New York: Harper Business, 1992).

Summary Point 10.8   **What Factors and Tools Encourage Creativity?**

- A questioning attitude allows employees to consider various alternatives and encourages creativity.
- National and organizational culture, structure, and leadership affect how new ideas are considered.

- Fear of taking risks prevents employees from being creative.
- Brainstorming and cooperative exploration are tools that managers can use to encourage individual creativity.

 GROUP DECISION MAKING

Groups and teams have more creative potential than individuals in organizations, especially when the task is complex. In addition, team decision making can be more effective than individual decisions because the open and supportive interaction of mature teams helps members define problems better. Also, the combined expertise of group members helps them develop and analyze more alternatives and solve problems in more novel and creative ways. What factors distinguish group and individual decision making and what are the tools that groups can use to make better decisions? We consider some of these next.

Special Features of Group Decision Making

Groups can rely on the same models of decision making as individuals. They should use a rational decision-making process to analyze situations and develop alternatives. They can consider the positive and negative aspects of decisions through linear models, and they can use intuition and experience when information is scarce and they face uncertain environments.

Hot ▼ Link

We discussed groups and their internal processes in chapter 7, pp. 229–64.

MANAGERIAL ADVICE
from the Experts

CREATIVITY IN ORGANIZATIONS

Managers benefit when their employees innovate. To encourage a creative, problem-solving mind-set, try some of the following techniques:

- Encourage interaction among employees by organizing formal and informal meetings within and across departments and creating cross-functional teams.
- Provide extensive information about the business and various problems that you and the organization face. To receive feedback, keep your door open, have a weekly meeting, start a bulletin board, publish a newsletter, create a Web page, or set up a hot line.
- Allow employees to try out new tasks and new assignments without fear of punishment. Rotate people to different positions, provide training in new areas, and encourage employees to take courses to expand their education.
- Encourage use of appropriate humor and shared laughter.
- Bring in creativity experts or share reading and video material on creativity; try out the exercises with your group.

Sources: Based on information in R. J. Sternberg and T. I. Lubart, *Defying the Crowd: Cultivating Creativity in a Culture of Conformity* (New York: Free Press, 1995); see also, R. Teitelbaum, "How to Harness Gray Matter," *Fortune* 135, no.11 (June 9, 1997): 168.

Similarly, decision heuristics and biases apply to groups just as they do to individual decision making. However, groups present a special challenge because of their processes and structure.

- Groups have *processes* that do not exist in individual decision making. For example, teams are subject to groupthink and conformity pressures.
- Groups and teams have *internal structures* and *roles* that affect the way members make decisions. For example, the presence of a leader or members focused on self-oriented roles affects the performance of teams.
- Groups develop *norms* that can help or hinder decision making. For example, a group may have norms for creativity and high performance that encourage good decision making.

In contrast to individuals, groups must manage group processes and dynamics; they must understand how group norms, culture, and development stage affect decisions. Group processes that compound decision-making difficulty include conformity, idiosyncrasy credit, and deviance. For instance, even a simple decision may be impossible to reach for a group that is in the conflict stage of development. Similarly, a decision that appears final may be challenged or blocked by a team member using her idiosyncrasy credit.

Managers must also recognize that group composition and roles affect decision making. Homogeneous teams may have less conflict, but they also may be less creative in their problem solving. When using groups to make decisions, managers need not only to support them with decision tools and train them in decision making, but also to be aware of how special group issues affect the decision process.

CAREER ADVICE
from the Experts

DEVELOPING FACILITATION SKILLS

Because teams make many decisions in organizations, good team facilitators are in demand. Having such facilitation skills can help secure a promotion or bring you to the attention of upper management. Facilitation skills include active listening, staying neutral, considering all positions, looking for patterns and similarities, bringing up points of agreement, and presenting win-win scenarios. To develop these skills, try to do the following:

- Volunteer to assist individuals who facilitate in organizations
- Observe outside group facilitators, such as trained focus group leaders, who may do marketing research in your company or at your school
- Practice your skills in all settings to help team processes and decision making
- Take company or outside training courses on facilitation

Source: J. Campbell, *Successful Facilitation for Team Trainees* (Clam Shell Publishers, 1997); C. Martin, *Facilitation Skills for Team Leaders* (Menlo Park, CA: Crisp, 1994).

Tools for Group Decision Making

Various group and team decision-making tools can help groups make better decisions. The common feature among the tools is their focus on increasing equal participation from all group members. They all aim to do the following:

- Reduce fear and conformity
- Discourage censorship by self or by others
- Increase the number and quality of the alternatives that the team develops

By providing a clear process for group decision making, these tools help groups that have not yet developed clear norms and processes. The tools allow for smooth group functioning and help groups reap some of the benefits of team decision making. We consider nominal group technique, Delphi, and group support systems next.

Nominal Group Technique   **Nominal group technique** (NGT) is a structured group process designed to generate and rank ideas. It is called *nominal* because the process actually reduces direct communication and interaction among team members during certain stages.[62] NGT proceeds this way. A small group of people is given a problem. Each group member individually writes down his or her alternatives. The alternatives are shared with the group and written down. Each is discussed and clarified without considering the author. The group then ranks the alternatives and votes on each of them. The process is repeated as often as necessary for the group to reach some agreement on the alternatives or solutions to the problem. Figure 10.6 illustrates the process.

The key to successful use of NGT is to limit interaction among group members in the early stages to prevent group conformity pressures. Furthermore, because the round-robin recording of ideas separates issues from people, the process reduces personal attacks and con-

Nominal group technique (NGT)
A structured group process of generating and ranking problem-solving ideas

FIGURE 10.6
Typical Nominal Group Technique Process

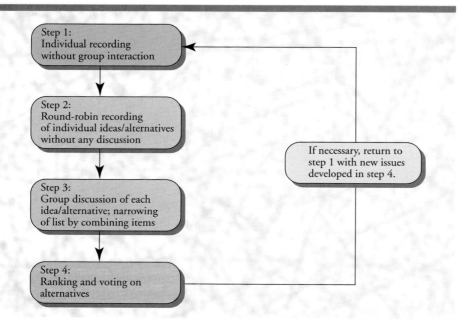

Step 1:
Individual recording without group interaction

Step 2:
Round-robin recording of individual ideas/alternatives without any discussion

Step 3:
Group discussion of each idea/alternative; narrowing of list by combining items

Step 4:
Ranking and voting on alternatives

If necessary, return to step 1 with new issues developed in step 4.

flicts. All group members have the same power and the same amount of input, thereby eliminating the potential negative effects of status and hierarchy. NGT encourages equal participation and helps build consensus.

Overall, NGT is an excellent decision-making tool, especially when large groups need to generate alternative solutions to problems. Its success depends to a great extent on the group leader's ability to manage the process well. Typically, an external person facilitates NGT to assure impartiality. The NGT facilitator usually leads but does not participate in the process of offering alternatives and ranking choices. Managers can use NGT in various stages. For instance, steps 1 and 2 may be completed before the group meets. The facilitator gets and records the ideas and presents them to the group, which then completes steps 3 and 4.

Delphi The *Delphi* technique of group decision making bypasses all face-to-face group meetings. **Delphi** is a structured group decision technique that obtains opinions about an issue through a series of formal surveys and rating scales.[68] A facilitator or a small group of people develops a questionnaire that asks the opinion of others about a certain topic. The survey is sent, either electronically or through regular mail, to a number of people who make individual anonymous responses. The facilitators summarize their responses and send back with another, more focused questionnaire. The results are once more summarized for the group. Although this process can be repeated a number of times, the second round is usually sufficient to clarify the issues.

Delphi technique
A structured group decision technique aimed at obtaining opinions about an issue through a series of formal surveys and rating scales

Consider the example of a department facing employee morale problems. Delphi can be used to inquire about the sources of the problem and to generate ideas for addressing them. The first survey is broad and explores many areas of dissatisfaction. It may include open-ended questions to allow for further input. The group receives the results along with another survey about the sources of dissatisfaction and low morale. The group can then use the final results as the basis for another round of Delphi focused on solutions or an NGT to generate alternatives.

Delphi has the following benefits:

- It can be used with large groups.
- It assures anonymity and reduces conformity pressure.
- It reduces interpersonal conflict.
- It is efficient and does not require lengthy meetings.
- It can make use of information technology tools such as e-mail.

In spite of the benefits of Delphi and NGT, neither can be used as the only decision-making tool. Both can support and help groups reach better decisions by reducing the potential for personal attacks and negative conflict. However, they do not replace the development of team processes. Groups must be allowed time to go through the stages of development; establish their own rules, norms, and procedures; and so forth. Their ability to develop several alternatives through NGT or Delphi alone does not make them a mature team. Furthermore, many situations require group members to work out issues openly and face-to-face.

Both techniques depend on the willingness of participants to share ideas and opinions and to trust that management will use their input appropriately.

A QUESTION OF ETHICS

Foul Play in Delphi   You suspect that the anonymous Delphi survey that you have completed through your company's e-mail is actually monitored by management. What are the ethical implications? What should you do?

Other Group Support Systems Organizations can use information technology to help group decision making. One type of technology is the group support system (GSS), which is technology that helps groups and teams become more efficient and effective. **Groupware** is a type of GSS. It is computer software specifically developed to help group members communicate, meet on-line, share ideas, exchange documents, work on data and documents simultaneously, and so forth. Other examples of GSS include **computer-aided decision systems** that ask participants to respond via computer to a number of standardized items. Managers and team members can use the instantly provided answers as the basis for further discussion or decision making.

GSS helps increase participation of group members in large groups. More ideas are generated, and instant feedback helps group efficiency. As with NGT and Delphi, these methods are tools to support other team decision-making processes and should not become the only means through which team members interact and develop solutions.

Groupware
Computer software that allows group members to communicate, share ideas, exchange documents, and work on data and documents simultaneously

Computer-aided decision systems
Systems that ask participants to respond to a number of standardized items through their computer. Answers are instantly fed back and can be used as the basis for further discussion or decision making

---

Summary Point 10.9   **What Are the Tools for Group Decision Making?**

- Nominal group technique (NGT) is a structured process designed to generate and rank ideas in a group.
- Delphi, a structured group decision technique, obtains opinions about an issue through a series of formal surveys and rating scales.
- Both NGT and Delphi reduce direct personal attacks and negative conflict and encourage wide participation in large groups.

- Decision tools help groups make better decisions but cannot replace the development of proper group and team processes.
- Other group support systems include groupware and computer-aided systems designed to increase group efficiency.

Decision Making *in Context*

As we investigated managerial decision making, we analyzed the role that national, ethnic, and organizational culture can play. Here, we briefly examine the relationship between decision making and four contextual factors: the environment, strategy, technology, and organizational structure.

A key decision that managers make is how they enact the organization's environment. That is, which environmental elements do they consider relevant to the organization? The enactment decision is critical because it strongly influences other decisions, such as these:

- What should the organization's mission, goals, and strategy be?
- Which organizational structure is most effective given its environment?
- What type of organizational culture best suits the organization's needs?

In fact, enactment is part of the strategic planning process. Leaders can and should rely on the models and tools discussed in this chapter to ensure that their enactment and other strategic decisions are optimal. The same decision-making processes, biases, heuristics, and cultural issues apply.

As we saw in the Change Challenge feature and Group Decision Making section, information technology affects organizational decision making. Such technology can track internal and external information and connect managers with constituents such as co-workers, suppliers, and customers. It can also affect the culture and structure of the organization. A business with little information technology, for instance, may have a culture in which people do not expect participative decision makeing because of the difficulty in sharing information quickly. If the organization lacks technology, it may not want or be able to allow telecommuting, a shamrock team structure, or other structures that depend on information access.

To stay flexible, managers should learn to use and manage high-tech decision-making tools to improve the efficiency and quality of their decisions. They should also be aware of the tools' limits, especially the potential for information overload and the belief that quantitative information tells the whole story. Similarly, managers need to make smart decisions about how much, when, and which information technology they and their employees should use.

Finally, the structure of an organization determines how and where decisions are made. It also affects creative decision making, as we noted in the chapter. In a centralized, hierarchical organization, managers control most of the decision-making power. In decentralized, flat organizations, employees at various levels make decisions. Team-based structures further spread decision-making power to groups at all levels.

For updated information on the topics in this chapter, Web exercises, links to related Web sites, an on-line study guide, and more, visit our companion Web site at:
http://www.prenhall.com/nahavandi

a Look Back at the

MANAGERIAL CHALLENGE

Philips Electronics

The world's third-largest electronics company was lagging when Cor Boonstra became CEO. Vowing to remake Philips and energize its financial performance, Boonstra methodically examined the entire corporation, piece by piece, gathering information to understand the situation better, define and diagnose the problems, and devise suitable alternatives. Like every other manager, Boonstra had to make decisions using less-than-perfect data drawn from internal and external sources. He had to rely on his intuition and previous experience (including 20 years at Sara Lee) to develop a turnaround strategy. And as an outsider entering the Philips management structure, he brought both objectivity and new framing approaches to the major decisions he faced.

At the end of his first full year as CEO, Boonstra held a news conference to report on how his initial objectives and decisions had affected the company's yearly results and to discuss plans for the upcoming year. He announced that Philips had become more profitable, meeting two of its three annual financial targets (and coming close to the third). He also explained his new corporate governance model, which established bottom-line responsibility for roughly 100 individual businesses within Philips.[69]

Although the company had made significant progress, the CEO still faced difficult decisions in the months ahead. He needed to reevaluate the company's manufacturing sites to find ways of cutting costs. In addition, he was concerned about overcapacity in certain product categories, which was hurting profitability. Finally, he had to craft a strategy for capturing a significant share of the thriving consumer electronics market.[70]

How Boonstra frames the current situation at Philips, as a crisis or not, will greatly affect his decisions about the company's current course. His personal risk propensity and creativity will also affect his decisions. He has proven so far that he can be patient and that he is willing to consider creative alternatives. Only time will tell whether his decisions will put Philips back on the track of profitability.

■ Point of View Exercises

You're the Manager: As a top manager for Philips's VCR products, you are responsible for making decisions about pricing, retail distribution, and advertising. Assume that the company is investing heavily in its consumer electronics products to capture market share. Which biases are most likely to influence your decisions?

You're the Employee: As an analyst assigned to the consumer products division, your job is to determine which markets offer the most sales and profit opportunity. Product managers use this information to prioritize the company's entry and investment in the markets you recommend. How might cognitive dissonance threaten your effectiveness in this role?

SUMMARY OF LEARNING OBJECTIVES

1. **Describe the rational, bounded rationality, linear, intuitive, and garbage can models of decision making.** The rational decision-making model aims at making the best possible decision through objective, orderly, and structured information gathering and analysis.

   The bounded rationality model of decision making acknowledges that there are a number of organizational and individual constraints to rational decision making that lead us to satisfice rather than optimize. The linear model of decision making improves decision-making accuracy by listing and assigning weights to the positive and negative aspects of each alternative.

   The intuitive model describes how managers make decisions based on intuition and past experiences. It can be useful when there is time pressure, and complete, objective information gathering is impossible.

   The garbage can model suggests that managers do not consider problems and solutions in a sequential, rational, and orderly manner. Instead they use information about events, people, alternatives, and opportunities in a haphazard way to generate ideas and potential solutions that may apply to the problem.

2. **Highlight the role of culture in decision making.** To understand the role of culture in decision making, managers must consider the following cultural elements: (1) individual or group goals, (2) whether group or individual decision making is used, (3) tolerance for ambiguity, (4) time orientation, (5) proactivity or fatalism, and (6) objectivity or subjectivity.

3. **Explain the effect of heuristics and biases in managerial decision making.** Decision heuristics and biases influence managerial decision-making processes and provide obstacles to objective decision making. Heuristics are rules and mental processes that we use to simplify decision making. They include availability, representation, anchoring and adjustment, and framing. Biases include escalation of commitment, cognitive dissonance, risk propensity, and relying on past experiences.

4. **Define creativity and specify ways managers can encourage it.** Creativity is the ability to combine ideas in new ways, to look at problems from many different angles, and to generate novel and useful alternatives. Characteristics of creative individuals include self-confidence and perseverance in the face of obstacles, willingness to take risks and to grow, openness to experience, and tolerance for ambiguity. Organizational factors in creativity are allowing a questioning attitude, national and organizational culture, fear of risk, a judgmental atmosphere, autocratic leadership, and rigid structures.

   The two major tools managers can use to encourage individual creativity are brainstorming and cooperative exploration. In brainstorming, individuals generate a large number of possible ideas without initially judging or evaluating them. Cooperative exploration requires individuals to consider a problem by taking different positions such as neutral, emotional, negative, positive, new solutions, and holistic rather than simply considering the positive and negative sides of issues.

5. **Review the special characteristics and tools of group decision making.** Although teams can rely on the same models of decision making as individuals, several special characteristics of teams make group decision making different. These include the issues of group processes and dynamics, group structure and composition, and group roles and norms.

   Nominal group technique (NGT) is a structured process aimed at generating and ranking ideas in a group. It reduces direct communication and interaction among team members during certain stages. Delphi is also a structured decision tool aimed at obtaining opinions about an issue through a series of formal surveys and rating scales. NGT and Delphi encourage sharing of ideas, equal participation, and thorough analysis of alternatives; help reduce interpersonal conflicts; and make teams more efficient in their decision making. Other team tools include computer-based groupware and group decision support systems (GSS) that use information technology tools to encourage people to share ideas and participate in decisions. These tools help improve group decision making but do not replace the development of group or team processes.

KEY TERMS

anchoring and adjustment, p. 355
availability, p. 354
bounded rationality model, p. 346
brainstorming, p. 364
cognitive dissonance, p. 358
computer-aided decision systems, p. 369
cooperative exploration, p. 364
creativity, p. 360

decision heuristics, p. 354
Delphi technique, p. 368
escalation of commitment, p. 356
framing, p. 356
garbage can model, p. 349
groupware, p. 369
intuitive decision making, p. 349
linear model, p. 348
nominal group technique, p. 367

nonprogrammed decisions, p. 354
programmed decisions, p. 354
propensity for risk, p. 359
rational decision making, p. 344
representation, p. 355
risk averse, p. 359
satisficing, p. 347

REVIEW QUESTIONS

1. Compare and contrast the five decision models presented in this chapter. What are the strengths and weaknesses of each?
2. Explain the effect of culture in decision making. List six questions managers should ask to ascertain the cultural effects.
3. List and describe the decision-making heuristics and biases that affect the way managers make decisions.
4. What are the elements of creativity?
5. How can managers encourage employees to be more creative?
6. Compare and contrast the tools for group decision making. When can each be used?

DISCUSSION QUESTIONS

1. Given the complexity and uncertainty of the business environment, when can managers rely on rational decision making? Does it depend on the type of decision they face? Explain.
2. How can managers use decision-making models to make better decisions?
3. How can knowledge of culture's effect on decision making help managers work more effectively with people from several cultures?
4. Should a manager be responsible for encouraging employee creativity? Explain your answer. Now take the opposite position and defend it.
5. What is the role of group decision-making tools such as NGT and Delphi in making teams effective? How should teams use them for maximum effect?

▶ **SELF-ASSESSMENT 10**
Myers-Briggs Type Inventory (MBTI)

Many organizations use the MBTI as a team building tool. The inventory is designed to assess the ways people gather and use information in their decision making and interpersonal relations.

The overall goal of this self-assessment is to identify your cognitive style and to provide you with information about what types of information you are more likely to pay attention to, gather, and use. There are no right or wrong answers. Please respond to the following 16 items. After you have completed all items, use the scoring key in Appendix 3 to identify your style.

PART I.   CIRCLE THE RESPONSE THAT COMES CLOSEST TO HOW YOU USUALLY FEEL OR ACT.

1. Are you more careful about
   - A. People's feelings
   - B. Their rights

2. Do you usually get along better with
   - A. Imaginative people
   - B. Realistic people

3. Which of these two is the higher compliment:
   - A. A person has real feeling
   - B. A person is consistently reasonable

4. In doing something with many other people, does it appeal more to you
   - A. To do it in the accepted way
   - B. To invent a way of your own

5. Do you get more annoyed at
   - A. Fancy theory
   - B. People who don't like theories

6. It is higher praise to call someone
   - A. A person of vision
   - B. A person of common sense

7. Do you more often let
   - A. Your heart rule your head
   - B. Your head rule your heart

8. Do you think it is worse
   - A. To show too much warmth
   - B. To be unsympathetic

9. If you were a teacher, would you rather teach
   - A. Courses involving theory
   - B. Fact courses

PART II.   CIRCLE THE WORD IN EACH OF THE FOLLOWING PAIRS THAT APPEALS TO YOU MORE.

10. A. Compassion   B. Foresight
11. A. Justice   B. Mercy
12. A. Production   B. Design
13. A. Gentle   B. Firm
14. A. Uncritical   B. Literal
15. A. Literal   B. Figurative
16. A. Imaginative   B. Matter of fact

PART III.   IDENTIFYING YOUR STYLE.

If your intuition score is equal to or greater than your sensation score, select *intuition*. If sensation is greater than intuition, select *sensation*. Select *feeling* if feeling is greater than thinking. Select *thinking* if thinking is greater than feeling. When thinking equals feeling, you should select feeling if a male and thinking if a female.

My style is (circle the two dimensions based on the instructions above)

Sensation **or** Intuition   Thinking **or** Feeling

FIGURE 10.7
Four Myers-Briggs Type Inventory Categories

Sources: Excerpted from U. C. U. Haley and S. A. Stumpf, "Cognitive Traits in Strategic Decision Making: Linking Theories of Personality and Cognition," *Journal of Management Studies* 26, no. 5 (1989): 477–97; T. Moore, "Personality Tests Are Back," *Fortune* (March 30, 1987): 74–82.

Thinking (T)

Sensation (S) | | Intuition (N)

Feeling (F)

Sensation Thinkers (ST)
Establish rules and regulations
Focus on facts and figures
Are decisive decision makers
Persevere on realistic goals
Focus on effectiveness and efficiency
Push others to get to the point
Give and receive concrete rewards
Are impatient with delays
Jump into action too quickly
Are tense when things don't go as planned

Intuitive Thinkers (NT)
Are architects of progress and ideas
See relationships among departments
Focus on possibilities and analyze objectively
Are change agents
Are responsive to creativity
Are straightforward and open
Enjoy intellectual activities
Enjoy problem solving
Are unaware of other's feelings
Judge others on intellectual achievements
Have unreasonable expectations

Sensation Feelers (SF)
Are pragmatic and methodical
Are troubleshooters and diplomats
Are good at working the system
Understand organizations well
Respond well to concrete ideas
Are predictable and easy to get along with
Reward outcome rather than effort
Are reluctant to accept change
Show overreliance on rules and regulations
Focus too much on present

Intuitive Feelers (NF)
Have personal charisma and commitment to others
Are good communicators
Seem comfortable with uncertainty and change
Are patient with complications
Are open to ideas and to change
Relate well to others
Seek social and personal contact
Need too much approval from others
Burn out and need periods of rest
Have trouble implementing ideas

PART IV.   INTERPRETING YOUR STYLE.

The MBTI indicates how people gather and use information, two key parts of the decision-making process. Each of the four styles tends to take a different view of problem solving, decision making, information use, time, and task accomplishment (see Figure 10.7). Each style has strengths and weaknesses, with no one style being best. The MBTI is used extensively in a number of organizations as part of team building to allow team members to assess their strengths and weaknesses.[71]

▶ TEAM EXERCISE 10
Survival

Sometimes group decision making is more effective than individual decision making. Research shows that if the decision is simple, it is beter to have one person responsible; however, if the problem is more complex, group decision making is more effective. In this exercise, you'll get a chance to compare the results of individual and group decision making.

THE SITUATION

You have gone on a Boundary Waters canoe trip with five friends to upper Minnesota and southern Ontario in the Quetico Provincial Park. Your group has been traveling the Saganagons Lake to Kawnipi Lake following through Canyon Falls and Kennebas Falls and Kenny Lake.

Fifteen to eighteen miles away is the closest road, which is arrived at by paddling through lakes and rivers and usually portaging (taking the land path) around numerous falls. Saganagons Lake is impossible to cross in bad weather, generally because of heavy rain. The nearest town is Grand Marais, Minnesota, sixty miles away. That town has plenty of camping outfitters, but limited medical help, so citizens rely on hospitals further to the south.

The terrain is about 70 percent land and 30 percent water, with small patches of land here and there in between the lakes and rivers. Bears are not uncommon in this region. It is now mid-May, when the daytime temperature ranges from about 25° to 70°, often in the same day. Nighttime temperatures can be in the 20s.

Rain is frequent and is life-threatening if the temperature is cold. It is unusual for the weather to stay the same for more than a day or two. Generally, it will rain one day and be warm and clear the next, with a third day windy—and it is not easy to predict what type of weather will come next. In fact, it may be clear and warm, rainy and windy, all in the same day.

Your group of six was in two canoes going down the river and came to a rapids. Rather than taking the portage route on land, the group foolishly decided to shoot the rapids by canoe. Unfortunately, everyone fell out of the canoes and some were banged against the rocks. Luckily no one was killed, but one person suffered a broken leg and several members had cuts and bruises.

Both canoes were damaged severely. Both were bent in half, one with an open tear of 18", while the other had two tears of 12" and 15" long. Both had broken gunwales (upper edges on both sides). You lost the packs that held the tent, most clothing, nearly all the food, cooking equipment, fuel, first aid kit, and flashlight. Your combined possessions include one jack knife, four canoe paddles, a pocketful of hard candies, five dollar bills, and 65 cents in change.

You had permits to take this trip, but no one knows for sure where you are and the closest phone is in Grand Marais. As you were scheduled back four days from now, it is likely a search party would be sent out in about five days (since you may have been delayed a day or so in getting back). Just now it has started to drizzle and it looks like rain will follow.

Your task now is to figure out how to survive in these unpredictable and possibly hazardous conditions until you can get help.

1. Introduction and individual ranking

Instructor gives brief background on case and asks students to rank the 14 items on the list in terms of survival value. The item considered most valuable should be ranked "1" while the least valuable should be ranked "14." Individuals should place their rankings on Table 1, column A.

2. Group discussion

In groups of 6–9 members come to a consensus on the ranking of the items. Use Table 1, column B for this. Members should not vote or horse trade, but rather should try to have everyone more or less agree on the ranking. When someone disagrees, members should try and listen carefully. When someone feels strongly, that person should attempt to use persuasive techniques.

3. Correct answers given

Instructor posts the correct answers and gives the reasons for these rankings, according to the experts. Students put correct rankings in column C of Table 1.

4. Computation of Table 1

    a. Compare your answer, listed under column A, with the correct answer, listed under column C. Subtract C from A in each row, taking the absolute value

Table 1

Rank order the following in terms of survival assistance, putting the most valuable as "1."

ITEMS	A Your ranking	B Group ranking	C Expert ranking	D (A–C) Individual error	E (B–C) Group error	F (A–B) Persuasion
Fanny pack of food—cheese, salami, gorp						
Plastic covered map of Boundary Waters						
Six PFD's—Personal Flotation Devices						
Two fishing poles, broken						
Set of clothes for three (wet)						
One yellow Frisbee						
Water purification tablets						
Duct tape, one 30′ roll						
Whiskey, one pint 180 proof						
Insect repellant, one bottle						
Matches, 30 dry						
Parachute cord, 35 feet						
Compass						
Six sleeping bags, synthetic, medium weight						

Individual Score (Total of D) _____

Group Score (Total of E)   _____

Persuasion Score (Total of F) _____

(do not count minus signs). That will be the individual error listed under column D. For example:

If you answered	and the correct answer was	the difference is
2	11	9
10	5	5
12	1	11

b. Total the numbers in column D (none of which should be negative numbers). This gives you your Individual Score.

c. Subtract column C from column B in each row, again using absolute values, to get the group error, which should be listed under column E.

d. Total the numbers in column E (none of which should be negative numbers). This gives you your Group Score.

e. Subtract the numbers in column B from column A and put the results (absolute value) in column F. This is your persuasion score, which measures how much you are able to influence other group members to your thinking. Spend a few minutes during your group discussion talking about the persuasion score. Who had the lowest (this person was the most persuasive) and who had the highest (this person was the least persuasive) scores?

Table 2

	Groups					
	1	2	3	4	5	6
Average Member Score						
Group Score						
Synergy						
Best Member Score						

5. Computation of Table 2

    a. Average Member Score
Add up the Individual Score (Step b, column D) of all group members and divide by the number of members in the group. Put this number in the indicated row.

    b. Group Score (Step d, column E)
Put this number in the indicated row.

    c. Synergy
If your Group Score is lower than your Average Member Score, then put "yes" in the column for Synergy. If your Group Score is higher than your Average Member Score, then put "no" in the column for Synergy.

    d. Best Member Score
This is the number of the member who has the lowest Individual Score. Put this score in the indicated column.

6. Group feedback (optional)

The group talks about how it did in terms of decision making, who was most persuasive, and so on.

7. Class discussion

The instructor leads discussion on group decision making and how each group did in this exercise, answering the following questions.

8. Group discussion

As a class, discuss the following questions:

1. To what extent did group discussion change accuracy of the answers?
2. Which behaviors helped or hindered the decision-making process?
3. What happened if a pesron had a very accurate Individual Score, but was not very persuasive in the group? Conversely, what if a person had a poor Individual Score and was very persuasive in the group?

Source: From Dorothy Marcic, *Organizational Behavior: Experiences and Cases*, 3d ed. (West, 1992). Copyright © 1992 West Publishing. Reprinted by permission of Southwestern College Publishing, a division of International Thompson Publishing, Inc., Cincinnati, OH 45227.

UP CLOSE

▶ **The Road to Hell Is Paved with Good Intentions**

John Baker, chief engineer of the Caribbean Bauxite Company stationed in the newly independent West Indian nation of Barracania, had been promoted to a new position in his native United States and was about to interview his successor—the able young Barracanian, Matthew Rennalls.

Baker, a 23-year veteran of the company, had spent the last two years grooming Rennalls as his successor. Rennalls, ten years younger than Baker, had received his engineering degree with honors from a U.S. university, and was the son of Barracania's minister of finance. He had been recruited as an assistant engineer through Caribbean Bauxite's affirmative action program, which had resulted in 18 Barracanians posted at mid-management positions.

Before the final interview, Baker reviewed the plusses and minuses of Rennalls's record. On the plus side were his technical ability, his enthusiasm, his willingness to take on new assignments, his constructive comments in meetings, and his popularity among the Barracanian employees. On the negative side were his racial consciousness and his sensitivity in his relations with white American employees.

Baker felt that Rennalls's race-consciousness had kept them from being closer friends than they were. They visited each other at home and played tennis together, but Baker still felt there was a barrier between them. Baker had not spoken with Rennalls about this in previous performance reviews, although he had heard complaints about Rennalls's attitude from American employees.

At the final interview, Baker said: "As you know, Matt, you will soon be sitting in this chair doing the job I am now doing. Perhaps I can give you some of the benefit of my age and experience. I'd like to review both the positive and negative aspects of your performance to encourage you and inspire you to improve.

"On the positive side, I have been most impressed by how you have applied your theoretical knowledge to the practical aspects of the job, and your input at meetings has always been helpful. From a technical point of view, there is no better candidate to succeed me at this job.

"On the negative side, I have noticed that you get along better with the Barracanian employees than with the Americans. It's important to relate well with your American

co-workers, Matt, especially as they will be in the more senior positions until the company has promoted more people of your caliber."

Rennalls replied, "Isn't it amazing how people can perceive you differently than you intend? I can assure you that my disputes with other employees have had nothing to do with their skin color. I have had problems with several poor performers. However, I am sorry to have created this false impression, and I will try to correct it as soon as possible. And I know the company intends to promote Barracanians as their experience warrants it. I am happy with my experience here, John—my father feels the same way—and I hope to stay with the company for many years."

Baker was inspired to continue: "You know, I'd like to mention another 'plus' on your record. You've been able to overcome a challenge I never faced. My ancestors have been part of this Western commercial environment for hundreds of years, but your forbears have had only 50 or 60 years to adjust to this culture. You and others like you should be congratulated for bridging this gap in such a short time, and I think the future of Barracania is brighter because of it."

Rennalls responded, "Again, I appreciate what you have said, and I thank you for your recognition of my own personal effort. I hope that more people will soon think as you do."

Baker left the interview buoyed by the cheerful note on which it had ended. However, the next morning there was a letter from Matthew Rennalls waiting for him at his desk:

"Dear Mr. Baker:

"I have always respected the advice of my elders. After our interview yesterday I considered the main points of our discussion to put your advice to best effect.

"The more I thought about it, the more furious I became. You insulted me and all Barracanians by claiming that our knowledge of modern living is only 50 years old while yours goes back 200 to 300 years—as if your materialistic culture could be compared with the spiritual values of ours. What right do you have to condescend to us?

"My father is as angry as I am, and he agrees that a company such as yours is no place for any self-respecting Barracanian.

"I feel ashamed and betrayed. Please accept this letter as my resignation, effective immediately."

Questions

1. What biases enter Baker's and Rennalls's decision-making processes?
2. What role does culture play in the interaction between the two men?
3. What should John Baker do next?

THE BIG PICTURE

▶ Kodak's Decision to Go Digital

When George Fisher took over as CEO of Eastman Kodak in 1993—the first outsider ever to hold that top position—the company's future was decidedly out of focus. Fisher had built a reputation as a star in turnaround strategy during his tenure as CEO at Motorola, where he led the high-tech company to new heights in profitability and productivity.[72] Now he faced an even greater challenge: positioning Kodak for profitable growth in an increasingly competitive global environment.

First, Fisher tackled Kodak's financial situation. He cut $7 billion of the company's debt by selling its drug, health, and chemical divisions. Next, he pushed hard for an array of new products to update Kodak's stodgy image. Perhaps his most controversial move, however, was the decision to emphasize digital imaging.[73] This technology uses a special camera-film system and allows electronic storage and manipulation of photographic images.

Although Fisher was enthusiastic about digital imaging—allocating $500 million yearly for research and development—widespread acceptance of the technology could mean the eventual end of traditional film products, which had long been Kodak's major moneymaker. So far, however, consumer reaction to digital imaging had only been lukewarm.

Nonetheless, Fisher decided to go ahead with the installation of thousands of digital imaging kiosks in U.S. retail stores to attract consumers who wanted to pull photos off the Internet, manipulate them, and create prints. To support this strategy, Kodak purchased a company that specializes in storing and transmitting photos on the Internet.[74] Meanwhile, global giants such as NEC, Sony, and Hewlett-Packard were heading in the opposite direction, developing products to allow consumers to work with digital images at home.[75]

Fisher and his top management team agreed that digital imaging is the future, so Kodak needed to move quickly to stake out a market-leading position. But the digital imaging strategy was costly: Kodak barely broke even in 1997, causing Fisher to slash $1 billion in costs and eliminate more than 10,000 jobs—still maintaining his focus on digital imaging.[76]

During his Motorola days, Fisher demonstrated his ability to focus on solutions and his acute market-sensitive intuition. He was an early champion of pagers and cellular phones, winning out over skeptics who thought those products would never catch on. Now, as CEO of Kodak, will Fisher's decisions put the company on track toward a more profitable future?

Questions

1. What decision-making models fit Kodak's highly competitive market?
2. What decision-making biases might be involved in decisions at Kodak?
3. Should Kodak stick to the tried and true where it has been successful or should it leap into an unknown risky market?

NOTES

1. C. P. Wallace, "Can He Fix Philips?" *Fortune* (March 31, 1997): 98–100; Business Wire, "National Academy of Recording Arts and Sciences Awards Philips Electronics Grammy for the Development of the CD," press release, March 2, 1998, accessed on-line at http://www.biz/yahoo.com/bw/980302/philips_e1_1.html.
2. Ibid., 98–99.
3. Ibid., 99.
4. Business Wire, "The Philips Group in 1997," press release, February 12, 1998, accessed on-line at http://biz.yahoo.com/bw/980212/philips_1.
5. Based on a case by S. A. Desai and E. N. Weiss, "Journey to Excellence: The Ritz-Carlton Hotel in Sydney, Australia," in A. A. Thompson and A. J. Strickland, III, *Strategic Management*, 10th ed. (Boston: Irwin/McGraw-Hill, 1995): 979–97.
6. Ibid.
7. Ibid.
8. Ibid., 993.
9. H. A. Simon, *Administrative Behavior* (New York: Free Press, 1957); H. A. Simon, "Altruism and Economics," *American Economic Review* (May 1993): 156–61.
10. M. Browne, *Organizational Decision-Making and Information* (Norwood, NJ: Ablex, 1993): 22–32.
11. J. G. March and H. A. Simon, *Organizations* (New York: Wiley, 1958).
12. For a summary, see R. M. Dawes, *Rational Choice in an Uncertain World* (Orlando, FL: Harcourt Brace Jovanovich, 1988): 202–27.
13. Ibid.
14. Ibid.
15. E. R. Duncan, "A Discriminant Analysis of Predictors of Business Failure," *Journal of Accounting Research* 10 (1972): 167–79.
16. For a summary of research on use of intuition in decision making, see W. H. Agor, *Intuition in Organizations* (Newbury Park, CA: Sage, 1989); O. Behling and N. L. Eckel, "Making Sense Out of Intuition," *Academy of Management Executive* 1 (1991): 46–47.
17. M. D. Cohen, J. G. March, and J. P. Olsen, "A Garbage Can Model of Organizational Choice," *Administrative Science Quarterly* (March 1971): 1–25.
18. For research supporting the garbage can model, see M. Mausch and P. LaPotin, "Beyond Garbage Cans: An A1 Model of Organizational Choice," *Administrative Science Quarterly* (March 1989): 38–67.
19. B. O'Reilly, "The Wreck of the Union Pacific," *Fortune* 137, no. 6 (March 30, 1998): 100.
20. Ibid., 94.
21. Ibid., 99.
22. Hofstede (1993).
23. K. H. Chung, "The Comparative Study of Managerial Characteristics of Domestic, International, and Governmental Institutions in Korea," paper presented at the Midwest Conference of Asian Affairs, Minneapolis, Minnesota, 1978.
24. E. W. Desmond, "Can Canon Keep Clicking?" *Fortune* 137, no. 2 (February 2, 1998): 98–104.
25. E. Lifson, "Camel Race in Berlin," *NPR Morning Edition*, National Public Radio, August 19, 1997.
26. March and Simon, *Organizations*; H. A. Simon, *The New Science of Management Decision* (New York: Harper and Row, 1960).
27. For a complete review of decision heuristics, see A. Tversky and D. Kahneman, "Judgment Under Uncertainty: Heuristics and Biases," *Science* 185 (1974): 1124–31.
28. Ibid.
29. Ibid.; S. Plous, *The Psychology of Judgment and Decision Making* (New York: McGraw-Hill, 1993).
30. The concept of framing was proposed by A. Tversky and D. Kahneman, "Framing of Decisions and the Psychology of Choice," *Science* 211 (1981): 435–58. For recent studies of the effects of framing, see K. Takemura, "Influence of Elaboration on the Framing of Decision," *Journal of Psychology* 128, no. 1 (1994): 33–39; K. J. Dunegan, "Framing, Cognitive Modes, and Image Theory: Toward an Understanding of a Glass Half Full," *Journal of Applied Psychology* 78, no. 3 (1993): 491–503.
31. R. Balu, "Orphan Brands Grow with New Parent," *Wall Street Journal*, April 2, 1998, B1, B14.
32. Ibid.
33. B. M. Staw, "The Escalation of Commitment to a Course of Action," *Academy of Management Review* 6 (1981): 577–87; M. H. Bazemann and A. Appleman, "Escalation of Commitment in Individual and Group Decision-Making," *Organization Behavior and Human Decision Processes* (Spring 1984): 141–52; B. M. Staw and J. Ross, "Behavior in Escalation Situations: Antecedents, Prototypes and Solutions," in L. L. Cummings and B. M. Staw (eds.), *Research in Organization Behavior*, vol. 9 (Greenwich, CT: JAI, 1988): 39–78; J. P. Walsh and C. M. Henderson, "Attributional Analysis of Decisions About Making Commitments," *Journal of Social Psychology* 129, no. 4 (1988): 533–49; D. A. Hantula and C. R. Crowell, "Intermittent Reinforcement and Escalation Processes in Sequential Decision-Making: A Replication and Theoretical Analysis," *Journal of Organizational Behavior Management* 14, no. 2 (1994): 7–36.
34. M. Meyer, "A Death Spiral?" *Newsweek* (July 28, 1997): 48–49.
35. G. Colvin, "The 1998 Don't-Get-It-All-Stars," *Fortune* (March 30, 1998): 169–70.
36. For a discussion of the factors in escalation of commitment, see J. Ross and B. M. Staw, "Organizational Escalation and Exit: Lessons from the Shoreham Nuclear Power Plant," *Academy of Management Journal* (August 1993): 701–32.
37. Colvin, "The 1998 Don't-Get-It-All-Stars," 170.
38. See J. Brockner, "The Escalation of Commitment to a Failing Course of Action: Toward Theoretical Progress," *Academy of Management Review* 17, no. 1 (1992): 39–61.
39. H. Garland, "Throwing Good Money After Bad: The Effect of Sunk Costs on the Decision to Escalate Commitment to Ongoing Projects," *Journal of Applied Psychology* 12 (1990): 728–32.
40. I. Simonson and B. M. Staw, "Deescalation Strategies: A Comparison of Techniques for Reducing Commitment to Losing Courses of Action," *Journal of Applied Psychology* 8 (1992): 419–26.
41. The concept of cognitive dissonance was first proposed by Leon Festinger, *A Theory of Cognitive Dissonance* (New York: Harper and Row, 1957). Examples of recent work supporting the concept and its application to a variety of situations include R. Harrison and J. G. March, "Decision-Making and Post-Decision Surprises," *Administrative Science Quarterly* (March 1984): 26–42.
42. For a recent study of risk propensity, see S. B. Sitkin and L. R. Weingart, "Determinants of Risky Decision-Making Behavior: A Test of the Mediating Role of Risk Perception and Propensity," *Academy of Management Journal* 38, no. 6 (1995): 1573–92.
43. E. Shapiro, "Brash as Ever, Turner Is Giving Time Warner Dose of Culture Shock," *Wall Street Journal*, March 24, 1997, A1, A8; A. Sharpe, "Used to Being Boss, Ted Turner Is Mulling His Time Warner Role," *Wall Street Journal*, November 27, 1995, A1, A5.
44. D. A. Blackmon, "Sunbeam Shares Dive as Investors Doubt Dunlap," *Wall Street Journal*, April 6, 1998, A5; see article by Al Dunlap himself, talking about his successes, in *Newsweek*, February 26, 1996, 48; also see T. Petzinger, "Does Al Dunlap Mean Business, or Is He Just Plain Mean?" *Wall Street Journal*, August 30, 1996, B1.
45. M. Brand, "Sunbeam Restructuring," *NPR Morning Edition*, National Public Radio, March 3, 1998.
46. For a detailed discussion of the definition of creativity, see M. A. Boden, "What Is Creativity?" in M. A. Boden (ed.), *Dimensions of Creativity* (Cambridge, MA: MIT Press, 1994): 75–117.
47. E. DeBono, *Serious Creativity: Using the Power of Lateral Thinking to Create New Ideas* (New York: Harper Business, 1992).
48. DeBono, *Serious Creativity*; T. M. Amabile, "A Model of Creativity and Innovation in Organizations," in B. M. Staw and L. L. Cummings (eds.), *Research in Organization Behavior*, vol. 10 (Greenwich, CT: JAI, 1988): 123–67; R. J. Sternberg and T. I. Lubard, *Defying the Crowd: Cultivating Creativity in a Culture of Conformity* (New York: Free Press, 1995).
49. P. E. Vernon, "The Nature-Nurture Problem in Creativity," in J. A. Glover, R. R. Ronning, and C. R. Reynolds (eds.), *Handbook of Creativity* (New York: Plenum, 1989): 93–110; H. J. Eysenck, "The Measurement of Creativity," in M. A. Boden (ed.), *Dimensions of Creativity* (Cambridge, MA: MIT Press, 1994): 199–242.
50. See T. R. Horton, *What Works for Me* (New York: Random House, 1986): 387–94.
51. T. T. Vogel, Jr., "Costa Rica's Sales Pitch Lures High-Tech Giants Like Intel and Microsoft," *Wall Street Journal*, April 2, 1998, A18.
52. Ibid.
53. A. Carrns and J. S. Hirsch, "Real-Estate Innovator Sees Future in Catering to Needs of the Elderly," *Wall Street Journal*, June 30, 1997, A1, A6.
54. R. J. Sternberg and T. I. Lubart, *Defying the Crowd: Cultivating Creativity in a Culture of Conformity* (New York: Free Press, 1995).
55. A. Muoio, "Life Is a Juggling Act," *Fast Company* (October–November 1997): 176.
56. K. Mieszkowski, "The Power of Public Relations," *Fast Company* (April–May 1998): 184, 196.

57. D. J. Burns and J. Brady, "A Cross-Cultural Comparison of the Need for Uniqueness in Malaysia and the United States," *Journal of Social Psychology* 132, no. 4 (1992): 487–95; K. Whitney, L. M. Sagrestano, and C. Maslach, "Establishing the Social Impact of Individuation," *Journal of Personality and Social Psychology* 66, no. 6 (1994): 1140–53.

58. J. Patrick, "What Works at Work?," *Fast Company* (February–March 1998): 140.

59. K. Szymanski and S. G. Harkins, "Self-Evaluation and Creativity," *Personality and Social Psychology Bulletin* 18, no. 3 (1992): 259–65, found that the potential for self-evaluation undermined creativity.

60. Z. Shapira, *Risk-Taking: A Managerial Perspective* (New York: Russell Sage Foundation, 1995).

61. R. A. Josephs, R. P. Larrick, C. M. Steele, and R. E. Nisbett, "Protecting the Self from the Negative Consequences of Risky Decisions," *Journal of Personality and Social Psychology* 62, no. 1 (1992): 26–37.

62. Cited in Shapira, *Risk Taking*, 130.

63. G. Wilson, *Problem Solving and Decision Making* (London: Kogan Page, 1993): 41.

64. Amabile, "A Model of Creativity."

65. R. Teitelbaum, "How to Harness Gray Matter," *Fortune* 135, no. 11 (June 9, 1997): 168.

66. DeBono, *Serious Creativity*.

67. A. L. Delbeq, A. Van de Ven, and D. H. Gustafson, *Group Techniques for Program Running* (Glenview, IL: Scott Foresman, 1975); J. B. A. Thomas, R. R. McDaniel Jr., and M. J. Dorris, "Strategic Issue Analysis: NGT + Decision Analysis for Resolving Strategic Issues," *Journal of Applied Behavioral Sciences* 25, no. 2 (1989): 189–200.

68. H. A. Linstone and M. Turoff, eds., *The Delphi Method: Techniques and Applications* (Reading, MA: Addison-Wesley, 1975).

69. Business Wire, "The Philips Group in 1997."

70. Ibid.

71. T. Moore, "Personality Tests Are Back," *Fortune* (March 30, 1987): 74–82.

72. Geoffrey Smith, "Can George Fisher Fix Kodak?" *Business Week* (October 20, 1997): 116.

73. Ibid., 116–20.

74. "Kodak to Buy 51 Percent of Picture Vision," Reuters, February 13, 1998.

75. Geoffrey Smith, "Kodak's Focus May Be Too Narrow," *Business Week* (November 24, 1997): 42.

76. Ibid.

USING POWER AND ORGANIZATIONAL POLITICS

LEARNING OBJECTIVES

1. Define power and identify cross-cultural differences in power, individual and organizational sources of power, and corruption of power.
2. Explain the role of empowerment in today's organizations.
3. Describe the political model of organizations, the factors that contribute to organizational politics, and political tactics.
4. Analyze the ways managers can use politics to benefit the organization.

MANAGERIAL CHALLENGE

Fidelity Investments

Ned Johnson III, chair of Fidelity Investments, the world's largest mutual fund company, was facing troubled times. The Boston-based company was founded by Johnson's father and remained under family control. Its enviable reputation for paying handsome returns on mutual funds had attracted $500 billion in assets from individual and institutional investors. By 1997, however, some of Fidelity's best-known funds lagged behind other funds in the high-flying performance of the bull market. More than 20 highly skilled fund managers had departed, and competition intensified as rivals nipped relentlessly at Fidelity's market share.[1]

To address this situation, Johnson made a series of key management changes. He named Robert C. Pozen to head the huge mutual fund division—and shifted his daughter Abigail Pierrepont Johnson into position as one of three senior vice presidents assisting Pozen. Industry observers saw this as a signal that the younger Johnson was being groomed as Fidelity's future chairperson, just as the elder Johnson had taken the reins from his father more than 20 years earlier.[2]

Like her father before her, Abby Johnson learned the mutual fund business from the ground up. She joined Fidelity in 1988 after graduating from Harvard Business School. Her first four assignments were in mutual fund management. Just months before moving into senior management, Johnson was put in charge of the computer system that handles research data for the company's investments. She retained that role when she became Pozen's assistant, and she added responsibility for supervising a cadre of portfolio managers—her former colleagues.[3] With the financial world watching, how would Abby Johnson handle power and politics at Fidelity Investments?

■ **Questions**

1. What sources of power might Abby Johnson draw on in her senior management role?
2. To what extent should Abby Johnson use empowerment as an option for managing Fidelity's portfolio managers?

Leaders and managers like Ned and Abby Johnson need power to influence others. Power helps managers fulfill their leadership responsibilities. It also affects relationships among people at all levels inside and outside the organization. As discussed in chapters 1 and 2, managerial power has changed considerably over the past 10 to 15 years. Managers delegate and empower others. Organizational structures have flattened, causing more people at each level to share power. Relationships—such as those among group or team members and with customers, contractors, and suppliers—are more important in some organizations than status and hierarchy.

These changes have altered the way organizations define and use power. Fluid coalitions and relationships are the core of the political process inside organizations. This chapter examines traditional and current views of power; its individual, team, and organizational sources; and its consequences. It also explores the use of politics in organizations.

 POWER

Power
The ability of a person to influence another

Authority
The power vested in a particular position, such as that of an office manager or human resource director

Hot ▼ Link

See the discussion on leadership substitutes and neutralizers in chapter 9, pp. 317–20.

The ability of one person to influence another is **power**. It is not the exclusive domain of leaders and managers. Individuals at all levels of an organization, as well as outsiders—namely, customers—have the ability to influence the behavior and attitudes of others. The terms *power, authority*, and *influence* are often used interchangeably, but each has a distinct meaning. **Authority** is power vested in a particular position, as with an office manager or human resource director. Many people in organizations have power based on factors such as expertise or access to information. Others have power because of their position in the organization. Finally, although the concepts of power and influence are closely related, they are not synonymous. A manager who has power may not be able to influence employees' behaviors because the employees do not respect her or because of various organizational factors, such as leadership neutralizers. Similarly, an individual without formal authority can still influence others.[4]

Power, authority, and influence are an integral part of organizations. The way power is acquired, used, and accepted may vary from one company to the next and from one culture to another. Nevertheless, all members of an organization use various forms of power to influence one another to achieve organizational and personal goals. In this section, we consider individual and organizational sources of power, the role of culture in the use of power, and the consequences of the abuse of power.

Sources of Power Related to Individuals

Managers and employees acquire power from several sources. The first set of sources relates to the individual. There are five sources of individual power: legitimate, reward, coercive, expert, and referent power.[5] We describe them in Table 11.1.

Table 11.1   SOURCES OF INDIVIDUAL POWER

Power Source	Description
Legitimate power	Based on a person's holding a formal position. Other people comply because of their belief in the legitimacy of the power holder.
Reward power	Based on a person's access to rewards. Others comply because of a desire to receive rewards.
Coercive power	Based on a person's ability to punish. Others comply because of fear of punishment.
Expert power	Based on personal expertise and knowledge in a certain area. Others comply because of their belief in the power holder's knowledge or skill.
Referent power	Based on a person's attractiveness to others. Others comply because they respect and like the power holder.

Five Sources of Individual Power   The first three power sources in Table 11.1, *legitimate, reward*, and *coercive* power, are position powers. An individual's access to them depends on the position that he or she holds in an organization. For example, the title that a person holds provides that person with legitimacy and, as a result, power to influence others. For example, Callaway Golf founder Ely Callaway has the title of chairperson. The title indicates that he presides over meetings of the board of directors, so he has legitimate power to decide which issues the board considers.

At first glance, most of us are more likely to listen to and comply with the company vice president than with our own department's manager. The **legitimate power** that comes with a position is further supported by symbols such as a big office, special parking, and so forth.

Along with legitimate power, many positions carry **reward power** because they give people access to resources they can use to *reward* others. For example, managers give or recommend raises and promotions. They can assign employees a better office, send them to a sought-after training program, authorize them to go to a business convention in Hawaii, and so forth. Having access to resources that others want is the source of reward power. The opposite of reward power is the **coercive power** to punish others. Because of the power of their position, managers can coerce or force others to do certain things. They can threaten disciplinary action, withdraw or withhold rewards, and threaten to fire employees.

Consider the example of Glaxo Wellcome and SmithKline Beecham, two giant pharmaceutical companies that called off their planned $70 billion merger. During the merger

Legitimate power
Based on a person holding a formal position. Others comply because of the belief in the legitimacy of the power holder

Reward power
Based on a person's access to rewards. Others comply because of the desire to receive rewards

Coercive power
Based on a person's ability to punish. Others comply because of the fear of punishment

Organizations use symbols such as size and location of office and furniture to convey the power of the person in the office.

talks, Glaxo chairperson Sir Richard Sykes apparently agreed to let Jan Leschly, SmithKline's CEO, become CEO of the merged company. In addition, one of the rewards that Sykes had promised his merger partners was the appointment of some SmithKline executives to key positions in the merged company. Then Sykes had a change of heart. He seemed to realize that with Leschly operating as CEO from Philadelphia, the center of reward and coercive power would shift from London, Glaxo's headquarters, to the United States. "Richard would have thought, 'Here I am based in London, with the real power in the U.S.,'" stated a Glaxo executive. "The Glaxo people woke up to the fact that SmithKline was running the show." According to other Glaxo executives, Sykes uses his power to reward and punish his top executives, sometimes unfairly. "Egos are taking precedence over future strategies," states Sean Lance, the former chief operating officer of Glaxo.[6] They accuse Sykes of trying to turn a merger of equals into a takeover by attempting to preserve his sources of power at the expense of the organization.

A QUESTION OF ETHICS

What Can You Ask Your Employees to Do for You?

Some managers have told employees that they will be subject to physical searches for missing office supplies, surprise drug tests, and video camera and computer screen monitoring. Legally, managers can monitor the daily activities of employees, but do you think these actions are ethical? In your opinion, which actions are and which ones aren't?

Although legitimate, reward, and coercive powers are vested in the individual, the individual has access to them because of the position he or she holds. The power disappears if the position is removed.[7] Examples of managers being sent to "Corporate Siberia" illustrate this point well. Once their position changes, they lose their means of influencing others. Sir Richard Sykes's fear of losing his position power was apparently one of the main reasons the Glaxo-SmithKline merger failed.

The last two sources of individual power—expert and referent power—are personal. Access to these two sources of power does not depend solely on the organization. In the case of **expert power**, the person has influence over others because he or she has some special expertise, knowledge, information, or skills that others need. People will listen to experts, follow their advice, and accept their recommendations. Other employees will bypass their formal manager to seek help from individuals who lack formal authority but have expertise. For example, a department's young computer expert has power in spite of her youth and inexperience.

Expert power
Based on personal expertise and knowledge in a certain area. Others comply because of the belief in the power holder's knowledge

Referent power
Based on a person's attractiveness to others. Others comply because of respect and liking for the power holder

As with expert power, **referent power** is not rooted in a person's position within an organization. Others listen to a person with referent power because they like and respect that person or are the person's friend. This type of power is the basis for charismatic and transformational leadership. Many charismatic leaders draw their power, especially early in their careers, almost entirely from their personal relationships with their followers. They are liked and admired for who they are and what they represent, not for their position in an organization.

Alan Greenspan, chairman of the Federal Reserve (Fed), is reputed to be the most powerful executive in the United States. He is an example of a leader with expert and referent power. As chairman, Greenspan has been able set policies to sustain low-to-moderate economic growth, assuring that the economy expands but does not overheat, thereby avoiding high inflation. In a 1996 survey of 1,000 CEOs of the largest U.S. companies, 96 percent wanted him reappointed as the leader of the Fed, an appointment that, of course, President Clinton made.[8]

Greenspan has tremendous legitimate power vested in the position of chairman of the Federal Reserve, but his sources of power mostly include his expertise (expert power), and powers of persuasion (referent power). He has no executive power, cannot implement a single decision, and has only a few staff people reporting to him. With his expert power, however, he is able to convince the U.S. president, Congress, and financial markets that his policies are in the best interest of the nation and devoid of politics. With his powers of persuasion, he is generally able to convince other Fed board members to support his inflation-fighting policies.

Because expert and referent powers do not depend on the organizational structure, they are more permanent and more effective sources of power for both managers and employees. They can also cause professional jealously. Consider an assistant manager in a department store who is popular with salespeople and customers alike, and who shows expertise and competence in doing her job. She brings new, creative ideas to her manager, and implements them when allowed. It is not surprising for that manager to feel threatened by someone who may appear to be performing better than he is.[9]

Most managers rely on several different individual sources of power. They may form personal relationships with their employees, use their charisma, demonstrate competence and expertise, gain access to information that both their employees and managers need, provide rewards and punishments, and establish legitimate power through their position and title. The more varied the sources of power, the more power a person will have to influence others.

Consequences of Individual Sources of Power

People's reactions to power depend on the sources of and manner in which power is used. In Figure 11.1, we show three of the most typical reactions to power and how they relate to sources of individual power.

Commitment means personal acceptance of the goals that a manager tries to achieve. It occurs when the influence process is welcome and accepted. Employees of a well-liked and highly respected manager who proposes changes in the work place are likely to accept new procedures. For instance, Dave Duffield, the CEO of PeopleSoft, a software company located in Pleasanton, California, is extremely popular with employees—so popular that employees have even put together a band called the Raving Daves. When Dave proposes changes, employees commit to them. "We're fast, nimble, and competitive, but we have a cuddly way about us," explains Duffield.[10]

Another potential reaction to power is compliance. In the case of **compliance**, although employees go along with the manager's request, there is no personal acceptance or commitment. Employees comply because they have to. For example, most of you are likely to accept minor changes in work processes that your manager imposes, regardless of whether you personally like the changes.

The third possible reaction to power is **resistance,** which means passive or active opposition to a manager's request. Some of the most dramatic examples of resistance occur in labor-management disputes that sometimes lead to strikes. In the summer of 1997, the Teamsters Union went on strike against United Parcel Service (UPS) because the union considered the company's use of part-time workers excessive and it did not want the company to change its policy concerning the union retirement fund. Both management and labor used their coercive power to resist the other party's demands.

As a general rule, a leader's or manager's power increases when employees have personal commitment. The use of expert and referent power is more likely to lead to commitment than the use of legitimate, reward, or coercive power.[11] However, many managers rely on compliance because building commitment takes too long and requires considerable interpersonal and persuasion skills. One of the elements of the team-based organizations and the participative management techniques described throughout the text is the shift away from position power to personal sources of power that can lead to higher commitment, satisfaction, and performance.[12]

To be effective, a person has to rely on the different sources of power and be skillful at using them at appropriate times to achieve both group and organizational goals. In addition to using individual sources of power, managers can also rely on organizational power sources. We review these next.

Hot ▼ Link
See discussions of charismatic leadership in chapter 9, pp. 321–26.

Commitment
Personal acceptance of the goals a manager is trying to achieve

Compliance
Employees go along with the manager's request but there is no personal acceptance or commitment

Resistance
Passive opposition, active opposition, or both to a manager's request

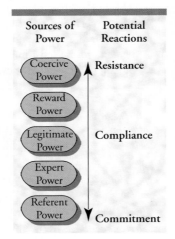

FIGURE 11.1
Potential Reactions to Sources of Power

CAREER ADVICE
from the Experts

CHANGING YOUR POWER
BASE THROUGHOUT YOUR CAREER

How you view and use power at different stages of your career changes.

- In the early stages of your management career, you must establish your expertise and develop extensive interpersonal networks by becoming known, volunteering for high-visibility tasks, and demonstrating your technical competence.
- If you intend to strike out on your own, try to maintain good relations with former managers. These relationships can be a valuable source of both power and resources for an entrepreneur who relies on contacts to make his or her business successful.
- In mid-career stages, when you have a stronger power base, the challenge is to demonstrate that you can use your power wisely and ethically to benefit the organization.
- In the later stages of your career, you should focus on letting go of power gracefully by training others to replace you.

Sources: J. P. Kotter, *Power and Influence* (New York: Free Press, 1985); see also H. Lancaster, "Managers Who Swim with the Big Fish Make It Pay," *Wall Street Journal*, April 9, 1996, B1.

Summary Point 11.1   **What Is Power and What Are Individual Sources of Power?**

- Power is the ability of one person to influence another, whereas authority is vested in a position.
- The five sources of power are legitimate, reward, coercive, expert, and referent.
- Legitimate, reward, and coercive power derives from the person's formal position in the organization. The source of expert and referent power is the individual.

- Three reactions to power are commitment, compliance, and resistance.
- Commitment is most likely to occur when people use expert or referent power. Resistance is likely to occur if a person relies too heavily on coercive power.

Organizational sources of power
Sources of power that managers or individuals derive from the structure of the organization. These sources depend on having access to and control of strategic contingencies

Strategic contingencies
Elements that are essential to the performance and effectiveness of an organization, a department, or a team

Sources of Power Related to the Organization

Although we separate individual and organizational sources of power, the differences between them are not always obvious. Individual sources of power depend on factors that an individual can acquire through a position or through specific actions that he or she takes. **Organizational sources of power** are sources of power for individuals that originate from the structure of the organization. These sources depend on having access to and control of strategic contingencies.[13] **Strategic contingencies** are elements that are essential to the performance and effectiveness of an organization, a department, or a team. In addition, individual sources of power explain how individuals acquire power. In contrast, organizational sources of power explain how individuals, departments, or teams acquire power in an organization. Table 11.2 presents the strategic contingencies that constitute sources of organizational power.

Table 11.2 STRATEGIC CONTINGENCIES AS SOURCES OF POWER

Strategic Contingency Factors	Description
Coping with uncertainty	People who help others deal with external uncertainty gain power. They do so by obtaining information, helping others interpret the information, predicting changes, or preventing changes from affecting the organization.
Centrality in the resource network	People who are central to information and resources that are essential to organizational performance gain power.
Dependency and substitutability	People on whom others depend to get their jobs done and who cannot be easily replaced gain power (similar to expert power).

Source: Based on information in D. J. Hickson, C. R. Hinnings, C. A. Lee, R. E. Scheneck, and J. M. Pennings, "A Strategic Contingencies Theory of Intra-Organizational Power," *Administrative Science Quarterly* 16 (1971): 216–29.

People who satisfy strategic contingencies make it easier for others in the organization to do their jobs and achieve their goals. Some departments and managers have better access to these sources of power than others. For instance, a group that focuses on analyzing a company's competitors and predicting their next strategic move *reduces uncertainty* for others in the organization. Similarly, any employee, manager, team, or department that has direct contact with customers can bring information to others and thereby reduce uncertainty. Marketing managers in most organizations have power that derives from their staff's interactions with customers and their access to data about customers' reactions to the company's products.

One organization that helps businesses gain a better understanding of their customers and thus reduces managers' uncertainty is Niehaus Ryan Group, Inc. This public relations firm provides customer data for its clients and helps them build a sustainable image in the market. Co-founder William Ryan helped Yahoo! create its successful public image. The Niehaus Ryan Group reduced uncertainty for managers at Yahoo! and gained power with its customers as a result.[14]

As some individuals or groups reduce uncertainty for others, they also become *central* to how the organization achieves its goals. In an organization that depends on a rare mineral to produce its goods, the person or department that negotiates with suppliers to purchase this mineral is central and can satisfy a strategic contingency. Therefore, this person or department is likely to have power.

Consider that chief financial officers (CFOs) play a central role in most organizations, especially during a merger. In 1995, John T. O'Neill, the CFO of toy maker Hasbro, became the center of media attention and a central figure in the fight against a hostile takeover by Mattel, its top competitor. Through his skills and knowledge, O'Neill gained access to the financial resources that enabled Hasbro to ward off Mattel's unfriendly overtures.[15]

The last source of organizational power is *dependency*.[16] If others depend on you and cannot replace your skills, expertise, and information easily, your power will increase. The database expert who custom designs an organization's management information system is assured of a job or at least of regular consulting because she cannot be replaced easily. Another example is the experienced administrative assistant assigned to a CEO. This person's thorough knowledge of the CEO's professional work and personal activities makes him difficult to replace. Therefore, knowledge and access to the CEO give him a great deal of power in the organization despite his low status and little legitimate or referent power.

Some organizational sources of power depend on personal skills; others rely on the position the person holds. For example, the ability to cope with uncertainty may result from having special expertise and knowledge, or from having access to information that others need. In the case of organizational sources of power, any activity that helps achieve the organization's mission gives an individual power. If customer focus is one of the organization's major goals, individuals who have direct customer contact will gain power.

At Canon, the Japanese copier and photographic equipment manufacturer, research and development (R&D) used to be central to the mission of the organization; now marketing is just as important. The head of the company's R&D division, Toru Takahashi, knows that his division needs to focus on customers' needs and wants. He states: "Engineers here used to think that they embodied what Canon was all about. I am trying to enlighten them with a more marketing-oriented approach."[17]

Summary Point 11.2   **What Are Organizational Sources of Power?**

- Organizational sources of power depend on strategic contingencies.
- Organizational sources of power include coping with uncertainty, centrality, and dependency.

- Individuals who engage in activities that further the organization's mission gain power.

The way managers use individual and organizational sources of power varies from one organization to another and from one person to another. The less hierarchical the organization, the less it will rely on formal power and the less formal the power will be. Two factors that strongly influence how we use power are national culture and gender.

Culture, Gender, and Power

Our culture and our social environment greatly influence our views of power. Remember that two major cultural values are power distance and power ascription. Because power is a central element of interpersonal relationships, its use differs widely from one culture to another.

Culture and Power   In low power-distance cultures, such as the United States and Australia, the difference in power between the highest and lowest levels of organizations and society is relatively small. Indicators of a low power-distance culture include employees calling managers by first name and socializing with managers outside of work. Conversely, in high power-distance cultures such as Mexico or Singapore, society attributes great power to leaders so managers are not supposed to make mistakes and do not interact much with employees. Employee participation is difficult to seek and Western models of participation are difficult to implement. Similarly, in some cultures, such as Malaysia and India, social status is the base of power. In other ascriptive cultures, expertise and competence are the sources of power.

A global manager must understand the cultural differences in power. A relaxed, low-key, open, and participative manager from a low power-distance culture who downplays power symbols is likely to be seen as weak and incompetent in a high power-distance culture. Similarly, a status-oriented manager from a high power-distance culture may seem overly authoritarian and unfriendly to employees from a low power-distance culture. Adjusting styles to match the culture is necessary for effective management.

Gender and Power   There has been a great deal of study of gender differences in the use of power. Some researchers and practitioners maintain that women are less hierarchical, more likely to encourage employee participation, and generally less likely to rely on organizational sources of power.[18] Others suggest that most women who reach the top levels of organizations and acquire considerable power have management styles indistinguishable from that of their male

Hot ▼ **Link**

We discussed power when we reviewed the research of Trompenaars and Hosftede in chapter 3, pp. 79–83.

Do women use power differently from men? Although some female executives are known for nurturing and supporting employees, others such as Jill Barad, CEO of Mattel, have a reputation of playing the corporate game according to a competitive—and some would say male-oriented—business culture.

counterparts. The research is inconclusive and personal case histories vary, as the following examples show.

Janice Gjertsen, head of Business Development at Digital City, one of the largest online local networks in New York City, states: "Men are oriented toward power, toward making fast decisions in a black-or-white mode. Women are more skilled at relationships. They see shades of gray and explore issues from different angles. . . . What's interesting is that the kinds of companies that we admire today are also those that depend increasingly on female attributes. We are in the relationship era."[19]

Wendy Luhabe, the managing partner of Bridging the Gap, an investment firm based in Auckland Park, South Africa, shares some of Gjertsen's views on gender and power. "Real power comes from within, not from your official position. And finally, the power to contribute—to make a difference in a fast-changing world—should never be confused with power over others."[20]

Harriet Rubin, founder and editor at large of Doubleday/Currency publishing giant, has the opposite view. "Women need to become more like men than men are. We need to become hyperaggressive and hyperdetermined—because business is about intense daring and a reckless abandon to succeed," she declares. "None of the 'female' techniques of getting ahead—networking, mentoring—really work. Women need to engage in more dramatic tactics, both as individuals and in groups."[21]

Jill Barad of Mattel, Irene Rosenfeld of Kraft Canada, Gail McGovern of AT&T, and Lois Juliber of Colgate Palmolive share some characteristics both among themselves and with their male counterparts. They all have a high degree of ambition and energy and are willing to play the game according to the terms established by the male business culture. All have accepted many transfers, worked interminable hours, taken on new challenges, and been willing to take risks. Many have made considerable personal sacrifices to become part of the top management team of their organizations.

Other women leaders, such as Jane Biering, a division vice president at Staples, pride themselves on being different. Biering attributes her success to her ability to develop a supportive, nurturing culture. Similarly, many women entrepreneurs start businesses with the goal of providing a better balance between work and family, both for themselves and their employees.[22]

Despite the inconclusive research as to how genders differ in their use of power, managers should recognize the possibility of divergent approaches and ascertain which approach works best, given the situation, to promote personal and organizational effectiveness.

Sexual Harassment and Power   Most researchers agree: Power is a key part of sexual harassment. **Sexual harassment** is unwelcome advances, requests for sexual favors, and other verbal and nonverbal behavior of a sexual nature.[23] Males can sexually harass females and vice versa, and members of the same sex can also harass each other. There are few hard-and-fast rules as to what constitutes sexual harassment, especially in cases that claim the harassment occurred because of a hostile environment. However, the U.S. Supreme Court has offered this guideline: The determination of sexual harassment should be based on what a reasonable person in the circumstances would and does perceive as abusive or hostile.

Sexual harassment
Unwelcome advances, requests for sexual favors, and other verbal and nonverbal behavior of a sexual nature

Most sexual harassment experts believe that the harassment occurs because of unequal power.[24] The person who initiates the sexual harassment is usually someone in a position of power over the other. This person can be a manager, a co-worker, or a powerful customer or outside vendor. Having power and influence allows that person to threaten and abuse implicitly or explicitly. A manager can punish or reward. A co-worker can withhold information or refuse to cooperate. A customer or vendor can complain about your performance or refuse to work with you.

Blatant examples of sexual harassment include directly asking for sexual favors in exchange for a job, a promotion, or other personnel-related outcomes. But is it harassment to tell an off-color joke during a lunch break in the coffee room? What about having adult magazines in the office or a calendar of nudes? By themselves, these occurrences probably do not constitute sexual harassment. However, an organization that allows such activity and others that are intimidating or abusive may have a *hostile work environment.*[25] The totality of the circumstances determines the answer. What might be appropriate in a Wall Street brokerage firm might not be suitable for a church organization. One off-color joke would not be, but a work place that allowed many other indecent, intimidating behaviors could be.

The Equal Employment Opportunity Commission in Washington reports that the number of sexual harassment cases filed with the agency increased by 150 percent between 1990 and 1996, to a total of 15,342.[26] To prevent legal action, organizations are training employees and managers to understand the dynamics of sexual harassment, to recognize such behaviors when they occur, and to stop them when they discover them. Many organizations turn to consultants to train managers to handle this difficult issue. Betsy Plevan, a partner at Proskauer Rose law firm, which specializes in sexual harassment, states: "When we do sexual harassment training workshops in companies, we ask people to look at different kinds of insensitive or abusive behavior and ask themselves, 'Is this appropriate for the workplace? Would you want your mother to hear about it?'"[27]

Managers who work overseas or with diverse and global employees face a particularly tough challenge. Views of what constitutes sexual harassment and whether it is acceptable differ considerably across cultures. For example, the French press was bewildered at how a personal matter between Supreme Court nominee Clarence Thomas and law professor Anita Hill could become a national scandal in Thomas's Senate confirmation hearings.

In countries where gender roles are highly differentiated and where women do not participate extensively in the workplace, traditional views of women's roles often make it difficult to recognize and address sexual harassment. Managers in many cultures continue to believe that sexual favors and behaviors are part of their rights.[28]

Understanding the dynamics of culture, gender, and power can help managers create a more productive working environment. For all its benefits and universal use in organizations,

Summary Point 11.3   **How Do Culture and Gender Affect Power?**

- The cultural value of power distance affects views of power and its use.
- The cultural value of achievement-ascription determines who holds power.

- Although organizational behavior researchers have studied the relationship between gender and power, the effects of gender differences are still uncertain.
- Power is a factor in sexual harassment.

---

power has a darker side that deserves attention. We next present the causes and consequences of as well as the remedies for the corruption of power.

The Dark Side of Power: Corruption

The old adage of "power corrupts and absolute power corrupts absolutely" applies to people in organizations. The corruption of power refers to a person who abuses power for personal gain. The power holder believes that he or she is not obliged to play by the same rules that apply to others in the organization. We look at the causes and consequences of and the potential remedies for corruption.

Causes and Consequences of the Corruption of Power   The cycle of power corruption starts when a person has a significant amount of power and access to resources with limited or no accountability to a higher authority. Figure 11.2 on the next page depicts the corruption cycle. Excessive

MANAGERIAL ADVICE
from the Experts

USING POWER AND INFLUENCE WISELY

Power, authority, and influence are crucial to a manager's ability to perform his or her job—even in today's less hierarchical organizations. Effective managers are aware of how to use power and influence carefully to achieve desired results. The following are some recommendations:

- When trying to influence your supervisor, rely on reasoning, rational persuasion, coalitions, and friendliness. Coercive, reward, or legitimate power is not likely to work with your manager.
- The most effective method of influence to use with colleagues is personal appeals; referent power works best in these cases.
- Keep in mind that neither your superiors nor your employees appreciate a power play based on higher authority, so use it sparingly.
- Building coalitions and developing friendships are effective at all levels; threats and coercion backfire at all levels. Rely on your referent power as often as you can.

Sources: D. Kipnis, S. M. Schmidt, C. Swaffin-Smith, and I. Wilkinson, "Patterns of Managerial Influence: Shogun Managers, Tacticians, and Bystanders," *Organizational Dynamics* (Winter, 1994): 62; also see G. Yukl and C. M. Falbe, "The Importance of Different Power Sources in Downward and Lateral Relations," *Journal of Applied Psychology* 76 (1991): 416–23.

A QUESTION OF ETHICS

How Should Managers Get Involved? | Managers often help define the line between personal and professional relationships. Office romances are commonplace; some involve employees of equal rank, and others are between managers and employees. Co-workers date, break up, marry, and divorce while continuing to work in the same teams and departments. In such cases, personal conflicts carry over to the workplace. Is it ethical for managers to establish policies that govern employee relationships with others in the organization? If such policies are established, how should managers monitor these relationships in an ethical way? Explain your answers.

power leads to increased distance between the power holder and others—for example, between a manager and employees. Managers have separate offices and parking areas, eat in special dining rooms, have limited contact with employees, and are generally protected from contact with those who have limited power. This separation is often explained by a legitimate need to protect the manager's valuable time. However, the distance that such a separation creates reduces the interaction between managers and employees, impedes the flow of information between them, and removes managers from the inner workings of their organizations.

The distance and separation from employees leads powerful managers to develop an inflated view of themselves.[29] After all, if they were not special, they would not have access to such privilege. As employees seek favors and need their managers' approval and support to get their job done, they comply with their managers' requests. They may flatter the managers in the hope of getting raises, promotions, or a special assignment. They may be afraid to give negative feedback or bad news that reflects badly on the manager. The compliance and flattery further inflate managers' view of themselves.

Because of the large disparity in power, employees may feel powerless so they become increasingly submissive and dependent. Their submissiveness and dependency is another factor that fuels power holders' inflated sense of power. Seeing employees show respect, obey, flatter, and comply provides the managers with a distorted view of their own abilities. Look at Richard M. Scrushy, the CEO of HealthSouth Corp., a multibillion-dollar healthcare company. He is also the CEO of MedPartners Inc., another giant health-related organization. This CEO of two major firms seems to have an inflated sense of power. For example, employees report that he uses fear to motivate, even "sending employees out of meetings if their ties are not straight."[30] How likely is any of his employees to question his ideas?

The last step in the corruption cycle is the consequences of corruption. They range from poor decision making to ethical violations. Isolated from others, overly confident, believing strongly in the correctness of their own judgment, power holders make decisions based on little or inaccurate information. They do not seek the employees' opinion because, by complying with their manager's every request, employees have already demonstrated to the manager that they are unable to make decisions on their own. The employees' flattery and submission, while inflating the managers' ego and providing short-term results, also lead managers to develop a low opinion of employees. As a result, the power holders rely increasingly on autocratic leadership and coercive and legitimate power to influence employees.

A final consequence of the power corruption cycle is for power holders to engage in unethical or illegal behaviors, or both.[31] Some managers devise their own rules, break the law, and engage in bribery and fraud. For example, in one of the most far-reaching cases of corruption and bribery in recent history, the officials of the Paris-based Credit Lyonnais bank were investigated by government officials in the United States, Italy, and France. The investigators discovered that Credit Lyonnais managers, Georges Vignon of France and Jacques Griffault of Italy, accepted bribes of up to $2 million from Giancarlo Parletti, a famous builder, to provide loans for his worldwide ventures. Mr. Parletti used the borrowed money to

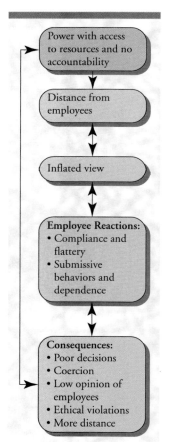

FIGURE 11.2
The Power Corruption Cycle

buy the MGM film studio in the United States. Credit Lyonnais, then the number one non-Japanese bank in the world, was rocked by the scandal and almost collapsed. All its executives, from the CEO to lower-level officials, were investigated. Investigators focused on bank managers with access to resources and the power to override the bank's regulations.[32] Initial reports indicated that Vignon and Griffault had too much unchecked power to do as they pleased.

Once the power corruption cycle starts, it feeds on itself. Employees become compliant and dependent because of their manager's power. However, managers attribute the compliance and submission to incompetence and an inability to make decisions. Therefore, they delegate fewer and fewer decisions and become increasingly autocratic. Similarly, the initial distance that excessive power creates increases in every step of the cycle. Both the managers' and the employees' behaviors create their own self-fulfilling prophecy.

The considerable power and privilege that we give business leaders and executives create an ideal climate for the development of corruption. Organizations can prevent the corruption that derives from excessive power in a number of ways.

Potential Remedies for the Corruption of Power   No magic formula can eliminate corruption due to excessive power. The closer managers are to the day-to-day activities of the organization and to employees and customers, the less potential there is for corruption. Organizations can prevent corruption of power by taking these steps:

1. *Increase contact between managers and employees.* Managers and employees should interact freely and frequently in formal and informal settings. Increased contact reduces artificial barriers, makes managers accessible, and allows information flow.
2. *Reduce employees' dependency on managers in two ways.*
   - *Set objective performance measures.* The less employees depend on their manager's judgment, subjective rating, and goodwill to receive raises, promotions, bonuses, good assignments, and so forth, the less they will flatter their manager. They will not comply as often.[33]
   - *Provide access to information and direct feedback.* Employees who have information about the organization and who receive direct feedback about their performance have more autonomy and do not have to rely on flattery and submission to win over managers.
3. *Monitor organizational culture and structure.* The most effective and most difficult solution to preventing power corruption is to change the culture and structure of organizations. The change should focus on performance, productivity, and customer service rather than on satisfying managers. The culture must encourage employees to address customers' rather than manager's needs.

Summary Point 11.4   **What Causes Power Corruption and How Can It Be Prevented?**

- A major cause of corruption is excessive power without accountability.
- Contributing and interrelated factors are a manager's distance from employees; inflated view of the self; and employee flattery, submissiveness, and dependency.
- Consequences are poor decision making, use of coercion, low opinion of employees, unethical or illegal actions, and distancing oneself from employees.
- Remedies for corruption include increased interaction with employees, a reduction of employee dependence on managers, and an open and performance-centered organization culture and structure.

Views and uses of power are changing in part because of the potential negative effects of power, changes in many organizations' structures, and the potential positive effects of sharing power.

The Potential Benefits of Empowerment

Bob Gavron, one of Britain's most successful entrepreneurs, supports empowerment through his leadership. Gavron founded St. Ives, the company that prints the glossy Condé Nast travel brochures and several other magazines. The St. Ives culture and structure reflect Gavron's management philosophy of giving responsibility to his employees. In return, he asks them to be responsible for their own actions. According to Gavron, St. Ives has been successful because of its empowered employees.[34] Similarly, executives of the Korean industrial giant Daewoo partly credit employee empowerment for their success in resurrecting a bankrupt Korean shipyard.[35]

As we discussed in chapters 1 and 2, empowerment is a growing practice in organizations. Figure 11.3 depicts the elements of empowerment. Empowerment allows employees at all levels of an organization to make more independent, autonomous decisions that allow the business to respond flexibly and rapidly to environmental demands.[36] In addition, empowerment can motivate employees by making their jobs more challenging and enriching, and providing them with a sense of accomplishment.

In spite of growing use and anecdotal accounts of the benefits of empowerment, research support has been mixed.[37] Although some studies indicate that empowerment may have a positive impact on job satisfaction, to date the effect on actual employee performance is not well established. The lack of clear research support may indicate that empowerment is not a significant fctor in work performance. However, it also may be due to many different definitions and ways in which managers implement the concept, making scientific measurement difficult.

To reap the benefits of an empowered workforce, an organization's leadership, culture, and structure must support and encourage power sharing. The leaders of an empowered organization need to remove bureaucratic obstacles and emphasize performance, trust in employees, and equitable rewards. The culture should encourage decision making and cooperation among employees at all levels. It should eschew power plays, displays of status, and autocratic managers. The

FIGURE 11.3
Elements of Empowerment

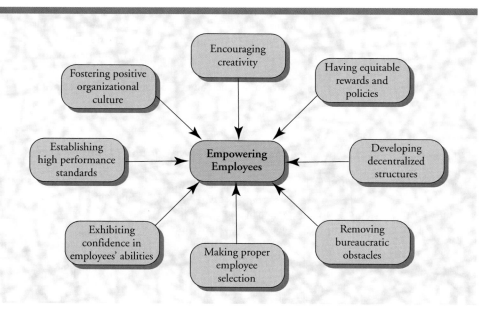

organization structure should be relatively flat, not vertical with centralized decision making. In fact, many organizations that use empowerment are partially or fully team based.[38]

An organization with a leader, culture, and structure that supports empowerment is Fastenal, a Minnesota-based manufacturer that markets and sells nuts and bolts in 620 stores in the United States and Canada. Fastenal CEO Bob Kierlin and president Will Oberton built a flat organization that distributes power to the employees who are closest to the customer. The culture of the organization is based on hard work, frugality, and loyalty. Kierlin outlines his management philosophy this way: "Just believe in people, give them a chance to make decisions, take risks, and work hard."[39]

In this empowered organization, Fastenal's local managers and assistant managers make many of the decisions that help provide customers with exemplary service. For example, when one customer needed a special stainless steel U-bolt, Keith Gleaves, the 24-year-old manager of a local store responded: "They weren't in stock, and none were coming in the next day. I drove to the hub at 2 A.M. to get them." Rich Schmidt of Machinery Services, who received the U-bolts, states: "As far as Fastenal goes, we never get told no."[40]

For Fastenal, the benefits of empowerment have been astonishing. Profits have risen 38 percent annually for the past five years, and the return to shareholders has been 39 percent annually, better than those of GE and Coke, two companies with some of the highest returns in the United States.

Empowerment does not mean that managers lack power. It means that the organization distributes power more equally among managers and employees. It also means that those with power rely more on personal as opposed to position power sources. This shift in the source of power can lead to more dedicated, committed employees who willingly perform and contribute to organizational effectiveness; however, it is not a cure-all and does not work in all organizations.

Summary Point 11.5   **How Can Organizations Reap the Potential Benefits of Empowerment?**

To reap the benefits of empowerment, the organization's leaders, culture, and structure should support power sharing.

- Leaders should emphasize high performance, trust in others, and equity.
- The culture should encourage distributed decision making and cooperation.

- The structure should be relatively flat with decentralized decision making.

As organizations decentralize, flatten, and become less hierarchical, managers, employees, team leaders, and team members at all levels rely on personal relationships, face-to-face negotiations, individual agreements, and coalitions to accomplish their tasks. These activities are part of politics in organizations, which we investigate next.

■ POLITICS IN ORGANIZATIONS

Most people associate organizational politics with shady, somewhat unethical dealings that allow people to get ahead because of whom they know rather than how they perform. These negative associations are only one part of politics in organizations. **Organizational politics** are activities that allow people in organizations to achieve goals without going through formal channels. Some political activities may be self-serving and even unethical; others serve the organization, and still others serve both.[41]

Organizational politics
Activities that allow people in organizations to achieve goals without going through formal channels

As long as personal agendas and goals are consistent with organizational goals, politics are simply an alternative method of doing things. When personal goals take precedence over organizational performance, politics can damage the organization. In the last part of this chapter, we explore the political model of organizations, factors that lead to politics, political tactics used in organizations, and ways to manage politics for the organization's benefit.

The Political Model of Organizations

The concepts discussed in this text are generally based on a model of organizations that assumes order, predictability, and some degree of control. These assumptions are most evident in the rational and linear decision-making models that we examined in chapter 10. With these models, organizational events and people's actions depend on clear processes and objectives. In contrast, the political model assumes that decision making and other organizational events are dynamic bargaining processes that depend on compromise and on satisfying multiple constituencies.[42]

Table 11.3 contrasts the rational and political models. The fundamental difference between the two approaches is that the rational model assumes it is possible to manage organizations in a logical, orderly fashion based on clear information, with specific, well-defined goals. The political model sees organizations as dynamic entities in which rules and processes change depending on the players, their goals, and the situations they face. Therefore, managers manage organizations through negotiations and coalitions among individuals and groups with differing goals.[43]

The key characteristics of the political model are decision-making processes based on short-term thinking, a continuous redefinition of problems, a consideration of many solutions simultaneously, and a failure to evaluate all alternatives and their consequences fully. Whereas the rational approach strives to consider all alternatives and their consequences, the political model suggests that people consider only certain alternatives based on their novelty and how much they deviate from existing policies. Similarly, managers do not consider all consequences fully; only those that appear immediately relevant receive attention. Because of the dynamic nature of organizations, the political approach suggests that problems are continually being redefined so that there is never one correct answer. Instead, managers must consider a series of plans to address the changing issues. Finally—again because of the dynamic nature of organizations—the political approach predicts that managers will develop short-term solutions.[44]

T a b l e   1 1 . 3   The Rational Model versus the Political Model

Organizational Features	Rational	Political
Goals	Clear and consistent for all groups	Unclear, often redefined, based on subgroups
Power bases	Legitimate and well known	Shifting and dynamic
Structure and control	Cenralized	Decentralized, dynamic, and shifting; control based on coalitions
Information	Accurate, widely shared with those who need it	Ambiguous, held as a source of power
Organizational processes	Well defined, logical, and rational	Ambiguous, dynamic, and contingent on situations and coalitions

Sources: Based on J. Pfeffer, *Power in Organizations* (Marshfield, MA: Pitman, 1981); E. F. Harrison, *The Managerial Decision-Making Process*, 3d ed. (Boston: Houghton Mifflin, 1987); M. Browne, *Organizational Decision Making and Information* (Norwood, NJ: Ablex, 1993).

Consider the example of Michael Ovitz, one of the entertainment industry's most famous deal makers. After he turned the Creative Artists Agency in Hollywood into the number one top-talent company in the industry, his friend Michael Eisner, CEO of Disney, hired him to be Disney's president. Eisner brought Ovitz to Disney in large part because of his legendary ability to negotiate and close deals. In other words, he was hired for his political skills.

Friends advised Ovitz to keep quiet for a year to learn about the Disney business before he started to challenge Disney's longtime executives. Never a team player, Ovitz ignored the advice and almost from the first day offended the company's powerful executives. His bullying negotiating style and lack of appreciation for those who helped him close deals quickly led to his demise at Disney. One acquaintance described his negotiating style as follows: "He tends to run over people. He created a lot of enemies over time."[45] The perception at Disney was that he was more interested in advancing his own agenda than helping the organization. Within a year, Eisner fired him. New York investment banker Herbert Allen said: "I think it's impossible to judge whether Michael would have been an effective executive. He's visionary, entrepreneurial, charismatic—but it has to be his show, and I think it should be a smaller show." Of course, Ovitz was well compensated for his one year of work at Disney. He received over $140 million in severance pay and stock options that may eventually net him over $300 million.[46] Michael Ovitz did not seem to consider carefully the consequences of his actions, and he failed to build a coalition among his employees to accomplish the task. His tactics seemed oriented to the short term, enriching himself rather than Disney, thus fitting the political model.

Summary Point 11.6   **What Is the Political Model?**

- Politics are activities that allow people in organizations to achieve goals outside formal channels.
- The political model suggests that organizations are dynamic systems in which
  1. information is scarce
  2. individuals and groups have diverse goals and interests

3. managers make decisions based on negotiation and formation of various coalitions that change from one issue to another
4. managers analyze problems, alternatives, and consequences based on individual goals rather than rational and systematic processes

---

How National and Ethnic Cultures Relate to Organizational Politics

National and ethnic cultures play a role in the use and acceptance of political behavior. The more a culture values rules, regulations, order, and logic, the less it will accept political behavior. Additionally, in ascriptive cultures such as India or Egypt, rewards can be based on non-performance factors that make the use of political processes acceptable.

The emotion-neutral dimension of Trompenaars's groupings also plays a role in the use of politics. Cultures that are based more on emotion accept a greater use of politics. In a neutral culture such as that of Japan, interaction is based on nonemotional objective factors as opposed to emotional bonds. In emotional cultures, such as those of Italy or France, subjective feelings and relationships enter into decisions more readily.[47]

In Japan, for example, Toyota has built a special relationship with its suppliers based on performance. Instead of holding its most valued manufacturing technology secret, Toyota has shared its knowledge widely so that its suppliers can improve. "It has consciously institutionalized a set of practices for transferring knowledge between itself and the suppliers, so that the whole group learns faster," states Wharton professor Jeffrey Dyer.[48]

Negotiations, which are inherently political, demonstrate how important cultural differences are. Research shows that cross-cultural negotiations can be riddled with misunder-

Hot ▼ Link

We discuss Trompenaars's groupings in chapter 3, pp. 79–80.

standing that arises in part from the use of power and politics. For example, Brazilians expect some degree of deception and therefore use it more themselves. They tend not to trust anyone in the early stages of negotiations.[49] This negotiation behavior occurs partly because of their perception of power and its importance in social and business relationships and partly because of the high context culture of Brazil. Brazilians expect those with power to use it fully. Therefore, during negotiation, they themselves use their power to gain an early advantage.

It is easy for Germans, who come from a low context culture and are therefore literal and rule bound, to misunderstand the Brazilians' motives. They are likely to interpret the Brazilians' political behavior as dishonest and deceitful rather than as a normal part of the negotiating process.

Culture also affects people's perceptions of what is and what is not political behavior. For example, touching is a normal part of social and business interactions in many Hispanic cultures in which personal space tends to be small. However, to Canadians or Swedes, who do not touch one another much because they place a large value on personal space, the physical gesture may look like a political ploy.

Overall, the political approach recognizes the dynamic nature of organizations and the complex individual and group goals that motivate people's behaviors. The role of power and influence outside the legitimate and hierarchical influence arena is key to the political model. For example, those who have expertise and information or access to various strategic contingencies use them to advance their own goals rather than share their power to satisfy organizational needs.

Summary Point 11.7   **How Does Culture Affect Political Behavior?**

- The more a culture values rules, regulations, order, and logic, the less the culture will accept political behavior.
- The more the culture is based on emotion (Trompenaars's emotional-neutral dimension), the more it accepts political behavior.

- Other cultural values, such as the value of personal space, affect whether people perceive or do not perceive behavior as political.

Neither the rational nor the political model fully explains how organizations function. Most organizations attempt to operate logically and rationally. However, in situations where systematic, rational decision making is impossible, individual power plays and goals operate. Next, we discuss conditions that encourage politics.

Conditions That Encourage Organizational Politics

As uncertainty in the organization increases, the usefulness of rational approaches decreases. Information becomes scarce, objectives change often, and goals often conflict, making careful analysis and predictions difficult. Under these conditions, political activity increases. In this section we explore how uncertainty in resource allocation, changes in coordination and integration, and new leadership encourage more political activity, as shown in Figure 11.4.

Uncertain Resource Allocation   Changes in any of the five contextual strategic forces, such as a company's environment or structure, affect the way organizations allocate resources. For example, as resources shrink or change due to competitive pressures, managers must negotiate their department's share. Deciding which department should get which resources, such as new personnel and equipment, office space, operation budgets, and salaries, are all difficult decisions when information is incomplete and inaccurate.

Top managers can make these decisions alone, trying to keep personal issues and agendas out of the deliberations. However, managers rarely have all the information they need to make such decisions by themselves. They need input from all departments about business needs, priorities, and objectives. The information exchange between top managers and departments leads to negotiation, give and take, and compromise, all of which are political activities.

Similar negotiations over resources occur when managers introduce new technology, change strategic direction, modify organizational structure, and alter culture. When Mercedes decided to build a factory for its new sport utility M-class vehicles in Vance, Alabama, the CEO of the factory, Andreas Renschler, chose a multicultural management team. The composition of the team was more diverse than Mercedes' typical group culture. Renschler appointed two Americans who had worked for GM, two Americans who had worked for Nissan, and four Germans who had worked in Mercedes plants in Germany. The eight members immediately started to argue about the design of the factory and how to allocate resources. "Duly noted by the Americans was the fact that the Germans' English improved markedly when they got annoyed." Despite the bickering, the team met the rigid timetable set by the headquarters in Stuttgart, Germany, designed the factory, and prepared a hiring plan for the workers.[50]

When an insurance company or a bank decides to restructure to be more efficient and more responsive to its customers, there is a good chance that the company will eliminate some jobs. Those who remain face new tasks, a redistribution of power and authority, and changes in the resources they have. Managers are supposed to make resource decisions based on the goal of increased performance and efficiency. However, this relatively clear goal is not enough to eliminate power struggles and individual agendas that focus on keeping jobs, departments, and pet projects. Because of the structural change, uncertainty increases so that the existing rules, procedures, and processes that guide decisions and behaviors no longer apply. As a result, managers and employees build new coalitions, negotiate, argue, and compete on a number of issues to ensure that they achieve their goals.

Changes in strategy, structure, technology, culture, or the environment typically alter how people coordinate and integrate their activities. The integration and coordination of activities is another factor that increases uncertainty and political activity.

Coordination and Integration The process of coordinating and integrating activities to achieve organizational goals requires political activity. For instance, managers have to negotiate the roles and activities that they or their employees will perform and the commitment they will give to each task. Team members, especially those in team-based organizations, also engage in political activities. This is because teams do not report to managers but must coordinate and integrate with other teams and departments to meet organizational objectives.

Changes in the environment, technology, strategy, structure, or culture may affect the way people coordinate and integrate activities. For instance, a structural change often means departments or divisions must merge and coordinate their activities in new ways. When two departments—or even two individuals—need to work together, they must make a number of joint decisions. Who does what? Who pays for various activities? Who makes decisions? How do they communicate? These are just a few issues that arise when people and departments have to coordinate their work. Some of these questions are simple; others are complex and involve issues of power, authority, goals, performance, and getting credit. There are no formal, standardized methods for resolving these issues.

Let's revisit the earlier example of the Mercedes factory in Vance, Alabama. The Germans had precise methods for coordinating and integrating activities. They had detailed plans for absolutely everything, including where to put down a hammer once a worker had finished using it. The American workers did not always like to be told how to do a job. Charlene Page, a team leader in the assembly plant, explains: "The Germans are very blunt and don't beat

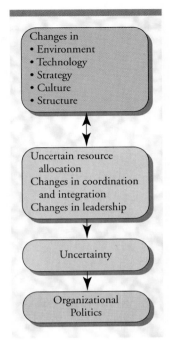

FIGURE 11.4
Factors in the Use of Politics

Hot ▼ Link

See chapter 8 for requirements of teams.

around the bush. You don't get politeness out of them about work. They might say, 'It looks real bad, and you're going to redo it.' They're such perfectionists."[51] The German CEO has a different perspective: "The Americans always want to hear that they're doing a good job." Because the Mercedes team had to coordinate activities, the Germans and Americans had to adapt to each other's culture. "It's the birth of a melting pot," says Renschler, the CEO.[52]

The last major factor in the use of organizational politics is leadership.

Leadership   When organizations face a new environment, major technological changes, and strategic, structural, and cultural redirection and change, one of their first actions is to look for new leadership. Hiring a new chief executive or a new manager creates uncertainty in organizations and leads to political activity.[53]

What happened to Motown Records is illustrative. After founder Berry Gordy started the business in the early 1960s, Motown achieved an enviable level of success that included 51 number one hits from 1964 to 1985. In 1988, he sold the company to MCA, who sold it to Polygram five years later. By then the label had produced only a handful of hits and was losing money.

In 1995, Andre Harrell, a flamboyant salesman from the Bronx, became CEO. He spent $200,000 on an ad campaign to promote himself, which irritated the artists. His lack of management experience quickly became a major problem for the staff. His self-described management style of "organized chaos" soon forced the Polygram executives to scrutinize his decisions. His staff ran around trying to figure out what he wanted because he tended to rush into projects. Meanwhile, the artists complained that he was not taking care of them and instead was promoting himself. Harrell admits: "I couldn't get into the artists' heads." The situation worsened when Polygram appointed three key executives to Harrell's management team, and Harrell decided to move the headquarters to New York from Los Angeles. Twenty-two months into the job, Polygram's CEO accepted Harrell's resignation. One industry expert mentions: "Andre was pretty much enamored of his own abilities. That was his undoing."[54]

In October 1997, George Jackson, a Harvard-educated film producer from Harlem became the CEO of the legendary Detroit record company.[55] His mandate was clear: reorganize Motown to become significantly smaller. "Motown will sign new artists and make new records. The plan is also to get it into its healthiest financial shape. Lean and mean—but as a full record company, not as a lesser thing," observed Polygram's Group CEO.[56] Jackson's appointment and the reorganization will significantly affect everyone in the organization. "George comes at the business from a different side than Andre. Andre is more of a purely creative executive, and George knows how to balance the business and the creative," explains Joycelyn Cooper-Gilstrap, senior vice president of Universal Musical Group.[57] "He understands the internalized discipline of running a business," states Danny Goldberg, Polygram's executive.[58] Jackson's appointment and plans are likely to decrease the level of illegitimate political activity at Motown.

As this example shows, changes in leadership create an opportunity to acquire power and resources. The resulting uncertainty allows politics to be introduced to replace the traditional relationships and processes that no longer apply.

Summary Point 11.8   **What Conditions Lead to the Use of Organizational Politics?**

- Uncertainty leads to more political activity.
- Uncertainty in resource allocation, often the result of changes in the contextual strategic forces, increases political activity.
- Changes in coordination and integration activities lead to more political activity.
- Leadership changes provide an opportunity for an increase in organizational politics.

Situations that lead to change in the strategic context of organizations create uncertainty and heighten political activity in organizations. Whether this political activity is beneficial or detrimental to the organization depends on the goals of the people involved, the methods they use to achieve their goals, and the way politics are managed in the organization. We consider various political tactics next, followed by a discussion of managing politics in organizations.

Political Tactics

Almost any activity in an organization can be considered political if the actors have a personal agenda. Generally, however, **political tactics** are those activities that fall outside the standardized, formal processes of the organization. Figure 11.5 presents the issues involved in determining the legitimacy of political tactics.

Political tactics
Activities outside the standardized, formal processes of the organization

Whether political tactics *are* legitimate depends on the goal of the person, how the activities affect others, and the overall fairness and equity of the actions. If a person engages in political actions to further organizational goals, if these actions do not harm others within and outside the organization, and if the actions are fair and equitable to all involved, the political actions are positive. However, if the goal is personal gain, others are harmed in the process, and the results are unfair, the political action is considered unethical.

Political actions that receive the most attention are the unethical ones. Most of us know of an unqualified person who was promoted because of personal connections, a subcontractor who won a contract because of his friendship with a manager, or an employee who was blamed for the manager's mistakes. Unfortunately, such events are part of organizational life. However, at least in some cases, one person's view of the events may not always be accurate. Think back to the Managerial Challenge. On the surface, it may seem that Abby Johnson's promotion to senior vice president of Fidelity's mutual fund division was unfair. After all, she is the boss's daughter. Those who work with her, however, may not view it that way because they are familiar with her dedication, skills, knowledge, and managerial style.

Moreover, determining the answers to the questions in Figure 11.5 is not easy. Not only are the answers subject to different points of view, but the person engaging in political activities can also manipulate the situation. So can those who disagree with the political activity. With these caveats in mind, we turn to four categories of political tactics: building relationships, controlling resources, image management, and blame and ingratiation.

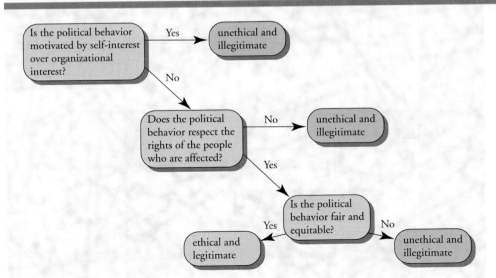

FIGURE 11.5
Legitimacy of Political Tactics

Sources: Based on S. P. Robbins, *Organizational Behavior: Concepts, Controversy, Applications* (Englewood Cliffs, NJ: Prentice Hall, 1996), 489; G. F. Cavanaugh, D. J. Moberg, and M. Vlasquez, "The Ethics of Organizational Politics," *Academy of Management Journal* (June 1981): 363–74.

Coalitions
Relationships with regard to specific issues

Alliances
General agreements of support among different individuals and groups

Networks
Broad, loose support systems

Hot ▼ Link

We discussed W. L. Gore in chapter 2, pp. 52–54.

Building Relationships   One set of political behavior involves developing relationships with others. Table 11.4 describes such relationships. **Coalitions** are relationships over specific issues. **Alliances** are general agreements of support among different individuals and groups, whereas **networks** are broad, loose support systems. In all three cases, people seek to influence others through various power bases such as using their expertise or friendship, threatening people with punishment, providing access to resources and information, and so forth. Successful coalitions, alliances, and networks are built on trust, openness, and respect. They create mutual obligations of support. These kinds of relationships are particularly important as organizations move toward loose structures where formal relationships are not clearly outlined.

Consider the example of W. L. Gore's lattice structure we presented in chapter 2. Employees enter the organization without a predetermined job title; they are expected to look around and find something they are interested in doing. In the process, they must identify senior and junior employees who can help and teach them. Being successful at W. L. Gore requires building relationships and involves political activity. The organization requires and sanctions such activities as they are essential to the achievement of goals.

Another significant relationship is the one that employees develop with their manager and other important and powerful people in the organization. Supporting one's manager and helping that person to be effective is more than performing the duties listed on a formal job description. The support might include taking on additional responsibilities when a colleague gets sick, correcting another employee's misperceptions of the manager's motivations, or letting others know how effective the manager is. This political behavior is beneficial to both the employee and to the organization.

The relationship-building activities depend on developing strong interpersonal relationships and personal bases of power. When undertaken with the interests of the organization in mind, these activities are key to managerial effectiveness and organizational performance.

Controlling Resources, Decisions, and Decision-Making Criteria   A second category of political behavior involves accumulating power through access to resources, decisions, and decision-making criteria. Individuals can accumulate this power by gaining expertise and making themselves or their department indispensable. For example, a team can provide others with key information about an industry and its competitors as a way of gaining power and influence. Joe Bomito, a consultant and team leader at Pfizer Pharmaceuticals, explains that teams need to gain the support of a powerful sponsor in the organization. "If you can show the boss that your team is doing something unique, something that will create a competitive advantage, the boss will want to become the de facto sponsor."[59]

Another method of acquiring power is to gain control of decision making and the decision-making processes and criteria. For instance, a CEO can gain control of board meetings

Table 11.4   BUILDING RELATIONSHIPS

Type of Relationship	Description
• Coalitions	Managers reach an agreement with a person or a group for cooperation over a specific issue
• Alliances	Managers reach a general agreement with a person or a group to support each other
• Networks	Broad and loose support systems with a large number of people who do not necessarily have a common interest
• Supportive Managerial Relationship	A strong relationship between manager and employee developed through support and performance

Team Challenge

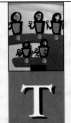

DEVELOPING A POWER BASE

Team members in organizations often complain that they lack the power to implement their ideas. Although many team-based organizations have changed their structure to address this issue, the majority of organizations that use teams haven't made adequate structural changes that provide teams with formal, legitimate power.[a] It is essential then for teams to learn to acquire and use power to be effective. Teams and team leaders can use strategic contingencies and politics to develop their power.

Team members must remember that organizations usually create teams to solve problems that individuals have been unable to solve. Therefore, teams can gain power when they reduce uncertainty for others in the organization. They can do this by bringing in information, predicting and forecasting the future, proposing novel solutions, and devising new products and services. Teams also gain power if they become central to an organization's resource and information networks. They can become central if they have powerful members and team sponsors or if they can negotiate for direct lines of communication to key personnel reporting to top-level executives. Finally, team members must volunteer to take on challenging and strategic issues and demonstrate that they are useful. They should focus on providing unique input that is not duplicated.

In addition to building power through the use of organizational sources, team members must work on developing relationships with other teams and individuals. By using politics actively and positively through coalition and network building, image management, and so forth, team members can gain the power they need to implement their ideas and achieve their goals.[b]

At PeopleSoft, a software company referred to in the sources of power section, teams become empowered by sharing information broadly. Teams receive a backpack full of computers and communication technology that allows them to keep in touch with the organization. Steve Zarate, the chief information officer, states: "If you have power, you also have responsibilities. If you have responsibilities, you need tools to get things done. We provide those tools." The teams at PeopleSoft are required to share all their information with everyone. Zarate insists that "everyone should know everything."[c] For instance, the members of the North American marketing team always have the latest information about a customer because the other teams are constantly updating the database. For PeopleSoft, information serves as the catalyst that empowers teams to do their jobs, to network with other teams, and to serve the customers.

a. J. R. Katzenbach and D. K. Smith, *The Wisdom of Teams* (New York: Harper Business, 1993).

b. A. Nahavandi and I. Aranda, "Restructuring Teams for the Re-Engineered Organization," *Academy of Management Executive* 8, no. 4 (1994): 58–68.

c. P. Roberts, "We Are One Company, No Matter Where We Are," *Fast Company* (April–May 1998): 125, 128.

by setting the agenda and controlling how much time will be spent on each issue. Another example is the manager who lets his employees make a decision after establishing clear criteria for what the decision-making process and criteria should entail.

A third method of influencing the decision-making processes is the selective use of data. For example, by presenting all the advantages and only a few disadvantages of an issue, people will often be able to persuade others to support their position. As is the case with relationship building, the control of resources and decision-making processes and criteria can be used either to benefit or to harm the organization.

Hot ▼ Link

We discussed image management in
chapter 5, pp. 171–74.

Image Management: Visibility and Avoidance   We explored image management in chapter 5. Managing one's image is an important political behavior. From the personal perspective, being seen as competent and credible is critical to a successful career. From an organizational perspective, it is important that managers notice competent and motivated employees, consider them for key projects, and groom them for promotions.

Image management also includes being assertive and willing to defend one's position without being overbearing and without using threats. An image of competence requires clearly stated arguments. Many managers and employees are highly competent and have good ideas and proposals. However, their chances of success are low if they simply wait quietly to be heard. Visibility and realistic self-promotion are necessary. Similarly, well-presented ideas must be forcefully defended, supported by a coalition of credible and powerful people, and clearly demonstrated to benefit the organization. All these aspects of image management involve positive political activities.

A less productive aspect of image management is avoiding association with tainted people—those who are considered deviants. Association with a deviant individual or group can damage one's career. However, how an organization defines deviance and how it manages those who do not conform to organizational norms are matters to consider before an individual decides to avoid deviants. To be successful, one should avoid close association with open revolutionaries. However, associating with creative individualists who agree with central norms but deviate from peripheral norms can be the source of innovation and creativity. The challenge is for managers to learn how to manage their relationship with subversive deviants, who on the surface are often in good standing. Avoiding them can damage one's image as much as associating with them can.

Blame and Ingratiation   The final category of political behavior is the one with the greatest potential for unethical behavior. This category includes blaming others for one's mistakes, openly attacking certain targets, and praising those who do not deserve it. None of these activities pass the ethical test questions posed in Figure 11.5. For instance, blaming others clearly does not respect their rights. Similarly, praising someone to gain favor when that person does not deserve it is not only unfair and self-interested, but it can also harm the organization by encouraging inflated self-image and corruption.

The next time you use the term *politics* to describe all that is shady and distasteful in the way your company makes decisions, remember that certain political behaviors can be useful in helping manage an uncertain environment. Also, consider how many political behaviors can benefit you and your organization. Politics is an integral, necessary part of organizational life; therefore, managers need to manage the political process so that it benefits the organization.

Summary Point 11.9   **What Political Behavior Is Legitimate and What Are Four Political Tactics?**

- The legitimacy of a person's political behavior is judged by whether the behavior is self-interested, whether it harms others, and whether it is fair.
- One political tactic is building relationships—such as coalitions, alliances, and networks—and supportive managerial relationships.
- A second political tactic, controlling resources and decision-making processes, involves developing expertise, mak-

ing oneself indispensable, and controlling decision-making criteria.
- Image management, another political tactic, includes making oneself visible and presenting oneself in the most positive light.
- Blaming, attacking, and ingratiation are the most negative political tactics.

Managing Political Behavior

Managing political behavior has two goals. First, managers should maintain and encourage the constructive relationship building, negotiation, and compromise that are key to an organization's ability to coordinate activities and be effective. Second, they should reduce negative, self-interested, destructive behaviors. Managers can use several approaches to accomplish this task:

- Create an open, supportive climate and culture that encourages frequent interaction and communication.
- Reduce uncertainty through information sharing.
- Develop and use consistent, clear, open, and fair processes, procedures, and rewards.
- Encourage cooperation and discourage unnecessary competition.
- Model and reward constructive behaviors.

These approaches are all part of other sound management techniques such as motivation and team building. As with many organizational issues, an open culture and proper role modeling from leaders and managers cannot be overemphasized. The political activity of negotiation, networking, coalition, and compromise will increase as organizations become more fluid and as power sources shift from legitimate, coercive, and reward power to expert and referent sources. Managers, employees, and team members need to recognize the potential benefits of and dangers to the organization of these conditions and behaviors and learn to use them appropriately.

Power and Politics *in Context*

Without power, managers could not influence employees nor guide them to achieve organizational goals. Without legitimate political behavior, organizations could not reach their goals as quickly or as effectively. In this section, we briefly examine the link between power and politics and the strategic planning process, organizational structure, and organizational culture.

The use of power and politics is particularly important when negotiating the mission, goals, and strategy of the organization. To formulate and implement the organization's strategy, managers use power to convince others to agree on and to implement strategies. Because the strategic planning process is complex and uncertain, the process is fertile ground for political behaviors. The success of managers and the organization depends on managers' ability to build coalitions, alliances, and networks to gain resources and to cooperate with others inside and outside the organization. At PeopleSoft, for instance, managers widely distribute information to make sure that politics do not prevent the employees from achieving the mission of the organization. Dave Duffield, the CEO, states, "If a competitor's strategy is right, it'll win. If our strategy is right, we'll win. We're not going to win or lose by keeping information secret."[60]

Developing and changing the structure of the organization also involves power in two ways. First, the structure determines the power distribution in the organization. In a traditional, hierarchical organization, power is concentrated at the top levels. In current structures, particularly in boundaryless and team-based organizations, employees at all levels have the power to make and implement decisions. Second, managers need power to make structural changes to stay in tune with their environment. In traditional structures, managers can rely on legitimate, reward, and coercive power. In current structures, managers and employees must rely on their ability to persuade based on their expertise and personal relationships with others inside and outside the organization.

Finally, culture at all three levels relates to managers' power. As discussed earlier, national and ethnic cultural values affect the way managers perceive and use power. Power and politics also affect the organization's culture. The manner in which a top manager uses power and politics helps form the culture of an organization. Contrast two earlier examples: Fastenal CEO Bob Kierlin and Richard Scrushy, CEO of Health South and MedPartners. Kierlin's use of referent power and empowerment fosters a supportive, open culture. Scrushy's reliance on fear sets the tone for an organizational culture that is tentative and distrustful.

For updated information on the topics in this chapter, Web exercises, links to related Web sites, an on-line study guide, and more, visit our companion Web site at:
http://www.prenhall.com/nahavandi

A Look Back at the

MANAGERIAL CHALLENGE

Fidelity Investments

When Abby Johnson was appointed one of three deputies assisting the head of Fidelity Investments' mutual fund division, she was able to draw power from her formal position as a member of senior management. Her legitimate power was derived, in part, from her higher station in the hierarchy created by her father, Ned Johnson, Fidelity's chairperson. Her reward power came from her ability to offer or recommend rewards such as promotions. And her coercive power came from the possibility that she would withdraw or withhold rewards or take disciplinary action against an employee under her supervision.

Johnson had two additional sources of power. First, she could claim expert power as a result of having demonstrated her skill at managing the portfolios of several Fidelity mutual funds. Second, she had referent power—and not just because of her relationship with her father. The younger Johnson has been described as modest and hard-working. Rather than use a heavy hand to direct the work of junior portfolio managers, she prefers to serve as a mentor, making suggestions and offering tips from her own experience.[61]

Johnson was also realistic about the importance of empowering portfolio managers, whose skill in buying and selling securities could determine their mutual funds' performance. Portfolio managers have a great deal of freedom as well as full access to resources, such as Fidelity's research database. With this autonomy, however, comes accountability. "There is a balance," Johnson stressed. "You need individual contributors who work as a team. You have to have your own opinion, but be accountable for your fund."[62] Every day brings new challenges to Fidelity's money management skills—and new opportunities for Johnson to use her power base and empowerment to support the success of the family business.

■ Point of View Exercises

You're the Manager: As a colleague of Abby Johnson, you share supervisory responsibilities for a group of portfolio managers at Fidelity. How do you think this would affect coordination and integration of activities within the mutual fund division?

You're the Employee: As a portfolio manager at Fidelity, you are uncertain of how the changes in supervision will affect the power and resources available to you and your peers. In this situation, what political activities might you undertake—and why?

SUMMARY OF LEARNING OBJECTIVES

1. **Define power and discuss cross-cultural differences in power, individual and organizational sources of power, and corruption of power.** Power is the ability of one person to influence another. There are five sources of individual power: legitimate, reward, coercive, expert, and referent. The basis for legitimate, reward, and coercion power is typically the organization; the basis for expert and referent power is the individual. Reactions to power range from acceptance and commitment to compliance to resistance. The more personal the source of power that is used, the more it is likely to lead to commitment rather than compliance or resistance.

   Organizational sources of power depend on access to and control of strategic contingencies, which refer to elements that are essential to the performance and effectiveness of an organization, a department, or a team. Individuals or groups who help others reduce or cope with uncertainty, those who are central to the resource or information networks, and those who cannot be replaced easily gain power.

   Numerous cultural values affect power. The cultural value of power distance impacts the views of power and its use. Who holds power is determined to a large extent by whether a culture is achievement oriented or ascriptive. Finally, researchers are divided on the role gender plays in the acquisition and use of power. However, power is a factor in sexual harassment.

   Power corruption refers to the abuse of power for personal gain and the sense that regular rules do not apply to the power holder. Contributing and interrelated factors are distance from others, inflated view of self, and employee flattery, submission, and dependence. Consequences are poor decision making, use of coercion, poor opinion of employees, unethical actions, and further distance from others. Solutions to corruption include an open culture, increased interaction with employees, reducing employee dependence on managers, and use of objective performance criteria.

2. **Explain the role of empowerment in organizations.** Empowerment involves giving away power to employees at all levels to allow them to make more independent, autonomous decisions. Its successful implementation requires a supportive culture, decentralized structures, and leaders who offer equitable rewards and procedures, have high performance standards, and trust employees.

3. **Describe the political model of organizations, the factors that contribute to organizational politics, and political tactics.** Organizational politics are activities that allow people to achieve goals outside the formal channels. The political model suggests that organizations function with poorly defined roles; shifting, dynamic, and uncertain power bases; and changing coalitions. It further assumes that decision making is based on short-term thinking, as managers continually redefine problems and consider many solutions simultaneously without fully evaluating all alternatives and their consequences.

   The use of politics increases as uncertainty increases. Such uncertainty is often due to changes in the environment, technology, strategy, structure, and culture of an organization. The legitimacy of political tactics is determined by whether the goals are personal or organizational, whether harm comes to various individuals, and whether the actions and outcomes are fair and equitable. Various political activities fall into the four categories of building networks and coalitions, controlling resources and decisions, managing image, and using blame and ingratiation.

4. **Analyze the ways managers can use politics to benefit the organization.** Managers can use political behavior to benefit the organization if they help create an open and supportive climate; reduce uncertainty through information sharing; ensure that processes, procedures, and rewards are consistent, clear, and fair; encourage cooperation and discourage unnecessary competition inside the organization; and model and reward constructive behaviors.

KEY TERMS

alliances, p. 404
authority, p. 384
coalitions, p. 404
coercive power, p. 385
commitment, p. 387
compliance, p. 387
expert power, p. 386

legitimate power, p. 385
networks, p. 404
organizational politics,
p. 397
organizational sources of
power, p. 388
political tactics, p. 403

power, p. 384
referent power, p. 386
resistance, p. 387
reward power, p. 385
sexual harassment, p. 392
strategic contingencies,
p. 388

REVIEW QUESTIONS

1. Compare and contrast power, influence, and authority.
2. Describe the individual and organizational sources of power and their consequences.
3. How does culture influence perception and the use of power?
4. Describe the power corruption cycle and outline the ways in which corruption can be prevented.
5. Compare and contrast the rational and political models of organizations.
6. Describe various political tactics and the way political activity can be managed for the organization's benefit.

DISCUSSION QUESTIONS

1. Why is power needed in organizations? What are the benefits and the disadvantages?
2. Why is power important to teams and how can managers help teams gain power?
3. How can managers and organizations encourage the ethical use of power?
4. Should managers encourage or discourage political behavior?
5. How can you train employees in the use of political behavior?

▶ SELF-ASSESSMENT 11
Views of Power

This self-assessment exercise will provide you with insight into your attitude regarding power. Indicate your reaction to each question by using the following scale:

1	2	3	4	5
Strongly Disagree	Somewhat Disagree	Neither Agree nor Disagree	Somewhat Agree	Strongly Agree

_____ 1. It is important for a leader to use all the power and status symbols the organization provides to be able to get his or her job done.

_____ 2. Unfortunately, with many employees, the only things that really work are threats and punitive actions.

_____ 3. To be effective, a leader needs to have access to many resources for rewarding subordinates when they do their job well.

_____ 4. Having excellent interpersonal relationships with subordinates is essential to effective leadership.

_____   5. One of the keys to a leader's influence is access to information.

_____   6. Being a friend of one's subordinates often reduces a leader's ability to influence them and control their actions.

_____   7. Leaders who are reluctant to punish their employees often lose their credibility.

_____   8. It is very difficult for a leader to be effective without a formal title and position within an organization.

_____   9. Rewarding subordinates with raises, bonuses, and resources is the best way to obtain their cooperation.

_____   10. To be effective, a leader needs to become an expert in the area he or she is overseeing.

_____   11. Organizations need to ensure that a leader's formal evaluation of subordinates is actively used in making decisions about them.

_____   12. Even in most enlightened organizations, a leader's ability to punish subordinates needs to be well preserved.

_____   13. Dismantling formal hierarchies and removing many leadership and status symbols have caused many leaders to lose their ability to influence their subordinates.

_____   14. A leader needs to take particular care to be perceived as an expert in his or her area.

_____   15. It is critical for a leader to develop his or her subordinates' loyalty.

INTERPRETATION

See Appendix 3 for a scoring key. Your total in each of the five categories indicates your attitude toward each of the individual power sources. What are your views? Which source of power do you use most often? What are the effects of your use of your preferred sources of power?

Source: A. Nahavandi, _The Art and Science of Leadership_ (Upper Saddle River, NJ: Prentice Hall, 1977): 92–93; adapted with permission.

▶ TEAM EXERCISE 11
Power Dynamics in Groups

PART I: SET UP

Students give a dollar bill to the teacher and are divided into three groups based on criteria established by the instructor. They are then assigned to their workplaces and instructed to read the rules and tasks below. The money is divided in thirds, two-thirds of it going to the top group, one-third to the middle group, and none to the bottom group.

PART II: RULES AND TASKS

Groups go to their assigned workplaces and complete their tasks.

Rules

    a. Members of the top group are free to enter the space of either of the other groups and to communicate whatever they wish, whenever they wish. Members of the middle group may enter the space of the lower group when they wish but must request permission to enter the top group's space (which the top group can refuse). Members of the lower group may not disturb the top group in any way unless specifically invited by the top. The lower group has the right to knock on the door of the middle group and request permission to communicate with them (which can also be refused).

b. The members of the top group have the authority to make any change in the rules that they wish, at any time, with or without notice.

Tasks

a. *Top Group:* Is responsible for the overall effectiveness and learning from the simulation and for deciding how to use the money.
b. *Middle Group:* Assists the top group in providing for the overall welfare of the organization and in deciding how to use its money.
c. *Bottom Group:* Identifies its resources and decides how best to provide for learning and the overall effectiveness of the organization.

PART III: DEBRIEFING

Each of the three groups chooses two representatives to go to the front of the class and discuss the following questions:

a. What occurred within and between the three groups?
b. What are some of the differences between being in the top group versus being in the bottom group?
c. What can we learn about power from this experience?
d. How accurately do you think this exercise reflects the reality of resource allocation decisions in large organizations?

Source: Lee Bolman and Terrence E. Deal, *Journal of Management Education* [formerly OBTR] 4, no. 3 (1979): 38–42. Copyright © 1979 by Sage Publications. Reprinted by permission of Sage Publications, Inc.

UP CLOSE

▶ Going Places

David Brooks was one of the most liked managers at Financial Security Investments. In an industry known for its cutthroat competitiveness, high employee turnover, low loyalty, and high employee mobility, the 20 brokers who reported to Brooks had surprisingly long tenures and strong loyalty to the company. They were all high performers with well-established clients who would deal only with them. They also displayed an unheard-of level of cooperation in helping one another, training new brokers, and supporting other areas of the company. Brooks's group had the lowest training costs and one of the best performance ratings among the five brokerage groups at Financial.

Brooks's brokers had nothing but praise for him. They described him as one of the fairest, toughest managers around. They said he really knew the business and took excellent care of his people. He provided them with extensive training, rewarded them fairly, supported them in their disputes with other departments and groups, and represented their interests well with upper management. They all knew he demanded excellent performance, but they also knew they could count on him to be flexible in accommodating their personal lives and the ups and downs that are an inherent part of the investment business.

Brooks had been with Financial for close to seven years. Within his first three years there, he had received four quick promotions, leading to his current appointment as group manager three years earlier. Brooks liked his job. Working with brokers and clients was exciting and always offered something new. He got along well with his manager, who praised him for his group's excellent performance and relied on him to train new brokers and to resolve problems in other parts of the company. However, Brooks felt that he was somehow stuck. His several recent requests for promotions and his two applications for higher-level positions had been denied. He became particularly frustrated when he compared himself with Leslie Baskin, who joined the company a year after he did and was now being made an associate vice president in the strategic division.

Like Brooks, Baskin had been a group manager and until the new promotion, she and Brooks had reported to the same division manager. Baskin had managed three different groups in a very short time period, which some attributed to the brokers' extreme dislike of her. Although her groups performed well enough, their turnover rate was high. In many ways they were much more like the rest of the industry than Brooks's group: They were fiercely competitive, cutthroat loners who cared only about themselves. Baskin herself matched that profile. She spent most of her time with upper management developing big accounts. She was always ready with a flashy proposal for the big projects. She managed to make her presentations when all the top executives were present. Although she never mentioned any of the people who had helped her put together her proposals, she always dropped the name of a few powerful people in her acknowledgments. She seemed to know the important people in the company, and she came through with some impressive clients. The fact that she rarely followed through and dumped her work on the other groups and the brokers seemed to escape the attention of upper management.

Brooks could not help but envy Baskin's success. He was also puzzled by how she had become successful given her actual performance. Yes, she had brought in some major clients, but overall her performance was lower than that of several other group managers, including himself. Her brokers disliked her and complained about her temper tantrums, her threats, her lack of support, and her unreasonable demands. Yet, she was going places.[63]

Questions

1. What are the sources of Brooks's and Baskin's power? What are their strengths and weaknesses?
2. What is your evaluation of the message the organization is sending by rewarding Baskin over Brooks? What are the implications of that message?
3. What do you think upper management should do?

THE BIG PICTURE

▶ The Turner and Levin Show at Time Warner

What is it like to work for someone else after being your own boss for over 30 years? Just ask Ted Turner, one of the world's most successful and well-known entrepreneurs. Over the course of three decades, he transformed a billboard business inherited from his father into Turner Broadcasting System, a vast entertainment powerhouse of television stations, cable networks, film libraries, sports teams, and other properties. In 1995, he sold his business to Time Warner and joined the media giant as a significant stockholder (with about 12 percent of the stock) and vice chairperson to Gerald Levin, the chairperson.[64]

At the time, Time Warner's stock was sagging and many criticized Levin for buying Turner Broadcasting. But Levin's acquisition involved much more than a collection of broadcast and cable properties: It also brought Turner into Time Warner's corporate power structure. The former entrepreneur—a longtime champion of frugal operations—immediately began crusading for cost cutting at every level. He was, for example, aghast at the fleet of six corporate jets and a helicopter. His constant prodding led to the sale of two jets and the helicopter.[65] He also pushed his employer to sell off the art masterpieces decorating the corporate headquarters in New York and continue the hunt for other ways to rein in expenses.[66]

Another of Turner's crusades was his campaign for cooperation rather than competition among Time Warner's corporate divisions. He protested loudly and vigorously after learning that one of the divisions had just signed a $50 million deal to sell movies to CBS, arguing that other Time Warner divisions should have been approached first. Ultimately, Turner's displeasure caused the division to back out of the arrangement.[67]

Active in civic and industry affairs, and a generous benefactor identified with many high-profile causes, Turner was accustomed to being in the spotlight. How would he and Gerald Levin get along? Industry observers noted that Turner's showy style was a good complement for Levin's lower-key demeanor. Just as important, Turner has been a strong backer of Levin—and the two have clearly enjoyed their collaboration. "I love working with Ted," Levin said recently. "He's one of the most interesting people on the planet." Turner was just as upbeat about the relationship: "We just have a ball together, but I try not to waste his time."[68]

Questions

1. What do you see as the sources of Ted Turner's power within Time Warner?
2. What effect is Turner having on the culture and political behavior at Time Warner?
3. Based on how Turner and Levin are running Time Warner, would you want to work there? Would you want to buy stock in the corporation? Explain your answers.

NOTES

1. David Whitford and Joseph Nocera, "Has Fidelity Lost It?" *Fortune* (June 9, 1997): 58–59, 61–62, 64, 66, 68, 70.
2. Ibid., 59.
3. Edward Wyatt, "Making Way for Fidelity's Heir Apparent," *New York Times*, February 15, 1998, sec. 3, pp. 1, 8–9.
4. For a detailed discussion of the influence process and influence tactics, see D. Kipnis, S. M. Schmidt, and I. Wilkinson, "Why Do I Like Thee: Is It Your Performance or My Orders?" *Journal of Applied Psychology* 66 (1980): 324–28; G. Yukl and C. M. Falbe, "Influence Tactics in Upward, Downward, and Lateral Influence Attempts," *Journal of Applied Psychology* 75 (1998): 132–40; G. Yukl and C. M. Falbe, "The Importance of Different Power Sources in Downward and Lateral Relations," *Journal of Applied Psychology* 76 (1991): 416–23.
5. J. R. P. French and B. H. Raven, "The Basis of Social Power," in D. Cartwright and A. Zander (eds.), *Group Dynamics*, 3d ed. (New York: Harper and Row, 1968).
6. J. Guyon, "A Mangled Merger," *Fortune* 137, no. 6 (March 30, 1998): 32.
7. For a discussion of power sources and their implications, see Yukl and Falbe, "The Importance of Different Power Sources."
8. T. Walsh, "CEOs: Greenspan by a Landslide," *Fortune* 133, no. 5 (March 18, 1996): 43.
9. H. Lancaster, "Standing Tall (But Not Too Tall) When You're No. 2," *Wall Street Journal*, May 21, 1996, B1.
10. P. Roberts, "We Are One Company, No Matter Where We Are," *Fast Company* (April–May 1998): 125; also see R. B. Lieber, "Why Employees Love These Companies," *Fortune* 137, no. 1 (1998): 73.
11. A. M. Rahim and M. Afzal, "Leader Power, Commitment, Satisfaction, Compliance, and Propensity to Leave a Job Among U.S. Accountants," *Journal of Social Psychology* 133, no. 5 (1993): 611–25.
12. Yukl and Falbe, "The Importance of Different Power Sources."
13. D. J. Hickson, C. R. Hinings, C. A. Lee, R. E. Scheneck, and J. M. Pennings, "A Strategic Contingencies Theory of Intra-Organizational Power," *Administrative Science Quarterly* 16 (1971): 216–29; G. R. Salancik and J. Pfeffer, "Who Gets Power—and How They Hold onto It: A Strategic-Contingency Model of Power," *Organizational Dynamics* (Winter 1977): 3–21.
14. K. Mieszkowski, "Branding Is Dead," *Fast Company* (April–March 1998): 190.
15. S. Barr, "Toy Story," *CFO* 12, no. 11 (November 1996): 54–62.
16. A. Pettigrew, *The Politics of Organizational Decision Making* (London: Tavistock, 1973).
17. E. W. Demond, "Can Canon Keep Clicking?" *Fortune* 137, no. 2 (February 2, 1998): 104.
18. J. B. Rosener, "Ways Women Lead," *Harvard Business Review* 68, no. 6 (1990): 119–25.
19. A. Muoio, "Women and Men, Work and Power," *Fast Company* (February–March 1998): 74.
20. Ibid., 82.
21. Ibid., 76.
22. J. B. White and C. Hymowitz, "Watershed Generation of Women Executives Is Rising to the Top," *Wall Street Journal*, February 10, 1997, A1, A6; *The Economist* (August 26, 1995): 59.
23. See *Jones v. Clinton*, ___ F. Supp. ___ (E.D.Ark. 1998).
24. J. M. Cleveland and M. E. Kerst, "Sexual Harassment and Perception of Power: An Underarticulated Relationship," *Journal of Vocational Behavior* (February 1993): 49–67.
25. A. Fisher, "After All This Time, Why Don't People Know What Sexual Harassment Means?" *Fortune* 137, no. 1 (1998): 156.
26. Ibid.
27. Betsy Plevan, quoted in Ibid.
28. For example, see W. Hollway and L. Mukurasi, "Women Managers in the Tanzanian Civil Service," in N. Adler and P. Izraeli (eds.), *Competitive Frontiers: Women Managers in a Global Economy* (Cambridge, MA: Blackwell, 1994): 344–50.
29. For detailed information regarding the causes and consequences of power corruption, see D. Kipnis, "Does Power Corrupt?" *Journal of Personality and Social Psychology*, 24 (1972): 33–41; C. Prendergast, "The Theory of 'Yes Men'," *American Economic Review* 83, no. 5 (1993): 757–70.
30. S. Jones, "Emergency Surgery for MedPartners," *Business Week* (March 9, 1998): 81.
31. For a discussion of the negative effects of power, see P. Block, *Stewardship: Choosing Service Over Self-Interest* (San Francisco: Berrett-Koehler, 1993).
32. D. McClintick, "The Bank Scandal That Keeps Growing," *Fortune* 136, no. 1 (July 7, 1997): 36–38.
33. See Prendergast, "The Theory of 'Yes Men'," and Block, *Stewardship*.
34. J. Bright, "How to Make a Mint from a Print," *Director* 47, no. 5 (1993).
35. "A Rescue at Sea in South Korea," *The Economist* (November 26, 1994): 81–82.
36. For detailed discussion of empowerment, see P. Black, *The Empowered Manager* (San Francisco: Jossey-Bass 1987); J. A. Conger and R. N. Kanungo, *Charismatic Leadership: The Elusive Factor in Organizational Effectiveness* (San Francisco: Jossey-Bass, 1988).
37. For examples in various industries and countries, see J. David, "Winners Share Goals but Methods Differ," *BRW* (international ed.) 4, no. 1 (1994): 34–35; D. Clutterbuck, "Clarify Your Purpose," *Managing Service Quality* (November 1993): 5–6.
38. See C. R. Leana, "Power Relinquishment versus Power Sharing: Theoretical Clarification and Empirical Comparison of Delegation and Participation," *Journal of Applied Psychology* (May 1987): 228–33; A. J. H. Thorlakson and R. P. Murray, "An Empirical Study of Empowerment in the Workplace," *Group and Organization Management* (March 1996): 67–83.
39. R. Teitelbaum, "Who Is Bob Kierlin—and Why Is He So Successful?" *Fortune* 136, no. 1 (December 8, 1997): 248.
40. Ibid., 246.
41. For definitions of organizational politics and discussion of its impact, see D. J. Vredenburgh and J. G. Maurer, "A Process Framework of Organizational Politics," *Human Relations* 37 (1984): 47–66; D. Yates Jr., *The Politics of Management* (San Francisco: Jossey-Bass, 1985); K. M. Kacmar and G. R. Ferris, "Politics at Work: Sharpening the Focus on Political Behavior in Organizations," *Business Horizons* (July–August 1993): 70–74.
42. M. Browne, *Organizational Decision Making and Information* (Norwood, NJ: Ablex, 1993): 33–42.
43. Ibid.; J. Pfeffer, *Power in Organizations* (Marshfield, MA: Pitman, 1981).
44. E. F. Harrison, *The Managerial Decision-Making Process*, 3d ed. (Boston, MA: Houghton-Mifflin, 1987): 83–84.
45. F. Rose, "Whatever Happened to Michael Ovitz?" *Fortune* 136, no. 1 (July 7, 1997): 124; also see "Disney's No. 2 Quits over Power Frustration," *Arizona Republic*, December 13, 1996, A8.
46. Rose, "Whatever Happened," 122.
47. F. Trompenaars, *Riding the Waves of Culture: Understanding Culture and Diversity in Business* (London: Nicholas Brealey, 1994).
48. A. Taylor, "How Toyota Defies Gravity," *Fortune* 136, no. 11 (December 8, 1997): 106.
49. For a detailed discussion of effect of culture in negotiations, see N. J. Adler, *International Dimensions of Organizational Behavior*, 2d ed. (Boston: PWS Kent, 1991): 179–221.
50. J. Martin, "Mercedes: Made in Alabama," *Fortune* 136, no. 1 (July 7, 1997): 154.
51. Ibid., 158.
52. Ibid., 152.
53. J. Gantz and V. V. Murray, "Experience of Workplace Politics," *Academy of Management Journal* 23 (1980): 237–51; Pfeffer, *Power in Organizations*.
54. R. S. Johnson, "Motown: What's Going On?" *Fortune* 136, no. 10 (November 24, 1997): 140.
55. Ibid., 133–40.
56. Ibid.
57. Ibid., 134–35.
58. Ibid., 135.
59. M. Fischetti, "Team Doctors, Report to ER!" *Fast Company* (February–March 1998): 177.
60. Roberts, "We Are One Company," 128.
61. Edward Wyatt, "Making Way for Fidelity's Heir Apparent," 1.
62. Ibid., 8.
63. This case is partially based on the results of research by F. Luthans, "Successful vs. Effective Managers," *Academy of Management Executive* 2, no. 2 (1988): 127–32.
64. Nelson D. Schwartz, "Suddenly, Jerry Levin's Stock Is Hot," *Fortune* (March 30, 1998): 106.
65. "Ted Turner's Management Consultant," *The Economist*, March 22, 1997: 86.
66. Schwartz, "Suddenly, Jerry Levin's Stock."
67. E. Shapiro, "Brash As Ever, Turner Is Giving Time Warner Dose of Culture Shock," *Wall Street Journal*, March 24, 1997: A1, A8.
68. Schwartz, "Suddenly, Jerry Levin's Stock," 106–108.

COMMUNICATING EFFECTIVELY

LEARNING OBJECTIVES

1. Explain the elements and process of communication and the functions of nonverbal communication.
2. Describe the different types and directions of organizational communication and identify the importance of external and strategic communication.
3. Discuss the barriers to and tools of effective communication.
4. Specify the role of technology in communication.
5. Highlight the importance of ethics in communication.

MANAGERIAL CHALLENGE

Avon Products

Avon Products has been reaching out to women one-to-one ever since Mrs. P. F. E. Albee, the first Avon Lady, started ringing doorbells in 1886. Door-to-door sales of cosmetics, fragrances, and other personal care products have always been the company's mainstay, accounting for about 98 percent of revenues. But 100 years later, Avon's environment is in flux—and the company is trying to keep up with the times.[1]

Throughout the 1980s, women entered the U.S. workforce in droves, leaving a shrinking pool of candidates to become doorbell-ringing Avon Ladies and even fewer women home to open the door when Avon rang. Just as bad, Avon's products were running up against the powerful brand images projected by Revlon and other competitors in the beauty business.[2]

Then Avon's management team recruited Andrea Jung in 1994 to become president of Avon's U.S. Product Marketing Group. A magna cum laude graduate of Princeton, Jung, 38, is fluent in Mandarin and a rising star in retail marketing. She was senior vice president at I. Magnin in San Francisco before moving to Neiman Marcus, where she served as executive vice president for women's apparel, cosmetics, accessories, and other product lines. At Avon, Jung's boss gave her the task of revitalizing the company's beauty products and, with the other members of the senior management team, exploring new ways to communicate effectively with women in its global markets.[3]

Jung is questioning the way women are portrayed in the media. She and her management team want to send a message that Avon takes women seriously, not as sex objects, not as men want to see women. She does not want a woman wearing Avon products to look "so made up [she has] no place to go," Jung declares.[4]

Jung enjoys building consensus among her team and making sure everyone's voice is heard. She makes an extra effort to listen to her team's suggestions and ideas. Recently, her Global Marketing team was having difficulty finding an appealing name for a new facial cream. Some team members wanted it to be called Vertical Lift, the rest Night Force. She and her team agreed to call it Anew Night Force Vertical Lifting Complex. After the decision she states jokingly: "It was like naming a child after your mother, your husband's mother, your grandmother, and your great aunt."[5]

■ Questions

1. What is Jung's style of communication?
2. How can she cut through the competitive noise and bring the company's message to customers outside the organization?

Andrea Jung is skilled at communicating with people inside and outside her company. As many effective managers are aware, she knows that many organizational woes result from communication problems. An organization relies on communication to inform employees and managers of its missions and goals, to direct and guide their behaviors and actions, to coordinate efforts, to clarify tasks, and to provide feedback. It is an integral part of all managerial activities at the micro, interpersonal level and at the macro, organizational level.

In this chapter, we explore the elements of communication and consider the importance of verbal and nonverbal communication. We examine the interpersonal, internal, and external levels of communication. Finally, we investigate the tools of effective communication.

■ ELEMENTS OF COMMUNICATION

Communication is the exchange of information between people. It is a continuous process in which one person sends a message to another who understands the meaning of that message and responds to it.[6] People are constantly communicating; they cannot help but communicate.[7] Communication is effective when the message is received and understood by the intended person with minimal distortions.

Elements of Organizational Communication

Figure 12.1 depicts the basic communication process. The sender creates a message, **encoding** it or putting it in a certain format to send to the receiver. The message can be sent through a variety of **media**, which are the methods of communication. These can include a written message, a phone conversation, face-to-face meetings, e-mail, and so forth. Before it reaches its intended receiver, *noise* can distort a message. **Noise** is all the factors that interfere with and distort communication. The intended receiver *decodes* and interprets the message. **Decoding**

Communication
The exchange of information between people; it occurs when one person understands the meaning of a message another person sends and responds to it

Encoding
The process by which the sender puts a message in a certain format to send to the receiver

Media
The methods of communication

Noise
All factors that interfere with and distort communication

Decoding
The process by which the receiver translated the sender's message into an understandable form

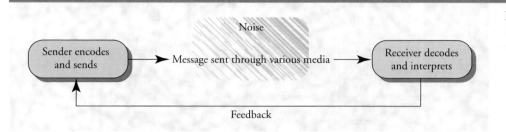

FIGURE 12.1
*The Process of
Communication*

is the process by which the receiver translates the sender's message into an understandable form. The receiver then provides feedback to the sender, indicating that a message was received and understood. The feedback closes the communication loop and completes the process. We consider the different elements of the communication process, giving special attention to non-verbal communication and culture.

The basic communication process is deceivingly simple. At any point in the process, a variety of distortions and obstacles can prevent effective communication. We look first at the functions and elements of organizational communication, including ethical and cultural issues that affect communication, and the levels and types of organizational communication. We then turn our attention to identifying the factors in effective communication.

Sender, Encoding, and Message The **sender** is the person who creates the communication and decides how to send it. For instance, a manager who wants to inform her team of policy changes regarding vacation time must decide how to send this message. She can write a memo, send a message via e-mail, announce the changes during a department meeting, or inform each employee in individual meetings. The choice of the communication medium affects the way others react to the message. On the one hand, if the new vacation policy is unpopular and controversial, employees may resent a memo outlining the policy without having the opportunity to discuss it. In that case, a department meeting or one-on-one meetings to discuss the effect on each employee may be more desirable than less personal media. On the other hand, if a manager must communicate an unpopular decision over which he has no control, it may be easier if he delivers the message through a formal memo without further communication.

Figure 12.2 presents the factors that affect the sender and message: the credibility and sensitivity of the sender, use of jargon, timing, and the selection of the medium. The credibility of the sender is the first communication factor that affects the sender and message. We

Sender
*The person who creates the
communication and decides
how it should be sent*

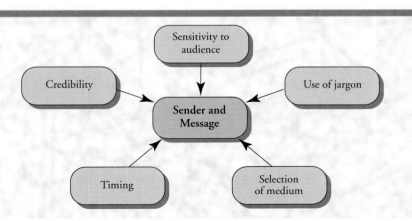

FIGURE 12.2
***Communication Factors
in Sender and Message***

are more likely to listen to and believe a person who has expertise or whom we trust. Second, the sender can be more effective by being sensitive to the needs of the audience or the people who will receive the message.

Third, the sender must present the message using the appropriate language with or without the use of **jargon**, which is language and terms that have a clear meaning among some groups but not others. Fourth, the message must be timed for maximum effectiveness. For example, a manager who decides to conduct performance reviews immediately after the organization announces impending layoffs will face hostile and inattentive employees. The reviews will be more effective if he delivers the message at a time when there is less tension.

Finally, the communication medium that managers select must fit the sender, the message, and the audience. A written communication takes longer but provides a permanent record and can help avoid misunderstandings. These factors explain why managers rely on written documentation to follow up on important verbal discussions ranging from an employee's performance review to contract negotiations with suppliers and customers. As opposed to written communication, verbal messages are faster and provide opportunities for immediate interaction and feedback. They are also richer as they involve nonverbal communication. Andrea Jung, profiled in the Managerial Challenge, relies on considerable face-to-face communication to interact with her employees, thereby building team cohesion.

Let's look at how the oil company British Petroleum (BP) decided to resolve a thorny morale problem through its choice of medium and sensitivity to its audience. BP's Thailand operation was doing poorly. Layoffs and cutbacks had demoralized its 2,000 Thai employees. British Petroleum's Thailand division head, John Mumford, decided to seek help from Pamela Mounter, a BP communication adviser. Together they designed a simple newsletter, written in Thai and custom-made for the local employees. The newsletter informed employees about the company's plans clearly and specifically. This clear communication from a credible source raised morale and reduced turnover so that the division eventually made a substantial profit.[8]

Receiver, Decoding, and Interpretation Once managers send a message, the intended receiver must understand it. A variety of factors influences the decoding process: the receiver's attention and emotional state, perceptual biases, and active participation in the communication. First, the receiver must pay attention to the message and must be in an open, receptive emotional state. For example, an employee will have trouble listening to and understanding his manager's communications when he is tired, upset, or angry.

Selective attention and perceptual biases further influence how people interpret a message. People do not pay attention to all information equally. Instead, they focus on novel and salient events. They also rely on stereotypes, haloes, or other biases to organize and interpret information, thereby introducing noise in the process. In general, to decode the message correctly, the receiver must be an active part of the communication process.

Feedback Once the receiver decodes the message, the communication process continues until the receiver gives feedback to the sender that she has understood the message. In effect, the receiver becomes the sender. The feedback can be the final step in the communication loop or a starting point for further communication. For instance, if the receiver has incorrectly interpreted the message, the sender must provide further clarification.

Noise All aspects of the communication process are subject to distortion and noise. The message may not be clear. The receiver may not be paying attention or may misinterpret the message, leading to poor decoding. Similarly, the feedback may be distorted or misunderstood, also leading to miscommunication. One of the basic challenges of communicating in organizations is to eliminate or at least reduce noise to allow for more effective communication.

Jargon
Language and terms that have a clear meaning among some groups but not others

Hot ▼ Link

We discussed selective attention and perceptual biases in chapter 5, pp. 154, 161–65.

Summary Point 12.1 **What Are the Elements of Communication?**

- The sender creates a message and encodes it or puts it in a certain format to send to the receiver through a variety of media.
- The credibility of the sender, sensitivity to the audience, use of jargon, selection of the medium, and timing are all important factors in communication.
- Noise can distort a message before reaches its intended receiver.

- The intended receiver decodes and interprets the message and provides feedback to the sender to indicate that the message was received and understood.
- Some factors that affect the decoding process are the receiver's attention and emotional state, selective attention and perceptual biases, and active participation.

Let's return to the BP example to see how an organization tried to meet this challenge. Mumford followed each newsletter with a bag lunch during which BP managers discussed issues and concerns face-to-face with their Thai employees. He used these lunches to receive feedback about his messages and to clarify any miscommunications.[9]

The basic communication process we presented typically applies to verbal communication. However, it also applies to messages we send without using the spoken or written word.

Nonverbal Communication

Nonverbal communication is communication that is sent without the use of the written or spoken word. Nonverbal communication plays a powerful role in the communication process. Even when we are not talking to others, we communicate with them through our facial expressions, body posture, tone of voice, use of touch, and the use of space and distance. The types of nonverbal communication that we discuss are facial expression (*occulesics*) and body posture (*kinesics*), tone of voice (*paralinguistics*), use of space (*proxemics*), and touching (*tactilics*).

Nonverbal communication
Communication that is sent without the use of the written or spoken word

Occulesics and Kinesics **Occulesics** consist of the facial expressions and eye contact we use to communicate. We use occulesics to convey a wide range of emotions and reactions. Our facial

Occulesics
Facial expressions and eye contact that we use to communicate

Our body language communicates a lot of information without the use of words. What does the body posture of these two people convey to you?

expressions and whether we do or do not look at people are among the primary ways we express how we feel. **Kinesics** is the study of bodies through posture, gesture, head movements, and so forth. The combination of facial expressions and body posture can send powerful nonverbal messages to those around us.

Facial expressions, eye contact, and the use of our bodies in communication vary greatly by culture.[10] For example, people from North America and Western Europe usually maintain steady eye contact when talking to one another; people from Asian and Native American cultures avoid direct eye contact, especially when talking to someone with a higher status.[11] People in the West consider steady eye contact as signaling honesty and openness; in contrast, people in the East tend to perceive it as a lack of respect. Similarly, in cultures that are high on the emotion dimension, such as France, the use of animated hand gestures while speaking is commonplace. In countries that are low on the emotion dimension, such as Britain and Japan, similar movements are considered overly and unnecessarily emotional. The Chinese perceive those same animated gestures as disrespectful.

Paralinguistics   The various vocal cues and other signals that accompany verbal messages are called **paralinguistics**. These include our tone of voice, volume, pitch, expression, and rate of speech.[12] How we speak has a strong impact on whether people listen to us, like us, or find us credible. We will pay attention to and understand a message delivered in a clear and confident tone of voice and at a moderate speed. We likely will ignore the same message delivered in a hesitant and garbled manner or spoken too fast or too softly.

Politicians and business executives alike make full use of paralinguistics by practicing their speeches and working with voice and communication coaches. Managers also take training seminars on language, appearance, and gestures to become more effective communicators. For example, when Michelle Martineau, manager of finance and development for Marriott Corporation, was asked to make a presentation in front of CEO Bill Marriott, the seminar she took on presentation skills gave her the added confidence she needed to be effective.[13] In the United States, communication consultants teach managers and other public figures how to eliminate their regional accents and improve their overall speech so they will appear more credible and competent.

National and ethnic cultural differences play an important role in paralinguisitics. Loud, confident North Americans or Australians sharply contrast with self-effacing, quiet Thai and Japanese. Gender differences also affect the use of paralinguistics. Generally, women speak less forcefully and use a less confident tone relative to men.[14] These differences can be a major impediment in business settings where projecting confidence is essential. To overcome this impediment, some business women work with voice coaches and communication consultants to deepen their voices, speak louder, and avoid hesitation. Jean Otte, founder of an organization that helps women improve their communication skills, states: "It's like being the new kid on the block. How do you get the boys to pass you the ball?"[15] She advises women to learn to incorporate in their communication style techniques that men appreciate.

Proxemics   **Proxemics** consists of the use of space and the distance between people. Our use of space changes depending on the type of relationship we have with people.[16] All people have a **personal space,** which is the area around them that they control. In effect, we surround ourselves with an invisible privacy bubble. Any violation of that space or bubble leads to personal discomfort. Imagine an employee who makes everyone uncomfortable because he stands too close when talking to them. What is your reaction when someone you do not know well reaches to pick lint from your jacket? People can feel the invasion of personal space so acutely that it leaves a lasting negative impression. Figure 12.3 shows the comfort zones of personal space in the United States.

In the United States, the *intimate zone* covers roughly a two-foot circle and is reserved for close family and friends. The *personal zone*, which extends to four feet, is accessible to friends and more distant family members. The *social zone*, which covers roughly twelve feet, is where most

Kinesics
The study of bodies through posture, gesture, and head movements

Paralinguistics
The various vocal cues and other signals that accompany verbal messages

Proxemics
The use of space and the distance between people

Personal space
The area around them that people control

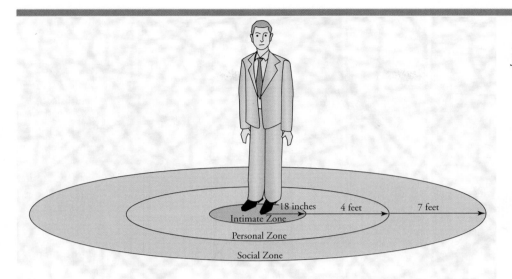

FIGURE 12.3
Zones of Personal Space for People from the United States

business interactions take place. The appropriate use of zones is essential to our ability to communicate comfortably with others. Stand too close and you may be perceived as inappropriate and rude. Stand too far away and you may be seen as distant, shy, and uncommunicative.

A personal space that is appropriate in one culture may be inappropriate in another.[17] Generally, people from Latin America, the Middle East, and Southern Europe tolerate closer distances than those from North America, Asia, and Northern Europe who need more personal space. Say, for instance, that a Saudi businessman inches closer to his German partner as they speak. The German will tend to back away. Both will be uncomfortable; the Saudi is likely to perceive the German as unfriendly and aloof, and the German will tend to see the Saudi as overly pushy and intimate. Cross-cultural differences in use of personal space can create conflict and prevent effective business communication.

In addition to personal space, we claim territories for ourselves. **Territories** are spaces over which we claim ownership and control. Our offices, lockers, and desks are all parts of our territory. We decorate and mark them in various ways to claim ownership of them. We use them to send messages about who we are and what is important to us.[18] Our *primary territory* is a space such as our homes. We fully recognize one another's primary territory and consider invasions serious matters. Our *secondary territories* are spaces we use regularly that we also share with others. Your seat in the classroom does not really belong to you, but you may become irritated if another student takes it. Similarly, you will feel uncomfortable if another employee takes your regular spot in the meeting room. Finally, we lay temporary claim to *public territories* that are shared by many. Examples of public territory include the entrance lobby of office buildings, restaurants, or stores. Although we do not expect to hold onto that space, we still will feel uncomfortable when others invade it.

Our offices are generally considered primary territory. We claim them by personalizing them, decorating them with personal items and pictures of our families or other important people and events. We place plaques and awards in visible places. Physicians decorate their offices with their diplomas to indicate their status and level of expertise.

Some organizations, such as many banks in the United States, replace personal offices with open, shared office spaces. Organizations that change offices from primary to secondary territory are usually trying to increase interaction and cooperation. However, even in open offices, employees attempt to make their space personal by arranging their furniture a certain way or decorating their glass partitions or desks.

Territories
Spaces over which we claim ownership and control

People claim their offices and other spaces as their own by personalizing them. Their use of space communicates clearly to others who they are.

A QUESTION OF ETHICS

Is Your Office Private?

Your boss uses her master key to enter your office when you are out to find a report she needs. While she is looking for the report, she finds a copy of a job application you have sent to another company and confronts you. What should you do? Did she act ethically? Explain.

Organizations consistently use space to send messages about their mission, their culture, and their values. Some organizational spaces are formal and dignified; others are relaxed. How a company decorates its public space, offices, and conference rooms sends a clear message about its culture. Dutch artist Jacqueline Hassink visited the offices of major corporations around the globe and found that the shape of their conference tables reflects the organizational culture. "When I first asked people for permission to photograph their meeting table, they were very surprised and confused. Then, as they thought about it, they suddenly realized the importance of the object. It is a symbol. It tells a lot about the company's view of management and power."[19] Hassink believes that round tables communicate a democratic culture, oval tables suggest a less democratic culture, and rectangular tables announce an autocratic culture.

Tactilics
Touching behaviors

Tactilics   Touching behaviors are known as **tactilics**. Because touching requires an invasion of someone's personal space, it can be a powerful form of communication. There are many stated and unstated norms with respect to touching others. Permission to touch is clearly tied to power in organizations. Those with power are generally allowed to touch those without power. For example, a manager can pat an employee on the back as encouragement, but an employee who touches her manager is likely to be considered as behaving inappropriately. In many Western cultures, it is unusual for employees at lower levels of a company to touch people at higher levels.

As U.S. organizations deal with sexual harassment issues, touching employees and co-workers—even in an apparently appropriate manner—has become a highly controversial issue. Inappropriate touching has been the major cause of action in several recent sexual harassment

Organizations such as Massachusettes General Hospital send powerful messages about who they are through how they arrange and decorate space. What message is its conference room conveying to you?

law suits.[20] Two of these cases were brought against Japanese auto manufacturer Mitsubishi and Manhattan brokerage firm Gruntal & Company. Female employees at both companies complained about male co-workers and managers groping and grabbing them. As a result of such incidents, many businesses have developed policies to regulate touching in the workplace.

Although the solution to the problem of touching in the workplace may seem simple, the issue is actually complex. Individual, gender, and cultural differences complicate perceptions about what is and is not appropriate touching.[21] For example, some nationalities, such as some in Latin America or the Middle East, are more comfortable with touching in the course of social interaction than the English or the Japanese. However, such touching typically occurs only between people of the same sex and with equal status. Similarly, in many cultures, women touch one another more than men. The appropriateness of touching is not only determined by culture—both national and subgroup—but also by context. A pat on the back may be inappropriate during a negative performance review in which an employee is angry, but the same gesture may be acceptable in a team meeting with many people present.

Most of us are aware of the power of our words to influence people and to enhance our image, but we tend not to be aware of our equally if not more powerful nonverbal behaviors and what we communicate through them. Nonverbal messages reinforce, undermine, or even negate the verbal ones. The management of nonverbal communication is therefore as important as the management of verbal communication. We next consider communication in organizations.

Summary Point 12.2   **What Are the Elements of Nonverbal Communication?**

- Occulesics consist of facial expressions and eye contact that we use to communicate.
- Kinesics is the study of bodies through posture and gestures.

- Paralinguistics are the various vocal cues and other signals that accompany verbal messages.
- Proxemics consist of the use of space and the distance between people.
- Tactilics involve touching behaviors.

COMMUNICATION IN ORGANIZATIONS

Communication networks
Formal and informal communication pathways and patterns

If we chart communication in an organization, we will see that it takes place at many different levels. People talk to their bosses, co-workers, colleagues, suppliers, and customers. People within and outside organizations are interconnected through a number of **communication networks,** which are formal and informal communication pathways and patterns. Figure 12.4 presents several typical communication networks. Traditional organizations rely on either the chain or the Y communication network. Team-based and boundaryless organizations encourage all-channel communication networks in which all parts of the units within an organization are interconnected. Such circle or all-channel communication networks closely resemble the informal, friendship-based patterns in which all members of a group communicate with one another.

Formal and Informal Communication

Formal communication networks
Networks that are designated by the organizational structure, charts, or other official documents

Informal communication networks
Networks that exist outside the official organizational networks

Formal communication networks are those designated by the organizational structure, charts, or other official documents. Examples include reporting relationships with one's manager and formal liaisons and integration mechanisms between and among departments. The most common type of formal communication in organization is communication downward with employees.

    Informal communication networks are those that exist outside the official organizational networks. These include communication among friends and allies, social groups, and cliques. Examples are the *grapevine*, an informal but organized network of communication, and the *old-boy network*, a closed group that uses information as a source of power. Informal networks develop for several reasons: to fill in gaps in organizational information, to satisfy social needs, to serve as a source of power, and to facilitate political activities.

    Informal networks develop to fill gaps in the formal communication networks. Employees who cannot get the information they need or want through formal channels obtain it through informal channels. In some cases, managers may not communicate information clearly enough or fast enough through formal channels. In other cases, they may willingly withhold information from employees. For instance, during mergers or restructuring, management often does not inform employees of impending layoffs to prevent panic or premature turnover. In these situations, employees obtain information through informal networks.

FIGURE 12.4
Communication Networks

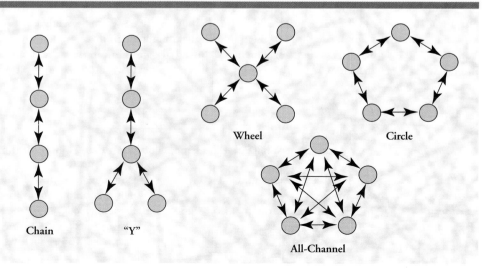

Chain   "Y"   Wheel   Circle   All-Channel

Informal networks further satisfy social needs because they provide a channel for social relationships at work. They also can be used as a source of power. Using the grapevine or an old-boy network to obtain valuable information and then disseminating it strategically can be an effective method of influencing others. In addition to satisfying the need for information, such activities are closely related to political behavior in which various activities take place outside formal channels. Managers and employees use informal networks for both legitimate and illegitimate political activities.

Informal networks are effective and powerful means of communication. Information travels faster and sometimes with less noise through an informal network in which there are many opportunities for feedback and two-way communication.[22] It can be costly for a manager to ignore informal networks or even try to disband them. People create these networks because they need more effective communication. Instead of ignoring or dismissing informal networks, managers can encourage or formalize them to improve organizational communication.

When Valley National Bank (VNB) of Arizona merged with Bank One of Ohio, VNB managers actively used communication to avoid misinformation about the merger. They acknowledged the employees' need for information by publishing a regular newsletter about the progress of the merger and by creating an information hotline for employees to call to get the latest news. Additionally, VNB managers provided updates about the mergers in meetings and informally whenever possible. These efforts to provide information about a stressful situation reduced destructive gossip and rumors.

Encouraging employees to offer anonymous feedback can be an effective use of informal communication. Anonymous messages may provide information about illegal or unethical activities that employees cannot communicate through the formal communication channels. For instance, Mark Willis, CEO of Times-Mirror Co., encourages employees to send anonymous e-mails in which they gripe about company policies. He then makes sure that the appropriate managers respond to the issues.[23]

Rite Aid Corporation, a large drugstore chain, is another company that uses informal networks to communicate serious issues to managers and to safeguard the anonymity of those who complain. Rite Aid has installed a voice-mail system that prepares a transcript of someone's message without revealing the caller's identity. The transcripts are sent to managers daily. Martin Grass, Rite Aid's CEO, reads these transcripts and claims that he and his managers "take each one seriously."[24]

Now that we have described formal and informal communication, we look at how communication flows in organizations.

Hot ▼ Link

We discussed sources of power and types of political activities in chapter 11, pp. 384–408.

Summary Point 12.3   **What Are Formal and Informal Communication Networks?**

- Formal communication networks are those that are designated by the organizational structure.
- Informal communication networks are those that exist outside official organizational networks.

- Informal networks can be used to fulfill social needs, to obtain information, to gain power, or to engage in political activities.

Direction of Communication

Organizational communication occurs in three general directions, as Table 12.1 describes. Communication flows *upward* when employees communicate with their managers and others above them in the hierarchy. Communication travels *downward* when managers communicate with those who report to them. Finally, communication flows *laterally* between co-workers. The basic communication process, the use of verbal and nonverbal messages, and the impact

Ta b l e 1 2 . 1   LEVELS OF COMMUNICATION

Level	Characteristics	Challenges
Upward	Information provided to higher levels of the organization in the form of analyses, reports, grievances, financial data, and so forth	• Maintain open channels and accept communication from below • Prevent selective filtering of news • Encourage participation and feedback to avoid isolation
Downward	Information provided from higher to lower levels. Typically includes instructions, goals, orders, peformance feedback, and so forth	• Watch for overutilization • Do not overburden employees • Avoid conflicting communication and keep messages clear • Encourage feedback
Lateral (horizontal)	Exchange of information to coordinate activities among people at the same level	• Recognize its importance • Do not dismiss as merely the activity of the grapevine • Provide more formal lateral communication channels

of culture exist when communication is occurring in all three directions. However, communication in each direction poses special challenges.

Upward Communication   Most organizations provide few formal ways for employees to communicate upward. Employees can send reports and other information, but this usually occurs only at the request of upper management. An array of staff, formal procedures, and well-established traditions often prevent those at lower levels from making contact with those at higher levels. Furthermore, employees are reluctant to inform managers of problems or complaints for fear of reprisals; the bearers of bad news often pay the price for their actions.[25] As a result, executives become increasingly isolated and the organization experiences what is known as the "mum effect" where only favorable information travels up.[26]

Poor and limited upward communication can slow decision-making processes, cause frustration, and lead to unhappy employees. The 1995 merger of Pharmacia AB of Sweden and Upjohn of Michigan resulted in a new pharmaceutical company, Pharmacia & Upjohn Inc.[27] To prevent managers from favoring either the Swedish or the American side of the organization, the company built a new headquarters in London, a neutral turf. All communication and decisions were rerouted through this headquarters.

The Swedes were the first to protest. Managers now had to send decisions that had taken a short time to make in Sweden or Italy, where Pharmacia has a major market presence, upward to headquarters in London for clearance. The headquarters' managers, who were only remotely familiar with the operational issues, soon became a major stumbling block for all staffing, drug introductions, and other daily decisions. "London calling" became a major joke for managers who did not like London's interference. "London was like an artificial limb," states Karl Olof Borg, manager of the research division in Milan, Italy.[28] Many talented people, frustrated with the process, left for other companies.

Downward Communication   Downward communication is the most common mode of formal communication in an organization.[29] Organizations have a number of ways through which managers and supervisors at all levels provide their employees with instructions, clarification, and direction. The challenge in downward communication is not to overburden employees with too many unclear or conflicting messages and to allow for two-way communication and feedback.[30]

Additionally, as information makes its way down the formal chain of command, it often loses accuracy and clarity. The result is that those who are charged with carrying out instructions do not have enough information to do so well. Overall, overreliance on downward communication can reduce employee motivation and deprive the organization of valuable information.

At Pharmacia & Upjohn, John Zabriskie, Upjohn's CEO before the merger, asked his managers to request more "accurate" accounting reports from the Italian division with every data point verified. That way, all departments under his control could send frequent updates to London on important matters. The Italians resented what they interpreted as mistrust and a sign of an American power play. Zabriskie's downward communications took a major toll on the company's various divisions and was one factor that led to his eventual resignation.[31]

A QUESTION OF ETHICS

Not Allowed to Tell | You are the manager of a large department in an organization that is restructuring. Your boss gives you a list of employees who will be laid off in the next month and specifically tells you not to share the information with them until the layoff time arrives. You know many of your employees will be hard hit and you would like to warn them. Should you communicate the confidential information to them? Is it ethical for you to do so? What are the consequences of your decision?

Lateral Communication Lateral communication is key to the integration of activities in organizations, yet many organizations do not formally recognize it and often dismiss it as "informal" and "simple gossip."[32] As a result, organizations do not provide mechanisms to foster it. The lack of lateral communication encourages managers to focus on their own goals and departments, sometimes at the expense of an organization's overall strategic goals. For example, the sales and manufacturing departments should work closely to ensure that clients get their products on time. Without effective lateral communication between these two departments, such integration is not possible.

British Petroleum's country managers are encouraging lateral communication among divisions located in multiple countries. Michel de Fabiani, manager of BP Oil France, stresses that open communication among divisions is essential for success. "It's when people don't understand or know the importance of an issue that you get gossip and leaks," Fabiani laments.[33] Fabiani has linked the marketing and production departments in his European territory to improve their daily communication. The departments are part of a network that allows scattered offices to communicate quickly and efficiently.

Organizations can improve all three levels of communication by encouraging two-way communication and increasing the number of formal and informal communication channels. To improve communication at all three levels, many organizations restructure so that they are more communication intensive.[34] One goal of boundaryless and team-based organizations is to increase the amount of accurate, timely, effective communication among different organizational levels. The by-products of increased communication include preventing executive isolation and employee alienation and improving motivation and the quality and speed of decision making. However, increased information also can be overwhelming and can cause frustration.

After the communication problems at Pharmacia & Upjohn became evident, the organization made structural changes to improve communication at all levels. Jan Ekberg, the interim CEO, has moved to an open communication style, a team-based structure, and a reliance on consensus.[35]

In addition to managing communications inside the organization, managers must also exchange information with external constituents. Next we consider external communication.

Summary Point 12.4   **What Are the Three Directions of Communication?**

- People in organizations communicate upward with their bosses and those who are above them in the hierarchy.
- They communicate downward with those who report to them.

- They communicate laterally with their co-workers.
- All three levels of communication can be improved by encouraging two-way communication and by increasing the formal and informal channels for communication.

External Organizational Communication

Organizations communicate with those outside the company to gather information and to project an accurate, desirable image. As open systems, organizations are in constant interaction with their external environment. Through communication, they create intelligence systems and build their image; they seek and send information. The active management of external communication falls in the domain of *public relations*. With the extensive use of information technology and the increased involvement of the media, people must actively manage their organization's communication with the outside. Figure 12.5 presents the different ways in which an organization communicates with the environment.

An organization uses four principal ways to create its public image:

- *Public relations (PR)*, which generally refers to the communication between an organization and its constituents. PR activities help create and maintain an

Change Challenge

360-DEGREE FEEDBACK

Over the last several decades organizations have changed their approach to employee career development. They have shifted from a guaranteed lifetime employment approach to one of helping employees stay current so they can find the next job when needed. As a result, organizations use new tools to increase employees' awareness of their strengths and weaknesses. Traditional performance reviews are downward communications, with an occasional opportunity for upward feedback.

A new method called "360-degree feedback" looks at information from all directions and all levels.[a] Bosses, co-workers, employees, customers, and other important constituents evaluate managers. Ultimately, the communication that managers receive comes from all directions. In the process, many hear information about themselves that is painful and difficult to accept. However, when implemented well, 360-degree feedback can provide managers with a much broader, accurate sense of their strengths and weaknesses. Organizations such as PepsiCo, Morgan Stanley, and PhotoDisc of Seattle actively use this method to improve managerial effectiveness.[b] At Levi Strauss, managers receive 360-degree feedback twice a year. The feedback results are tied to their annual pay increases.[c]

a. R. Lepsinger and A. D. Lucia, *The Art and Science of 360-Degree Feedback* (San Francisco: Pfeiffer, 1997).

b. M. Marcetti, "Pepsi's New Generation of Employee Feedback," *Sales and Marketing Management* 128, no. 8 (1996): 38–40; S. Gruner, "Feedback from Everyone," *Inc.* 19, no. 2 (1997): 102–104.

c. S. Sherman, "Levi's," *Fortune* 135, no. 9 (1997): 104–18.

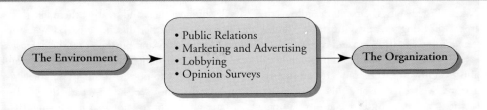

FIGURE 12.5
*Methods of Communica-
tion with the Environment*

Based on G. L. Kreps,
Organizational Communication (New
York: Longman, 1986): 242–58.

identity, ensure organizational survival by predicting what the environment will be, and increase organizational effectiveness.[36]

- *Marketing and advertising* are activities that are closely related to public relations. However, they focus on specific products or services rather than on overall organizational image.
- *Lobbying* helps establish relationships and influence powerful external constituents. Information about the organization is used in the development of such relationships.
- *Surveys* to learn about public opinion and the marketing of products and services are major sources of information about the external environment. Such information is essential in strategic planning.

Summary Point 12.5   **What Is External Organizational Communication?**

- Public relations, marketing and advertising, lobbying, and surveys create an organization's public image.

- PR activities help organizations present their mission to the public and thus communicate with the external environment.

External Strategic Communication

Before the advent of broadcast media, the Internet, and other media that easily connect large groups of people, organizations were better able to control and manage their communication with the external environment. Those days are gone forever. As a result, managers must learn to communicate and handle information strategically to support the organization's mission and goals.

Communicating the basic mission and strategy of the organization is the first step in managing external communication. Every mission and strategy should carry a communication component that serves the following functions:[37]

- Anticipates public debate about the organizational mission
- Clarifies issues that will require management attention
- Clarifies the communication objectives and the activities that support them
- Provides a communication plan

The overall goal of strategic communication is to tie information obtained from the environment to an organization's mission and goals, and to communicate information about the organization back to the environment in an accurate and positive manner.

Consider the case of Nike in Asia and how it mismanaged information. Nike was reluctant to run a PR campaign in Asia to answer questions about its treatment of workers. Nike subcontracts the manufacturing of its shoes to companies in Vietnam and Indonesia. For some time, local newspapers in Asia have been making allegations of worker abuse and low wages in Nike facilities. Cara Pincombe, an Australian visiting Vietnam, was surprised to hear tour operators describe Nike's alleged abuses. One guide "told us they were bashing workers and treating them like slaves. It was shocking," recalls Pincombe.[38] These allegations were further disseminated via Web sites. The result was talk shows and cartoonists ridiculing the company and putting it on the defensive.

Nike claims that it immediately corrected the few instances where there were some abuses. However, the company admits that it did not tell the public about these corrective actions. Martha Benson, Nike's spokesperson in Asia, does not see the benefits of producing "a slick corporate public-relations campaign. We are about sports, not manufacturing 101." Greg Rushford, a PR expert, claims that Nike is the victim of "lousy PR" and miscommunication. "Nike's putting a small Band-Aid on a large wound," states Aviva Diamond, president of PR firm Blue Streak.[39] Nike has not managed its strategic communication. That is, Nike was unprepared to respond to the charges and had no plans to counteract the negative claims with a response based on facts and figures.

How Can Managers Communicate Strategically?

A manager is leaving his office around 6:00 P.M. one evening and as he walks to his car, a reporter and film crew from the local TV station approach. The reporter asks if she can get the manager's reaction to a breaking story about the multimillion-dollar sexual harassment lawsuit just filed against his company. What should the manager do? How should he react? That depends in part on company media policies (many firms insist that all media contacts be handled by a communication specialist) and on whether the organization trains managers in handling media encounters.

If the organization allows managers to have media contact, those managers should keep two points in mind. First, think about the public relations consequences for the entire organization. Second, prepare to understand the medium, the audience, the message, and the risks. Advice from specialists, training for managers, and skills development for managers can help in the preparation process.

The Public Relations Perspective   Whereas large organizations often have public relations departments or outside specialists who plan and execute external communication, managers are often responsible for such activities in smaller companies. One way to learn about public relations consequences is to perform journalistic functions in your organization. These functions include understanding the news value of events and preparing statements based on organizational mission, objective, and accurate information.[40] Another method is to establish positive long-term relationships with members of the media. These relationships give managers the opportunity to learn about public relations and to persuade media members how and when to publicize their organizations.

Finally, individual managers can now acquire technical skills that were once the domain of public relations professionals and graphic designers. Desktop publishing and the proliferation of production businesses such as Kinko's and AlphaGraphics mean that managers can produce their own newsletters, press releases, brochures, and flyers to manage the image of their department or organization more easily.

Meeting the Press   Large corporations often train their executives or designate an official spokesperson to handle media contacts. For instance, after many public relations blunders, Nike hired consultants who understood the local Vietnamese and Indonesian culture to prepare a PR campaign. Nike's goal was to respond to future problems immediately by staying in touch with local journalists "who understand the context," and won't "apply Western standards to local wages," declares Benson.[41] These journalists are not likely to criticize Nike's subcontractors and may instead mention that Nike is keeping thousands of workers employed in Asia.

Managers of smaller firms may not have access to such specialists or training, yet they still need to develop the skills to communicate with the press in a professional and effective

Table 12.2   MEETING THE PRESS

Guideline	Description and Examples
State your most important position first.	Make a clear statement of your most important issue first without referring to secondary issues. *"My company will not be taking any action on this issue. Let me explain the reasons. . . ."*
Take the public's perspective.	View the problem from the public's and the reporter's points of view and address issues and answer questions with those views in mind. *"Our company would like to give our union the raise they have requested. However, the increase will have to be passed on to customers and we do not think that is in their best interest."*
Use "I" rather than "we" whenever possible.	Speak in personal terms to humanize the company. *"I have never personally faced any problems in the 10 years I have worked for this company."*
There is no "off the record."	Do not say anything that you do not want quoted, as off-the-record statements can be used without attributing them directly to a specific person.
Do not repeat a question if it contains questionable language you do not approve.	Do not use the reporter's offensive words or expressions in answering the question. The question is not quoted; the answer is. *In response to a question that asks why the company is polluting the environment and killing an endangered bird species, "My company has an impeccable record of environmental safety," is a better choice than "We are not polluters and bird killers."*
Tell the truth, be direct, and do not exaggerate.	Stick to facts that you can support, answer questions directly, and watch for your own accuracy.
Keep your cool and avoid an argument.	Keep the tone professional; realize that the reporter is doing his or her job and is looking for an angle. *"My company has spent three million dollars in Alaska alone last year to ensure that our manufacturing process does not pollute the water supply."*

Source: Based on C. Burger, "How to Meet the Press," in *The Articulate Executive: Orchestrating Effective Communication* (Boston: Harvard Business Review, 1993): 69–81.

manner.[42] Table 12.2 summarizes the general guidelines for communicating with the media strategically. Thorough preparation about the organizational mission, the strategic communication plan (if one exists), the questions to anticipate, and so forth are first steps. Next, as basic as this may seem, managers need to adjust their communication to the type of media involved. A radio interview will not capture nodding of the head, a skeptical look, or body posture. Words and vocal tone become crucial. Finally, managers should learn to respect media members' expertise and goals in asking questions.

To communicate effectively within organizations and with external constituents, managers must develop several communication tools. We review these tools next.

Summary Point 12.6   **What Is Strategic Communication?**

- Communicating the basic mission and strategy of the organization is the first step in the management of external communication.
- Every mission and strategy should carry a communications component.
- The communications component should anticipate public debate about the organizational mission, clarify issues that will require management's attention, clarify communication objectives and the activities that support them, and provide a communication plan.
- To handle media contacts effectively, managers should consider the public relations perspective and prepare to meet with media members through consultation with specialists, training, or skills development.

TOOLS OF EFFECTIVE COMMUNICATION

The communication process involves a number of complex factors. Not only does the sender have to send the message accurately, but she must remove barriers, monitor nonverbal messages, control distractions, and ensure her credibility. All these elements make communicating even a simple message highly challenging. On the positive side, the ability to communicate well is not a stable and unchanging personality trait. Because it is a skill, managers can learn to communicate more effectively. We analyze the four factors in effective communication. These include the removal of barriers to communication, active listening, giving effective feedback, and building credibility.

Barriers to Effective Communication

The first element in effective communication is for managers to remove as many barriers or noise as possible. Some barriers relate to our biased perceptual process and need to be addressed on an individual and personal level. Other barriers are organizational and require a broader systems approach.

Individual Barriers: Perceptual Biases   In chapter 5, we discussed the perceptual process and the various biases that affect how we gather, organize, and interpret information about others. These biases allow us to be efficient by making quick decisions. However, they also lead us to stop gathering information. If we have already made up our minds, we stop paying attention. In

---

CAREER ADVICE
from the Experts

LEARNING NEW SKILLS

Demonstrating the ability to learn new skills and improving on existing ones can mean the difference between landing or not landing a job or promotion.

- Become aware of your strengths and weaknesses and seek opportunities to observe and reflect on your own behaviors.
- Try to be motivated to change your current skills level. Wanting to change or learn is key.
- Learn about alternative behaviors. What are some new behaviors you can adopt to replace less effective ones?
- Set goals that are specific, measurable, achievable, reasonable, and have a time frame. Starting small can help you stay motivated.
- Create opportunities to test and practice new skills by enlisting help from friends, family members, trusted colleagues, and managers.
- Reward, correct, and start over.

Sources: D. A. Kolb, I. M. Rubin, and J. M. McIntyre, *Organizational Psychology: Readings on Human Behavior in Organizations,* 4th ed. (Englewood Cliffs, NJ: Prentice Hall, 1984); S. Robbins, *Training in Interpersonal Skills* (Upper Saddle River, NJ: Prentice Hall, 1996).

communication, the lack of attention and the tendency to make quick judgments based on biases prevent full understanding of the message.

Suppose for a moment that a manager has a strong negative prejudice against an ethnic group based on her belief that its members are lazy and unmotivated. The manager will pay scant attention to an employee's explanation as to why he didn't meet his goals if he is a member of that ethnic group. She will not listen to his suggestions for improving work processes and will lose the opportunity to improve quality in her department. Her stereotyping prevents effective communication. Similarly, other perceptual biases—such as halo and primacy-recency effects, the fundamental attribution error, or the self-serving bias—all provide noise that garbles, changes, or in other ways affects the message and impedes effective communication.

Our need for consistency and the power of the self-fulfilling prophecy further affect the communication process. The sender changes his or her message based on biases, thereby limiting the way the listener can react and provide feedback. The listener, faced with a certain message, provides a response that confirms the sender's expectations. These individual barriers to communication can be managed by awareness, seeking objective data and confirmation whenever possible, and practicing the active listening skills that we describe later in this section.

Organizational Barriers   The structure and culture of an organization can act as barriers to effective communication. In particular, a rigid hierarchical structure that limits and dictates how information is shared can prevent the flow of information and the delivery of an honest, accurate message. Think back to the Pharmacia & Upjohn merger example. Recall that the imposition of a structure that prevented local managers from communicating effectively with their overseas counterparts led to communication problems. An executive vice president in London, Goran Ando, acknowledged that a structure that forced everyone to communicate through headquarters garbled the communication process.[43]

In addition to the new structure being a barrier, the cultural differences at Pharmacia created severe communication barriers. In the Italian operation of Pharmacia, Swedish managers claimed that they often had to leave the room "just so . . . the Italians would speak out honestly." The Italians' respect for authority prevented them from speaking candidly in front of their managers. When the Americans entered the scene after the merger, the addition of a third culture made the communication problems worse. The new CEO is breaking down communication barriers by changing the organization's rigid structure to one that is decentralized.[44] The new structure allows for a free flow of information and encourages the communication needed to support consensus-based decision making.

Formal lines of reporting and a clear hierarchy can help information flow in an orderly way. However, in certain circumstances formal systems also can prevent effective communication because they slow down the communication process, cause frustration, or lead to self-censorship and negative political activities.

Another powerful organizational barrier to effective communication is strong *status differences*. As the power differences between the higher and lower levels of organizations increase, the flow and amount of information decrease. Information is distorted or not shared accurately through a variety of mechanisms and sometimes because of corruption. Even in flat organizations, access to the CEO and other top executives is typically restricted for those at lower levels.

One goal of team-based and boundaryless organizations is to reduce status differences and to allow vital information from the bottom of the organization—which often includes information about customers—to flow freely and accurately to all other levels.

A final organizational barrier to effective communication is time. Effective communication requires time and attention. As managers rush to meet their next deadline or tackle an emerging crisis, they fail to follow the basic rules of effective communication. They send garbled, unclear messages, do not pay attention to perceptual biases, do not follow through, and

Hot ▼ Link

We discussed perceptual biases in chapter 5, pp. 161–65.

Hot ▼ Link

See chapter 11 for a discussion of power corruption, pp. 393–96.

so forth. Building enough time to ensure that managers deliver messages well and accurately is an important challenge both internally and externally.

The communications problems surrounding the start-up of the EuroDisney theme park in Paris were due in part to cultural issues and time pressure.[45] Disney failed to provide an effective PR campaign that would tell the public about the park's mission. For months before the park opened, the French press demonized it as an invasion of the American culture. Disney managers, busy with the construction, failed to communicate effectively to the public that 51 percent of EuroDisney was owned by the French government. In effect, the French public was the largest shareholder of the business.

Summary Point 12.7   **What Are Barriers to Effective Communication?**

- Individual barriers include perceptual biases that act as noise to prevent effective communication.
- Awareness and use of objective data can help remove individual barriers.

- Organizational barriers include organizational culture and structure, status differences, and time.

Active Listening

Active listening
Process whereby the listener assumes a conscious and dynamic role in the communication process through a variety of behaviors and actions

In addition to minimizing individual and organizational barriers to effective communication, managers need to focus on active listening. In **active listening**, the listener assumes a conscious and dynamic role in the communication process through a variety of behaviors and actions. The active listener focuses intently on both the sender and the message.[46] He shows empathy and understanding for the other person and accepts responsibility for ensuring effective communication.[47] The elements of active listening are these:

- Be silent.
- Avoid distractions and focus on the message.
- Avoid formulating an answer while the other person is talking, and do not evaluate the message until it is complete.
- Use appropriate nonverbal signals such as eye contact, head nods, and facial expressions.
- Ask questions and paraphrase the message to ensure understanding.

The active listener hears the whole message without interpretation and judgment. She is effective by listening not only to the spoken message but also to the nonverbal cues that the sender uses to communicate emotions and feelings.

One factor that managers need to consider is the effect of culture on how others listen. As we learned in our discussion of nonverbal behavior, for many Westerners and particularly for North Americans, sustained eye contact is a sign of listening. Native Americans and many Asians are uncomfortable with such direct contact. A Western manager can easily misinterpret his Asian employee's unwillingness to look at him as a sign of inattention rather than as a sign of respect. Similarly, whereas active listening requires asking questions and paraphrasing, such behaviors may be difficult in cultures with high power distance.

BP manager John Mumford, who instituted newsletters and bag lunches to improve communication with Thai workers, faced a communication problem, partially because of cultural differences. The Thai culture is high in power distance. Informal, direct interaction and communication among people with different levels of power does not come easily to the workers. To resolve the problem, Mumford asked everyone who had a birthday that month to show up for lunch. He mentions that this was "the only way to get the fork-lift drivers and accountants in the same room."[48]

Effective Feedback

Communicating with people about their behavior or job performance is a challenging task. **Feedback** is information about some behavior and its effect. Managers not only provide their employees with feedback regarding their performance, but they also give feedback to clients and customers about numerous matters.

    For many, giving positive feedback is easy. We enjoy telling others they are doing well and that we appreciate their work and effort. When we receive positive feedback, it is easy to be an active listener. Giving negative feedback that points out errors, mistakes, and areas of weakness is more difficult. When we hear negative information about ourselves, we often become defensive, try to formulate an answer, and find excuses—all while the other person is still talking to us. In short, we stop actively listening to the message. However, accurate positive *and* negative feedback are pivotal to motivation and learning.[49]

    People cannot change their behavior if they are not aware of its effects and consequences. The person providing feedback can take several steps to ensure effective communication:[50]

- The sender should focus on specific behaviors that are clearly documented instead of on vague statements about personality or attitudes.
- The feedback should be job related and professional rather than personal.
- The feedback should address behaviors that are under the person's control rather than on factors the person cannot change or control.
- The feedback should occur as closely in time to the offending behavior as possible.
- The sender must ensure that the receiver understands the feedback fully.

    As with active listening, what is considered appropriate feedback is culture specific. Whereas organizations encourage U.S. managers to give direct, timely feedback to their employees, the same advice is likely to get the Middle Eastern or Asian manager in trouble. In such community-oriented cultures, where saving face is important, feedback is acceptable only when given in the most subtle and roundabout ways.

    Additionally, people from high-context cultures are likely to read between the lines and pick up subtle messages in communication to a much higher degree than people from low-context cultures, thereby reducing the need for direct feedback. For example, a manager should clearly and specifically inform an employee from a low-context culture such as Germany about what mistakes she made and how to correct them. The same manager must be much more soft-spoken and maybe even deliver the negative feedback through a third person when working with an employee from a high-context culture such as Thailand.

Supportive Communication

A general element in effective communication is supportive communication. **Supportive communication** is honest and accurate interpersonal communication that focuses on building and enhancing relationships. Table 12.3 outlines the attributes of supportive communication. Active listening and effective feedback both contribute to it, so the guidelines we offer for supportive communication may not apply in all cultures. In supportive communication, the receiver is able to hear the message and understand it while the sender receives accurate feedback, allowing for clear two-way communication.

    Supportive communication tries to create an environment in which people can communicate, discuss, and disagree over issues without resorting to personal attacks or hidden agendas. Sharing thoughts and feelings honestly while recognizing that the other person has a

Feedback
Information about performance or some behavior and its effect

Hot ▼ Link
We discussed high- and low-context cultures in chapter 3, pp. 76–77.

Supportive communication
Honest and accurate interpersonal communication that focuses on building and enhancing relationships

T a b l e   1 2 . 3   ATTRIBUTES OF SUPPORTIVE COMMUNICATION

Attribute	Examples
Oriented to the problem, not the person	"Let's figure out what the problem is and solve it," rather than, "You have caused the problem."
Descriptive, not evaluative	"This is what happened and how I reacted to it," rather than, "Your actions were wrong and intended to hurt others."
Specific, not general	"You came late to the last three team meetings," rather than, "You are always late."
Two-way, not one-way	"This is how I see the issue. What is your point of view?" rather than, "I have looked at the problem and come up with the solution."
Open and integrative, not final	"My points are related to yours and build on them," rather than, "This is my position."
Reflecting feelings accurately, not hiding them	"This really upset me and I would like to know why it happened," rather than, "There is nothing wrong, don't worry."
Validating, not demeaning the other's viewpoint	"We seem to disagree but I do see where you are coming from," rather than, "You make no sense; this is too complicated for you to understand."

legitimate and worthwhile point of view are at the core of supportive communication.[51] For example, when using supportive communication, a manager describes the facts related to an employee's performance as objectively as possible, avoiding accusations, and focusing on the employee's behavior. The description also includes an explanation of the manager's own reaction to the employee. Finally, the manager suggests several alternatives for improvement while being prepared and willing to discuss the employee's suggestions.

Another aspect of supportive communication is to validate the other person's views and feelings, confirming that they are worthy and competent.[52] To achieve this goal, one must avoid statements that convey superiority over the other person. To illustrate, the use of jargon, putdowns, or language that the other person does not understand are all likely to make the other person feel inferior. Additionally, being rigid, appearing to have all the answers, and showing indifference toward the other person's point of view further invalidate the other person's views and feelings.

Reducing noise and communicating with others effectively require that all the communicating individuals accept the responsibility of reducing barriers by being aware of their perceptual biases, actively listening, giving feedback, and generally communicating in a supportive manner. Additionally, organizations should provide the organizational culture, climate,

---

Summary Point 12.8   **What Are the Elements of Active Listening, Effective Feedback, and Supportive Communication?**

- In active listening, the listener plays a conscious and dynamic role in the communication process through a variety of behaviors and actions.
- Feedback is information about some behavior and its consequences. Effective feedback is fact based, timely, and focused on behaviors.

- Both active listening and feedback vary from one culture to another.
- Supportive communication is honest and accurate interpersonal communication that aims at building and enhancing relationships.

structure, and resources to help individuals communicate. The use of technology in communication is one such organizational factor.

 TECHNOLOGY AND COMMUNICATION

Technology and various telecommunication tools have changed our access to information and the way we communicate. In some cases, the use of technology supports and enhances existing communication patterns. In others, technology changes the communication process so much that it creates new challenges. In this section we consider the effect of electronic mail, the Internet, and group support systems on communication in organizations.

Electronic Mail

In the United States, consumer use of electronic mail, or **e-mail**—messages and communication distributed via telecommunication software—has jumped from 5 million people in 1992 to 55 million in 1997. Some projections set the number of users at around 115 million by the year 2000.[53] In addition to consumer use, a large number of internal company e-mail systems connect people in all parts and at all levels of organizations. Looked at simply, e-mail makes communication faster and easier. On a more complex level, the presence of e-mail in organizations changes issues of access to information thereby affecting organizational structure, decision making, and power.

E-mail
Messages and communication via computers and various communication software

Fifteen years ago, if an employee wanted to discuss a problem or present an innovative idea to the CEO, she had to convince secretaries, administrative assistants, and maybe her own manager that she needed to see the president. Her chance of meeting the CEO to discuss the idea personally was slim. If her idea ever made its way up the hierarchy, it was distorted, sanitized, changed, and perhaps even attributed to someone else. Today, the same employee can simply send an e-mail with an attached proposal to the CEO who receives her message with minimal distortion. The added benefit or danger is a clear paper trail to give her credit or blame.

Because e-mail does not follow the formal hierarchical structure of an organization, it can change that structure. Quick and easy access to this communication medium has the potential to change coordination and integration of activities, reporting relationships, and communication with suppliers and customers. E-mail and other group support systems are tools that have contributed to the flattening of organizations.

Along with easy access and efficiency in communication, e-mail creates challenges for organizations. A written mistake, insult, or sign of anger sent to a large number of people in the department can seriously damage a career. Learning to manage e-mail and teaching managers and employees e-mail etiquette are essential. Knowing how to protect confidentiality while using e-mail is also a skill that managers must master.

Consider the case of UOP against Andersen Consulting. UOP, a petroleum-processing technology firm, hired Andersen Consulting to design a new computer system for its operations. Five years later, UOP fired the consulting firm and filed a $100 million lawsuit for breach of contract and fraud. UOP provided reams of e-mail messages showing Andersen consultants knew that the system would not work and the time frame was not achievable. Most important, the e-mail trail provided evidence that Andersen consultants were calling each other incompetent and evaluating their own work as sub-par. One consultant, David Craigmile, wrote about a colleague working on the UOP project: "He should be taking classes at a community college, not charging for this." Copies of all these e-mails were found in UOP's mainframe system. Robert Price, a managing partner at Andersen Consulting in Chicago, states, "We believe this is an isolated case. We have never experienced anything like this, and we fully expect to win this case in court."[54] As this incident shows, managers who are ill-prepared to deal with communication technology can harm organizational effectiveness.

The Internet and Other Communication Options

The Internet (also known as the World Wide Web or the Web) has become a valuable tool for organizations to use in communicating with their environment. Companies create Web pages that users around the world can access quickly and easily. Through Web pages, customers can order products on-line, complain about a company's services, ask questions, research the company's mission and strategy, and seek clarification about future products. Five to ten years ago, only a handful of organizations had Web sites. Now a majority either has or is developing one.

One key reason for this proliferation is the ease with which a company can provide information to current or potential stakeholders. Furthermore, the Internet allows users to access information almost immediately. Questions that once required hours of research may now be answered quickly if the user has the right search tools and accesses reliable sources. However, as with any new technology, the Internet has its disadvantages.[55] One significant problem is the quality of information that it offers.

Evaluating the Quality of Information   So much information travels through the Internet that users often have difficulty evaluating the quality of the information passed from source to source. Frequently, publicity statements and rumors about organizations are reported as fact. Because of the speed of the Internet, a rumor can be spread around the world even before the company is aware of it or contacted for verification. In that small window of time, thousands of people may accept the questionable information as fact. Take Nike's situation. Five Web sites seemed to be the source of the rumors about Nike's labor problems. These sites "serve as a clearinghouse" for the attacks on Nike, explains Vada O. Manager, the company's senior PR manager.[56] Although there was some truth to the stories, ample evidence suggests that issues were exaggerated.

Why are people allowed to spread inaccurate information? No journalistic standards govern what does and does not get distributed over the Web. In contrast to a Web story, a typical journalist must check and verify facts before publishing the accounts as news. Because of the speed and volume of Internet information, organizations should train managers to think critically about the source and quality of the information so they can separate fact from fiction.

The Effect of Expanding Communication Options   The Internet is a technological tool, similar to a cellular or satellite telephone, that gives people another option for communicating. Managers and employees can access the Internet through their personal computers and be in touch with their offices, headquarters, or any other location. The technology allows workers flexibility to work at home or to send files, messages, and drafts of reports to their offices while on the road.

A product from Centrepoint Technology, called Concero Switchboard, not only allows users to hook up to the Internet from home, but it can also manage their regular phone calls, faxes, cell phones, speakers, and modems. All can be connected to the PC, offering the user an array of 47,000 combinations of features and options.[57]

The quick access to information and increase in connectedness poses challenges and opportunities for organizations. Because consumers can buy directly from the seller, many sales divisions (such as Avon's) face the challenge of retaining customers or redefining their mission and strategy. For example, auto companies plan to allow consumers to custom-order cars directly from the manufacturer via the Internet. If the plan succeeds, the car dealership industry will have to concentrate more on after-sales service than on sales. As an example of opportunity, however, the Internet has helped put corporations of different sizes and from different regions on a more equal footing. Any business large or small can advertise a service on the Web and sell its products globally.

A small Indonesian telephone company, Pasifik Satelit Nusantara, has started to install satellite phones in the remotest parts of Indonesia, such as in the west Java village of Cidaun.

Small companies such as Indonesia's Nusantara are able to compete with giants such as Motorola by relying on state-of-the-art technology that allows them to connect remote parts of the world with business hubs.

Nusantara is competing with Motorola's Iridium satellite system, soon to operate around the globe. John Windolf, Iridium's head of advertising, acknowledges the company's strategy of being present everywhere: "The business traveler will be Iridium's prime mover, but the developing world is a substantial market as well."[58] Technology is allowing Nusantara to compete with the much larger Motorola.

The Internet is opening many doors through which organizations can communicate with their environment. It also allows employees to communicate with their organizations more easily when they are away from the office.

Group Support Systems

We discussed the role of various group support systems (GSS) in chapter 10. GSS allow many different people to speak, listen, and share data and information at the same time. They include various types of communication hardware and software that can be used to connect team members. When GSS are available, groups are likely to use them and, at the very least, have better access to information.[59] GSS can make group processes more efficient and increase group performance, particularly in large groups.[60] Information flows faster and is shared more broadly. For example, groups can perform brainstorming to generate new ideas or use the nominal group technique (NGT) not only faster but also with anonymity, thereby preventing self- or other types of censorship.[61]

Research indicates that GSS generally improve communication, especially in large groups; however, excessive reliance on technology at the expense of face-to-face communication

Summary Point 12.9   **What Effect Does Technology Have on Communication?**

- E-mail and other technologies make communication faster and easier and affect structure, decision making, and power in organizations.
- The main purpose of the Internet is to provide an easy and efficient method by which companies can commu-

nicate with anyone, anywhere. Evaluating the quality of the information is a key challenge for Internet users.
- GSS allow many different people to speak, listen, and share data and information at the same time; they can make group processes more efficient if managed well.

can depersonalize the group's communication process. Individual members may feel as though they are merely one data point in the GSS network. Additionally, the rich nonverbal cues available in face-to-face communication are lost when communication is by computer. Overall, a well-managed GSS combined with extensive opportunities for face-to-face interaction can greatly improve the communication process and contribute to more effective decision making.

 ## ETHICS IN COMMUNICATION

Managers who communicate with others within or outside the organization typically face ethical issues. The manager who is asked to keep vital information confidential or not to share data with customers or suppliers because of trade secrets may face an ethical issue if she considers leaking the information. On a grander scale, employees and managers who have knowledge of their company's violations of ethics or social responsibility must either live with their conscience or communicate the information externally and put their careers in jeopardy. Table 12.4 presents three categories of unethical communication.

There are three standards or rules of ethical communication within and outside an organization:[62]

- *Honesty.* Truthful communication should entail not only reporting facts and figures accurately and precisely but also providing people with information regarding expectations, decisions, processes, and judgments that affect their work and careers. Additionally, honesty should be modeled and clearly expected as a basic standard of upward and lateral communication.
- *Refraining from doing harm.* Organizations that do not communicate information about the potential dangers of their products are violating this rule.
- *Fairness and justice to internal and external stakeholders.* The organization's communication must attempt to be fair to its constituents.

Note that these ethical standards of communication also determine the appropriateness of political activities in organizations. Let's see how they apply to an actual company. Global Marketing Group (GMG) provided dishonest information to customers. Founded by Eric Christian Ralls, a student in Arizona, the company advertised on the Internet that for a small fee it would send customers a low-cost credit card. GMG advertising assured that cards were issued by offshore banks and that no credit checks were needed. The company charged $25 per month for the card. Any customer who recruited a friend to apply got a finder's fee in addition to a portion of the fees the friend paid. If that friend recruited others, the original customer would receive a portion of their monthly fees as well. The system

Table 12.4   CATEGORIES OF UNETHICAL COMMUNICATION

Unethical Communication	Description and Examples
Managers knowingly provide inaccurate information to employees.	Unclear performance expectations; false restructuring and layoff information; recruiting with false information
Dishonest information about the organization is given to outsiders.	Hiding information about harmful products or illegal activities; deceptive advertising; overpricing; altering records
Managers use inappropriate influence and control.	Price fixing; bribery; industrial espionage; insider trading and stock manipulation

was similar to illegal pyramid schemes, with later customers losing their investment if the company failed.

Ralls's resume, posted on the Internet, stated that he had a master's degree from the Thunderbird School of International Management, thus proving his level of expertise in international investment. Thunderbird officials say that he never received his degree. After being questioned by reporters, Ralls moved to Grand Cayman Island.[63] Apparently, no applicant has received a card and GMG refuses to disclose which offshore banks it has partnered with to issue them. Ralls admits that there are inaccuracies on the company's Web site but blames the companies that created the Web site for the mistakes. The whole company seems to have been built on a fraudulent scheme. GMG's communication was inaccurate, it did harm, and it was unfair to its customers, thereby violating all three rules of ethical communication.

Summary Point 12.10   **What Are the Ethics in Communication?**

- Interpersonal, internal, or external organizational communication may all give rise to ethical situations.

- Being honest, refraining from doing harm, and being fair are the standards for ethical behavior in communication.

Communication *in Context*

We have already discussed the importance and impact of communication on contextual factors in several sections in this chapter. Here, we more closely examine the link between communication and structure, organizational culture, and technology.

First, the structure of the organization can be both an advantage and an impediment to communication processes inside organizations. On the one hand, a formal structure can clarify communication patterns, thereby easing the flow of information. On the other hand, the same formal structure can impede the flexibility that encourages individuals and departments to interact and communicate freely. Additionally, organizational structure can increase or decrease status, hierarchy, and distance between people, thereby affecting the communication flow and pattern. Managers must pay attention to the structure to assure that it supports the communication needs of the organization's mission, goals, and strategy.

Organizational culture also determines how managers communicate within and outside the organization. Managers need to use a contingency approach to decide which organizational culture best meets the communication needs of the business. Some organization cultures encourage open communication to make them more responsive to the environment. In other organizations, managers control information distribution as they see fit, such as those in a firm that deals with highly sensitive information. Similarly, organizational culture affects how the organization communicates with its outside constituents. Some organizations form cooperative partnerships with their suppliers and customers and share information openly. Others treat outsiders cautiously and communicate only minimally with them.

Finally, today's ever-changing technology is a central factor in the way we share meaning and exchange information. The advent of information technology tools has not only affected the speed and accessibility of information but has also changed how we interact and communicate with others. People must manage and use technology to assure that it supports organizational and individual performance.

Consider the links between communication, structure, organizational culture, and technology at Connor Formed Metal Products. Connor is a small California-based company that makes metal stamps, springs, and wire forms. The business had a crucial communication problem: Managers could not accurately estimate the time it took to get orders ready for delivery, so they couldn't communicate a specific delivery date to customers. Inaccurate estimates caused dissatisfied customers and stress in the organization.[64] The company president, Robert Sloss, asked his 200 employees to find a solution. The employees tweaked the existing systems several times and discovered that each solution led to several new problems.

What ensued was a complete overhaul of a number of organizational functions to allow managers, employees, and customers to communicate directly and efficiently. Cross-functional teams of employees from sales, marketing, production, engineering, and design meet regularly to discuss every order. Employees and managers together designed a shop floor information system that allows employees access to rapid, on-line, detailed information on demand. Much of the currently available information was previously available only to managers. Perhaps more important, each employee can now enter upgrades in the system and modify the manufacturing process. They often put a "shop hold" on the system, meaning that the production process stops until a manager meets with the employee to listen to concerns and suggestions, address the problem, and then remove the hold allowing the production to resume.

Other innovations include inviting Connor customers to visit the plant and meet and directly work with the actual team that will manufacture their product. For their part, Connor employees travel to customers' organizations regularly to find out how they use their products and identify problems they may have. The more open culture, the flatter structure, and the information system promote productive communication between managers and employees and between Connor and its customers. The payoff is improved customer service, higher job satisfaction, and stronger productivity.

Robert Sloss believes that knowledge is a crucial factor in today's organizations. It therefore must be shared quickly with employees to allow the company to respond to its rapidly changing environment.

 For updated information on the topics in this chapter, Web exercises, links to related Web sites, an on-line study guide, and more, visit our companion Web site at:
http://www.prenhall.com/nahavandi

A L o o k B a c k a t t h e

MANAGERIAL CHALLENGE

Avon Products

Avon's beauty brands were definitely in need of a makeover when Andrea Jung joined the company in 1994. Noise from competitors' brand advertising was interfering with the firm's product messages. And with the rise in two-career families, the company was having difficulty recruiting more Avon Ladies to sell its products, even as fewer women were at home to answer the door. To support future sales growth, Jung had to help Avon get back in touch with a market whose needs and lifestyles were changing.

Actively listening to customers helped Jung and her managers develop a strategy to communicate Avon's leadership as a company that takes women seriously instead of treating them as sex objects. Through marketing, advertising, and public relations, she portrayed Avon as a maker of world-class beauty products for the wide-ranging needs of today's women. New products with new names plus a new advertising campaign all helped to reinforce the image of a more contemporary, more upscale Avon. The company also expanded internationally, boosting sales by building a network of Avon Ladies and boutiques in China, Russia, and other growing markets.[65]

Avon still had to move beyond its traditional door-to-door sales approach to open a dialogue with customers at home and at work using additional media. Supplementing the messages it was sending through advertising media and its Avon representatives, the company encouraged customer feedback through a toll-free telephone line, catalog sales, a World Wide Web presence, and new retail outlets. When Jung was promoted to president in 1998, she sought to boost Avon's credibility as a market-leading beauty brand by opening an image center—part store, part spa—in Manhattan's exclusive Trump Tower shopping atrium. "This is the image makeover, part two," she explained. "This is a statement. It will define Avon."[66] The next few years will continue to test the effectiveness of Avon's ongoing communication strategy.

■ Point of View Exercises

You're the Manager: As a manager working for Andrea Jung, you sometimes hear from Avon representatives who want to know the truth about rumors they have heard through the grapevine. What should you do about this informal network? What can you do to correct rumors that are false?

You're the Employee: As an Avon representative, you are an independent contractor who sells Avon products to customers. You want to find out whether the company is planning to boost its catalog and Internet sales efforts, which you fear will cut into your sales and commissions. What kind of upward communication might you use to get an informed response to your question? Why?

SUMMARY OF LEARNING OBJECTIVES

1. **Explain the elements and process of communication and the functions of nonverbal communication.** Communication, a continuous process, is the exchange of information and meaning between people. It occurs when one person understands and responds to a message sent by another. Communication is considered effective when the sender's message reaches the intended person with minimal distortions. We communicate considerable amounts of information through nonverbal communication without the use of words. We use facial expressions and eye contact (occulesics), body posture and gesture (kinesics), vocal cues and other signals that accompany verbal messages (paralinguistics), and space and the distance between people (proxemics). National culture has a great impact on how people use and interpret nonverbal communication.

2. **Describe the different types and directions of organizational communication and identify the importance of external communication.** Formal communication networks are those that are designated by the organizational structure. Informal communication networks are those that exist outside the official organizational networks. They develop to fill gaps in the formal communication networks. People in organizations communicate upward with those who are above them in the organization structure. They communicate downward with those who report to them, and they communicate laterally with their co-workers. The basic communication process, the use of verbal and nonverbal messages, and the impact of culture are present when people are communicating in all three directions.

   In addition to internal communication, successful organizations communicate with their environment to obtain information and to project an accurate and desirable image about their activities. Public relations, marketing and advertising, lobbying, and surveys about public opinion and the marketing of products and services are major sources of information about the external environment.

3. **Discuss the barriers to and tools of effective communication.** Managers communicate effectively by first removing as many of barriers or as much of the noise as possible. Some barriers occur because of perceptual biases, so they need to be resolved on an individual, personal level. Other barriers are organizational and require a broader systems approach. In active listening, the listener takes on a conscious and dynamic role in the communication process through a variety of behaviors and actions.

   Tools of effective communication include active listening, effective feedback, and supportive communication. The active listener is intently focused on the sender and the message. Feedback is information about some behavior and its effect. Supportive communication is honest and accurate interpersonal communication that is focused on building and enhancing relationships.

4. **Specify the role of technology in communication.** New technology requires us to rethink how we communicate. Although e-mail makes communication faster and easier, it also affects structure, decision making, and power. The Internet has become a valuable tool for organizations to use in communicating with their environment because it makes information available to users immediately. The major challenge for users is evaluating the quality of the information. Teams also rely on technology to communicate more effectively. Group Support Systems allow many different people to speak, listen, and share data and information at the same time. The use of GSS can make group processes more efficient and increase group performance, particularly in large groups.

5. **Highlight the importance of ethics in communication.** The three standards of ethical communication inside and outside an organization are honesty, refraining from doing harm, and fairness.

KEY TERMS

active listening, p. 436
communication, p. 418
communication networks,
    p. 426
decoding, p. 418
e-mail, p. 439
encoding, p. 418
feedback, p. 437
formal communication
    networks, p. 426

informal communication
    networks, p. 426
jargon, p. 420
kinesics, p. 422
media, p. 418
noise, p. 418
nonverbal communication,
    p. 421
occulesics, p. 421
paralinguistics, p. 422

personal space, p. 422
proxemics, p. 422
sender, p. 419
supportive communication,
    p. 437
tactilics, p. 424
territories, p. 423

REVIEW QUESTIONS

1. What are the major elements of communication?
2. What is strategic communication?
3. Describe the barriers to effective communication.
4. What are the new technologies that are affecting communication?
5. List and explain the three principles of ethical communication.

DISCUSSION QUESTIONS

1. Explain how managers can change the direction of communication in their organizations.
2. Discuss the importance of being media savvy.
3. How important is it for managers to be able to give effective feedback?
4. How can the Internet affect the patterns of internal and external communication in an organization?
5. Discuss the importance of ethics in communication.

▶ SELF-ASSESSMENT 12
Communicating Supportively

Please respond to the following questions by using the 1 through 6 rating scale that follows. Your answers should reflect your attitudes and behavior as they are now, not as you would like them to be. This instrument is designed to help you discover your level of competency in communicating supportively. See Appendix 3 for a scoring key.

1	2	3	4	5	6
Strongly disagree	Disagree	Slightly disagree	Slightly agree	Agree	Strongly agree

_____ 1. I reinforce other people's sense of self-worth and self-esteem in my communication with them.

_____ 2. I convey genuine interest in the other person's point of view, even when I disagree with it.

_____ 3. I don't talk down to those who have less power or less information than I do.

_____ 4. I convey a sense of flexibility and openness to new information, even when I feel strongly about it.

_____ 5. I strive to identify some area of agreement in a discussion with someone who has a different point of view.

_____ 6. My feedback is always specific and to the point rather than general or vague.

_____ 7. I don't dominate conversations with others.

_____ 8. I take responsibility for my statements and point of view by saying, "I think" instead of "they think."

_____ 9. When discussing someone's problem, I usually respond with a reply that indicates understanding rather than giving advice.

_____ 10. When asking questions of others in order to understand their viewpoints better, I generally ask "what" questions instead of "why" questions.

_____ 11. I hold regular, private meetings with people I work and/or live with.

Source: Adapted from D. A. Whetten and K. S. Cameron, _Developing Management Skills_, 3d ed. (Reading, MA: Addison-Wesley, 1995): 242–43. Copyright © 1995, 1991, 1984, Addison-Wesley Educational Publishers, Inc. Reprinted by permission of Addison Wesley Longman.

▶ TEAM EXERCISE 12
One-Way and Two-Way Communication

This exercise is designed to demonstrate the differences between one-way and two-way communication.

STEP 1: FORM GROUPS

Form groups of three. Randomly select two pairs from your group; the third member will act as an observer. Decide which pair will go first. In each pair, randomly select a sender and a receiver. Your instructor will provide each group with a set of pictures.

STEP 2: FIRST EXERCISE

The sender will verbally describe a set of pictures to the receiver, without showing it to the receiver. The receiver will reproduce the pictures on a piece of paper. Neither may ask questions or request information. The sender should limit nonverbal cues as much as possible.

Once finished, the observer will score the receiver's reproductions based on criteria provided by the instructor.

STEP 3: SECOND EXERCISE

The sender will verbally describe a set of pictures to the receiver without showing it to the receiver. The receiver will reproduce the pictures on a piece of paper. Both sender and receiver can ask questions, request information, and provide as many nonverbal cues as necessary, while avoiding drawing the picture in the air to show the receiver. Once finished, the observer will score the receiver's reproductions based on criteria provided by the instructor.

STEP 4: COMPARISON AND DISCUSSION

In your groups discuss the following:

1. Which set was more accurately reproduced? Why?
2. Which exercise was more satisfying and comfortable? Why?
3. What are the implications for organizational communication?

UP CLOSE

▶ E-Mail Abuse

Randy Burton was very proud of having introduced an efficient and easy-to-use e-mail system to his 50-person department. The system connected all employees, managers, and supervisors as well as several customers and suppliers. It included several conferences to which people could contribute and allowed for the posting of private messages, synchronous chats, and the sending and sharing of data in a wide variety of formats. As employees quickly embraced the system, the use of written memos declined.

One of the most common uses of the system was the exchange of information and ideas in the professionals' conference known as "Pro Con." A message posted on the conference was automatically sent to the 30 professionals who worked in the department. The issues posted ranged from requests for information, to meeting announcements, to controversial discussions of the organization's diversity policies.

On a typical day, 20 to 30 messages were posted on Pro Con, each new message sounding a beep and leading to a red flag on the employees' desktops. Less than half these messages conveyed meaningful information. Although employees could send personal detailed responses to "Pro Con" messages, most simply pushed the general response key. As a result, the majority of messages read something like: "I agree," "Me too," "I'll be there," "OK with me," and "Sounds good." The crowded desktops and the constant beeping irritated many employees who regularly told others how to use the various features to prevent these problems.

More seriously, several discussions of controversial issues led to highly personal and nasty attacks on various individuals. When opinions were expressed, people quickly formed camps. It was almost as though the different camps competed to see who could send the most messages on the conference the fastest. In some cases, people in offices and cubicles next door to one another would exchange message after message in response without once having a face-to-face conversation. Several employees' requests to maintain a professional tone and not to personalize discussions were met with ridicule. They were accused of being "prissy" and of playing thought police.

Burton had received numerous requests to intervene. He was reluctant to do so because the Pro Con was a very convenient tool in spite of the problems. His inclination was to give it time. He was encouraged to see that the number of messages in the past three months had dwindled to fewer than 10 a day. Burton's assistant Eddie Gonzales pointed out that the meaningless two- to three-word acknowledgments were still there and that only four or five employees seemed to be using the system. The rest simply read messages without responding.

A recent discussion provided a case in point. Steve Eagleton, a professional employee who had been the source of many of the personal attacks, sent a proposal to change work procedures. It was immediately supported by three of his colleagues who praised his creativity and initiative. One other employee suggested that the issue required a face-to-face meeting but was quickly shouted down by messages accusing her of being antiquated and wanting to block innovation. She was never heard from again. The other 20 or so professionals never responded to the proposal. All the department members were talking about the proposal in the hallways. Few supported it. After two weeks, Eagleton took his proposal to Burton and requested that it be implemented. He noted that the department had had the opportunity to review, discuss, and change it through the Pro Con and cited the positive response on Pro Con as evidence of support.

Questions

1. If you were Burton, what would you do? Would you implement the idea?
2. What are the advantages and disadvantages of the e-mail system as implemented?
3. How has it encouraged/impeded communication? Why?
4. What can be done to improve the communication system?

THE BIG PICTURE

▶ Communication at the Crossroads for Levi Straus

What happens when blue jeans are no longer red hot? That was the situation facing Robert Haas, CEO of Levi Strauss. The San Francisco-based apparel firm's revenues were stagnant and teen buyers were defecting to other fashion brands, despite the introduction of new products and clever marketing initiatives. Haas knew that the company needed major changes to reverse the slide in Levi's share of the jeans market, which had slipped from a healthy 31 percent to just 19 percent in only seven years.[67]

Attacking the problem, Haas made two announcements in 1997 that sent shock waves throughout the company. First, he called for an initial round of 1,000 layoffs; nine months later, he shuttered 11 plants and laid off another 6,000 employees. What brought Levi's to this crossroads? Busy with the launch of new clothing lines and a leveraged buyout that added $3.3 billion in corporate debt, the firm "became less attentive in our hiring, staffing, and cost-control efforts," said the CEO. "Management, including myself, all share responsibility."[68]

By any measure, Levi's had performed well under Haas's leadership. Since he became CEO in 1984, the privately held company's total market value had increased 14-fold; net income had grown 18-fold; and sales had tripled. But Haas sought more than financial performance: he also wanted to forge a strong bond between the company and its employees. To do so, he championed the adoption of an "Aspirations Statement" emphasizing teamwork, recognition, diversity, openness, ethics, and trust.

Translating these tenets into action required careful communication. All Levi's managers had to attend week-long courses in leadership, diversity, and decision making. At the end of each course, participants were asked to determine whether their units were abiding by the aspirational values—and to identify any gaps between the aspirations and actual operations. This extensive training helped spread the values throughout the company, supported by a 360-degree feedback evaluation system tying management bonuses to measures of aspirational behavior.

Starting at the top, organizational communication emphasized collaboration and teamwork. Haas told his top managers, "I don't have the answers, and you don't either. We've got to listen, be open to influence."[69] Although decision making in teams took more time, the company benefited from greater commitment to implementation. Lines of communication were open in every direction, and the Aspirations Statement made employees feel empowered and valued. Then Haas announced the layoffs and plant closings—and Levi's faced new internal communication challenges as it geared up to boost sales and market share.

Questions

1. What contextual strategic forces influence Levi's communication with employees? Be specific.
2. How do you think news of the layoffs affected Levi's informal communication networks?
3. If you were the manager of a plant that remained open after others closed, what are two communication strategies you could use to rebuild trust and encourage interchange of ideas among employees at every level?

NOTES

1. Betsy Morris, "If Women Ran the World It Would Look a Lot Like Avon," *Fortune* 136, no. 2 (July 21, 1997), accessed online at http://bigmouth .pathfinder.com/@@JLQij7AeTAMAQFmF/fortune/1997/970721/avo.html.

2. Ibid.

3. "Avon Senior Management: Andrea Jung," (n.d.), Avon Products Web site, accessed on-line at http://www.avon.com/about/financial/keypeople/gbc/jung.html.

4. Morris, "If Women Ran the World," 78.

5. Ibid., 79.

6. G. L. Kreps, *Organizational Communication: Theory and Practice* (New York: Longman, 1986): 27.

7. P. Watzlawick, J. Beavin, and D. Jackson, *Pragmatics of Human Communication* (New York: Norton, 1967).

8. S. Murray, "BP Alters Atmosphere Amid Turnaround," *Wall Street Journal*, September 17, 1997, A19.

9. Ibid.

10. L. H. Chaney and J. S. Martin, *Intercultural Business Communication* (Englewood Cliffs, NJ: Prentice Hall, 1995), provide a detailed discussion of the influence of culture on communication.

11. S. Thiederman, *Bridging the Cultural Barriers for Corporate Success* (New York: Lexington Books, 1991).

12. Kreps, *Organizational Communication*, 47.

13. K. J. Rottenberger, "Can Anyone Become a More Effective Communicator?" *Sales and Marketing Management* 112, no. 9 (1992): 60–66.

14. D. Tannen, *You Just Don't Understand* (New York: Ballantine, 1990); D. Tannen, *That's Not What I Meant* (New York: Ballantine, 1986).

15. L. Himelstein, "How Do You Get the Boys to Pass You the Ball?" *Business Week* (February 17, 1997): 70.

16. E. T. Hall, *The Hidden Dimension* (Garden City, NY: Doubleday, 1966): 107–22.

17. V. P. Richmond, J. C. McCroskey, and S. K. Payne, *Intercultural Relationships: Nonverbal Behavior in Interpersonal Relations*, 2d ed. (Englewood Cliffs, NJ: Prentice Hall, 1991): 291–310.

18. For work on use of territory see I. Altman, *The Environment and Social Behavior* (Monterey, CA: Brooks/Cole, 1975).

19. E. Calonius, "Tables of Power," *Fortune* 135, no. 8 (April 28, 1997): 147.

20. K. D. Grimsley, "Women, Mitsubishi Take Case to Mediation," *Washington Post*, May 21, 1997, C13; T. J. Lueck, "Brokerage Pays $750,000 in Harassment Case," *New York Times*, May 7, 1997, B9.

21. R. E. Axtell, *Gestures* (New York: Wiley, 1991).

22. Kreps, *Organizational Communication*, 203–5.

23. J. S. Lublin, "Dean Boss: I'd Rather Not Tell You My Name, But . . ." *Wall Street Journal*, July 18, 1997, B1.

24. Ibid.

25. L. P. Stewart, "Whistle Blowing: Implications for Organizational Communication Scholars," paper presented at the meeting of the International Communication Association, Acapulco, Mexico, May 1980.

26. A. Vogel, "Why Don't Employees Speak Up?" *Personnel Administration* 30 (1967): 18–24.

27. R. Frank and T. M. Burton, "Cross-Border Merger Results in Headaches for a Drug Company," *Wall Street Journal*, February 4, 1997, A1, A12.

28. Ibid.

29. The importance of downward communication was emphasized by early management theorists such as C. I. Barnard, *The Functions of the Executive* (Cambridge, MA: Harvard University Press, 1938); M. Weber, *The Theory of Social and Economic Organization* (1909; reprint trans. A. Henderson and T. Parson; New York: Oxford University Press, 1948); H. Fayol, *General and Industrial Management* (1916; reprint, London: Pitman, 1949).

30. For a discussion of the levels of communication, see Kreps, *Organizational Communication*; for challenges of downward communication, see W. Davis and J. R. O'Connor, "Serial Transmission of Information: A Study of the Grapevine," *Journal of Applied Communication Research* 5 (1977): 61–72.

31. Frank and Burton, "Cross-Border Merger."

32. Kreps, *Organizational Communication*.

33. Murray, "BP Alters Atmosphere," A19.

34. S. R. Axley, *Communication at Work: Management and the Communication-Intensive Organization* (Westport, CT: Quorum, 1996).

35. Frank and Burton, "Cross-Border Merger."

36. J. E. Grunig and T. Hunt, *Managing Public Relations* (New York: Holt, Rinehart, and Winston, 1984); L. A. Velmans, "Public Relations: What It Is and What It Does: An Overview," in B. Cantor (ed.), *Experts in Action: Inside Public Relations* (New York: Longman, 1984): 1–6; "Opening the Japanese Market to Washington Apples," *Agri-Marketing* (April 1996): 62–65.

37. A. Ferguson, *Mastering the Public Opinion Challenge* (Burr Ridge, IL: Irwin, 1994): 259–60.

38. S. Marshall, "Labor Problems in Asia Hurt Nike's Image," *Wall Street Journal*, September 26, 1997, B18.

39. Ibid.

40. D. M. Dozier, L. A. Grunig, and J. E. Grunig, *Manager's Guide to Excellence in Public Relations and Communication Management* (Mahwah, NJ: Lawrence Erlbaum, 1995): 57–58.

41. Marshall, "Labor Problems."

42. For a discussion of the difference among different media, see M. B. Goodman, "Corporate Communication and Meeting the Press," in M. B. Gordon (ed.), *Corporate Communication: Theory and Practice* (Albany, NY: State University of New York Press, 1994): 259–65.

43. Frank and Burton, "Cross-Border Merger," A12.

44. Ibid.

45. P. Gumble and R. Turner, "Mouse Trap," *Wall Street Journal*, March 10, 1994, A1; J. Huey, "Eisner Explains Everything," *Fortune* (April 17, 1995): 45–68.

46. D. Antonioni, "Practicing Conflict Management Can Reduce Organizational Stressors," *Industrial Management* 37, no. 5 (1995): 7–8.

47. C. R. Rogers and R. E. Farson, *Active Listening* (Chicago, IL: Industrial Relations Center, University of Chicago, 1976).

48. Murray, "BP Alters Atmosphere."

49. R. E. Coffey, C. W. Cook, and P. L. Hunsaker, *Management and Organizational Behavior* (Burr Ridge, IL: Austin Press/Irwin, 1994).

50. See J. E. Jones and W. Bearley, *360 Feedback: Strategies, Tactics, and Techniques for Developing Leaders* (Amherst, MA: HRD Press, 1996): 12–13; S. Robbins, *Training in Interpersonal Skills* (Upper Saddle River, NJ: Prentice Hall, 1996): 73–75.

51. For discussion of various aspects of supportive communication, see J. R. Gibb, "Defensive Communication," *Journal of Communication* 11 (1961): 121–28; J. Brownell, *Building Active Listening Skills* (Englewood Cliffs, NJ: Prentice Hall, 1986); M. E. Schnake, M. P. Dumler, D. S. Cochran, and T. R. Barnett, "Effects of Differences in Superior and Subordinate Perception of Superiors' Communication Practices," *Journal of Business Communication* 27 (1990): 37–50.

52. For a detailed discussion of validation in supportive communication, see D. A. Whetten and K. S. Cameron, *Developing Management Skills*, 3d ed. (New York: HarperCollins, 1995): 261–63.

53. J. G. Auerback, "Getting the Message," *Wall Street Journal*, June 16, 1997, R22.

54. E. MacDonald, "E-Mail Trail Could Haunt Consultant in Court," *Wall Street Journal*, June 19, 1997, B1.

55. For a discussion of the impact of communication technology, see the work of Claude Fischer, cited in G. C. Hill, "Bringing It Home," *Wall Street Journal*, June 16, 1997, R1, R4.

56. Marshall, "Labor Problems."

57. M. Himowitz, "A Command Center for Your Home Office," *Fortune* 137, no. 4 (March 2, 1998): 198.

58. J. Lee, "Satellite Phone Service Takes Off in Indonesia," *Fortune* 137, no. 5 (March 16, 1998): 154.

59. G. P. Huber, "A Theory of the Effects of Advanced Information Technologies on Organizations' Design, Intelligence, and Decision Making," *Academy of Management Review* 15, no. 1 (1990): 47–71.

60. A. R. Dennis and R. B. Gallupe, "A History of Group Support Systems Empirical Research: Lessons Learned and Future Directions," in L. M. Jessup and J. S. Valacich, *Group Support Systems: New Perspectives* (New York: MacMillan, 1993): 59–77.

61. Anonymity in GSS has been researched extensively. For some examples, see L. M. Jessup, T. Connolly, and J. Galegher, "The Effects of Anonymity on Group Process in an Idea-Generating Task," *MIS Quarterly* 12, no. 3 (1990): 313–21; J. S. Valacich, A. R. Dennis, and J. R. Nunamaker, Jr., "Group Size and

Anonymity Effect on Computer-Mediated Idea Generation," *Small Group Research* 23, no. 1 (1992): 49–73.

62. R. C. Batchelder, "Applied Management Ethics Training at Lockheed–California Company," in D. G. Jones (ed.), *Doing Ethics in Business: New Venture in Management Development* (Cambridge, MA: Oelgeschlager, Gunn & Hain, 1982): 45–57.

63. S. Frank, "Inside a Get-Rich-Quick Plan on the Web," *Wall Street Journal*, July 9, 1997, B1, B4.

64. Based on "The Powerful Combination of Ownership and Participation," *Employment Bulletin and Industrial Relations Digest* 11, no. 1 (1997): 1–2.

65. Morris, "If Women Ran the World," 78–79.

66. Mark Lewis, "Avon's Jung Plants Flag on Fifth Avenue," *Yahoo! News*, February 21, 1998, accessed on-line at http://204.71.177.76/text/headlines/980221/business/stories/avon_1.html.

67. Based on information from Stratford Sherman, "Levi's: As Ye Sew, So Shall Ye Reap," *Fortune* (May 12, 1997): 104–18; see also "Week in Review," *San Francisco Business Times*, November 10, 1997; and Linda Himelstein, "Levi's Is Hiking Up Its Pants," *Business Week* (December 1, 1997): 70, 75.

68. Stratford, "Levi's," 105.

69. Ibid., 115.

MANAGING CONFLICT AND NEGOTIATING

LEARNING OBJECTIVES

1. Explain the views and types of conflict and the role of culture in conflict.
2. Describe individual conflict management styles.
3. Identify the sources of conflict and methods of managing conflict.
4. Discuss the role of culture in negotiation, negotiation processes, and ethical practices.
5. Identify negotiating strategies and common errors.

CHAPTER OUTLINE

Understanding and Managing Conflict

Negotiating

Managing Conflict and Negotiating in Context

MANAGERIAL CHALLENGE

Arthur Andersen and Andersen Consulting

When Arthur Andersen established his namesake accounting firm in 1913, he certainly did not anticipate the deep-seated conflict that has simmered for more than a decade between the accountants and the consultants. Originally, the firm provided traditional auditing and tax services to corporate clients. After computers entered the corporate world, Andersen professionals began to offer technology-related consulting services as well.

For a long time, the profits from accounting and consulting projects went into a single pot, to be divided by all the partners, regardless of their specialty. In the late 1980s, the consulting side was achieving impressive growth and profit gains, yet the pot still had to be shared by all partners, even those in the slower-growing accounting side of the business.[1] Responding to pressure from the consulting partners, the firm established Andersen Consulting in 1989 as a separate division, retaining the Arthur Andersen name for the accounting division.[2]

The divisions continued to share expenses such as training, but now each held onto 85 percent or more of its profits to divide among its own partners. Up to 15 percent of each division's profits could be tapped by the other. Once in the early 1990s, Andersen Consulting received an influx of Arthur Andersen's profits. Otherwise, the money tended to flow out of consulting, which rankled the consultants.[3]

Andersen Consulting was thriving as its pursuit of technology projects with corporate giants paid off. Slower growth in accounting led Arthur Andersen to compete for consulting assignments in management strategy, legal issues, and corporate finance. When the accounting side started pursuing technology projects with mid-sized companies the consulting division began to balk. By 1997, the rift had widened to such an extent that the two divisions could not even agree on who should run the combined organization.[4]

■ Questions

1. What is causing the conflict between Arthur Andersen and Andersen Consulting?
2. How can each side manage the conflict?

Arthur Andersen and Andersen Consulting are locked into destructive conflict. A significant part of a manager's job is to manage and resolve conflict among employees. Some conflicts are interpersonal and related to individual styles, preferences, and goals. Others are caused by organizational factors. Still others emanate from disagreements with outsiders regarding supplies, products, and services. But are they all destructive? Not always. Effective managers learn to negotiate conflicts and disagreements and to use them as a source of creativity.

This chapter focuses on understanding the nature and sources of conflict in organizations and on developing strategies to manage conflict so that it can have a positive effect on organizations. The chapter also investigates the elements and methods of negotiation.

■ UNDERSTANDING AND MANAGING CONFLICT

When people with different goals and interests work together, the potential for disagreement is always present. The Managerial Challenge highlights how the partners at Andersen Consulting and Arthur Andersen disagreed over turf and how to distribute each division's contribution. **Conflict** is a process in which people disagree over significant issues, thereby creating friction between parties. Any situation in which opposition or argument occurs because of differing goals and values is a conflict.[5] For conflict to exist, several factors must be present:

Conflict
A process in which people disagree over significant issues, thereby creating friction between parties

- People have opposing interests, thoughts, perceptions, and feelings.
- Those involved in the conflict recognize the existence of the different points of view.
- The disagreement is ongoing rather than a singular occurrence.
- People with opposing views try to prevent each other from accomplishing their goals.

Conflict can be a destructive force in a team or an organization.[6] However, it can also be beneficial when used as a source of renewal and creativity. This section explores views, consequences, and types of conflict and the effect of culture on conflict. We also investigate individual differences in handling conflict, sources of conflict, and methods for managing conflict.

Before we begin, note that we use the terms *conflict* and *competition* interchangeably, as many people do, although the precise meanings of the two terms differ. **Competition,** the rivalry between individuals or groups over an outcome that both seek, can be a source of conflict. Note that in competition there is a winner and a loser. With conflict, people can disagree over issues and outcomes, but they can cooperate so that no one loses or wins.

Competition
The rivalry between individuals or groups over an outcome that both seek

Views of Conflict

There are two general views of conflict. The first assumes that conflict is dysfunctional and detrimental to organizations. It holds that the struggle over incompatible goals prevents people and organizations from being productive and reaching their potential. The second view suggests that conflict is a natural part of organizational life that can help improve the quality of decision making and increase effectiveness.

Conflict: Dysfunctional or Beneficial? Management theorists such as Taylor developed the view that conflict is dysfunctional and destructive. They viewed conflict as a threat to managerial authority and a waste of time. Other research used to support this view shows that conflict causes unnecessary stress, reduces communication and group cohesion, and prevents employees from focusing on their tasks. These arguments are easily understood when one thinks of the destructive effects of infighting, intense animosity, and personality conflicts in a company.

In many instances, however, conflict can have a positive effect, particularly when it is based on issues rather than personalities.[7] In such cases, conflict has the potential to enhance problem solving and creativity.[8] Encouraging employees to present and discuss their different points of view allows for a thorough consideration of alternatives, solutions, and their consequences. These discussions are at the heart of effective decision making. Additionally, conflict can increase motivation and provide the necessary energy to complete a task.

The Middle Ground As with most of the organizational processes discussed so far, conflict is neither all good nor all bad. Some levels and types of conflict are healthy; others are not. Figure 13.1 shows how moderate levels of conflict stimulate creative decision making and prevent groupthink and apathy. Very low conflict levels lead to complacency and stagnation. Extreme levels, especially if based on individual rather than organizational goals, are detrimental to the organization, causing dysfunctional behavior.[9] The level and type of conflict determine whether it is beneficial or detrimental to the organization.

Managers should expect intelligent, well-trained, and motivated employees to disagree over a variety of issues. In fact, when employees agree easily on how to approach any issue of importance to a company, it signals trouble. By the same token, disagreement over trivial

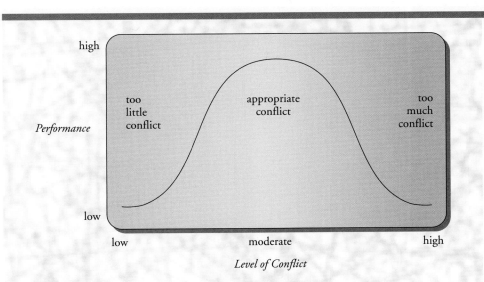

FIGURE 13.1
Conflict and Performance

Source: L. D. Brown, *Managing Conflict of Organizational Interfaces* (Reading, MA: Addison Wesley, 1986), Figure 1.1, p. 8. Adapted with permission.

issues is dysfunctional and destructive. Proper management of conflict is at the heart of growth, creativity, and change.

Consider the example of Elizabeth Goth, 34, a fifth-generation member of the Bancroft family that owns most of Dow Jones and publishes the *Wall Street Journal*. She has been quietly questioning the performance of the company's CEO, Peter Kann, and its president, Ken Burenga. She claims that the main reason the shares of the famous organization are lagging is that the board of directors has not put enough pressure on the two to perform. "There is a history with this company," she states. "We have had questionable outcome after questionable outcome in various business levels."[10] While she still cares for Kann as a friend, she questions his competence. "He'd be a great uncle, father, friend," she claims. However, it really bothers her "that my family has let its affection for Peter take precedence over the need to hold his feet to the fire."[11] Members of the board of directors have severely criticized Goth for airing the issue in public. However, many industry observers believe that the root of Dow Jones' problems is its failure to deal with conflict openly.[12]

Consequences of Conflict

Hot ▼ Link

We discussed group cohesion in chapter 7, pp. 245–50.

Clearly, conflict has both positive and negative consequences, as we see in Figure 13.2. On the positive side, all of us have experienced the exhilaration and energy that come from competing. Competition and conflict can motivate people and inspire them to focus on the task. Involvement in conflict or competition brings group members closer together and leads to increased discussions of various issues and alternatives. When outside conflict or competition occurs, group members band together and brainstorm to find creative solutions. This process increases group cohesion and effectiveness.

Companies can use competition with other companies as a way of reducing internal conflict and focusing the employees' energies on outside competitors. Scott McNealy, the CEO of Sun Microsystems, has used the company's main product, a programming language called Java, as a means of focusing his organization on competitor Microsoft. A sophisticated product, Java enables different computers to understand each other's programming language, making it simple to have access to the Internet, for example. McNealy uses every opportunity to poke fun at Bill Gates of Microsoft. McNealy's goal is to stop "Bill Gates' centrally planned economy."[13]

FIGURE 13.2
Consequences of Conflict

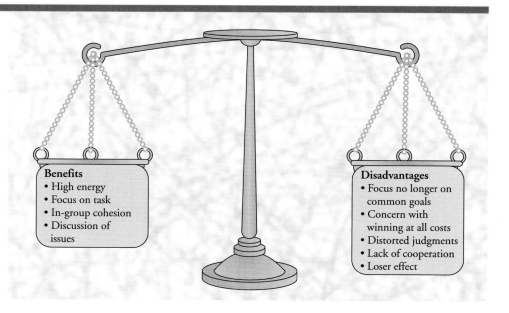

Benefits
- High energy
- Focus on task
- In-group cohesion
- Discussion of issues

Disadvantages
- Focus no longer on common goals
- Concern with winning at all costs
- Distorted judgments
- Lack of cooperation
- Loser effect

One of his favorite puns: "In a world without fences, who needs Gates?" is intended to show Java's superiority in competing with Microsoft's Windows products.[14] In response, Microsoft's engineers respond that Java is "a moderately interesting programming language."[15] The competition between Sun and Microsoft is a strong motivating factor for Sun employees.

Despite its potential benefits, conflict has drawbacks as well. Individuals, teams, or departments that are in conflict and competition may *lose sight of the common goal* and focus on winning at any cost. They withhold important information and resources from one another and sabotage one another's work. A focus on winning at all costs is damaging, whether the conflict is internal or involves outside competitors.

In Japan, competing companies manage to set aside their differences for the good of the overall economy. Such a level of cooperation is rare in the United States, where each company looks out for itself, fighting against national and international competitors. The value of individualism partly explains the existing system of competition in the United States. Moreover, antitrust laws prevent U.S. competitors from banding together to resolve issues. Because Japan does not have similar laws, its companies are free to form alliances and collectively compete with foreign competitors.

Another negative consequence of conflict is distorted judgments that lead to lack of cooperation and even more conflict. When we conflict with another person or group, we tend to perceive them negatively, describe them by using unflattering stereotypes, and pay attention only to negative information. Biased by the conflict, we focus on all that is bad and ignore or distort all that is good. Because we see the "others" as incompetent, disloyal, and so forth, there is little incentive to cooperate, an attitude that fuels further conflict.

Finally, when conflict leads to winners and losers, losers are demoralized and demotivated. Consider an organization that sets up a competition among five teams for the design of a new service. The team that wins receives accolades and rewards; the losers are ignored or even punished. At the outset of the competition, all teams may be strongly motivated to win, so they work hard on their task. However, when the manager announces the winner, the remaining four teams lose their motivation to contribute. This *loser effect* harms long-term relationships and overall organizational performance.

Organizations can prevent the loser effect if they plan effectively. An organization could, for instance, set up the competition just described so that members of the losing teams help implement the winning design. IBM used this method to develop one of its most successful computers. After the teams presented their concepts to top management, the group debated which system to use. The discussion became so heated that one observer rhetorically stated: "There was blood all over the floor."[16] After top management selected the winning design, Fred Brooks, head of systems planning for the Poughkeepsie, New York, division and his key personnel knew they had lost the competition. To their surprise, however, top management asked them to contribute to producing and marketing the product. Newly energized, Brooks and his team contributed so much to the new system that he eventually led the effort.[17]

Summary Point 13.1   **What Are the Views and Consequences of Conflict?**

- Conflict is a process in which people disagree over significant issues, thereby creating friction between parties.
- Some theorists view conflict as dysfunctional; others view it as positive. Most believe that conflict is detrimental at low and high levels and beneficial at moderate levels.

- Positive consequences of conflict include high energy and a focus on the task, group cohesion, and open discussion of issues.
- Negative consequences of conflict include losing sight of common goals, focusing on winning at all costs, displaying distorted judgment and a lack of cooperation, and encouraging the loser effect.

Types and Levels of Conflict

Intrapersonal conflict
An internal conflict because one's goals, values, or roles diverge

Table 13.1 summarizes the four types of conflict. **Intrapersonal conflict** is a person's internal conflict. It occurs because the individual holds divergent goals, values, or roles.[18] For example, a father who wants both to be heavily involved in his young children's school activities and to be on the corporate fast track may experience intrapersonal conflict. School involvement means that the father must devote significant time and energy outside of work. Being on the fast track requires long hours, personal sacrifice, and considerable travel. This father's goals, values, and roles with respect to fatherhood and family conflict with his role as a manager.

Interpersonal conflict
Conflict due to differences in goals, values, and styles between two or more people who are required to interact

Interpersonal conflict refers to conflict that arises because two or more people who are required to interact have different goals, values, or styles. Interpersonal conflict, which occurs often in organizations, can be problematic for managers. Because such conflict typically revolves around personal differences rather than organizational goals, the potential negative impact is high.

In 1997, Dale Sundby wanted to form PowerAgent, a company that specialized in personalized Internet advertising. Sundby's business idea attracted several powerful investors. However, in just ten months and after spending $22 million, the idea died. Interpersonal conflict between Sundby and PowerAgent board member Barry Sullivan (who was also vice president of Internet and Electronic Services for EDS) was part of the reason.[19]

What went wrong? Apparently, Sullivan and other board members did not like the way Sundby spent money. When Sundby asked for more, Sullivan at first agreed to bring in an additional $10 million investment from EDS. "Barry assured us that it would go through smoothly and quickly," Sundby states.[20] However, Sullivan then told Sundby that EDS was not going to invest but would lend the money to PowerAgent. In exchange, EDS wanted the right to use PowerAgent's technology. The conflict escalated. Sundby eventually sued EDS and Sullivan, claiming that they never intended to provide support but planned instead to bankrupt him so they could steal his idea. He accused Sullivan of masquerading as a partner so that he and EDS could defraud PowerAgent.[21]

Intragroup conflict
Conflict within a work group over goals and work procedures

Intragroup conflict refers to conflict within a work group over goals and work procedures. This type of conflict can be extremely detrimental to group cohesion. The conflict may occur because members disagree about goals, procedures, and norms, or how to handle deviants. Some intragroup conflict is healthy, but when it is intense, unresolved, and unmanaged, intragroup conflict eventually interferes with a group's ability to function effectively. For example, PowerAgent's board of directors grappled with intragroup conflict. When the business was still a going concern, the members disagreed over whether the company should launch three products simultaneously or one at a time. The former strategy was expensive but had stronger potential. Some directors wanted the company to take the risk. Others wanted the company to lay off a third of its employees and scale back its big promotion campaign.[22]

Table 13.1   TYPES OF CONFLICT

Type of Conflict	Description
Intrapersonal	Within a person, because he or she is motivated to engage in two or more activities that are incompatible
Interpersonal	Between two or more people who interact and have incompatible goals, styles, and values
Intragroup	Within the members of a group, who disagree over group goals, activities, or processes
Intergroup	Among different groups, departments, or divisions that disagree over tasks, resources, and information

Finally, **intergroup conflict** occurs when groups within and outside an organization disagree on issues. Intergroup conflict is usually about broad organizational issues such as resource allocation, access to information, and system-related processes. For instance, departments in most organizations face conflict over the allocation of resources during budget negotiations, each vying for a larger share of the pie. Or key departments may disagree as to how a product should be designed or marketed.

PowerAgent's marketing team, for example, felt the software developers had designed a poor-quality product that needed more work before the launch. One manager hired to market the product states: "I took one look at the product right after getting there and said, 'You've got to be kidding. We can't launch anything that looks like this. This is awful. Awful.'" However, neither the developers nor Sundby agreed. "Dale had a certain arrogance that we were going to force ad agencies to do it our way because we were going to be the game in town," recalls a former PowerAgent employee.[23]

Intergroup conflict occurs at different organizational levels. Figure 13.3 depicts these levels. **Horizontal conflict** takes place between departments or groups at the same level of the organization. As departments integrate their activities to achieve organizational goals, they may disagree over schedules, quality, efficiency, and so forth. Sales and production departments often conflict over production and delivery schedules. Salespeople promise customers certain delivery dates without double-checking the production schedule. When the sales force learns of product delays, conflict results.

Vertical conflict occurs between groups at different levels of the hierarchy. It typically involves broad organizational issues of control and power. A production department may have a conflict with top executives over the allocation of resources for raises. Another vertical conflict may occur because managers want autonomy to stay flexible and responsive to local customers' needs but headquarters wants to control and standardize procedures to monitor costs.

Intergroup conflict
Conflict that occurs when groups within and outside the organization disagree on various issues

Horizontal conflict
Conflict that takes place between departments or groups at the same level of the organization

Vertical conflict
Conflict between groups at different levels of the organization

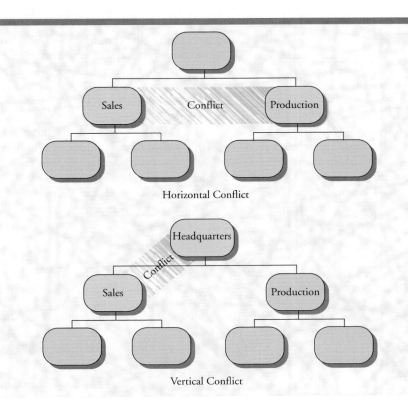

FIGURE 13.3
Levels of Intergroup Conflict

Summary Point 13.2   **What Are the Types and Levels of Conflict?**

- There are four different types of conflict: intrapersonal, interpersonal, intragroup, and intergroup.

- Horizontal intergroup conflict occurs between departments and groups at the same level; vertical intergroup conflict takes place between groups at different hierarchical levels.

Local U.S. 7-Eleven store managers faced this kind of conflict with their Japanese owner, Ito-Yokado Co. The Japanese headquarters insisted on installing a new information system to improve store efficiency and profitability. The local store managers countered that the system curtailed their ability to respond to customers' needs and gave headquarters too much control.[24]

National Culture, Organizational Culture, and Conflict

One factor that determines how people handle and view conflict is culture at both the national and organizational levels. Some cultures are more tolerant and accepting of conflict than others, who tend to view it as a sign of trouble. Any cross-cultural contact has the potential for conflict because people from different cultures have different values and goals. Any difference in goals or values can lead to conflict, so we cannot identify all those differences here. However, let's look at the degree to which the culture values competition by examining the difference between individualistic and collectivist cultures.

People in individualistic cultures such as that of the United States value and encourage competition. In collectivist cultures, characteristic of many Asian and Latin American countries, people focus on the community and consensus. Thus, in collectivist cultures, managers discourage competition to reduce conflict.

These contrasting cultural values may help explain the conflict in the 7-Eleven example. The collectivist values of the Japanese executives clashed with the individualistic American store managers. The Japanese headquarters may have urged standardization in part to discourage competition. The U.S. managers probably resisted its control to allow for individual practices that better served customers, even if that meant competing with other 7-Eleven stores. The 7-Eleven CEO, Toshifumi Suzuki, ignored American managers' objections. He states: "American 7-Elevens don't have a choice: It's either adopt our plans or die."[25] The overall good of the organization takes precedence over individual stores' desire for flexibility.

The culture of an organization can act in much the same way as national culture. An organization based on individual achievement and competition will encourage conflict, whereas one based on cooperation and group consensus is likely to discourage conflict. Furthermore, because of the leader's impact on culture, the leader's conflict management style—which we discuss in the next section—can affect how the organization as a whole views and manages conflict.

Summary Point 13.3   **What Are Some Effects of National and Organizational Culture on Conflict?**

- Cross-cultural contact has the potential for conflict because, by definition, people from different cultures often have different values and goals.
- The national cultural value of individualism-collectivism affects tolerance of conflict. Cultures that value individualism are more tolerant of conflict than those from collectivist cultures.
- The organizational culture affects how employees view and manage conflict.

Individual Conflict Management Styles

Because of the importance and consequences of interpersonal conflict, researchers have developed several models for understanding how different individuals handle it.[26] Two dimensions are used to identify different conflict management styles. The first is concern for self; the second is concern for others. **Concern for self** refers to the extent to which a person focuses on satisfying his or her own needs. **Concern for others** is the degree to which a person wants to satisfy the needs of others.[27] Figure 13.4 depicts how the combination of these two dimensions creates five conflict management styles: integrating, obliging, dominating, avoiding, and compromising. To identify your conflict management styles, take Self-Assessment 13.1.

The Five Conflict Management Styles If you have a high concern for your own and others' needs, your dominant conflict management style is *integrating*, also called problem solving. People with an **integrative style** focus on collaboration, openness, and exchange of information. They prefer to analyze conflict issues thoroughly and openly with all parties. Those with integrative styles confront issues head on, focus on problem solving and finding a win-win solution.[28] Sara Levinson, president of NFL Properties, appears to have an integrating style. She describes herself: "Indeed, I will be brash enough to suggest that the culture of NFL Properties has changed under my leadership—and changed for the better. Now the emphasis is on sharing ideas, communicating them throughout the company, and reaching common goals."[29]

The person with an **obliging style** of dealing with conflict focuses on the needs of others while sacrificing or ignoring his own needs. The style is also called accommodating or smoothing. Those with an obliging style resolve conflict by focusing on similarities, playing down differences, and setting aside their own goals.

The person with a **dominating style** of conflict resolution has a low concern for others and a high concern for self. The style is also known as forcing or competing because people who use it see conflict as a competition in which their primary goal is to win. Dominating people resolve conflict by imposing their will through formal power or any other available means. This approach creates a win-lose situation that can, in the long run, exacerbate rather than resolve conflicts.

In the Dow Jones conflict discussed earlier, William (Billy) C. Cox III joined his cousin Elizabeth Goth in her battle to change the company. While Elizabeth Goth was more low key, Billy was highly confrontational in his crusade. He stated unequivocally that his goal was to replace the CEO and the president at all costs and that he would not rest until it happened. "[CEO] Peter Kann and [President] Ken Burenga have to go. That's the only way this com-

Concern for self
The extent to which a person focuses on satisfying his or her own needs

Concern for others
The degree to which a person wants to satisfy the needs of others

Integrative style of conflict management
High concern for self and for others and focus on collaboration, openness, and exchange of information

Obliging style of conflict management
Low concern for self, high concern for others, and focus on the needs of others while sacrificing or ignoring personal needs

Dominating style of conflict management
High concern for self, low concern for others, and focus on advancing own goals at any cost

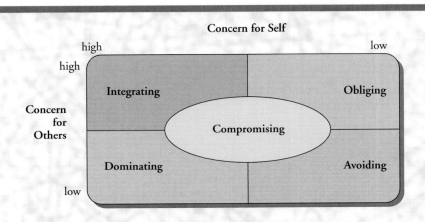

Concern for Self

FIGURE 13.4
Conflict Management Styles

▶ **SELF-ASSESSMENT 13.1**
Conflict Management Styles

Knowing one's predominant style of conflict management and learning to develop other styles are valuable skills for managers.

Instructions: For each of the items listed next, indicate how often you rely on that tactic by circling the appropriate number. If you do not work, think of another group setting and replace the term *co-workers* with *group members*.

CONFLICT-HANDLING TACTIC	RARELY				ALWAYS
1. I argue my case with my co-workers to show the merits of my position.	1	2	3	4	5
2. I negotiate with my co-workers so that a compromise can be reached.	1	2	3	4	5
3. I try to satisfy the expectations of my co-workers.	1	2	3	4	5
4. I try to investigate an issue with my co-workers to find a solution that will be acceptable to everyone involved.	1	2	3	4	5
5. I am firm in pursuing my side of the issue.	1	2	3	4	5
6. I attempt to avoid being put on the spot and try to keep my conflict with co-workers to myself.	1	2	3	4	5
7. I hold on to my solution to a problem.	1	2	3	4	5
8. I use give and take so that a compromise can be reached.	1	2	3	4	5
9. I exchange accurate information with my co-workers so that we can solve the problem together.	1	2	3	4	5
10. I avoid open discussion of my differences with co-workers.	1	2	3	4	5
11. I accommodate the wishes of my co-workers.	1	2	3	4	5
12. I try to bring all our concerns out in the open so that the issues can be resolved in the best possible way.	1	2	3	4	5
13. I propose a middle ground to break deadlocks.	1	2	3	4	5
14. I go along with the suggestions of my co-workers.	1	2	3	4	5
15. I try to keep my disagreements with my co-workers to myself to avoid hard feelings.	1	2	3	4	5

Scoring Key:

Integrating Item Score	Obliging Item Score	Dominating Item Score	Avoiding Item Score	Compromising Item Score
4. _____	3. _____	1. _____	6. _____	2. _____
9. _____	11. _____	5. _____	10. _____	8. _____
12. _____	14. _____	7. _____	15. _____	13. _____
Total = _____	Total = _____	Total = _____	Total = _____	Total = _____

My primary conflict-handling style is _____ (category with highest score)
My backup conflict-handling style is _____ (category with second highest score)

Source: M. A. Rahim, "A Measure of Styles of Handling Interpersonal Conflict," *Academy of Management Journal* (June 1983): 368–76. Reprinted with permission of the Academy of Management, P.O. Box 3020, Briar Cliff Manor, NY 10510-3020, via Copyright Clearance Center, Inc.

pany is going to turn itself around."[30] His dominating style earned him titles like "loose cannon—a flake."[31] Billy Cox focused on accomplishing his goals.

Individuals with a low concern for themselves and for others' needs have an **avoiding** conflict style. They approach conflict by suppressing, setting aside, and ignoring the issues. By avoiding conflict, they satisfy neither their own nor other people's goals. People who avoid conflict may not acknowledge its existence and refuse to address or deal with issues. For instance, some managers avoid dealing with sexual harassment complaints, hoping that the issue dies from neglect. Yet, by avoiding conflict resolution they put the organization, the complaining parties, and their own careers in jeopardy.

People with a **compromising** style try to achieve a reasonable middle ground so that all parties win. They explore issues to some extent and move to a give-and-take position where there are no clear losers or winners. Everybody ends up with something, but not everything he or she wants. Compromising focuses on negotiation and diplomacy. It satisfices rather than optimizes. Managers who use this style can be successful in reaching an agreement. However, because the goal is agreement not results, it can lead to negative results in certain circumstances.

Christopher Hemmeter is a 58-year-old developer who attempted to build the largest casino in the world in downtown New Orleans.[32] He declared that the casino would bring over $1 billion a year in revenues and would revive downtown New Orleans. He made so many promises to so many people that involved compromise that the deal fell through. For instance, to secure the exclusive right to lease the property, Hemmeter capitulated to the city council's request that he not have any hotels, restaurants, or retail shops in the casino. That way, he wouldn't compete with downtown New Orleans service providers. To further satisfy the politicians, he promised to give the city 30 percent of the casino's revenues—at least twice as much as any other casino in the country. These compromises meant the deal became unprofitable for Harrah's Entertainment, his business partner. After spending more than $900 million on the venture, Harrah's finally declared the casino bankrupt and closed its doors.[33]

Which Style Is Best? Which conflict style works best depends on the situation. Managers should take a contingency approach and match the style with the situation. Table 13.2 summarizes the situations in which each style should and should not be used. Note that although conflict management style may have a basis in personality, it is not considered a permanent personality trait. Rather, it is a behavioral style related to managing conflict. As such, people can practice and learn new styles, thereby expanding their ability to handle different conflict situations.

Managers must consider several factors before deciding which conflict management style is appropriate:

- *Complexity of the problem and the need for long-term solutions:* Complex problems require thorough problem solving and input from many parties, thus making either integrating or compromising more appropriate approaches.
- *Time:* When it is critical to resolve the conflict quickly, lengthy analyses and debates are inappropriate so dominating or obliging may be the best conflict style.
- *Importance of the issue:* Managers must not waste their time resolving trivial conflicts. Some conflicts are better left alone either because they are simply unimportant or because they cannot be resolved.
- *Power of the various parties:* Those who have considerable power can use most styles easily. Employees with low power often do not have the option of dominating or even pushing for integration. Similarly, managers cannot use a dominating style with those who have more power than they do.

Failure to adjust conflict styles can harm others and the organization. The shareholders and CEO of Northstar Health Services found this out the hard way. Thomas Zaucha, the CEO of this small health-service company, asked his friend Steven Brody to join the Northstar Health

Avoiding style of conflict management
Low concern for self and others and focus on suppressing, setting aside, and ignoring the issues

Compromising style of conflict management
Moderate concern for self and others and focus on achieving a reasonable middle ground where all parties win

Hot ▼ Link

We discussed satisficing and optimizing in chapter 10, pp. 344–47.

Table 13.2   USING DIFFERENT CONFLICT MANAGEMENT STYLES

Conflict Management Style	When to Use	When Not to Use
Integrating	When issues are complex and require input and information from others When commitment is needed When dealing with strategic issues When long-term solutions are needed	When there is no time When others are not interested or do not have the skills When conflict occurs because of different value systems
Obliging	When the issues are unimportant to you When your knowledge is limited When there is long-term give and take When you have no power	When others are unethical or wrong When you are certain you are correct
Dominating	When there is no time When issues are trivial When any solution is unpopular When others lack expertise When issues are important to you	When issues are complex and require input and information from others When working with powerful competent others When long-term solutions and commitment are needed
Avoiding	When issues are trivial When conflict is too high and parties need to cool off	When a long-term solution is needed When you are responsible for resolving the conflict
Compromising	When goals are clearly incompatible When parties have equal power When a quick solution is needed	When there is an imbalance in power When the problem is complex When long-term solutions are needed When conflict is rooted in different value systems

Sources: Based on M. A. Rahim, "A Measure of Styles of Handling Interpersonal Conflict," *Academy of Management Journal* (June 1983): 368–76; M. A. Rahim, *Managing Conflict in Organizations*, 2d ed. (Westport, CT: Praeger, 1992).

board to provide his financial expertise. Soon, however, Zaucha and Brody started to feud over management matters; interventions from other directors only made matters worse. Eventually, the conflict resulted in nasty letter campaigns, accusations of illegal corporate activities, and a shouting match that would have turned into a fistfight if the police had not intervened.

Brody and Zaucha both used the dominating style to manage their dispute. The style was not appropriate because both had power, the management issues were strategic and complex, and the problems needed long-term solutions. Neither used an integrative or compromising conflict management style that would have been appropriate in this situation. What happened as a result? Employees were distracted from doing their jobs and banks and suppliers refused to deal with Northstar until it resolved its boardroom fracas. Before the conflict, Northstar stock was worth $10 a share. Afterward, the price dropped to 75 cents.[34]

Summary Point 13.4   What Are Individual Conflict Management Styles?

Concern for self and concern for others determine an individual's conflict management style.

- Integrating, obliging, dominating, avoiding, and compromising are the five basic individual styles of conflict management.
- Each style has strengths and weaknesses and each is appropriate in different types of situations.

- Even though people tend to have a primary conflict management style, individuals can learn to use other styles well.

CAREER ADVICE
from the Experts

MANAGING CONFLICT

Although everyone has a primary conflict management style, we can learn to use all five styles.

- Be aware of your primary style and understand the situations in which it is most effective.
- Develop a thorough understanding of the other styles and the situational elements that make them appropriate.
- Select situations in which you can practice different styles without losing too much. Find conflicts where your mistakes won't matter.
- Enlist trusted co-workers and friends to observe you and provide you with feedback.
- Practice other styles as often as possible and keep track of your progress.

Sources: Based on information in M. A. Rahim, *Managing Conflict in Organizations*, 2d ed. (Westport, CT: Praeger, 1992).

Organizational Sources of Conflict

Organizational sources of conflict are those events or factors that cause goals to differ. Many of us experience what we label "personality conflicts" at work. We attribute these to individual personality quirks or cultural differences, we try to ignore them, or we deal with them the best we can. As long as personality conflicts do not interfere with work, they are not an organizational source of conflict.

In this section, we investigate five sources of organizational conflict: goal incompatibility, differentiation, interdependence, uncertainty and resource scarcity, and a competitive reward system. Figure 13.5 depicts these organizational sources of conflict.

Goal Incompatibility and Differentiation   Goal incompatibility is the source of many conflicts. One organizational factor that exacerbates goal incompatibility is differentiation among departments.[35] For example, in a functional organization each department has its own goals and pro-

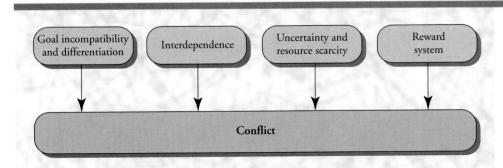

FIGURE 13.5
Organizational Sources of Conflict

Hot ▼ Link

We discussed functional structures and differentiation in chapter 2, pp. 54–55.

cedures. The goal of employees in research and development (R&D) is to design the most creative and advanced product possible. Meanwhile, the goal of the production department is to achieve maximum efficiency and quality. When R&D makes innovative design changes, it interferes with the production department's efficiency and ability to deliver quality products that it has perfected through repetition. Conflict between the two departments results.

Other examples of differentiation that can cause conflict include conflicts between legal departments and various managers, and conflicts between marketing and production or engineering. The legal department's goal is typically risk management, which is sometimes different from simple, sound management. Marketing and sales want to address every customer need and may overpromise, whereas engineering feels more limited in the choice of product variations.[36]

Interdependence
The extent to which employees depend on others to get their work done

Interdependence   A second source of organizational conflict is **interdependence,** which is defined in OB as the extent to which employees depend on others to get their work done. As long as people with different goals can stay away from one another, there is little conflict. The conflict arises when interdependence is high. Consider three shifts of assembly line workers, each of which picks up where the previous one leaves off. Each group's actions affect the others. Their disagreements over work procedures, cleanup, organization of the workplace, and so forth will to lead to conflict because of their interdependence. Interdependence forces interaction and requires give and take, which is difficult when there are conflicting goals.

Uncertainty and Resource Scarcity   Recall that the components of uncertainty are change and complexity. An increase in change and complexity creates conflict in organizations because environmental uncertainty makes it difficult for managers to set direction clearly. They lack information about ways to handle rapid change, so they often change employee goals.

Similarly, when resource scarcity prevents some employees, teams, or departments from achieving their goal, there will be interpersonal and interdepartmental conflict.[37] Cost-cutting activities are examples of the effect of resource scarcity. As resources dwindle and the organization has to make do with less, individuals, work teams, and departments compete over those limited resources. As money became scarce at PowerAgent, for example, the production department managers insisted that all the available resources go to design and production of several products. Marketing wanted the resources invested in the product it felt had the most potential.[38]

Reward System   The last source of organizational conflict is the reward system.[39] If managers reward competition and set up a win-lose environment for their employees, they will increase conflict in their organizations. For example, most organizations give raises and promotions on a competitive basis. At Citicorp, managers are told that only 10 percent of their employees can get the top ranking regardless of performance. This reward system encourages competition among employees for limited spots and thus creates conflict. Other examples of potentially conflict-producing practices include recognition of individual achievements, such as employee of the month, or major awards that are given on a competitive basis in many organizations.

Summary Point 13.5   **What Are the Sources of Organizational Conflict?**

- Goal incompatibility and differentiation
- Interdependence

- Uncertainty and resource scarcity
- Competitive reward system

Moderate conflict is likely to provide benefits to the organization, whereas too much or too little conflict can be detrimental. Managers, then, should learn to handle conflict management effectively. Next, we present several actions that managers can take to reduce or encourage conflict as needed.

Managing Conflict

To manage conflict effectively, the organization should maintain a moderate level of conflict through prevention and reduction or through an increase or stimulation of conflict. Table 13.3 presents two approaches to conflict management. Managers may target behaviors or attitudes to manage conflict.[40] The *behavioral* approach does not delve into the roots of the conflict or analyze its sources. The goal is simply to stop the behavior causing the conflict. The results are often short term and are useful if the conflicting parties are not interdependent so that they can limit or avoid interaction. The *attitudinal* approach addresses the roots of conflict by focusing on emotions, beliefs, and behaviors. It is more time-consuming than the behavioral approach, but has the potential for a long-term resolution. Managers should use the attitudinal approach when conflicting parties have to work together—such as in a self-managed team or between members of production and engineering departments.

If conflict is too high, managers may want either to prevent or reduce conflict. We examine how to prevent and reduce conflict next.

Preventing and Reducing Conflict

Table 13.4 summarizes different methods of conflict prevention and reduction. As the table shows, the prevention and reduction methods can use either the behavioral or the attitudinal approach.

Behavioral Methods of Conflict Prevention and Reduction

What should a manager do if her employees are in constant conflict over a variety of issues? First, she can refer to the professional conduct section in the company policies and procedures manual. Say that she finds several statements about cooperation and respect for others. In a department meeting, she can discuss these statements with her employees and tell them that company policy requires them to work cooperatively. She may also move several employees' offices away from one another or transfer others to another department. Finally, she may make threats about the consequences of not following her directions.

The manager is using *enforcement of rules and policies* and *separation* as methods of resolving conflict. The source of the conflict is not addressed and employees do not develop the skills to address their differences. The manager has not developed a long-term solution; the conflict is simply suppressed. These tactics are appropriate when the individuals or groups do not have to work together. They also can be used successfully if the conflict is over trivial issues and "time off" can help cool tempers.

Table 13.3   TWO APPROACHES TO MANAGING CONFLICT

Behavioral Approach	Attitudinal Approach
• Focus: changing individuals' behaviors	• Focus: changing individuals' attitudes (beliefs, feelings, and behaviors)
• Relatively quick	• Time-consuming
• Short-term effects	• Potential long-term resolution
Examples: Keep conflicting parties separate; enforce policies and procedures	Examples: Build teams; rotate employees to other teams or departments

Table 13.4   CONFLICT PREVENTION AND REDUCTION METHODS

Method (B = Behavioral; A = Attitudinal)	Appropriateness	Consequences
Enforcing rules (B)	• Addresses trivial issues • Gives immediate results	• Quick results • Causes of conflict not addressed • No long-term change • Conflict likely to reemerge
Separation (B)	• Keeps conflicting parties apart • Used for situations where there is no interdependence	• Quick results • Causes conflict; reasons not addressed • No long-term change • Conflict likely to reemerge
Clear tasks (B)	• Ambiguity and uncertainty are the cause of conflict • Task can be clarified	• Quick results • No long-term changes
Common enemy or competition with outside (B or A)	• Used when competition with the outside is part of organizational goals	• Increased in-group cohesion • Source of conflict not addressed; can recur once outside threat is gone
Member rotation (A)	• Used when there is interdepartmental conflict • Used when skill cross-training is needed	• Increased empathy for others • Flexibility in work assignments • Short-term increase in training costs • Long-term change
Increasing resources and rewarding cooperation (B or A)	• Used when resources are available • Used when conflict is created by competition	• Conflict resolution as long as resources are available • Source of conflict not addressed • Can lead to long-lasting change
Team-building, problem solving, and organizational development (A)	• Conflict is complex, with major impact • Used when there is time • Used when long-term solutions are sought	• Long-term change • Sources of conflict addressed • Skill development • Requires considerable use of time and resources

In addition to enforcing rules and separation, *clarifying tasks* can help reduce conflict. This behavioral method is effective when the conflict is caused by a lack of clarity concerning work procedures or goals.

Attitudinal Methods of Conflict Reduction and Prevention   Compared to the behavioral approaches, attitudinal methods of conflict resolution aim not only at changing people's behavior but also at changing how they think (cognition) and feel (emotion) about the conflict and one another. Attitudinal approaches try to find and resolve the root causes of the conflict. This approach tends to result in longer-term resolution compared to the behavioral approach.

One method of conflict reduction that applies the attitudinal approach is to find a common enemy or to compete with another group outside the organization. The focus on an outside enemy or group can help pull conflicting parties together. For instance, two departments that are fighting may join forces to ensure that their new product gets to market before their competitors' products. In the process, they come to think, feel, and behave differently about each other. Similarly, two companies engaged in intense domestic competition may join forces to fight a global competitor. Boeing and McDonnell Douglas have competed for many years in the commercial and defense airplane industry. Yet Boeing purchased McDonnell Douglas in 1997 so that the combined companies could compete more effectively with the European airframe manufacturer, Airbus.

The presence of an outside enemy does not fully address the source of a conflict, but it increases interaction and cohesion, eases internal tension, and provides an opportunity for the conflicting parties to focus on common goals rather than on differences.

Rotating members among departments achieves a similar goal. Employees who rotate to other departments learn to look at conflict from varying points of view. This new perspective and the increased interaction with other employees provide opportunities for the conflicting parties to discuss and resolve their differences. Rotation has the added benefit of increasing an organization's flexibility in work assignments. As employees learn different skills, they can fill in for one another as needed.

Managers can further resolve conflict by *increasing internal resources* so that individuals and departments do not have to compete for them. A related approach is to allocate resources in a manner that precludes pitting one individual or department against another. For example, managers can fund any project that merits funding regardless of which department proposed the project.

Another method of conflict resolution is full-scale intervention through *team building*. The various methods of team building that we discussed in chapter 8 can be used to resolve conflict. Through building trust, respect, and support; clarifying goals; and similar methods, managers can help increase group cohesion and reduce conflict. Similarly, teaching individuals and groups problem-solving skills can help them manage conflict. They can discuss seemingly incompatible goals by relying on rational decision-making models, Nominal Group technique, brainstorming, or other methods presented in chapter 10. Team building and problem solving both focus on long-term solutions and can be time consuming.

Along with team building, managers use **organizational development (OD),** which is defined as making wholesale change in an organization by addressing issues at the individual, group, *and* organizational levels. As we will discover in chapter 14, OD uses various team-building techniques in addition to numerous diagnostic and problem-solving tools that analyze a broad range of organizational problems. For the purpose of this discussion, you need to know that team building and OD are appropriate methods of dealing with complex and deep-rooted conflict. They require a considerable investment of time and resources, but they also have the potential for long-term change, skills development, and long-lasting effectiveness. We next look at ways managers can stimulate conflict.

Hot ▼ Link

For a discussion of team building, see chapter 8, pp. 279–85; for a description of group decision methods, see chapter 10, pp. 365–69.

Organizational development (OD)
Wholesale change in an organization by addressing issues at the individual, group, and organizational levels

Increasing or Stimulating Conflict   Managers may face situations in which they must stimulate conflict to prevent employee complacency and groupthink and to encourage creativity.[41] The three methods for stimulating conflict are introducing change, increasing task ambiguity and competition, and creating interdependence. The key is to focus on issues rather than personal feelings.

First, managers can stimulate conflict by *introducing change* to a team or department. New members, new rules, new tasks, and new leadership all force employees out of their comfortable routines. Change requires thinking of procedures and relationships in a new way and leads to varying degrees of conflict.

Second, managers can *increase task ambiguity*. This method is closely related to introduction of change. Just as clarifying tasks prevents and reduces conflict, uncertainty stimulates it. Managers can assign tasks for which there are no clear requirements, instructions, or procedures so that employees need to discuss and debate such issues. Not having a clear path or well-established procedures generally leads to disagreement, creates conflict, and increases creativity.

Another method of stimulating conflict is *creating interdependence among employees and departments*. Depending on others to perform tasks requires interaction, a consideration of other perspectives, and negotiation of incompatible goals and approaches. Managers can create interdependency to varying degrees. For example, they can divide tasks in different parts and give each part to different teams or assign complex tasks that no one person or department can complete without help from others.

A QUESTION OF ETHICS

How Much Conflict Is Ethical?

You feel that creativity in your department is low, so you decide to form a team to shake things up. You select employees who seem complacent and match them with some aggressive go-getters to tackle a complex project. However, reports indicate that conflict in the team is intense. One employee asks to be pulled off the team, claiming that the conflict is too stressful. Should you intervene? Explain your answer.

This was partly the plan at Dow Jones. Elizabeth Goth and Billy Cox wanted Kann and Burenga fired, partly because a project named Rolling Thunder failed. Burenga conceived the project to design new products and update the technology in the organization. He formed three interdependent teams, each with a different goal. A steering committee coordinated their efforts. "I thought at first that Burenga might be able to pull this off. I thought he would come in here and set goals. But it never happened," states a frustrated Dow Jones executive. The steering committee felt lost: "It was 80 percent debating and 20 percent doing something," reports a committee member.[42] The result was chaos and "total confusion." The $650 million project was soon nicknamed "Rolling Blunder" and Burenga scrapped it.

In contrast to interdependence, which stimulates conflict by requiring increased interaction, *increasing competition* leads to decreased interaction. This method is a relatively simple way to stimulate conflict to reap its creativity and motivational benefits.

Regardless of which method a manager uses, he or she must keep conflict at a constructive level by using a combination of conflict resolution and conflict stimulation methods. We now turn our attention to one of the most useful skills a manager can have in resolving conflict: negotiation. Conflict and negotiation go hand in hand. No matter what method managers use to resolve or stimulate conflict, a certain amount of negotiation is necessary to convince all parties that the chosen solution is the right one.

Summary Point 13.6   **What Are the Ways to Manage Conflict Effectively?**

- Conflict reduction or prevention can use the behavioral or the attitudinal approach to manage conflict.
- Behavioral conflict reduction and prevention methods include enforcing rules, separating employees, assigning clear tasks, having a common enemy and outside competition, and increasing resources and rewarding cooperation.

- Attitudinal conflict resolution methods include having a common enemy, rotating employees, increasing resources, and team building and OD.
- Managers can stimulate conflict through introduction of change, increasing task ambiguity, and creating interdependence or competition.

 NEGOTIATING

Negotiation
Process by which two or more parties reach a mutually agreeable arrangement to exchange goods and services

Whether you manage a small department, own your own business, head a major corporation, or hold an entry-level sales position in a company, you must know how to negotiate. **Negotiation** is a process whereby two or more parties reach a mutually agreeable arrangement to exchange goods and services.[43] It is one of the most commonly used, beneficial skills managers can develop. The global business environment, the diverse workforce, rapid pace of change, and shift toward teams and empowerment require managers to hone their negotiation skills. In this section, we discuss the impact of culture on negotiation, present a model for negotiation, highlight its ethical issues, identify common mistakes made in negotiations, and discuss several individual and third-party negotiation strategies.

Culture

Globalization has increased the frequency of cross-cultural negotiations. Given that negotiation involves exchange, interaction, and communication, culture's impact on this process is significant. Knowing how culture affects negotiations and having information about another party's culture allow for better planning, preparation, communication, and exchange.[44]

The various cultural dimensions discussed in chapter 3 all affect the process of negotiation. Managers from masculine cultures are likely to emphasize assertiveness and independence, see negotiation as a competition, and focus on winning at all costs. Managers who value uncertainty avoidance will tend to rely too much on quick, easy, and available solutions that hinder the creative process of the search for new solutions. For example, cultures that are comfortable with uncertainty (low uncertainty avoidance), characteristic of several Scandinavian and North American countries, are likely to take a creative, problem-solving approach to negotiations. On the other hand, cultures that avoid uncertainty (for example, the culture of China) are likely to emphasize bureaucratic rules and established procedures and rituals when negotiating.

The power-distance and individuality-collectivism dimensions further affect the negotiation process. Low power distance will likely lead to open sharing of ideas and cooperative behaviors in negotiations whereas individualism will put the task before the relationship and emphasize self-interest. Managers from collectivist cultures will concentrate on building cohesion, saving face, and minimizing conflict. Negotiators from individualistic cultures will tend to make decisions on their own during negotiations; those from collectivist cultures will seek their group's input before making any concessions.[45]

High and low context is another cultural dimension that influences negotiations. Managers from high-context cultures rely on the context, various nonverbal cues, and situational factors to communicate with others and to understand the world around them. Managers from low-context cultures are likely to use verbal and written messages to understand others and situations.[46] As a result, negotiators from low-context cultures, such as Germany or Canada, pay attention to what is said and written and want clear, formal written documentation of all agreements. Those from high-context cultures, such as Korea or Vietnam, will look for subtle, nonverbal cues, read between the lines, and operate on trust and on implicit agreements.

Some of Trompenaars's cultural dimensions provide further insight into cross-cultural negotiations. Negotiators from emotional cultures such as Italy may upset their British counterparts with a show of emotion. Negotiators from a present-based culture such as the United States

Cross-cultural negotiations, such as the one between Israeli and Egyptian U.N. representatives, are fertile ground for misunderstanding and conflict. A manager's knowledge of cultural differences can help avoid unnecessary conflict.

and Germany will have a present and future orientation whereas Mexicans will consider the past as an integral part of their negotiations. Moreover, being from a diffuse culture, the Mexican manager will be more likely to carry other relationships and interactions to the negotiating table; the North American or Australian manager will tend to focus more on the current exchange.

These cultural differences can add considerable confusion and conflict to an already difficult and complex business negotiation. In addition to national cultural differences, many ethnic, gender, and individual variations affect the style and process of negotiation. Skilled negotiators take these factors into account during all phases of negotiations and change their approach and style accordingly to reach agreements.

Radha Basu is an international manager whose job is to negotiate software design for Hewlett-Packard (H-P). She runs teams of software engineers and marketers in the United States, England, Germany, India, Australia, Japan, and Switzerland. As each team develops software for its local markets, she negotiates with customers to ensure a fair return for H-P. She can be found negotiating on the phone with Japanese clients, their lawyers, H-P's Japanese lawyers, software engineers, her Asian teams, and production people from H-P's Singapore plant. Basu was born and raised in India and has worked in Germany and the United States. She brings a wealth of cultural and international experience to her day-to-day negotiations. She is informal when necessary, formal when called for, respectful with male counterparts from countries with clearly differentiated gender roles, and soft-spoken yet inquisitive with her employees. She uses her sense of humor to deflect thorny cultural differences in negotiations.

Basu's soft-spoken style causes confusion among H-P's German engineers. Her preference for the word *should* instead of *must* has led them to think they have a choice when, in fact, they do not. Although she recognizes the confusion her message may cause and knows her intent would be clearer if she simply told them what to do, she confesses, "I can't get that word off my tongue."[47]

Elements and Phases of Negotiations

All negotiations share four common elements:[48]

- The parties involved are in some way interdependent.
- The parties are in conflict over goals or processes.

Radha Basu, international manager and skilled negotiator for Hewlett-Packard, predicts that more companies in the computer industry will have to conduct global negotiations to succeed.

- The parties are motivated and capable of influencing one another.
- The parties believe they can reach an agreement.

These four elements come into play at different stages in the negotiation process.

Figure 13.6 outlines the phases of negotiation. The first phase is *preparation*. It is by many accounts one of the most important steps in the negotiation process.[49] Preparation includes gathering factual information about issues and alternatives; acquiring information about the other party's style, motivations, personalities, and goals; and analyzing the location, setting, and tone of the negotiating meeting. Intense preparation not only leads to a better outcome but also reduces the anxiety of negotiating. For example, Basu prepares by developing intricate knowledge of the products and the parties to the negotiation.

The second phase is the *presentation* of initial offers and demands, either orally or in writing. Increasingly, managers implement this phase by using various information technology tools. Effective verbal and nonverbal communication skills and effective self-presentation and image management play an essential role in presentation.[50] Managers must carefully monitor their voices, eye contact, use of time and space, and active listening skills to ensure their credibility.

Cultural differences play a part in the presentation of initial offers and demands. For example, Arabs and other Middle Easterners often make extreme initial demands, fully expecting to back down later. Germans stick to facts, objective offers, and what they perceive to be realistic demands. Similarly, Mexicans see the presentation of the initial offer as an opportunity to demonstrate their rhetorical skills and lofty principles whereas Swedes make unemotional, fact-based presentations that may be perceived by their Mexican counterparts as showing disinterest or lack of preparation. Because the presentation phase of negotiation depends heavily on communication skills, and culture significantly influences communication, this second phase of negotiation presents many opportunities for cross-cultural conflict and misunderstanding.

The third phase is the actual *bargaining* in which managers use various negotiating strategies to reach an agreement. They can use their preparation regarding facts and people to strengthen their position further or to change it to accommodate the situation and the offers and demands of the other party. Here, the communication skills of active listening, giving feedback, and persuasion once again come into play. It is particularly important during this phase to stick to the issues, remain calm, and allow for an objective discussion and evaluation of the process.

The final *agreement* phase closes the negotiation process. Negotiators reiterate the discussions, verbal agreements, and written notices, and they summarize them. They then put the agreement into a format that is acceptable to both parties. In some cultures, a handshake is enough to formalize a deal. This is particularly true in a high-context culture in the Middle East and Latin America. In low-context cultures, such as Germany or the United States, negotiators require formal, precise, legal documents before an agreement becomes official. An additional part of the final phase of negotiation is the follow-up where parties meet either in a business setting or socially to confirm the agreement and clarify any additional issues.

The process of negotiation is continuous. Once an agreement is reached, negotiations over clarifications and implementation are likely to start the process over. Additionally, one party can stop the negotiation at any stage, forcing all to restart the process.

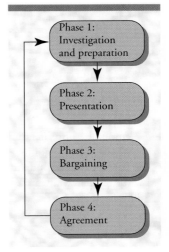

FIGURE 13.6
Phases of Negotiation

Hot ▼ Link

See our discussion of elements of communication in chapter 12, pp. 418–25.

A QUESTION OF ETHICS

| *How Should You Handle the Information?* | During your company's negotiations with a Malaysian supplier, you inadvertently stumble upon a sheet of paper the Malaysian team left on the table. It contains their negotiating strategy and pricing information. What should you do with the information? |

Summary Point 13.7   **How Does Culture Affect Negotiations and What Are the Steps and Phases of Negotiation?**

- Negotiators from masculine cultures, with their emphasis on assertiveness and independence, may see negotiation as a competition and focus on winning at all costs.
- Negotiators from cultures that avoid uncertainty will emphasize bureaucratic rules, established procedures, and rituals in negotiations.
- Power-distance, individuality-collectivism, emotion, and time-orientation dimensions further affect the negotiation process.

- All negotiations have four common elements: Parties are interdependent, conflict exists, the parties can influence each other, and an agreement is possible.
- Negotiation has four phases: preparation, presentation of offers, bargaining, and agreement.

Ethics and Negotiation

Negotiating to get what you need raises a number of ethical dilemmas. Should you always tell the truth? Should you be up front and reveal your game plan? What can you ethically not tell? These are difficult questions that arise regularly in all negotiations. What follows are some typical unethical behaviors that occur during negotiations:[51]

- *Selective disclosure:* Negotiators highlight positive information and downplay or fail to mention negative information.
- *Misrepresentation:* Negotiators misstate facts or their position; for example, they misrepresent the lowest price they are willing to accept.
- *Deception and lying:* Negotiators give the other party factually incorrect information or information that leads to incorrect assumptions or conclusions.
- *False threats and false promises:* Negotiators provide misinformation about actions that you might take and concessions that they may be willing to make.
- *Inflicting direct or indirect harm:* Negotiators intentionally sabotage the other party's chances of success.

Any of these violations is likely to occur in negotiations. The last two, giving false information and inflicting harm, are the most severe ethical violations, although how a negotiator ranks the others depends on his values and morals, the national and organizational cultures, the presence of formal rules and regulations, and the severity of the consequences of the unethical behavior. The individual negotiators often determine whether a behavior is unethical. Table 13.5 offers tips for monitoring ethical behavior.

Table 13.5   **WATCHING FOR ETHICS IN NEGOTIATIONS**

Advice	Explanation
Learn from your mistakes.	We all have committed ethical violations; learn from them.
Do you like what you see?	Evaluate your own behavior and strategies. Can you live with yourself?
What does the other person see?	Consider how you appear to your opponent and other observers. Are you projecting an image that you like?

Source: Based on information in J. K. Murnighan, *The Dynamics of Bargaining Games* (Englewood Cliffs, NJ: Prentice Hall, 1991): 201–2.

Summary Point 13.8   **What Are Ethical Considerations in Negotiation?**

- All negotiations have the potential for serious violation of ethics.
- Ethical violations include selective disclosure, misrepresentation, lying, threats, and harming the other party.

- Negotiators' personal values and culture affect their ethical behavior.

Common Mistakes in Negotiation

Whether we are buying a car, negotiating a raise with our boss, or working on a multimillion-dollar deal with a skilled negotiator from halfway across the globe, we face common obstacles. One of the most common is the fear that we may be *conceding too much* and therefore lose face, either because we appear to give in too easily or because we make a major blunder. While we worry about how we look to the other side, we simultaneously believe that we are more reasonable and rational than they are. These fears distort our judgment and add to a number of other common mistakes we make while negotiating. Table 13.6 describes the major mistakes negotiators make.

Perceptual biases and decision heuristics are the sources of many of the negotiating mistakes described in Table 13.6. Because negotiation involves social perception and decision making, it is subject to the biases in our perceptual process and to various decision-making heuristics. Selective attention and other perceptual filters and biases, such as stereotypes and halo effects, affect our perceptions of ourselves and of the other parties in negotiation. Additionally, how we frame decisions and the anchors we use to make our initial offers affect the content of our negotiation.

Overconfidence stems from lack of information and misperception concerning the correctness of our position. Considerable research shows that we underestimate our chances of being wrong.[52] Similarly, lack of information and not using expert information cause the winner's curse. For instance, consider a first-time car buyer who makes an offer on a car primarily based on what he can afford. If the seller quickly accepts his offer, the buyer will likely feel

Hot ▼ **Link**

For presentation of perceptual biases see chapter 5, pp. 161–70; for decision heuristics, see chapter 10, pp. 354–56.

Table 13.6   MISTAKES IN NEGOTIATION

Mistake	Description	Causes
Irrational escalation of commitment	Continuing a selected course of action beyond what is considered rational and in spite of contrary information	• Wanting to win at all costs • Impression management (ego) • Decision heuristics and perceptual biases
Mythical fixed pie	"What is good for the other side is always bad for us"	• Lack of creativity in problem solving • Competitiveness
Winner's curse	Making a quick high offer and feeling cheated when the offer is accepted quickly	• Lack of information • Lack of expertise • One party having more information than the other
Overconfidence	Overestimating your ability to be correct	• Use of high anchors and adjustment • Lack of information • Distorted self-perception

Source: Based on discussions in M. H. Bazerman and M. A. Neale, *Negotiating Rationally* (New York: Free Press, 1992).

cheated because, compared to the buyer, the seller has considerable information about the actual worth of the car. The buyer could avoid the winner's curse by doing research about the price of the car, shopping around, checking consumer information, planning the negotiation, or asking for help from a more experienced car buyer. Various government regulations and consumer guarantees further aim at preventing the winner's curse.[53]

Negotiators can avoid many common negotiating mistakes through awareness and preparation—which are the basic tools of effective negotiations. Bill Richardson, former U.S. Ambassador to the United Nations, is a skilled negotiator who has negotiated with many foreign countries on behalf of the United States. "You have to be a good listener. You have to respect the other side's point of view. Certainly you want to have a goal. You want to come out of a meeting with something, even if it's only a second meeting. And basically you have to use every single negotiating technique you know—bluster, reverence, humor," Richardson advises.[54]

The various methods of avoiding biases and using decision heuristics described in chapters 5 and 10 apply to perception and decision making in negotiating situations. Some of the tools managers can use are careful and thorough data collection, use of objective data and linear models rather than global judgments, and reliance on expert opinion and advice. "I talk to people who know the guy I'll be negotiating with. I talk to scholars, . . . experts, journalists," Richardson says.[55]

Summary Point 13.9   **What Are the Common Negotiating Mistakes and How Can Managers Avoid Them?**

- Escalation of commitment, fixed pie, winner's curse, and overconfidence are some of most common mistakes managers make in negotiation.

- Being aware of the issues, full preparation, and relying on expert opinion can reduce the chance of making mistakes.

Negotiation Strategies

In addition to preparing carefully and avoiding mistakes, competent negotiators need to be ready to use a variety of other skills and qualities that we list here.[56]

1. *Creativity:* A good negotiator is creative and able to look at issues and problems from a number of angles.
2. *Versatility and flexibility:* Closely related to creativity is the ability to change course when needed. Effective negotiators are able to think quickly and change strategies as the situation demands.
3. *Control:* Negotiators need to be aware of what they can and cannot control. Among things they can control are their presentation, preparation, behavior, and strategies. Factors that are beyond a negotiator's control are the other party's perceptions, reactions, and strategies. Managers should focus on factors they can control.
4. *Motivation:* A good negotiator is aware of her motivation. She must know her goals and her limits.
5. *Ability to say no:* A negotiator must be able to refuse the deal the other party offers if it does not match his goals. He must be prepared and able to walk away if an agreement cannot be reached.

Next, we consider general elements of various negotiating strategies, followed by an examination of individual and third-party negotiation strategies.

MANAGERIAL ADVICE
from the Experts

BECOME A BETTER NEGOTIATOR

- Set goals and targets ahead of time, include minimum acceptable levels and ideals for each issue, and identify areas where you have leverage.
- Know yourself: Develop your own negotiating style and standards of behavior and stick with them.
- Prepare extensively by getting the facts and information about the other party's style, motivation, and strategies, and by practicing.
- Separate people and issues; keep your cool and stay professional.
- Be aware of the negotiation setting and climate and adjust your behavior accordingly.
- Be creative and open to new ideas.
- Don't compete for the sake of competing.
- When it's over, don't harp on what could have been; learn from your mistakes and move on.

Sources: Based on information in R. Fisher, W. Ury, and B. Patton, *Getting to Yes: Negotiating Agreement Without Giving In* (New York: Penguin, 1991); also see J. K. Murnighan, *Bargaining Games: A New Approach to Strategic Thinking in Negotiations* (New York: Morrow, 1992); D. W. Hendon, R. A. Hendon, and P. Herbig, *Cross-Cultural Business Negotiations* (Westport, CT: Quorum, 1996).

General Elements of Negotiating Strategies   Four factors apply to all negotiation strategies. Table 13.7 summarizes these four techniques: focus on substantive issues, maintain a positive climate, remain flexible, and be aware of and use power effectively. The underlying theme of these four is preparation.

Specific Individual Negotiation Strategies   Negotiation strategies are either "win-win" or "win-lose." The traditional view of negotiation (which corresponds to the classical view of conflict described earlier in the chapter) sees negotiation as a zero-sum game in which one party's gain

Table 13.7   TECHNIQUES FOR ALL NEGOTIATION STRATEGIES

Technique	Description
• Focus on the substantive issues.	Success depends on focusing on the real issues and not getting sidetracked by irrelevant and unimportant factors.
• Keep the climate positive.	Even when strong conflict and disagreement exist, success is more likely if the interactions remain positive and personal attacks are not used.
• Remain flexible.	Keep options open as long as possible and do not rush to close substantial or procedural issues.
• Manage the balance of power.	The parties' power is an essential element of negotiation. Be aware of and use various sources of power wisely to persuade and influence.

Source: Based on information in W. Mastenbroek, *Negotiate* (Oxford, UK: Basil Blackwell, 1989).

Distributive negotiation
Zero-sum negotiation in which one party's gain always leads to the other's loss; the rewards and outcomes are divided unequally among the parties

always leads to the other's loss. This view is called **distributive negotiation** because the rewards and outcomes are divided unequally among the parties.

Michael Price is a mutual funds manager who invests small investors' money in large company stocks. Price buys stocks of U.S. corporations through his company, Heine Securities, holds them until their value increases, and then sells them at a profit.[57] He has a unique strategy for dealing with underperforming companies. If the stock price of one of the companies in which he has invested does not increase, Price calls the CEO and demands that the CEO "unlock the value" in the company. He is willing to meet with the CEO and engage in a long discussion and negotiations over how the CEO will increase the stock price. Typically, the CEO agrees to cut costs and to restructure, usually resulting in thousands of layoffs. If, however, the CEO balks at Price's demands, Price often launches a shareholder's fight to replace the CEO.

What is unique about Price's strategy is that it forces CEOs to negotiate with him personally over how they manage their organizations. As a shareholder, he wields his power and forces the company to change even if the CEO and the top executives are reluctant to make those changes. For example, Price was the force behind the merger of Chase Manhattan Bank with Chemical Bank.

Although Chase Manhattan was thriving as one of the biggest banks in the world and was not for sale, its stock price had not increased as much as the stock of other major banks. Enter Michael Price. He first bought $100 million of Chase stocks and then demanded a meeting with Chase's CEO, Tom Labrecque, during which Price demanded that Chase sell many of its divisions and get rid of its nonperforming assets. Labrecque responded that Chase would remain on its current course and promised that within two years Chase's stock price would increase substantially. Not good enough! After lunch, Price started buying additional shares of "undervalued" Chase stocks. Within three weeks, he held a $375 million stake in Chase.

A month later, during Chase Manhattan's annual meeting, Michael Price rose and challenged Tom Lebrecque to "Unlock the value or let someone else do it for you." Within three months, Tom Lebrecque announced that Chase had agreed to let Chemical Bank purchase Chase and to maintain the valuable Chase name. The reorganization of the two banks led to 12,000 layoffs. Price's investment in Chase increased by a cool $500 million.[58]

Michael Price uses a domineering conflict management style and relies on *firm competition* as his negotiation strategy. His ability to be successful with these approaches depends on his access to power based on his stock ownership. His reputation further allows him to use such strategies successfully. His style fits his level of power and his purely financial goals of increasing stock prices to benefit the shareholders.

Michael Price, president of Heine Securities, relies on forcing and competition when he negotiates. His goal is to get the best financial deal for himself and his shareholders.

Integrative negotiation approaches offer a win-win scenario in which parties try to reach an agreement that benefits them both even if each does not achieve all its goals. Although integrative strategies create a positive climate by eliminating winners and losers, they are not easily implemented. They require considerable motivation, creativity, and patience. Ms. Basu, the Hewlett-Packard manager, views negotiation from an integrative perspective. By staying within certain parameters, she and her client both win. Basu wins the contract and her client wins by buying a high-quality product at a reasonable price from a reputable company.

When selecting a negotiating strategy, managers must consider two factors. First, they must determine the importance of the relationship with the other party. Does the manager want to establish a positive, long-term relationship with the other party? Do the other party's thoughts and feelings matter to the manager? Is it important that the other party leave the negotiation satisfied and happy? If the answer to these questions is yes, the relationship with the other negotiating party is important and must be preserved.

Second, managers must ascertain the importance of the outcome.[59] Is this an important deal? Does this agreement affect organizational performance? Does it affect the manager's career success and chances of promotion? If the answer to these questions is positive, then the outcome of the negotiation is important. The manager must therefore assure that she achieves her goals. The combination of these two factors leads to the four negotiating strategies illustrated in Figure 13.7.

Trusting Collaboration   Trusting collaboration involves cooperation, give-and-take and compromise, and collaborative problem solving to achieve a win-win outcome. Negotiators use this strategy when both the relationship and the task outcome are important.[60] Both parties can share motives, ideas, and goals openly as they want to reach a mutually acceptable agreement that promotes long-term relationships and continued cooperation. Using trusting collaboration is essential in team environments where conflict is inevitable and negotiation essential. Team members are interdependent and they value the outcome and the relationship with others. Their goal therefore should be to negotiate issues and differences using a collaborative strategy. When using trusting collaboration, managers must do the following:

- Use a neutral setting where both parties are comfortable.
- Take turns making offers.
- Explain and clarify their reasons and motives.
- Offer an honest consideration and appraisal of their own and the other party's positions.
- Be willing to yield on some issues.

Integrative negotiation
Win-win scenario in which parties try to reach an agreement that benefits all, even if each party does not achieve all its goals

---

Is the substantive outcome important?

	yes	no
Is the relationship outcome important? — yes	**Trusting Collaboration** • Openness • Cooperation • Win-win • Problem solving	**Open Subordination** • Openness • Yielding • Yield-win • One-way acceptance
Is the relationship outcome important? — no	**Firm Competition** • Aggressive • Forcing issues • Win-lose • Imposing solution	**Active Avoidance** • No interaction • Refusal to negotiate • No-win • No solution

FIGURE 13.7
Four Negotiating Strategies

Source: Based on G. T. Savage, J. D. Blair, and R. L. Sorenson, "Consider Both Relationships and Substance When Negotiating Strategically," *Academy of Management Executives* (February 1987): 37–47.

Firm Competition   Managers who do not care about the relationship with the other party but value the task outcome can use firm competition. It is an aggressive win-lose strategy in which managers concentrate on imposing their own party's solution. Using firm competition as a negotiating strategy requires access to power, organizational support, and the willingness to forgo future relationships. Michael Price used firm competition as his negotiating strategy with the CEO of Chase Manhattan Bank.

Tactics in firm competition include the following:

- Imposing negotiation location
- Presenting one's offers first
- Refusing to consider or discuss the other party's issues
- Exaggerating one's own position and the extent to which one has made concessions
- Yielding little or not at all on terms.

Open Subordination   When the task or substantive outcomes are not important but the relationship is, negotiators can select open subordination as a negotiation strategy. It involves yielding to the other party on all or most points and openly accepting his solutions. Open subordination may be the only option when managers do not have much power or leverage to negotiate. However, they can also use this strategy when they have power but want to create goodwill or reduce hostilities when conflict is high. For instance, it is important for many start-up operations and small businesses to have a well-known client. Thus, the small business owners accept the demands of this client, however unreasonable, to gain access to other, similar high-profile customers.

Tactics of open subordination include these:

- Letting the other party present all offers.
- Making high offers and low demands.
- Magnifying the other party's concessions while downplaying one's own.
- Conceding to other party's demands.

Active Avoidance   Active avoidance involves refusing to negotiate as the negotiator does not care about either the task outcome or the relationship. In this case one neither seeks to win nor lose. The individual is simply not a party to the exchange and interaction. Often, managers avoid getting involved in negotiations because they have no stake in the results.

To determine which of the four strategies to use, managers must consider the situation. Furthermore, their conflict management styles and their personalities may lead to a preference for certain strategies. For example, if a manager's primary interpersonal conflict management style is domineering, he is likely to use firm competition as a negotiating strategy, just as Michael Price did. Similarly, an integrating person is likely to prefer trusting collaboration. Personal style and preferences notwithstanding, managers should apply the strategy that best fits the relationship and task outcomes they seek.

Third-Party Strategies   When two parties cannot reach agreement in their negotiations, they may seek the help of a third party to resolve their differences. Third-party intervention and negotiation strategies can take four forms, as described in Table 13.8.[61] The first two strategies, *conciliation* and *consultation*, focus on improving interpersonal relations to allow for later discussion of substantive issues. Typically, the conciliator is a person both parties trust, whereas the consultant has some formal facilitation training that he applies to help the negotiation.

Conciliation and consultation are informal processes; *mediation* and *arbitration* are formal third-party interventions. Mediation involves consideration of both interpersonal and substantive issues; it includes formal evaluation of parties' positions and relies on persuasion

Team Challenge

NEGOTIATING IN TEAMS

When a team from one company negotiates an agreement with a team from another company, team members tend to lose control and make too many concessions. Here are some guidelines to follow:

- *Train all team members in the art of negotiating.*
- *Give each team member an acceptable range for making concessions ahead of time.*
- *Train each member to check back with the whole team before making major concessions.*
- *Do not allow team members to make concessions while the other parties remain silent; long silences are pressure tactics, particularly in cross-cultural negotiations.*
- *Instruct team members to stop the negotiation and meet with each other as often as possible to reformulate their strategy.*
- *Ensure that the entire team understands that final offers from one team member do not mean a final offer from the whole team.*
- *Instruct team members always to leave time at the end of a negotiating session to reexamine the whole agreement.*

and reasoning to bring the two parties together. Mediators propose solutions and process changes. However, negotiating parties are not obligated to accept them. Finally, arbitration is a legally binding process in which a formal arbitrator is called to impose a final solution. Both mediation and arbitration are used to resolve labor management disputes.

In 1996, during the dispute between American Airlines' managers and employees, a government mediator tried to help the two sides reach agreement to avoid employee strikes. When the mediation failed and the two parties refused to submit their claims to arbitration,

Table 13.8   THIRD-PARTY NEGOTIATION STRATEGIES

Strategy	Description	Appropriateness
Conciliation	Trusted third party helps in improving communication and cooling off emotions	When emotional issues are getting in the way of working on substantive issues
Consultation	Trained facilitator helps resolve interpersonal conflicts and offers suggestions for process and climate improvement	When deadlock is related to interpersonal conflict and unclear rules and processes
Mediation	Trained mediator uses reasoning, persuasion, and negotiation with parties to suggest solutions	When new ideas are needed and deadlock exists over both interpersonal and substantive issues
Arbitration	Formal trained arbitrator with power and authority recognized by both parties imposes a solution or selects one party's final offer	When there is urgency to resolve conflict and all other methods have failed

As a means of negotiating disputes, owners and players who cannot agree on salary terms submit the dispute to an impartial arbitrator who makes a final, binding decision.

the president of the United States intervened and eventually a collective bargaining agreement was signed. Another example of formal third-party intervention is the formal arbitration in baseball labor disputes. The players' labor agreement requires owners and players who cannot agree on a fair salary to submit their dispute to an arbitrator. The arbitrator makes a final and binding decision.

Managing conflict and negotiating agreements are daily activities for managers in today's organizations. Some conflicts and negotiations occur among individuals and deal with personal factors. Others are caused by broad organizational factors and require organizational-level change and negotiation. In managing conflicts and negotiations, the ability to remain objective, to focus on issues rather than personalities, and to be flexible and creative is essential. The temptation to be competitive—just for the sake of winning—often detracts from the objective of reaching an acceptable agreement. Furthermore, successful conflict management and negotiation require considerable preparation and particular awareness of cultural differences and how they affect behavior.

Summary Point 13.10   **What Are Negotiation Strategies?**

- Creativity, flexibility, motivation, awareness, and the ability to say no are key to successful negotiation.
- Setting goals, establishing minimum acceptable levels for the final agreement, not getting personal, and focusing on substantive issues are essential.
- The distributive approach leads to win-lose results; the integrative approach leads to win-win results.

- Managers can use trusting collaboration, firm competition, open subordination, and active avoidance as negotiating strategies.
- Conciliation, consultation, mediation, and arbitration are third-party interventions.

Managing Conflict and Negotiating *in Context*

Even though most of us experience conflict on a personal level, the organizational context plays a key role in how we manage conflict. Culture, structure, and strategy are key to managing conflict and effective negotiation. Although culture strongly affects the management of conflict and negotiation processes, structure has the greatest impact on conflict. Also, negotiation is integral to the strategic process.

As we discussed throughout the chapter, culture affects how we perceive and handle conflict and influences negotiating styles and strategies. Therefore, managers must be aware of their own, their employees', and their external business partners' culture when dealing with conflict and negotiating agreements. Additionally, organizational culture strongly influences both processes. The culture of some organizations tolerates and encourages conflict whereas other organizations view open disagreement as a sign of disloyalty and trouble. The way a manager deals with conflict should dovetail with the organization's culture.

One way managers can manage conflict is through the structure of the organization, namely departmentation, formalization, hierarchy, centralization, and span of control. Managers can rotate employees, combine goals, and encourage departments either to cooperate or compete.

Finally, deciding an organization's strategy requires constant negotiation among top managers and with other internal and external constituents, including financial institutions, governmental agencies, and community groups. Strategic concerns increasingly require international negotiations and agreements. A case in point is Ms. Basu of Hewlett-Packard, who negotiates with clients from numerous countries and resolves conflicts among employees in her multicultural teams while keeping the overall growth strategy of her organization in mind.[62]

For updated information on the topics in this chapter, Web exercises, links to related Web sites, an on-line study guide, and more, visit our companion Web site at:
http://www.prenhall.com/nahavandi

A L o o k B a c k a t t h e

MANAGERIAL CHALLENGE

Arthur Andersen and Andersen Consulting

By any standard, the level of conflict between accountants and consultants at Arthur Andersen was entirely too high. This horizontal conflict was not resolved by establishing two separate divisions for accounting and consulting. Andersen Consulting, the consulting side, continued to grow more rapidly than Arthur Andersen, the accounting side. Even after an overhaul, the reward system used to divide profits among partners remained a major source of conflict between the two. And as both sides sought ways of achieving higher growth, differentiation contributed to the intensifying conflict about perceived overlap in services and clients. Still, the two sides voted to remain siblings rather than separate.[63]

In mid-1997, the partners had to vote on who would replace the departing CEO. Jim Wadia, Arthur Andersen's managing partner, did not receive the two-thirds majority needed to take office as CEO, nor did George Shaheen, Andersen Consulting's managing partner. Finally, the board of directors selected W. Robert Grafton as interim CEO.[64]

The conflict publicly erupted at the end of 1997 when Andersen Consulting sent out a news release charging that Arthur Andersen had violated its agreement by trying to sign up the same clients sought by Andersen Consulting. The accounting side saw things differently: They insisted that they had not agreed to stay away from consulting. After both sides escalated their efforts, George Shaheen requested independent arbitration to resolve the issues. By February 1998, the divisions were presenting their arguments at the International Chamber of Commerce in Paris.[65]

Money was definitely at issue. Under the partnership agreement, a departing group was supposed to pay the remaining partners an amount equal to 150 percent of annual revenues—as much as $9 billion in the case of Andersen Consulting.[66] Small wonder that settling the fate of the two divisions could take years.

■ Point of View Exercises

You're the Manager: As a partner at Andersen Consulting, you manage a number of associates, nonpartners who work with you on client projects. This morning, one of your best associates approached you with questions and concerns about the rift between Andersen Consulting and Arthur Andersen. You want to reassure this associate so she will remain with the firm and feel motivated to continue her outstanding performance. How should you respond?

You're the Employee: As an associate at Andersen Consulting, you work on client projects under the supervision of a partner. The ongoing conflict between Andersen Consulting and Arthur Andersen has provoked questions from employees at client organizations where you perform consulting services. How should you respond?

SUMMARY OF LEARNING OBJECTIVES

1. **Explain the views and types of conflict and role of culture in conflict.** Conflict is a process in which people with incompatible goals struggle. Whereas low and high levels of conflict are detrimental for organizations, a moderate level of conflict can stimulate creativity and eliminate complacency.

   The four different types of conflict are intrapersonal (conflict within one's self), interpersonal (conflict between two or more people), intragroup (conflict within a group), and intergroup (conflict among groups). Horizontal intergroup conflict occurs between departments and groups at the same level; vertical intergroup conflict takes place between groups at different hierarchical levels.

   Because people from different cultures have contrasting values and goals, cross-cultural contact has a strong potential for conflict. Any two cultural values that differ may cause the conflict. For instance, the national cultural value of individualism-collectivism affects how well people tolerate conflict.

2. **Describe individual conflict management styles.** Concern for self and concern for others are the determinants of an individual's conflict management style. Integrating is defined as concern for self and others. Dominating is concern for self, but not others. Obliging is concern for others, but not for self, and avoiding is defined as concern for neither self nor others. Each style has strengths and weaknesses and each is appropriate in different types of situations.

3. **Identify the sources of conflict and methods of managing conflict.** Goal incompatibility and differentiation are two of the major sources of conflict in organizations. Interdependence among the departments and teams also leads to conflict. Uncertainty and resource scarcity, as well as the presence of a competitive reward system, are major contributors to conflict in organizations.

   To manage conflict, managers either prevent or reduce conflict when levels are too high or stimulate conflict when levels are too low. Conflict reduction or prevention can take place at a behavioral level with a focus on changing simple behaviors or at an attitudinal level with the focus on addressing the root of conflict. Conflict can be stimulated through introduction of change, increase in ambiguity and competition, and creation of interdependence.

4. **Discuss the role of culture in negotiation, negotiation processes, and ethical practices.** National and organizational culture can affect negotiations because each negotiating party's motivation, outlook, and strategies depend in part on that party's values. Masculinity, power distance, collectivism, and high-low context are national cultural values that affect how managers negotiate.

   Negotiations have four common elements: Parties are interdependent, some degree of conflict exists among the parties, they can influence each other, and agreement is possible among the parties. The four phases of negotiation are preparation beforehand, presentation of offers as the opening position, bargaining among the parties, and agreement. Negotiation is a process that can stop at any time or begin again.

   Negotiations have the potential for serious violation of ethics by each of the parties involved. Some ethical errors are selective disclosure of information, misrepresentation of facts and positions, lying about issues and the data, and threatening and harming the other party.

5. **Identify negotiating strategies and common errors.** Escalation of commitment, fixed pie, winner's curse, and overconfidence are some of most common mistakes parties make in negotiation. Intensive preparation and being aware of the issues will reduce the chance of making costly mistakes. If issues become overwhelming, relying on expert opinion can

reduce mistakes in negotiation. Creativity, flexibility, motivation awareness, and the ability to say no are keys to successful negotiation. The distributive approach to negotiation leads to win-lose results, whereas the integrative approach leads to win-win results. The importance of the relationship and the outcome are combined to yield four negotiation strategies: trusting collaboration, firm competition, open subordination, and active avoidance. Conciliation, consultation, mediation, and arbitration are third-party negotiation options.

KEY TERMS

avoiding style of conflict management, p. 463
competition, p. 454
compromising style of conflict management, p. 463
concern for others, p. 461
concern for self, p. 461
conflict, p. 454
distributive negotiation, p. 478

dominating style of conflict management, p. 461
horizontal conflict, p. 459
integrative negotiation, p. 479
integrative style of conflict management, p. 461
interdependence, p. 466
intergroup conflict, p. 459
interpersonal conflict, p. 458

intragroup conflict, p. 458
intrapersonal conflict, p. 458
negotiation, p. 470
obliging style of conflict management, p. 461
organizational development (OD), p. 469
vertical conflict, p. 459

REVIEW QUESTIONS

1. Compare and contrast the two major views of conflict.
2. Describe the five individual conflict management styles and the situations in which each should be used.
3. Explain the ways managers can manage conflict.
4. Present the various models of negotiation and explain when each applies.
5. Identify the common mistakes people make when negotiating.
6. Explain the effect of culture on negotiation.

DISCUSSION QUESTIONS

1. What is the role of conflict in organizational performance?
2. To what extent should a manager take culture into consideration when managing conflict?
3. Under which conditions is it appropriate for a manager to stimulate conflict? What are the ethical implications?
4. What can managers do to learn to negotiate better?
5. Which negotiation strategies are most effective in team-based organizations? Why?

▶ SELF-ASSESSMENT 13
Avoiding Mistakes in Negotiation

Before you engage in any negotiation, rate yourself and the party with whom you are negotiating on these questions. For each question circle the response that describes your position and your estimate of your negotiating partner's position. See Appendix 3 for a scoring key.

QUESTIONS	MY POSITION		OTHER PARTY'S POSITION	
1. Are you negotiating mostly to support and justify an earlier action or decision?	Yes	No	Yes	No
2. What is good for me is automatically bad for the other person and vice versa.	Yes	No	Yes	No
3. Are you overconfident about your own judgment?	Yes	No	Yes	No
4. Do you have all the relevant information?	Yes	No	Yes	No
5. Have you used objective and rational data to establish your initial offers and demands?	Yes	No	Yes	No
6. Are you overrelying on easily available information and ignoring less accessible data?	Yes	No	Yes	No
7. Have you considered all the possible alternatives and positions in the negotiation?	Yes	No	Yes	No
8. Have you considered your opponent's needs and goals?	Yes	No	Yes	No

Source: Adapted from M. H. Bazerman and M. A. Neale, *Negotiating Rationally* (New York: Free Press, 1992): 172–73. Copyright © 1992 by Max H. Bazerman and Margaret A. Neale. Adapted with permission of the Free Press, a division of Simon & Schuster.

▶ TEAM EXERCISE 13
The Blind Partnership Game

All students are randomly given a number by their instructor. These numbers indicate each person's worth. The numbers by themselves are useless. They are valuable only if two people combine their numbers; only then can the wealth be counted. The game will be played for several rounds with new numbers given out at each round. At the end of each round each person's wealth will be recorded. Winners are those with high numbers at the end of the final round.

THE GAME
For each round, once you receive your number you must find a partner with whom to negotiate, combine, and then split your total wealth. The round ends when all students have reached their agreement.

RULES
1. Anyone can bargain with any other individual.
2. You do not know what is considered a high or a low number.
3. Your final worth (your winning) depends on your partnership agreement.
4. You can say your number, but you *may not show your paper*; you therefore cannot prove that you are telling the truth.
5. You must negotiate how to split your wealth *before* you know for sure what your partner's number is (before you see that person's paper or show yours).
6. Your agreement should be expressed in terms of fractions or percentages rather than actual numbers.

Example: Your number is 100. You find a partner who tells you that she has 80. You can decide to split this evenly (half for each) or each just take out what you brought in, or some other combination (for example, 60% for you and 40% for your partner).

Sources: This exercise is based on one described in J. K. Murnighan, *Bargaining Games: A New Approach to Strategic Thinking in Negotiations* (New York: Morrow, 1992): 51–53; J. K. Murnighan, *The Dynamics of Bargaining Games* (Upper Saddle River, NJ: Prentice Hall, 1991): 36–37. Reprinted by permission of Prentice-Hall, Inc.

UP CLOSE

▶ **"We Are So Happy to Be Able to Accommodate You"**

Jennifer Mannion and her husband Randy Garcia moved to the small company town in the Midwest about six months ago, after Randy accepted a very attractive high-level accounting position at Alpha. Jennifer was disappointed at not having found a good position in the area. With an MBA in marketing and several years' experience in sales and consumer and marketing research, Jennifer had excellent credentials and experience. She had not considered Alpha because she felt uncomfortable working in the same company as Randy.

Anna Kim, the Alpha marketing director, called Jennifer almost immediately after Randy showed her Jennifer's résumé. Anna was excited at the prospect of having someone with Jennifer's skills and wanted Jennifer to work on several projects as an independent contractor. Jennifer accepted. Six months later, Anna offered Jennifer the full-time position of assistant director.

Jennifer was ready to sit down and talk to Anna about her job offer. Jennifer liked the people in the marketing department and her previous reservations about working at Alpha had dissipated. She felt that she was regaining some control over her career. The salary for the position was about 20 percent below the market average, even for this rural area—and several areas of responsibility were not clear. Jennifer was also interested in learning about other areas of marketing and wanted to clarify her need for flexibility from the outset. She collected data to back up her requests for a higher salary and developed several alternative job descriptions based on conversations with previous colleagues around the country. She did her homework and was eager to talk to Anna.

Her meeting with Anna was disappointing. Anna avoided talking about the offer. When Jennifer began discussing the salary and presenting her market data, Anna said, "You seem to fit well with our department. And we are so happy to be able to accommodate you and Randy and find a position for you. I think the salary is just fine." Anna further referred to how difficult it was for dual-career couples to find good positions in this area. Anna agreed to several minor things that Jennifer wanted, but she made no adjustments in the position description and would not clarify the responsibilities. The more Jennifer proposed alternatives and solutions and tried to discuss changes, the more Anna closed up and made small talk.

After meeting for nearly an hour, Jennifer left feeling that all her preparation had been wasted. The position was still attractive and she really did not have any viable alternatives at this point, but her enthusiasm was gone. Anna's words "we are so happy to accommodate you," kept ringing in her ears. Did they really want her here? How did others view her position? Did she really want to work with Anna? She knew Alpha would be lucky to have someone with her skills and experience join them. She was perfect for the job. Yet maybe she should just commute and go someplace where she would be valued.

Questions

1. What are Jennifer's and Anna's conflict and negotiation styles?
2. How would you evaluate the negotiation meeting between the two women?
3. If you were Jennifer, what would you do?

THE BIG PICTURE

▶ The United States versus Microsoft

Has Microsoft, the gigantic software maker led by Bill Gates, been violating antitrust laws by acting like a monopoly? This issue was at the heart of the conflict between Microsoft and the U.S. Justice Department in the spring of 1998. The government had been tangling with Microsoft for years over the overwhelming market dominance of the Microsoft Windows operating system. Now the conflict intensified as Microsoft prepared to ship its Windows 98 software package—complete with built-in Internet browser—on June 25.

The Justice Department charged that Microsoft was breaking the law by bundling its Internet Explorer program with Windows 98, which put makers of competing Web browsers such as Netscape Navigator at a serious disadvantage. "What cannot be tolerated—and what antitrust laws forbid—is the barrage of illegal, anticompetitive practices that Microsoft uses to destroy its rivals and to avoid competition," said Joel Klein, the Justice Department's top trust buster.[67]

For its part, Microsoft waged a public relations war against the government's charges, stressing the consumer benefits of new Windows innovations and arguing that its bold tactics were entirely legal. "We are free to continue to compete as aggressively as the little guy as long as we compete according to the rules," said William Neukom, the company's senior vice president for law and corporate affairs. "If the competitors are bruised, that's the nature of competition."[68]

In early May 1998 both sides met in Washington, D.C., to try to negotiate a settlement. Microsoft delayed sending master copies of its software to computer manufacturers as it continued to negotiate. In exchange, the government temporarily delayed the filing of antitrust lawsuits. Microsoft said it was willing to consider some concessions, including allowing computer makers to decide whether the Windows screen is the first to appear when the PC is switched on.[69]

But the main battleground was Internet software. To ensure competition among Web browsers, the government suggested that Microsoft either include Netscape's rival Navigator software with Windows or remove its own Internet Explorer from the desktop. Neither option was acceptable to Microsoft. "It's a little like asking us to include three cans of Pepsi with every six-pack of Coke," Gates said of the proposal.[70]

Despite hours and hours of discussion, talks finally broke down when Microsoft took back some concessions it had previously made.[71] The Justice Department quickly filed suit, even as Microsoft began shipping Windows 98 to computer makers. The legal maneuvering could go on for years, with the future of antitrust regulation in a high-tech world very much at stake.

Questions

1. What types of conflict can you identify in this case?
2. How did the importance of the outcome affect the strategy of Microsoft and Justice Department negotiators?
3. If you were running Microsoft, would you have accepted either of the government's proposals for opening competition among Web browsers? Explain your answer.

NOTES

1. David Whitford, "Arthur, Arthur . . ." *Fortune* (November 10, 1997): 169.
2. Melody Petersen, "How the Andersens Turned into the Bickersons," *New York Times*, March 15, 1998, sec. 3, pp. 1, 13.
3. "Spouse Trouble: Management Consulting," *Economist* (June 7, 1997): 64.
4. Howard Banks, "House Divided," *Forbes* (November 3, 1997): 344.
5. For a detailed discussion of conflict, see M. A. Rahim, *Managing Conflict in Organizations*, 2d ed. (Westport, CT: Praeger, 1992); K .W. Thomas, "Conflict and Negotiation Processes in Organizations," in M.D. Dunnette and L. M. Hough (eds.), *Handbook of Industrial and Organizational Psychology*, vol. 3, 2d ed. (Palo Alto, CA: Consulting Psychologists Press, 1992): 651–718; S. Robbins, *Managing Organization Conflict: A Nontraditional Approach* (Englewood Cliffs, NJ: Prentice Hall, 1974).
6. C. R. Schwenk, "Conflict in Organizational Decision Making: An Exploratory Study of Its Effects in For-Profit and Not-For-Profit Organizations," *Management Science* 36 (1990): 436–48; K. W. Thomas and W. H. Schmidt, "A Survey of Managerial Interest with Respect to Conflict," *Academy of Management Journal* (June 1976): 315–18.
7. Robbins, *Managing Organizational Conflict*; S. Robbins, "Conflict Management and Conflict Resolution Are Not Synonymous Terms," *California Management Review* 21, no. 2 (1978): 67–75.
8. E. DeBono, *Serious Creativity Using the Power of Lateral Thinking to Create New Ideas* (New York: Harper Busienss, 1992).
9. L. D. Brown, *Managing Conflict of Organizational Interfaces* (Reading, MA: Addison Wesley, 1986).
10. J. Nocera, "Attention, Dow Jones: Ms. Goth Wants Results Now!" *Fortune* 137, no. 4 (March 2, 1998): 109.
11. Ibid., 124.
12. Ibid., 108–24.
13. B. Schlender, "The Adventures of Scott McNealy, Javaman," *Fortune* 137, no. 7 (October 13, 1997): 72.
14. Ibid., 78.
15. Ibid.
16. J. B. Quinn, "The IBM 360 Decision: From Triumph to a New Industry," in H. Mintzberg and J. B. Quinn, *The Strategy Process*, 3d ed. (Upper Saddle River, NJ: Prentice Hall, 1996): 224.
17. Quinn, "The IBM 360 Decision," 220–38.
18. A. E. Reichers, "Conflict and Organizational Commitments," *Journal of Applied Psychology* 71 (1986): 508–14.
19. M. Warner, "A Tale from the Dark Side of Silicon Valley," *Fortune* 137, no. 7 (April 13, 1998): 92.
20. Ibid., 96.
21. Ibid., 92–96.
22. Ibid.
23. Ibid., 96.
24. N. Shirouzu and J. Bigness, "7-Eleven Operators Resist System to Monitor Managers," *Wall Street Journal*, June 16, 1997, B1.
25. Ibid., B3.
26. Early research about conflict management style dates back to work by Mary Parker Follett and to Blake and Mouton. See, for example, M. P. Follett, "Constructive Conflict," in H. D. Metcalf and L. Urwick (eds.), *Dynamic Administration: The Collected Papers of Mary Parker Follett* (1926; reprint, New York: Harper & Row, 1940): 30–49; R. R. Blake and J. S. Mouton, *The Managerial Grid* (Houston: Gulf, 1964).
27. These two dimensions are based on research by Thomas and Schmidt, "Survey of Managerial Interest," and later fully developed by M. A. Rahim and T. V. Bonoma, "Managing Organizational Conflict: A Model for Diagnosis and Intervention," *Psychological Reports* 44 (1979): 1323–44.
28. H. C. M. Prien, "Stijlen van conflicthantering [Styles of handling conflict]," *Nederlands Tijdschrift voor de Psychologie* 31 (1976): 321–46.
29. A. Muoio, "Women and Men, Work and Power," *Fast Company* (February–March 1998): 80.
30. Nocera, "Attention, Dow Jones," 109.
31. Ibid., 122.
32. P. Elkind, "The Big Easy's Bad Bet," *Fortune* 136, no. 11 (December 8, 1998): 162–76.
33. Elkind, 165–66.
34. C. Adams, "At Northstar Health, CEOs Come and Go, but Problems Endure," *Wall Street Journal*, June 20, 1997, A1, A10.
35. E. Neilsen, "Understanding and Managing Intergroup Conflict," in Jay W. Lorsch and Paul R. Lawrence (eds.), *Managing Group and Intergroup Relations* (Homewood, IL: Irwin and Dorsey, 1972): 329–43.
36. Warner, "Tale from the Dark Side."
37. L. R. Pondy, "Organizational Conflict: Concepts and Models," *Administrative Science Quarterly* 12 (1968): 296–320.
38. Warner, "Tale from the Dark Side."
39. M. Deutsch, "The Effects of Cooperation and Compensation upon Group Process," in Dorwin Cartwright and Alvin Zander (eds.), *Group Dynamics* (New York: Harper & Row, 1968): 461–82.
40. Neilsen, "Understanding and Managing Intergroup Conflict."
41. R. A. Cosier and C. R. Schwenk, "Agreement and Thinking Alike: Ingredients for Poor Decisions," *Academy of Management Executive* (February 1990).
42. Nocera, "Attention, Dow Jones," 119.
43. See M. H. Bazerman and M. A. Neale, *Negotiating Rationality* (New York: Free Press, 1992): 1–2; R. N. Lebow, *The Art of Bargaining* (Baltimore: Johns Hopkins University Press, 1996): 1–2, for definitions of negotiation.
44. D. W. Hendon, R. A. Hendon, and P. Herbig, *Cross-Cultural Business Negotiations* (Westport, CT: Quorum, 1996).
45. See ibid. for extensive discussion and examples of cross-cultural issues in negotiation.
46. For discussion of the concept of high and low context, see M. Munter, "Cross-Cultural Communications for Managers," *Business Horizons* (May–June 1993): 69–78.
47. G. P. Zachary, "Globe-Trotters," *Wall Street Journal*, September 18, 1997, R10.
48. D. A. Lax and J. K. Sebenius, *The Manager as Negotiator* (New York: Free Press, 1986).
49. R. Fisher, W. Ury, and B. Patton, *Geting to Yes: Negotiating Agreement Without Giving In* (New York: Penguin, 1991); S. Kozicki, *The Creative Negotiator* (Pyrmont, NSW, Australia: Gower, 1993).
50. J. Ilich and B. Schindler-Jones, *Successful Negotiating Skills for Women* (Reading, MA: Addison Wesley, 1993).
51. R. J. Lewicki, "Lying and Deception: A Behavioral Model," in M. H. Bazerman and R. J. Lewicki (eds.), *Negotiating in Organizations* (Beverly Hills: Sage, 1983).
52. For examples of studies, see S. E. Taylor and J. D. Brown, "Illusion and Well-Being: A Social Psychologic Perspective," *Psychological Bulletin* 103 (1988): 193–210; R. E. Nisbett and L. Ross, *Human Inference: Strategies and Shortcomings of Social Judgment* (Englewood Cliffs, NJ: Prentice Hall, 1980).
53. Bazerman and Neale, *Negotiating Rationally*, 49–52.
54. J. Martin, "How to Negotiate with Really Tough Guys," *Fortune Advisor 1997* (New York: Fortune Books, 1997): 110–13.
55. Ibid., 111.
56. For tips on creative negotiation, see S. Kozicki, *The Creative Negotiator* (Pyrmont, NSW, Australia Grover, 1993).
57. A. E. Serwer, "Mr. Price Is on the Line," *Fortune* 134, no. 11 (December 9, 1996): 70–88.
58. Ibid.
59. G. T. Savage, J. D. Blair, and R. L. Sorenson, "Consider Both Relationships and Substance When Negotiating Strategically," *Academy of Management Executive* (February 1989): 37–47.
60. The following presentation of each strategy and their implications is based on ibid.
61. R. J. Fisher, *The Social Psychology of Intergroup and International Conflict Resolution* (New York: Springer-Verlag, 1990); Bazerman and Neale, *Negotiating Rationally*.
62. Zachary, "Globe-Trotters."
63. "Spouse Trouble."
64. Banks, "House Divided."
65. Peterson, "How the Andersens," 3.
66. Whitford, "Arthur, Arthur," 169, 174.
67. Steve Lohr, "U.S. vs. Microsoft: Government Sets the Stage," *New York Times*, May 19, 1998.
68. John Markoff, "Defiant Gates Defends His Business Practices," *New York Times*, May 19, 1998.
69. Joel Brinkley, "Antitrust Talks with Microsoft Are Called Off," *New York Times*, May 17, 1998, p. 25.
70. Markoff, "Defiant Gates."
71. Brinkley, "Antitrust Talks," p. 1.

MANAGING CHANGE

LEARNING OBJECTIVES

1. Identify and analyze the external and internal forces for change in organizations, the influence of culture on change, and the various types of change.
2. Summarize the causes and methods of overcoming resistance to change.
3. Describe Lewin's force field analysis and Nadler's systems model, the process of change, and the role of change agents.
4. Specify how organizations deal with unplanned change.
5. Describe the concepts and methods of organization development and explain the principles, obstacles, and requirements of learning organizations.

MANAGERIAL CHALLENGE

DaimlerChrysler

When Jurgen Schrempp was named CEO of Daimler-Benz in mid-1995, the German automaker had swerved into unprofitable territory. Renowned for its excellent design and engineering, the Mercedes car division had lost sales because of high prices, undistinguished models, and global competition. Although the company was the world's largest truck maker, sales in that division were also stalled. In addition, the company was still struggling to digest the diverse software, aerospace, and electronics businesses it had acquired as part of a 1980s plan to become an "integrated technology company."[1] The plan failed. The business units were incompatible and ended up draining valuable resources from the Mercedes division. As a result, mainly due to lack of resources, the new Mercedes models looked very much like the old ones, and loyal customers were turning to BMW and Lexus. And profitability was a real problem. In 1993 and 1994, Daimler reported only minimal profits—followed by a loss of nearly $4 billion for 1995.[2]

CEO Schrempp brings an extensive knowledge of Daimler's operations, gained during his years of rising through the ranks. He began as a young apprentice mechanic at Mercedes and then moved into management, tackling assignments in Germany, South Africa, and the United States. By the time he took over the chief executive position, he had learned to make difficult decisions, including the decision to allow one of his unprofitable acquisitions to go bankrupt rather than continue its immense losing streak.[3]

Revamping the entire Daimler organization for improved profitability is a daunting task. To succeed, Schrempp has to win the support of the powerful unions, which hold 9 seats on the corporation's 20-member governing board. He also has to steer Mercedes out of its sales slump. In the United States alone, its car sales plummeted more than 40 percent from their peak in 1991 to their low point in 1996. Finally, he must find ways to transform Daimler into a faster-moving, more responsive corporation.

The company's merger with Chrysler is one strategy designed to change Daimler-Benz.[4] Chrysler makes light trucks and moderately priced cars that complement Daimler's line of heavy trucks and luxury cars. The new company, named Daimler Chrysler AG, will further open the North American market to the German auto maker. Schrempp will run the company and states: "Remember that Mercedes has a 1 percent market share in the U.S., and Chrysler has a 1 percent market share in Europe. . . . We help Chrysler in Europe, and Chrysler can help us in the U.S."[5]

■ **Questions**

1. What internal and external forces were prompting Jurgen Schrempp to change Daimler-Benz?
2. What else could he do to spur effective change and renew success for the company?

If today's only constant is change, then organizations and their managers must develop the skills to anticipate, assess, deal with, and implement change effectively. Daimler Chrysler, like many other companies around the world, is struggling to reinvent itself to keep up with change. Unfortunately, developing the skills needed for change is difficult because almost everyone resists change. It's also challenging because change can be positive, negative, or a combination of both, so managers must develop the analytical skills to assess and predict the effects of change.

This chapter offers basic information that can help you to learn how to learn about the process of change, its effects, and its implementation. We examine the forces and types of change and some factors that heighten and lessen resistance to change. We also investigate two change theories and guidelines for managing change successfully through organizational development and learning organizations.

 FORCE AND TYPES OF CHANGE

Organizational change
The transformation of or adjustment to the way an organization functions

Organizational change is the transformation of or adjustment to the way an organization functions. All organizations undergo some degree of change on a continual basis. Managers correct and adjust work procedures, hire new employees, redo forms, create new positions, eliminate old ones, and so forth. However, organizations face many additional pressures to change, such as new competitors, technology, or customer demands. As a result, organizations are learning to deal with myriad types of change.

Compared with organizational change, **innovation** is the use of various skills and resources to create an idea, product, or service that is new to an organization's industry or market.[6] Innovation leads to new business that did not previously exist. Although innovation typically involves change, change can occur without innovation.

Consider, for example, the innovation of liquid clothes detergent. Procter & Gamble (P&G) introduced the product in 1992 with the intention of limiting its production and keeping its price high.[7] However, the product changed the detergent industry as competitors flooded the market with lower-priced liquid detergents. In response, P&G now devotes a large section of its limited-capacity production plant in Lima, Ohio, to the production of liquid detergent. P&G's innovation not only changed the industry, but forced unplanned and unwanted change on the company itself, as it was not ready to deal with the success of its own product and the quick response of its competitors.

In this section, we consider the external and internal forces for change, the role of culture in change, and the types of changes that organizations typically face.

Forces for Change

When do organizations change? What are the factors that lead managers to plan changes? The forces for change are both external (in the environment) and internal (in the processes and people inside a company). Figure 14.1 depicts the forces for change. **External forces** for change are those factors that are part of an organization's general and business environments. **Internal forces** for change arise from inside the organization. They are issues related to the internal functioning of organizations.

External Forces Changes in the general environment—such as cultural, social, or political changes—often force organizations to respond. Demographic changes in an organization's workforce and customer base typically require an adjustment to the organizational culture and strategy. For example, both McCormick Spice and Avon, companies discussed in earlier chapters, have seen their profits shrink partly as a result of women entering the workforce. These organizations have changed course to survive.

Changing social trends can also pressure organizations to change. In many Western nations, for instance, consumers demand environmentally safe products. As a result, companies not only engage in active public relations campaigns to demonstrate their environmental responsibility, but they also create safe, environment-friendly products. Take Ecover, a small company from Belgium that competes with the likes of Procter & Gamble and Lever Bros. Co. Recognizing that one-third of all household pollution comes from cleaning products, its competitive edge is its environmentally safe cleaning supplies—from laundry powder and dishwashing liquids to car wax. Its products are made only from natural soaps and renewable raw materials; its factory operates on natural energy sources such as wind and solar energy. The

Innovation
The use of various skills and resources to create an idea, product, or service that is new to an organization's industry or market

Hot ▼ Link

We explained the general and business environments in chapter 2.

External forces for change
Those factors that are part of an organization's general and business environment

Internal forces for change
Forces that arise from inside the organization that relate to the internal functioning of organizations

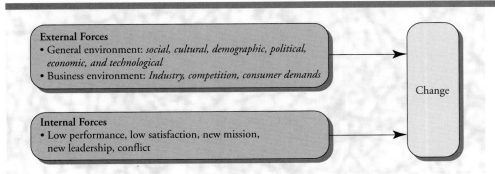

FIGURE 14.1
Forces for Change

External Forces
• General environment: *social, cultural, demographic, political, economic, and technological*
• Business environment: *Industry, competition, consumer demands*

Internal Forces
• Low performance, low satisfaction, new mission, new leadership, conflict

Change

Changes in consumer tastes and concerns create many opportunities for new businesses to address those needs. Tom's of Maine has built its business on addressing the concerns of those who feel responsible for the environment.

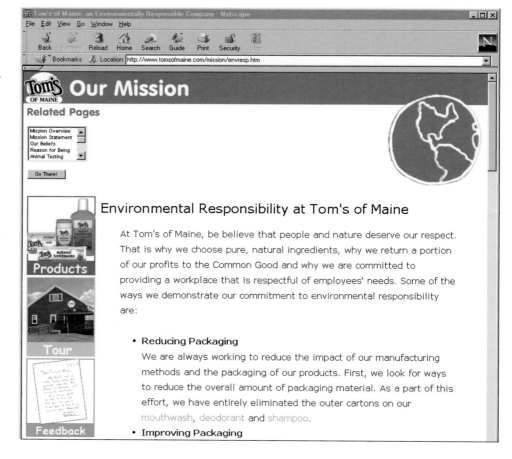

company's strategy has been to launch its products in Western European countries, such as the Netherlands, where consumer concern for the environment is high. Its sales are evidence of its success—over $30 million a year.[8]

Political forces in the general environment also cause change in organizations. As governments change labor laws, financial regulations, and ownership requirements, organizations respond by changing their internal procedures. For instance, for many years India had strict labor laws that did not allow companies to lay off employees without the government's permission, which the government rarely granted.[9] This strict regulation made it difficult for multinational companies such as Siemens of Germany and Philips of the Netherlands to operate in India. Recently, the Indian government decided to loosen this regulation by declaring that although layoffs are still prohibited, workers can be "retired" with "buyout" compensation packages. The change in the Indian government policy has allowed more flexibility in human resource policies and led many companies to "retire" employees by giving them a lump-sum compensation.[10]

Other external forces for change occur in the business environment. Organizations have to react to changes in their industry, stay ahead of their competition, and respond to their customers. As we saw in the Managerial Challenge, new industry competitors and customer demands pressured Daimler-Benz to change its products and marketing and merge with Chrysler. Similarly, retailers and the fashion industry respond to changes in the tastes of teenage consumers. As teen tastes shift, organizations must change whole product lines. The retail and fashion industries must further respond to consumers' demands for low prices by finding ways to hold down costs. Moving manufacturing to developing countries where labor costs are lower has allowed many clothing firms such as Liz Claiborne and Ann Taylor to stay competitive.[11]

Internal Forces Organizations must address internal forces for change. Although the internal forces for change are often closely related to external factors, they can be considered separately. First among the internal forces is low performance in the form of poor quality or inefficiency. As sales decrease, customer complaints rise and an organization loses its market share to competitors, leading to a need for change. Similarly, low employee satisfaction, high turnover or absenteeism, and increasing internal conflicts all create internal pressures for change. Managers and employees who perceive that the organization as a whole or their department or team is not performing as well as it can will make a variety of changes to close the **performance gap**—the difference between expected and actual performance.

Performance gap
The difference between expected and actual performance

Whirlpool, a Michigan-based appliance maker, cut 10 percent of its worldwide workforce, closed several plants in Europe, and pulled out of two joint ventures in China because managers did not think the company was performing as well as it should. The company is trying to manage its lack of productivity in some of its operations in Europe and Asia. Whirlpool's CEO, David R. Whitman, states: "We are taking steps to align the organization with the marketplace realities of our industry. While difficult, these changes are necessary to reach the level of operating performance our employees, customers and shareholders expect."[12]

Other internal forces for change include a new mission and new leadership. These two forces do not always occur together; however, they are often closely related. Organizations often find new leaders to implement a new mission. For example, when Pepsi-Cola North America, the largest unit of PepsiCo Inc., appointed Philip A. Marineau president and CEO, it intended to change its strategy, culture, and structure. Marineau is one of the few outsiders brought into a leadership post at PepsiCo. "The most positive aspect is that the people at Pepsi brought in an outsider—it shows that they're ready to play the game differently," observes Tim Pirko, president of a beverage consulting company.[13] After months of searching, AT&T also brought in an outsider CEO to change the way it conducts business.[14]

New CEOs often change the way an organization functions by changing its mission. The new publisher of the *Los Angeles Times*, Mark Willes, is a good example.[15] He wants to transform the newspaper from a relatively conservative publication into one that reflects the city's multicultural community. He has asked the editors to propose ideas for new community-based features. Willes's goal is for the paper to take an active role in improving the quality of life in Los Angeles while increasing circulation by 50 percent as soon as possible. Reaching these objectives will require major organizational changes.

The Influence of Culture

As pressure for change increases from inside and outside the organization, not all managers react and respond in the same way. Some perceive the pressure as a threat; others see it as a business opportunity. One factor that determines the way people perceive pressures for change is culture. We discuss the effect of organizational culture on change when we examine the concept of learning organizations. From a broader perspective, however, national cultural values of tolerance for ambiguity, and perception and use of time affect managers' perceptions of change.

In cultures of countries such as Greece, Guatemala, Portugal, or Japan where people do not easily tolerate uncertainty and ambiguity, pressure for change is seen as a threat and is either ignored or carefully planned and managed. The Japanese manage change through extensive and detailed long-term planning and forecasting. The Japanese Ministry of International Trade and Industry (MITI) targets certain industries for growth and supports them with

Hot ▼ Link

We discussed cultural values of tolerance for ambiguity and perception of time in chapter 3.

financial backing and a reduction of red tape. Typically MITI supports these industries until they are established internationally.[16] These thorough strategic planning activities help the Japanese view change as less of a threat.

Countries such as Malaysia and Thailand also have centralized planning agencies that coordinate growth and investment in target industries. One purpose of these planning efforts is to reduce uncertainty and ambiguity. At the other end of the ambiguity/tolerance dimensions are the cultures of Sweden, the United States, and Canada where change is tolerated more readily because of its potential opportunities. The short-term rather than long-term orientation in most U.S. business plans is partially a result of the society's relative tolerance of uncertainty.

The relationship to and perception of time further affect how managers implement change. Present-oriented cultures, where time is linear, are likely to react relatively quickly to change and focus on short-term planning. The short-term orientation leads to a state of constant change. Past and future-oriented cultures are less likely to react quickly to change. For example, in the late 1980s and early 1990s, the economies of many developed countries were in a state of recession. Many parts of Europe and Asia were unable to recover as quickly as the United States, mainly because their businesses rely on government programs for support. Changes in regulations take a long time because of the political process and thus are of no immediate help to businesses in crisis. Meanwhile, quick reactivity and focus on the present allowed U.S. businesses to recover and flourish.

In Denver, Colorado, many corporations went bankrupt during the recession of the 1980s. However, the growth of technology companies quickly brought new capital and thousands of new jobs to the city. In 1997, President Clinton selected Denver as the location for an economic summit of the leaders of the richest nations in the world to showcase the robustness of the U.S. economy. Other nations trying to imitate the United States in this regard often find culture to be an obstacle. Business analysts suggest that "to match America's dynamism, they must overcome significant differences in culture, history, and geography. While Americans tend to embrace change for its own sake, Europeans and Japanese tend to mistrust it."[17]

The short-term orientation and focus on immediate results also has disadvantages. The focus on quarterly results can prevent managers from making the long-term investments that are essential to organizational growth.[18]

Summary Point 14.1   What Are Forces for Change and the Influence of Culture?

- External forces for change include elements of the general and business environments.
- Internal forces for change are low performance, low employee satisfaction, a new mission, and changes in leadership.

- Culture affects views and management of change through the values of uncertainty avoidance and the perception of time.

Types of Change

Change tends to be stressful and is usually met with some resistance. However, different types of changes affect people to different degrees. Change that is sudden and drastic is more likely to cause stress and resistance, whereas gradual and programmed change is easier to manage.

Planned change
Change that occurs when managers or employees make a conscious effort to change in response to a specific problem

Planned and Unplanned Change   Some changes in organizations are carefully planned and executed; others happen randomly without specific preparation by those it affects. **Planned change**

occurs when managers or employees make a conscious effort to change in response to a specific problem. It is programmed and expected. Examples include the introduction of a new information management system, changes in accounting procedures, changes in product packaging, and strategic human resource plans.

Unplanned change occurs randomly and spontaneously without the specific intention of addressing a problem. For example, the merger between Daimler-Benz and Chrysler is an unplanned change for their competitors in the auto industry. Examples of other unplanned changes are raw material shortages due to political shifts, cutbacks due to competitors' actions or innovations, and natural disasters such as El Niño–related weather changes that affect the production schedule of the movie industry in California.

Evolutionary and Revolutionary Change   Some changes happen slowly and affect the organization more gradually. Other changes are sudden and result in fast adjustments in organizational functioning. The pace of each type of change is different.

Evolutionary Change   Gradual, incremental change is called **evolutionary change**. The stages of change are identifiable and narrowly focused so that members of the organization do not feel sudden shifts. They are able to adjust various work processes and structures in small stages to close the performance gap or reach their desired goals. Evolutionary change can be either planned or unplanned. For example, unplanned evolutionary change occurs when employees adjust their work habits to improve quality in minor ways on a regular basis to address unforeseen problems. Planned evolutionary or **convergent change** is the result of a specific and conscious action to make changes in an organization. It occurs when the organization fine-tunes its strategy, structure, and systems.[19]

Convergent change is common. Companies refine their procedures and standards, hire managers who can do things a bit better; and clarify rules, structures, and relationships all the time. During convergent change, managers make sure that everyone continues to follow the existing mission and holds the same values and beliefs. The major shortcoming of this type of change is that it can make an organization complacent. Managers start to think their organization is immune to major environmental changes and instead concentrate on fine-tuning only. IBM, GM, and Montgomery Ward became complacent in the late 1970s and 1980s because of this sense of immunity. After decades of dictating the norms of competition in the computer industry, their incremental fine-tuning could not keep them competitive. Many smaller, more flexible competitors had better and less expensive products on the market and consumers were no longer willing to pay more for their brand names.

An example of evolutionary change is the implementation of total quality management (TQM) programs. An inherent component of TQM is continuous improvement, which requires continuous and incremental changes to all processes.[20] Several typical elements of TQM are quality circles as well as cross-functional and self-managed teams.

Wainwright Industries Inc. is a small business that has benefited from the implementation of incremental change and TQM. The company makes stamped and machined products for the automotive and aerospace industries. It has the potential to cause major pollution. However, by gradually and continuously identifying sources of pollution, switching to water-based systems, and using organic lubricants and coolants, Wainwright has reduced its pollution to zero. The organization has highly motivated employees who cooperate with suppliers to identify and reduce sources of pollution. Wainwright has been so successful that it received the U.S. Department of Commerce Malcolm Baldrige award for its outstanding quality and achievements.[21]

Revolutionary Change   Change that is rapid and dramatic is called **revolutionary change** or **frame-breaking change**.[22] It carries with it a sense of urgency and crisis. In some cases, revo-

---

Unplanned change
Change that occurs randomly and spontaneously without the specific intention of addressing a problem

Evolutionary change
Change that is gradual and incremental

Convergent change
Planned evolutionary change that is the result of specific and conscious action to make changes in an organization

Hot ▼ Link

We discussed TQM in chapter 1, p. 10, and quality circles, cross-functional teams, and self-managed teams in chapter 8, pp. 273–77.

Revolutionary change or frame-breaking change
Change that is rapid and dramatic

MANAGERIAL ADVICE
from the Experts

IMPLEMENTING TQM PRINCIPLES

Edwards W. Deming is known as the founder of TQM principles in both Japan and the United States. Some principles he recommends to implement total quality management are listed here:

- Drive out fear (of failure, and of speaking out).
- Be open to new philosophies and willing to lead your team in change.
- Do not depend on others for quality control and inspections; be responsible for the quality of the product or service as you build or deliver it.
- Train employees extensively on the job.
- Leaders should help people do their job better (quality), not just supervise and control them.
- Avoid blaming employees for poor quality. Look at work processes and training instead and fix the problem without blame.
- Involve everyone in the change. Change and quality are everyone's job.

Sources: E. W. Deming, *Out of Crisis* (Cambridge, MA: MIT Press, 1989); M. Walton, *The Deming Management Method* (New York: Perigee, 1990).

lutionary change is planned; in others, it is a response to crisis. Companies that undertake major restructuring are examples of revolutionary organizational change. Instead of making gradual adjustments to its structure, an organization decides to make a drastic change in the way it organizes its employees. Other revolutionary changes result from reengineering efforts that redesign work processes.

At times, organizations must completely reinvent how they conduct their business. Frame-breaking change becomes necessary because of a major shift in the environment. For example, when one company introduces a newer, faster, and less expensive computer component or model, all its competitors may have to shift to the new technology to survive. Organizations that are not able to reinvent their missions, values, cultures, and processes to respond to revolutionary changes in the environment do not last.

When the environment for the U.S. airline industry changed after major deregulation in the 1970s, low-cost carriers such as Southwest Airlines mushroomed, forcing the whole industry to redefine itself. Deregulation was an environmental jolt that required frame-breaking change for those airlines that were inefficient. A similar situation exists in Europe where European Union deregulation is forcing major changes in the airline industry. Some companies, such as British Airways, have successfully adjusted; others, such as Air France, are struggling because of resistance from unions, a well-entrenched bureaucracy, and the potential negative social effects of restructuring.

Daimler-Benz underwent frame-breaking change to entirely reengineer its work processes to introduce its new line of Mercedes sport utility vehicles in the United States in 1997. After losing ground to competing products such as the Jeep Cherokee and the Ford Explorer, Mercedes built a state-of-the-art production facility in Vance, Alabama. The result is the production of a low-cost, high-quality vehicle. Starting at around $35,000, the new

Mercedes is able to compete effectively with American and Japanese brand-name sport-utility vehicles (SUVs). The high initial demand for this product has resulted in a nine-month waiting list for buyers.[23] The new Mercedes is the product of revolutionary change. It could not have been built simply by changing existing Mercedes products. The Chrysler acquisition further allows Daimler to compete in the SUV market.

Innovation often leads to revolutionary changes both inside and outside organizations. Only a few years ago, no one used the Internet, owned a cell phone, or had a small satellite dish at home. Each of these innovations led to the creation of new industries. Today, numerous companies market their products on the Internet and compete in the cell phone business; and numerous satellites belonging to major firms orbit the earth to bring satellite TV and other communication technology to customers. Each of these companies employs thousands of people in newly designed jobs with new work processes and structures.

In spite of the publicity that product and service innovations receive, successful innovation is rare and requires considerable resources and patience. By some estimates, less than 15 percent of all research and development projects lead to successful products or services. To be a successful innovator, an organization has to make considerable changes to its processes, culture, and structure. Whether it involves restructuring, reengineering, or product innovation, revolutionary change causes stress as organizations undergo considerable redirection.

Changing Elements Within Organizations As organizations change to adapt to external and internal forces they can change four elements described in Table 14.1. The way the four organizational elements fit within the open system view of organizations is shown in Figure 14.2. When managers change people either by hiring new employees or by training their existing workforce to learn new skills, they are changing one of the major inputs into organizations. Changing technology, administration, and management practices affect how inputs are transformed into outputs. Finally, new products or services or changes to existing ones affect an organization's output. The changes in an organization's input, processes, and outputs both affect and are affected by the environment.

Although we have presented the four change elements as separate entities, they are closely interrelated. Changes in any one element engender changes in some or all the others.

Hot ▼ Link

We presented the open system model of organizations in chapter 1, pp. 15–16.

Table 14.1   CHANGING ELEMENTS WITHIN ORGANIZATIONS

Organizational Element	Description and Examples
Technology	Changes in the way inputs are transformed into outputs
	Examples: machinery, tools and computers, accounting procedures, work processes, how services are delivered to clients
Product or service	Changes in the product or service that is delivered to customers
	Examples: new product, changes in old product, new service, customized product or service
Administration and management	Changes in how companies are organized and managed, including changes in mission, culture, structure, policies, and management style
	Examples: new mission and strategy, new reward systems, empowerment, use of team-based structures, outsourcing
People or human resources	Changes in employee behaviors, skills, and attitudes, as well as personnel changes
	Examples: training for customer focus and quality service, forming teams, new leadership, new employees

FIGURE 14.2
Change and the Open System

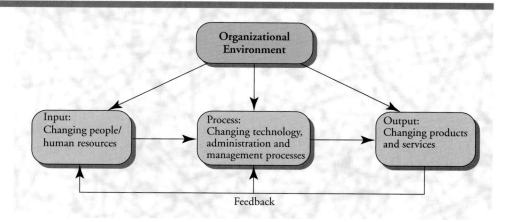

For example, the introduction of a new data-based management system (a change in technology) requires employee training, which is a change in people. The new database may also link several previously independent departments or teams, thereby creating opportunities for interaction and the need for more integration and coordination, which are administrative changes.

The different elements in organizations can change spontaneously or through planning. They also can change slowly and incrementally or be revolutionized by drastic reengineering. In all cases, any type of change will lead to some resistance. We consider the causes of resistance to change and methods of overcoming it next.

Summary Point 14.2   **What Are the Types of Organizational Change?**

- Planned change occurs as a result of a conscious effort by managers or employees to respond to a specific problem; it is programmed and expected.
- Unplanned change occurs randomly and spontaneously without a specific intention to address a problem.
- Evolutionary or convergent change is gradual, incremental, and has a narrow focus.

- Revolutionary or frame-breaking change is rapid and dramatic and carries a sense of urgency and crisis.
- Organizational elements that change to adapt to the environment include technology, products, administration and management, and human resources.

 RESISTANCE TO CHANGE

One of the major causes of stress is change. Even positive changes such as receiving a promotion or getting married can create anxiety and lead to stress. Minor organizational changes often require a brief period of adjustment. However, large-scale changes in work routines, requirements, or rewards typically require a long adjustment period. All changes, especially large-scale ones, meet with some resistance.

Employees who are comfortable with a certain routine may resist new procedures. For example, even the installation of a new and better computer system or software may cause complaints from employees who think it is not worth the time to learn new programs. They may be slow in their learning, refuse to go to training, or even sabotage the new system.

Causes of Resistance

Resistance to change is both an individual and an organizational issue. As we see in Figure 14.3, organizational, group, and individual factors cause resistance to change.

Organizational Factors   The tendency for an organization as a whole to resist change so as to maintain the status quo is **organizational inertia**. Companies that suffer from inertia become rigid and inflexible and cannot adapt to their environment or to internal demands for change.[24] Internal power struggles, poor decision-making processes (including poor perception), a narrow functional focus, and a generally bureaucratic structure and culture all contribute to inertia and prevent organizations from changing when they need to.[25]

The classic example of inertia is IBM. While IBM was doing very well in the large computers and servers market, it was losing about $300 million a year in the home PC product line. The IBM culture responded well to any changes affecting the large computers, but it was not nimble enough to respond to rapid changes in the home PC market. The IBM PC Aptiva was loaded with software that consumers did not want and was priced higher than competing brands. When consumers compared prices, they could find a PC similar to the Aptiva for $700 less. As one buyer put it: "The reputation of IBM, in my opinion, is worth a maximum premium of $100."[26] IBM's bureaucratic structure delayed decision making and prevented the company from responding quickly enough in the dynamic PC market to increase its market share.

An organization's culture and reward systems can either encourage or discourage resistance to change. A culture that fosters trust and cooperation can prepare employees to expect or instigate change, especially if employees are not punished for good-faith mistakes, are rewarded for trying new ideas, and are given proper training to adjust to the changes.[27] Companies such as Sony, Royal Dutch/Shell, GE, Disney, and Toyota actively promote and reward innovation and flexibility.[28]

Sony's culture supports innovation in product development. Royal Dutch/Shell's culture promotes the most talented employees and allows them leeway to innovate. GE is relentless in

Organizational inertia
The tendency for an organization as a whole to resist change and want to maintain the status quo

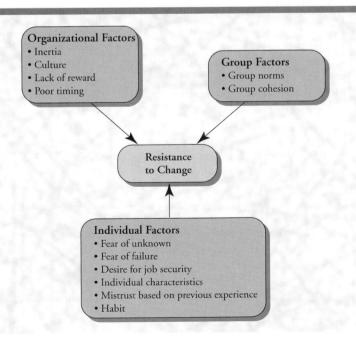

FIGURE 14.3
Causes of Resistance to Change

Sony's managers and CEO encourage innovation in product development. Here, CEO Norio Otiga shows off a Sony Mini Disc, a system that uses a 2.5-inch disc. Sony's innovative, creative culture helps the organization manage change effectively.

shaking up its divisions to encourage change. Disney CEO Michael Eisner explains the company's culture as follows: "We create a new product—a book, a movie, something—every five minutes, and each one has to be superb. Our goal is to do it better every time out."[29] Finally, Toyota's culture promotes "smart engineering," a practice that encourages employees to participate in the development of new methods, continuously reduce costs, and offer higher quality, thereby providing better values to customers.[30] Employee involvement and participation can considerably reduce resistance to change.[31]

A final organizational factor that leads to resistance is the timing of change. As employees are asked to adapt and adjust to a multitude of situations, their patience and tolerance are taxed. For example, after having gone through a major restructuring, employees may strongly resist a simple update to the computer system that they use, even though the change is positive and affects them only minimally. Thinking about the order and the timing of planned change can help managers avoid unnecessary resistance.

Hot ▼ Link

We discussed group norms and group cohesion in chapter 7, pp. 243–51.

Group Factors Two group-related factors affect resistance to change, as Figure 14.3 shows: group norms and group cohesion. Recall that group norms determine how group members behave. Peripheral norms can change relatively easily, whereas central norms are difficult to change. Because central norms involve the group's identity, any change in them is likely to be resisted. Group members will actively work to preserve their group and protect one another.[32] To illustrate, assume that a group has well-established central norms regarding respect for leaders and centralized decision making. Its members will not adjust easily to shared leadership and decentralized decision making because these will be perceived as threats to the group's identity.

Similarly, strong group cohesion can affect acceptance of change. Let's say that an organization with strong group cohesion reengineers to change from a functional structure to a cross-functional team structure. Although the cohesive functional groups have been disbanded, the members' attraction to one another and their desire to stick together will cause resistance to the new structure. Just as group cohesion can work against change, it can also work for change. A cohesive group that wants to implement change can typically overcome individual members' resistance through peer pressure for conformity.

Team Challenge

CHANGING TEAM MEMBERS' PARTICIPATION

Managers have recently noticed that team members are reluctant to speak out and do not contribute as much as they should to group discussions and decision making. Some reasons that team members do not participate are listed next:[a]

- *An expert is present so everyone defers to him or her.*
- *A compelling argument is made by one person, so others do not share their views.*
- *People lack the self-confidence to speak up.*
- *Conformity pressures exist.*
- *The decision being made is trivial.*
- *A threatening climate exists.*

Changing the level of team members' participation in decision making is essential. Without input from all, the benefit of team decision making is lost. Here are some suggestions for remedying the situations:

- *Adjust the team's membership, size, and mix of expertise.*
- *Have well-defined goals and frame issues appropriately.*
- *Set a positive, productive tone for the team.*
- *Monitor the team's progress and encourage self-management.*

a. Based on P. W. Mulvey, J. F. Veiga, and P. M. Elsass, "When Teammates Raise a White Flag," *Academy of Management Executive* 10, no. 1 (1996): 40–49.

Individual Factors People resist change because they fear its consequences. Their comfortable routines are disrupted. They must change habits, a hard task in that it requires learning new, unfamiliar ways to perform a job. They face novel situations. They have to learn new skills and are uncertain about their ability to master them. All these factors make change threatening to individuals. Furthermore, some individuals feel economic insecurity, are risk averse, are relatively closed to new experiences, or have developed a mistrust of management and organizational change because of prior negative experiences. For example, if someone was laid off because of reengineering in her previous job, she will resist reengineering in her current job in spite of assurances that her job is secure.

Individual characteristics can also be a key factor in resisting change. Some people accept change more easily than others because of their culture, personality, and prior experiences. For example, younger executives with less tenure in organizations tend to be more open to change.

The combination of organizational, group, and individual factors can provide formidable resistance to change in organizations. Managers should expect some resistance, even to the smallest and simplest change. They should therefore have a plan to manage resistance.

Dealing with Resistance

Increased communication and information are basic requirements for dealing with resistance to change. Fear of the unknown, loss of job security, and mistrust are considerably reduced through

A QUESTION OF ETHICS

Cooperating with Resistance

Your supervisor wants you to implement her pet project, a new reporting system that will help many members of the organization, but not your department. In fact, it will add extra time to your employees' already overloaded work schedules. You protested in the managers' meetings, but no one felt your concerns were important enough to override the project. When you explain the new reporting system in your department meeting, you can sense there will be resistance. Is it ethical for you to turn a blind eye to employees who don't do the reporting? What if the employees fail to make daily reports as required but make them once every other week or once a month? Should you turn a blind eye to "mistakes" in the reporting process? Do your answers depend on the importance of the project to the organization? Explain.

extensive, open, and supportive communication. Additionally, timing change properly and providing rewards for the adoption and implementation of a change are basic issues that managers must consider. Table 14.2 presents specific methods for dealing with resistance to change.

Each of the methods presented in Table 14.2 can be used to deal with multiple causes of resistance:

- *Education and communication* provide information through various communication methods including face-to-face meetings, newsletters, and announcements. They can reduce fear of the unknown, build trust, and help diminish group resistance.
- *Participation and involvement* rely on input from all those affected by the change to design and implement it. These methods can be particularly effective in pre-

Table 14.2 METHODS FOR DEALING WITH RESISTANCE TO CHANGE

Method	When to Use	Advantages	Disadvantages
Education and communication	When there is lack of information and fear of the unknown	Once persuaded, people will often help with the implementation of change	Time-consuming when many people are involved
Participation and involvement	When managers do not have all the necessary information or when others have power	Participation leads to commitment	Time-consuming; risk inappropriate change being implemented
Facilitation and support	When people are resistant because of adjustment factors (such as fear)	The only option for adjustment problems	Time-consuming; high risk of failure
Negotiation and agreements	When there can be winners and losers and different groups have considerable power	Can be a relatively easy way to deal with resistance	Can be expensive and lead to further negotiation
Manipulation and cooptation	When nothing else works or other options are too expensive and time-consuming	Relatively quick and inexpensive	Can lead to mistrust and resentment over being manipulated; high potential for unethical behaviors
Explicit and implicit coercion	When there is no time and managers have considerable power	Can be fast and effective in the short term with all types of resistance	Can lead to resentment and have only short-term impact

Source: Based on J. P. Kotter and L. A. Schlesinger, "Choosing Strategies for Change," *Harvard Business Review* 57 (March–April 1979): 111. Copyright © 1979 by the President and Fellows of Harvard College. All rights reserved.

venting cohesive teams from resisting change. Once the team accepts involvement in the change, its cohesion helps speed up acceptance and facilitates implementation.

- *Facilitation and support* require active listening and supportive communication along with counseling and support for individuals. These methods are highly effective in reducing fear and mistrust when dealing with individual resistance to change.
- *Negotiation and agreement* recognize the role and power of others in the success of the change effort and offer incentives and trade-offs in exchange for acceptance of change. They are effective when dealing with powerful individuals and cohesive teams.
- *Manipulation and cooptation* reduce resistance to change by focusing employees' attention on some other factors or by simply bribing them to cooperate. These methods cannot be effective in the long run.
- *Coercion* relies on force to push acceptance of change. Although quick and applicable in all situations, coercion does not build commitment and can eventually backfire.

Managers can implement change successfully by using a combination of these methods. The first step in all cases is to understand the cause of resistance. You have probably noticed that none of the methods we described addresses organizational inertia. Dealing with organizational inertia and cultural factors in resistance to change requires broad organizational activities. We address these shortly when we discuss organizational development and learning organizations. We turn next to the models and processes of planned change.

Summary Point 14.3   **What Are Causes and Methods of Overcoming Resistance to Change?**

- The causes of resistance to change consist of organizational, group, and individual factors.
- Organizational inertia is an organization's tendency to resist change to maintain the status quo. The culture of an organization can be a major factor in inertia.
- Two group-related factors that effect resistance to change are group norms and group cohesion.

- Individuals resist change because they fear its consequences, their comfortable routines are disrupted, they face unfamiliar situations, they have to learn new skills and are uncertain about their ability to master them, and they are risk averse.
- To handle resistance, managers must first understand its causes, then select a method to overcome it.

MODELS AND PROCESSES OF PLANNED CHANGE

Understanding how the process and elements of change function helps managers to plan and implement change. In this section we examine two models of the planned change process and the typical elements of that process as well as the role of *change agents*.

Lewin's Force Field Analysis of Change

In the 1950s, social psychologist Kurt Lewin proposed a theory of organizational change that continues to influence current thinking.[33] Lewin's force field analysis proposes that organizations contain forces that drive change and forces that resist change. When these two forces are balanced, the organization maintains its status quo. When the forces for change are stronger than those that resist change, managers overcome inertia and implement changes. Lewin further suggests that change takes place in a three-stage process.

Unfreezing
Stage in Lewin's force field model of change during which existing practices and behaviors are questioned and motivation to change develops

Three Stages of Change   According to Lewin, the first stage of change is **unfreezing,** which means that existing practices and behaviors are questioned and the motivation to change develops. Unfreezing involves dissatisfaction with current performance and management practices. Becoming aware of the need for change reduces the forces that resist change and strengthens those that support it. Consider the case of Sears Roebuck in bringing change to a poorly performing organization.[34]

For more than two decades, Sears lost business to retailers such as Wal-Mart and department stores such as Robinsons-May. Sears repeatedly reorganized without positive results. It appeared that customers had no reason to shop at Sears any longer. A new management team, however, reversed the negative trends. Anthony Rucci, Sears's chief administrative officer and "chief learning officer," surveyed employees to find out their perception of the company. The results shocked him. Employees thought that Sears earned about 45 cents on every dollar of sales when in fact it earned only 1.7 cents. Next, he surveyed Sears's customers and found that they felt Sears treated them badly. Sears's employees were also surprised to find out how poorly they were perceived by their customers. Rucci concluded that employees had no idea how badly the organization was hurting and therefore had no reason to make or accept changes. His role at Sears has been to educate the employees about the need for change. He wants them to be economically literate to know the consequences of each sale lost due to customer dissatisfaction.[35]

The second stage of Lewin's model is the *change* itself. In this stage new practices and policies are implemented and new behaviors are learned. As we discussed earlier in the chapter, change can involve technology, people, products, services, or management practices and administration. In the change stage, various work processes are transformed.

For instance, at Sears, after learning how dissatisfied customers were, Rucci instituted a training program to educate, motivate, and empower the 300,000 employees to develop and share ideas on how to change the organization to make it more customer driven. Rucci readily shares information so that employees can see the consequences of their actions on the bottom line. The company has made numerous structural changes to be more flexible and less top-heavy. Rucci explains: "We have built an empirical model that says that unless you have a trained, literate, motivated, competent work force, and give them decision-making authority, you don't get satisfied customers no matter how good the merchandise is."[36] The results of all these efforts? Sears has doubled the amount it earns on each dollar of sales, and its customer satisfaction ratings have improved slightly.

Under Anthony Rucci's leadership, Sears has been slowly reinventing itself to be more responsive to its customers and more profitable.

The final stage of Lewin's model is **refreezing**, during which the newly learned behaviors and freshly implemented practices are encouraged and supported to become part of employees' routine activities. Key factors in the refreezing stage are coaching, training, and the use of appropriate reward systems. Returning to the Sears example, Anthony Rucci predicts that soon a portion of every employee's pay will be pegged to the company's financial performance. He wants managers to remove barriers to employees' performance and to remind them repeatedly that they work for customers. He states, "We have to keep repeating the basics while getting better at empowering our people. A lot of that is just getting us managers out of their way. When people get a chance to accomplish something themselves, they build self-esteem."[37]

Lewin's model of change has four key characteristics:

- It emphasizes the importance of recognizing the need for change and being motivated to implement it.
- It acknowledges the inevitable presence of resistance to change.
- It focuses on people as the source of learning and change.
- It highlights the need to support new behaviors.

Refreezing
Stage in Lewin's force field model during which the newly learned behaviors and freshly implemented practices are encouraged and supported and become part of employees' routine activities

Nadler's Systems Model

David Nadler has proposed a model of change that uses a broad systems view of organizations.[38] According to Nadler, any change has a ripple or domino effect throughout an organization. The systems model suggests that to implement change managers must consider four elements:

- *Informal organizational elements* are factors such as communication patterns, leadership, and power.
- *Formal organizational elements* are formal organizational structures and work processes.
- *Individuals* are individual employees and managers, their individual characteristics, styles, attitudes, abilities, weaknesses, and so forth.
- *Tasks* are the assignments that managers and employees have.

In accordance with a systems view of organizations, change in any of these four elements leads to changes in others. For example, when a new CEO joins a company, she likely will create major and minor change throughout the organization. Similarly, an internal travel department's new company policy for travel reimbursement affects all employees and managers. Changing the criteria and requirements for hiring or promotion affects how individuals do their tasks, how they interact and organize to do their job, and how they communicate and supervise employees.

Changes in the system finally lead to new or transformed outputs. As an illustration, changes due to a new CEO's strategic leadership may increase investors' confidence in the company and lead to an increase in stock prices. The new travel reimbursement policy makes operations more efficient and saves the company money. The new criteria for hiring and promotion may slow down the staffing process and cause a problem in staffing various departments.

Summary Point 14.4   **What Are the Elements of Lewin's and Nadler's Models of Planned Change?**

- Lewin's force field analysis proposes that all organizations contain forces that drive change and forces that resist change.
- The three stages of change are unfreezing, change, and refreezing.

- Nadler proposes a model of organizational change based on the systems view of organizations. It assumes that change is a process in which inputs become outputs and change in any part of the system has the potential to affect all other parts.

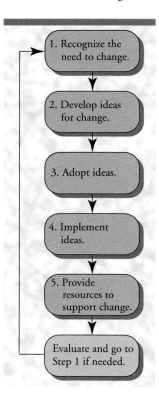

FIGURE 14.4
The Process of Planned Change

Process of Change

Whether through an analysis of forces for and against change or through understanding how organizational systems react during change, planned change follows the general process outlined in Figure 14.4. The process has six steps: recognize the need to change, develop ideas for change, adopt ideas, implement ideas, provide resources to support change, and evaluate.

The first step in the process is for managers and employees to recognize their dissatisfaction with current levels of performance. There may be a performance gap or managers may perceive that the organization is not taking advantage of an opportunity.[39] Recognition of the need to change starts the process of unfreezing described in Lewin's model.

The second step in the change process is to develop alternatives and ideas for change. Ideas can come from managers, employees, or customers. Any process that encourages participation and creativity is helpful in developing plans and ideas for addressing existing problems. For example, managers can use the decision-making models discussed in chapter 10. Furthermore, if those who will be most affected by the change are involved and participate in the development of alternatives and ideas, they are more likely to be motivated and committed to changing.

The next two steps are adoption and implementation of the change plan. These two steps are similar to Lewin's change phase. The final two steps—allocation of resources to make the change and evaluation—support the implementation phase. Organizations need to devote human, financial, and operational resources to ensure that the change is successful. Managers must train and reward employees, update technology and management styles, and so forth.

The planned change process is a continuous, dynamic loop. After managers and employees implement a change, they evaluate its effectiveness to assess whether the performance gap has closed. Did the change achieve its goals? Are customers satisfied? Is the organization more efficient? Are employees more motivated? If not, the change process starts over with the recognition of a need for change.

Returning to the Sears example, top management unveiled a three-step plan to make Sears a "compelling place to shop, work, and invest." The first part of this plan addresses the way Sears's employees should treat customers. The second part addresses how employees' morale and motivation must be raised so they will want to work at Sears. The final part of the plan focuses on how the organization will make sure Sears's shareholders get a good return on their investment. Managers have specific benchmarks to measure each of these goals and chart the company's progress in achieving them. In addition, Sears has drafted learning maps to visually display the ways the business is changing. The company encourages employees to use the maps to discuss changes in their work environment. Sears is hoping that the information on customer satisfaction combined with reinforcement from management on the three goals will make it a more productive and profitable organization.[40]

The process of change can originate at and be implemented by different levels within the organization. **Top-down change** is initiated and planned by managers at the top of the organization. Managers then charge employees at other levels with implementing the change and managing its effects. Top-down change fits well with hierarchical and traditional command-and-control organizations. It tends to force rapid change. The initial change at Sears was primarily top down.

Bottom-up change is initiated, planned, and implemented by employees at low levels of the organization. Although it typically involves issues that affect lower-level employees, as predicted by Nadler's systems model of change, its impact eventually spreads throughout the organization. Bottom-up change elicits considerably more involvement and participation by employees, thereby reducing the likelihood of their resisting. However, unless upper-level

Top-down change
Change initiated and planned by managers at the top of the organization

Bottom-up change
Change initiated, planned, and implemented by employees at low levels of the organization

managers are fully involved in planning the change, they may not support it or provide necessary resources to implement it fully.

Boundaryless and team-based organizations rely on bottom-up change, which encourages empowerment and employee responsibility. Employees at all levels are encouraged to identify problems and develop and implement solutions. Management empowers them with the authority and the responsibility for decision making and implementation. In a supportive organizational culture, the bottom-up approach can be both rapid and effective.

Change Agents

As organizations adopt ideas for change, individuals must accept responsibility for overseeing their implementation. **Change agents** are individuals who are experts at managing change and are charged with its implementation. Change agents can come from within the organization or be external consultants. External change agents benefit from not being involved with internal organizational politics and therefore having more credibility. However, internal change agents have considerably more knowledge about the organization and its needs and can plan and implement unique ideas. Organizations use a variety of internal change agents:

- **Idea champions** are employees who either volunteer or are assigned to focus on leading the change effort by overcoming resistance and obtaining necessary support and resources. They are also called *institutional entrepreneurs* or intrapreneurs. The best idea champions are employees who have developed a personal interest in the success of a new idea and have credibility within the organization. Many organizations use idea champions formally. For example, Ford and Chrysler both used Hal Sperlich as an idea champion to develop their minivans.[41]
- **Innovation departments** are formal departments in the organizational structure that are assigned the task of research and development of new ideas. The technical aspect of their job involves the development of ideas while the softer aspect involves preparing people for change. At Xerox Corp., for example, such departments develop and test new ideas and then follow them through to manufacturing.[42]
- **Venture teams** are temporary task forces or teams formed to develop ideas or carry out a change. The whole team acts as idea champions. Usually these teams have specific objectives and timetables. DuPont uses these teams to create and market new products and bring innovation and change to its organization. The teams are typically given only two weeks to make a "go" or "no go" decision on an idea. If the decision is to move forward, new teams form to start the project.[43]
- *Independent business units* are another type of change agent. If a new idea is risky and perhaps unrelated to the company's current business, an independent business unit is formed to develop and market it. For example, Hewlett-Packard created such a unit to develop and market its printers. When the idea first surfaced, Hewlett-Packard thought that printers were risky ventures unrelated to its core business of hardware and software design. By creating a separate business unit to develop its printers, Hewlett-Packard reduced its chances of damaging its name if the venture failed. The separate unit also had the advantage of being able to make quick decisions without constantly relying on approval from headquarters.[44] As it turned out, printers have become one of the most successful products Hewlett-Packard has ever developed.

Change agents
Individuals who are experts at managing change and are charged with its implementation

Idea champions (institutional entrepreneurs or intrapreneurs)
Employees who either volunteer or are assigned to focus on leading the change effort by overcoming resistance and obtaining necessary support and resources

Hot ▼ Link

We discussed intrapreneurship in chapter 1, pp. 25–26.

Innovation departments
Formal departments in the organizational structure that are assigned the task of research and development of new ideas

Venture teams
Temporary task forces or teams that are formed to develop ideas or carry out a change

Summary Point 14.5   **What Are the Elements of the Change Process and What Are Change Agents?**

- The first step in the change process is for managers and employees to recognize their dissatisfaction with current levels of performance.
- The second step is to develop alternatives and ideas for change.
- The next two steps are adoption and implementation of the change plan, which are similar to Lewin's change phase.

- After a change is implemented, its effectiveness is evaluated to assess whether the performance gap has closed.
- The process of change can originate and be implemented either from the top or the bottom.
- Organizations have developed a variety of formal internal change agents, including idea champions, innovation departments, venture teams, and independent business units.

DEALING WITH UNPLANNED CHANGE

We have reviewed models that illustrate the ways managers can plan and implement change. However, many organizations are forced to manage unplanned changes. The labor market changes. Unions go on strike. Competitors surprise you with an innovative product or service, or your predictions that the market is going in one direction prove wrong. How can an organization respond to these changes? Organizations can ignore the problem, assume the worst possible scenario and respond to the changes with all available resources, or take a middle-of-the-road position.

Managing unplanned change falls in the domain of *crisis management*. A crisis occurs when managers substantially misread the environment or are surprised by a competitor's actions. For instance, think back to Procter & Gamble's lack of preparation for its competitors' price strategies in the liquid laundry detergent market. As a result, P&G had to alter its production plans and devote much needed plant capacity to producing more liquid detergent. The problem had an upside: The company became more efficient in producing liquid detergents because it did not want to lose money on each sale.

Crisis also occurs when successful organizations become bureaucratic and rigid. Success breeds arrogance and complacency. In an environment of success, managers become less vigilant or ignore danger signs. Leo Burnett, an advertising agency with a long track record of success, created such well-known campaigns as United Airlines' "friendly skies" and the Pillsbury Doughboy. Its list of clients included other major companies such as Disney, Miller Brewing Company, and McDonald's. The company was a "world-class model of customer service and creativity." But its fortune has changed. United Airlines CEO Jerry Greenwald decided to give his company's account to Fallon McElligott, a small and highly innovative ad agency. Miller Brewing followed suit, switching its Miller Light account to Fallon. Leo Burnett's CEO was shocked and surprised by the move: "We were blind-sided."[45] Apparently, the ad agency had failed to meet customer needs and was relying on its long-standing relationships with clients. In losing the United Airlines account, CEO Fizdale notes: "They wanted to transform the airline. We still wanted to make ads. We didn't see that their needs had changed."[46] The loss of these major accounts has brought a sense of crisis to the Leo Burnett ad agency.

Once crises occur, it is difficult to control them. The cost to the organization, its human resources, and its various stakeholders is likely to be high. Organizations can manage unplanned change by taking the following actions before a crisis develops:[47]

- Avoid allowing the organization to become rigid, inflexible, formal, and hierarchical.
- Infuse moderate amounts of irrationality, unreliability, informality, and spontaneity into the organization. These characteristics prevent complacency.

- Instead of taking a defensive posture in the case of a crisis, go on the offensive with a new strategy.
- Replace top managers to bring in fresh ideas, methods, missions, and visions.
- Experiment continuously with new products, markets, technologies, structures, people, and methods.

A QUESTION OF ETHICS

| *Pay for Performance* | During the restructuring of organizations, top managers usually receive hefty salaries and severance packages, whereas employees are simply laid off. In contrast, the CEO of Union Carbide has tied his salary to the company's performance by agreeing to forfeit one year's pay if the organization misses its performance targets.[48] Should an executive's salary be tied to performance? What are the ethical implications for the executives and for shareholders? |

Summary Point 14.6   **How Do Companies Deal with Unplanned Change?**

- Organizations are forced to manage unplanned changes.
- Crisis occurs when managers misread the environment, are surprised by a competitor's actions, or when successful organizations become complacent.

- Unplanned change can be managed by avoiding rigid structures, introducing frequent change and moderate uncertainty, going on the offensive with new strategies, and changing leadership, products, and markets often.

ORGANIZATIONAL DEVELOPMENT AND LEARNING ORGANIZATIONS

Since the 1960s, management researchers and practitioners have paid special attention to models of managing planned change. By preparing organizations for planned change, these methods also can make managing unplanned change easier. Two issues are obvious. The hardest types of change and the most important ones are those that involve changing people and culture. No product or administrative or technological change can succeed if people do not support it. No organization can transform itself by simply changing management systems and structures. Deep-rooted assumptions and practices must be transformed as well. We next explore the concept of organizational development, which focuses on changing people, and the principles of organizational learning, which focus on wholesale cultural transformation and continuous improvement and growth.

Organizational Development

Organizational development (OD) is a discipline devoted to the implementation of systemwide planned change with a focus on people, organizational structure, and culture.[49] OD applies knowledge from different behavioral sciences such as psychology and sociology to improve organizational performance.

Principles and Steps   The goal of OD is to implement successful long-term planned change to which employees are committed. It aims to educate; change beliefs, assumptions, and attitudes; and transform behaviors.[50] Figure 14.5 presents the OD general principles. The *commitment to long-lasting change* in people and organizations, a *humanistic approach* that involves empowerment and cooperation, the use of *action research tools* to improve management practice, and a *focus on process* are at the heart of OD.

Organizational development (OD)
A discipline devoted to the implementation of systemwide change with a focus on people and organizational climate

FIGURE 14.5
Organizational Development Principles

The guiding principles translate into the OD process, which requires substantial time, resources, and commitment from the organization. Table 14.3 describes OD steps. The steps are often combined, but together they represent OD's action research orientation in which the focus is on employee involvement, careful and complete data gathering, open feedback and participation, and the development of joint solutions to implement change. Because OD considers all organizational aspects and systems, its success depends heavily on organizational commitment to its principles and methods. No OD effort can succeed without management support.

OD Methods   The aim of OD methods is to help the organization and its members unfreeze undesirable behaviors and practices, reduce resistance, adopt new attitudes and assumptions, and learn new behaviors.[51] The five OD methods that we review are survey feedback, sensitivity training, process counseling, team building, and the Managerial Grid®.

Table 14.3   **ORGANIZATIONAL DEVELOPMENT STEPS**

Steps	Description
Entry	Management recognizes the need for change and seeks the help of internal or external OD specialists to address problems.
Contracting	After a general evaluation of the problems, the OD specialists reach agreement with management about goals, expectations, and processes.
Diagnosis	OD specialists conduct extensive information gathering through one-on-one interviews, group meetings, questionnaires, review of existing documents, and so forth to diagnose the source of problems.
Feedback	OD specialists analyze and summarize data for the organization. Feedback and recomendations are presented and further clarification and suggestions are sought.
Planning Change	Based on the information gathered and feedback, a plan is devised to address the problems; commitment from the organization is sought.
Intervention	The change plan is implemented, leading to an intervention or change in the organization. Commitment from all members of the organization is essential.
Evaluation	The intervention is evaluated through a variety of methods, including surveys and interviews, and the need for further intervention is assessed.

Source: W. Burke, *Organizational Development*, 2d ed. (Reading, MA: Addison Wesley, 1994).

Survey Feedback   The use of surveys to assess employee attitudes, organizational climate, and differences in perceptions is **survey feedback**. The results help the organization identify and clarify problem issues in a systematic way that avoids personal attacks. It is one of the most-used OD techniques, often conducted independently by OD program specialists. Survey feedback provides efficient, relatively quick access to information from a broad group of employees. The key to the success of survey feedback is designing a reliable, valid survey that addresses relevant issues. The survey results should then help members spot potential problem areas and provide an impetus to positive, democratic discussion about ways to improve or rectify problems.

Sensitivity Training and Counseling   The OD method of using face-to-face unstructured small-group interaction to provide people with insight into themselves is known as **sensitivity training**. Its goal is to develop self-awareness and improve interpersonal interaction. The focus is on honesty, openness, and learning to share personal feelings and insights.[52] The newly developed skills and insights that employees gain from this training help them in their daily interactions at work. Companies also use individual counseling to provide employees with increased insight and self-awareness to help them in their work relationships.

Process Consultation   A common complaint from managers is that they have a general sense that something is hindering employee performance but they can't identify the specific problem. **Process consultation** involves an internal or external facilitator who works with individual managers to help improve their work relationships and processes. The facilitator observes the manager, provides feedback, discusses the manager's strengths and weaknesses, and helps the manager analyze interpersonal and individual process problems at work. Unlike sensitivity training and survey feedback, the aim is not to solve the organization's problems but to offer insight into how the manager can change to solve his or her problems.

Team Building   Team building includes various activities that help to develop trust and cohesion and promote effective, efficient working relationships in teams. The principles of sensitivity training are often a theme in team building as members are encouraged to share ideas and concerns openly and develop common understanding and solutions. Some popular team-building methods include survival exercises, white-water rafting, and mountain climbing.

Survey feedback
The use of surveys to assess employee attitudes and organizational climate with the goal of addressing issues identified through the survey results

Sensitivity training
Face-to-face, unstructured small-group interaction used to provide members insight about themselves and help them develop self-awareness

Process consultation
Facilitators working with managers on the job to identify problems and help improve relationships and processes

Hot ▼ Link
We discussed team building in chapter 8, pp. 279–86.

Many organizations use outdoor adventures and group activities to develop trust and cohesion in their teams. Playfair Inc. of Berkeley, California, develops team training exercises. Here, Playfair founder Matt Weinstein (right) and colleagues experiment with an exercise they developed—designing a sculpture of craft materials that symbolizes the firm's mission.

Numerous organizations such as firefighting units, police departments, and bomb squads use weekend teaming to enhance the level of understanding and sharing in their teams. Nike, H-P, Motorola, Boeing, and thousands of other organizations do the same.

Managerial Grid® One of the most-used OD methods is the Managerial Grid® developed by Robert Blake and Jane Mouton.[53] The grid focuses on teaching managers to increase their concern for people and their concern for production which, according to the theory, are both essential for organizational performance.

Does OD work? Research findings are mixed and the methodology of many studies appears flawed. However, an overall review of findings suggests that the positive effects of changes in organizational processes are more evident than changes in individuals.[54] Because OD involves a variety of different methods and techniques, it is not always possible to evaluate each method's impact or their combined overall effectiveness. Furthermore, OD is practice oriented and always theory driven, making it even harder to test.[55]

In addition, some methods such as sensitivity training and the Managerial Grid® have lost their popularity for more pragmatic reasons—the expense and the time it takes to implement them. However, the OD themes of focusing on people, viewing organizations as systems, and using action research as the basis for change continue to be used in many change efforts in organizations. Like any other change effort, OD requires strong support from the organization's leadership.[56]

Summary Point 14.7   **What Is Organizational Development?**

- Organizational development (OD) is a discipline devoted to the implementation of systemwide change with a focus on people and the organizational climate.

- OD principles include commitment to long-term change and a humanistic approach, action research, and a focus on developing effective internal processes.
- OD methods include survey feedback, sensitivity training, process consultation, and team building.

Learning Organizations

As many organizations struggle with the need for revival or survival, they understand the importance of changing their cultures in fundamental ways.[57] Companies in the United States and other Western countries fight to renew themselves and remain flexible and able to compete with innovative entrepreneurial firms. Their survival and that of other organizations depends on their ability to handle carefully planned change and to change continually. In his book *The Fifth Discipline*, Peter Senge proposes the concept of *learning organizations* to address the importance of flexibility and the ability to learn, adapt, change, and create continuously.[58]

Learning organizations
Organizations in which people continually expand their capacity to create, where innovation and cooperation are nurtured, and where knowledge is transferred throughout the organization

Learning organizations are organizations in which people continually expand their capacity to create, where innovation and cooperation are nurtured, and where knowledge is transferred throughout the organization. The learning organization learns and creates faster than its competitors and this ability becomes a major competitive advantage. Learning organizations do not simply manage planned change; their goal is to become a place where creativity, flexibility, adaptation, change, and learning are everyday processes and thus an integral part of the culture.[59]

The Five Disciplines The five disciplines that form the core of learning organizations are summarized in Table 14.4. The disciplines focus on people and organizations' ability to learn new approaches and new behaviors by understanding their existing patterns, developing new patterns through thinking together, and supporting and encouraging the use of the new patterns.

Table 14.4   THE FIVE DISCIPLINES OF LEARNING ORGANIZATIONS

Discipline	Description
Personal mastery	Continually clarifying and developing personal goals and visions and developing special levels of proficiency
Mental models	Being aware of existing mental models and developing new ones based on openness and inquiry
Building a shared vision	Binding people through a common identity and a common picture of the future that builds commitment rather than compliance
Team learning	Developing synergy and the ability to think together by suspending assumptions
Systems thinking	Being bound by invisible fabrics and interrelated actions; all people and issues are connected

Sources: P. M. Senge, "Creating Learning Communities," *Executive Excellence* 14, no. 3 (1997): 17–18; P. M. Senge, "Leading Learning Organizations," *Training and Development* 50, no. 12 (1995): 36–37; P. M. Senge and J. D. Sterman, "Systems Thinking and Organizational Learning: Acting Locally and Thinking Globally in the Organization of the Future," *European Journal of Operations Research* 59, no. 1 (1992): 137–40; P. M. Senge, *The Fifth Discipline: The Art and Practice of the Learning Organization* (New York: Doubleday, 1990).

The binding theme of the five disciplines is the fifth one: *systems thinking*. Being able to see the interrelationship among people and among organizational elements—rather than considering linear cause-and-effect chains—is essential to understanding how organizations function. The systems view allows for integration of all the other disciplines. Senge suggests: "At the heart of learning organizations is a shift of mind—from seeing ourselves as separate from the world to connected to the world, from seeing problems as caused by someone or something 'out there' to seeing how our own actions create the problems we experience. A learning organization is a place where people are continually discovering how they create their reality. And how they can change it."[60]

Organizational Learning Disabilities   A variety of factors prevent organizations from reaching their potential and from learning to adapt, create, and be flexible. All these factors, shown in Figure 14.6, stem from an absence of systems thinking. Instead, the organization considers jobs, tasks, events, practices, and behaviors as isolated rather than interrelated.[61]

The *functional and operational boundaries* that define clear jobs and separate different people are one of the first blocks to learning. Tasks, functions, and jobs are isolated. The boundaries in turn lead employees to see themselves as isolated rather than part of a whole and teach them not to care about other parts.

Two other organizational learning disabilities are *ignoring gradual change* and *focusing on events*. When organizations focus only on sudden changes and specific events, they ignore gradual change. They also look for specific and clear causes to problems rather than considering systemwide obstacles. Because the organizations do not consider gradual processes and the inter-

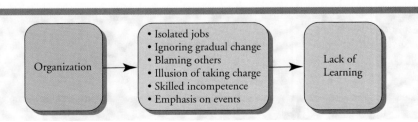

FIGURE 14.6
Blocks to Learning in Organizations

relatedness of events, they do not adapt or learn well. Associated with these two factors is the tendency for managers to *take charge* and jump into action. This is particularly true in the cultures of the United States or Germany where proactiveness and gaining control over the environment are valued. Rather than observing and learning, managers aggressively attack issues.

A consequence of this proactive approach is the tendency to *blame others* for problems. Identifying internal or external enemies who are the cause of a company's problems prevents it from carefully and thoughtfully considering its contributions to the problems. A final organizational learning disability is *skilled incompetence*. Generally, an organization strives to hire the most skilled people and rewards them for finding answers and solving problems. The organization considers them experts. As a result, they may learn not to admit mistakes or ignorance. Because they do not admit their mistakes, they do not ask questions, cannot learn, and slowly become skilled but incompetent managers. The lack of inquiry prevents people from seeing the real issues.

Consider the case of Advanced Micro Devices (AMD) and its CEO Jerry Sanders. Under his leadership the company has tried twice to compete with Intel with its K5 and K6 chips and has failed. Each time Sanders has blamed others for his failures. To make matters worse, AMD's board of directors has rewarded him with higher pay, even though the company's stock price keeps declining. AMD exhibits the symptoms of organizational learning disability. Rather than looking for system-oriented solutions internally—and perhaps a new CEO—the company has concentrated on selling products that have proven failures in the market.[62]

Applying the Five Disciplines Organizations can use Peter Senge's five disciplines to become learning systems. Table 14.5 highlights the factors that contribute to learning in organizations.

CAREER ADVICE
from the Experts

LEARNING BUSINESS LANGUAGES

As we learn new skills and gain more business experience, experts urge us to learn to speak many "languages."

- Learn to speak all the functional languages of a business, including accounting, marketing, production, and so forth. Coursework and reading can provide a foundation. Personal interaction in all fields can further build your linguistic skills.
- Volunteer for assignments in various divisions so that you learn about the whole organization rather than just one part.
- Change divisions formally or accept interesting challenges from other firms. Even though these lateral shifts may mean demotions or lower salaries in the short run, the potential payoff of cross-training is high.
- Set learning goals and monitor your progress carefully, making adjustments as needed.
- Above all, focus on learning from both your own and others' successes and failures.

Sources: Based on H. Lancaster, "Learn 'Languages' and You Will Always Land on Your Feet," *Wall Street Journal*, October 24, 1997, B1; also see T. Peters, *The Pursuit of Wow!* (New York: Vintage, 1994).

Table 14.5   FACTORS THAT ENCOURAGE
              LEARNING IN ORGANIZATIONS

Factor	Description
Openness to new ideas	Willingness to question everything and to use all available tools to explore new ideas
Local solutions	Allowing each person, team, or department to find and implement its own solutions without concern for standardization
Time for learning	Providing managers with time and resources to learn new ideas and try them out; focus on long-term results
Stewardship	Leading organizations through providing direction, guidance, and service to others rather than command and control

Many of these factors are already being applied in organizations that have adopted team-based and boundaryless structures and implemented empowerment. The first step in becoming a learning organization is to be *open to new ideas*, which involves not only encouraging participation in decision making but displaying a willingness to question one's assumptions and acquiring the skills required to do so.[63] Critical thinking, creativity skills, the application of scientific testing methods, such as those used in TQM, and learning to distinguish between facts and generalizations are all skills that one can use to remain open to learning.

The second factor is allowing for the *development of local solutions* and local ideas.[64] Instead of controlling from the top and imposing ideas developed by a few managers, employees and managers at all levels develop and implement their own solutions. Empowerment imposed from the top misses its target, as does forcing the creation of teams where they are not needed, or imposing a structure that does not fit a department's environment or strategy. Having local solutions reduces what is traditionally considered management control. The kind of control managers exercise should be a shared vision that guides all actions as opposed to controlling employees' every action.

All employees and managers should be given *time and opportunities to learn*, reflect, train, and develop new skills and new competencies. Most organizations readily recognize the need for technical training. Few, however, recognize the need for time to analyze, reflect, and simply think. Research tells us that managers do not have time to reflect, they tend simply to move from crisis to crisis.[65] Unfortunately, organizations still have not addressed this issue as they continue to demand and reward quick actions.

Finally, learning organizations require a new form of leadership. Some have called it *stewardship*.[66] **Stewards** are leaders who develop a general vision while remaining partners with their employees and customers and concentrating on serving them to help them accomplish goals.[67] They may be unseen and are often unappreciated. They set general directions, help develop a shared vision, continue to contribute as individuals, and give up much of the power and privilege traditionally associated with organizational leaders and managers.

Herman Miller, the world's largest furniture maker, practices the principles of learning organizations. CEO Ed Simon explains his mission-driven belief in learning organizations: "I see organizational learning as learning how to accept, embrace, and seek change."[68] Herman Miller uses internal practices that encourage creativity in its furniture designs. It is known for empowering employees, using a flat structure that deemphasizes status, and having a single-minded focus on respect for and training of employees. Ed Simon believes that for his organization to be creative, it "requires a new paradigm, a new model of how organizations work—organizations that operate in a continual learning mode, creating change."[69]

Stewards
Leaders who develop a general vision while remaining partners with their employees and customers and concentrating on serving them to help them accomplish their goals

---

Summary Point 14.8   **What Are Learning Organizations?**

- Learning organizations are organizations where people continually expand their capacity to create, where innovation and cooperation are nurtured, and where knowledge is transferred throughout the organization.
- The five disciplines of learning organizations are personal mastery, mental models, a shared vision, team learning, and systems thinking.

- Organizational learning disabilities include having isolated jobs, blaming others, ignoring gradual change, following a tendency to take charge and emphasize events, and allowing skilled incompetence.
- Openness, encouraging local solutions, providing time for learning and reflection, and implementing new leadership all encourage learning in organizations.

Change *in Context*

Implementing change is one of the biggest challenges managers face. Change in any part of the organization has a ripple effect that spreads to other parts. It is therefore essential for managers at all levels to think about change in a systemwide strategic fashion. To implement change successfully, managers must actively manage all five contextual strategic forces: the environment, technology, strategy, structure, and culture. We offer some highlights for managers to keep in mind as they step back to see how change affects the entire organization.

The environment, crowded with competitors and customers whose demands change often, spurs organizations to change. As a result, reading the environment accurately and recognizing the need for change is essential. Being aware of globalization and the impact of culture is one key challenge. Another is focusing on rapidly changing technologies. Changes in technologies trigger commensurate changes in how organizations transform their inputs into outputs and how they serve customers. The explosion of information technology along with revolutionary and innovative uses of computers in manufacturing and service delivery are changing how people work and what they can achieve. Successful organizations and effective managers understand and incorporate these changes as they address their customers' needs.

Managers must change their strategies, structures, and cultures in response to environmental and technological pressures for innovation and change. They must devise new missions, reorganize people, and change their assumptions and values. Ignoring any one of the strategic forces for any length of time can be disastrous at worst. At best, it hampers organizational flexibility, adaptability, and responsiveness.

If managers design organizations that continuously learn, adapt, and change, there will be less need for frame-breaking change. For the most part, revolutionary change becomes necessary when managers enact their environment poorly or misconceive the organization's mission and strategy. Revolutionary change, of course, often requires a change of management, so it is in managers' best interest to pay attention to the effect of change on the context of the organization.

McDonald's, the world's largest restaurant and for many around the world a key symbol of U.S. pop culture, has struggled for many years to implement change successfully. The company has experienced considerable international growth partly because of its ability to take culture into consideration (for example, vegetarian burgers in India).

The global success and flexibility have not been matched inside the United States, where McDonald's has lost market share to Burger King and other fast-food chains. As a result

McDonald's franchise owners have not been happy with the company's growth plans.[70] Franchisees also have struggled with their lack of autonomy to respond to local customers and competitors. Because McDonald's is based on extensive standardization that assures uniform quality, the company has been reluctant to provide increased autonomy. McDonald's has not yet been able to adjust its strategies and structure to respond to internal and external pressures for change.

The company's culture and leadership seem to provide a barrier to change. McDonald's CEO, Michael Quinlan, states: "Do we have to change? No, we don't have to change. We have the most successful brand in the world."[71] Warren Berris, a respected leadership professor at the University of Southern California, blames the company's leadership for its lack of flexibility. He observes that "this board is so stale, it's hard to imagine it asking the right questions."[72]

In spite of an unwillingness to change its strategies, structure, and culture, the company has tried to respond to customer demands for healthier foods and the increased taste for ethnic foods by test marketing carrot sticks, pasta, chicken fajitas, and McLean Deluxe hamburgers. None has been successful.

McDonald's provides an excellent example of a successful and well-established organization that struggles with discovering the type and level of change it can introduce and implement effectively. Its success in some areas along with its less than stellar record in others illustrate the considerable challenge today's managers face in managing change.

For updated information on the topics in this chapter, Web exercises, links to related Web sites, an on-line study guide, and more, visit our companion Web site at:
http://www.prenhall.com/nahavandi

A Look Back at the

MANAGERIAL CHALLENGE

DaimlerChrysler

Jurgen Schrempp faced a bumpy road ahead when he took the wheel as CEO of Daimler-Benz in 1995. But a formidable combination of external and internal forces propelled the CEO toward plans for change. Externally, the worldwide recession and foreign exchange problems of the early 1990s had hampered global vehicle sales. Also, the company had not done well against the updated styling, lower prices, and customer-friendly services offered by competing luxury cars such as Lexus and Acura. Another external factor was the accelerating demand for sport utility vehicles—which Mercedes did not offer.

Internally, poor sales and lower-than-expected profits were extremely powerful forces for change. Daimler's 1980s "integrated technology" strategy had led to acquisitions in other industries, but these acquisitions were never successfully blended into the overall organization. The appointment of Schrempp as CEO became a new internal force for change.

Knowing that he needed the support of Daimler's unions to reduce resistance to upcoming changes, the CEO negotiated new union contracts that provided job protection for several years. He also created an incentive plan allowing all 140,000 employees to qualify for bonuses based on their contribution to company profitability. In exchange, the union made concessions on wages and work rules.[73]

In other changes, Schrempp sliced off a layer of top management, sold off a number of unprofitable business units—significantly reducing the workforce—and began promoting "value-driven management" with higher goals for improved performance.[74] Just as important, his product and pricing changes resulted in more affordable Mercedes cars, the marketing of a new sport utility model, and the creation of a two-seat Smart car specifically for the European market. These changes raised sales to record levels, putting Daimler back on the road to steady profits.[75]

Then Schrempp planned the merger with Chrysler in 1998, bringing major, long-term changes to the company. The Daimler of 1998 is very different from the one Schrempp inherited in 1995, and it will be for the foreseeable future.

■ Point of View Exercises

You're the Manager: As an assembly line supervisor in the Mercedes plant in Tuscaloosa, Alabama, you oversee employees who work on the M-class sport utility vehicle models. In keeping with Schrempp's "value-driven management" initiative, you want to set higher goals for improved performance in your area. What resistance to bottom-up change might you encounter among your employees?

You're the Employee: As an assembly line worker in Tuscaloosa, you are being asked to participate in setting and meeting higher goals for improved performance. What would you tell management to do to make you more comfortable with the changes that are coming? For example, in what ways would you like to be involved with the decisions that will be made?

SUMMARY OF LEARNING OBJECTIVES

1. **Identify and analyze the external and internal forces for change in organizations, the influence of culture on change, and the various types of change.** Organizational change is the transformation of or adjustment to the way an organization functions. External forces for change are those factors that are part of an organization's business environment and cultural context. Internal forces arise from inside the organization and issues related to the internal functioning of organizations. National cultural values of tolerance for ambiguity and perception and use of time affect how managers view and manage change.

    Planned change occurs as a result of conscious effort from managers or employees in response to a specific problem. Unplanned change occurs randomly and spontaneously without specific intention to address a problem. Evolutionary or convergent change is gradual, incremental, narrow in focus, revolutionary or frame-breaking change is rapid and dramatic, and carries a sense of urgency and crisis. Organizational elements that are changed to adapt to the environment include technology, product, administration and management, and human resources.

2. **Summarize the causes and methods of overcoming resistance to change.** The causes of resistance to change are divided among organizational, group, and individual factors. Organizational culture and organizational inertia, the tendency to oppose change and to maintain the status quo, can result in such inflexibility that the organization cannot change. Two group-related factors that affect resistance to change are group norms and group cohesion. Individuals resist change because they fear its consequences, their comfortable routines are disrupted, they face unfamiliar situations, they have to learn new skills and are uncertain about several individual differences.

3. **Describe Lewin's force field analysis and Nadler's systems model, the process of change, and the role of change agents.** Lewin's force field analysis proposes that organizations have forces that drive change and forces that resist change. The forces interact in three stages of unfreezing, change, and freezing. Lewin's model recognizes change as an ongoing process that depends on people's acceptance. Nadler proposes a model of organizational change that uses a broad systems view of organizations. Accordingly, change in any part of the system always triggers change in other parts.

    The steps in planned change are recognizing the need for change, developing alternatives and ideas for change, adoption and implementation of the change plan, and evaluating the change.

    The process of change can originate and be implemented either from the top or the bottom. Organizations use internal change agents to promote and implement change. These change agents include idea champions, innovation departments, venture teams, and independent business units.

4. **Specify how organizations deal with unplanned change.** Organizations are forced to manage unplanned changes and manage crises that occur when managers misread the environment or are surprised by a competitor's actions, or when successful organizations become arrogant and complacent. Unplanned change can be managed by avoiding rigid structures, introducing frequent change and moderate uncertainty, going on the offensive, and changing leadership, products, and markets often.

5. **Describe the concepts and methods of organization development and the principles, obstacles, and requirements of learning organizations.** Organizational development (OD) is a discipline devoted to the implementation of systemwide change with a focus on people and organizational climate. Its principles include commitment to long-term change and a humanistic approach, action research, and focus on developing effec-

tive internal processes. OD methods include survey feedback, sensitivity training, process consultation, and team building.

Learning organizations are organizations where people continually expand their capacity to create, where innovation and cooperation are nurtured, and where knowledge is transferred throughout the organization. The five disciplines of learning organizations are personal mastery, mental models, building a shared vision, team learning, and systems thinking. Openness, encouraging local solutions, providing time for learning and reflection, and implementing new leadership all encourage learning in organizations.

KEY TERMS

bottom-up change, p. 508
change agents, p. 509
convergent change, p. 497
evolutionary change, p. 497
external forces for change,
  p. 493
idea champions (institutional entrepreneurs or
  intrapreneurs), p. 509
innovation, p. 493
innovation departments,
  p. 509

internal forces for change,
  p. 493
learning organizations,
  p. 514
organizational change,
  p. 501
organizational
  development, p. 511
organizational inertia,
  p. 501
performance gap, p. 495
planned change, p. 496

process consultation, p. 513
refreezing, p. 507
revolutionary change for
  frame-breaking change,
  p. 497
sensitivity training, p. 513
stewards, p. 517
survey feedback, p. 513
top-down change, p. 508
unfreezing, p. 506
unplanned change, p. 497
venture teams, p. 509

REVIEW QUESTIONS

1. List the internal and external factors that force organizations to change.
2. Compare and contrast planned and unplanned and evolutionary and revolutionary change.
3. Why do organizations and people resist change and what methods can managers use to overcome resistance to change?
4. List the different types of internal change agents organizations use.
5. What do Lewin's and Nadler's models for planned change teach managers?
6. How do organizations deal with unplanned change?
7. Compare and contrast the principles and goals of OD and learning organizations.

DISCUSSION QUESTIONS

1. To what extent can today's organizations prevent change?
2. Should managers encourage planned and evolutionary change to prevent unplanned and revolutionary change? Why? Why not?
3. Which methods of overcoming resistance to change are most useful in today's team-based organizations? Why? What are the implications?
4. To what extent do you think the principles of learning organizations can be implemented in organizations today? What are the obstacles that managers may face?

▶ **SELF-ASSESSMENT 14**
Developing Creativity

Being open to change is to a great extent a function of being creative. Although creativity is partly a personality trait, individuals can enhance their personal creativity in several ways. Rate each statement according to how well it applies to you by using the following scale: 1 = never; 2 = some of the time; 3 = always. See Appendix 3 for a scoring key.

1.	My life is so hectic, I have no time to pay attention to anything new.	1	2	3
2.	I set daily goals for myself and focus on getting them done.	1	2	3
3.	I put in considerable effort to do something well when I do it.	1	2	3
4.	I have clear priorities about what is important to me and what is not.	1	2	3
5.	I look for ways of making things I enjoy more complex and challenging.	1	2	3
6.	I know what I like and don't like in life.	1	2	3
7.	I face problems head-on and look for solutions immediately.	1	2	3
8.	I am disorganized and feel that my schedule is out of control.	1	2	3
9.	I often surprise others with my unexpected actions or words.	1	2	3
10.	My office/home is organized in a way that calms me and supports my activities.	1	2	3
11.	I rarely follow through on things that spark my interest.	1	2	3
12.	I keep routine things simple so that I have energy to focus on what is important.	1	2	3
13.	I make time for relaxation and reflection.	1	2	3
14.	I approach problems by trying to develop as many solutions as possible before I try to solve them.	1	2	3
15.	I stop and look at unusual things, people, and events around me.	1	2	3

Source: Developed based on information in M. Csikszentmihalyi, *Creativity: Flow and the Psychology of Discovery and Invention* (New York: HarperPerennial, 1996).

▶ **TEAM EXERCISE 14**
Analyzing and Planning for Change

This exercise is designed to provide you with the experience of analyzing the need for change in a given situation and conducting basic planning for the change.

PART I: FORM TEAMS AND SELECT A PROBLEM

In teams of three to five members, select a problem (organizational or personal) that one team member faces that requires change. Potential examples include the following: the people you supervise take long breaks; the group you belong to in one of your classes is unfocused; the spring program committee that you lead at your child's school cannot decide on anything; customers are ignored and mistreated, and so on. Note that each of these problems—and any you are likely to identify—involves many different individual and organizational issues we have discussed in the book.

PART II: ANALYZE THE SITUATION

- Write a brief description of the problem.
- Verbally restate the problem in as many ways as you can.
- Consider all the positive and negative aspects of the problem.
- Consider all the related issues.
- Agree on a final description of the problem.

PART III: PLAN FOR CHANGE

- Identify as many alternative solutions as you can without evaluating each (brainstorming).
- Evaluate each solution carefully; consider its positive and negative aspects, whether it can work, and so on.
- Select one solution as the best; it does not have to be perfect, just the best one based on your team's analysis.
- Decide on the strategy you will use to implement your solution. Issues you need to consider:
  - The people and resources you need to implement your idea
  - The major obstacles to implementation
  - Key people (idea champions) and resources that can help you implement
  - Training needs
  - Costs
  - Timetable
  - How to measure success

PART IV: PRESENTATION

Each team will make a five- to ten-minute presentation of the results of their analysis and planning.

UP CLOSE

▶ Pushing the Sales Team into the Twenty-First Century

The five-person industrial sales team at Link USA, a long-distance phone services company, was responsible for selling phone systems and long-distance services to small- and medium-size companies. Team members, who had been working together for several years, had turned their skills and methods into a fine art. They not only performed well and reached all their goals, but they also supported one another through training and customer support. Although they were on commission and thus intensely competitive, they were also good friends and socialized outside work.

The team had developed a comfortable routine. Because members were on the road often, they were rarely in the office during regular hours. They often came in at night and on weekends to work and catch up with one another. Although Link USA had an extensive electronic database system for tracking customers, the sales team still relied on notes and oral communication to keep track of clients. The system worked well within the team, but others inside the company could not always get the information they needed.

Billing services in particular was always complaining about the team's secrecy, lack of cooperation, and unwillingness to use proper procedures. The accounting manager, Terry Sanchez, said of the team: "They sign all these new accounts and new features and don't bother to tell us or enter them properly into the system. We find out about it too late, and then get blamed for not being on top of things. We are an information company. Should we not have our internal information process straightened out?"

The complaints got so loud that Glen Bartolo, CEO of USA Link, intervened. After discussion with the information systems people and marketing managers and with help from an outside consultant, a state-of-the-art client-tracking system was selected to help the team. The system was high-tech, jazzy, easy to use, and effective. It had been used successfully in other companies. Bartolo loved it. Data could be entered by writing on the screen with a special pen or through the key pad, then immediately transferred to the company through phones. The system also had several handy features such as client notes that allowed reps to make personal comments about their clients.

Each salesperson received a minicomputer notepad and two hours of training. The whole team showed up, finished the course, and stated that they were excited about the new system, which was to be implemented immediately. Two weeks later, no data had been entered through any of the computers. The sales team leader, Travis Andersen, assured Bartolo and other managers that team members were just adjusting and would be using it soon. Six weeks after the initial training, it became obvious that instead of entering data quickly as had been the goal, the team members were using the system once every few weeks and only when they were in the office.

The information systems (IS) and marketing managers met with the sales team. The youngest member of the sales team, Jennifer Lee, was the first to speak out: "The system is really cute and cool and kind of easy to use. But it just is not worth my time; I can do things quicker without it." Andersen added: "What we really need is access to a fax to just send in orders. We don't need this stuff." When the IS manager pointed out that all the forms were already on the system and could simply be filled out, Andersen complained that it took too long and was too complicated. Another team member could not understand why they had to enter so much data that no one else needed. If accounting wanted things faster, he said, all they had to do was ask. When she was told that she was rarely in during regular hours, she still insisted that she was always just a phone call away, that her customers had no trouble finding her, and she could not understand why accounting had problems. The meeting was adjourned, with the team members making vague commitments to make better use of the new system.

The sales team met after work that day at the local coffee shop. They complained about the rest of the company not understanding their job and being too wrapped up in high-tech equipment to focus on the customer. Lee was particularly upset that no one seemed to care what they or their customers needed. Diane Nugyen, another member summarized everyone's feeling: "We make sure that we take care of our customers. That's how we get the accounts and that's how we keep them. Management likes that, but they don't care how we get there. They are all wrapped up in their high-tech stuff. They just don't know what we need and what it takes to keep making our customers happy. The secret to our success is not a few cute notes on a fancy note pad! We need a better product and faster customer service, so we can sell even more."

Questions

1. What are the causes of the sales team's resistance to change?
2. If you were brought in as a consultant what would you do now?

THE BIG PICTURE

▶ Following a Legend at Coca-Cola

When M. Douglas Ivester was named CEO of Coca-Cola in 1997 after the untimely death of Roberto Goizueta, he became the steward of one of the world's best-known brands. Hand-picked by Goizueta as his successor, Ivester was replacing a leader whose accomplishments can only be described as "legendary." In 16 years as CEO, Goizueta had spearheaded a massive global expansion that increased Coca-Cola's market value from $4 billion in 1981 to an astounding $145 billion by 1997.[76] Now that Ivester had been tapped to run the company, employees and stockholders alike wondered what changes he would make.

Ivester joined Coca-Cola in 1979 as an auditor and rose steadily through the ranks to become chief financial officer. During the 1980s, he served first as the president of Coca-Cola's European unit and then as the president of the North American division. Settling into the CEO position, Ivester knew that his knowledge of marketing was limited, but he made it his business to learn. In the months following his appointment, he scheduled a series of one-on-one sessions with internal experts who briefed him on marketing, legal issues, child care, and other topics.

Ivester's fiercely competitive nature was a definite asset in the soft drink industry, where Coca-Cola was being targeted by global giants such as Pepsi-Cola as well as smaller local firms. He staked out his company's leadership position several years ago when he told an audience of soft-drink managers: "I want your customers. I want your space on the shelves. I want your share of the consumer's stomach. And I want every single bit of beverage growth potential that exists out there."[77]

Some industry analysts and competitors questioned Ivester's aggressive tactics, noting that rivals might be entirely shut out of many larger retail outlets if the chains signed exclusive contracts with Coca-Cola. Meanwhile, Ivester pushed ahead with the company's strategy of working with larger bottlers to maximize economies of scale within the vast bottling and distribution system. He also encouraged new product ideas while working toward even higher soft drink sales all over the world.

No matter what changes Ivester made in the months and years ahead, he clearly recognized that the future success of Coca-Cola was based, in large part, on the groundwork laid by Goizueta. In announcing higher company earnings soon after his appointment as CEO, Ivester stated: "It's a great legacy to build on, and gives us all great strength—and enviable capabilities—for 1998 and beyond."[78] Change was inevitable, but would Ivester follow a planned and measured path, or would he completely restructure the company in preparation for new competitive initiatives?

Questions

1. What internal and external forces for change seemed to have the greatest influence on Coca-Cola after Ivester's appointment as CEO?
2. Why do you think Coca-Cola was able to avoid a period of crisis after Roberto Goizueta's unexpected death from lung cancer?
3. If you were Ivester, would you choose evolutionary change or frame-breaking change to strengthen Coca-Cola's competitive position? Explain your answer.

NOTES

1. Alex Taylor, "'Neutron Jurgen' Ignites a Revolution at Daimler-Benz," *Fortune* (November 10, 1997): 144–52.
2. Ibid.
3. Ibid.
4. A. Taylor III, "Gentlemen, Start Your Engines," *Fortune* 137, no. 11 (June 8, 1998): 138–46.
5. Ibid., 144.
6. R. L. Daft, "Bureaucratic versus Nonbureaucratic Structure in the Process of Innovation and Change," in S. B. Bacharach (ed.), *Perspectives in Organizational Sociology: Theory and Research* (Greenwich, CT: JAI, 1982): 129–66; R. A. Burgelman and M. A. Maidique, *Strategic Management of Technology and Innovation* (Homewood, IL: Irwin, 1988).
7. T. Parker-Pope, "Boom in Liquid Has P&G Scrambling," *Wall Street Journal*, September 25, 1997, B1.
8. "Save the Planet: Getting Clean, Staying Green," *Glamour* (October 19, 1996), accessed on-line at www.ecomat.com/Glamour_mag.html; "Gunter Pauli Cleans Up," *Fast Company* (November 1993), accessed on-line at www.fastcompany.com.
9. J. Karp, "Firms Find Loosening in India's Labor Practices," *Wall Street Journal*, October 13, 1997, A16.
10. Ibid.
11. "Fortune 1000," *Fortune* 138, no. 8 (April 27, 1998): F45.
12. C. Quintanilla and J. Carlton, "Whirlpool Unveils Global Restructuring Effort," *Wall Street Journal*, September 19, 1997, A3.
13. N. Deogun, "PepsiCo Looks to Outsider Marineau to Supply New Ideas and Inspiration," *Wall Street Journal*, September 25, 1997, B11.
14. J. J. Keller, "AT&T Board Faces Many Twists and Turns in Search for New CEO," *Wall Street Journal*, October 13, 1997, A1, A6.
15. F. Rose, "In Los Angeles, *Times*'s Willes Starts Overhaul," *Wall Street Journal*, September 25, 1997, B1, B6.
16. P. Evan, "Japan's Green Aid," *China Business Review* 21, no. 4 (1994): 39–44; G. Copplestone, "MITI Cuts Japan Loose," *Management Today* (January 1995): 44–49.
17. J. M. Schlesinger, "U.S. Company Shows Foreign Nations Ways to Grow Much Faster," *Wall Street Journal*, June 16, 1997, A1, A12.
18. M. A. Hitt, R. A. Hoskisson, and R. D. Ireland, "A Mid-Range Theory of the Interactive Effects of International and Product Diversification on Innovation and Performance," *Journal of Management* 20 (1994): 297–326.
19. See M. L. Tushman, W. H. Newman, and E. Romanelli, "Convergence and Upheaval: Managing the Unsteady Pace of Organizational Evolution," *California Management Review* (Fall 1986).
20. For a presentation of general TQM principles, see E. W. Deming, *Out of Crisis* (Cambridge, MA: MIT Press, 1989).
21. "Small Firm Praised for Big E-Policies," *Environment Today* 5, no. 11 (1994): 11.
22. Tushman, Newman, and Romanelli, "Convergence and Upheaval."
23. V. Reitman, "With Mercedes's New M-Class, Make That M for Mania," *Wall Street Journal*, October 9, 1997, B1, B9.
24. M. T. Hannon and J. Freeman, "Structural Inertia and Organizational Change," *American Sociological Review* 49 (1994): 149–64.
25. For discussion of factors that contribute to inertia, see L. E. Greiner, "Evolution and Revolutions Organizations Grow," *Harvard Business Review* (July–August 1972): 37–46; R. M. Kanter, *When Giants Learn to Dance: Mastering the Challenges of Strategy* (New York: Simon & Schuster, 1989).
26. R. Narisetti, "IBM to Revamp Struggling Home-PC Business," *Wall Street Jorunal*, October 13, 1997, B1, B6.
27. A. S. Judson, *Changing Behavior in Organizations: Minimizing Resistance to Change* (Camdrige, MA: Basil Blackwell, 1991).
28. A. Fisher, "The World's Most Admired Companies," *Fortune* (October 27, 1997): 220–40.
29. Ibid., 234.
30. K. Mieskowski, "The Power of Public Relations," *Fast Company* (April–May 1998): 192.
31. W. A. Pasmore and M. R. Fagans, "Participation, Individual Development, and Organizational Change: A Review and Synthesis," *Journal of Management* (June 1992): 375–97.
32. Judson, *Changing Behavior.*
33. K. Lewin, *Field Theory in Social Science* (New York: Harper and Row, 1951).
34. S. Sherman, "Bringing Sears into the New World," *Fortune* 136, no. 7 (October 13, 1997): 183–84.
35. Ibid.
36. Ibid., 184.
37. Ibid.
38. D. A. Nadler, "Concept for the Management of Organized Change," in M. L. Tushman and N. L. Moore (eds.), *Reading in Management Innovation*, 2d ed. (Cambridge, MA: Ballinger, 1988): 718–31.
39. The description of the change process is based on information presented in R. Daft, *Organization Theory and Design*, 3d ed. (St. Paul, MN: West, 1989).
40. Sherman, "Bringing Sears."
41. See R. A. Burgelman and L. R. Sayles, *Inside Corporate Innovation* (New York: Free Press, 1986).
42. Examples cited in T. L. Wheelen and J. D. Hunger, *Strategic Management and Business Policy* (Reading, MA: Addison-Wesley, 1998): 275–77.
43. S. McMurray, "DuPont Tries to Make Its Research Wizardry Serve the Bottom Line," *Wall Street Journal*, March 27, 1992, A1, A4.
44. S. K. Yoder, "How H-P Used the Tactics of the Japanese to Beat Them at Their Game," *Wall Street Journal*, September 1994, A1, A6.
45. P. Sellers, "Leo Burnett: Undone by an Upstart," *Fortune* 135, no. 10 (May 26, 1997): 99.
46. Ibid., 100.
47. This section is based on W. H. Starbuck, A. Greve, and B. L. T. Hedberg, "Responding to Crisis," *Journal of Business Administration* (Spring 1978), and in H. Mintzberg, J. B. Quinn, and J. Voyer, *The Strategy Process* (Englewood Cliffs, NJ: Prentice Hall, 1995): 387–94.
48. T. Ewing, "Carbide CEO to Forfeit Pay if Goals Missed," *Wall Street Journal*, September 25, 1997, A3.
49. For a complete discussion of organization dveelopment, see W. L. French and C. H. Bell Jr., *Organizational Development,* 5th ed. (Englewood Cliffs, NJ: Prentice Hall, 1995).
50. W. Bennis, *Organizational Development: Its Nature, Origins and Perspectives* (Reading, MA: Addison Wesley, 1969).
51. T. G. Cummings and C. G. Worley, *Organizational Change and Development* (Minneapolis–St. Paul, MN: West, 1993).
52. Sensitivity training was developed in the 1940s and is also known as encounter groups or T-groups. For information about their use in management, see J. P. Campbell and M. D. Dunnette, "Effectiveness of T-Group Experiences in Managerial Training and Development," *Psychological Bulletin* 70 (1968): 73–104.
53. R. R. Blake and J. S. Mouton, *The New Managerial Grid* (Houston: Gulf, 1978).
54. J. I. Porras and P. J. Robertson, "Organization Development: Theory, Practice, and Research," in M. D. Dunnette and L. M. Hough (eds.), *Handbook of Industrial and Organizational Psychology*, 2d ed., vol. 3 (Palo Alto, CA: Consulting Psychologists Press, 1992), 719–822; R. A. Guzzo, R. D. Fette, and R. A. Katzell, "The Effects of Psychologically Based Intervention Programs on Worker Productivity: A Meta-Analysis," *Personnel Psychology* 38 (1985): 275–91.
55. French and Bell, *Organization Development*, 326–34.
56. P. Rogers, J. E. Hunter, and D. L. Rogers, "Influence of Top Management Commitment on Management Program Success," *Journal of Applied Psychology* (February 1993): 151–55.
57. P. Bate, *Strategies for Cultural Change* (Oxford, UK: Butterworth-Heinemann, 1994).
58. See P. M. Senge, *The Fifth Discipline: The Art and Practice of the Learning Organization* (New York: Doubleday, 1990), for original presentation of the concepts of learning organizations.
59. For an excellent review of the various literature contributing to learning organizations, see M. Easterby-Smith, "Disciplines of Organizational Learning: Contributions and Critiques," *Human Relations* 50, no. 9 (1997): 1085–2006. For a critique of the field, see E. W. K. Tsang, "Organizational Learning and the Learning Organization: A Dichotomy Between Descriptive and Prescriptive Research," *Human Relations* 50, no. 1 (1997): 73–87.
60. Senge, *The Fifth Discipline,* 12–13.
61. P. M. Senge, "Creating Learning Communities," *Executive Excellence* 14, no. 3 (1997): 17–18; P. M. Senge, "Leading Learning Organizations," *Training and Develoment* 50, no. 12 (1995): 36–37; P. M. Senge and J. D. Sterman, "Systems

Thinking and Organizational Learning: Acting Locally and Thinking Globally in the Organization of the Future," *European Journal of Operations Research* 59, no. 1 (1992): 137–40; P. M. Senge, *The Fifth Discipline: The Art and Practice of the Learning Organization* (New York: Doubleday, 1990).

62. C. Colvin, "The 1998 Don't-Get-It All-Stars," *Fortune* (March 30, 1998): 169–70.

63. Senge, "Creating Learning Communities"; Senge, "Leading Learning Organizations"; Senge, *The Fifth Discipline.*

64. P. Block, *Stewardship: Choosing Service over Self-Interest* (San Francisco, CA: Berret-Koehler, 1993).

65. H. Mintzberg, "The Manager's Job: Folklore and Fact," *Harvard Business Review* (July–August 1975): 49–61.

66. Block, *Stewardship.*

67. L. C. Spears, *Reflections on Leadership: How Robert K. Greenleaf's Theory of Servant-Leadership Influenced Today's Top Management Thinkers* (New York: Wiley, 1995).

68. Senge, *Fifth Discipline.*

69. Ibid., 349.

70. S. Branch, "What's Eating McDonald's?" *Fortune* 136, no. 7 (October 13, 1997): 122–25.

71. D. Leonhardt, "McDonald's: Can It Regain Its Golden Touch?" *Business Week* (March 9, 1998): 73.

72. D. Leonhardt, "They Don't Bite the Hand That Feeds Them," *Business Week* (March 9, 1998): 76–77.

73. Taylor, "Neutron Jurgen," 146, 148.

74. Ibid.

75. Bill Vlasic, "German Carmakers in the Fast Lane," *Business Week* (April 13, 1998): 78–82.

76. N. Deogun, "Can His Successor, Douglas Ivester, Refresh Coca-Cola?" *Wall Street Journal*, October 20, 1997, B1, B5; David Greising, "What Other CEOs Can Learn from Goizueta," *Business Week* (November 3, 1997): 38.

77. N. Deogun, "PepsiCo Hoping to Cut Coke's Lead in Restaurant Sales," *Wall Street Journal*, October 30, 1997, A6.

78. Coca-Cola Publicity Release, Coca-Cola Web site, January 28, 1998.

► Organizational Processes at Jagged Edge

"Our image is central to us. We have to control what goes out to the public and create the right image between hard and soft."[1] Controlling the JEMG image is one of Paula Quenemoen's major responsibilities. From the Salt Lake City office, Paula and Brad Barlarge gather and provide information to magazines, shoot their own photos, create news releases, cajole other media to mention JEMG, and use direct, clear language to project the JEMG image of serious but fashionable mountain gear.

A similar emphasis on communication exists inside the organization. The Quenemoens share information freely with their top management team. A monthly press release keeps everybody informed of the latest developments. The group has a formal meeting once a week, and Paula particularly is pushing for expanded use of e-mail. Constant communication keeps Paula and Brad in touch with the rest of JEMG even during winter months when traveling the seven hours to Telluride is often difficult.

Shared communication is the basis of most decisions at JEMG. Margaret Quenemoen says, "It's rare for me to just make decisions. We talk about things. We decide what we will do. We look at historical information and our numbers." Margaret believes that the group generates its best ideas during informal gatherings where formal titles don't matter. In making decisions the group tends to concentrate on how JEMG can improve rather than on external competitors. "We don't really look at our competitors. Why would they know what to do? We just concentrate on what we can do."[2]

The open communication and shared information are inevitable given the close relationships and considerable informal interaction among employees and managers at JEMG. Such extensive informal interaction sometimes creates a challenge for accomplishing formal tasks. Paula struggles to maintain some distance from her employees, who are also her friends and her climbing partners. She enjoys being the "good guy and making people feel good and empowering them," but she is also aware that she needs to play the "bad guy when things are not happening."[3]

At JEMG a person's expertise and standing in mountain sports is key. For example, Brad Barlarge, one of the youngest managers, is recognized by everyone in the company for his considerable mountain climbing expertise. Josh Lear is introduced not only as the merchandising manager but also as one of the top two snowboarding instructors in Telluride. David Potter, the vice president, not only shares the owners' vision, but is one of the most athletic members of JEMG's staff. Erlend Greulich states, "I make sure that I do everything well. My employees can then say, 'I respect him.'"[4]

Mountaineering continues to play a role in other interactions as well. Interpersonal conflicts and disagreements are resolved as they would be during an expedition. People talk things out, figure out what needs to be done as quickly as possible, and move on. There is no time to drag their feet. Tim O'Neill, the buyer, resolves disagreements by putting on what he calls "clinics" in which he keeps everyone informed and educates them about what needs to be done. Few issues appear to fester long because people realize that inaction due to disagreement prevents the group from continuing its journey and reaching the top.

Compared to the constant challenge and unpredictability of their dangerous extreme sports, the daily challenges of business seem nearly stress-free to the people of Jagged Edge. When asked about managing change, Paula Quenemoen states, "Change is easy. Things are often overwhelming, always changing, always evolving. What needs to be done is obvious."[5] Margaret has a similar view: "Change is just one step at a time. We have slow change daily. Opportunities always come up."[6] Others echo this almost nonchalant attitude toward change. Greulich states, "Change is the focus of our culture."[7] The company's business plan is replete with statements about being on the edge, dealing with challenges, and expanding personal limits.[8]

Interestingly, Margaret Quenemoen is facing challenge from her sister and others in the organization in her efforts to expand and grow the organization by introducing summer sports gear such as golf jackets. Paula's reaction to the idea was a disgusted grimace, laughter, and a simple "you've got to be kidding—golf at the Jagged Edge?" Margaret, however, appears serious. The market for winter gear is limited and the company wants to grow.

Questions

1. How are communication and decision making linked at Jagged Edge?

2. What factors contribute to how conflict and change are managed?

3. What factors explain the resistance to moving into sports such as golf? How can the obstacles be overcome, and how would the change affect the company?

Notes

[1] Interview with Paula Quenemoen, June 8, 1998.

[2] Interview with Margaret Quenemoen, June 4, 1998.

[3] Interview with P. Quenemoen.

[4] Interview with Erlend Greulich, June 8, 1998.

[5] Interview with P. Quenemoen.

[6] Interview with M. Quenemoen.

[7] Interview with E. Greulich.

[8] JEMG's business plan.

EFFECTIVENESS: THE PERSON-ORGANIZATION FIT

LEARNING OBJECTIVES

1. Explain effectiveness, discuss the role of culture in its definition, and highlight the importance of the person-organization fit.
2. Review the antecedents, consequences, and management of organizational stress and career management, two individual effectiveness issues.
3. Compare and contrast the various current views on organizational effectiveness.
4. Describe how to create a fit between the person and the organization.

MANAGERIAL CHALLENGE

Olmec Toys

Yla Eason was thinking about both personal and professional goals when she founded Olmec Toys in 1985. A Harvard MBA and former *New York Times* reporter, she was working as a financial editor when her young son brought up the subject of superheroes. "I was concerned when my three-year-old told me he wanted to be a He-Man but couldn't because He-Man was white," she said. "I felt that if my son couldn't fantasize about himself as a superhero, just because he was black, his color may interfere with other career objectives."[1]

Eason scoured stores for the kind of action figures her son wanted. When she found that none were available, she decided to make her own. Naming her company 'Olmec' after an ancient tribe of Aztec Indians who dealt with African traders, she first created Sun Man, an action figure for boys, followed by Menelik and Imani, African prince and princess dolls dressed in kente cloth fashions.[2]

Starting Olmec Toys represented a major life change for Eason—a change that challenged her relationship-building and leadership skills. As a small business owner trying to crack the multibillion dollar toy industry, she needed to convince both retailers and consumers of the value of her product. "There was no such thing as ethnic marketing when we started," explained Eason. "Major toy companies had never gone after this market, so it was tremendously difficult for us at first."[3]

But when a giant toy maker began selling its own black doll in 1991, retailers quickly took notice. More competition meant more stress for Eason. It also showed that she was on the right track. She realized: "There is definitely a market for these products."[4]

■ Questions

1. What stakeholders should Easton consider as she continues to build her business?
2. How could she improve organizational effectiveness by integrating her individual mission, values, and goals with her company's strategy and direction?

The entrepreneurial track that Eason has taken is increasingly becoming an option for people who want to make a significant impact in business and achieve personal success. The goal of all managers is to run an effective organization. For their part, individuals want to perform well and be effective on both a personal and an organizational level. All the topics discussed throughout this book deal with the effective management of people and organizations. We strive to increase quality, to design flexible structures, to create responsive cultures, to motivate employees and help them achieve their potential, to create innovative and productive teams, to improve decision-making processes, to use power appropriately, to communicate clearly, and to manage change well. All these activities and management processes relate to personal and organizational effectiveness.

This chapter focuses on understanding the different approaches to and aspects of individual and organizational effectiveness. We also address an emerging effectiveness issue: Organizational and individual effectiveness depends on the fit between the person and the organization. We concentrate on the issue of fit by first defining effectiveness, then considering personal effectiveness in terms of managing stress and building a successful career, and finally reviewing the current views of organizational effectiveness.

■ WHAT IS EFFECTIVENESS?

Effectiveness
State attained when a person or an organization reaches its planned destination and achieves its goals

What does it mean for a person or an organization to be effective? On both a personal and an organizational level, **effectiveness** means a person or an organization reaches the planned destination and achieves the goals. The mission and goals may include improved efficiency or improved work quality, customer satisfaction, stronger innovation, or increased employee satisfaction.

Each individual and organization has different goals. For some individuals, for instance, the goal may be to become a success. Note that effectiveness is closely linked to success; both terms refer to achieving one's purpose. However, success implies gaining fame and prosperity whereas effectiveness does not (unless fame and fortune are the goals).

Similarly, each organization has different goals. SunAmerica, a company that specializes in investing annuities, concentrates on efficiency. Its founder and chairperson, Eli Broad (which rhymes with *road*), has hired many employees who are willing to work hard for high financial rewards. The employees qualify for generous stock options if they achieve high performance standards and meet or beat their goals. A frugal man, Broad has created a cost-saving culture that employees share. Because everyone is an owner, all employees monitor each

Being effective means different things to different companies. Eli Broad of SunAmerica *(center)* believes that his company is effective if it is efficient. At WorldCom, effectiveness is growth.

other. They frown on individuals who do not perform, waste company resources, or play politics. "We're brutal at getting on employees who don't carry their weight," says Deborah Gero, a SunAmerica employee. The organization has been very effective in achieving its mission. Its profits have increased from $39 million in 1990 to over $270 million in 1996, and its stock price has soared by 5,000 percent during the same period.[5]

Compare SunAmerica's efficiency goal to WorldCom's focus on growth. WorldCom, a telecommunication organization based in Jackson, Mississippi, acquired MCI in a $37 billion deal in 1998.[6] Bernie Ebbers, WorldCom's CEO, has bought 40 companies in the last ten years, vaulting the company to number 33 on the Fortune 500 list. WorldCom has become the number one carrier of Internet traffic by controlling over 40 percent of the Internet networks. Ebbers's strongest skill is his ability to close deals that make strategic sense for his company. Many have called it luck. He has another opinion: "I'm a person who believes that life isn't a *comme ci, comme ça* type of thing. I believe that there is a plan for our lives and for our participation in the world. How could one company be so dang lucky? I mean it's pretty hard to explain, isn't it?"[7] Ebbers's growth goal is designed to provide a vast array of voice and data telecommunication services to its clients worldwide.[8] For WorldCom, being effective means continued growth.

Culture and Effectiveness

People from different cultures have different values, so their goals differ as a result. For example, the concept of self-actualization, which has long been part of the Western definition of motivation and effectiveness, is not a prevalent goal in collectivist cultures, such as those of Singapore or Costa Rica, because they tend to value community rather than individual achievement. In such cultures, individuals forgo personal freedoms and goals for the good of their clan or community.

The cultural value of masculinity is another factor in how people view effectiveness. In masculine cultures, self-reliance and independence are at the core of individual effectiveness. In the United States, psychological definitions of mental health often include the concept of independence. A person who is mentally healthy, then, should be independent. However, the focus on independence is less meaningful in feminine cultures where nurturing and dependence are valued. Therefore, an effective and successful person in a masculine culture will be independent and autonomous, whereas dependence on others in a feminine culture may signal effectiveness. Additionally, the acquisition of material goods is an inherent part of effectiveness in masculine cultures such as Korea but less so in feminine cultures such as Sweden.[9]

Finally, the way a culture views time affects the way people define effectiveness. In present-oriented cultures, as in the United States and Australia, people's time frame for being effective and successful is short. They are impatient about getting results and achieving goals as quickly as possible. In cultures with a circular time orientation, the time frame for effectiveness is longer. The Japanese tend to take a long-term view of career success so employees who work for the same company for decades, slowly rising through the ranks, may be deemed highly effective. North Americans, however, tend to expect results within a few years and are willing to change jobs to succeed.

Summary Point 15.1   **What Is Effectiveness and How Does Culture Affect It?**

- Effectiveness means achieving goals.
- Each individual and organization has different goals, so they will define effectiveness differently.

- Cultural differences in individualism, masculinity, and time orientation affect definitions of effectiveness.

People and organizations can be effective and successful in many domains. People may have successful relationships, be respected leaders in their community, or be effective volunteer organizers for their favorite charity. Organizations may provide a high return on investment to shareholders, be recognized for their social responsibility, or admired for their concern for employees.

In this chapter, we first focus on personal effectiveness at work and then consider organizational effectiveness. Organizations cannot be effective without individuals who are productive and who achieve work-related goals. However, organizations are not effective simply by having productive employees. Managers must be able to integrate and coordinate all their employees' efforts and outputs to create a whole that is greater than the sum of the parts. The key to this synergy is having a fit between the person and the organization.

Throughout the text, we explored topics that address individual effectiveness, especially in part II. Next, we consider two additional individual determinants of personal effectiveness in organizations: stress and career management. We then turn our attention to organizational effectiveness and the person-organization fit.

 INDIVIDUAL EFFECTIVENESS

Ultimately, individual effectiveness is related to long-term happiness. In the narrower context of organizational behavior, individual effectiveness refers to a person's work-related performance and career. Underlying both issues of individual effectiveness are the ideas of integration and fit. Lack of fit between what people value and who they are and the mission and goals of the organization in which they work leads to frustration and stress. Similarly, career success, to a great extent, depends on being able to mesh personal career goals with organizational goals.

Stress

Stress
An individual physiological and psychological response to perceived environmental threats

Stressors
Environmental threats perceived by an individual

Do you often feel overwhelmed by work? Do you feel a sense of dread as you commute to work or school? Do you wake up about as tired as you were when you went to sleep? If you answered yes to these questions, you are experiencing stress. Take Self-Assessment 15.1 to measure your level of stress.

Definition   **Stress** is an individual physiological and psychological response to perceived environmental threats.[10] These environmental threats are called **stressors**. Although most of us

▶ **SELF-ASSESSMENT 15.1**
Are You Stressed?

To assess your stress level, use the scale below to find out how often you have experienced the symptoms of stress.

0 = NEVER;   1 = OCCASIONALLY;   2 = FREQUENTLY;   3 = ALWAYS OR NEARLY ALWAYS

1.	Anxious and nervous	0	1	2	3
2.	Fatigued, disinterested, and apathetic	0	1	2	3
3.	Irritable and frustrated	0	1	2	3
4.	Accident prone	0	1	2	3
5.	Increase in drug or alcohol intake	0	1	2	3
6.	Emotional outbursts and hostility	0	1	2	3
7.	Unable to make decisions	0	1	2	3
8.	Poor concentration and short attention span	0	1	2	3
9.	Hypersensitive to criticism and wanting to cry at the smallest problem	0	1	2	3
10.	Insomnia	0	1	2	3
11.	Hot and cold flashes and/or increased sweating	0	1	2	3
12.	Increased heart rate and shortness of breath	0	1	2	3
13.	Frequent headaches	0	1	2	3
14.	Digestion problems (heartburn, constipation, diarrhea)	0	1	2	3
15.	Unexplained rashes	0	1	2	3

Scoring Key

It is not the total score that is important, but the number of items on which you score 2 or 3. If you are showing more than 4 or 5 items with scores of 2 or 3, it is likely that you are having some stress-related problems.

Source: Based on T. Cox, *Stress* (Baltimore: University Park Press, 1978); S. Cartwright and C. L. Cooper, *Managing Workplace Stress* (Thousand Oaks, CA: Sage, 1997).

welcome some level of challenge and some threats from our environment, excessive and constant challenges and threats cause stress. The **general adaptation syndrome (GAS)** describes the three stages that individuals go through when they respond to stressors and try to adapt to them.[11] Figure 15.1 depicts the three GAS stages.

1. **Alarm** is the first physical reaction that occurs when a person feels threatened because he or she perceives and recognizes stressors. The body reacts to the threat by increasing respiration, blood pressure, and heart rate; by dilating pupils; and by tensing muscles. People who are roller-coaster fans readily recognize these reactions which they experience when they realize the drop is about to happen. If stressors continue to be present, the second stage of GAS starts.

2. **Resistance** occurs when a person fights the threat. The initial alarm passes and the individual prepares to resist the stressors physically and psychologically. Initially, the person has plenty of energy as he or she finds a variety of ways to deal with the situation. If the threat continues, however, tension and fatigue set in. The individual's resistance eventually wears down and he or she moves to the final stage of the GAS.

General adaptation syndrome (GAS)
A model that describes the three stages that individuals go through when responding to stressors and trying to adapt to them

Alarm
The first GAS stage; includes a physical reaction that occurs when the person feels threatened because he or she perceives and recognizes stressors

Resistance
The second GAS stage; occurs when one fights the threat

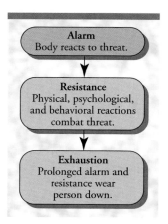

FIGURE 15.1
General Adaptation Syndrome

Exhaustion
The third GAS stage; results from long-term exposure to stressors

3. **Exhaustion** results from long-term exposure to stressors. Continuous and unsuccessful resistance to stressors wears down the individual. All of us have limits in terms of the degree of alarm and resistance we can handle before our physical and mental defenses eventually collapse.

Continued and prolonged exposure to stressors puts people in a continual GAS cycle where they experience alarm and resistance. Even when the stressors are managed successfully, people eventually lose their ability to cope and become exhausted and unable to function. Self-Assessment 15.1 includes many of the major symptoms of stress.

Stress has *physiological*, *psychological*, and *behavioral* components. The physiological component includes physical reactions such as increases in heart rate, breathing, blood pressure, and arousal. The psychological component includes anxiety, irritability, fear, and depression. The behavioral component includes verbal outbursts, hostility, drug and alcohol abuse, and violence.

Consequences   Today's typical workplace puts heavy demands on workers and managers. When stress thwarts our ability to perform, we may feel helpless and angry.[12] The stress from layoffs; plant closings; job insecurity; demands for increased efficiency, quality, and innovation; and the constant need to change and learn new skills all come at a substantial personal cost for employees and managers. One estimate of the cost of stress in the United States through absenteeism, health insurance claims, and lost productivity is $150 billion per year.[13] By one estimate 60–90 percent of medical office visits are for stress-related symptoms.[14] Studies in Norway attribute a staggering cost to stress-related sickness and work accidents.[15] In the United Kingdom, stress-related heart disease is estimated to cause 21 percent of all absenteeism.[16]

In Japan, work stresses due to fierce competition and an intense sense of responsibility and loyalty to the company have been blamed for death by overwork, or *karoshi*. The estimated yearly number of deaths in Japan due to karoshi is around 10,000.[17] Workers complain about working too hard, wanting to call in sick, and simply needing more sleep.[18] To reduce stress and basically to force employees to work less, Japan's prime minister has proposed legislation to reduce work hours.[19] Work stress is a worldwide phenomenon with a tremendous impact on a person's ability to be productive and effective and on an organization's effectiveness.

Stress has been linked to five types of problems. *Physiological* problems include elevated blood pressure and a fast-beating heart. *Behavioral* effects include alcoholism and moodiness; *psychological* reactions are such things as fatigue and anxiety. The fourth type of stress-related problems are *cognitive*. They include forgetfulness and indecisiveness. Finally, stress has *organizational* consequences such as job dissatisfaction, absenteeism, and turnover.[20]

Burnout
Feelings of exhaustion and a sense of powerlessness leading to apathy and psychological withdrawal

Burnout   In the extreme, stress leads to **burnout**, which is characterized by feelings of exhaustion and a sense of powerlessness that leads to apathy and psychological withdrawal. Left unchecked, burnout creates a sense of despair.

Burnout both at home and in the workplace destroys a person's motivation to be involved in any activity. It is particularly common in jobs that involve interaction with other people. Those who experience burnout often work long hours without a break. Rob Kulat, an entrepreneur, explains how he developed burnout: "I have been starting work early, then working nights and over the weekend. I extend my maniacal pace to cutting the lawn, cleaning on the weekend, making it a time of exhaustion, not relaxation. My exercise and diet regimen has slipped, speeding the spiral toward burnout. My breaking point came during an overseas business trip."[21]

Health Problems   Lack of job satisfaction and stress are linked to overall lack of satisfaction with life.[22] More seriously, several major physical and psychological health problems are consistently linked to stress. Among them are coronary heart disease, which accounts for over half the deaths in the United States, and depression. Another consequence is drug and alcohol abuse, which affects both individual and organizational effectiveness and performance.[23]

The future of organizations clearly includes continued change and demands for higher productivity and more efficiency. Vincent DiBianca, an industry expert, notes that the pace of work in today's organizations is much faster than ever before: "It's frenetic, it's disorienting, the pace is relentless."[24] Often, the more challenging the work, the more stress the work causes. Some degree of challenge and stress is needed to energize most of us. Not enough challenge bores us; too much creates undue stress. The key is to find a middle ground where the challenge is sufficient to motivate us without being overwhelming. Recognizing, understanding, and managing stress are a personal and an organizational necessity.

Factors That Influence Stress Figure 15.2 summarizes the factors that cause stress. Although any one of the items listed in Figure 15.2 can by itself lead to major stress, most of us face more than one of these stressors before we experience symptoms of stress.

Individual Factors Individual sources of stress stem from our personalities or from events in our personal lives. The primary source is life changes.[25] We all know that negative changes, such as the loss of a loved one, lead to stress. What we do not always acknowledge is that any change in our life, even when it is positive—such as getting married or moving to a new house—carries the potential for stress. Classic research by Holmes and Rahe showed that those who experienced more changes, both good and bad, experienced more symptoms of stress and were more likely to have health problems.[26]

Table 15.1 presents life events as they relate to stress and their rankings. Life change units (LCUs) are the amount of stress a person experiences during a period of time. LCUs are calculated by adding the mean value for all the stressors a person has experienced. Those experiencing LCUs of under 150 points were not heavily affected. Those who had LCU scores between 150 and 300 points had a 50 percent chance of developing health problems the following year. The likelihood increased to 70 percent for those with LCU scores of over 300.

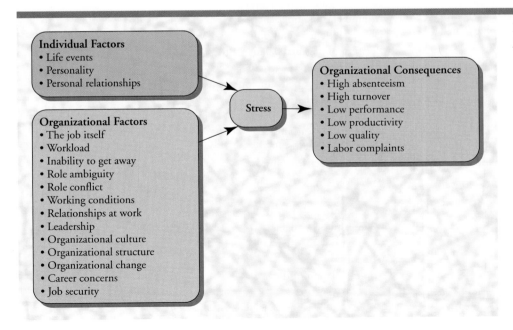

FIGURE 15.2
Factors in Stress

Table 15.1   LIFE CHANGES

Rank	Life Event	Mean Value
1	Death of a spouse	100
2	Divorce	73
3	Marital separation	65
4	Jail term	63
5	Death of close family member	63
6	Personal injury or illness	53
7	Marriage	50
8	Fired at work	47
9	Marital reconciliation	45
10	Retirement	45
11	Change in health of family member	44
12	Pregnancy	40
13	Sex difficulties	39
14	Gain of new family member	39
15	Business readjustment	39
16	Change in financial state	38
17	Death of a close friend	37
18	Change to different line of work	36
19	Change in number of arguments with spouse	35
20	Mortgage over $10,000	31
21	Foreclosure of mortgage or loan	30
22	Change in responsibilities at work	29
23	Son or daughter leaving home	29
24	Trouble with in-laws	29
25	Outstanding personal achievement	28
26	Spouse beginning or stopping work	26
27	Beginning or ending school	26
28	Change in living conditions	25
29	Revision of personal habits	24
30	Trouble with boss	23
31	Change in work hours or conditions	20
32	Change in residence	20
33	Change in schools	20
34	Change in recreation	19
35	Change in church activities	19
36	Change in social activities	18
37	Mortgage or loan less than $10,000	17
38	Change in sleeping habits	16
39	Change in number of family get-togethers	15
40	Change in eating habits	15
41	Vacation	13
42	Christmas	12
43	Minor violation of the law	11

Source: T. H. Holmes and R. H. Rahe, "The Social Readjustment Rating Scale," *Journal of Psychosomatic Research* (1967): 213–18. Used with permission.

Not everyone who experiences change becomes ill. A factor that moderates the effect of life changes and affects stress is personality. As you may remember, the Type A concept was originally developed to identify an independent risk factor in coronary health problems. A Type A person's need for and attempts at gaining control lead him or her to experience a higher amount of stress. If you are a Type A, your perception of change, daily events, and irritations, such as being held up in traffic, not making a deadline, being interrupted while you are working, or not receiving the shipment you need to finish your work, are likely to be major sources of stress. To the Type Bs, similar events are less irritating as these people do not feel constant threats to their ability to control.

Another personality factor that has been linked to stress and its effects is **hardiness**.[27] Individuals who are hardy believe they have control over their lives, are committed to their activities, and treat change as a challenge rather than a threat. Research indicates that hardy individuals resist stress and its negative effects better than nonhardy people.

Various other personal factors in stress, such as financial problems, family troubles, abusive relationships, addictions, and so forth can be both a source and a consequence of stress. In addition, social isolation and a sense of being alone have been linked to stress and many physiological and psychological problems, such as depression and heart attack.[28]

Organizations are recognizing the role of personal stress factors in the workplace and many are providing their employees with assistance to deal with problems ranging from addiction and substance abuse to bankruptcy and elder and child care. Marriott Corporation, the international hotel chain with 135,000 employees, has instituted a number of such programs to improve its employees' and the company's effectiveness. Marriott reported close to 100 percent yearly turnover in its hourly workers. Personal problems such as unreliable child care and lack of knowledge of English were two of the major reasons for the high turnover rate. Specifically, workers faced problems, such as acquiring housing, that they could not resolve because of cultural differences or lack of language proficiency.

To help employees manage the personal stress that affected organizational effectiveness, Marriott contracted with a company called Associate Resource Line in Philadelphia.[29] That company provides Marriott employees access to resources and a variety of services through its many bilingual employees. Employees can call the company to discuss problems, seek out housing opportunities, locate child care centers in their area, and so forth. Resource Line employees make follow-up calls to ensure that problems are solved. Marriott further provides parenting, language, and citizenship classes as well as child vaccination programs for its employees. The company reported a drop in stress and absenteeism that helped justify the cost of the programs.

Hot ▼ Link

We discussed Type A in chapter 4, pp. 122–25.

Hardiness
An individual trait that indicates the degree to which people believe they have control over their lives, they are committed to their activities, and they treat change as a challenge rather than a threat

A QUESTION OF ETHICS

Stress Programs for All?	Although many companies are instituting stress management programs, unions—particularly those representing the hospitality industry—accuse management of hypocrisy because almost 30 percent of workers are part-timers and receive no benefits. Unions claim that stress reduction programs do little to improve those workers' actual conditions. What should the ethical position be for management in dealing with part-time employee stress? Should management take a different ethical position for part-time versus full-time workers? What about temporary employees who are working the same number of hours as full-time employees?

Many other companies address individual sources of stress through various programs. The Home Depot provides prenatal health screening and education to its 26,000 female employees.[30] L. L. Bean has a program to teach its 8,000 employees how to prevent back prob-

Organizations such as Symmetrix, a consulting firm in Massachusetts, are recognizing that individual sources of stress affect their employees' productivity and are therefore helping their workers manage stress better through meditation.

lems, while SmithKline Beecham Corp. offers breast cancer and mammography programs. Adolph Coors Co. helps its employees with lifestyle-induced health problems through wellness classes and training.[31] All these programs recognize that individual stressors affect work behavior and performance.

Organizational Factors   A recent five-year study of stress in the workplace released by the Families and Work Institute found that increased job pressures are a major source of stress.[32] The results indicate that job stress contributes more to low productivity than do personal stressors. Therefore, managers must be aware of the organizational, job-related stress factors.

Not all jobs are created equal. Some are inherently more stressful than others. Being an air traffic controller, working in a hospital emergency room, washing skyscraper windows in New York City, working in the pit on Wall Street, and managing a large number of people are all stressful jobs.[33] Some jobs, particularly those in which one has responsibility for others and those where one is pulled in many different directions, are more stressful than others. Management is such a job. Increasingly, managers are finding their jobs overwhelming and stressful.[34] They are caught between lower and higher levels, supervise too many people from too many different areas, work excessively long hours, have little job security, and experience little opportunity for promotion.

Another organizational factor in stress is the work load. The official 40-hour work week in the United States is, in reality, considerably longer than 40 hours, especially for many managers and other professionals. A recent survey showed that working hours increased from 43.3 hours a week in 1997 to 47.1 in 1998. Additionally, one-third of those surveyed reported taking work home on evenings and weekends compared to only 25 percent doing so 10 years ago.[35] For managers and others in professional-level positions, working 60 hours or more is often the norm. In one major corporation in Southern California, there is an informal race among the managers to see who gets to the office first on Saturdays and Sundays and occupies the parking space closest to the building.

It is therefore not surprising that work overload is one of the major sources of stress (see Figure 15.2). Having too much work causes stress, and negatively affects the individual's relationships inside and outside the work sphere. Workaholics who take their computer to bed and their fax and cell phone to the beach when they're on vacation face angry and frustrated family members.[36] Brenda Frost, training coordinator at Washington Mutual Bank in Seattle feels that her work stress affects her personal life: "You get to a point where you just can't do it all. It's a circle. I am a vegetable at home, and I'm a lot more scattered at work."[37]

Another factor that causes stress is the inability to get away because of information technology. Pagers, cell phone, faxes, and e-mail do not allow people to get away from their work. An administrative assistant to a high-ranking executive was disciplined by her boss for having turned off her pager on a Saturday. The boss was working at a conference and could not understand why her assistant was unavailable.

Another organizational stressor is **role conflict**, which refers to the contradictory roles an individual plays.[38] The conflict is often between home and work roles. Brenda Frost of Seattle's Washington Mutual Bank feels guilty because work is so overwhelming that she gives her 4-year-old a video to watch just to have some time to herself.[39] In her opinion, this behavior means she's not living up to her image of a good mother. Role conflict can also be between different roles at work. For example, the manager who is expected to enforce organizational rules that she believes do not benefit her customers or employees experiences role conflict. Her role as an enforcer conflicts with her role as a motivator.

Role ambiguity is lack of clarity about the role one is playing. Not having a clear job description or not knowing the performance expectations are both examples of role ambiguity. Working in teams in which each person's role is not clear and leadership is shared can be another source of role ambiguity. Employees who are used to being assigned to a task and told what to do by a manager may experience confusion and stress when they work in self-managed teams and do not have such direction.

Poor working conditions, ranging from a noisy and dirty work environment to exposure to dangerous equipment, are another organizational stress factor.[40] A corollary stress factor is *relationships* with co-workers, customers, subordinates, and others at work. Working in ineffective teams, having unsupportive colleagues, dealing with difficult employees, managing unresolved conflict, and similar conditions all create a stressful work environment due to relationship issues. As organizations increase the use of groups and teams, people who previously could work alone are forced to work and interact with others, creating more potential for conflict and stress.

Leadership is another aspect of work relationships. Having a supervisor whose management and leadership styles do not fit one's needs and personality is a tremendous source of stress. Whether one requires more direction, fewer instructions, more participation, or simply a more supportive boss, the mismatch between what people expect of their manager and what he provides is stressful.

Deborah Risi left the corporate life mainly because of bad leadership. After working for many years at Apple, Pacific Bell, Cullinet Software, and other companies, she decided to open her own consulting firm. She provides marketing strategy advice to large organizations such as Oracle, Cisco Systems, and Sun Microsystems and is successful in her trade. "I looked back on my work history and realized that I had never felt really, really good about it. I had maybe one boss I could both respect and learn from. I was tired of working incredibly hard for companies that lacked leadership and didn't share my values," Risi declares.[41]

Culture is yet another organizational stressor. We discussed the importance of culture and climate in chapter 3. Organizations with cultures of control, hostility, and suspicion contribute to employee stress.[42] Supportive cultures that encourage trust and cooperation help reduce pressure and stress.[43] Fair *policies* and open processes further affect stress levels. Similarly, top-down and hierarchical *structures*, in which employee participation is discouraged and communication is formal, are more likely to create stress than are flat and participative structures.

Finally, concerns about *career progress* and *job security* are key organizational stressors. Reengineering, restructurings, and layoffs have changed traditional career paths; long-term

Role conflict
Conflict caused when the individual plays contradictory roles

Role ambiguity
Conflict due to the lack of clarity about the role one is expected to play

employment is now the exception rather than the rule. A large number of employees and managers face uncertain job and career futures, a situation that adds to stress.

The list of organizational stressors is neither complete nor universal. Every organization is different. Most important, every individual reacts differently to different situations. What one person considers overload may be a challenge to another person. A loose and participative culture may cause stress for someone who needs order and structure or be a source of motivation for one who enjoys and seeks autonomy.

Clearly, stress is an interaction between the person and the situation. Managing individual sources of stress is a personal responsibility. Managers cannot control the individual sources of stress. However, they can help their employees manage it better. Managers also have the ability and the responsibility to control organizational sources of stress.

Managing Stress   Eliminating all stress from one's life is neither possible nor desirable. It is impossible because stress comes from threats and challenges in our environment that are often outside our control. It is not desirable because some stress is necessary to keep us motivated and interested. However, the appropriate level of stress differs from one person to another.

CAREER ADVICE
from the Experts

HANDLING AN ABUSIVE BOSS

Many of us have had bad bosses. However, there are managers who cross the line from bad to abusive by screaming profanities, deceiving, terrorizing, and humiliating their employees. Other managers rule with an iron fist, watching their employees' every move and acting in irrational and arbitrary ways. The latter type of abuse is often unnoticed by others and sometimes goes unpunished by the organization. If you are unlucky enough to have one of these bosses, what can you do to protect yourself?

- Recognize abuse and clearly differentiate it from tough work standards. Tough is fair and humane; abuse is personal and cruel.
- Seek support from other employees; do not isolate yourself and suffer in silence.
- Monitor your own behavior to make sure you are not abusing others (domino effect).
- Adapt some of your own behaviors to avoid the abuse. For example, stay away, avoid your manager at certain times of the day, and keep written records.
- Use the bottom line to get the boss to change: "Your behavior is costing us money and productivity."
- Give the manager specific, work-related examples of unacceptable behavior.
- Follow available organizational processes to complain to higher levels or to human resources.
- Get out if you can! Ask for a transfer or look for another job.

Sources: H. A. Hornstein, *Brutal Bosses and Their Prey* (New York: Riverhead, 1996); M. Loeb, "The Bad Boss Gets a New Life," *Fortune* 33, no. 10 (May 27, 1996): 192–93; S. Caudron, "The Boss from Hell," *Industry Week* 244, no. 16 (September 4, 1995): 12–18.

Managing stress to maintain it at a healthy level benefits the individual physically and psychologically, allowing for a more productive life. The organization benefits by preventing absenteeism, turnover, and poor performance. A stress management program should have the following characteristics:[44]

- Identify the major individual and organizational stressors and learn how to control them.
- Identify individual employees' stress tolerance levels.
- Communicate with employees about the consequences of stress and educate them about the symptoms of negative stress.
- Develop realistic goals for changing attitudes, modifying behaviors, and acquiring skills to manage stress.
- Develop individualized assistance programs.
- Increase employee control over the work environment.

There are two methods for managing stress to increase personal and organizational effectiveness. The obvious one is to reduce the individual and organizational sources of stress. The second method is to build individual resistance to stressors.

Reducing Sources of Stress   Individual employees and their managers can both reduce sources of stress. Individuals can actively reduce the number of stressors. *Limiting changes* helps reduce stress. For example, whenever possible, you can monitor the types and numbers of changes that you are experiencing. You may want to avoid setting your moving dates before a major holiday, especially if you are also graduating from college at about the same time.

Individuals can reduce personality and personal relationship stressors by seeking counseling, changing dysfunctional behaviors such as alcohol and drug abuse and violence, and learning new skills. Similarly, individuals can reduce organizational stressors related to role ambiguity and conflict by clarifying their personal values and setting priorities. For example, an employee who is stressed because of the dual pressures of caring for an aging parent while working 50-hour work weeks can reduce his level of stress by clarifying his central values and priorities. Another suggestion to help clarify goals is to write a personal mission statement. As it does for an organization, an individual mission statement provides direction, clarifies priorities, focuses a person's attention on goals, and helps the person through difficult decisions by providing guiding principles.[45]

Managers have considerable control over organizational sources of stress. As one strategy, they can conduct a stress audit, which is an assessment designed to ascertain the level and sources of stress in the organization. Managers can then address the specific stressors through individual action or changes in organizational policies and practices. Various managerial tools that we have discussed throughout the text, ranging from motivation and goal setting to team building, decision making, conflict management, and communication can all be used to reduce stress.

Managers can further review their employees' workload and set priorities and goals to help them manage excessive work. They can reduce role ambiguity and conflict by clarifying job descriptions, negotiating with employees, and communicating their expectations more clearly.[46] In fact, some managers put themselves in their employee's shoes for a day to realize how unreasonable the workload is.[47]

Problems with working conditions, although often costly, are relatively easy to address. Managers can replace outdated, dangerous equipment, repair ventilation systems, provide more privacy by changing the office design, reduce noise, strictly enforce safety regulations, and so forth.

Managers can further reduce organizational stressors by helping employees improve relationships at work through team building, conflict management, and negotiation. Managers and leaders can be trained to use appropriate methods and processes. If major intervention is needed, managers can concentrate on changing organizational cultures and structures through organizational development efforts, reengineering, or other large-scale organizational change programs. In these situations, small gestures and events are not enough. Barbara Feuer, an organizational psychologist, states: "When you have an unhealthy, unhappy environment, a company picnic is almost an insult."[48] Change needs to take place at the cultural and structural levels. Finally, managers must address job security and career concerns.

Employee assistance programs (EAP)
Organizational programs that help employees address personal as well as organizational problems

Specific tools organizations use to reduce stress include improved communication, more participative structures and cultures, and matching employees to tasks and jobs. Another powerful tool is **employee assistance programs (EAP)**, which are programs that help employees address personal as well as organizational problems. In addition to offering counseling and training, EAPs give referrals to outside counselors. A Canadian survey of 1,000 employers indicates that the use of EAPs increased from 36 percent to 48 percent from 1990 to 1993, demonstrating their increased popularity.[49]

Why the increase? Companies are recognizing that although employees may experience problems that are not work related, these problems still affect their productivity and effectiveness at work. Helping employees reduce stress, regardless of the source, can benefit the organization.

Organizations have developed a variety of additional methods to reduce stress. At S. C. Johnson & Sons, in Racine, Wisconsin, employees and managers engage in water-gun fights, lunchtime aerobics, and massages during breaks. Another firm, Hill & Knolton, based in Los Angeles, California, bought tickets to the Los Angeles Philharmonic breakfast concert for all its employees.[50] Health care insurance company Cigna relies on more traditional methods by offering stress-reduction training for its employees. The training includes meditation, stretching, and the use of upbeat music.[51] Johnson and Johnson's "Live for Life Program" provides resources to create a healthy workplace by concentrating on health-related education and practices. The company's top managers strongly support the program to integrate healthy practices into all aspects of the culture and practices at Johnson and Johnson.[52] The purpose of these programs is to reduce stress while also building the individual's stress resistance to increase both individual and organizational effectiveness.

Building Resistance to Stress   Many of the sources of stress simply cannot be eliminated or reduced. A manager's job is stressful. In fact, some studies have found that middle managers are the most stressed workers in the organization, mainly because they are often caught in the middle of people and issues.[53] Organizations cannot avoid reorganization and change. There will always be more work than employees can handle and funds for hiring help will always be limited. Stress is an integral part of working.

As a complement to or substitute for reducing or removing the source of stress, employees and managers can learn to build resistance to stress. This approach focuses on the individual, although organizational programs can help people build such resistance.

To build resistance, individuals should find an activity that allows them to get away and gain perspective. Francesca Luzuriaga, executive vice president of Mattel, is a hardworking, globe-trotting manager who practices ballet to reduce her stress. She states: "The harder I work, the more I need to dance. When I miss a few days, my secretary says, 'go dance!' If I don't, I get hyperactive, and I drive the people I work with nuts."[54] Mike Bonsignore, the CEO of Honeywell, does deep-sea diving and photography to reduce stress. He states: "It's wondrous and weightless down there. It's as close to meditation as I get—me in my purest form."[55]

The primary method for developing resistance to stress is to build the body's ability to fight the alarm stage. This is achieved through physical and mental health. A healthy diet and exercise are an integral part of resistance. Factors related to mental health include relaxation, meditation and biofeedback, and the development of social support.

Mattel executive Francesca Luzuriaga and Honeywell CEO Mike Bonsignore have both found unique and personal ways to manage their stress. What do you do?

Relaxation trains a person to be calmer and to reduce arousal. Learning to relax reduces the harmful effects of the alarm stage of the GAS by slowing breathing and heart rates and lowering blood pressure. *Meditation*, which involves sitting with closed eyes and focusing on a repetitive message for about 20 minutes, achieves similar results. *Biofeedback* shows people their amplified physical responses. Seeing how their bodies react teaches people to control their physical reactions better during stressful times.

Having a strong *social support network* is yet another way to build resistance to stress.[56] A social support network is a group of people who provide support, comfort, encouragement, and assistance through a variety of means. Some of us rely on our family for social support. Others seek the support of friends, religious groups, or other formal and informal groups. Individuals who have and actively use a social support network benefit from improved health and quality of life.[57] They do not feel isolated and therefore reduce a major stressor. Given that we spend a considerable amount of our time at work, co-workers can be an excellent source of support. For example, working in a cohesive team, in addition to performance benefits, can help a person manage stress.

Being able to manage stress well is a key factor in individual effectiveness. People who are stressed cannot focus well and work toward their goals. For organizations, appropriate levels

Summary Point 15.2   **Stress, Its Sources, and How It Can Be Managed**

- Stress is an individual physiological and psychological response to perceived stressors.
- Stress takes place in three stages called the general adaptation syndrome (GAS). The stages are alarm, resistance, and exhaustion.
- Individual sources of stress stem from individual personality or events in our personal lives.

- Organizational stressors are the job itself, working conditions, role conflict and ambiguity, and relationships with supervisors and co-workers.
- Stress can be managed through reduction of stressors or by building resistance.

of stress mean higher satisfaction, lower absenteeism, and an opportunity for workers to be productive and effective. At the core of stress is the issue of lack of control. People who feel powerless and who do not have control experience stress. Providing employees with increased control over events, then, is at the heart of managing stress.[58] We next consider the management of careers as the second factor in individual effectiveness.

Building a Successful Career

Long-term effectiveness involves building a successful career. Both the individual and the organization are responsible for managing and building a person's career, but the responsibilities of both are quite different from what they were several decades ago. For instance, most of the responsibility is now on the individual employees' shoulders. Many new employees and baby boomers define success as achieving personal goals and experiencing a sense of personal accomplishment, rather than moving up the corporate ladder in record time.[59] We investigate career trends in the twenty-first century, explore the typical career stages, and discuss special career challenges for women.

Careers in the Twenty-First Century   Dating back to the 1950s, organizations had a simple contract with their employees: "Work hard and deliver and we will keep you employed and secure." This contract started to disappear in the mid-1980s and is now all but gone in most U.S. companies. A new contract with different elements is taking its place.

Figure 15.3 presents the key elements of careers in the twenty-first century. Increasingly today's organizations are neither capable of nor interested in managing their employees' careers totally. Individuals must assume this *responsibility*.[60] Andy Grove, Intel executive and management guru states: "The sad news is, nobody owes you a career. You own it as a sole proprietor."[61]

Continuous learning is another essential factor in effective careers. Individuals must keep abreast of technological changes and new management methods. Although few organizations accept responsibility for career management, many are committed to helping their employees learn. The organizational commitment to learning reflects another feature of the new employment contract: *employability*.[62] Rather than promising to employ people for life, today's orga-

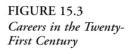

FIGURE 15.3
Careers in the Twenty-First Century

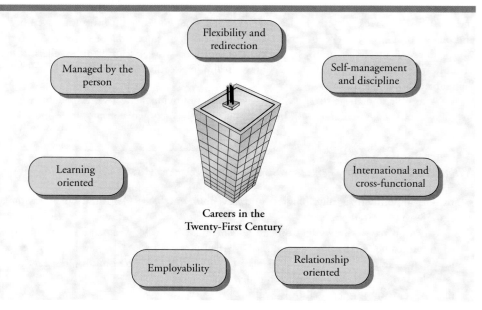

nizations are committed to training and educating their employees so that they will continue to remain marketable and employable.[63] For example, the Calvert Group, an investment firm in Bethesda, Maryland, reimburses its employees for taking any kind of course.[64]

Because each of us is the sole proprietor of our career, we should keep several factors in mind. First, because of changing organizational structures, the use of groups and teams, and the implementation of boundaryless and virtual organizations, *building and maintaining cooperative relationships* with internal and external constituents are essential.[65] Negotiating agreements, managing conflict productively, and developing long-term ties are a necessity.

Second, each individual needs to build his or her *cross-cultural and cross-functional experiences*. Knowledge of different areas of an organization and of global business helps people manage the complex and diverse relationships in today's organizations.

A QUESTION OF ETHICS

New Jobs or Irresponsibility?	Organizations are shifting the responsibility for career success to employees. Is this trend a necessary new reality or does it indicate that managers and organizations are shirking their social responsibilities? Does an organization have an ethical responsibility to help its employees manage their careers? Does an employee have any ethical responsibility to stay loyal to an organization that does help to manage his or her career?

The last two factors individuals must consider in managing their careers are *flexibility* and sufficient *self-management and discipline* to control and manage their own careers and work.[66] The ability to adapt quickly depends partly on having a broad base of knowledge and skills and partly on individual style and personality. Developing self-management skills is akin to self-leadership discussed in chapter 9. With the flattening of organizations and the use of self-managed teams, managers and supervisors no longer control employee behaviors. Therefore, self-motivation, discipline, and the ability to set priorities and establish a balance among various activities are individual rather than organizational requirements.

Despite the lack of long-term employment, many people find ways to stay with the same company through cross-functional training, which builds confidence and expands skills. Consider the career of Thomas Filipski, who has spent 16 years at Cotter & Co. He has held several jobs in the company, starting in the accounting department, moving to the mergers and acquisitions area, then to regional marketing, and recently to inventory management. He has built a network of people at Cotter who believe in his ability to get the job done. He always seeks out the tough assignments that no one else will touch. "If you're confident, you seek out the mess, the tangled string of yarn or the new, nobody's-got-a-clue-how-we're-going-to-do-it situation," advises career expert Paul Zellner.[67]

Bob Shamberg is another executive with a long tenure in one company, having spent 26 years at Sears managing very different marketing ventures and departments. He confesses to reengineering his own job every few years. He is also taking financial management classes. Shamberg explains, "Everything I do has significant financial implications and that's a gap in my background and experience."[68]

Thinking about career success in the next century requires that we understand the fundamental changes organizations are experiencing. As structures and management practices change, the meaning of a successful career and individual effectiveness also changes. We must learn to view our careers in a new light.[69]

Career Stages Careers are typically divided into three broad stages that are described in Table 15.2. Each stage presents special challenges for the individual and the organization.

T a b l e   1 5 . 2   CAREER STAGES AND CHALLENGES

Career Stage	Individual Challenge	Organizational Challenge
Starting out: Younger employees	• Defining interests • Finding challenging career	• Adjusting to generational differences • Providing appropriate challenges • Making room for newcomers
Established career: Middle-age employees	• Staying motivated and employed • Avoiding plateaus and stagnation • Finding source of rejuvenation	• Maintaining technical skills • Providing growth in flat organizations • Providing job security and employability
Approaching retirement: Older employees	• Managing retirement • Keeping active and productive • Finding new interests	• Planning for retirement • Replacing talent and experience • Planning for successors

Early Career   The major concern for workers in their twenties and early thirties is to find a career that is interesting and challenging, and can satisfy their needs. Employees just entering the workforce are the baby busters who thus far have exhibited concerns for quality of work life and personal and family well-being. Those who went to grade school in the 1990s—already called Generation Y—will be entering the workforce in record numbers between 2008 and 2010. They will be competing with the aging baby boomers and the baby busters for resources and jobs.[70]

Managers working with new generations must accommodate their needs and recognize their uniqueness to help them become productive and effective. Involving them in decision making and providing them with broad access to information about their jobs and company processes are key to managing these workers successfully. Generation Y and the baby busters have grown up seeing their parents lose jobs due to layoffs, restructurings, and delayerings; consequently, their organizational loyalty is low. Thus, managers face the challenge of keeping them interested.

Middle Career   A large number of managers and employees in mid-career have themselves been laid off and restructured. People in the middle of their careers expect some stability and security to support their adolescent and college-age children. Additionally, many face career stagnation. **Plateauing** refers to the leveling off of a career without further opportunities for growth. As organizations remove layers and flatten their structures, traditional promotions and career ladders disappear, leaving many in mid-career with limited prospects. Those who are laid off must find new careers.

For those who remain, the growing workload, survivor guilt, and a sense of having been betrayed all lead to lack of motivation. They stay with organizations without any interest, motivation, or commitment because they feel trapped and because they have invested too much to leave.[71]

The major individual and organizational challenge at this stage is to redefine career tracks and find innovative, creative ways to redirect and rejuvenate careers. Jim Simon, a 46-year-old communication specialist, has redefined his career a number of times.[72] After receiving a liberal arts degree in 1973, he began his career by writing newspaper articles, then got a job in a state agency after which he joined a ballet company as marketing manager. He finally went to work at TRW, the highly diversified financial services and manufacturing company, as an executive. He learned to speak the languages of all the functional areas of business, including marketing, finance, and operations. He differentiated himself by always stating his personal philosophy and acting decisively.

Plateauing
The leveling off of a career without further opportunities for growth

MANAGEMENT ADVICE
from the Experts

SABBATICALS TO REVIVE EMPLOYEES

Sabbaticals, or extended paid and unpaid leaves, have long been a staple in the academic world. They are designed to provide faculty an opportunity to explore new ideas and to rejuvenate and revive slumping motivation and careers. Several business organizations such as Intel, Federal Express, Xerox, America West Airlines, and Tandem offer some form of extended leave to their employees to help them energize their careers or learn new skills.

- Offering a sabbatical is a good strategy in this age of decreasing employee loyalty and burnout.
- Consider sabbaticals long-term investments in your most valuable employees.
- Plan sabbaticals carefully to benefit both individual growth and company interests.
- Encourage employees to explore career options, but also expect them to come back with increased skills and fresh perspectives to benefit the company.
- The manager and employee should jointly consider who will substitute for the employee and how that substitute will handle work while the employee is away.

Sources: H. Lancaster, "Sabbatical Can Help You Improve Your Job or Spur a New Career," *Wall Street Journal*, February 13, 1996, B4; J. Robinson, "The Big Break," *Escape* (July 1997): 18–19.

Although Simon lost his job when TRW reorganized, he is undaunted. He believes his varied experiences make him valuable to many companies. But he will not work for just any organization. He says he is looking for an organization with "enough of the right specs."[73]

Late Career   In the United States, male life expectancy is 72; female life expectancy is 79.[74] The average person can expect to live to age 75. As we live longer, our careers are extending. Many baby boomers will have active careers well into their retirement years. By 2030, the baby boomers of the 1990s will be senior citizens and form a large and powerful segment of the population.

Both now and in the future, the challenge of managing late careers is to find ways to retire with security and ways to continue to be productive and grow. Organizations must deal with the financial aspects of retirement through managing retirement funds and offering their employees options and training to manage their retirement. Additionally, managers must replace retiring employees and plan for the succession of important executives. Many organizations face the challenge of finding a replacement for successful executives who are approaching retirement age.

Think back for a moment to the success of SunAmerica and its CEO, Eli Broad. At 64, Broad is approaching retirement age but has no plans to retire yet. However, the company needs to be prepared for the inevitable. A SunAmerica executive Barry Munitz articulates the company's dilemma clearly: "Eli is such a strong figure. Microsoft without Bill Gates, GE without Jack Welch—that's the challenge we face."[75] Effective organizations plan for succession carefully.

Although managing these career changes is the responsibility of both organizations and individuals, as is the case with other career management issues, the active management of

Longevity in life means that careers are likely to lengthen. Hal Wright is an example. He continues to write, edit, and deliver his newspaper from his airplane at age 93.

careers increasingly falls on individual employees' shoulders. As organizations struggle to address individual needs and manage a diverse workforce, individual employees can build effective careers by actively communicating their needs to and negotiating agreements with their managers so they can find ways to achieve both personal and organizational goals.

Special Considerations: Helping Women Be Effective in Organizations   All employees need help, support, and mentoring to build successful careers. Good management techniques are gender- and colorblind. However, women face challenges on several fronts that their male counterparts encounter less frequently. Though we address these issues in the framework of gender differences, the topics and techniques can apply to all workers, regardless of gender, age, or ethnicity.

One issue that women must confront and overcome in building their careers is basic *gender discrimination* in a variety of areas. The average salary of women is still less than 75 percent of the salary of their male counterparts. In a recent survey of the accounting profession by the Institute of Management Accounting and *Management Accounting* magazine, female accountants earned $8,622 less than their male counterparts.[76] This male "premium" is evident even after the results are adjusted for management levels, years in the field, education levels, and professional certification. The results indicate that "there is evidence of potential wage/salary discrimination by gender."[77]

In the publishing business, where only a few women hold the position of CEO, female employees have sued employers for discrimination and have won major settlements. For example, in 1986 Macmillan Publishing agreed to pay more than $1.9 million to settle a wage discrimination suit brought by four of its female employees; the settlement covered close to 1,500 women who worked at Macmillan. In the *Publisher's Weekly* salary survey of 1994–95, only 7 women appeared among the top 70 highest-paid publishing executives. Publishing is not alone in having few women in top positions. A survey of the 500 largest organizations in the United States found that just over 2 percent of women held the titles of executive vice president and above, and that only 2 percent of women were among the top five executives earning the highest salaries in their firms.[78]

The U.S. Department of Labor has been documenting some of the other obstacles to women's progress in organizations.[79] A 1990 Department of Labor study found that although women are present in lower- and middle-management positions, they do not have access to the jobs and experiences that are required for upper-level management. For example, women (when compared to men) do not receive broad cross-functional training. Instead, organiza-

Change Challenge

DUAL-CAREER COUPLES AND OTHER NOVELTIES

I t used to be the norm for a company to transfer its employees to a new location and expect their families to pack up and follow. However, numerous employees are now part of dual-career couples in which both partners are professionals. In some cases, a spouse is unwilling to relocate and risk jeopardizing his or her career. In other cases, employees want to scale back the hours they spend on their careers to enjoy personal activities or to spend more time raising children or caring for aging parents. Many organizations also have to deal with co-workers who are in committed relationships.[a]

Some managers consider these new career issues a problem, worrying about their negative effect on fast-track careers and potential conflicts of interest. There is also some evidence that men pay a penalty in terms of salary and promotion when they are part of a dual-career couple.[b] Nonetheless, solutions to these problems exist. Organizations such as Sara Lee, Dow Chemicals, and Hoechst Celanese are meeting the challenge and actively managing work-family issues. They are achieving these goals by promoting successful role models who juggle work and family, providing job flexibility, and helping in situations where one spouse is transferred by paying for lost income. Dow Chemical helped Ann Judge's husband set up his own business after she was transferred. Sara Lee has several highly visible working mothers in executive positions, and Hoechst helps working parents temporarily reduce their hours to juggle family responsibilities.[c]

Recognizing and creatively managing and accommodating the career needs of a diverse workforce is an inevitable change in today's organizations. Companies that successfully achieve this goal not only stand a better chance of retaining valued employees but also enhance their public image, which can further attract high-quality employees and managers.

a. H. Lancaster, "How Co-Workers Who Marry Can Both Stay on the Fast Track," *Wall Street Journal*, September 23, 1997, B1.

b. B. Morris, "Is Your Family Wrecking Your Career?" *Fortune* 135, no. 5 (1997): 70–90.

c. S. Shellenbarger, "Some Firms Manage to Ease Family Duties and Aid Promotions," *Wall Street Journal*, December 13, 1995, B1.

tions assign them to traditionally female areas such as human resource management. Another area in which women receive less exposure than men is global and international experience. Although experience in these areas is essential for obtaining upper-management positions, women are often excluded from consideration for key foreign assignments. Eventually, as a result of narrow focus and lack of international experience, when the time comes for promotion, women in middle-level management are indeed not ready to be promoted.

Another obstacle that women face in building their careers is the "superwoman" syndrome, creating the belief that women can pursue high-powered fast-track careers while also burdened with the majority of household and child and elder-care responsibilities.[80] The superwoman is expected to be perfect at the office, at home, and in the community, excelling in every role she plays in life. She also often suffers from stress overload. Professor Sharon Hays of the University of Virginia is one of the many who claim that for women to be successful and effective, society must change its views so that parenting and household responsibilities are more evenly divided between men and women.[81]

Women must also make decisions regarding their work and career goals. A survey of 300 career women between the ages of 35 and 49, conducted jointly by the research firm Yankelovich Partners and *Fortune* magazine, found that 87 percent of the women surveyed had considered making major changes in their lives and careers or were considering such changes.[82] Many decisions related to whether continuing to work was worth it. The survey indicated that men rarely face such dilemmas. They simply expect to continue working. As Yla Eason of Olmec Toys shows, many women leave their corporate jobs at the height of their careers to open their own businesses, pursue altruistic causes, or follow drastically different careers.

Shoya Zichy, for example, used to be a vice president at American Express. She left the job to pursue painting, but later returned as a counselor to other women executives. She observes, "Here were all these extremely talented women. I started asking myself, 'Why are so many of these brilliant women burning out?'"[83] It seems that many women decide halfway through their careers that they need to redefine their vision, their goals, and their professional lives. Many are not willing to play the corporate game any more—unless they can define their own rules so that the jobs fit their needs and goals.

The myth is that these women leave their careers to be at home with their children; actually, most leave to pursue alternative careers. In a survey of its high-potential female employees, managers at Deloitte & Touche, a major accounting and consulting company, were surprised to find that 90 percent of those leaving were moving to other companies. Only a few were planning to stay home to care for small children.[84]

Francoise Jeanpierre, an MBA with Fulbright credentials, left an international banking job to build her own entrepreneurial firm. The trend of women finding different paths to success is very familiar to her. She states: "This is a far richer and more diverse issue than can be classified by glass ceiling or work-family. It is an array of creative choices by people who reinvent themselves."[85] Ann Clurman, a partner at Yankelovich, a firm specializing in public opinion survey, agrees: "There is some kind of profound something going on—a reassessment, a rethinking, a big gulp, whatever. It has to do with self-image and the workplace. And I find this astonishing."[86]

Decisions to leave work for alternative careers inevitably carry some degree of dissonance, which is often intensified by mixed cultural messages about the role of women in society. Although they now have a choice of working, many cultures continue to expect them to be primarily wives and mothers. The fact that a choice even exists for women appears to be a benefit for them in the view of many male managers who feel trapped in their jobs with no option but to work. However, the choice increases the pressure that many women feel.[87]

Brenda Barnes's resignation as head of PepsiCo's North American beverage business in 1997 provides a vivid example of the challenges many women face. As one of America's highest-ranking businesswomen, many considered Barnes a role model. One of her stated reasons for quitting was the toll that her job took on her personal life, her husband, and her three children.[88] Some women were envious that she could afford to resign; others lamented her quitting as a setback for all working women. Barnes left after a highly successful, 22-year career. In spite of such a successful career, for issues of balance between family and work to be the focus of discussion is evidence of the continued challenge that women face.

Solutions   Organizations and individuals can take several actions to help women overcome career obstacles:

- Women need to find mentors or learning partners for specific areas rather than concentrating on finding a mentor who will guide them through their whole career.[89]

- Men and women need training to understand gender differences in style and approaches to work and the impact of these differences on how we perceive others and how we make decisions.
- Success must be redefined to fit the needs of diverse employees. The traditional definitions that emphasize money and status do not always satisfy the career goals of many women.[90]
- Both women and men should be offered flexible schedules that allow them to manage their personal lives more competently.

As opposed to finding an organization that fits with their values, many women find that starting their own business is the ideal alternative. One-third of all small businesses in the United States are owned by women.[91] By 1995, women-owned businesses in the United States employed about three-quarters as many employees as did the all Fortune 500 firms.[92] Since 1994, the number of these businesses has increased by 43 percent to 7.7 million.

Women continue to start businesses at twice the rate by men.[93] An interesting note is that the success rate of women-owned businesses in the United States is consistently higher than that of businesses owned by men. Some experts attribute this phenomenon to careful planning and calculated risk taking.[94] Whatever the reason, the success of women-owned businesses indicates that contrary to stereotypes, women are fully capable of managing business organizations effectively. And, as the number of women leaving corporate life to start or join small companies shows, the lack of person-organization fit is often the cause of their frustration in many corporate settings.

Managing stress and building a successful career are two central elements of individual effectiveness at work. There are, however, a number of other elements that contribute to individual effectiveness. Individual effectiveness depends to a great extent on the right fit between individual needs and organizational goals. We now consider the topic of organizational effectiveness and the issue of fit in determining individual and organizational effectiveness.

Summary Point 15.3   **How We Can Manage Our Careers**

- Characteristics of careers in the twenty-first century include taking individual responsibility, being flexible, building relationships, focusing on learning, gaining cross-cultural and cross-functional experience, and being employable.
- The three career stages are early, middle, and late. Each presents specific individual and organizational challenges.
- Special challenges that women face in managing their careers include gender discrimination, lack of access to

  career-building experiences, and social pressures for continuing traditional roles.
- Factors that help women build successful careers are mentors, training, entrepreneurship, and redefining success to provide a better fit between the person and the organization.

TRENDS IN ORGANIZATIONAL EFFECTIVENESS

A partial list of definitions of organizational effectiveness includes productivity, efficiency, profit, growth, readiness, high employee morale, and flexibility.[95] Other components of effectiveness are an organization's ability to use its environmental resources and respond to external demands.[96] Because of the complexity and variety of views, it is difficult to develop a single definition of effectiveness. We define **organizational effectiveness** as an organization's

Organizational effectiveness
An organization's ability to maintain smooth internal functioning and external adaptability while achieving its goals

ability to maintain smooth internal functioning and external adaptability while achieving its goals. The various approaches to effectiveness focus on different parts of organizational systems. To be effective, an organization must acquire the resources it needs, process them efficiently and effectively, and deliver the outcomes its environment values.[97] Figure 15.4 depicts the link between views of organizational effectiveness and open systems.

System resource approach
Definition of organizational effectiveness that focuses on how well an organization acquires and uses resources from the environment

The **system resource approach** to effectiveness focuses on how well an organization acquires and uses resources from the environment.[98] It considers the input side of open systems in terms of the organization's bargaining position in acquiring inputs and scarce valuable resources. Based on this approach, an organization is effective if it can acquire needed resources successfully. For instance, a university that is able to attract good students, hire high-quality faculty, and receive a good share of the state's budget to continue its operations is considered effective.

Internal process approach
Definition of organizational effectiveness that focuses on internal organizational processes including efficiency, employee satisfaction, management practices, and communication

The **internal process approach** focuses on internal organizational processes including efficiency, employee satisfaction, management practices, and communication.[99] For example, an organization that produces computers at better quality and at lower cost than another is more efficient. Based on the internal process approach, an organization is also effective if its employees are motivated and satisfied, there is good communication internally, and so forth.

Goal approach
Looks at the amount and quality of outputs in terms of goods or services

The **goal approach** to effectiveness looks at the amount and quality of outputs in terms of goods or services. An organization is effective if it achieves its various output goals of production, quality, service, and customer satisfaction. In some sense, the goal approach can encompass the other two approaches as the goals can be the effective acquisition of resources (inputs), employee motivation and communication, or efficiency (process). The goal approach focuses on the output component of open systems.

No single approach to organizational effectiveness is complete. Each provides a view of how an organization is performing, and it is appropriate and useful in some situations. Given the complexity of defining and measuring effectiveness and the many new forms, missions, and designs of organizations, it is no surprise that companies are developing numerous ways to evaluate how well they are doing.

Stakeholders, Quality, and Flexibility

Organizations are increasingly considering their relationship with stakeholders as a key factor of effectiveness. Remember that stakeholders are any group that has an interest or a stake in the organization. They include investors, employees, managers, suppliers, governments, customers, and communities. The **constituency approach** to effectiveness states that organizations are effective if they address the needs of their key stakeholders.[100]

Constituency approach
An organization is effective when it addresses the needs of its key stakeholders

One particular group of constituents many organizations consider vital is customers. Being responsive to customers' needs is a major organizational concern. Since the 1980s, being close to customers and serving their needs have become an integral part of the definitions of

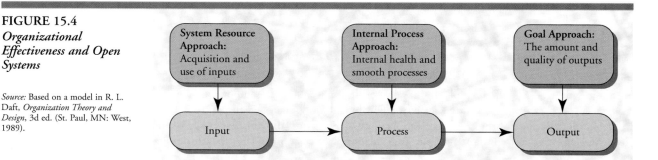

FIGURE 15.4
Organizational Effectiveness and Open Systems

Source: Based on a model in R. L. Daft, *Organization Theory and Design*, 3d ed. (St. Paul, MN: West, 1989).

organizational effectiveness.[101] An expanded view of customers includes not only the obvious external customers who buy products or use services but internal customers as well. **Internal customers** are employees who depend on a person or a department for products and services. To illustrate, the internal customers of a human resource department are all the managers and employees who use its services. The production department can consider as its internal customers the employees of both the research and development and the sales departments.

Internal customers
Employees who depend on a person or a department for products and services

Using customers as a focal point provides a broad perspective on organizational effectiveness as it includes collaboration, communication, efficiency, and many other factors that are key to performance.[102] For example, Boeing is ranked as one of the world's most-admired companies, partly because it is so effective in getting its customers involved in designing and customizing its aircraft. The company is also aware of the needs of its managers, employees, shareholders, and the community. For Boeing, effectiveness means making sure that the needs of all of its constituents are balanced.

Knight-Ridder, the second largest newspaper company in the United States and owner of 29 daily papers (including the *Philadelphia Inquirer* and the *Miami Herald*), achieved what appeared to be an impossible feat. CEO James Batten and President Tony Ridder confronted the challenges posed by declining readership of print media and the exponential growth of electronic information services. They pushed their conservative and well-entrenched news organization to redefine itself.

More than 300 employees became involved in an initiative aimed at increasing readership. Nonhierarchical teams debated, researched, and analyzed how to face the challenges. The effort, called 25/43 because it targeted readers between the ages of 25 and 43, lead to a redefinition of the traditional mission of a news organization. As a result of customer focus groups and extensive research and discussion, Knight-Ridder newspapers now focus as much on the relevance of their articles as on the quality of their news. Their papers introduced shorter, more accessible articles and columns about topics such as parenting and environmental tips.

For Knight-Ridder, the customer has become an obsession. Robert Singleton, the company's chief financial officer, states: "We were telling our people we want to build another *USA Today*. We want you to try to be more relevant to the community."[103]

Some companies focus on community stakeholders, so they view safeguarding the environment as one element of their effectiveness. British Petroleum is ranked number one among the oil companies for responsibly using environmental resources. CEO John Browne states: "You have to be responsive to the communities where you operate, and you can—as long as you perform extremely well for shareholders."[104]

Another current focus of effectiveness is quality. This focus has roots in the Total Quality Movement (TQM) of the 1980s, which advocates such practices as the use of teams, monitoring customer satisfaction, just-in-time inventory and delivery, statistical control methods, and cost-of-quality monitoring. A distinguishing feature of TQM is the concept of **kaizen** or continuous improvement.

Kaizen
Continuous improvement

Although many of the specific steps and technical practices of TQM are no longer being implemented, the core theme of quality continues to dominate organizational performance. It is much less expensive for companies to build a high-quality product than it is to constantly repair one that is of low quality. When auto manufacturers recall hundreds of thousands of vehicles because of a low-quality part, their prestige and their customers' loyalty is on the line. Customers always ask, "Couldn't you have done it right the first time?" The quality issue becomes more critical when a product's failure puts customers' lives in danger. If a drug manufacturer's product fails, thousands of patients suffer. If a Boeing airplane is faulty, the risk of physical harm to customers becomes severe. As a result of the risks and benefits, most companies consider quality part of their definition of effectiveness.

Finally, more organizations consider flexibility and adaptability crucial to organizational effectiveness. New structures such as virtual organizations and the extensive use of outsourc-

Hot ▼ Link

We discussed learning organizations in chapter 14, pp. 514–18.

ing are just a few examples of the trend toward flexibility. The concept of learning organizations directly addresses issues of flexibility and adaptability. To be effective, organizations should be able to learn and quickly adapt to a new environment.

Consider Coca-Cola's recent reorganization decision. Recognizing that foreign operations generated over 80 percent of the company's revenues, Coke reorganized its foreign bottling operations. The company did this in spite of heavy criticism from industry observers, who did not see the need to rock a successful boat. However, Roberto Goizueta, Coke's late CEO, considered the reorganization pivotal to preparing his company for the future. His proactive approach allowed Coke to be flexible and adaptable during his term in office and played a key part in Coke's selection as the "No. 1 company in the world in product quality, attracting and developing new talent, and overall global effectiveness."[105]

Summary Point 15.4   **What Are the Elements of the Open System, Stakeholder, and Quality Approaches to Organizational Effectiveness?**

- An effective organization acquires the resources it needs, processes them well, and delivers high-quality outputs to its environment.
- The constituency approach to effectiveness states that organizations are effective if they address the needs of their key stakeholders.

- Key stakeholders include internal and external customers.
- A focus on quality is one of the major aspects of organizational effectiveness in today's organizations.
- Being flexible and adaptable are requirements for organizations if they are to remain effective.

Identifying the Best Companies: Benchmarking

Benchmarking
The process of establishing performance and effectiveness standards and criteria by using companies identified as excellent models

How can managers tell how well their organizations are doing compared to their competition or to other successful companies? The answer for many organizations is to establish benchmarks. **Benchmarking** is the process of establishing performance and effectiveness standards and criteria by using companies identified as excellent as models. Managers and other business people can benchmark their company's overall performance against "best-run" companies and those with the "best practices." The business and the academic press regularly present lists of best practices based on survey and interview results.[106] These results are then used to benchmark or establish performance and effectiveness standards and criteria. Additionally, organizations can benchmark best practices in their own industries. For example, Federal Express is highly effective in delivering packages. DuPont is renowned for manufacturing chemicals. J. P. Morgan is ranked number one in creativity in banking. Pfizer is renowned for the quality of its pharmaceutical products. 3M is admired for its ability to innovate.[107]

What do the benchmarks tell us apart from the organizations that are the most admired? Common threads among exceptional companies are their attention to human resource practices, their strong relationships with those inside and outside the organization, and their ability to learn and adapt.

The attention to human resource practices and the strong established relationships with those inside and outside the organization help admired companies manage people well. They hire the right people, train them effectively, and then allow them to flourish. Jack Welch, the CEO of General Electric, personally interviews all candidates for the top 500 positions at GE. He states, "My whole job is picking the right people."[108]

Employee involvement (EI) programs
Programs that concentrate on increasing employee participation in decision making and employee empowerment

Many of these admired companies also focus on quality and employee involvement. In an extensive longitudinal study started in 1987, researchers at the University of Southern California regularly tracked the use of employee involvement and TQM programs in several hundred major companies.[109] **Employee involvement (EI) programs** concentrate on increasing employee participation in decision making and employee empowerment. They include such methods as information sharing, group decision making, and the use of teams, empowerment, profit sharing, and stock option plans. The study results show that the adoption of EI and TQM programs has clear positive benefits on performance, profitability, competitiveness, and employee satisfaction.[110]

Another common thread among these exceptional companies is their ability to learn and adapt. Sony has become one of the world's most effective companies because of its adaptability. Its new CEO, Nobuyuki Idei, is a courageous risk taker who has revamped the company. He has reorganized its board of directors, restructured major divisions, hired talented people, and improved the company's already innovative products. Sony's ability to learn and adapt has earned it the enviable position of being the most admired company in Asia.[111]

At PIPSA, a large Mexican paper manufacturer, CEO Rene Villarreal, a Yale Ph.D., is trying to bring the principles of learning to his organization. His chief learning officer (CLO), Raul Cicero, states: "People have to believe that the time they spend learning is productive. They also have to believe that what they do matters." Villarreal says, "Creating knowledge workers is easy if you're a software company filled with Ph.D.s. It's more difficult in a company of manual laborers." He believes that managers need to respect each employee's learning style and willingness to share his or her knowledge. "As long as you're interested in learning and can transfer knowledge, you're a good source of intellectual capital," he declares.[112]

The characteristics of today's excellent companies closely match those of effective individuals. Both are focused on building relationships and on learning. Both need to be flexible and adaptable and to be able to adjust to quick changes in our complex global business environment.

Summary Point 15.5   What Is Benchmarking?

- Benchmarking establishes performance and effectiveness standards and criteria by identifying high-performing companies and their characteristics.
- Common threads among exceptional companies are their attention to human resource practices through the establishment of employee involvement and TQM programs, establishing relationships inside and outside the organization, and their ability to learn and adapt.

CREATING A FIT BETWEEN THE PERSON AND THE ORGANIZATION

At the heart of personal and organizational effectiveness is a sense of being able to contribute and being able to make a difference.[113] As individuals, we are most fulfilled when we make a significant contribution to our organization, our community, or our family. It is important that what we do matters. Similarly, organizations achieve their potential when they make a positive impact in the lives of their varied stakeholders and constituents.

The opportunity and ability to contribute can happen only if there is a fit between what people want to achieve and what their organization wants to achieve. Fit has been defined in two ways:[114]

- *Compatibility:* Hiring employees whose values and goals match those of the organization, thereby strengthening and reinforcing the company's existing culture and increasing cohesion.[115]
- *Diversity:* Hiring employees who are different from the organization in order to extend the fit and provide diversity.[116]

Each approach has advantages and disadvantages, leading to the conclusion that organizations must combine them to be effective. Managers must strengthen their central cultural values and look for diversity on peripheral values. Additionally, younger organizations may need to find people who are compatible, whereas more established organizations can benefit from an infusion of diverse employees.[117]

Creating a fit between the person and the organization goes even further. It is not that organizations must find people who are either similar or different. Instead, to create fit, every manager and every employee must continuously consider how to encourage and make meaningful contributions that can simultaneously satisfy personal and organizational needs. Here are some general guidelines for managers and employees:

- Be clear on your own and the organization's central and peripheral values. As a potential employee, know your priorities and where you have flexibility. As a manager, be aware of what is key to organizational survival, what cannot be compromised, and the areas where there may be flexibility.
- When looking for a job or hiring a new employee, actively and thoroughly explore common values and areas of differences. How is the person similar or dissimilar to the organization? These issues should not be the only decision-making factor because few people and organizations always have the luxury of choice. However, awareness of the similarities and differences is a necessary starting point.
- When a new person joins the organization, work on finding common ground and developing compatibility to allow the person to develop a sense of belonging. Few of us are committed and motivated when we feel like outsiders. Managers and employees should both consider adjusting to accommodate the other person.
- Emphasize each employee's uniqueness and allow him or her to develop it in ways that contribute to the organization. For example, an efficiency-focused department may benefit from a new employee's marketing and public relations skills and build the expertise into department goals.
- As an employee, be ready to reevaluate your priorities and change. As a manager, be willing to push your organization to change and be ready to lead the change if needed to create a better fit. The constant adjustment and flexibility to new situations is part of both personal and organizational learning.

Creating a fit between the person and the organization allows both to be effective. Creating this fit is a dynamic, two-way process in which both parties are ready and willing to consider new ideas, explore new methods, and change as needed. In other words, the person-organization fit is about learning and growing, both of which are at the heart of effectiveness.

Effectiveness *in Context*

Everything is connected. Effectiveness at the individual and organizational levels is a complex, multifaceted concept. Whether an individual or an organization is effective depends on many factors. Much of early management practice and theory assumed that we could study issues and factors in isolation and establish their linkages and relationships. Such an approach has value, particularly when one is learning a discipline, as we saw demonstrated in every chapter of this book. Some examples include the study of individual factors that motivate people and the study of individuals and group decision-making factors. However, it is important to understand the dynamism of all factors as they affect the organization as a system.

The desired outcome of all the processes we have discussed is effectiveness and performance. In organizations, individual and overall organizational effectiveness are inseparable. People and organizations are part of one, large, seamless entity.[118] Although separating the ways one influences the other helps our understanding and makes a complex system more accessible, the process of influence and interaction is continuous and dynamic. Organizations and people are part of and tied to their environment, which includes all the organizational, technological, and cultural elements we discussed.

Effectiveness for both individuals and organizations comes from fit and integration. Individual missions, values, and goals have to fit and integrate with the organization's strategic forces. Organizations and people have to fit and integrate with their environment. Without such fit and integration there can be no effectiveness.

Sue Burish is an entrepreneur who designs training programs. After working for numerous companies—including Southern Pacific Railroad, Crocker Bank, and Raychem Corp., a large electronic manufacturer—she decided her personal and organizational lives did not mesh. "In traditional companies people don't believe in themselves. How they act is so frequently not who they are. They put on masks for eight hours and then take them off when they're done," she claims. She complains about a lack of stability in organizations; that is why she left to start her own business. "I have been riffed, merged, and bankrupted into unemployment. I used to think that what I needed to do was balance my life, keep my personal and professional lives separate. But I discovered that the real secret is integration. I integrate my work into my life. I don't see my work as separate from my identity," Burish declares.[119] Her new approach means that although she works hard she finds more value in her work and an increase in her personal and professional effectiveness.

The person-organization fit may not always be perfect, but with adjustment people and organizational goals can support one another. To increase the chances of success, employees, managers, and organizations should actively and continuously work to align individual, organizational, and environmental forces.

For updated information on the topics in this chapter, Web exercises, links to related Web sites, an on-line study guide, and more, visit our companion Web site at:
http://www.prenhall.com/nahavandi

A Look Back at the

MANAGERIAL CHALLENGE

Olmec Toys

Founding Olmec Toys to make and market ethnic dolls and action figures was only the first step for Yla Eason, a mother and entrepreneur determined to create suitable toys as positive role models for her young son. To capture even a tiny percentage of the lucrative U.S. toy market, she had to get Sun Man, Imani, and Menelik onto store shelves across the country, not an easy task for a pioneering firm. More doors opened for Olmec Toys after a major toy maker began offering a black doll in 1991—but the competitive environment heated up as well.

To stay ahead of her rivals, Eason concentrated on understanding the needs and interests of children, a major stakeholder group for any toy company. "We pay a lot of attention to what kids are doing and what the street trends are," she explained. Studying these trends led Olmec to introduce Hip Hop Kids, a line of dolls with names like "B. Boy Smart" dressed in up-to-the-minute street styles.[120] The company also teamed up with Playskool to create Kids of Color, soft dolls made with kente cloth designed specifically for infants.

All of Olmec's products have been designed with its young stakeholders firmly in mind. "We hope our toys help kids feel good about themselves, because that's the essential first step in achieving anything," said Eason. "We mean our products to be a form of identity by helping kids understand their own image and cultural heritage."[121]

Starting with the personal goal of finding a role model toy for her son, Eason has fused individual and organizational performance by building her company around her own mission, values, and goals. With annual sales of nearly $10 million, Olmec Toys has grown into the largest minority-owned toy maker in the United States—and earned Eason a prestigious Business Enterprise Award for translating social responsibility into profitability.[122] The personal-organizational fit at Olmec results in both personal and organizational effectiveness.

■ Point of View Exercises

You're the Manager: As Olmec Toys' distribution manager, you are responsible for getting more shelf space in more retail outlets for your dolls and action figures. Which of the three effectiveness approaches is the most appropriate for your situation? How can you apply the basics of this approach to measure and improve your department's effectiveness?

You're the Employee: As a shipper in the distribution department, you pack and send shipments of toys to U.S. retailers. Company growth has increased your workload and you feel more stressed than when you first joined the company last year. Realistically, what steps can you take to reduce the stress without quitting this job?

SUMMARY OF LEARNING OBJECTIVES

1. **Explain effectiveness, discuss the role of culture in its definition, and highlight the importance of the person-organization fit.** On both a personal and an organizational level, effectiveness is about achieving goals. Individuals or organizations that reach goals are effective. Cultural differences in individualism, masculinity, and time orientation affect specific definitions of effectiveness. In all cultures, however, the fit between individual needs and goals and organizational mission and goals are key to both individual and organizational effectiveness.

2. **Review the antecedents, consequences, and management of organizational stress and career management, two individual effectiveness issues.** Stress is an individual's physiological, psychological, and behavioral response to environmental stressors. Life changes and events, personality, and various relationships are part of individual factors in stress. Organizational stressors include the job, workload, role problems, working conditions, relationships at work, organizational culture and structure, and concern with career issues.

   Stress impacts the individual's psychological and physical health and affects organizational performance through increased absenteeism, turnover, and lower productivity and quality. Both the individual and the organization have a part in managing stress by either trying to reduce or eliminate sources of stress or by building the individual's resistance to stress.

   Careers in the next century will require individuals to take full responsibility to continue to learn and be flexible, to focus on building relationships, to gain global knowledge, and to be self-directed. At the early career stages, organizations need to deal with generational differences and face the challenge of providing interesting careers for young employees. At the mid-career stage, plateauing or stagnation is a major concern as both the individual and the organization find ways to reenergize careers in the face of diminished opportunity for promotion. In later stages, secure retirement and smooth succession and transition are major concerns.

   Women face particular challenges in building their careers as they continue to battle gender discrimination and conflict regarding women's roles. Such challenges can be overcome through organizational support, training for both men and women, and redefinition of careers in novel and flexible ways.

3. **Compare and contrast the various current views on organizational effectiveness.** Effective organizations acquire resources, process them efficiently, and deliver high-quality products and services to their environment. Current approaches to organizational effectiveness focus on how the organization satisfies its key stakeholders, particularly its internal and external customers. In addition, organizations are continuing their single-minded focus on quality and the ability to be flexible and adaptable as primary indicators of effectiveness.

   Benchmarking is the process of establishing performance and effectiveness standards and criteria. Increasingly, the practices of companies that are ranked as excellent and "best run" are used as models by others. Common threads among the best-run companies are their use of employee involvement programs and their focus on learning and flexibility.

4. **Describe how to create a fit between the person and the organization.** In organizations, individual and overall organizational effectiveness are inseparable. People and organizations are parts of an integrated whole. If a person fits into the organization, the individual and the organization can be more effective. Individual missions, values, and goals have to fit and integrate with the organization's context, structure, and strategy. In addi-

tion, organizations and people have to fit and integrate with their environment. To create fit, managers and employers must assess how to encourage and make meaningful contributions that can satisfy both personal and organizational needs. They need to understand the individual and the organizational values, how those values are similar and dissimilar, and find common ground to allow employees to develop a sense of belonging and ways to contribute, and how to adjust to change through learning.

KEY TERMS

alarm, p. 535
benchmarking, p. 556
burnout, p. 536
constituency approach, p. 554
effectiveness, p. 532
employee assistance program (EAP), p. 544
employee involvement (EI) programs, p. 556

exhaustion, p. 536
general adaptation syndrome (GAS), p. 535
goal approach, p. 554
hardiness, p. 539
internal customers, p. 555
internal process approach, p. 554
kaizen, p. 555

organizational effectiveness, p. 553
plateauing, p. 548
resistance, p. 535
role ambiguity, p. 541
role conflict, p. 541
stress, p. 534
stressors, p. 534
system resource approach, p. 554

REVIEW QUESTIONS

1. What is effectiveness and what role does culture play in how people view effectiveness?
2. What are the sources and consequences of stress? What can individuals and organizations do to help manage stress?
3. What are key career challenges in the next century? What can you do to prepare yourself better for a successful career?
4. When is an organization effective?
5. Compare and contrast the different approaches to organizational effectiveness.

DISCUSSION QUESTIONS

1. How can global managers accommodate the needs of their diverse workforce when it comes to defining success and effectiveness?
2. What is the link between stress and the person-organization fit?
3. As a manager, how can you help your employees manage their careers successfully? What is the employee's responsibility?
4. How has the focus of organizational effectiveness changed over the years? Do you find the shift appropriate? Why? Why not?
5. Discuss how the fit between the person and the organization leads to effectiveness.

▶ **SELF-ASSESSMENT 15**
Key Questions for Managing Your Career

The questions below will help you assess how well you are managing your career. (If you don't yet have a career-oriented job, think of your role in your educational institution or in another setting that is helping you to further your career.) See Appendix 3 for a scoring key.

Use the following rating scale to answer the questions:

    1 = NEVER OR ALMOST NEVER TRUE   2 = SELDOM TRUE
    3 = USUALLY TRUE   4 = ALWAYS OR ALMOST ALWAYS TRUE

1. I add value to my job and company rather than simply pass on existing information.   1   2   3   4
2. I am always looking for ways to make things better at work.   1   2   3   4
3. I am aware of and informed about what is going on in my company and in my industry.   1   2   3   4
4. I continually look for opportunities to learn new skills.   1   2   3   4
5. I am on the lookout for and volunteer for global assignments.   1   2   3   4
6. I am continually trying out new ideas and new technologies at work.   1   2   3   4
7. I actively look for opportunities to work with people who are in different areas.   1   2   3   4
8. I am building a large network of professional contacts inside and outside the organization.   1   2   3   4
9. I know my priorities and I have a clear sense of what is important to me in life.   1   2   3   4
10. My success in life only partially depends on my job.   1   2   3   4

Sources: Based on A. S. Grove, "A High-Tech CEO Updates His Views on Managing and Careers," *Fortune* 132, no. 6 (1995): 229–30; H. Lancaster, "Learn 'Languages' and You'll Always Land on Your Feet," *Wall Street Journal*, October 24, 1997, B1.

▶ **TEAM EXERCISE 15**
Career Goals and Interviews

One of the most common questions asked in job interviews is "What are your career and life goals?" Being able to answer such a question clearly can make the difference between getting and not getting the job. The purpose of this exercise is to provide you with practice in identifying and presenting your career goals in interviews.

PART I: WRITING DOWN YOUR GOALS
Write a paragraph stating your career and life goals. The statement should be general enough to fit different situations. It should reflect your personal values and priorities. Consider both short-term (1 to 2 years) and long-term (5 years and beyond) goals.

PART II: GROUP INTERVIEWS
In groups of three, take turns presenting your career goals in a mock interview setting. In each round, one person presents and two act as interviewers. The interviewers should challenge the candidates and force them to think on their feet. Remember to maintain a professional atmosphere. The interviewers then provide feedback and advice to the candidates on how to clarify the goals.

PART III: CLASS PRESENTATION
Each team should present the major sticking points they saw and any general advice they developed as a result of their interviews (what works and what does not).

UP CLOSE

► ## Western Central University Tries to Define Effectiveness

Western Central University (WCU) is an urban state university that offers upper-division undergraduate and several professional graduate programs such as master's degrees in nursing, education, and business administration. The College of Business (COB) has nearly 1,500 students including 500 part-time MBA students. The COB student body is composed of a majority of working adults at both the graduate and undergraduate levels. Ninety percent of the MBAs and over 60 percent of the undergraduates work full time, and their average age is 26.

Dean Linda McNair joined the COB three years ago with a focus on benchmarking and defining educational outcomes for the college. She strongly believes that her college should be run like a business. She states: "We get limited resources from the state. We need to identify our customers and serve them well. We need to become lean and efficient. There is no room for waste; we simply don't have enough resources to offer a lot of different majors and electives. We need to focus." To that end, McNair pushed through a curriculum revision that eliminated all majors, replacing them with specializations that require fewer credits. The courses are lockstep, with only two electives allowed in each major. McNair hired several part-time faculty and is increasing the course offerings on the Internet and adding TV courses. Creating a general major was primarily a response to the input of several business leaders who consistently stated that they really did not care about the majors. Rather, they wanted well-educated generalists who could be trained.

The faculty approved the curriculum changes by a narrow margin. Implementation of the new programs has been slow and many faculty have expressed concern about its potential effects. Nancy Durant, a management faculty members, muses: "This whole talk of efficiency in education may make economic sense, but I am not sure if education is about efficiency or quality. Are we supposed to just get people out of here as soon as we can, or are we here to give them a quality education?" One of the MIS faculty, Charlie Garcia, teaches one of the on-line courses. "The course is full and is going well. It is MIS

and we are using the technology. However, I just can't really take care of my students. We can't discuss anything really in depth; the on-line chats are not the same as the face-to-face classroom discussions. Students are learning the basics, but not a whole lot more. They do sound happy though." The finance faculty, whose major was eliminated, complain: "We know about efficiency in finance, but our role is to add value to our students and our community. This can't be done by hiring part-timers and offering TV courses."

Another major debate among the faculty is who the customer is. One group considers the students the primary customers. A marketing faculty member states, "These are not 18-year-old freshmen who aren't sure of what they want. Our students are mostly working adults who pay for their own education. They are the customer." That view is also shared by the student services staff and advisers in the college. An accounting faculty member disagrees: "Our students don't always know what is good for them. If you left it up to them, they would just want easy courses to graduate. The true customer is the business community that hires our students. We need to cater to their needs." An ethics professor takes the argument one step further by suggesting that the role of the university is to educate truly productive citizens.

The business students' association president summarized the students' views in a letter to the dean. The students' major concerns are the lack of electives, few choices of majors, the lack of sufficient sections of different courses offered, poor career services, and unavailability of part-time faculty. The students' overriding concern is the fact that recruiters come to campus looking for students with specific majors; without such majors, WCU students are at a disadvantage.

Questions

1. What effectiveness measures should the COB use?
2. Who are the COB's customers and constituents?
3. If you were the dean, what would you do?

THE BIG PICTURE

▶ **Working Hard to Improve Working Conditions**

Linda Chavez-Thompson has been working hard to improve the lot of workers throughout the United States for more than 30 years. Elected as executive vice president of the AFL-CIO in 1995, she became the highest-ranking woman in the country's labor movement—and gained a new, more powerful platform from which to campaign for workers rights.

The daughter of a sharecropper who served as a union steward, Chavez-Thompson vividly remembers looking for a summer job in Lubbock, Texas, when she was 10 years old. The only work she could find was hoeing cotton alongside her parents, which paid 30 cents an hour for a 10-hour day.[123] After that early introduction to the world of work, she began her professional career in 1967 as a secretary for the Laborers' International Union. She soon became active in union organizing and rose through the ranks to the position of international vice president of the American Federation of State, County and Municipal Employees Union, with responsibility for political and legislative action, educational programs, and other activities.

After she was elected to the AFL-CIO position, Chavez-Thompson continued to demonstrate her stakeholder focus by listening and responding to workers from all walks of life. "It's not just the members," she said. "We're also working for those who have no representation, who have no voice." One group that was particularly responsive to her outreach efforts was working women. "In the past, women felt they weren't part of making changes, that their opinions weren't sought out," she said.[124] To this group,

Chavez-Thompson was more than a top union official: She was also a highly visible role model for career success.

Chavez-Thompson was keenly aware of the career-stalling effects of corporate downsizing. In AFL-CIO town meetings around the country, she called for companies to be held publicly accountable for providing suitable wages, benefits, safe working conditions, and—ultimately—employee loyalty. At the same time, she believed that her organization should publicize the achievements of companies that have built especially solid relationships with employees, their internal customers.

In addition to serving on several national boards and councils, Chavez-Thompson added yet another challenging responsibility in 1997: serving on the president's Race Advisory Board. "What I am looking forward to is taking this issue off the back burner and putting it on the front burner," she explained. "Certainly, someone has to do something before [the issue of race] becomes a total crisis."[125]

Questions

1. How might Chavez-Thompson define effectiveness in terms of her executive position at the AFL-CIO?
2. What effect do you think Chavez-Thompson's outside activities might have on her career?
3. If you were in Chavez-Thompson's position, what would you say about shifts in the contract between companies and employees?

NOTES

1. Courtenay Haris, "Dolls for Kids of Color," *PriceCostco Connection* (1995), accessed on-line at http://www.pricecostco.com/pcc/profile/pr795d.htm.
2. City of Richmond, "Olmec Toys—A Bright Star in the Business Community," (1997): accessed on-line at http.//www.ci.richmond.va.us/active/9705/aolmectoys.
3. Harris, "Dolls for Kids of Color."
4. Maggie Jackson, "Doing Right Thing Can Be Good for Profits," *The Standard-Times* (New Bedford, MA), February 19, 1997, accessed on-line at http://www.s-t.com/daily/02-97/02-19-97/a066bu03.
5. J. Martin, "Eli Broad Runs Things His Way," *Fortune* 136, no. 7 (October 13, 1997): 177–80.
6. A. Kupfer, "MCI Worldcom: It's the Biggest Merger Ever. Can It Rule Telecom?" *Fortune* 137, no. 8 (1998): 119–28.
7. Ibid., 120.
8. Ibid., 126.
9. J. P. Alston, "Wa, Guanxi, and Inhwa: Managerial Principles in Japan, China, and Korea," *Business Horizons* 32, no. 2 (1989): 28–29.
10. M. T. Matteson and J. M. Ivancevich, *Controlling Work Stress* (San Francisco: Jossey-Bass, 1987).
11. The multistage view of stress was proposed by H. Seyles, *The Stress of Life* (New York: McGraw-Hill, 1976).
12. H. Levinson, "When Executives Burn Out," *Harvard Business Review* 74, no. 4 (1996): 152–63.
13. R. Karasek and T. Theorell, *Healthy Work: Stress, Productivity and the Reconstruction of Working Life* (New York: Wiley, 1990).
14. A. Perkins, "Medical Costs: Saving Money by Reducing Stress," *Harvard Business Review* (November–December 1994): 12.
15. P. Lunde-Jensen, "The Costs of Occupational Accidents and Work-Related Sickness in Nordic Countries," *Janus* 18, no. 4 (1994): 25–26.
16. S. Cartwright and C. L. Cooper, *Managing Workplace Stress* (Thousand Oaks, CA: Sage, 1997).
17. A. Rowley, L. do Rosario, and S. Awanohara, "Ease Up, Japan: What's In It for Us? A Dying Breed," *Far Eastern Economic Review* 155, no. 31 (August 6, 1992): 52–59.
18. F. A. Palumbo and P. A. Herbig, "Salaryman Sudden Death Syndrome," *Employee Relations* 16, no. 1 (1994): 54–62.
19. C. M. Solomon, "If You're Feeling Overworked, Just Think About How the Japanese Feel," *Personnel Journal* 72, no. 6 (1993): 58–60.
20. P. L. Perrewe and F. A. Vickory, "Combating Job Stress," *Training and Development Journal* (April 1988): 84–85.
21. S. Shellenbarger, "Some Readers Saw the Burnout Coming, and Many Empathized," *Wall Street Journal*, July 9, 1997, B1.
22. T. A. Judge and S. Watanabe, "Another Look at the Job Satisfaction–Life Satisfaction Relationship," *Journal of Applied Psychology* 78, no. 6 (1993): 939–48.
23. D. Ganster and J. Schaubroeck, "Work Stress and Employee Health," *Journal of Management* (June 1991): 235–42; S. Boeck and M. E. Mulling, "Drug Abuse on the Job," *USA Today*, February 25, 1997, A1.
24. T. D. Schellhardt, "Want to Be a Manager?," *Wall Street Journal*, April 4, 1997, A1, A4.
25. T. H. Holmes and R. H. Rahe, "The Social Readjustment Rating Scale," *Journal of Psychosomatic Research* (1967): 213–18.
26. Ibid.
27. S. C. Kobasa, "Conceptualization and Measurement of Personality in Job Stress Research," in J. J. Hurrell Jr., L. R. Murphy, S. L. Sauter, and C. L. Cooper (eds.), *Occupational Stress: Issues and Development in Research* (New York: Taylor & Francis, 1988): 100–9.
28. M. Castleman, "Close Social Ties Keep Body, Mind Together," *New York Times*, reported in the *Arizona Republic*, September 1, 1996, A2.
29. Based on a report in "All Things Considered," National Public Radio, January 2, 1997.
30. G. Levenworth, "Prevention Strategies Pay Off," *Business and Health* 13, no. 3 (1995): 28–33.
31. S. M. Holmes, M. L. Power, and C. K. Walter, "A Motor Carrier Wellness Program: Development and Testing," *Transportation Journal* 35, no. 3 (1996): 33–45.
32. M. Jackson, "Job Rated Top Inducer of Stress, Study Finds: Demand at Work Hurting Home Life and Office Life," *Arizona Republic*, April 15, 1998, E1, E3.
33. For an example of the impact of stress on medical doctors, see "Stress Drives Doctors to Drink and Drugs," *IRS Employment Review* (May 1996): 5559.
34. T. D. Schellhard, "Off the Ladder: Want to Be a Manager? Many People Say No, Calling the Job Miserable," *Wall Street Journal*, April 4, 1997, A1, A4.
35. Jackson, "Job Rated Top Inducer," E3.
36. S. Shellenbarger, "People Are Working Harder—and Taking More Heat for It," *Wall Street Journal*, February 26, 1997, B1.
37. Jackson, "Job Rated Top Inducer," E1.
38. For a discussion of role issues in stress, see J. M. Ivancevich and M. T. Matteson, *Stress at Work* (Glenview, IL: Scott Foresman, 1980); S. S. Nandram and B. Kandermans, "Integrating Domains of Work Stress and Industrial Relations: Evidence from Five Countries," *Journal of Organizational Behavior* 14, no. 5 (1993): 415–31; K. Williams and G. M. Alliger, "Roles Stressor, Mood Spillover, and Perceptions of Work-Family Conflict in Employed Parents," *Academy of Management Journal* 37, no. 4 (1994): 837–68.
39. Jackson, "Job Rated Top Inducer," E1.
40. C. L. Cooper and M. J. Smith, *Job Stress and Blue Collar Work* (New York: Wiley, 1985).
41. D. Pink, "Free Agent Nation," *Fast Company* (December–January 1998): 132.
42. J. T. Sauter, S. Hurrell, and C. L. Cooper, *Job Control and Worker Health* (New York: Wiley, 1989).
43. L. T. Thomas and D. C. Ganster, "Impact of Family Supportive Work Variables on Work-Family Conflict and Strain: A Control Perspective," *Journal of Applied Psychology* 80, no. 1 (1995): 6–15.
44. S. M. Crampton, J. W. Hodge, J. M. Mishra, and S. Price, "Stress and Stress Management," *S.A.M. Advanced Management Journal* 60, no. 3 (1995): 10–20.
45. H. Lancaster, "Getting Your Goals for Life and Work Down in Writing," *Wall Street Journal*, October 14, 1997, B1.
46. W. F. Joyce, V. E. McGee, and J. W. Slocum Jr., "Designing Lateral Organizations: An Analysis of the Benefits, Costs, and Enablers of Nonhierarchical Organizational Forms," *Decision Sciences* 28, no. 1 (1997): 1–15.
47. S. Reese, "Pushing Productivity Past the Breaking Point," *Business and Health* 15, no. 4 (1997): 31–36.
48. Ibid., 34.
49. A. M. Downey, "Fit to Work," *Business Quarterly* 61, no. 2 (1996): 69–74.
50. Reese, "Pushing Productivity."
51. E. McShulskis, "Stress Reduction in the Workplace," *HR Magazine* 41, no. 8 (1996): 24.
52. Downey, "Fit to Work."
53. Crampton et al., *Stress*; A. B. Fisher, "Welcome to the Age of Overwork," *Fortune* (November 30, 1992): 64–71; K. Hall and L. K. Savery, "Tight Rein, More Stress," *Harvard Business Review* (January–February 1986): 1162–64.
54. P. Sellers, "The Boss's Other Life," *Fortune* 136, no. 10 (November 24, 1997): 160.
55. Ibid., 159.
56. For some examples of the positive effect of social support, see R. Karambayya and A. H. Reilly, "Dual Earner Couples: Attitudes and Actions in Restructuring Work for Family," *Journal of Organizational Behavior* 13, no. 6 (1992): 585–601; S. Parasuram, J. H. Greenhaus, and C. S. Granrose, "Role Stressors, Social Support, and Well-Being Among Two-Career Couples," *Journal of Organizational Behavior* 13, no. 4 (1992): 339–56; M. R. Manning, C. N. Jackson, and M. R. Fusilier, "Occupational Stress, Social Support, and the Costs of Health Care," *Academy of Management Journal* 39, no. 3 (1996): 738–46.
57. J. S. Anderson, "Stress and Burnout Among Nurses: A Social Network Approach," *Journal of Social Behavior and Personality* 6, no. 7 (1991): 251–72.
58. Thomas and Ganster, "Impact of Family"; S. C. Thompson, A. Sobolew-Shubin, M. E. Galbraith, and L. Schwankovsky, "Maintaining Perceptions of Control: Finding Perceived Control in Low-Control Circumstances," *Journal of Personality and Social Psychology* 64, no. 2 (1993): 293–304.
59. D. T. Hall and P. H. Mirvis, "The New Career Contract: Developing the Whole Person at Midlife and Beyond," *Journal of Vocational Behavior* 47 (1995): 269–89.
60. K. R. Brousseach, M. J. Driver, K. Eneroth, and R. Larsson, "Career Pandemonium: Realigning Organizations and Individuals," *Academy of Management Executive* 10, no. 4 (1996): 52–66.
61. A. S. Grove, "A High-Tech CEO Updates His Views on Managing and Careers," *Fortune* 132, no. 6 (1995): 229.

62. G. Dutton, "Nurturing Employees on the Bottom Line," *HR Focus* (September 1997): 1–3.
63. D. T. Hall, "Protean Careers of the 21st Century," *Academy of Management Executive* 10, no. 4 (1996): 8–15.
64. Dutton, "Nurturing Employees."
65. B. B. Alfred, C. C. Snow, and R. E. Miles, "Characteristics of Managerial Careers in the 21st Century," *Academy of Management Executive* 10, no. 4 (1996): 17–27.
66. Ibid.
67. H. Lancaster, "Employees Still Find Corporate Loyalty Has Its Rewards," *Wall Street Journal*, April 6, 1996, B1.
68. Ibid.
69. For a discussion of how we need to change the language we use to define career issues, see M. B. Arthur and D. M. Rousseau, "A Career Lexicon for the 21st Century," *Academy of Management Executive* 10, no. 4 (1996): 28–39.
70. E. Graham, "When Terrible Twos Become Terrible Teens," *Wall Street Journal*, February 5, 1997, B1, B4.
71. K. D. Carson and P. P. Carson, "Career Entrenchment: A Quiet March Toward Occupational Death," *Academy of Management Executive* 11, no. 1 (1997): 62–75.
72. H. Lancaster, "Learn 'Languages' and You'll Always Land on Your Feet," *Wall Street Journal*, October 24, 1997, B1.
73. Ibid.
74. R. Weiss, "Aging: New Answers to Old Questions," *National Geographic* 192, no. 5 (1997): 2–31.
75. Martin, "Eli Broad," 180.
76. K. E. Reichardt, "Salaries 1995," *Management Accounting* 77, no. 12 (1997): 20–29.
77. Ibid., 27.
78. G. Feldman, "Breaking Through the Glass Ceiling," *Publishers Weekly*, vol. 244:31 (1997): 82–90.
79. See the Glass Ceiling Commission study in http.//www.ilr.cornell.edu/library/e_archive/GlassCeiling.
80. P. Brook, "Superwoman Goes Home," *Saturday Night* 111, no. 5 (1996): 30–38.
81. See G. Stuttaford, *Publishers Weekly* 243, no. 38 (1996): 64, review of S. Hays, *The Cultural Contradiction of Motherhood* (New Haven, CT: Yale University Press, 1996).
82. B. Morris, "Executive Women Confront Midlife Crisis," *Fortune* 132, no. 6 (September 18, 1995): 60–86.
83. Ibid., 62.
84. Ibid.
85. Ibid., 68.
86. Ibid., 65.
87. B. O'Reilly, "Men at Midlife: Crisis? What Crisis," *Fortune* 132, no. 6 (1995): 72; also see B. Morris, "Is Your Family Wrecking Your Career?" *Fortune* 135, no. 5 (March 17, 1995): 70–90.
88. N. Deogun, "Top PepsiCo Executive Picks Family over Job," *Wall Street Journal*, September 24, 1997, B1, B10; S. Shellenbarger, "Woman's Resignation from Top Pepsi Post Rekindles Debates," *Wall Street Journal*, October 8, 1997, B1.
89. H. Lancaster, "How Women Can Find Mentors in a World with Few Role Models," *Wall Street Journal*, April 11, 1997, B1.
90. Morris, "Executive Women."
91. S. D. Esters, "Conning Studies Female Entrepreneurs," *National Underwriter* 101, no. 40 (1997): 47–48.
92. Morris, "Executive Women."
93. "The Feminine Factor," *Internal Auditor* 54, no. 5 (1997): 48–49.
94. Esters, "Conning Studies," 48.
95. For a discussion of various views of organizational effectiveness, see J. P. Campbell, "On the Nature of Organizational Effectiveness," in P. S. Goodman and J. M. Pennings (eds.), *New Perspectives on Organizational Effectiveness* (San Francisco: Jossey-Bass, 1977): 36–41; K. S. Cameron and D. A. Whetten, *Organizational Effectiveness: A Comparison of Multiple Models* (New York: Academic Press, 1982). Other examples can be found in organizational theory textbooks such as R. H. Miles, *Macro Organizational Behavior* (Glenview, IL: Scott Foresman, 1980); S. P. Robbins, *Organizational Theory: Structure, Design, and Applications* (Englewood Cliffs, NJ: Prentice Hall, 1987).
96. J. Pfeffer, "Power and Resource Allocation in Organizations," in B. M. Staw and F. Salancik (eds.), *New Directions in Organizational Behavior* (Chicago: St. Clair, 1977).
97. See R. L. Daft, *Organization Theory and Design*, 3d ed. (St. Paul, MN: West, 1985): 98–99.
98. J. B. Cunningham, "A Systems-Resource Approach for Evaluating Organizational Effectiveness," *Human Relations* 31 (1978): 631–56; E. Yuchtman and S. E. Seashore, "A System Resource Approach to Organizational Effectiveness," *Administrative Science Quarterly* 11 (1967): 377–95.
99. J. B. Cunningham, "Approaches to the Evaluation of Organizational Effectiveness," *Academy of Management Review* 2 (1977): 463–74; W. Evan, "Organization Theory and Organizational Effectiveness: An Exploratory Analysis," *Organization and Administrative Sciences* 7 (1976): 15–28.
100. J. Pfeffer and G. Salancik, *External Control of Organizations* (New York: Harper & Row, 1978).
101. T. J. Peter and R. H. Waterman Jr., *In Search of Excellence: Lessons from America's Best-Run Companies* (New York: Harper & Row, 1982), were among the first to identify responsiveness to customers as key to organizational effectiveness.
102. For a recent ranking of excellent companies, see A. Fisher, "The World's Most Admired Companies," *Fortune* 136, no. 8 (October 27, 1997): 220–40.
103. N. A. Wishart, J. J. Elam, and D. Robey, "Redrawing the Portrait of a Learning Organization: Inside Knight-Ridder, Inc.," *Academy of Management Executive* 10, no. 1 (1996): 7–20.
104. Fisher, "The World's Greatest," 240.
105. Ibid., 228.
106. This trend started with Peters and Waterman, *In Search of Excellence*, and continues through articles in the business press and recent books such as J. Fitz-Ens, *The Eight Practices of Exceptional Companies: How Great Organizations Make the Most of Their Human Assets* (New York: Amacom, 1997).
107. Fisher, "The World's Greatest."
108. Ibid., 232.
109. E. E. Lawler III, S. A. Mohrman, and G. E. Ledford Jr., *Creating High Performance Organizations: Practices and Results of Employee Involvement and Total Quality Management in Foreign 1000 Companies* (San Francisco: Jossey-Bass, 1995).
110. For summary information on the relationship of EI and TQM to organizational outcomes, see ibid., 72, 77.
111. Fisher, "The World's Greatest."
112. E. Matson, "You Can Teach This Old Company New Tricks," *Fast Company* (October–November 1997): 44–45.
113. G. Dutton, "The Re-Enchantment of Work," *Management Review* (February 1998): 51–54.
114. G. N. Powell, "Reinforcing and Extending Today's Organizations: The Simultaneous Pursuit of Person-Organization Fit and Diversity," *Organizational Dynamics* (Winter 1998): 50–61.
115. Among proponents of the compatibility argument is T. J. Peters and R. H. Waterman Jr., *In Search of Excellence: Lessons from America's Best Run Companies* (New York: Harper & Row, 1982); for studies about compatibility, see J. A. Chatman, "Matching People and Organizations: Selection and Socialization in Public Accounting Firms," *Administrative Science Quarterly* 36 (1991): 459–84.
116. Proponents of the diversity arguments include T. Cox and S. Blake, "Managing Cultural Diversity: Implications for Organizational Competitiveness," *Academy of Management Executive* 5, no. 3 (1991): 45–56.
117. Powell, "Reinforcing and Extending."
118. D. K. Banner and T. E. Gagne, *Designing Effective Organizations: Traditional and Transformational Views* (Thousand Oaks, CA: Sage, 1995); M. J. Wheatley, *Leadership and the New Science: Learning About Organization from an Orderly Universe* (San Francisco: Berrett Koehler, 1994).
119. D. Pink, "Free Agent Nation," *Fast Company* (December–January 1998): 134.
120. Harris, "Dolls for Kids of Color."
121. Ibid.
122. Jackson, "Doing Right Thing."
123. Leyla Kokmen, "Bringing New Life into AFL-CIO," *Seattle Times* (May 17, 1996): accessed on-line at http://www.seattletimes.com/sbin/iarecord?NS-search-set=/352b8/aaaa0059i2b85b7&NS-doc-offset=3&.
124. Ibid.
125. Michael A. Fletcher, "Clinton Names Advisory Panel to Address U.S. Racial Divide," *Washington Post*, June 13, 1997, A2.

VIDEO CASE 5

ON LOCATION!

▶ The Person-Organization Fit at Jagged Edge

A person's and an organization's effectiveness and success stem from a fit between the goals of the person and those of the organization. Nowhere is this concept better represented than at Jagged Edge.

The Quenemoens created a company so they could do what they love best and provide a service to a sport that is their passion. Margaret states, "This is what we are."[1] Paula echoes the sentiment: "Work is an extension of what we do. Our products have evolved through our own use."[2] Tim O'Neill, JEMG's buyer, is almost poetic when asked about the issue: "Climbing fulfills my body and my spirit. Working here grounds me. It gives me a sense of worth. I have the feeling of kindred spirit. The Jagged Edge is my extended family."[3]

A large part of JEMG's success can be attributed to the company's ability to attract employees who share a common passion in life. Everybody loves mountain sports. These sports define who they are as individuals. For many of the employees, there is no other alternative in life. Many of them lived in poverty, sacrificing all simple amenities to be able to do the extreme sports that they love. Several JEMG managers, including Margaret herself, report having lived in their car for periods of time. JEMG provides a means for all of them to make a living at something that is their passion and to continue to pursue their passion. Margaret states, "Our goal is to be successful. We are in an industry we love, and down the road we will make a good living as a benefit."[4]

Finding such a perfect fit is rare. Maintaining it may be one of the biggest challenges JEMG faces. Currently, managers make every effort to match individual needs with company goals. For example, after hiring Josh Lear, Margaret was so impressed with his abilities and what she considered to be a great fit with the company that she moved him around

until she found the merchandising position at which he is currently excelling. Greulich also talks about finding the "perfect match" for employees so that they can do what they love while helping the company. He remembers how Tim O'Neill's love of traveling was one factor that led to him becoming a buyer for the company. "He needed to take trips, so he became the buyer. It's a perfect fit."[5]

Finding the right fit for everyone keeps employees satisfied with their jobs. When things get out of control and difficult to manage, the folks at Jagged Edge simply head for the mountains. They hike, climb, bike, or kayak. They can take time off simply because the weather is perfect for their sport. They still are responsible for their job, but each manager, including the owners, share a passion for the sports and understand the burning desire to go out on that "perfect powder day."

The Quenemoens themselves find release in their sport, although they feel the enormous pressure of running a business in a competitive world. When asked how stress affects her, Margaret states, "I bite my nails, and I do activities to let off steam."[6] The Jagged Edge people rely on the mountain sport metaphor to manage their stress and their career. They simply take things one step at time, learn from their mistakes, and continue the journey until they reach their goal.

If the past helps predict the future, even partially, the Jagged Edge Mountain Gear Company has a bright future ahead. The Quenemoens' goal of "becoming a nationally recognized competitor" in their industry seems near. Margaret is most concerned about the company's ability to continue growing. Paula worries about unforeseen obstacles that have kept other companies with similarly good products from succeeding in the past. She also worries about becoming "corporate."

Questions

1. What factors create the person-organization fit at Jagged Edge? What are the results of such a fit? What are the potential problems with such good fit?
2. What major challenges do you think the company faces?
3. What do you think the company can do to prepare for these challenges?

Notes

[1] Interview with Margaret Quenemoen, June 4, 1998.

[2] Interview with Paula Quenemoen, June 8, 1998.

[3] Interview with Tim O'Neill, June 8, 1998.

[4] Interview with M. Quenemoen.

[5] Interview with Erlend Greulich, June 8, 1998.

[6] Interview with M. Quenemoen.

APPENDIX 1:
The History of Management Ideas

Although several thousand years ago historians, philosophers, and social scientists discussed the nature of people, groups, and social institutions, it was not until the industrial revolution of the late nineteenth century that the scientific study of organizations began. In this appendix, we review the evolution of management and organization behavior theory, considering the classical and humanistic viewpoints.[1] We also focus on early studies of motivation that help inform our current understanding of organizational behavior. We close with a brief overview of dominant approaches to the current study of organizational behavior.

 THE CLASSICAL VIEWPOINT

The first formal study of management dates back to the industrial revolution of the nineteenth century. As scientific discoveries such as the steam engine allowed for mass production of goods, large factories replaced individual artisans. These large factories posed new challenges for owners. Large numbers of workers had to be managed, trained, controlled, and motivated. These workers had to have the right tools and a ready supply of materials.

To address these problems, managers began to rely on rational, scientific approaches similar to those used to invent factory machines. The early theories concentrated on training workers to become as efficient as machines. Several later theories introduced the importance of people in effective management.

Scientific Management

The early study of management focused on applying scientific principles to managing organizations. The phrase **scientific management** indicates the application of scientific principles to management practice.

Frederick Taylor   Frederick Winslow Taylor (1856–1915) is known as the father of scientific management. In 1889 Taylor, an engineer for Bethlehem Steel, analyzed the problem of **soldiering**, defined as the process of workers deliberately working under capacity.[2] Taylor hypothesized that three factors caused soldiering: workers' fear of losing their jobs if each produced more, inappropriate wages and incentives that did not encourage high production, and a reliance on rules of thumb in operations and production.

Scientific management
Early approach to management using scientific principles to manage people and organizations

Soldiering
The process of workers deliberately working under capacity

571

Table A.1   TAYLOR'S SCIENTIFIC MANAGEMENT PRINCIPLES

1. Each task should be studied scientifically to determine the best way to perform it.
2. Workers should be carefully, scientifically selected and trained to perform tasks.
3. Management and workers should cooperate to ensure efficient production.
4. Management should be responsible for planning. Workers should implement management's plans.

Using scientific methods, Taylor precisely measured the movements, tools, and processes that workers used to unload iron from rail cars and load steel onto them. These time and motion studies suggested that each worker was capable of loading 47.5 tons per day instead of the average 12.5. Taylor further devised a wage incentive plan that recommended a 30 to 100 percent increase in wages to encourage workers to meet the new goal. The application of scientific principles at Bethlehem Steel led to a considerable increase in production. Table A.1 summarizes Taylor's proposed scientific management principles that served as the basis for early scientific management.

Frank and Lillian Gilbreth   Two other influential thinkers of the scientific management era were the husband-and-wife team of Frank and Lillian Gilbreth. Frank Gilbreth (1868–1924) is famous for his pursuit of efficiency and finding the "one best way" to do anything. Lillian Gilbreth (1878–1972) obtained her doctorate in psychology and focused her attention on the human aspects of work. The Gilbreths pioneered the time and motion studies that Taylor and other researchers implemented. After Frank's death in 1924, Lillian continued her work alone as one of the first female contributors to the field of management.

Many scientific management concepts that Taylor and the Gilbreths proposed were strongly criticized for encouraging worker exploitation, workforce reductions, overspecialization, and monotonous work. Despite the criticism, many managers adopted these ideas. The influence of scientific management is still evident in management areas such as training and job design.

Administrative Scientific Management Principles

Administrative approach
Early management approach focused on helping managers coordinate organizational activities

In contrast to scientific management principles that concentrated on increasing worker productivity and efficiency, the **administrative approach** to scientific management focused on helping managers coordinate and manage various organizational activities. The major contributors to the administrative approach were German sociologist Max Weber, French industrialist Henri Fayol, American behaviorist Mary Parker Follet, and American management theorist Chester Barnard.

Bureaucracies
Impersonal authority- and efficiency-driven organizations first proposed as ideal by Max Weber

Max Weber's Bureaucracies   Although the term *bureaucracy* currently has a negative connotation, Max Weber (1864–1920) developed the idea of bureaucracies, another aspect of scientific management, to improve management practices. **Bureaucracies** are impersonal organizations based on clear authority, responsibility, formal procedures, and separation of management and ownership.[3] Weber observed that family-operated organizations, then common in Europe, took care of their owner families often at the expense of fairness, efficiency, and effectiveness. Weber proposed the idea of bureaucracies to counteract the policies and procedures of family-owned businesses. Table A.2 summarizes the elements of bureaucracies.

Weber's idea offered a way to eliminate the practices of social privilege and favoritism prevalent in family-owned organizations, and it encouraged a sense of order that allowed managers to run organizations efficiently and smoothly. Weber's influence on organizational behavior is most evident in the areas of organization theory, design, and structure.

Table A.2   ELEMENTS OF WEBER'S IDEAL BUREAUCRACIES

Elements	Description
Well-defined hierarchy	Well-defined lines of authority where each person reports to supervisors at higher levels. The hierarchy allows for clear responsibility and accountability.
Specialization	Jobs are broken down into well-defined, clear tasks to allow workers to become experts at their job.
Formal written policies and procedures	Written policies and procedures regulate all worker activities and ensure uniformity.
Technical competence	Technical competence and merit rather than personal relationships are the basis for hiring, job assignments, and career advancement.
Separation of ownership and management	Professional managers rather than owners should run the organization to ensure focus on efficiency and fairness.

Source: Based on M. Weber, *The Theory of Social and Economic Organizations*, transl. A. M. Henderson and T. Parsons (New York: Free Press, 1947).

Henri Fayol   Theorist Henri Fayol (1841–1925) identified five basic management functions that are still an integral part of management theory and practice: planning, organizing, commanding, coordinating, and controlling.[4] In addition, Fayol developed fourteen management principles based on his work with the Comambault mining group. The six most significant principles follow:

- *Unity of command:* Each person should report to only one supervisor.
- *Division of labor:* People should specialize in specific activities to become more efficient.
- *Fairness and equity:* Employees should be remunerated fairly and equitably, and treated with humanity and kindness.
- *Discipline and order:* The organization should be run smoothly and efficiently based on discipline, order, and good organization.
- *Scalar chain of command:* Organizations must have a clear chain of authority that includes all employees.
- *Teamwork and subordination of individual interests:* Management must encourage harmony and teamwork and not allow the interest of one employee to prevail over those of the whole organization.

Mary Parker Follet   Social scientist Mary Parker Follet (1868–1933) highlighted the importance of worker participation and conflict reduction in organizations.[5] Many of her views contrasted sharply with the scientific management approach because she focused on the importance of people, group dynamics, ethics, and the appropriate use of power. She advocated problem solving and conflict management through the use of solutions that could satisfy all involved parties, not just the manager. Her views foreshadowed many current OB principles, such as empowerment and teamwork.

Chester Barnard   Although Chester Barnard (1889–1961) never completed his degree at Harvard, he became a highly influential management thinker because of his 1938 classic book *The Functions of the Executive*.[6] One of his most outstanding contributions is the idea of **acceptance of authority,** meaning that subordinates must be willing to accept a manager's

Acceptance of authority
Management's authority depends on subordinates' willingness to accept it

authority for a manager to be effective. Barnard also believed that managers should communicate clearly and understand the informal organization.

The early management theories provided managers with the tools to manage workers and employees at a time when large organizations and the concept of management were fairly new. Parker Follet and Barnard's views became the basis for the humanistic approach to management, a departure from the scientific management approach.

◼ HUMANISTIC VIEWPOINT

Industrial engineers who conducted time and motion studies at the Hawthorne plant of the Western Electric Company sparked the development of the humanistic approach. This approach focuses on providing people with growth opportunities and challenge. In this section, we explore the findings of the Hawthorne studies and the human relations movement.

The Hawthorne Studies

The Hawthorne studies started as a typical scientific management efficiency study. Researchers Elton Mayo and Fritz Roethlisberger, interested in the effect of lighting on productivity, conducted a series of illumination studies. They manipulated lighting levels in an electric relay production plant. To the researchers' surprise, productivity improved independent of the level of illumination. In one case, workers who complained that they could barely see still managed to perform better than before the study began.[7]

Hawthorne effect
People change their behavior when they are observed

Researchers concluded that factors other than lighting affected performance, and they set out to assess which work conditions had the greatest impact. After considering pay, rest period, length of workday, and several other factors, they concluded that the new supervisors—the researchers in this case—were the primary factor in performance. This finding, known as the **Hawthorne effect,** suggested that the attention from being singled out for study changes a person's behavior.

Further studies by the Hawthorne team of researchers established that workers value their informal social relationships at work and rely on group norms to restrict their productivity output to a level that is beneficial to the group members. The study results created a revolution in management thinking.

In spite of several serious flaws in the Hawthorne studies and their methodologies, and the possible errors in their analyses and conclusions, their impact has been undeniable.[8] The Hawthorne studies shifted the focus of management thought from efficiency and technical work aspects to social relationships.

Human Relations Movement

Human relations movement
Management approach focused on the human and social dimensions of work

The human relations movement became the primary approach to management from the 1930s to the 1970s. Interest in the human and social dimensions of work distinguishes the **human relations movement.** Managers who adopt this approach should demonstrate care and concern for their employees and provide them with cooperative, collaborative environments that encourage growth. Abraham Maslow and Douglas McGregor are two major theorists of the human relations movement.

Abraham Maslow Psychology professor Abraham Maslow (1908–1970) had a great impact on management thinking through his hierarchy of needs theory. His theory is based on three principles. First, Maslow believed that people always have unsatisfied needs. Second, he assumed that humans direct all their actions at fulfilling those needs. Third, Maslow proposed that human needs are organized in a hierarchy with physiological, safety, and security needs at the bottom; social needs for belonging and love and esteem in the middle; and self-actualization needs at the top.[9]

According to Maslow, people move from the bottom of the hierarchy to the top in an orderly sequence. Unsatisfied needs are a source of frustration and stress; satisfied needs stop driving behavior. In addition, Maslow suggested that people try to move up the hierarchy of needs to achieve self-actualization.

Despite only limited support, Maslow's theory has had great impact by helping managers understand that individuals have different needs that drive their behaviors at different times.[10] His theory focused attention away from satisfying lower-level needs to concentrating on higher-level needs such as challenge and growth.

Douglas McGregor   Industrial management professor Douglas McGregor (1906–1964) recognized the limitations of focusing only on developing good cooperative relationships with workers. As a result of his studies, McGregor proposed the Theory X and Theory Y of management as presented in Table A.3.[11]

McGregor's Theory X matches the scientific management assumptions, while Theory Y follows the human relations approach. McGregor suggested that by implementing management principles based on Theory Y, managers could capitalize on people's natural desire to grow and learn. According to McGregor, management should provide a supportive and challenging environment in which individuals achieve their potential. Maslow's hierarchy of need and McGregor's Theory X and Theory Y are some of the most well-known management concepts and have had a major impact on management practice.

Current approaches to organizational behavior continue to reflect the influence of both the scientific management and the human relations eras. Some of the earliest organizational behavior theories focused on understanding human motivation. We next present a historical perspective of motivation theory.

 EARLY VIEWS OF MOTIVATION

Because of the key role of motivation on performance in organizations, management scholars have devoted significant attention to understanding what motivates people to work. In the following section, we consider two early motivation theories that influence current motivation theories.

Table A.3   THEORY X AND THEORY Y OF MANAGEMENT

Theory X	Theory Y
People dislike work and try to avoid it	Working is a natural part of life and people will engage in work with pleasure
People must be forced to work and must be controlled	People are self-directed and internally motivated to work
People seek security, do not want responsibility and therefore want to be directed	People have imagination and creativity, are eager to learn, grow, and accept responsibility
Organizations and managers must control and direct workers	Organizations and managers must help workers achieve their potential

Source: D. McGregor, *The Human Side of Enterprise* (New York: McGraw-Hill, 1960).

Herzberg's Two-Factor Theory

In the 1950s Frederick Herzberg suggested that workers who are satisfied with their work have the internal motivation to work hard.[12] Similar to Maslow, Herzberg proposed that different needs drive people's behavior. However, Herzberg found that two entirely different sets of factors lead to job dissatisfaction and job satisfaction. His theory is therefore called the two-factor theory.

Hygiene factors
Based on Herzberg's theory, factors that lead to dissatisfaction

According to the two-factor theory, job dissatisfaction results from **hygiene factors** or **dissatisfiers,** which are factors such as salary, job security, working conditions, supervision, and company policies. When hygiene factors are poor—pay is low, working conditions poor, supervisors incompetent, and so forth—workers will be dissatisfied with their work. However, providing better hygiene factors does not necessarily lead to motivation to work. For example, when workers are well paid and have safe working conditions, they are no longer dissatisfied, but they are not necessarily motivated to work.

Motivators
Based on Herzberg's theory, factors that lead to satisfaction, motivation, and performance

The second set of factors is **motivators,** which include the job itself, achievement, responsibility, and growth opportunities. According to Herzberg, these motivators drive job satisfaction and performance. Managers must remove dissatisfiers to ensure that workers' basic needs are satisfied. They then must concentrate on motivators to increase motivation to work.

Herzberg's concepts are used widely and have had considerable impact on management practice worldwide. Although, as was the case with Maslow's work, there has been only limited research support for the theory, the two-factor theory has further helped focus attention on needs that are important in the workplace. Particularly, the focus on the job content continues to be a central issue today.

McClelland's Theory of Needs

Theorist David McClelland proposed that motivation stems from three basic needs: achievement, power, and affiliation, described in Table A.4.[13]

Individuals with a high need for achievement like responsibility, take calculated risks, and seek feedback in their performance. Their desire to do things better than others is their distinguishing characteristic.[14] High achievers like challenge, so they avoid easy or impossible tasks. Those with a high need for power are driven to control and influence others. They can use the need either positively to inspire and lead others or negatively to dominate. They want to have an impact and are often competitive. Finally, people with a high need for affiliation concentrate on developing social relationships and being liked by others, sometimes at the expense of task accomplishment.

Treating McClelland's three needs as central individual differences can help managers understand their own and other people's behaviors. Some research indicates that the most effective managers have moderate need for achievement, a high need for power, and a low need for affiliation.

Understanding human needs continues to be part of our views of motivation. To provide a complete picture, current approaches consider other individual difference characteristics and include a broad variety of job-related and organizational factors.

Table A.4   McClelland's Theory of Needs

Needs	Description
Need for Achievement (nAch)	The drive to reach goals, excel, and succeed
Need for Power (nPow)	The drive to control and influence others
Need for Affiliation (nAff)	The drive to have friends and close interpersonal relations

CURRENT APPROACHES: SYSTEMS AND QUALITY

Current views of organizations and motivation are complex and strongly dominated by holistic, systems-oriented, and contingency assumptions. The **systems view** sees organizations as a complex collection of interrelated parts working toward a common purpose. The **contingency view** suggests that what works in managing people and organizations depends on a number of contingencies. Therefore, managers must take a broad view of their organizations and understand the individual, job-related, and organizational processes that interact to lead to individual behavior and performance.

In addition to a complex, holistic view of people and organizations, OB researchers and practitioners also focus on quality. Quality experts W. Edward Deming (1900–1993) and Joseph Juran of the United States and Kaoru Ishikawa of Japan have advocated precise measurement of processes, empowerment, worker participation, use of teams, and a concentration on providing quality products and services to internal and external customers.[15] Armand Feigenbaum further proposed the concept of total quality management, which became the basis for many management practices in the 1980s and 1990s.[16]

Current views of management reflect the complexity of global organizations and recognize the challenge of managing individuals with diverse needs.

Systems view
Organizations are a complex collection of interrelated parts

Contingency view
Effective management of organization and people depends on various contingency factors

---

NOTES

1. For a complete history of management, see D. A. Wren, *The Evolution of Management Thought,* 2d ed. (New York: Wiley, 1979).
2. F. W. Taylor, *Principles of Scientific Management* (New York: Harper & Brothers, 1911).
3. M. Weber, *The Theory of Social and Economic Organizations,* ed. T. Parsons, transl. A. M. Henderson and T. Parsons (New York: Free Press, 1947).
4. H. Fayol, *Industrial and General Administration* (Paris: Dunod, 1916).
5. M. P. Follet, *The New State: Group Organization: The Solution of Popular Government* (London: Longmans, Green, 1918); and M. P. Follet, *Creative Experience* (London: Longmans, Green, 1924).
6. C. I. Barnard, *The Functions of the Executive* (Cambridge, MA: Harvard University Press, 1938).
7. E. Mayo, *The Human Problems of an Industrial Civilization* (New York: Macmillan, 1933); F. J. Roethlisberger and W. J. Dickson, *Management and the Worker* (Cambridge, MA: Harvard University Press, 1939); and R. G. Greenwood, A. A. Bolton, and R. A. Greenwood, "Hawthorne a Half Century Later: Relay Assembly Participants Remember," *Journal of Management* 9 (1983): 217–31.
8. For a critique of the Hawthorne studies and its conclusions, see A. Carey, "The Hawthorne Studies: A Radical Criticism," *American Sociological Review* (June

1967): 403–16; J. A. Sonnenfeld, "Shedding Light on the Hawthorne Studies," *Journal of Occupational Behavior* (April 1985): 111–30.
9. A. H. Maslow, *Motivation and Personality* (New York: Harper & Row, 1954).
10. For some early studies supporting Maslow's hierarchy, see L. W. Porter, "A Study of Perceived Need Satisfaction in Bottom and Middle Management Jobs," *Journal of Applied Psychology* (February 1961): 1–10; and L. W. Porter, *Organizational Pattern of Managerial Job Attitudes* (New York: American Foundation For Management Research, 1964).
11. D. McGregor, *The Human Side of Enterprise* (New York: McGraw-Hill, 1960).
12. F. Herzberg, B. Mausner, and B. Snyderman, *The Motivation to Work* (New York: John Wiley & Sons, 1959).
13. D. C. McClelland, *The Achieving Society* (New York: Van Nostrand Reinhold, 1961); D. C. McClelland, "Business Drive and National Achievement," *Harvard Business Review* (July–August 1962): 99–112.
14. McClelland, *The Achieving Society.*
15. M. Walton, *Deming Management at Work* (New York: Putnam, 1990); and J. M. Juran, "Made in U.S.A.: A Renaissance in Quality," *Harvard Business Review* 71 (1993): 42–50.
16. A. V. Feigenbaum, "How Total Quality Counters Three Forces of Internal Competitiveness," *National Productivity Review* 13 (1994): 327–30.

APPENDIX 2:
Research Methods
in Organizational Behavior

How do managers assess why production is low, which methods improve quality more, why employees are unmotivated, and which training program is best? Managers who must find the answers to these questions on a regular basis often rely on scientific findings and methods. Scientific methods allow managers to make consistent decisions based on objective data and findings. Those who understand the scientific process and its methods can evaluate research findings more effectively and, when appropriate, can collect their own data.

In this appendix we investigate the elements of the scientific process, explain basic research terminology, explore the difference between causation and correlation, and compare and contrast types of data collection methods. We close with a discussion of the ethical issues involved in research.

■ THE SCIENTIFIC PROCESS

The scientific process involves the systematic testing of hypotheses through data collection. Its purpose is to explain various events. The process relies on the cycle of *observation*, *prediction*, *testing*, and *measurement*. For example, a manager who wants to find out why her department is rife with conflict can start observing her employees, interviewing them, and sending out questionnaires. She may also visit her local library or university library to read books and research articles about the cause of conflict in organizations. Through observation she will develop several hypotheses about the cause of the conflict. A **hypothesis** is an educated guess or conjecture about a certain behavior or the relationship between events. The manager's hypotheses will allow her to make predictions about the cause of the conflict. For example, she may develop two hypotheses: (1) the reward system encourages competition rather than cooperation, and (2) inappropriate lateral communication causes conflict.

Hypothesis
An educated guess about a behavior or the relationship between events

The next step is testing the hypotheses. First, we can design a research study to test hypotheses. For instance, our manager could implement a new reward system that rewards cooperation. She also could put in place new communication procedures that encourage lateral communication. These changes allow her to test her hypotheses. Once she has made the changes, she must measure the level of conflict in her department through observation, interviews, surveys, and so forth, and compare it to the original level.

Managers use the scientific process to find answers based on systematic analysis rather than on hunches, which are subject to many biases. The scientific approach and its methods allow managers to establish what they know with a degree of certainty and to be aware of the limits of their knowledge.

 BASIC TERMINOLOGY

To communicate research findings, scientists rely on specific terminology. Next, we review key research terms and their definitions.

Theory

Theory
A model that systematically explains and predicts relationships or behaviors

A **theory** is a model that systematically explains and predicts the relationship between events or behaviors. It clarifies how and why things happen. This book presents many theories or models of organizational behavior. These models explain what motivates people, what makes teams effective, what factors affect leadership, conflict, communication, and stress, and so forth. Each theory contains many different interrelated hypotheses about certain relationships. For example, Fiedler's contingency model of leadership, discussed in chapter 9, proposes that leadership effectiveness is a function of the match between the leader's style and the leadership situation. The theory also proposes several hypotheses about when certain styles of leadership are most effective.

As you may have noticed throughout the text, organizational behavior theories on the same topic may differ because the assumptions, predictions, and explanations vary. For example, the Normative Decision Model of leadership predictions conflict with the predictions of Fiedler's contingency model because the assumptions of the two models differ. The former assumes that a leader can change his or her behavior at will, and the latter doesn't. Such differences are the strength of the scientific process. Because OB deals with human behavior, completely accurate prediction of every behavior and event is impossible. As a result, we are rarely able to establish the single best theory or model. Through continued testing and theory development, we refine and revise our models of human behavior at work and build our knowledge.

Independent Variables

Independent variable
Hypothesized cause of an event or behavior

Scientists call the events, behaviors, or objects they measure and manipulate *variables*. An **independent variable** is the hypothesized cause of a certain event or behavior. For example, chapter 15 indicates that scientists believe work overload, life changes, personality factors, and role conflict cause stress. These four factors, then, are independent variables. Similarly, OB theorists who explore the reasons for increased group cohesion select the independent variables of more interaction and group homogeneity (see chapter 7).

Dependent Variables

Dependent variable
The effect of an independent variable

A **dependent variable** is the effect of an independent variable. Continuing our example from chapter 15, stress is the effect of work overload, life changes, personality factors, and role conflict. Stress is the dependent variable, and work overload, life changes, personality factors, and role conflict are the independent variables. As another example, the ability or inability to delegate is one of the suggested effects of having strong Type A personality traits. Delegation ability is the dependent variable and having strong Type A personality traits is the independent variable.

Moderating Variables

Moderating variable
A variable that affects the relationship between an independent variable and a dependent variable

A **moderating variable** changes or affects the relationship between an independent variable (the cause) and a dependent variable (the effect). Moderating variables are important in OB because few cause-and-effect relationships are simple. For example, money (the cause) can increase motivation (the effect) in some but not all people. The moderating variables between money and motivation may be personality traits, values, or career stage. For example, a person who values wealth may be more motivated by financial gains than a person who values personal happiness. Throughout the text, we discuss how culture moderates many hypotheses in OB. For instance, participation in decision making may lead to higher job satisfaction or higher performance in cultures that have low power-distance but not necessarily in those with high power-distance.

 EVALUATING RESEARCH FINDINGS

Now that we have explored the meaning of hypotheses, theories, and the different variables, how can we evaluate whether research findings apply to the organizational issue and whether they are accurate? The answer to these questions is highly complex. To begin, we explore three factors: selection and formation of the research study group, reliability, and validity.

Random Selection and Control Group

Selection of research study participants is a crucial research evaluation issue. Say you read a study about a new reward system that increases worker productivity. You are ready to implement the program in your company when you discover that all the study subjects were high-potential employees with excellent performance. Does your opinion of the effectiveness of the new system change?

It should. We cannot tell whether the reward system or the high potential of the employees made the difference in the outcome. The study violated the basic scientific requirement of random assignment. **Random assignment** requires that studies avoid systematic bias in selecting study participants. Everyone must have the same chance of being selected. Say that a follow-up study evaluating the new reward system corrects for the original problem by randomly selecting a group of employees regardless of their potential. The follow-up study has no systematic bias in its selection process. The new study finds that everyone who received the new rewards improved his or her performance by at least 5 percent. Should you adopt the new system?

Random assignment
Assures that all participants have equal chance of being selected

The answer is, not yet. Other factors such as a better economy, a new product line, modernized equipment, or new leadership may have caused the productivity increase. How can we isolate the cause of the increase in productivity? We randomly select a **control group**, which is a group of study participants who receive the same treatment as the original study group except for one key element. In our case, the control group would not participate in the new reward system. In medical research to test the effects of a new drug, control groups receive a placebo while the experimental group receives the drug being tested. We measure both the control group and the experimental group before and after the study. If there is a change in the experimental group, then researchers can conclude that the intervention, be it the reward system or the new drug, is the cause of the change.

Control group
A group who receives the same treatment as the research group except for the key independent variable(s)

Having random assignment and a control group allows researchers to establish with some confidence that the independent variable causes the change in the dependent variable they are measuring.

Reliability

Researchers and managers must be confident that the changes they are observing are not due to unreliable methods and measures. **Reliability** is the consistency of measurement. For example, experts often challenge the reliability of personality tests. Some theorists are critical of measures such as the self-assessments in chapter 4. They claim the final score may depend on too many outside factors such as mood, time of day, and level of hunger for the test to be rea-

Reliability
Consistency of measurement

sonably consistent and reliable across time and place. A reliable measure is not affected by extraneous factors but measures what it is supposed to measure consistently across time and place. Although 100 percent reliability is rarely possible when measuring any human activity and behavior, the goal is to develop measures that have a high degree of reliability.

Validity

Internal validity
The extent to which a measure actually measures what it is supposed to

The final issue to consider in evaluating research is validity. **Internal validity** refers to the extent to which a measure actually measures what it is supposed to. A measure can be reliable without being internally valid. For example, do the various tests that employers administer to prospective employees actually measure work-related behaviors? Do they accurately measure integrity, honesty, ability to work with others, leadership qualities, and so forth? Many measures are not internally valid and managers should rely on them with caution. Similarly, many personality tests are reliable, such as those used in the Big Five personality traits (see chapter 4). However, research indicates that they are not valid measures of work-related behaviors, so managers should avoid using them to make employment decisions.

External validity
The extent to which findings apply to other groups

External validity refers to whether the findings or results apply to other groups or only to the group in the study. If the results can be generalized, the research has external validity. For example, experts criticize many findings in psychological research because the studies rely on a sample of college freshmen, whose reactions are not necessarily representative of all age groups and other categories. As a result, researchers should not generalize the results.

Having random assignment and a control group and using reliable and valid measures increase a researcher's ability to make predictions. Managers must learn to evaluate research findings based these factors to ensure good decision making.

▮ CORRELATION AND CAUSATION

The goal of scientific processes and methods is to describe and predict how events relate to one another. Therefore, research in management and organizational behavior establishes relationships between events. For example, we know from years of research that there is a relationship between satisfaction and performance (see chapter 6). However, the direction of the relationship is not always clear. Does satisfaction cause performance, or does performance cause satisfaction?

Causality
A relationship in which the cause precedes the effect

Correlation
The strength of the relationship between two variables

Causality refers to the relationship between events in which the direction of the cause-and-effect relationship is clear. The independent variable causes changes in the dependent variable. **Correlation** refers to the strength of the relationship between two events without establishing a direction of the cause-and-effect relationship. We know a correlation between satisfaction and performance exists, but researchers still debate causality—which variable is the cause and which is the effect.

Researchers calculate the correlation between two variables through a correlation coefficient that ranges from −1.00 (a perfect negative correlation) to 0 (no correlation) to +1.00 (a perfect positive correlation). A negative correlation indicates that two variables vary in opposite directions. For example, increased communication relates to decreased conflict. A positive correlation indicates that two variables vary in the same direction—that is, increased competition is related to increased conflict. Management researchers rarely, if ever, find perfect positive or negative correlation. Instead, they can establish a range of strong-to-weak correlations between variables.

Although organizational behavior research has identified many relationships among various variables, it is more difficult to establish causality. Managers should understand the difference between correlation and causality. Furthermore, they should not assume that a strong correlation implies causality.

HOW TO COLLECT DATA: RESEARCH DESIGNS

Researchers and managers can use a variety of methods or research designs to collect data about events.

- A *case study* is a detailed description and analysis of one organization, department, event, or person. Case studies typically rely on in-depth interviews and observation. They provide considerable detail about one case. Examples are the Managerial Challenges that open each chapter in this book.
- *Surveys* are a series of questions posed in questionnaires or interviews. They typically include a large number of general questions with set answers. They provide a large amount of information without going into much depth. They allow researchers to establish general relationships. Examples include political opinion surveys and satisfaction surveys conducted in many organizations.
- *Field experiments* are experiments conducted in real-life settings. They include some specific change or manipulation introduced into an organization. The researcher then measures the effects of the change. Field experiments provide specific information about the effect of a change and also help researchers establish causation. Examples include introduction of a new training program, reward system, or production method.
- *Laboratory experiments* are experiments done in controlled artificial environments designed to replicate real situations as closely as possible. Researchers use them to gather specific information about the effect of a change and to establish causation. Examples include psychological experiments on stress that measure the effect of loss of control or the use of a specific type of leadership style in small groups.

As Table A.5 shows, the four research designs have advantages and disadvantages. When assessing research results based on each research design method, managers must be aware of the strengths and weaknesses of each type.

Table A.5   SRENGTHS AND WEAKNESSEES OF THE FOUR RESEARCH DESIGNS

	Case Studies	Surveys	Field Experiments	Laboratory Experiments
Internal Validity	high to low	high, if well-designed	moderate to low	very high
External Validity	very low	high, if sample well-selected	high to moderate	moderate to low
Cost	variable	moderate	high to moderate	moderate to low
Advantages for Managers	learning example and starting point for further investigation	large amount of general data	realistic information about specific effect of certain programs	precise information about specific issues
Disadvantages for Managers	can lead to tendency to overgeneralize based on one case; information provided is limited to case writer's perspective	no in-depth information; overuse without further follow-up provides little detail	findings may not be applicable outside of setting; effect of other factors is difficult to assess	artificial setting; findings may not be applicable outside of lab setting

ETHICAL CONSIDERATIONS

A final issue to consider in scientific research is ethics. Ideally, researchers provide the people they are studying or surveying full information, protect their rights to privacy, and explain possible risks. For example, a consultant who is conducting research about organization climate and satisfaction should inform the employees he is interviewing or surveying how the data will be used, who will have access to it, whether they are guaranteed confidentiality, and so forth. The goal should be to obtain information that is objective and accurate without violating individual rights and without embarrassing or harming people who participate.

APPENDIX 3:
Scoring Keys for
Self-Assesment Exercises

▶ **SELF-ASSESSMENT 1**
Is It Time to Consider a Career Move?

Give yourself 1 point if you have answered yes to questions 1, 3, 4, 6, 7, 8, 9, and 10, and 1 point if you have answered no to questions 2 and 5. A score of less than four indicates that your current job is not ideal and you should consider other job options seriously. A score between five and seven indicates that you need to keep your eyes open for internal changes and external opportunities. A score between eight and ten indicates that your current position is both stable and challenging and has good potential. In addition to your score, consider that you may need to keep your current job for personal reasons (for example, you need the money while you finish school), in spite of less than ideal circumstances.

▶ **SELF-ASSESSMENT 2**
Personal Acceptance of Change

What do your responses reveal about how you deal with change? As you look at each item, note the difference between the number you placed in column A (resistance to change) and the number in column B (acceptance of change). A large difference (4 is the maximum possible) indicates that your ability to accept change is high.

1. Which changes did you strongly resist at first, but now accept? Think of as many reasons as possible for why you now accept these changes. Identifying these reasons may help you identify your strengths in acceptance of change.
2. Based on your responses, do you consider yourself to be open to change, or do you find change difficult to deal with?
3. Are there any events that you strongly resisted and that you now have difficulty accepting? Seek to identify the reasons for your nonacceptance. As you compare strongly resisted events that you accept with those you do not, you may find valuable clues to your ability to cope with change in your life.

▶ **SELF-ASSESSMENT 3**
Are You Globally Aware?

Reverse your scores for questions 4, 7, 9, and 12 (1 = 5, 2 = 4, 4 = 2, 5 = 1). Add all your scores for the 12 questions. The minimum score is 12; the maximum is 60. A score of 12 to 20 indicates that you are not globally aware and do not have a lot of competencies in the global management area. A score of 21 to 40 indicates moderate levels of awareness and global competencies. A score above 41 indicates a high amount of global awareness and competencies.

   Being a globally competent and aware manager includes having a global perspective, knowledge of other cultures, customs, and languages, being flexible, comfortable with change, and willing to learn, having a positive view of cultural differences, and having global and cross-cultural experiences.

▶ **SELF-ASSESSMENT 6**
Goal Setting

Add your scores for the following items for each goal.

	GOAL #1		GOAL #2		GOAL #3
Specific		*Specific*		*Specific*	
Items 1 and 2:	_____	Items 1 and 2:	_____	Items 1 and 2:	_____
Measurable		*Measurable*		*Measurable*	
Items 3 and 4:	_____	Items 3 and 4:	_____	Items 3 and 4:	_____
Achievable		*Achievable*		*Achievable*	
Items 5 and 6:	_____	Items 5 and 6:	_____	Items 5 and 6:	_____
Reasonable		*Reasonable*		*Reasonable*	
Items 7 and 8:	_____	Items 7 and 8:	_____	Items 7 and 8:	_____
Time frame		*Time frame*		*Time frame*	
Items 9 and 10:	_____	Items 9 and 10:	_____	Items 9 and 10:	_____
Overall score:	_____	*Overall score:*	_____	*Overall score:*	_____

The maximum score for each area is 10. The maximum overall score is 50. The closer you are to the upper end of the scale, the better is your goal setting.

▶ **SELF-ASSESSMENT 7**
Assertiveness

   Sum up your answers to items 1, 4, 7, 10, 13, and 16.
   Enter your **Passive** score here: _____.
   Sum up your answers to items 2, 5, 8, 11, 14, and 17.
   Enter your **Aggressive** score here: _____.
   Sum up your answers to items 3, 6, 9, 12, 15, and 18.
   Enter your **Assertive** score here: _____.

For each scale, you should have a score between 6 and 24.

▶ SELF-ASSESSMENT 8
Individual Responsibility in Developing Trust

The statements represent the five elements needed to develop trust in teams.

Open communication: add up your scores on items 4,10, and 12: _____
Integrity: add up your scores on items 6, 8, and 11 : _____
Respect and support: add up your scores on items 7, 9, and 14: _____
Fairness and equity: add up your scores on items 2, 5, and 13: _____
Competence and hard work: add up your scores on items 1, 3, and 15: _____

Building trust in teams depends on each member's accepting responsibility for his or her own behavior. What area do you need to work on? For each group, 3 is the lowest and 15 is the highest score.

▶ SELF-ASSESSMENT 9
Are You a Team Leader?

Reverse score items 2, 5, 6, 8, and 9 (1 = 5, 5 = 1). Add your score on all items. Maximum possible score is 50. The higher the score, the more team leadership skills you have.

▶ SELF-ASSESSMENT 10
Myers Briggs Type Inventory

To categorize your responses to the questionnaire, count one point for each response on the following four scales and total the number of point recorded in each column

Sensation	Intuition	Thinking	Feeling
2B. _____	2A. _____	1B. _____	1A. _____
4A. _____	4B. _____	3B. _____	3A. _____
5A. _____	5B. _____	7B. _____	7A. _____
6B. _____	6A. _____	8A. _____	8B. _____
9B. _____	9A. _____	10B. _____	10A. _____
12A. _____	12B. _____	11A. _____	11B. _____
15A. _____	15B. _____	13B. _____	13A. _____
16B. _____	16A. _____	14B. _____	14A. _____
Totals: _____	_____	_____	_____

▶ SELF-ASSESSMENT 11
Views of Power

1. Reverse scoring for items 6 (1 = strongly agree, 5 = strongly disagree)
2. Legitimate power: Add items 1, 8, and 13   Total: _____
   Reward power: Add items 3, 9, and 11   Total: _____
   Coercive power: Add items 2, 7, and 12   Total: _____
   Referent power: Add items 4, 6, and 15   Total: _____
   Expert power: Add items 5, 10, and 14   Total: _____

▶ SELF-ASSESSMENT 12
Communicating Supportively

Add your scores on the 11 items. Compare your scores against the maximum of 66 and against the scores of other students in your class. Where are your strengths? Your weaknesses?

▶ SELF-ASSESSMENT 13
Mistakes in Negotiation

For each of the eight questions reconsider your position and strategy if you have answered "no." You can improve your chances of rational negotiating by auditing your position on these items. Being aware of possible biases in your opponent can help you anticipate and prepare for problems.

▶ SELF-ASSESSMENT 14
Developing Creativity

Reverse scores for items 1, 7, 8, and 11 (1 = 3, 2 = 2, 3 = 1). Add up your scores for the 14 items. The minimum score is 14; the maximum is 45. A score above 30 indicates that you are undertaking many activities that enhance personal creativity. Consider the items where you have scored 1 and develop plans for improvement.

▶ SELF-ASSESSMENT 15
Key Questions for Managing Your Career

If you have answered 3 or 4 (usually or always true) to 7 or more of the questions, you are very aware of issues that will affect your career in the twenty-first century. Review the items that you answered 1 or 2 and set goals for improvement.

GLOSSARY

A

Ability A natural talent to do something mental or physical

Acculturation The process of diverse groups working together and resolving differences to greater or lesser degrees

Active listening Process whereby the listener assumes a conscious and dynamic role in the communication process through a variety of behaviors and actions

Actor-observer difference The tendency to rely more on external attributions when explaining our own actions

Agreeableness A person's general friendliness, courtesy, and the degree to which she or he is trusting and liked by others

Alarm The first GAS stage; includes a physical reaction that occurs when the person feels threatened because he or she perceives and recognizes stressors

Alliances General agreements of support among different individuals and groups

Anchoring and adjustment The process whereby we select a starting point for a decision and adjust our thinking based on our first anchor or starting point

Assimilation The smaller minority group willingly gives up its culture and adopts the culture of the more dominant group

Attention stage of perception The selection of stimuli, cues, and signals to which we will pay attention

Attitudes A stable pattern of response toward particular people, objects, or situations that a person has

Attribution process The process of assigning a cause to a behavior

Authority The power vested in a particular position, such as that of an office manager or human resource director

Autocratic decision style A decision style whereby the leader makes a decision with little or no involvement from followers

Automation The process of replacing human resources with machines

Autonomy The degree to which a person can make independent decisions and act without having to check with a supervisor

Availability A tendency to pay attention to information we remember because it is so accessible

Avoiding style of conflict management Low concern for self and others and focus on suppressing, setting aside, and ignoring the issues

B

Behavioral approach Considers behaviors that leaders undertake to be effective

Behavioral cues Cues that signal what behaviors and actions are expected and appropriate

Behavioral method A performance evaluation method that focuses on work-related behaviors

Behavioral zone of comfort A range of behaviors that come naturally and easily and feel comfortable to perform because they reflect individual characteristics

Benchmarking The process of establishing performance and effectiveness standards and criteria by using companies identified as excellent models

Bottom-up change Change initiated, planned, and implemented by employees at low levels of the organization

Boundaryless organization A structure designed to reduce or remove obstacles to free interaction among departments and people, and between different organizational levels

Bounded rationality model Decision-making model that assumes numerous organizational and individual factors restrict rational decision making

589

Brainstorming A creative process in which individuals generate a large number of ideas without censorship

Bureaucracy Organization with a highly formalized, specialized, standardized, centralized structure with many layers and hierarchical reporting relationships

Burnout Feelings of exhaustion and a sense of powerlessness leading to apathy and psychological withdrawal

Business environment Customers, competitors, human resources, suppliers, financial institutions, governmental regulations, the economy, and technology

C

Central norms Rules of behavior that are essential to the group's identity, goals, and survival

Change agents Individuals who are experts at managing change and are charged with its implementation

Channeling, or confirmatory hypothesis testing The process by which we limit people's interactions with us so their behaviors support our expectations

Charisma The ability to appeal to others' emotions and form profound and powerful bonds

Closure The process of filling in missing information to understand a stimulus

Coalitions Relationships with regard to specific issues

Coercive power Based on a person's ability to punish. Others comply because of the fear of punishment

Cognitive dissonance The result of holding inconsistent or conflicting beliefs and attitudes

Cohesion (also called cohesiveness) The degree to which group members are attracted to the group and to one another

Commitment Personal acceptance of the goals a manager is trying to achieve

Communication The exchange of information between people; it occurs when one person understands the meaning of a message another person sends and responds to it

Communication networks Formal and informal communication pathways and patterns

Competence The ability and expertise to perform one or more tasks well

Competition The rivalry between individuals or groups over an outcome that both seek

Complex task One that has many different elements and potential solutions

Compliance Employees go along with the manager's request but there is no personal acceptance or commitment

Compromising style of conflict management Moderate concern for self and others and focus on achieving a reasonable middle ground where all parties win

Computer-aided decision systems Systems that ask participants to respond to a number of standardized items through their computer. Answers are instantly fed back and can be used as the basis for further discussion or decision making

Conceptual skills The ability to analyze various situations, solve problems, and learn

Concern for others The degree to which a person wants to satisfy the needs of others

Concern for self The extent to which a person focuses on satisfying his or her own needs

Conflict A process in which people disagree over significant issues, thereby creating friction between parties

Conformity The process of abiding by the group norms

Conscientiousness A personality dimension of reliability and dependability, being careful and organized, and being a person who plans

Consideration Leadership behaviors that aim at creating mutual trust and respect with followers

Constituency approach An organization is effective when it addresses the needs of its key stakeholders

Consulation (C) A decision style whereby the leader consults with followers but makes the final decision

Contingency approach A view of management suggesting that what works depends, or is contingent, on the situation

Contingency rewards Rewards contingent upon performance

Continuous improvement A practice in which everyone engages in activities needed to improve the quality of products or services on an ongoing basis

Controlling The process of monitoring, measuring, and evaluating employees' performance based on the set goals

Convergent change Planned evolutionary change that is the result of specific and conscious action to make changes in an organization

Cooperative exploration Creativity tool that requires individuals to consider a problem by taking different positions

Creativity (also divergent thinking or lateral thinking) The ability to link or combine ideas in novel ways

Cross-departmental teams Teams of members from different departments that are formed to address a specific problem either within a particular work unit or within the whole organization

Cross-functional task forces Teams whose members are from different functional areas with different expertise designed to provide broad perspective

Cross-functional teams Teams of people from different departments

Cultural diversity Differences due to individual and group factors such as ethnicity, religion, gender, age, physical attributes, sexual orientation, regional differences, and so forth

Culture The values commonly held among a group of people

D

Decision heuristics The tendency to make mental shortcuts while making decisions

Decoding The process by which the receiver translated the sender's message into an understandable form

Deculturation The process of forcing one group to give up its culture entirely without fully allowing it to adopt the culture and practices of the dominant group

Delphi technique A structured group decision technique aimed at obtaining opinions about an issue through a series of formal surveys and rating scales

Deviants Individuals who do not conform to the group and deviate from the norms

Distributive negotiation Zero-sum negotiation in which one party's gain always leads to the other's loss; the rewards and outcomes are divided unequally among the parties

Diversity audits Evaluations of the organization's diversity performance and suggestions for future action

Dominating style of conflict management High concern for self, low concern for others, and focus on advancing own goals at any cost

E

E-mail Messages and communication via computers and various communication software

Effectiveness State attained when a person or an organization reaches its planned destination and achieves its goals

Emotional stability A person's level of anxiety, depression, and general emotional insecurity

Employee assistance programs (EAP) Organizational programs that help employees address personal as well as organizational problems

Employee involvement (EI) programs Programs that concentrate on increasing employee participation in decision making and employee empowerment

Empowerment Giving power to employees at various levels of the organization

Enactment The process of identifying relevant environmental elements to define the environment of the organization

Encoding The process by which the sender puts a message in a certain format to send to the receiver

Environment All external factors that have the potential to affect the organization

Environmental complexity The number of elements an organization has to consider in its enactment process

Environmental uncertainty Unpredictability in the environment

Equity A sense that something is fair, just, and impartial. In motivation equity refers to perceiving that your inputs and outputs are balanced

Escalation of commitment Continuing a course of action in the face of negative information

Ethics A person's concept of right and wrong

Evolutionary change Change that is gradual and incremental

Exemplary leadership Leadership theory that underscores the importance of the leader setting an example for followers

Exhaustion The third GAS stage; results from long-term exposure to stressors

Expatriates Individuals who leave their own country to work

Expert power Based on personal expertise and knowledge in a certain area. Others comply because of the belief in the power holder's knowledge

Expert systems Computer systems and software designed to help decision makers improve the quality and efficiency of their decisions

External forces for change Those factors that are part of an organization's general and business environment

External or situational attributions The process of assigning a cause to the behavior that is related to factors external to the person

Extroversion/introversion The degree to which people enjoy socializing, seek and enjoy the company of others, and express their feelings and emotions openly. Extroverts have strong tendencies toward socializing; introverts have weak tendencies

F

Facilitation The leader focuses on freeing the team from obstacles to allow the team to reach the goals it has set

Feedback Information about performance or some behavior and its effect

Formal communication networks Networks that are designated by the organizational structure, charts, or other official documents

Formal groups Groups that have prescribed goals that satisfy organizational needs

Framing The process of placing a situation in context before making a decision

Functional structure One in which people who perform the same function are in the same groups, teams, or departments

Fundamental attribution error The tendency to underestimate situational factors and overestimate personal factors when making attributions about others' actions

G

Garbage can model Decision-making model that assumes managers use information about events, people, alternatives, and opportunities haphazardly to generate ideas and potential solutions to problems

General adaptation syndrome (GAS) A model that describes the three stages that individuals go through when responding to stressors and trying to adapt to them

General environment Societal, demographic, and cultural trends; the political climate; and historical and religious influences

Globalization The interconnectedness of people and organizations around the world

Goal approach Looks at the amount and quality of outputs in terms of goods or services

Group Two or more people who interact in an organized manner to perform a task or activity to achieve a common goal

Group (G) A decision style whereby the leader relies on group consensus to make the decision

Groupthink Poor decision making that results from group cohesion

Groupware Computer software that allows group members to communicate, share ideas, exchange documents, and work on data and documents simultaneously

H

Halo effect A perceptual bias in which one characteristic creates a positive impression that becomes the central factor around which all other information is selected, organized, and interpreted

Hardiness An individual trait that indicates the degree to which people believe they have control over their lives, they are committed to their activities, and they treat change as a challenge rather than a threat

Heterogeneous cultures Cultures that have many different subcultures

Heterogeneous groups Groups with members who have many differences

High-context cultures Cultures that rely heavily on the context, nonverbal cues, and situational factors to communicate with and understand others

Homogeneous cultures Cultures that have only one or very few subcultures

Homogeneous groups Groups with members who have a number of similarities

Horizontal conflict Conflict that takes place between departments or groups at the same level of the organization

Human Resource Management (HRM, also known as or personnel management) The procedural, technical, and legal aspects of recruiting, placement, training, evaluation, and development of the employees of an organization

Human skills The ability to work with and through others to achieve results

Hybrid structure Combines the functional and product structures

I

Idea champions (institutional entrepreneurs or intrapreneurs) Employees who either volunteer or are assigned to focus on leading the change effort by overcoming resistance and obtaining necessary support and resources

Idiosyncrasy credit A process that allows cohesive groups to be creative by giving credit to conforming members who can then use the accumulated credits to deviate from the group

Impression management The act of consciously, carefully monitoring and managing the impression we make on others

Individualism/collectivism The extent to which individuals or closely knit social structure such as the extended family are the basis for social systems

Informal communication networks Networks that exist outside the official organizational networks

Informal groups Groups that exist because of members' common interests, social ties, or friendship

Information technology Communication hardware and software that allows people to interact with one another

Ingratiation The process of presenting another person in a positive light

In-group Followers who have a high-quality relationship with the leader

Initiation of structure Leadership behaviors concerned with defining and organizing the task to help followers achieve the goals

Innovation The use of various skills and resources to create an idea, product, or service that is new to an organization's industry or market

Innovation departments Formal departments in the organizational structure that are assigned the task of research and development of new ideas

Instrumental values The means, or instruments, that people believe they should use to reach the terminal values

Integration The smaller minority group preserves its uniqueness but also adopts some of the values of the dominant group

Integrative negotiation Win-win scenario in which parties try to reach an agreement that benefits all, even if each party does not achieve all its goals

Integrative style of conflict management High concern for self and for others and focus on collaboration, openness, and exchange of information

Interactionist view A view suggesting that heredity and the environment interact to influence the development of individual differences

Interdependence The extent to which employees depend on others to get their work done

Intergroup conflict Conflict that occurs when groups within and outside the organization disagree on various issues

Internal customers Employees who depend on a person or a department for products and services

Internal forces for change Forces that arise from inside the organization that relate to the internal functioning of organizations

Internal or personal attributions The process of assigning a cause to the behavior that is related to internal factors

Internal process approach Definition of organizational effectiveness that focuses on internal organizational processes including efficiency, employee satisfaction, management practices, and communication

Interpersonal conflict Conflict due to differences in goals, values, and styles between two or more people who are required to interact

Interpretation and judgment stage of perception The clarification and translation of organized information to allow for the attribution of meaning

Intragroup conflict Conflict within a work group over goals and work procedures

Intrapersonal conflict An internal conflict because one's goals, values, or roles diverge

Intrapreneurship The drive, creativity, and flexibility that characterize small entrepreneurial firms within a large business

Intrinsic motivation Motivation resulting from factors that are not affected by external rewards

Intuitive decision-making model Decision-making model that assumes managers make decisions by relying on past experience and their personal assessment of a situation

J

Jargon Language and terms that have a clear meaning among some groups but not others

Job satisfaction The general attitude that people have about their jobs

K

Kaizen Continuous improvement

Kinesics The study of bodies through posture, gesture, head movements

Knowledge workers Employees whose value for the organization is their expertise and knowledge

L

Law of effect People repeat behaviors that bring them satisfaction and pleasure, and stop those that bring them dissatisfaction and pain

Leader Person who influences individuals and groups in an organization, helps them establish goals, guides them toward achievement of those goals, and allows them to be effective as a result

Leader-member relations (LMR) In Fiedler's Contingency model, refers to cohesion of the group and the quality of interaction between the leader and follower and among group members

Leading Motivating and encouraging employees to perform work on schedule, helping to resolve conflict, and ensuring that employees coordinate efforts to achieve company goals

Learning organizations Organizations in which people continually expand their capacity to create, where innovation and cooperation are nurtured, and where knowledge is transferred throughout the organization

Learning theory An approach to understanding and predicting human behavior that focuses on learning behaviors

Least preferred co-worker (LPC) scale Scale used in Fiedler's Contingency model to determine whether the leader has a *task* or *relationship* orientation

Legitimate power Based on a person holding a formal position. Others comply because of the belief in the legitimacy of the power holder

Linear model A model in which the decision maker lists positive and negative factors of each decision alternative and assigns each factor a numerical weight

Locus of control A personality trait that indicates an individual's sense of control over his or her life, the environment, and external events

Low-context cultures Cultures that focus on explicit verbal and written messages to understand people and situations

M

Machiavellian personality An individual's willingness to manipulate others for personal gain and to put self-interest above the interest of the group

Management by objectives Focuses on setting goals, monitoring progress, and giving feedback and correction

Management by exception Leadership style whereby the leader only interacts with followers or intervenes when things go wrong

Management philosophy The system of values about the nature of people and organizations and how the organization should conduct business

Management team (administrative team) Team of managers and supervisors from different work units with the goal of coordination of administrative and managerial tasks to achieve organizational goals

Manufacturing firms Business organizations that produce tangible goods

Masculinity The amount of value placed on assertiveness, material goods, ambition, and independence

Matrix structure Uses project teams of both functional specialists and product/project specialists

Mechanistic organization An organization that has centralized decision making and formal, standardized control systems

Media The methods of communication

Membership fluidity The extent to which the team membership is stable

Mission A statement of the organization's purpose and reason for existence

Motivating potential score Indicator of the challenge level of a job, made up of skills variety, task identity, task significance, autonomy, and feedback

Motivation A state of mind, desire, energy, or interest that translates into action

N

National culture A set of values and beliefs shared by people within a nation

Needs related to things that are lacking and are desired

Negative reinforcer An unpleasant outcome preceeding a behavior aimed at encouraging a certain behavior

Negotiation Process by which two or more parties reach a mutually agreeable arrangement to exchange goods and services

Networks Broad, loose support systems

Neutralizers Situations and factors that make the leader's actions irrelevant

Noise All factors that interfere with and distort communication

Nominal group technique (NGT) A structured group process of generating and ranking problem-solving ideas

Nonverbal messages Communications sent without using language

Nonprogrammed decisions Novel, nonroutine decisions that are made infrequently

Nonverbal communication Communication that is sent without the use of the written or spoken word

Norms Shared rules and expectations about group members' behaviors

O

Obliging style of conflict management Low concern for self, high concern for others, and focus on the needs of others while sacrificing or ignoring personal needs

Occulesics Facial expressions and eye contact that we use to communicate

Open systems Complex systems made up of interrelated parts that continuously interact with one another and with their external environment

Openness to experience A tendency toward being curious, creative, and broad-minded

Organic organization Organization with a low degree of formality, specialization, and standardization; decentralized decision making; and well-integrated activities

Organizational behavior (OB) The study of how people behave in organizations and how organizations structure their human resources to achieve goals

Organizational behavior modification (OB Mod) The application of learning principles to manage organizational behavior

Organizational change The transformation of or adjustment to the way an organization functions

Organizational chart A diagram of the basic structure of the organization

Organizational culture The set of values, norms, and beliefs shared by members of an organization

Organizational development (OD) A discipline devoted to the implementation of systemwide change with a focus on people and organizational climate

Organizational effectiveness An organization's ability to maintain smooth internal functioning and external adaptability while achieving its goals

Organizational inertia The tendency for an organization as a whole to resist change and want to maintain the status quo

Organizational politics Activities that allow people in organizations to achieve goals without going through formal channels

Organizational rewards Positive outcomes that organizations provide individuals

Organizational socialization The process by which employees learn about the culture of an organization

Organizational sources of power Sources of power that managers or individuals derive from the structure of the organization. These sources depend on having access to and control of *strategic contingencies*

Organizations Groups of two or more people who cooperate and coordinate their activities in a systematic manner to reach goals

Organization stage of perception The organization of information that the perceptual filter allowed through during the attention stage

Organization Theory (OT) The study of organizational processes at the macro level of analysis

Organizing The process of assigning tasks, establishing procedures, and setting deadlines to reach the goals

Outcome approach A performance evaluation method that considers the results employees achieve

Out-group Followers who do not have a quality relationship with the leader

Outsourcing The process of hiring outsiders to do various tasks

Overjustification The tendency to make external attributions about our own behaviors when an external reward is given

P

Paralinguistics The various vocal cues and other signals that accompany verbal messages

Perception The mental process of selecting those cues and stimuli that we pay attention to

Perceptual biases Perceptual distortions, often caused by cognitive shortcuts, that lead to mistakes

Perceptual filter The process of letting some information in while keeping out the rest

Performance gap The difference between expected and actual performance

Peripheral norms Rules of behavior that support central norms but aren't central to the group's identity or task

Personal space The area around them that people control

Personality A stable set of physical and psychological characteristics that makes each person unique

Phenomenal absolutism Believing that what you perceive is objective reality

Physical perception The process of gathering and interpreting information about physical objects

Planned change Change that occurs when managers or employees make a conscious effort to change in response to a specific problem

Planning The process of setting goals and deciding on how to allocate resources to achieve those goals

Plateauing The leveling off of a career without further opportunities for growth

Political tactics Activities outside the standardized, formal processes of the organization

Portfolio career A career in which employees develop a portfolio of accomplishments in different companies that keeps them employable

Position power (PP) In Fiedler's Contingency model, refers to the leader's official power and influence over subordinates to hire, fire, reward, or punish

Positive reinforcer A pleasant outcome that follows a desired behavior and is aimed at encouraging the behavior

Power The ability of a person to influence another

Power distance The size of the gap between those who have a lot of power and those who have little power

Primacy effect A tendency to overemphasize early information

Process consultation Facilitators working with managers on the job to identify problems and help improve relationships and processes

Process teams Teams that do not have departmental affiliation and that function independently to undertake broad organizational-level process improvements

Product or divisional structure One that groups people by the products or services they work on

Programmed decisions Routine decisions that have clearly outlined procedures

Propensity for risk An individual's tolerance for risk

Proxemics The use of space and the distance between people

Punishment A negative event that occurs after an undesirable behavior and is aimed at stopping that behavior

Pygmalion effect, or self-fulfilling prophecy The process by which one's expectations and perceptions become reality because of the strength of the original expectations

Q

Quality circles Small work groups of eight to ten volunteers from a common work area who meet to find solutions to specific problems about the quality of work processes, products, or services

R

Rate of change The speed at which various elements in the environment change

Rational decision-making model A decision-making model that assumes decisions are based on objective, orderly, structured information gathering and analysis

Recency effect A tendency to overemphasize the most recent information rather than earlier data

Reengineering Redesigning an organization around basic processes to become more effective and more efficient

Referent power Based on a person's attractiveness to others. Others comply because of respect and liking for the power holder

Refreezing Stage in Lewin's force field model during which the newly learned behaviors and freshly implemented practices are encouraged and supported and become part of employees' routine activities

Reinforcement theory Theory that recommends rewarding and encouraging desirable behaviors, and punishing and discouraging undesirable ones by providing an organizational environment and response pattern that will guide proper behavior

Reinforcer An outcome or event that increases the likelihood of a behavior occurring again

Relationship motivation (high LPC) The person is primarily motivated by interpersonal relations

Relationship roles (maintenance roles) Roles that aid the social interaction among group members

Relativist ethical view A belief that what is right or wrong depends on the situation or the culture

Representation The process of evaluating an event without comparing it to others or comparing situations that are not similar

Resistance Passive opposition, active opposition, or both to a manager's request

Resistance The second GAS stage; occurs when one fights the threat

Restructuring Changing the way the human resources of an organization are organized

Revolutionary change or frame-breaking change Change that is rapid and dramatic

Reward power Based on a person's access to rewards. Others comply because of the desire to receive rewards

Risk-averse Tending to avoid risk

Role ambiguity Conflict due to the lack of clarity about the role one is expected to play

Role conflict Conflict caused when the individual plays contradictory roles

Roles Specific formal or informal activities that each person performs in the group

S

Salient cues Those cues that are somehow so striking that they stand out

Satisficing The process of making a decision that is satisfactory but not necessarily optimal

Schemas Mental patterns that people apply to explain certain situations and events

Selective attention The process of paying attention to some, but not all, physical and social cues

Self-managed teams (SMTs) Process teams of employees who have full managerial control over their own work

Self-monitoring The degree to which people are capable of reading and using cues from the environment to determine their own behavior

Self-oriented roles Roles focused on satisfying the individual member's needs

Self-perception theory A theory suggesting that people make attributions about themselves by looking at their own behavior

Self-presentation The actions we take to control the impressions we present

Self-promotion An impression management tactic in which one presents positive information about oneself to appear competent

Self-serving bias A person's tendency to accept credit for success and reject blame for failures

Sender The person who creates the communication and decides how it should be sent

Sensitivity training Face-to-face, unstructured small-group interaction used to provide members insight about themselves and help them develop self-awareness

Separation The smaller minority groups advocate separation from the dominant culture and refuse to interact and exchange cultural elements

Service firms Business organizations that deliver a service rather than a tangible product

Sexual harassment Unwelcome advances, requests for sexual favors, and other verbal and nonverbal behavior of a sexual nature

Shamrock team Team that combines a small group of core permanent members, part-time members, and outside subcontractors or consultants

Similar-to-me effect A perceptual bias that leads us to develop a liking for a person that we perceive is similar to us or to quickly dislike those who are different

Situational control (sit con) In Fiedler's Contingency model, the combination of LMR, TS, and PP that indicates the amount of the leaders has over the situation

Skill An acquired talent that a person develops related to a specific task

Skill variety Refers to the number of different skills used to do a job

SMART goals Specific, measurable, achievable, reasonable, and have a time frame

Social facilitation Occurs when individuals work harder in the presence of others

Social loafing People work less hard when their individual contribution to a task cannot be measured

Social perception The process of gathering, selecting, and interpreting information about how we view ourselves and others

Stakeholders Individuals and groups who have some interest or stake in the organization

Stereotype A generalization about an individual based on one's perception of the group of which the person is a member

Stewards Leaders who develop a general vision while remaining partners with their employees and customers and concentrating on serving them to help them accomplish their goals

Strategic contingencies Elements that are essential to the performance and effectiveness of an organization, a department, or a team

Strategic Management The study of how upper management sets the general course for the business and how it uses human, financial, and operational resources to achieve company goals

Strategic management process The combined processes of strategy formulation and implementation

Strategy How a business achieves its mission and goals

Strategy formulation The process of forging a cohesive, integrated set of strategies designed to deal with the environment and achieve the business mission and goals

Strategy implementation Actions the organization takes to execute its strategies

Stress An individual physiological and psychological response to perceived environmental threats

Stressors Environmental threats perceived by an individual

Strong organizational culture A culture that is well defined; members from different parts of the organization are aware of its components, most members accept its core values and assumptions, and most behave in ways that are consistent with it

Structure How people are organized to achieve the company's mission

Subculture A group in an organization that may agree with the organization's basic assumptions and core values but have many distinct values and behaviors

Substitutes Situational or individual factors that replace the leader's actions

Superleadership A process of leading people to lead themselves

Supportive communication Honest and accurate interpersonal communication that focuses on building and enhancing relationships

Survey feedback The use of surveys to assess employee attitudes and organizational climate with the goal of addressing issues identified through the survey results

SWOT analysis An analysis of a company's internal *s*trengths and *w*eaknesses and the *o*pportunities and *t*hreats in the organization's environment

Synergy The process of combining two or more actions that results in an effect that differs from the total of the individual actions

System resource approach Definition of organizational effectiveness that focuses on how well an organization acquires and uses resources from the environment

T

Tactilics Touching behaviors

Task complexity The extent to which the team's task is intricate and consists of different interrelated parts

Task identity The extent to which the job allows a person to identify with it or feel that he or she owns the outcome

Task motivation (low LPC) The person is primarily motivated by task accomplishments

Task roles Roles that relate to the task the group is performing

Task significance The importance of a job to the organization or to the wider community

Task structure (TS) In Fiedler's Contingency model, refers to the degree of clarity a task has

Team building Activities aimed at improving the internal work and relationship processes of teams

Team manager/facilitator A team member who is responsible for helping the team move forward but is not single-handedly responsible for the outcome

Teams Mature groups with highly interdependent members who are fully committed to a common goal

Technical skill The know-how to perform a certain task

Technology The knowledge, tools, techniques, and processes used to create the goods and services of an organization

Terminal values Goals for behavior or for a certain state of affairs that a person would like to achieve

Territories Spaces over which we claim ownership and control

360-degree feedback A technique in which managers receive feedback about their behaviors, style, and performance from all organizational levels including bosses, peers, and subordinates

Top-down change Change initiated and planned by managers at the top of the organization

Total Quality Management (TQM) A management concept that focuses on customer satisfaction through continuous improvement of business processes

Trait approach Aimed at identifying individual characteristics such as demographic factors or personality traits that distinguished leaders from followers

Trait method A performance evaluation method in which managers rate employees on individual personality traits

Transactional leadership Leadership activities that involve an exchange between leader and follower and deal with day-to-day leadership activities of taking care of task and motivating followers

Transformational leadership Leadership activities that deal with planning and implementing major changes in organizations and aim to transform organizations

Type A A personality trait evidenced when a person tries to do more in less and less time in an apparently tireless pursuit of everything

U

Uncertainty avoidance The extent to which uncertainty is tolerated and finding absolute truths is important

Unfreezing Stage in Lewin's force field model of change during which existing practices and behaviors are questioned and motivation to change develops

Universalist view of ethics A belief that all activities should be judged by the same standards, regardless of the situation or culture

Unplanned change Change that occurs randomly and spontaneously without the specific intention of addressing a problem

V

Value conflict Disagreement among values that an individual holds or between individual and organizational values

Value system The way a person's values are organized and prioritized

Values Stable, long-lasting beliefs and preferences about what is worthwhile and desirable

Venture teams temporary task forces or teams that are formed to develop ideas or carry out a change

Vertical conflict Conflict between groups at different levels of the organization

Virtual organizations Organizations that function with a limited, relatively small core of permanent employees and facilities

Visionary leadership Leadership theory that emphasizes the leader's role in creating and articulating an inspiring vision for followers

W

Weak organizational culture A culture that is not well defined, or one with which there is not much agreement or behavior consistent with what is defined

Work teams Groups created either to deal with issues that require input from more than one person or to generate commitment from employees

PHOTO CREDITS

ABOUT THE AUTHOR
Page xxi: Abdi Neghabat.

CHAPTER 1
Pages 1, 29: Courtesy Starbucks Coffee Company; page 13: Courtesy of Talent Alliance, Photo by Phil Degginger; page 19: Yves Logghe/AP/Wide World Photos; page 26: Tom Wagner/SABA Press Photos, Inc.; page 27: Teri Stratford.

CHAPTER 2
Pages 35, 66: Marty Katz/New York Times Pictures; page 43: Courtesy of 3D Systems; page 52: Courtesy of Walt Ennis, W. L. Gore & Associates, Inc.

CHAPTER 3
Pages 73, 100: Les Stone/Sygma; page 93: James Schnepf/James Schnepf Photography, Inc.; page 95: James Schnepf/Liaison Agency, Inc.

CHAPTER 4
Pages 111, 141: Jonathan Daniel/Allsport Photography (USA), Inc.; page 125, 133: Mojgan B. Azimi Photography.

CHAPTER 5
Pages 149, 180: Jillian Edelstein/SABA Press Photos, Inc.; page 152: William Vandivert/James Carr; page 157: Greg Miller Photography; page 162: Jim Cooper/AP/Wide World Photos; page 168: Chris Hartlove Photography.

CHAPTER 6
Pages 189, 219: Ed Quinn/SABA Press Photos, Inc.; page 193: Kingston

Technology Company/Co-Founders John Tu & David Sun; page 196: Jonathan Daniel/Allsport Photography (USA), Inc.; page 212: Kistone Photography.

CHAPTER 7
Pages 229, 256: Neal Peters Collection/ Paramount/NPC; page 232: Stuart Franklin/Magnum Photos, Inc.; page 238: Courtesy Rosenbluth International; page 240: Jacqueline Hassink.

CHAPTER 8
Pages 265, 291: Courtesy Shirley Kirshbaum & Associates, NYC; page 270: Harry How/Allsport Photography (USA), Inc.; page 287: Courtesy SEI Investments; page 289: Roger Tully/Lucent Technologies.

CHAPTER 9
Pages 299, 332: Kistone Photography; page 303: Arthur Ourand/Courtesy Ethama Institute, Los Gatos, CA; page 322: Richard Vogel/AP/Wide World Photos; page 324: Richard Drew/AP/Wide World Photos.

CHAPTER 10
Pages 343, 371: Gilles Mingasson/Liaison Agency, Inc.; page 350: Cook/Jenshel; page 352: Greg Girard/Contact Press Images Inc.; page 361: Courtesy Meditrust Corporation; page 362: Wayne Sorce.

CHAPTER 11
Pages 383, 408: FPG International LLC; page 385: Michael Newman/PhotoEdit;

James Schnepf/Liaison Agency, Inc.; page 391: Dana Fineman/Sygma.

CHAPTER 12
Pages 417, 445: AP/Wide World Photos; page 421: FPG International LLC; page 424: Mark Richards/PhotoEdit; Frank Herholdt/Tony Stone Images; page 425: Stock Boston; page 441: Bob Sacha Photography.

CHAPTER 13
Pages 453, 484: Mark Hess/Newborn Group; page 471: Liaison Agency, Inc.; page 472: Courtesy the Hewlett-Packard Company; page 478: Suzanne Opton; page 482: Eric Miller/AP/Wide World Photos.

CHAPTER 14
Pages 491, 520: Michael Latz/AP/Wide World Photos; page 502: Richard Drew/AP/ Wide World Photos; page 506: Michael L. Abramson Photography; page 513: Robert Holmgren/Robert Holmgren Photography.

CHAPTER 15
Pages 531, 560: Marty Lederhandler/AP/ Wide World Photos; page 533: John Barr/AP/Wide World Photos; page 540: Bob Sacha Photography; page 545: Peter Sibbald/ Peter Sibbald Photography; page 550: Karen Kasmauski/Matrix International, Inc.

INDEX

INTERNATIONAL EXAMPLES AND NATIONAL CULTURE COVERAGE IN

 AFGHANISTAN:
chapter 9

 AUSTRALIA:
chapters 2–3, 5, 10–13, 15

 BRAZIL:
chapters 2, 5, 11

 BELGIUM:
chapter 14

 CANADA:
chapters 1, 3, 8, 11, 13–15

 PEOPLE'S REPUBLIC OF CHINA:
chapters 1, 3–4, 6-7, 9, 12–13

 COSTA RICA:
chapters 3, 10, 15

 DENMARK:
chapters 1–2, 8

 EGYPT:
chapters 3, 10–11

 FRANCE:
chapters 1, 3, 5–6, 8, 10–14

 GUATEMALA:
chapter 14

 GERMANY:
chapters 1, 3–4, 6, 8–14

 GREAT BRITAIN:
chapters 1, 3, 5, 6–9, 11–12, 15

 INDIA:
chapters 1, 3, 7, 9–11, 14

 INDONESIA:
chapters 1, 3, 12

 IRAN:
chapters 1, 9

 IRELAND:
chapter 3

 ISRAEL:
chapter 7

 ITALY:
chapters 1, 3–4, 11–12

 JAPAN:
chapters 1–4, 6–15